8-1 (a) Gross profit percentage, Year 1, 33%
8-2 (a) (1) Inventory, FIFO, $32,740
8-3 (a) (2) Inventory, LIFO, $247,520
8-4 (a) Cost percentage, 55%
8-5 (b) Cost percentage, 75%
8-6 (b) Cost of goods sold, Sept., $6,250
Case 8-1 (b) Gross profit, $9,800
Case 8-2 No key figure

9-1 (a) Total cost of equipment, $191,354
9-2 Depreciation for Year 2: (b) $47,200; (c) $48,000
9-3 Depreciation for Year 2: (b) $70,400; (c) $72,000
9-4 New truck, book value Aug. 15, $16,000
9-5 (a) (2) Loss on trade-in of plant assets, $3,000;
(d) New truck, basis for income tax purposes, $14,300
9-6 (c) Accumulated depletion, $2,232,000
9-7 No key figure
Case 9-1 (a) Total depreciation for first three years:
Bay, $37,500; Cove, $68,463
Case 9-2 (b) Adjusted net income, $15,600

Part Three (a) Total assets: Alpine, $499,900;
Nordic, $486,300; (b) Revised cumulative
net income: Alpine, $195,000; Nordic, $219,000

10-1 No key figure
10-2 No key figure
10-3 No key figure
10-4 (c) Total current liabilities, $112,552
10-5 No key figure
10-6 (b) Payroll taxes expense, $1,644
10-7 (b) FICA taxes deducted from earnings of
employees, $9,595.20
Case 10-1 No key figure
Case 10-2 No key figure

11-1 (c) Accrued bond interest expense, $200,000
11-2 (b) (1) Net bond liability, $8,826,000
11-3 (c) (1) Premium on bonds payable, $248,000
11-4 (b) Net long-term liability, $5,840,400

11-5 (a) Carrying value of bonds, June 30, 1990:
$9,417,000
11-6 (a) Carrying value of bonds, June 30, 1990:
$8,272,600
11-7 (c) Bond interest expense (a) $261,000,
(b) $248,000
11-8 (d) Lease payment obligation, $40,184
Case 11-1 No key figure
Case 11-2 No key figure

12-1 (b) Withdrawals, $12,300
12-2 (a) (3) Share to Martin, $39,000
12-3 (a) Share to Partner B, $188,000
12-4 (b) Total assets, $277,800
12-5 Stockholders' equity, (a) $363,000;
(b) 6,320,000
12-6 Stockholders' equity, $843,500
12-7 (b) Total assets, $1,008,200
12-8 No key figure
12-9 Case A, Stockholders' equity, $1,143,000
Case 12-1 No key figure
Case 12-2 No key figure

13-1 Income before extraordinary items, $1,820,000
13-2 (a) Net income, $1,070,000
13-3 (a) Net income, $265,000
13-4 Stockholders' equity Dec. 21, $4,728,000
13-5 Stockholders' equity Dec. 31, $743,600
13-6 (b) Stockholders' equity, $7,376,900
13-7 (b) Cash January 31, $60,350
13-8 No key figure
Case 13-1 (a) Net income, $2,600,000
Case 13-2 No key figure

Part Four No key figure

14-1 No key figure
14-2 Net cash used by investing activities, $(6,000)
14-3 Net cash flow from operating activities,
$467,000

(continued on back flap)

FINANCIAL ACCOUNTING

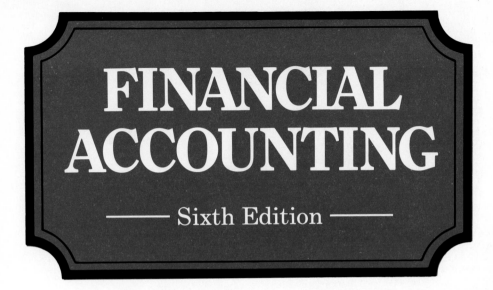

FINANCIAL ACCOUNTING

—— Sixth Edition ——

Robert F. Meigs
SAN DIEGO STATE UNIVERSITY

Walter B. Meigs
UNIVERSITY OF SOUTHERN CALIFORNIA

McGraw-Hill Publishing Company

New York   St. Louis   San Francisco   Auckland   Bogotá
Caracas   Hamburg   Lisbon   London   Madrid   Mexico   Milan
Montreal   New Delhi   Oklahoma City   Paris   San Juan
São Paulo   Singapore   Sydney   Tokyo   Toronto

FINANCIAL ACCOUNTING

2 3 4 5 6 7 8 9 0 V N H V N H 8 9 3 2 1 0 9

ISBN 0-07-041842-X

This book was set in Century Schoolbook by Progressive Typographers, Inc.
The editors were Robert D. Lynch and Edwin Hanson; the production supervisor was Salvador Gonzales.
Part-opening photo credits: Part 1, G. Contorakes; Part 2, Palmer/Kane, Inc.,
Gabe Palmer; Part 3, Luis Villota; Parts 4 and 5, Comstock.
Von Hoffmann Press, Inc., was printer and binder.

Library of Congress Cataloging-in-Publication Data

Meigs, Robert F.
　　Financial accounting.

　　Walter B. Meig's name appears first on the rev. 5th ed.
　　Includes index.
　　1. Accounting.　　I. Meigs, Walter B.　　II. Title.
HF5635.M492　　1989　　　　　657　　　　88-9132
ISBN 0-07-041842-X

Contents

Preface   xxi

Part One   The Accounting Cycle

Chapter 1   Accounting: the language of business   3

WHAT IS ACCOUNTING?   4

*The purpose and nature of accounting. The functions of an accounting
system. Communicating accounting information—who uses accounting
reports. The distinction between accounting and bookkeeping. The work of
accountants. The public accounting profession—the CPA. Private
accounting. Governmental accounting. Generally accepted accounting
principles (GAAP). Development of generally accepted accounting
principles—the FASB. Profitability and solvency: key financial objectives.
Accounting as the basis for business decisions. Internal control. Forms of
business organization.*

FINANCIAL STATEMENTS: THE STARTING POINT IN THE
STUDY OF ACCOUNTING   15

*The balance sheet. The concept of the business entity. Assets. Liabilities.
Owners' equity. What is capital stock? The accounting equation. Effects of
business transactions upon the balance sheet. Effect of business
transactions upon the accounting equation.*

USE OF FINANCIAL STATEMENTS BY OUTSIDERS   27

*Bankers and other creditors. CASE IN POINT. Owners. Others
interested in financial information.*

END-OF-CHAPTER REVIEW   28

*Summary of chapter learning objectives. Key terms introduced or empha-
sized in chapter 1. Demonstration problem for your review. Solution to
demonstration problem.*

ASSIGNMENT MATERIAL   31

Review questions. Exercises. Problems. Business decision cases.

Chapter 2   Recording changes in financial position   42

The role of accounting records.

THE LEDGER   43

*The use of ledger accounts. Debit and credit entries. Recording
transactions in ledger accounts: illustration. Running balance form of
ledger account. The normal balance of an account. Sequence and
numbering of ledger accounts.*

THE JOURNAL   52

*Why use a journal? The general journal: illustration of entries. Posting.
Ledger accounts after posting.*

THE TRIAL BALANCE   59

Uses and limitations of the trial balance. Locating errors. Dollar signs.

THE ACCOUNTING CYCLE: AN INTRODUCTION   61

Manual and computer-based systems: a comparison.

END-OF-CHAPTER REVIEW   65

*Summary of chapter learning objectives. Key terms introduced or
emphasized in chapter 2. Demonstration problem for your review.
Solution to demonstration problem.*

ASSIGNMENT MATERIAL   70

Review questions. Exercises. Problems. Business decision cases.

Chapter 3   Measuring business income   82

*Retained earnings. Net income. The time-period principle. Revenue.
Expenses. Dividends. Debit and credit rules for revenue and expense.*

Recording revenue and expense transactions: an illustration. The journal. The ledger. The trial balance. Adjusting entry for depreciation expense. The adjusted trial balance.

FINANCIAL STATEMENTS   99

The income statement. Statement of retained earnings. The balance sheet. Income statement and retained earnings statement: a link between two balance sheets.

CLOSING THE ACCOUNTS   103

After-closing trial balance. Sequence of procedures in the accounting cycle. Accounting procedures in a computer-based system. Dividends — declaration and payment. Accrual basis of accounting versus cash basis of accounting.

END-OF-CHAPTER REVIEW   111

Summary of chapter learning objectives. Key terms introduced or emphasized in chapter 3. Demonstration problem for your review. Solution to demonstration problem.

ASSIGNMENT MATERIAL   116

Review questions. Exercises. Problems. Business decision cases.

Chapter 4   Completion of the accounting cycle   129

Accounting periods and financial statements. Transactions affecting more than one accounting period.

ADJUSTING ENTRIES: A CLOSER LOOK   130

Types of adjusting entries. Characteristics of adjusting entries. Apportioning recorded costs. Apportioning unearned revenue. Recording unrecorded expenses. Recording unrecorded revenue. Adjusting entries and the accrual basis of accounting.

THE WORK SHEET   141

Preparing the work sheet. Uses for the work sheet. Work sheets in computer-based systems. The accounting cycle. Preparing monthly financial statements without closing the accounts. Reversing entries.

END-OF-CHAPTER REVIEW 158

Summary of chapter learning objectives. Key terms introduced or empha-sized in chapter 4. Demonstration problem for your review. Solution to demonstration problem.

ASSIGNMENT MATERIAL 162

Review questions. Exercises. Problems. Business decision cases.

Part one: comprehensive problem   A Friend With A Truck, Inc. 176

Part Two   Merchandising Concerns, Internal Control, and Accounting Systems

Chapter 5   Accounting for purchases and sales of merchandise 181

MERCHANDISING COMPANIES 181

Revenue from sales. Sales returns and allowances. Sales discounts. Cost of goods sold. The periodic inventory system. Beginning inventory and ending inventory. Purchases of merchandise. Shoplifting and inventory "shrinkage" losses. Income statement for a merchandising company. Analyzing the income statement. Work sheet for a merchandising busi-ness. Financial statements. Closing entries. Summary of merchandising transactions and related accounting entries. Sales taxes. Perpetual inventory systems. CASE IN POINT.

CLASSIFIED FINANCIAL STATEMENTS 199

The purpose of balance sheet classification. Current ratio. Working capital. Classification and format of income statements. Multiple-step income statements. Single-step income statements.

END-OF-CHAPTER REVIEW 204

Summary of chapter learning objectives. Key terms introduced or empha-sized in chapter 5. Demonstration problem for your review. Solution to demonstration problem.

ASSIGNMENT MATERIAL   208

Review questions. Exercises. Problems. Business decision cases.

Chapter 6   Internal control and accounting systems   219

THE SYSTEM OF INTERNAL CONTROL   219

*Accounting controls and administrative controls. Relationship between
the accounting system and the system of internal control. Guidelines to
achieving strong internal control. The role of business documents. Recording purchase invoices at net price. Limitations and cost of internal control.*

TAILORING AN ACCOUNTING SYSTEM TO THE NEEDS OF
A LARGER BUSINESS   229

*Special journals. Sales journal. Controlling accounts and subsidiary
ledgers. Purchases journal. Cash receipts journal. Cash payments journal.
The general journal. Showing the source of postings in ledger accounts.
Reconciling subsidiary ledgers with controlling accounts. Variations in
special journals.*

COMPUTER-BASED ACCOUNTING SYSTEMS   245

*Recording retail sales — computers reduce the work. Advantages of
computer-based systems. CASE IN POINT.*

END-OF-CHAPTER REVIEW   246

*Summary of chapter learning objectives. Key terms introduced or empha-
sized in chapter 6. Demonstration problem for your review. Solution to
demonstration problem.*

ASSIGNMENT MATERIAL   250

Review questions. Exercises. Problems. Business decision cases.

Part two: comprehensive problem   Crestline Lumber Co.   264

Part Three   Accounting for Assets

Chapter 7   Cash and accounts receivable   269

CASH   269

*The need for internal control. Cash receipts. CASE IN POINT. Cash
disbursements. Petty cash. Bank statements. Reconciling the bank
statement.*

ACCOUNTS RECEIVABLE   280

*Uncollectible accounts. The Allowance for Doubtful Accounts. Writing off
an uncollectible account receivable. Recovery of an account previously
written off. Monthly estimates of credit losses. Direct charge-off method.
Credit card sales. Analysis of accounts receivable. Internal controls for
receivables.*

NOTES RECEIVABLE   289

*Nature of interest. Accounting for notes receivable. CASE IN POINT.
Discounting notes receivable.*

END-OF-CHAPTER REVIEW   295

*Summary of chapter learning objectives. Key terms introduced or empha-
sized in chapter 7. Demonstration problem for your review. Solution to
demonstration problem.*

ASSIGNMENT MATERIAL   299

Review Questions. Exercises. Problems. Business decision cases.

Chapter 8   Inventories   311

*Inventory defined. Periodic inventory system versus perpetual inventory
system. The matching principle as applied to inventories. Inventory
valuation and the measurement of income. Importance of an accurate
valuation of inventory. Taking a physical inventory. The year-end cutoff
of transactions. Passage of title to merchandise. Pricing the inventory.
Cost basis of inventory valuation. Inventory valuation methods. Consist-*

ency in the valuation of inventory. The environment of inflation. Inventory profits. The lower-of-cost-or-market rule (LCM). CASE IN POINT. Estimating ending inventory and cost of goods sold. The gross profit method of estimating ending inventory. The retail method of estimating ending inventory. Internal control of inventories. CASE IN POINT. Perpetual inventory system. Internal control and perpetual inventory systems. CASE IN POINT. Perpetual inventory records. Need for an annual physical inventory.

END-OF-CHAPTER REVIEW   337

Summary of chapter learning objectives. Key terms introduced or emphasized in chapter 8. Demonstration problem for your review. Solution to demonstration problem.

ASSIGNMENT MATERIAL   340

Review questions. Exercises. Problems. Business decision cases.

Chapter 9   Plant and equipment, depreciation, and intangible assets   352

PLANT AND EQUIPMENT   353

Plant and equipment — a stream of services. Major categories of plant and equipment. Determining the cost of plant and equipment. Capital expenditures and revenue expenditures. CASE IN POINT.

DEPRECIATION   357

Allocating the cost of plant and equipment over the years of use. Depreciation not a process of valuation. Accumulated depreciation does not consist of cash. Causes of depreciation. Methods of computing depreciation. Revision of depreciation rates. Depreciation and income taxes. Inflation and depreciation. Historical cost versus replacement cost.

DISPOSAL OF PLANT AND EQUIPMENT   366

Gains and losses on disposal of plant and equipment. Gains and losses for income tax purposes. Trading in used assets on new.

NATURAL RESOURCES   369

Accounting for natural resources.

Ex 3, 8
2.
Prob
9

INTANGIBLE ASSETS   370

*Characteristics. Operating expenses versus intangible assets. Amortiza-
tion. Depreciation, depletion, and amortization — a common goal. Goodwill. Patents. Trademarks and trade names. Franchises. Copyrights.
Other intangibles and deferred charges. Research and development
(R&D) costs.*

END-OF-CHAPTER REVIEW   376

*Summary of chapter learning objectives. Key terms introduced or empha-
sized in chapter 9. Demonstration problem for your review. Solution to
demonstration problem.*

ASSIGNMENT MATERIAL   379

Review questions. Exercises. Problems. Business decision cases.

Part three: comprehensive problem   Alpine Village and
Nordic Sports   389

Part Four   Accounting for Liabilities and Owners' Equity

Chapter 10   Current liabilities and payroll accounting   393

*The nature of liabilities. Timely recognition of liabilities. CASE IN
POINT. Current liabilities. Accounts payable.*

NOTES PAYABLE   396

*Notes payable issued to banks. Notes payable with interest charges
included in the face amount. Comparison of the two forms of notes payable. Loss contingencies. CASE IN POINT.*

PAYROLL ACCOUNTING   403

*Internal control over payrolls. CASE IN POINT. Deductions from
earnings of employees. Social security taxes (FICA). CASE IN POINT.
Federal income taxes. Other deductions from employees' earnings.*

Employer's responsibility for amounts withheld. Payroll records and procedures. Payroll taxes on the employer. Distinction between employees and independent contractors.

END-OF-CHAPTER REVIEW   410

Summary of chapter learning objectives. Key terms introduced or emphasized in chapter 10. Demonstration problems for your review. Solution to demonstration problem.

ASSIGNMENT MATERIAL   415

Review questions. Exercises. Problems. Business decision cases.

Chapter 11   Bonds payable, leases, and other liabilities   422

BONDS PAYABLE   422

What is a bond issue? Tax advantage of bond financing. Accounting entries for a bond issue. The concept of present value. The present value concept and bond prices. CASE IN POINT. CASE IN POINT. Bonds sold at a discount. Amortization of bond discount. Bonds sold at a premium. Year-end adjustments for bond interest expense. Straight-line amortization: a theoretical shortcoming. Effective interest method of amortization. Retirement of bonds payable. Bond sinking fund. Conversion of bonds payable into capital stock. Conversion of bonds from the investor's viewpoint. CASE IN POINT.

LEASES   441

Operating leases. Capital leases.

OTHER LONG-TERM LIABILITIES   443

Mortgage notes payable. Pension plan.

END-OF-CHAPTER REVIEW   444

Summary of learning objectives. Key terms introduced or emphasized in chapter 11. Demonstration problem. Solution to demonstration problem.

ASSIGNMENT MATERIAL   447

Review questions. Exercises. Problems. Business decision cases.

Chapter 12   Ownership equity: single proprietorships, partnerships, and corporations   455

SINGLE PROPRIETORSHIPS   456

Accounting for the owner's equity in a single proprietorship. Closing the accounts. Financial statements for a single proprietorship.

PARTNERSHIPS   458

Significant features of a partnership. Advantages and disadvantages of a partnership. Limited partnerships. The partnership contract. Partnership accounting. Partnership profits and income taxes. Alternative methods of dividing partnership net income. Other aspects of partnership accounting.

CORPORATIONS   466

What is a corporation? Advantages of the corporate form of organization. Disadvantages of the corporate form of organization. Formation of a corporation. Authorization and issuance of capital stock. Par value. Market price of common stock. Stock issued for assets other than cash. No-par stock. Preferred stock and common stock. Characteristics of preferred stock. CASE IN POINT. Market price of preferred stock. CASE IN POINT. The underwriting of stock issues. Subscriptions to capital stock. Donated capital. Stockholder records in a corporation. Retained earnings or deficit. Balance sheet for a corporation illustrated.

END-OF-CHAPTER REVIEW   483

Summary of chapter learning objectives. Key terms introduced or emphasized in chapter 12. Demonstration problem for your review. Solution to demonstration problem.

ASSIGNMENT MATERIAL   487

Review questions. Exercises. Problems. Business decision cases.

Chapter 13   Corporations: a closer look   497

REPORTING THE RESULTS OF OPERATIONS   498

Developing predictive information. Reporting unusual items — an illustration. Continuing operations. Discontinued operations. CASE IN POINT. Extraordinary items. Changes in accounting principle. Earnings per share. Primary and fully diluted earnings per share.

OTHER TRANSACTIONS AFFECTING STOCKHOLDERS'
EQUITY   505

*Cash dividends. Dividend dates. Liquidating dividends. Stock dividends.
Stock splits. Retained earnings. Prior period adjustments. Treasury stock.
Recording purchases of treasury stock. Reissuance of treasury stock.
Statement of stockholders' equity. Book value per share of common stock.
Illustration of a stockholders' equity section.*

INVESTMENTS IN CORPORATE SECURITIES   518

*Marketable securities. Accounting for marketable securities. Marketable
debt securities (bonds). Marketable equity securities (stocks). Gains and
losses from sales of investments. Balance sheet valuation of marketable securities. CASE IN POINT. Lower-of-cost-or-market.*

END-OF-CHAPTER REVIEW   523

*Summary of chapter learning objectives. Key terms introduced or empha-
sized in chapter 13. Demonstration problem for your review. Solution to
demonstration problem.*

ASSIGNMENT MATERIAL   527

Review questions. Exercises. Problems. Business decision cases.

Part four: comprehensive problem
Review Session   537

Part Five   Special Report and Analysis of Accounting Information

Chapter 14   Measuring cash flows   543

STATEMENT OF CASH FLOWS   544

*Purpose of the statement. Example of a statement of cash flows. Classifi-
cation of cash flows. Critical importance of cash flow from operations.
Approaches to preparing a statement of cash flows.*

PREPARING A STATEMENT OF CASH FLOWS:
AN ILLUSTRATION   549

*Additional information. Cash flows from operating activities. Cash
payments for merchandise and for expenses. Differences between net
income and net cash flow from operations. Cash flows from investing activities. Cash flows from financing activities. Relationship of the cash flow
statement to the balance sheet. The statement of cash flows: a second look.*

END-OF-CHAPTER REVIEW   560

*Summary of chapter learning objectives. Key terms introduced or empha-
sized in chapter 14. Demonstration problem for your review. Solution to
demonstration problem.*

ASSIGNMENT MATERIAL   564

Review questions. Exercises. Problems. Business decision cases.

Chapter 15   Analysis and interpretation of financial statements   575

*What is your opinion of the level of corporate profits? CASE IN POINT.
Some specific examples of corporate earnings . . . and losses. Sources of
financial information. Comparative financial statements. Tools of analysis.
Dollar and percentage changes. CASE IN POINT. Trend percentages.
Component percentages. Ratios. Comparative data in annual reports of
major corporations. Standards of comparison. Quality of earnings. Quality
of assets and the relative amount of debt. Impact of inflation. Illustrative
analysis for Seacliff Company. Analysis by common stockholders. Return
on investment (ROI). Leverage. Analysis by long-term creditors. Analysis
by preferred stockholders. Analysis by short-term creditors. Summary of
analytical measurements.*

END-OF-CHAPTER REVIEW   599

*Summary of chapter learning objectives. Key terms introduced or empha-
sized in chapter 15. Demonstration problem for your review. Solution to
demonstration problem.*

ASSIGNMENT MATERIAL   603

Review questions. Exercises. Problems. Business decision cases.

Part five: comprehensive problem   American Home Products Corporation   615

Chapter 16   Income taxes and business decisions   628

Tax Reform Act of 1986. Tax planning versus tax evasion. The critical importance of income taxes. The federal income tax: history and objectives. Classes of taxpayers.

INCOME TAXES: INDIVIDUALS   632

Cash basis of accounting for income tax returns. Tax rates. Income tax formula for individuals. Total income and gross income. Deductions to arrive at adjusted gross income. Deductions from adjusted gross income. Personal exemptions. Taxable income — individuals. Capital gains and losses. The tax liability. Quarterly payments of estimated tax. Tax returns, tax refunds, and payment of the tax. Computation of individual income tax illustrated. Alternative Minimum Tax. Partnerships.

INCOME TAXES: CORPORATIONS   644

Taxation of corporations. Corporation tax rates. Taxable income of corporations. Illustrative tax computation for corporation. Accounting income versus taxable income. Alternative accounting methods offering possible tax advantages. Interperiod income tax allocation.

TAX PLANNING   650

Form of business organization. Tax planning in the choice of financial structure. CASE IN POINT. Tax shelters.

END-OF-CHAPTER REVIEW   654

Summary of learning objectives. Key terms introduced or emphasized in chapter 16. Demonstration problem for your review. Solution to demonstration problem.

ASSIGNMENT MATERIAL   659

Review questions. Exercises. Problems. Business decision cases.

Appendix A   Applications of present value   667

The concept of present value. Present value tables. Selecting an appropri-
ate discount rate. Discounting annual cash flows. Discount periods of less
than one year. Accounting applications of the present value concept.

ASSIGNMENT MATERIAL   674
Problems.

Appendix B   Investments for purposes of control   676

The equity method.

CONSOLIDATED FINANCIAL STATEMENTS   678
Parent and subsidiary companies. Growth through the acquisition of
subsidiaries. CASE IN POINT. Financial statements for a consolidated
economic entity. Methods of consolidation. Consolidation at the date of
acquisition. Intercompany eliminations. Acquisition of subsidiary's stock
at a price above book value. Less than 100% ownership in subsidiary.
Consolidated income statement. Accounting for investment in corporate
securities: a summary.

ASSIGNMENT MATERIAL   688
Problems.

Appendix C   International accounting and foreign currency translation   692

What is international accounting? Foreign currencies and exchange rates.
Accounting for transactions with foreign companies. Currency fluctuations
—who wins and who loses? Consolidated financial statements that
include foreign subsidiaries.

ASSIGNMENT MATERIAL   701
Review questions. Problems.

Appendix D   Accounting for the effects of inflation   704

What is inflation? Profits — fact or illusion? CASE IN POINT. Two approaches to "inflation accounting." Disclosing the effects of inflation in financial statements.

"INFLATION ACCOUNTING" — AN ILLUSTRATION   708

Net income measured in constant dollars. Interpreting the constant dollar income statement. Gains and losses in purchasing power. Interpreting the net gain or loss in purchasing power. Net income on a current cost basis. Interpreting a current cost income statement. Expressing comparative data in dollars of constant purchasing power. Interpreting comparative data stated in constant dollars.

ASSIGNMENT MATERIAL   715

Review questions. Exercises. Problems.

Index   723

Preface

A new edition provides authors with an opportunity to add new material, to condense the coverage of topics that have declined in relative importance, to reorganize portions of the book to improve instructional efficiency, and to refine and polish the treatment of basic subject matter. We have tried to do all these things in this sixth edition.

The environment of accounting is changing fast, and the shift toward computers, the increasing public interest in income tax policies, and the growing importance of international business activity affect the goals and content of an introductory text in accounting. In order to function intelligently as a citizen as well as in the business community, every individual needs more than ever before an understanding of basic accounting concepts. Our goal is to present accounting as an essential part of the decision-making process for the voter, the taxpayer, the government official, the business manager, and the investor.

This edition, like the preceding ones, is designed for use in the first college-level course in accounting. In this course, instructors often recognize three groups of students: those who stand at the threshold of preparation for a career in accounting, students of business administration who need a thorough understanding of accounting as an important element of the total business information system, and students from a variety of other disciplines who will find the ability to use and interpret accounting information a valuable accomplishment. During the process of revision, we have tried to keep in mind the needs and interests of all three groups.

NEW FEATURES IN THIS EDITION

In the text

1 Comprehensive Review Problems for each of five parts in the textbook. (The text is organized into five parts, each consisting of from two to four related chapters.) These problems illustrate the major concepts introduced in each part. For example, the Comprehensive Problem for Part One is a "mini-practice set," covering the entire accounting cycle. The Comprehensive Problem for Part Five asks students to analyze the financial statements of a well-known corporation. Partially filled-in working papers are provided for these problems in the Working Papers supplement.

2 Introductory level coverage of the new Statement of Cash Flows.

3 Coverage of the historic Tax Reform Act of 1986, including the effects of the Act upon individuals and corporations.

4 A new chapter on current liabilities and payroll accounting.

5 A new appendix on accounting for the effects of inflation, emphasizing the FASB's new guidelines for voluntary disclosure.

6 Chapter learning objectives integrated into the text material through marginal notations and summaries at the end of each chapter.

7 More than 70 new Exercises, Problems, Business Decision Cases, and Comprehensive Problems. In addition, most of the exercises and problems carried forward from the prior edition have been revised.

8 In each chapter, a new first exercise emphasizing accounting terminology. This exercise is coordinated with similar exercises in the *Test Bank* and the *Study Guide.*

9 Increased emphasis upon accounting theory and generally accepted accounting principles throughout the text.

10 Careful shortening of the text, which now contains 16 chapters rather than 17. The content of many individual chapters also has been revised and shortened.

New features in the supplemental package

1 *General Ledger Software and Applications,* produced by CYMA/McGraw-Hill.

2 *Accounting/Lotus Connection,* by E. James Meddaugh. Software, data, and instructions for working accounting problems with Lotus 1-2-3.

3 An enlarged *Study Guide,* now providing thorough explanations of the reasoning behind the correct answer to each multiple-choice question. Also features many new questions and exercises, with solutions now at the end of each chapter.

4 *Computer Tutorial* — a computer-based test bank for use by students. Includes a wide variety of objective questions and exercises for each chapter in the text. For all objective questions, the software provides students with immediate feedback explaining why their answers are right or wrong.

5 A greatly expanded *Test Bank,* available as a printed manual or in computer-based formats.

6 An expanded set of *Teaching Transparencies,* now in color.

FEATURES CARRIED FORWARD FROM PRIOR EDITIONS

Special qualities that are carried forward from prior editions include:

1 Depth of coverage. Topics are covered in a depth that will qualify the student for subsequent course work in accounting.

2 Accuracy in all problem material and solutions. All problems, solutions, and examination materials have been developed and tested first-hand by the authors in their own classes for introductory accounting students. This personal attention to accuracy is supplemented by independent testing by other accounting faculty.

3 Perspective — careful effort throughout the text and problems to utilize current and realistic prices, interest rates, and profit levels.

4 People-oriented problems which depict the complex decisions that must be made by men and women acting as managers, investors, and in other roles.

5 Abundant problem material, including review questions, exercises, problems, and Business Decision Cases. In addition, each chapter contains a glossary of key terms and a demonstration problem to assist students in developing skill in analyzing and solving accounting problems.

6 Checklist of key figures for problems and Business Decision Cases included on the inside cover pages of the textbook.

7 Coverage of computer-based accounting systems integrated into the early "accounting cycle" chapters.

8 Frequent use of real business examples — termed *Cases in Point* — to illustrate key accounting concepts.

9 The most thorough coverage of income taxes found in an introductory level textbook. Our coverage of income taxes emphasizes basic concepts likely to remain relevant for many years to come.

10 An appendix featuring an introductory level discussion of international accounting and foreign currency translation, complete with problem material.

11 Careful integration into the text and problem material of recent pronouncements of the Financial Accounting Standards Board.

12 The most comprehensive package of supplementary materials available for any financial accounting textbook.

NEW AND EXTENSIVELY REVISED CHAPTERS

In terms of chapter content, this sixth edition represents our most extensive revision to date. The text contains two new chapters, yet is one chapter shorter. Two chapters have been condensed into one; chapter content and sequence have been rearranged, and many new topics are discussed.

Chapter 5, "Accounting for Purchases and Sales of Merchandise," has been extensively revised. The new format is shorter and, we believe, more effective. In a revised Chapter 6, we now discuss in one place the related topics of internal control and accounting systems.

In Chapter 7, we have shortened the text by condensing into one chapter the related topics of cash, accounts receivable, and notes receivable. We have moved the discussion of marketable securities, formerly included in this chapter, to follow our discussions on bonds payable and capital stock.

An all-new Chapter 10 covers in one place the various types of current liabilities, including accounts payable, notes payable, and payrolls. The topic of loss contingencies also is covered in this chapter.

We have moved the chapter on bonds payable and other long-term liabilities (now Chapter 11) to precede the chapters on owners' equity. This change enables us to discuss the major balance sheet topics in "balance sheet order."

Chapter 13, "Corporations: A Closer Look," has been extensively revised. This chapter covers many special corporate reporting topics, such as discontinued operations, earnings per share, stock dividends, and stock splits. We have tried to shorten and to clarify our discussion of each topic, while increasing our emphasis upon the proper interpretation of these events by the users of financial statements. In keeping with these goals, we have added to this chapter a brief discussion of marketable securities. This addition enables us to explain the effects of many stockholders' equity transactions from the viewpoints of both the issuing corporation and the investor.

We actually unveiled our new Chapter 14, "Measuring Cash Flows," in our Revised Fifth Edition. This chapter covers in an introductory manner the all-new Statement of Cash Flows—a fundamental change in basic financial reporting requirements.

A discussion of our revised chapters is never complete without addressing the dynamic topic of income taxes. We have integrated throughout the textbook the latest income tax concepts and regulations. In addition, our extensively revised Chapter 16 presents income tax concepts which, stemming from the Tax Reform Act of 1986, are likely to form the framework of income taxation for many years to come. We regard our introductory-level coverage of income taxes as a unique strength of this textbook.

SUPPLEMENTARY MATERIALS

A distinguishing characteristic of this textbook is the wide variety of supplementary learning and teaching aids for students and instructors. All these materials, with the exception of the computerized supplements, were prepared personally by the authors of the textbook.

For students

1 *A self-study guide.* The **Study Guide** enables students to measure their progress by immediate feedback. This self-study guide includes a summary of the highlights of each chapter and an abundance of objective questions and short exercises. Answers to all questions and exercises are provided immediately following each chapter. As an additional study aid, the reasoning behind the answer to each multiple-choice question is explained in detail. This guide provides a useful review for students before classroom discussions and examinations.

2 *Working papers.* A soft-cover book of partially filled-in working papers of the problems, Business Decision Cases, and Comprehensive Problems is published separately from the text. These work sheets provide for each problem, Business Decision Case, and Comprehensive Problem the appropriate type of columnar paper. In addition, problem headings and "given" data have been filled in to save students much of the mechanical pencil-pushing inherent in problem assignments.

3 *Computer Tutorial.* Using objective questions and exercises from our Study Guide, this computer-based supplement allows students to test themselves on any chapter. For objective questions, the tutorial provides immediate on-screen explanations of why incorrect answers are wrong, along with page references to discussions in the textbook. To assist in solving exercises, the tutorial includes a built-in calculator and numerous "help screens."

4 *Manual practice set.* The manual practice set available with our preceding edition has been completely revised. Designed for use after completing Chapter 6 of the text, the *World Premieres, Inc.,* practice set is bound in two separate books, making it easier for students to journalize transactions, post entries, and prepare financial statements. The purpose of this manual practice set is to acquaint students with the flow of information through an accounting system and to allow them to perform personally each step in the accounting cycle.

5 *Computerized practice set.* The *Candlelight Restaurant Supply, Inc.,* practice set accompanying this sixth edition allows students to experience hands-on operation of a computer-based accounting system.

   This computerized practice set has a unique instructional feature that identifies any erroneous input. If an error is made in analyzing a transaction, the computer responds with hints and help statements until the transaction is recorded correctly. Thus, any printed computer output generated by the student represents a correct solution to the practice set. The practice set is accompanied by a special instruction booklet for the student.

6 *CYMA/McGraw-Hill* An educational version of a leading *general ledger software* package. The narrative of transactions and chart of accounts for our manual practice set, *World Premieres, Inc.,* is provided for use with this software. However, the software is extremely flexible; it may be used to work most accounting cycle problems, and to maintain personal accounting records or those of a small business.

7 *Checklist of key figures for problems.* This list appears on the front and back inside covers of this book. The purpose of the checklist is to aid students in verifying their problem solutions and in discovering their own errors.

Supplements for instructors

1 *Solutions manual.* A comprehensive manual containing answers to all review questions, exercises, problems, Business Decision Cases, and Comprehensive Problems contained in the text, along with a complete solution to the manual practice set.

   In the development of problem material for this book, special attention has been given to the inclusion of problems of varying length and difficulty. By referring to the time estimates, difficulty ratings, and problem descriptions in the *Solutions Manual,* instructors can choose problems that best fit the level, scope, and emphasis of the course they are offering.

2 *An instructor's guide.* This separate manual includes the following three sections for each chapter of the textbook:

a A brief topical outline of the chapter listing in logical sequence the topics the authors like to discuss in class.

b An assignment guide correlating specific exercises and problems with various topics covered in the chapter.

c Comments and observations.

The "Comments and observations" sections indicate the authors' personal views as to relative importance of topics and identify topics with which some students have difficulty. Specific exercises and problems are recommended to demonstrate certain points. Many of these sections include "Asides," introducing real-world situations (not included in the text) that are useful in classroom discussions.

Also included in the Instructor's Guide are sample assignment schedules, ideas for using each element of the supplemental package, solutions to the parallel sets of *Achievement Tests* and *Comprehensive Examinations,* and solutions to the computer-based practice sets.

3 Two parallel sets of *Achievement Tests* and *Comprehensive Examinations.* Each set consists of four Achievement Tests with each test covering three or four chapters; the Comprehensive Examination covers the entire text and may be used as a final examination.

4 *An enlarged test bank.* With an abundance of true-false questions, multiple-choice questions, and short exercises organized on a chapter-by-chapter basis, this supplement is a valuable resource for instructors who prepare their own examinations.

5 *Transparencies of solutions to exercises, problems, and cases.* This visual aid enables instructors to display by overhead projector the complete solution to every numerical exercise, problem, Business Decision Case, and Comprehensive Problem in the text. The transparencies now use a bold typeface for greater clarity.

6 *Teaching transparencies.* A large number of transparencies have been produced for use in the classroom to illustrate various accounting concepts and procedures. These transparencies all differ from the illustrations appearing in the textbook and are enhanced by the use of color.

CONTRIBUTIONS BY OTHERS

We want to express our sincere thanks to the many users of the preceding editions who offered helpful suggestions for this edition. Especially helpful was the advice received from the following reviewers:

Sarah L. Adams, California State University–Chico
Gyan Chandra, University of Miami
J. V. Colmie, Thomas Nelson Community College
Wai P. Lam, University of Windsor (Canada)
Leonard Lederich, Hostos Community College
Mary A. Ferrara-Meigs, San Diego State University

Deborah Payne, University of Texas
Manuel A. Tipgos, University of Kentucky

We are most appreciative of the expert attention given this book and its many supplements by the editorial staff of McGraw-Hill, especially Bob Lynch and Ed Hanson.

Our special thanks go to Virginia Bakay, University of Nevada – Las Vegas, and Audrie M. Beck, Towson State University, for assisting us in the proof stages of this edition by reviewing the end-of-chapter problems and text examples for accuracy.

The assistance of Beth Ann Olmstead, Char Garrett, and Rosemary Savage was most helpful in preparation of the manuscript of both the text and supplements.

We also are grateful to the Financial Accounting Standards Board which granted us permission to quote from FASB Statements, Discussion Memoranda, Interpretations, and Exposure Drafts. All quotations are copyrighted © by the Financial Accounting Standards Board, High Ridge Park, Stamford, Connecticut 06905, U.S.A. and are reprinted with permission. Copies of the complete documents are available from the FASB.

Robert F. Meigs
Walter B. Meigs

FINANCIAL ACCOUNTING

Part One	The accounting cycle
Chapter 1	Accounting: the language of business
Chapter 2	Recording changes in financial position
Chapter 3	Measuring business income
Chapter 4	Completion of the accounting cycle

In these first four chapters, the continuing example of Greenhill Real Estate is used to illustrate the concepts of accrual accounting for a small, service-type business. Accounting for a merchandising concern will be introduced in Part Two.

Chapter 1
Accounting:
the language of business

CHAPTER PREVIEW

This introductory chapter explores the nature of accounting information and the environment in which it is developed and used. We emphasize the uses of accounting reports, the services performed by accountants, and the institutions which influence accounting practice. A basic financial statement — the balance sheet — is illustrated and discussed. We explain the nature of assets, liabilities, and owners' equity; and why a balance sheet always "balances." Attention is focused upon the set of standards called ***generally accepted accounting principles.*** Specific accounting principles introduced in Chapter 1 are the concept of the business entity, the cost principle, the objectivity principle, the going-concern assumption, and the stable-dollar assumption. We also introduce Greenhill Real Estate, a company used as a continuing example throughout the first four chapters. In Chapter 1, the activities of Greenhill illustrate the effects of business transactions upon the balance sheet.

After studying this chapter you should be able to meet these Learning Objectives:

1 Define accounting and explain the purpose of an accounting system.
2 Describe the work of CPAs and other accountants.
3 Explain the phrase "generally accepted accounting principles."
4 Explain the function of the FASB.
5 State two basic financial objectives of every profit-oriented business.
6 Describe a balance sheet; define assets, liabilities, and owners' equity.
7 Discuss the accounting principles involved in asset valuation.
8 Indicate the effects of various transactions upon the balance sheet.

WHAT IS ACCOUNTING?

1 Define
accounting and
explain the
purpose of an
accounting
system.
Some people think of accounting as a highly technical field which can be understood only by professional accountants. Actually, nearly everyone practices accounting in one form or another on an almost daily basis. Accounting is the art of measuring, describing, and interpreting economic activity. Whether you are preparing a household budget, balancing your checkbook, preparing your income tax return, or running General Motors, you are working with accounting concepts and accounting information.

Accounting has often been called the "language of business." Such terms as assets, liabilities, revenue, expense, cash flow, inventory turnover, and earnings per share are but a few examples of technical accounting terms widely used in the business community. Every investor, manager, and business decision maker needs a clear understanding of accounting terms and concepts. At the end of each chapter in this book, the first exercise is devoted to enhancing your knowledge of accounting terminology.

We live in an era of accountability. Although accounting has made its most dramatic progress in the field of business, the accounting function is vital to every unit of our society. An individual must account for his or her income, and must file income tax returns. Often an individual must supply personal accounting information in order to buy a car or home, to qualify for a college scholarship, to secure a credit card, or to obtain a bank loan. Large corporations are accountable to their stockholders, to governmental agencies, and to the public. The federal government, the states, the cities, the school districts: all must use accounting as a basis for controlling their resources and measuring their accomplishments. Accounting is equally essential to the successful operation of a business, a university, a fraternity, a social program, or a city.

In every election the voters must make decisions at the ballot box on issues involving accounting concepts. Therefore, some knowledge of accounting is needed by all citizens if they are to act intelligently in meeting the challenges of our society. This book will help you develop your knowledge of accounting and your ability to use accounting information in making economic and political decisions.

The purpose and nature of accounting

The underlying purpose of accounting is to provide financial information about an economic entity. In this book the economic entity we concentrate upon is a business enterprise. Business executives and managers need the financial information provided by an accounting system to help them plan and control the activities of the business. For example, management needs answers to such questions as the profitability of each department of the business, the adequacy of the company's cash position, and the trend of earnings. Thus, accounting is the connecting link between decision makers and business operations. To repeat this basic concept, the goal of the accounting system is to provide useful information to decision makers.

Financial information about a business is also needed by *outsiders.* These outsiders include owners, bankers, other creditors, potential investors, labor unions, the government, and the public, because all these groups have supplied money to the business or have some other interest in the business that will be served by information about its financial position and operating results. Remember that every individual as well as every business must make economic decisions about the future. Therefore, everyone needs some understanding of accounting as a basis for making sound decisions.

The functions of an accounting system

An accounting system consists of the methods and devices used by an entity to keep track of its financial activities and to summarize these activities in a manner useful to decision makers. To achieve these goals, an accounting system may make use of computers and video displays as well as handwritten records and reports printed on paper. In fact, the accounting system for any sizable business is likely to include all these records and devices. Regardless of whether the accounting system is simple or sophisticated, three basic steps must be performed as data concerning financial activities are collected and processed—the data must be *recorded, classified,* and *summarized.*

Step 1—recording financial activity. The first function of an accounting system is to create a systematic record of the daily business activity, in terms of money. For example, goods and services are purchased and sold, credit is extended to customers, debts are incurred, and cash is received and paid out. These *transactions* are typical of business events which can be expressed *in monetary terms,* and must be entered in accounting records. The mere statement of an intent to buy goods or services in the future does not represent a transaction. The term *transaction* refers to a completed action rather than to an expected or possible future action.

The recording of a transaction may be performed in many ways, such as writing with a pen or pencil, entering data through a computer keyboard, or passing machine-readable price tags over an optical scanner.

Of course, not all business events can be measured and described in monetary terms. Therefore, we do not record in the accounting records such events as the death of a key executive or a threat by a labor union to call a strike.

Step 2—classifying data. A complete record of all business activities usually amounts to a huge volume of data—too large and diverse to be useful to decision makers such as managers and investors. Therefore, the data must be classified into related groups or categories of transactions. For example, grouping together those transactions in which cash is received or paid out is a logical step in developing useful information about the cash position of a business.

Step 3 — summarizing the data. To be useful to decision makers, accounting data must be highly summarized. A complete listing of the sales transactions of a company such as Sears, for example, would be too long for anyone to read. The employees responsible for ordering merchandise need sales information summarized by product. Store managers will want sales information summarized by department, while Sears' top management will want sales information summarized by store. Outsiders, such as the company's stockholders and the Internal Revenue Service, probably will be most interested in a single sales figure which represents the total sales of the entire company.

These three steps we have described — recording, classifying, and summarizing — are the means of creating accounting information. However, the accounting process includes more than the **creating** of information. It also involves **communicating** this information to interested parties and **interpreting** accounting information to help in the making of specific business decisions.

Often we will want to compare the financial statements of Company A with those of Company B. From this comparison, we can determine which company is the more profitable, which is financially stronger, and which offers the better chance of future success. You can benefit personally by making this kind of analysis of a company you are considering investing in — or going to work for.

Communicating accounting information — who uses accounting reports

An accounting system must provide information to managers and also to a number of outsiders who have an interest in the financial activities of the business enterprise. The major types of accounting reports which are developed by the accounting system of a business enterprise and the parties receiving this information are illustrated in the diagram on the next page.

The persons receiving accounting reports are termed the **users** of accounting information. The type of information that a specific user will require depends upon the kinds of decisions that person must make. For example, managers need detailed information about daily operating costs for the purpose of controlling the operations of the business and setting reasonable selling prices. Outsiders, on the other hand, need summarized information concerning resources on hand and information on operating results for the past year to use in making investment decisions, imposing income taxes, or making regulatory decisions.

As shown in the preceding diagram, **financial statements** are the main source of financial information to persons outside the business organization, and also are of great importance to management. The basic purpose of financial statements is to assist decision makers in evaluating the financial strength, profitability, and future prospects of a business. Thus, management, the owners, bankers, the IRS, and other outside groups have a direct interest in financial statements.

Apart from financial statements, other types of accounting reports include income tax returns, reports to regulatory agencies, and management reports.

The Internal Revenue Service (IRS) requires businesses and individuals to file annual income tax returns designed to measure taxable income. **Taxable income**

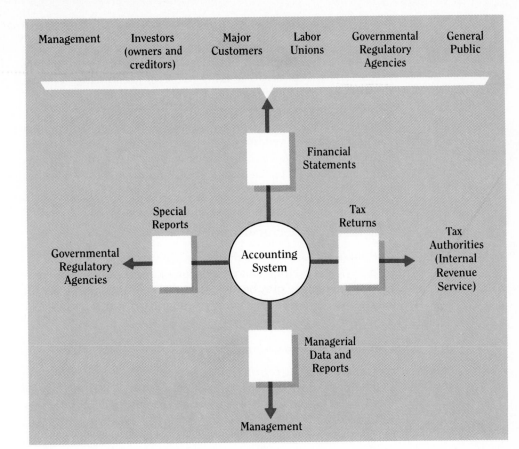

is a legal concept defined by laws which are frequently modified or changed. Thus, the rules used in preparing income tax returns may vary from one year to the next. In general, however, there is a close parallel between income tax laws and the financial concepts underlying financial statements.

Certain types of business, such as banks and telephone companies, are regulated by government agencies. These regulated companies are often required to file special types of accounting reports specifically tailored to the needs of the regulatory agency. In large part, however, reports to regulatory agencies are based upon the same accounting principles as are financial statements.

The management of a business organization needs much detailed accounting data for use in planning and controlling the daily operations of the business. Management also needs specialized accounting information for long-range planning and for major decisions such as the introduction of a new product or the modernizing of an older plant. Accounting information being provided to managers need not conform to the rules for preparing financial statements. Rather, it should be tailored to the managers' specific information needs.

The distinction between accounting and bookkeeping

Persons with little knowledge of accounting may fail to understand the difference between accounting and bookkeeping. **Bookkeeping** means the recording of transactions, the record-making phase of accounting. The recording of transactions tends to be mechanical and repetitive; it is only a small part of the field of accounting and probably the simplest part. Accounting includes not only the maintenance of accounting records, but also the design of efficient accounting systems, the performance of audits, the development of forecasts, income tax work, and the interpretation of accounting information. A person might become a reasonably proficient bookkeeper in a few weeks or months; however, to become a professional accountant requires several years of study and experience.

The work of accountants

Accountants tend to specialize in a given subarea of the discipline just as do attorneys and members of other professions. In terms of career opportunities, the field of accounting may be divided into three broad areas: (1) the public accounting profession, (2) private accounting, and (3) governmental accounting.

The public accounting profession — the CPA

2 Describe the work of CPAs and other accountants.

Certified public accountants are independent professional persons comparable to attorneys or physicians, who offer accounting services to clients for a fee. The **CPA certificate** is a license to practice granted by the state on the basis of a rigorous examination and evidence of practical experience. All states require that candidates pass an examination prepared and graded on a national basis twice each year by the American Institute of Certified Public Accountants. Requirements as to education and practical experience differ somewhat among the various states.

Auditing. The principal function of CPAs is auditing. How do people outside a business entity — owners, creditors, government officials, and other interested parties — know that the financial statements prepared by a company's management are reliable and complete? In large part, these outsiders rely upon **audits** performed by a CPA firm which is **independent** of the company issuing the financial statements.

To perform an audit of a business, a firm of certified public accountants makes a careful study of the company's accounting system and gathers evidence both from within the business and from outside sources. This evidence enables the CPA firm to express its professional **opinion** as to the fairness and reliability of the financial statements. Persons outside the business, such as bankers, and investors who rely upon financial statements for information, attach great importance to the annual **audit report** by the CPA firm.

Income tax services. In making business decisions, executives consider the income tax consequences of each alternative course of action. The CPA is often called upon for "tax planning," which will show how a future transaction such as the acquisition of expensive new equipment may be arranged in a manner that will hold income taxes to a minimum amount. The CPA may also be retained to prepare the federal and state income tax returns. To render tax services, the CPA must have extensive knowledge of tax statutes, regulations, and court decisions, as well as a thorough knowledge of accounting.

Management advisory services. Many CPA firms offer their clients a wide range of management consulting services. For example, a CPA firm might be engaged to study the feasibility of installing a computer-based accounting system, of introducing a new product line, or of merging with another company. The fact that business executives often seek their accountants' advice on a wide range of business problems illustrates the relevance of accounting information to virtually all business decisions.

Private accounting

In contrast to the CPA in public practice who serves many clients, an accountant in private industry is employed by a single enterprise. The chief accounting officer of a medium-sized or large business is usually called the **controller** in recognition of the use of accounting data to control business operations. The controller manages the work of the accounting staff. He or she is also a part of the top management team charged with the task of running the business, setting its objectives, and seeing that these objectives are met. Among other positions held by accountants in a business organization are assistant controller, chief accountant, internal auditor, plant accountant, systems analyst, financial forecaster, and tax accountant.

In a large business, the work of accountants may be divided into such areas as:

1 *Financial accounting.* Financial accounting develops and communicates accounting information for internal use by management and also for external use by persons outside the business, such as owners, bankers, creditors, the IRS, and other government agencies. A principal purpose of financial accounting is the preparation of financial statements in accordance with the generally accepted accounting principles discussed later in this chapter.

   To appreciate the importance of financial accounting and published financial statements, consider the millions of investors who own stock in IBM, General Electric, and other large companies. Financial accounting provides these millions of interested outsiders with information about the safety and the profitability of their investments. Financial statements may be viewed as the end product of financial accounting. In this book, we concentrate upon financial accounting.

2 *Internal auditing.* The internal auditing staff is responsible for evaluating the system of internal control to ensure that accounting reports are reliable, that the company's resources are safeguarded against theft or wasteful use, and that company policies are followed consistently at all levels of the business.

3 *Tax accounting.* As the laws defining taxable income have become more complex, both internal accountants and independent public accountants have devoted more time to problems of taxation. Although many companies rely largely on CPA firms for tax planning and the preparation of income tax returns, large companies also maintain their own tax departments.

4 *Cost accounting.* Knowing the cost of a particular product is vital to the efficient management of a business. For example, an automobile manufacturer needs to know the cost of each type of car produced. Knowing the cost of each manufacturing process (such as painting an automobile) or the cost of any business operation (such as an employee training program) is also essential to making sound business decisions. The phase of accounting concerned with collecting and interpreting cost data is called cost accounting.

5 *Forecasting.* A forecast (or budget) is a plan of financial operations for some future period expressed in monetary terms. By using a forecast, management is able to make comparisons between planned operations and actual results achieved. A forecast provides each division of the business with a specific goal, and thus gives management a means of measuring the efficiency of performance throughout the company.

6 *Management accounting.* An accounting system provides information for both external and internal use. The external reporting function has already been touched upon in our discussion of a CPA firm's independent audit of annual financial statements. The *internal* reporting function of an accounting system gives managers information needed for daily operations and also for long-range planning. Developing the types of information most relevant to specific managerial decisions and interpreting this information is called *management accounting* or *managerial accounting.* In short, management accounting is used by insiders rather than by outsiders. Both cost accounting and forecasting are often viewed as elements of management accounting. Keep in mind that financial accounting and managerial accounting are not two entirely separate disciplines. Much managerial accounting information is actually financial accounting information, rearranged to suit a particular managerial purpose.

Certificate in Management Accounting. The Institute of Management Accounting offers a program leading to a Certificate in Management Accounting. This certificate is a recognition of an individual's knowledge and competence in management accounting. To qualify, one must pass a professional examination and meet specified standards as to education and professional experience.

Governmental accounting

Government officials rely on accounting information to help them direct the affairs of their agencies just as do the executives of corporations. However, accounting for governmental activities requires a somewhat different approach because the objective of earning a profit is absent from government agencies. Every agency of government at every level (federal, state, and local) must have accountants in order to carry out its responsibilities. Universities, hospitals, churches, and other not-for-profit institutions also follow a pattern of accounting that is similar to governmental accounting.

Internal Revenue Service. One of the governmental agencies which perform extensive accounting work is the Internal Revenue Service (IRS). The IRS handles the millions of income tax returns filed by individuals and corporations, and frequently performs auditing functions relating to these income tax returns and the accounting records on which they are based.

Securities and Exchange Commission. Another governmental agency deeply involved in accounting is the Securities and Exchange Commission (SEC). The SEC establishes requirements regarding the content of financial statements and the reporting standards to be followed. All corporations which offer securities for sale to the public must file annually with the SEC audited financial statements meeting these requirements.

Generally accepted accounting principles (GAAP)

3 Explain the phrase "generally accepted accounting principles."

To understand financial statements, one must first understand generally accepted accounting principles. These are the "ground rules," developed over a long span of years by the accounting profession. The purpose of these broad basic rules is *to guide* accountants in measuring and reporting the financial events that make up the life of a business. Briefly stated, generally accepted accounting principles are the accounting standards and concepts used in the measurement of financial activities and the preparation of financial statements.

If accountants consistently prepare financial statements in conformity with generally accepted accounting principles, then the current year's financial statements can be compared fairly with prior years' statements, and with the financial statements of other companies. When financial statements are comparable because they are all prepared under the same rules, then investors, bankers, and financial analysts can make better decisions in allocating capital to the most promising companies. The efficient allocation of capital is essential to the successful working of our national economy. To summarize, we need a well-defined body of accounting principles to guide accountants in preparing financial statements that are reliable, understandable, and comparable.

In this chapter we will discuss five generally accepted accounting principles: the business entity concept, the cost principle, the going-concern assumption, the objectivity principle, and the stable-dollar assumption. These and other generally accepted accounting principles will be considered further at many points throughout this book.

Development of generally accepted accounting principles — the FASB

4 Explain the function of the FASB.

Research to develop accounting principles which will keep pace with changes in the economic and political environment is a major activity of professional accountants and accounting educators. In the United States four groups which have been influential in the improvement of financial reporting and accounting practices are the Financial Accounting Standards Board, the American Institute of Certified Public Accountants, the Securities and Exchange Commission, and the American Accounting Association.

Of special importance in establishing generally accepted accounting principles is the Financial Accounting Standards Board, known as the FASB. The FASB consists of seven full-time members, including representatives from public accounting, industry, and accounting education. In addition to conducting extensive research, the FASB issues *Statements of Financial Accounting Standards,* which represent authoritative expressions of generally accepted accounting principles.

Note that the FASB is part of the private sector of the economy and not a government agency. The development of accounting standards in the United States has traditionally been carried on in the private sector although the government, acting through the SEC, has exercised great influence on the FASB and other groups concerned with accounting research and standards of financial reporting.

The contribution of the FASB and the other groups mentioned above will be considered in later chapters. At this point we merely want to emphasize that accounting is not a closed system or a fixed set of rules, but a constantly evolving body of knowledge. As we explore accounting principles and related practices in this book, you will become aware of certain problems and conflicts for which fully satisfactory answers are yet to be developed. The need for further research is apparent despite the fact that present-day American accounting practices and standards of financial reporting are by far the best achieved anywhere at any time.

Profitability and solvency: key financial objectives

5 State two basic financial objectives of every profit-oriented business. The management of every business must keep foremost in its thinking two primary objectives. The first is to earn a profit. The second is to stay solvent, that is, to have on hand sufficient cash to pay debts as they fall due. Profits and solvency, of course, are not the only objectives of business managers. There are many others, such as providing jobs for people, protecting the environment, creating new and improved products, and providing more goods and services at a lower cost. It is clear, however, that a business cannot hope to accomplish these objectives unless it meets the two basic tests of survival — operating profitably and staying solvent.

A business is a collection of resources committed by an individual or group of individuals, who hope that the investment will increase in value. Investment in any given business, however, is only one of a number of alternative investments available. If a business does not earn as great a profit as might be obtained from alternative investments, its owners will be well-advised to sell or terminate the business and invest elsewhere. A business that continually operates at a loss will eventually exhaust its resources and be forced out of existence. Therefore, in order to operate successfully and to survive, the owners or managers of an enterprise must direct the business in such a way that it will earn a reasonable profit.

Business concerns that have sufficient cash to pay their debts promptly are said to be *solvent.* In contrast, a company that finds itself unable to meet its obligations as they fall due is called *insolvent.* Solvency must be ranked as a primary objective of any enterprise, because a business that becomes insolvent may be forced by its creditors to stop operations and end its existence.

Accounting as the basis for business decisions

How do business executives know whether a company is earning profits or incurring losses? How do they know whether the company is solvent or insolvent, and whether it probably will be solvent, say, a month from today? The answer to both these questions in one word is *accounting.* Accounting is the process by which the profitability and solvency of a company can be measured. Accounting also provides information needed as a basis for making business decisions that will enable management to guide the company on a profitable and solvent course.

For specific examples of these decisions, consider the following questions. What prices should the firm set on its products? If production is increased, what effect will this have on the cost of each unit produced? Will it be necessary to borrow from the bank? How much will costs increase if a pension plan is established for employees? Is it more profitable to produce and sell product A or product B? Should an investment be made in new equipment? All these issues call for decisions that should depend, in part at least, upon accounting information. It might be reasonable to turn the question around and ask: What business decisions could be made intelligently *without* the use of accounting information? Examples would be hard to find.

We have already stressed that accounting is a means of measuring the results of business transactions and of communicating financial information. In addition, the accounting system must provide the decision maker with *predictive information* for making important business decisions in a changing environment.

Internal control

Business decisions of all types are based at least in part upon accounting information. Management needs assurance that the accounting information it receives is accurate and reliable. This assurance comes from the company's *system of internal control.*

A system of internal control consists of all the measures taken by an organization for the purposes of (1) protecting its resources against waste, fraud, and inefficiency; (2) ensuring accuracy and reliability in accounting and operating data; (3) securing compliance with company policies; and (4) evaluating the level of performance in all divisions of the company. In short, a system of internal control includes all of the measures designed to assure management that the entire business operates according to plan.

In performing an audit of financial statements, CPAs always study and evaluate the company's system of internal control. The stronger the system of internal control, the more confidence the CPAs can place in the reliability of the financial statements and accounting records.

A basic principle of internal control is that no one person should handle all phases of a transaction from beginning to end. When business operations are so organized that two or more employees are required to participate in every transaction, the possibility of fraud is reduced and the work of one employee gives assurance of the accuracy of the work of another. The principal reason for many business documents and accounting procedures is to achieve strong internal control. Therefore, we shall discuss various internal control concepts and requirements throughout our study of accounting.

Forms of business organization

A business enterprise may be organized as a *single proprietorship,* a *partnership,* or a *corporation.*

Single proprietorship. A business owned by one person is called a single proprietorship. Often the owner also acts as the manager. This form of business organization is common for small retail stores and service enterprises, for farms, and for professional practices in law, medicine, and public accounting. The owner is personally liable for all debts incurred by the business. From an accounting viewpoint, however, the business is an entity separate from the proprietor.

Partnership. A business owned by two or more persons voluntarily associated as partners is called a partnership. Partnerships, like single proprietorships, are widely used for small businesses and professional practices. As in the case of a single proprietorship, a partnership is not legally an entity separate from its owners; consequently, a partner is personally responsible for the debts of the partnership. From an accounting standpoint, however, a partnership is a business entity separate from the personal activities of the partners.

Corporation. A business organized as a separate legal entity with ownership divided into transferable shares of capital stock is called a corporation. Capital stock certificates are issued by the corporation to each stockholder showing the number of shares he or she owns. The stockholders are free to sell all or part of these shares to other investors at any time, and this ease of transfer adds to the attractiveness of investing in a corporation.

Persons wanting to form a new corporation must file an application with state officials for a corporate charter. When this application has been approved, the corporation comes into existence as a *legal entity* separate from its owners. The important role of the corporation in our economy is based on such advantages as the ease of gathering large amounts of money, transferability of shares in ownership, limited liability of owners, and continuity of existence. In this book we shall use the corporate form of organization as our basic model, along with some specific references to single proprietorships and partnerships.

FINANCIAL STATEMENTS: THE STARTING POINT IN THE STUDY OF ACCOUNTING

The preparation of financial statements is not the first step in the accounting process, but it is a convenient point to begin the study of accounting. The financial statements convey to management and to interested outsiders a concise picture of the profitability and financial position of the business. Since these financial statements are in a sense the end product of the accounting process, the student who acquires a clear understanding of the content and meaning of financial statements will be in an excellent position to appreciate the purpose of the earlier steps of recording and classifying business transactions.

The two most widely used financial statements are the **balance sheet** and the **income statement.**[1] Together, these two statements (perhaps a page each in length) summarize all the information contained in the hundreds or thousands of pages comprising the detailed accounting records of a business. In this introductory chapter and in Chapter 2, we shall explore the nature of the balance sheet, or statement of financial position, as it is sometimes called. Once we have become familiar with the form and arrangement of the balance sheet and with the meaning of technical terms such as **assets, liabilities,** and **owners' equity,** it will be as easy to read and understand a report on the financial position of a business as it is for an architect to read the blueprint of a proposed building. (We shall discuss the income statement in Chapter 3.)

The balance sheet

6 Describe a balance sheet; define assets, liabilities, and owners' equity.

The purpose of a balance sheet is to show the financial position of a business **at a particular date.** Every business prepares a balance sheet at the end of the year, and most companies prepare one at the end of each month. A balance sheet consists of a listing of the assets and liabilities of a business and of the owners' equity. The following balance sheet portrays the financial position of Vagabond Travel Agency, Inc., at December 31.

VAGABOND TRAVEL AGENCY, INC.
Balance Sheet
December 31, 19___

Balance sheet shows financial position at a specific date

Assets		Liabilities & Stockholders' Equity		
Cash	$ 40,500	Liabilities:		
Notes receivable	50,000	Notes payable	$ 26,000	
Accounts receivable	62,500	Accounts payable	36,000	
Supplies	2,000	Income taxes payable	18,000	
Land	100,000	Total liabilities	$ 80,000	
Building	90,000	Stockholders' equity:		
Office equipment	5,000	Capital stock	$225,000	
		Retained earnings	45,000	270,000
Total	$350,000	Total		$350,000

[1] A third financial statement, called a **statement of cash flows,** will be discussed later.

Note that the balance sheet sets forth in its heading three items: (1) the name of the business, (2) the name of the financial statement "Balance Sheet," and (3) the date of the balance sheet. Below the heading is the body of the balance sheet, which consists of three distinct sections: assets, liabilities, and stockholders' equity. The remainder of this chapter is largely devoted to making clear the nature of these three sections.

Another point to note about the form of a balance sheet is that cash is always the first asset listed; it is followed by receivables, supplies, and any other assets that will soon be converted into cash or consumed in operations. Following these items are the more permanent assets, such as land, buildings, and equipment.

The liabilities of a business are always listed before the owners' equity. Each type of liability (such as notes payable, accounts payable, and income taxes payable) should be listed separately, followed by a total figure for liabilities.

The concept of the business entity

The illustrated balance sheet refers only to the financial affairs of the business entity known as Vagabond Travel Agency, Inc., and not to the personal financial affairs of the owners. Individual stockholders may have personal bank accounts, homes, automobiles, and investments in other businesses; but since these personal belongings are not part of the travel agency business, they are not included in the balance sheet of this business unit.

In brief, *a business entity is an economic unit which enters into business transactions that must be recorded, summarized, and reported. The entity is regarded as separate from its owner or owners;* the entity owns its own property and has its own debts. Consequently, for each business entity, there should be a separate set of accounting records.

Assets

Assets are economic resources which are owned by a business and are expected to benefit future operations. Assets may have definite physical form such as buildings, machinery, or merchandise. On the other hand, some assets exist not in physical or tangible form, but in the form of valuable legal claims or rights; examples are amounts due from customers, investments in government bonds, and patent rights.

One of the most basic and at the same time most controversial problems in accounting is determining the dollar values for the various assets of a business. At present, generally accepted accounting principles call for the valuation of assets in a balance sheet at *cost,* rather than at appraised market values. The specific accounting principles supporting cost as the basis for asset valuation are discussed below.

7 Discuss the accounting principles involved in asset valuation.

The cost principle. Assets such as land, buildings, merchandise, and equipment are typical of the many economic resources that will be used in producing income for the business. The prevailing accounting view is that such assets should be recorded at their cost. When we say that an asset is shown in the balance sheet at its *historical cost,* we mean the dollar amount originally paid to acquire the asset; this amount may be very different from what we would have to pay today to replace it.

For example, let us assume that a business buys a tract of land for use as a building site, paying $100,000 in cash. The amount to be entered in the accounting records as the value of the asset will be the cost of $100,000. If we assume a booming real estate market, a fair estimate of the sales value of the land 10 years later might be $250,000. Although the market price or economic value of the land has risen greatly, the accounting value as shown in the accounting records and on the balance sheet would continue unchanged at the cost of $100,000. This policy of accounting for assets at their cost is often referred to as the *cost principle* of accounting.

In reading a balance sheet, it is important to bear in mind that the dollar amounts listed do not indicate the prices at which the assets could be sold, nor the prices at which they could be replaced. One useful generalization to be drawn from this discussion is that a balance sheet does *not* show "how much a business is worth."

The going-concern assumption. It is appropriate to ask *why* accountants do not change the recorded values of assets to correspond with changing market prices for these properties. One reason is that the land and building being used to house the business were acquired for *use* and not for resale; in fact, these assets cannot be sold without disrupting the business. The balance sheet of a business is prepared on the assumption that the business is a continuing enterprise, a "going concern." Consequently, the present estimated prices at which the land and buildings could be sold are of less importance than if these properties were intended for sale.

The objectivity principle. Another reason for using cost rather than current market values in accounting for assets is the need for a definite, factual basis for valuation. The cost for land, buildings, and many other assets purchased for cash can be rather definitely determined. Accountants use the term *objective* to describe asset valuations that are factual and can be verified by independent experts. For example, if land is shown on the balance sheet at cost, any CPA who performed an audit of the business would be able to find objective evidence that the land was actually valued at the cost incurred in acquiring it. Estimated market values, on the other hand, for assets such as buildings and specialized machinery are not factual and objective. Market values are constantly changing and estimates of the prices at which assets could be sold are largely a matter of personal opinion. Of course at the date an asset is acquired, the cost and market value are usually the same because the bargaining process which results in the sale of an asset serves to establish both the current market value of the property and the cost to the buyer. With the passage of time, however, the current market value of assets is likely to differ considerably from the cost recorded in the owner's accounting records.

The stable-dollar assumption. Severe inflation in several countries in recent years has raised serious doubts as to the adequacy of the conventional cost basis in accounting for assets. When inflation becomes very severe, historical cost values for assets simply lose their relevance as a basis for making business decisions. Much consideration has been given to the use of balance sheets which would show assets at current appraised values or at replacement costs rather than at historical cost.

Accountants in the United States by adhering to the cost basis of accounting are implying that the dollar is a **stable unit of measurement,** as is the gallon, the acre, or the mile. The cost principle and the stable-dollar assumption work very well in periods of stable prices, but are less satisfactory under conditions of rapid inflation. For example, if a company bought land 20 years ago for $100,000 and purchased a second similar tract of land today for $500,000, the total cost of land shown by the accounting records would be $600,000. This treatment ignores the fact that dollars spent 20 years ago had far greater purchasing power than today's dollar. Thus, the $600,000 total for cost of land is a mixture of two kinds of dollars with very different purchasing power.

After much research into this problem, the FASB required on a trial basis that large corporations report supplementary data showing current replacement costs and price-level adjusted data. However, after a few years, the cost of developing and disclosing such information in financial statements was judged to be greater than the benefits provided. Consequently, the disclosure requirement was eliminated. At the present time, the stable-dollar assumption continues in use in the United States — perhaps until challenged by more severe inflation sometime in the future.

Accounting concepts are not as exact and unchanging as many persons assume. To serve the needs of a fast-changing economy, accounting concepts and methods must undergo continuous evolutionary change. As of today, however, the cost basis of valuing assets is still the generally accepted method.

The problem of valuation of assets is one of the most complex in the entire field of accounting. It is merely being introduced at this point; in later chapters we shall explore carefully some of the valuation principles applicable to the major types of assets.

Liabilities

Liabilities are debts. All business concerns have liabilities; even the largest and most successful companies find it convenient to purchase merchandise and supplies on credit rather than to pay cash at the time of each purchase. The liability arising from the purchase of goods or services on credit is called an **account payable,** and the person or company to whom the account payable is owed is called a **creditor.**

A business concern frequently finds it desirable to borrow money as a means of supplementing the funds invested by the owner, thus enabling the business to expand more rapidly. The borrowed funds may, for example, be used to buy merchandise which can be sold at a profit to the firm's customers. Or, the borrowed money might be used to buy new and more efficient machinery, thus enabling the company to turn out a larger volume of products at lower cost. When a business borrows money for any reason, a liability is incurred and the lender becomes a creditor of the business. The form of the liability when money is borrowed is usually a **note payable,** a formal written promise to pay a certain amount of money, plus interest, at a definite future time.

An *account payable,* as contrasted with a *note payable,* does not involve the issuance of a formal written promise to the creditor, and it does not call for payment of interest. When a business has both notes payable and accounts payable, the two types of liabilities are shown separately in the balance sheet, with notes payable usually listed first. A figure showing the total of the liabilities should also be inserted, as shown by the illustrated balance sheet on page 15.

The creditors have claims against the assets of the business, usually not against any particular asset but against the assets in general. The claims of the creditors are liabilities of the business and have priority over the claims of owners. Creditors are entitled to be paid in full even if such payment should exhaust the assets of the business, leaving nothing for the owners.

Owners' equity

The owners' equity in a corporation is called *stockholders' equity.* In the following discussion, we will use the broader term "owners' equity" because the concepts being presented are equally applicable to the ownership equity in corporations, partnerships, and single proprietorships.

The owners' equity in a business represents the resources invested by the owners. The equity of the owners is a *residual claim* because the claims of the creditors legally come first. If you are the owner of a business, you are entitled to whatever remains after the claims of the creditors are fully satisfied. Thus, owners' equity is equal to the total assets minus the liabilities. For example, using the data from the illustrated balance sheet of Vagabond Travel Agency, Inc.:

Vagabond has total assets of..	$350,000
And total liabilities amounting to	80,000
Therefore, the owners' equity must equal......................................	$270,000

Suppose that Vagabond borrows $20,000 from a bank. After recording the additional asset of $20,000 in cash and recording the new liability of $20,000 owed to the bank, we would have the following:

Vagabond now has total assets of...	$370,000
And total liabilities are now..	100,000
Therefore, the owners' equity still is equal to...................................	$270,000

It is apparent that the total assets of the business were increased by the act of borrowing money from a bank, but the increase in total assets was exactly offset by an increase in liabilities, and the owners' equity remained unchanged. The owners' equity in a business *is not increased* by the incurring of liabilities of any kind.

Increases in owners' equity. The owners' equity in a business comes from two sources:

1 Investment by the owners
2 Earnings from profitable operation of the business

Only the first of these two sources of owners' equity is considered in this chapter. The second source, an increase in owners' equity through earnings of the business, will be discussed in Chapter 3.

Decreases in owners' equity. Decreases in owners' equity also are caused in two ways:

1 Distribution of cash or other assets by the business to its owners
2 Losses from unprofitable operation of the business

Both causes of decreases in owners' equity will be considered in Chapter 3.

Owners' equity in corporations and single proprietorships. The ownership equity of a corporation consists of two elements: capital stock and retained earnings, as shown in the following illustration:

For a Corporation

Equity of stockholders . . .

Stockholders' equity:

Capital stock $1,000,000
Retained earnings.   278,000
    Total stockholders' equity $1,278,000

The $1,000,000 shown as *capital stock* represents the amount invested in the business by its owners. The $278,000 of *retained earnings* represents the portion of owners' equity which has been accumulated through profitable operation of the business. The corporation has chosen to retain this $278,000 in the business rather than to distribute these earnings to the stockholders as *dividends.* The total earnings of the corporation may have been considerably more than $278,000, because any earnings which were paid to stockholders as dividends would not appear on the balance sheet. The term *retained earnings* describes only the earnings which were *not* paid out in the form of dividends.

A single proprietorship is not required to maintain a distinction between invested capital and earned capital. Consequently, the balance sheet of a single proprietorship will have only one item in the owners' equity section, as illustrated below:

For a Single Proprietorship

. . . equity of a single proprietor

Owner's equity:

John Smith, capital. $30,000

What is capital stock?

As previously mentioned, the caption *capital stock* in the balance sheet of a corporation represents the amount invested by the owners of the business. When the owners of a corporation invest cash or other assets in the business, the corporation issues in exchange shares of capital stock as evidence of the investor's ownership equity. Thus, the owners of a corporation are termed *stockholders.*

The basic unit of capital stock is called a **share,** but a corporation may issue capital stock certificates in denominations of 1 share, 100 shares, or any other number. The total number of shares of capital stock outstanding at any given time represents 100% ownership of the corporation. Outstanding shares are those in the hands of stockholders. The number of shares owned by an individual investor determines the extent of his or her ownership of the corporation.

Assume, for example, that Draper Corporation issues a total of 5,000 shares of capital stock to investors in exchange for cash. If we assume further that Thomas Draper acquires 500 shares of the 5,000 shares outstanding, we may say that he has a 10% interest in the corporation. Suppose that Draper now sells 200 shares to Evans. The total number of shares outstanding remains unchanged at 5,000, although Draper's percentage of ownership has declined to 6% and a new stockholder, Evans, has acquired a 4% interest in the corporation. The transfer of 200 shares from Draper to Evans had **no effect** upon the corporation's assets, liabilities, or amount of stock outstanding. The only way in which this transfer of stock affects the corporation is that the list of stockholders must be revised to show the number of shares held by each owner.

The accounting equation

A fundamental characteristic of every balance sheet is that the total figure for assets always equals the total of liabilities plus owners' equity. This agreement or balance of total assets with the total of liabilities and owners' equity is one reason for calling this financial statement a **balance sheet.** But **why** do total assets equal total equities? The answer can be given in one short paragraph:

The dollar totals on the two sides of the balance sheet are always equal because these two sides are **merely two views of the same business property.** The listing of assets shows us what things the business owns; the listing of liabilities and owners' equity tells us who supplied these resources to the business and how much each group supplied. Everything that a business owns has been supplied to it by the creditors or by the owners. Therefore, the total claims of the creditors plus the claims of the owners equal the total assets of the business.

The equality of assets on the one hand and of the claims of the creditors and the owners on the other hand is expressed in the equation:

Fundamental accounting equation

$$\text{Assets} = \text{Liabilities} + \text{Owners' Equity}$$
$$\$350,000 = \quad \$80,000 \quad + \$270,000$$

The amounts listed in the equation were taken from the balance sheet illustrated on page 15. A balance sheet is simply a detailed statement of this equation. To emphasize this relationship, compare the balance sheet of Vagabond Travel Agency, Inc., with the above equation.

To emphasize that the owners' equity is a residual element, secondary to the claims of creditors, it is often helpful to transpose the terms of the equation, as follows:

Alternative form of accounting equation

$$\text{Assets} - \text{Liabilities} = \text{Owners' Equity}$$
$$\$350,000 - \quad \$80,000 \quad = \$270,000$$

Every business transaction, no matter how simple or how complex, can be expressed in terms of its effect on the accounting equation. A thorough understanding of the equation and some practice in using it are essential to the student of accounting.

Regardless of whether a business grows or contracts, this equality between the assets and the claims against the assets is always maintained. Any increase in the amount of total assets is necessarily accompanied by an equal increase on the other side of the equation, that is, by an increase in either the liabilities or the owners' equity. Any decrease in total assets is necessarily accompanied by a corresponding decrease in liabilities or owners' equity. The continuing equality of the two sides of the balance sheet can best be illustrated by taking a brand-new business as an example and observing the effects of various transactions upon its balance sheet.

Effects of business transactions upon the balance sheet

8 Indicate the effects of various transactions upon the balance sheet.

Assume that John Green, Susan Green, and R. J. Hill organized a corporation called Greenhill Real Estate. A charter was obtained from the state authorizing the new corporation to issue 18,000 shares of capital stock with a par value of $10 a share.[2] John and Susan Green each invested $72,000 cash and R. J. Hill invested $36,000. The entire authorized capital stock of $180,000 was therefore issued as follows: 7,200 shares to John Green, 7,200 shares to Susan Green, and 3,600 shares to R. J. Hill. The three stockholders each received a stock certificate as evidence of his or her ownership equity in the corporation.

The planned operations of the new business call for obtaining listings of houses and commercial property being offered for sale by property owners, advertising these properties, and showing them to prospective buyers. The listing agreement signed with each property owner provides that Greenhill Real Estate shall receive at the time of sale a commission equal to 6% of the sales price of the property.

The new business was begun on September 1 with the deposit of $180,000 in a bank account in the name of the business, Greenhill Real Estate. The initial balance sheet of the new business then appeared as follows:

GREENHILL REAL ESTATE
Balance Sheet
September 1, 19__

Assets		Stockholders' Equity	
Cash.........................	$180,000	Capital stock	$180,000

Beginning balance sheet of a new business

Purchase of an asset for cash. The next transaction entered into by Greenhill Real Estate was the purchase of land suitable as a site for an office. The price for the

[2] Par value is the amount assigned to each share of stock in accordance with legal requirements. The concept of par value is more fully explained in Chapter 11.

land was $141,000, and payment was made in cash on September 3. The effect of this transaction on the balance sheet was twofold: first, cash was decreased by the amount paid out; and second, a new asset, Land, was acquired. After this exchange of cash for land, the balance sheet appeared as follows:

GREENHILL REAL ESTATE
Balance Sheet
September 3, 19__

Assets		Stockholders' Equity	
Cash	$ 39,000	Capital stock	$180,000
Land	141,000		
Total	$180,000	Total	$180,000

Balance sheet totals unchanged by purchase of land for cash

Purchase of an asset and incurring of a liability. On September 5 an opportunity arose to buy a complete office building which had to be moved to permit the construction of a freeway. A price of $36,000 was agreed upon, which included the cost of moving the building and installing it upon Greenhill Real Estate's lot. As the building was in excellent condition and would have cost approximately $60,000 to build, it was considered a very fortunate purchase.

The terms provided for an immediate cash payment of $15,000 and payment of the balance of $21,000 within 90 days. Cash was decreased $15,000, but a new asset, Building, was recorded at cost in the amount of $36,000. Total assets were thus increased by $21,000, but the total of liabilities and owners' equity was also increased as a result of recording the $21,000 account payable as a liability. After this transaction had been recorded, the balance sheet appeared as follows:

GREENHILL REAL ESTATE
Balance Sheet
September 5, 19__

Assets		Liabilities & Stockholders' Equity	
Cash	$ 24,000	Liabilities:	
Land	141,000	Accounts payable	$ 21,000
Building	36,000	Stockholders' equity:	
		Capital stock	180,000
Total	$201,000	Total	$201,000

Totals increased equally by purchase of building on credit

Note that the building appears in the balance sheet at $36,000, its cost to Greenhill Real Estate. The estimate of $60,000 as the probable cost to construct such a building is irrelevant. Even if someone should offer to buy the building from Greenhill for $60,000 or more, this offer, if refused, would have no bearing on the balance sheet. Accounting records are intended to provide a historical record of *costs actually incurred;* therefore, the $36,000 price at which the building was purchased is the amount to be recorded.

Sale of an asset. After the office building had been moved to Greenhill Real Estate's lot, the company decided that the lot was larger than was needed. The adjoining business, Carter's Drugstore, wanted more room for a parking area; so, on September 10, Greenhill sold a small, unused corner of the lot to Carter's Drugstore for a price of $11,000. Since the selling price was computed at the same amount per foot as the corporation had paid for the land, there was neither a profit nor a loss on the sale. No down payment was required, but it was agreed that the full price would be paid within three months. By this transaction a new asset in the form of an account receivable was acquired, but the asset Land was decreased by the same amount; consequently, there was no change in the amount of total assets. After this transaction, the balance sheet appeared as shown below:

GREENHILL REAL ESTATE
Balance Sheet
September 10, 19__

	Assets		Liabilities & Stockholders' Equity	
No change in totals by sale of land at cost	Cash .... $ 24,000		Liabilities:	
	Accounts receivable 11,000		Accounts payable .... $ 21,000	
	Land 130,000		Stockholders' equity:	
	Building 36,000		Capital stock 180,000	
	Total $201,000		Total $201,000	

In the illustration thus far, Greenhill Real Estate has an account receivable from only one debtor and an account payable to only one creditor. As the business grows, the number of debtors and creditors will increase, but the Accounts Receivable and Accounts Payable accounts will continue to be used. The additional records necessary to show the amount receivable from each debtor and the amount owing to each creditor will be explained in Chapter 6.

Purchase of an asset on credit. A complete set of office furniture and equipment was purchased on credit from General Equipment, Inc., on September 14 for $5,400. As the result of this transaction the business owned a new asset, Office Equipment, but it had also incurred a new liability in the form of Accounts Payable. The increase in total assets was exactly offset by the increase in liabilities. After this transaction the balance sheet appeared as follows:

GREENHILL REAL ESTATE
Balance Sheet
September 14, 19__

	Assets		Liabilities & Stockholders' Equity	
Totals increased by acquiring asset on credit	Cash .... $ 24,000		Liabilities:	
	Accounts receivable 11,000		Accounts payable .... $ 26,400	
	Land 130,000		Stockholders' equity:	
	Building 36,000		Capital stock 180,000	
	Office equipment 5,400			
	Total $206,400		Total $206,400	

Collection of an account receivable. On September 20, cash in the amount of $1,500 was received as partial settlement of the account receivable from Carter's Drugstore. This transaction caused cash to increase and the accounts receivable to decrease by an equal amount. In essence, this transaction was merely the exchange of one asset for another of equal value. Consequently, there was no change in the amount of total assets. After this transaction the balance sheet appeared as follows:

GREENHILL REAL ESTATE
Balance Sheet
September 20, 19__

Totals unchanged by collection of a receivable

Assets		Liabilities & Stockholders' Equity	
Cash	$ 25,500	Liabilities:	
Accounts receivable	9,500	Accounts payable	$ 26,400
Land	130,000	Stockholders' equity:	
Building	36,000	Capital stock	180,000
Office equipment	5,400		
Total	$206,400	Total	$206,400

Payment of a liability. On September 30 Greenhill paid $3,000 in cash to General Equipment, Inc. This payment caused a decrease in cash and an equal decrease in liabilities. Therefore the totals of assets and equities were still in balance. After this transaction, the balance sheet appeared as follows:

GREENHILL REAL ESTATE
Balance Sheet
September 30, 19__

Totals decreased by paying a liability

Assets		Liabilities & Stockholders' Equity	
Cash	$ 22,500	Liabilities:	
Accounts receivable	9,500	Accounts payable	$ 23,400
Land	130,000	Stockholders' equity:	
Building	36,000	Capital stock	180,000
Office equipment	5,400		
Total	$203,400	Total	$203,400

The transactions which have been illustrated for the month of September were merely preliminary to the formal opening for business of Greenhill Real Estate on October 1. During September no sales were arranged by the company and no commissions were earned. Consequently, the stockholders' equity at September 30 is shown in the above balance sheet at $180,000, unchanged from the original investment on September 1. September was a month devoted exclusively to organizing the business and not to regular operations. In succeeding chapters we shall continue the example of Greenhill Real Estate by illustrating operating transactions and considering how the net income of the business can be determined.

Effect of business transactions upon the accounting equation

The balance sheet of a business is merely a detailed expression of the accounting equation, Assets = Liabilities + Owners' Equity. To emphasize the relationship between the accounting equation and the balance sheet, let us now repeat the September transactions of Greenhill Real Estate to show the effect of each transaction upon the accounting equation. Briefly restated, the seven transactions were as follows:

Sept. 1 Issued capital stock in exchange for $180,000 cash invested in the business by the stockholders.

3 Purchased land for $141,000 cash.

5 Purchased a building for $36,000, paying $15,000 cash and incurring a liability of $21,000.

10 Sold part of the land at a price equal to cost of $11,000, collectible within three months.

14 Purchased office equipment on credit for $5,400.

20 Received $1,500 cash as partial collection of the $11,000 account receivable.

30 Paid $3,000 on accounts payable.

The table below shows the effects of each of the September transactions on the accounting equation. The final line in the table corresponds to the amounts in the balance sheet at the end of September. Note that the equality of the two sides of the equation was maintained throughout the recording of the transactions.

	Assets					= Liabilities	+ Owners' Equity
	Cash	+ Accounts Receivable	Land	+ Building	+ Office Equipment	= Accounts Payable	+ Capital Stock
Sept. 1	+$180,000						+$180,000
Sept. 3	−141,000		+$141,000				
Balances	$ 39,000		$141,000				$180,000
Sept. 5	−15,000			+$36,000		+$21,000	
Balances	$ 24,000		$141,000	$36,000		$21,000	$180,000
Sept. 10		+$11,000	−11,000				
Balances	$ 24,000	$11,000	$130,000	$36,000		$21,000	$180,000
Sept. 14					+$5,400	+5,400	
Balances	$ 24,000	$11,000	$130,000	$36,000	$5,400	$26,400	$180,000
Sept. 20	+1,500	−1,500					
Balances	$ 25,500	$ 9,500	$130,000	$36,000	$5,400	$26,400	$180,000
Sept. 30	−3,000					−3,000	
Balances	$ 22,500 +	$ 9,500 +	$130,000 +	$36,000 +	$5,400 =	$23,400 +	$180,000

USE OF FINANCIAL STATEMENTS BY OUTSIDERS

Through careful study of a company's financial statements, an outsider with a knowledge of accounting can gain an understanding of the financial position of the business and become aware of significant changes since the date of the preceding balance sheet. Bear in mind, however, that financial statements have limitations. Only those factors which can be reduced to monetary terms appear in the balance sheet. Let us consider for a moment some important business factors which are not set forth in financial statements. Perhaps a competing store has just opened for business across the street; the prospect of intensified competition in the future will not be described in the balance sheet. As another example, the health, experience, and managerial skills of the key people in the management group are extremely important in the success of a business, but these qualities cannot be measured and expressed in dollars in the balance sheet.

Bankers and other creditors

Bankers who have loaned money to a business or who are considering making such a loan are vitally interested in the balance sheet of the business. By studying the amount and kinds of assets in relation to the amount and payment dates of the liabilities, a banker can form an opinion as to the ability of the business to pay its debts promptly. The banker gives particular attention to the amount of cash and of other assets (such as accounts receivable) which will soon be converted into cash, and then compares the amount of these assets with the amount of liabilities falling due in the near future.

The banker is also interested in the amount of the owners' equity, as this ownership capital serves as a protecting buffer between the banker and any losses which may befall the business. Bankers seldom are willing to make a loan unless the balance sheet and other information concerning the prospective borrower offer reasonable assurance that the loan can and will be repaid promptly at the maturity date.

Another important group making constant use of balance sheets consists of the credit managers of manufacturing and wholesaling firms, who must decide whether prospective customers are to be allowed to buy merchandise on credit. The credit manager, like the banker, studies the balance sheets of customers and prospective customers for the purpose of appraising their debt-paying ability. Credit agencies such as Dun & Bradstreet, Inc., make a business of obtaining financial statements from virtually all business concerns and appraising their debt-paying ability. The conclusions reached by these credit agencies are available to business managers willing to pay for credit reports about prospective customers.

● **CASE IN POINT** ● A recent article in *Business Week* identified the top 100 fastest growing small companies and posed the following question: "What do these companies have in common?" The answer given was "A strong balance sheet."

Owners

The financial statements of corporations listed on the stock exchanges are eagerly awaited by millions of stockholders. A favorable set of financial statements may cause the market price of the company's stock to rise dramatically; an unfavorable set of financial statements may cause the bottom to fall out of the market price. Current dependable financial statements are one of the essential ingredients for successful investment in securities. Of course, financial statements are equally important in a business organized as a single proprietorship or as a partnership. The financial statements tell the owners just how successful the business has been and also summarize in concise form its present financial position.

Others interested in financial information

In addition to owners, managers, bankers, and merchandise creditors, other groups making use of accounting data include financial analysts, governmental agencies, employees, investors, and writers for business periodicals. Some very large corporations have more than a million stockholders; these giant corporations send copies of their annual financial statements to each of these many owners. This wide distribution of financial statements marks an increasing awareness of the impact of corporate activities on all aspects of our lives and of the need for greater disclosure of information about the activities of business corporations.

The purpose of this discussion is to show the extent to which a modern industrial society depends upon accounting. Even more important, however, is a clear understanding at the outset of your study that accounting does not exist just for the sake of keeping a record or in order to fill out income tax returns and various other regulatory reports. These are but auxiliary functions. If you gain an understanding of accounting concepts, you will have acquired an analytical skill essential to the field of professional management. ***The prime and vital purpose of accounting is to aid decision makers in choosing among alternative courses of action.***

END-OF-CHAPTER REVIEW

Summary of chapter learning objectives

1 Define accounting and explain the purpose of an accounting system.

Accounting is the art of measuring, describing, and interpreting economic activity. The purpose of an accounting system is to develop accounting information about an economic entity and communicate this information to decision makers.

2 Describe the work of CPAs and other accountants.

Certified public accountants offer a variety of accounting services to the public for a fee. These services include auditing, income tax services, management advisory services, and small business services. Private accountants, in contrast to CPAs, work for a single company. Their responsibilities include designing accounting systems, cost accounting, financial forecasting, tax work, and internal auditing. Accountants also work for governmental agencies, such as the IRS and the SEC. These governmental accountants perform functions similar to those of private accountants, and also such special functions as auditing income tax returns.

3 Explain the phrase "generally accepted accounting principles."
Generally accepted accounting principles are the concepts, principles, and "ground rules" used in the preparation of financial statements.

4 Explain the function of the FASB.
The Financial Accounting Standards Board issues *Statements of Financial Accounting Standards,* which are authoritative expressions of generally accepted accounting principles. The FASB is a part of the private sector, not a governmental agency.

5 State two basic financial objectives of every profit-oriented business.
Two basic financial objectives of every profit-oriented business are (1) operating profitably, and (2) remaining solvent.

6 Describe a balance sheet; define assets, liabilities, and owners' equity.
A balance sheet is a financial statement showing the assets, liabilities, and owners' equity in a specific business entity. Assets are economic resources owned by the business; liabilities are the debts or financial obligations of the business, and owners' equity is the owners' *residual interest* in the business (equal to the excess of assets over liabilities).

7 Discuss the accounting principles involved in asset valuation.
Most assets are valued in accordance with the *cost principle.* This generally accepted accounting principle indicates that the valuation of assets in a balance sheet should be based upon historical cost, not upon current market value. Two other accounting principles supporting the valuation of assets at cost are the *going-concern assumption* and the *objectivity principle.*

8 Indicate the effects of various transactions upon the balance sheet.
A transaction which increases total assets also must increase either total liabilities or owners' equity. Similarly, a transaction which decreases total assets must decrease either total liabilities or owners' equity. Some transactions increase one asset while decreasing another; such transactions do not change the total amounts of assets, liabilities, or owners' equity.

Key terms introduced or emphasized in chapter 1

Accounting equation. Assets equal liabilities plus owners' equity. $A = L + OE$.

American Institute of Certified Public Accountants (AICPA). The national professional association of certified public accountants (CPAs). Carries on extensive research and is influential in improving accounting standards and practices.

Assets. Economic resources owned by a business which are expected to benefit future operations.

Auditing. The principal activity of a CPA firm. Consists of an independent examination of the accounting records and other evidence relating to a business to support the expression of an impartial expert opinion about the reliability of the financial statements.

Balance sheet. A financial statement which shows the financial position of a business entity by summarizing the assets, liabilities, and owners' equity at a specific date.

Business entity. An economic unit that enters into business transactions. For accounting purposes, the activities of the entity are regarded as separate from those of its owners.

Certificate in Management Accounting (CMA). A designation granted to persons who have demonstrated competence in management accounting by passing an examination and meeting educational requirements.

Certified public accountants (CPAs). Independent professional accountants licensed by a state to offer auditing and accounting services for a fee.

Corporation. A business organized as a separate legal entity and chartered by a state, with ownership divided into transferable shares of capital stock.

Cost principle. The widely used concept of valuing assets for accounting purposes at their original cost to the business.

Dividend. A distribution of cash by a corporation to its stockholders.

Financial accounting. The area of accounting which emphasizes measuring and reporting the financial position and operating results of a business entity in conformity with generally accepted accounting principles.

Financial Accounting Standards Board (FASB). An independent group which conducts research in accounting and issues authoritative statements as to proper accounting principles and methods for reporting financial information.

Financial statements. Reports which summarize the financial position and operating results of a business (balance sheet and income statement).

Generally accepted accounting principles (GAAP). The accounting concepts, measurement techniques, and standards of presentation used in financial statements. Examples include the cost principle, the going-concern assumption, and the objectivity principle.

Going-concern assumption. An assumption by accountants that a business will continue to operate indefinitely unless specific evidence to the contrary exists, as, for example, impending bankruptcy.

Internal control. All measures used by a business to guard against errors, waste, and fraud; to assure the reliability of accounting data; to promote compliance with all company policies; and to evaluate the level of performance in all divisions of the company.

Liabilities. Debts or obligations of a business. The claims of creditors against the assets of a business.

Management accounting. The area of accounting which emphasizes developing and interpreting accounting information relevant to specific managerial decisions.

Owners' equity. The excess of assets over liabilities. The amount of the owners' investment in a business plus profits from successful operations which have been retained in the business.

Partnership. A business owned by two or more persons voluntarily associated as partners.

Retained earnings. That portion of stockholders' equity resulting from profits which have been retained in the business rather than distributed as dividends.

Securities and Exchange Commission (SEC). A governmental agency which reviews the financial statements and other reports of corporations which offer securities for sale to the public. Works closely with the FASB and the AICPA to improve financial reporting practices.

Single proprietorship. An unincorporated business owned by one person.

Solvency. Having enough money to pay debts as they fall due.

Stockholders' equity. The owners' equity in a corporation.

Transactions. Business events which can be measured in money and which are entered in accounting records.

Demonstration problem for your review

The accounting data (listed alphabetically) for Crystal Auto Wash at September 30, 19__, are shown below. The figure for Cash is not given but it can be determined when all the available information is assembled in the form of a balance sheet.

Accounts payable...............	$14,000	Land	$68,000
Accounts receivable.............	800	Machinery & equipment	65,000
Buildings	52,000	Notes payable	29,000
Capital stock	50,000	Retained earnings..............	99,400
Cash...........................	?	Supplies	400
Income taxes payable	3,000		

Instructions. Prepare a balance sheet at September 30, 19__.

Solution to demonstration problem

CRYSTAL AUTO WASH
Balance Sheet
September 30, 19__

Assets		Liabilities & Stockholders' Equity		
Cash.........................	$ 9,200	Liabilities:		
Accounts receivable............	800	Notes payable		$ 29,000
Supplies......................	400	Accounts payable		14,000
Land	68,000	Income taxes payable.........		3,000
Buildings	52,000	Total liabilities		$ 46,000
Machinery & equipment	65,000	Stockholders' equity:		
		Capital stock........	$50,000	
		Retained earnings ...	99,400	149,400
Total	$195,400	Total		$195,400

ASSIGNMENT MATERIAL

Review questions

1 In broad general terms, what is the purpose of accounting?

2 Why is a knowledge of accounting terms and concepts useful to persons other than professional accountants?

3 What is meant by the term **business transaction?**

4 What are financial statements and how do they relate to the accounting system?

5 Explain briefly why each of the following groups is interested in the financial statements of a business:
a Creditors
b Potential investors
c Labor unions

6 Distinguish between **accounting** and **bookkeeping.**

7 What is the principal function of certified public accountants? What other services are commonly rendered by CPA firms?

8 Private accounting includes a number of subfields or specialized phases, of which cost accounting is one. Name three other such specialized phases of private accounting.

9 The following questions relate to the term, **generally accepted accounting principles:**
   a What type of accounting reports should be prepared in conformity with these principles?
   b Why is it important for these principles to be widely recognized?
   c Where do these principles come from?
   d List two examples of generally accepted accounting principles which relate to the valuation of assets.

10 Is the Financial Accounting Standards Board (FASB) a government agency? What is its principal function?

11 One primary objective of every business is to operate profitably. What other primary objective must be met for a business to survive? Explain.

12 Information available from the accounting records provides a basis for making many business decisions. List several examples of business decisions requiring the use of accounting information.

13 What are the objectives of a company's system of internal control?

14 State briefly the purpose of a balance sheet.

15 Define assets. List several examples.

16 Define liabilities. List several examples.

17 Ray Company was offered $300,000 cash for the land and buildings occupied by the business. These assets had been acquired five years ago at a price of $200,000. Ray Company refused the offer, but is inclined to increase the land and buildings to a total valuation of $300,000 in the balance sheet in order to show more accurately "how much the business is worth." Do you agree? Explain.

18 Explain briefly the concept of the **business entity.**

19 State the accounting equation in two alternative forms.

20 The owners' equity in a business arises from what two sources?

21 Why are the total assets shown on a balance sheet always equal to the total of the liabilities and the owners' equity?

22 Can a business transaction cause one asset to increase or decrease without affecting any other asset, liability, or the owners' equity?

23 If a transaction causes total liabilities to decrease but does not affect the owners' equity, what change, if any, will occur in total assets?

24 Give examples of transactions that would:
   a Cause one asset to increase and another asset to decrease without any effect on the liabilities or owners' equity.
   b Cause both total assets and total liabilities to increase without any effect on the owners' equity.

Exercises

Exercise 1-1
Accounting terminology

Listed below are nine technical accounting terms introduced in this chapter.

Objectivity	Solvent	Audit
GAAP	Liabilities	Internal control
Retained earnings	FASB	Owners' equity

Each of the following statements may (or may not) describe one of these technical terms. For each statement, indicate the accounting term described, or answer "None" if the statement does not describe correctly any of the terms.

a A residual amount equal to total assets minus total liabilities.
b Unable to pay debts as they come due.
c The "ground rules" for presenting accounting information in financial statements.
d A government agency with authority to set requirements as to the content of financial statements and the reporting standards used by corporations offering securities for sale to the public.
e A system comprising all the measures designed to assure management that the entire business operates according to plan.
f An organization in the private sector of the economy which conducts accounting research and issues authoritative statements on generally accepted accounting principles.
g A term relating to asset valuations that are factual and can be verified by independent experts.

Exercise 1-2
Preparing a balance sheet

The following balance sheet of Golden Parachute is incorrect because of improper headings and the misplacement of several accounts. Prepare a corrected balance sheet.

GOLDEN PARACHUTE
August 31, 19__

Assets		Owners' Equity	
Capital stock	$ 50,000	Accounts receivable............	$ 37,800
Cash.........................	10,900	Notes payable	75,600
Building	48,200	Supplies......................	1,400
Automobiles..................	16,500	Land	27,000
Retained earnings.............	16,200		
Total	$141,800	Total	$141,800

(handwritten note in margin: Payable key to liability)

Exercise 1-3
Preparing a balance sheet

The items included in the balance sheet of Coin Machines at December 31, 19__, are listed below in random order. You are to prepare a balance sheet (including a complete heading). Arrange the assets in the sequence shown in the balance sheet illustrated on page 15 and include a figure for total liabilities. You must compute the amount for capital stock.

Land	$95,000	Office equipment...............	$ 3,400
Accounts payable	14,600	Building	70,000
Accounts receivable............	18,900	Cash..........................	12,100
Capital stock	?	Notes payable	70,000
Retained earnings..............	24,800		

Exercise 1-4
Using the accounting equation

Compute the missing amount in each of the following:

	Assets	=	Liabilities	+	Owners' Equity
a	$195,000		$114,000		? *81,000*
b	?		69,000		$ 50,000 *119,000*
c	410,000		?		202,000 *101,000*

(handwritten answers: 81,000; 119,000; 101,000)

Exercise 1-5
Using the
accounting
equation

a The assets of Atom Company total $235,000 and the owners' equity amounts to $70,000. What is the amount of the liabilities? $165,000

b The owners' equity of Party Game Corp. appears on the balance sheet as $95,000 and is equal to one-third the amount of total assets. What is the amount of liabilities? $290,000

c The assets of Hot Line Phones amounted to $75,000 on December 31, 1990 but increased to $105,000 by December 31, 1991. During this same period, liabilities increased by $25,000. The owners' equity at December 31, 1990 amounted to $50,000. What was the amount of owners' equity at December 31, 1991? Explain the basis for your answer.

Exercise 1-6
Effects of
business
transactions

For each of the following categories, state concisely a transaction that will have the required effect on elements of the accounting equation.

a Increase an asset and increase a liability.
b Decrease an asset and decrease a liability.
c Increase one asset and decrease another asset.
d Increase an asset and increase owners' equity.
e Increase one asset, decrease another asset, and increase a liability.

Exercise 1-7
Effects of
business
transactions

Several business transactions of Pizza Parlor are listed below:

a Issued capital stock in exchange for cash.
b Purchased a pizza oven for cash.
c Purchased a delivery truck at a price of $12,000, terms $1,500 cash and the balance payable in 24 equal monthly installments.
d Paid a liability.
e Borrowed money from a bank.
f Sold land for cash at a price equal to its cost.
g Sold land for cash at a price in excess of its cost.
h Sold land for cash at a price less than its cost.
i Collected an account receivable.

Indicate the effects of each of these transactions upon the total amounts of the company's assets, liabilities, and owners' equity. Organize your answer in tabular form, using the column headings shown below and the symbols + for increase, − for decrease, and NE for no effect. The answer for transaction (a) is provided as an example:

Transaction	Assets	Liabilities	Owners' Equity
(a)	+	NE	+

Exercise 1-8
Effects of
business transac-
tions on total
assets

The following transactions represent part of the activities of Moon Corporation for the first month of its existence. Indicate the effect of each transaction upon the total assets of the business by use of the appropriate phrase: "increase total assets," "decrease total assets," "no change in total assets."

a Issued capital stock in exchange for cash.
b Purchased a typewriter for cash.
c Purchased a delivery truck at a price of $12,000, terms $2,000 cash and the balance payable in 24 equal monthly installments.
d Paid a liability.
e Borrowed money from a bank.
f Sold land for cash at a price equal to its cost.
g Sold land on account (on credit) at a price equal to its cost.

     h Sold land for cash at a price in excess of its cost.
     i Sold land for cash at a price less than its cost.
     j Collected an account receivable.

Problems

Problem 1-1
Preparing a balance sheet, computing retained earnings

Listed below in random order are the items to be included in the balance sheet of Mystery Mountain Lodge at December 31, 19__ .

Accounts receivable............	$ 6,200	Furnishings	$ 47,800
Cash........................	27,900	Snowmobiles.................	15,700
Income taxes payable	5,800	Notes payable	242,000
Accounts payable.............	51,600	Equipment	18,400
Capital stock	180,000	Land	140,000
Buildings	296,000	Retained earnings.............	?

Instructions. You are to prepare a balance sheet at December 31, 19__, using a sequence for assets similar to the illustrated balance sheet on page 15. (After "Building," you may list the remaining assets in any order.) Include a proper heading and a figure for total liabilities. The amount for Retained Earnings must be computed. Remember that the figure for total assets should appear on the same line as the amount for the total of liabilities and stockholders' equity.

Problem 1-2
Preparing a balance sheet; effects of a change in assets

¡HERE COME THE CLOWNS! is the name of a traveling circus. The ledger accounts of the business at June 30 are listed below in alphabetical order.

Accounts payable..............	$17,400	Notes payable	$120,000
Accounts receivable............	8,900	Notes receivable..............	2,400
Animals......................	56,040	Props and equipment...........	39,720
Cages........................	16,420	Retained earnings.............	75,100
Capital stock	50,000	Salaries payable	6,500
Cash.........................	?	Tents........................	42,000
Costumes.....................	11,280	Trucks & wagons	70,560

Instructions

    a Prepare a balance sheet by using these items and computing the amount of cash at June 30. Organize your balance sheet similar to the one illustrated on page 15. (After "Accounts Receivable," you may list the remaining assets in any order.) Include a proper balance sheet heading.

    b Assume that late in the evening of June 30, after your balance sheet had been prepared, a fire destroyed one of the tents, which had cost $11,200. The tent was not insured. Explain what changes would be required in your June 30 balance sheet to reflect the loss of this asset.

Problem 1-3
Explaining effects of business transactions

Five selected transactions of Cannon Corporation are summarized in the table below. The effect of each transaction upon the accounting equation is shown, and also the new balance of each item in the equation. For each of the transactions (a) through (e), you are to write a sentence explaining the nature of the transaction. For example, the explanation of transaction (a) could be as follows: Received $1,500 cash from collection of accounts receivable.

		Assets				=	Liabilities	+	Owners' Equity
	Cash +	Accounts Receivable +	Land +	Building +	Office Equipment =		Accounts Payable +		Capital Stock
Balances	$3,000	$9,000	$35,000	$55,000	$3,000		$12,000		$93,000
(a)	+1,500	−1,500							
Balances	$4,500	$7,500	$35,000	$55,000	$3,000		$12,000		$93,000
(b)					+800		+800		
Balances	$4,500	$7,500	$35,000	$55,000	$3,800		$12,800		$93,000
(c)	−1,200						−1,200		
Balances	$3,300	$7,500	$35,000	$55,000	$3,800		$11,600		$93,000
(d)	−300				+900		+600		
Balances	$3,000	$7,500	$35,000	$55,000	$4,700		$12,200		$93,000
(e)	+5,000								+5,000
Balances	$8,000 +	$7,500	+ $35,000 +	$55,000 +	$4,700 =		$12,200 +		$98,000

Problem 1-4
Recording effects
of business
transactions
The items making up the balance sheet of Travel Connection, Inc., at December 31 are listed below in tabular form similar to the illustration of the accounting equation on page 26.

		Assets			=	Liabilities		+	Owners' Equity
	Cash +	Accounts Receivable +	Automobiles +	Office Equipment =	Notes Payable +	Accounts Payable +			Capital Stock
Balances	$9,500	$58,400	$9,000	$3,800	$20,000	$25,200			$35,500

During a short period after December 31, Travel Connection had the following transactions:

(1) Bought office equipment at a cost of $5,700. Paid cash.
(2) Collected $4,000 of accounts receivable.
(3) Paid $1,200 of accounts payable.
(4) Borrowed $10,000 from a bank. Signed a note payable for that amount.
(5) Purchased an automobile for $10,500. Paid $3,000 cash and signed a note payable for the balance of $7,500.

Instructions

a List the December 31 balances of assets, liabilities, and owners' equity in tabular form as shown above.
b Record the effects of each of the five transactions in the tabular arrangement illustrated above. Show the totals for all columns after each transaction.

Problem 1-5
Preparing a
balance sheet;
effects of business
transactions

The balance sheet items for Gremlin Auto Wash (arranged in alphabetical order) were as follows at August 1, 19__ :

Accounts payable	$ 4,000	Equipment	$26,000
Accounts receivable	300	Land	40,000
Building	20,000	Notes payable	46,000
Capital stock	25,000	Retained earnings	18,700
Cash	4,600	Supplies	2,800

During the next two days, the following transactions occurred:

Aug. 2 Issued 7,500 shares of $2 par value capital stock in exchange for $15,000 cash.
　　3 Equipment was purchased at a cost of $9,000 to be paid within 10 days. Supplies were purchased for $500 cash from another car-washing concern which was going out of business. These supplies would have cost $900 if purchased through normal channels.

Instructions

a Prepare a balance sheet at August 1, 19__ . Include a proper heading.
b Prepare a balance sheet at August 3, 19__ . Include a proper heading.

Problem 1-6
Preparing a bal-
ance sheet for a
single proprietor-
ship; discussion
of accounting
principles

Hollywood Scripts is a service-type enterprise in the entertainment field, and its owner, Bradford Jones, has only a limited knowledge of accounting. Jones prepared the balance sheet below, which, although arranged satisfactorily, contains certain errors with respect to such concepts as the business entity and asset valuation. Note that Hollywood Scripts is a *single proprietorship.*

HOLLYWOOD SCRIPTS
Balance Sheet
November 30, 19__

Assets		Liabilities & Owner's Equity	
Cash	$　940	Notes payable	$ 67,000
Notes receivable	2,900	Accounts payable	29,800
Accounts receivable	2,465	Total liabilities	$ 96,800
Land	70,000	Owner's equity:	
Building	54,326	Bradford Jones, capital	63,080
Office furniture	6,848		
Other assets	22,401		
Total	$159,880	Total	$159,880

In discussion with Jones and by inspection of the accounting records, you discover the following facts:

(1) One of the notes receivable in the amount of $700 is an IOU which Jones received in a poker game about two years ago. The IOU bears only the initials B.K. and Jones does not know the name or address of the maker.
(2) Office furniture includes an antique desk purchased November 29 of the current year at a cost of $2,100. Jones explains that no payment is due for the desk until January and therefore this debt is not included among the liabilities.
(3) Also included in the amount for office furniture is a typewriter which cost $525 but is not on hand, because Jones gave it to a son as a birthday present.

(4) The "Other assets" of $22,401 represents the total amount of income taxes Jones has paid the federal government over a period of years. Jones believes the income tax law to be unconstitutional, and a friend who attends law school will help Jones recover the taxes paid as soon as he completes his legal education.

(5) The asset land was acquired at a cost of $34,000, but was increased to a valuation of $70,000 when a friend of Jones offered to pay that much for it if Jones would move the building off the lot.

Instructions

a Prepare a corrected balance sheet at November 30, 19__ .

b For each of the five numbered items above, use a separate numbered paragraph to explain whether the treatment followed by Jones is in accordance with generally accepted accounting principles.

Problem 1-7
Preparing a balance sheet; discussion of accounting principles

Mary McBryan is the founder and manager of Old Town Playhouse. The business, which is organized as a corporation, needs to obtain a bank loan to finance the production of its next play. As part of the loan application, McBryan was asked to prepare a balance sheet for the business. She prepared the following balance sheet, which is arranged correctly, but contains several errors with respect to such concepts as the business entity and the valuation of assets, liabilities, and owners' equity.

OLD TOWN PLAYHOUSE
Balance Sheet
September 30, 19__

Assets		Liabilities & Stockholders' Equity		
Cash	$ 18,600	Liabilities:		
Accounts receivable	156,200	Accounts payable		$ 4,600
Props and costumes	1,800	Salaries payable		28,200
Theater building	13,500	Total liabilities		$32,800
Lighting equipment	8,500	Stockholders' equity:		
Automobile	12,000	Capital stock	$10,000	
		Retained earnings	20,000	30,000
Total	$210,600	Total		$62,800

In discussions with McBryan and by reviewing the accounting records of Old Town Playhouse, you discover the following facts:

(1) The amount of cash, $18,600, includes $12,000 in the company's bank account, $2,100 on hand in the company's safe, and $4,500 in McBryan's personal savings account.

(2) Accounts receivable include $6,200 owed to the business by Artistic Tours. The remaining $150,000 is McBryan's estimate of future ticket sales from September 30 through the end of the year (December 31).

(3) McBryan explains that the props and costumes were purchased several days ago for $14,800. The business paid $1,800 of this amount in cash and issued a note payable to Actors' Supply Co. for the remainder of the purchase price ($13,000). As this note will not be paid until January of next year, it was not included among the company's liabilities.

(4) Old Town Playhouse rents the theater building from Kievits International at a rate of $1,500 per month. The $13,500 represents the rent paid through September 30 of the current year. Kievits International acquired the building seven years ago at a cost of $126,000.

(5) The lighting equipment was purchased on September 26 at a cost of $8,500, but the stage manager says that it isn't worth a nickel.

(6) The automobile is McBryan's personal car, a 1979 Jaguar XJ12, which she purchased two years ago for $9,600. She recently saw a similar car advertised for sale at $12,000. She does not use the car in the business, but it has a personalized license plate which reads "PLAHOUS."

(7) The accounts payable include business debts of $3,700 and the $900 balance of McBryan's personal Visa card.

(8) Salaries payable includes $25,000 offered to Mario Dane to play the lead role in a new play opening next December and also $3,200 still owed to stage hands for work done through September 30.

(9) When McBryan founded Old Town Playhouse several years ago, she invested $10,000 in exchange for 20,000 shares of capital stock. She is unsure of the meaning of the term, "retained earnings." However, Live Theatre, Inc., recently offered to buy her business for $30,000. Therefore, she listed the $20,000 difference between this offer and the amount of her original investment as retained earnings.

Instructions

a Prepare a corrected balance sheet for Old Town Playhouse at September 30, 19___ . You will have to compute the amount of retained earnings necessary to bring the total of liabilities and stockholders' equity into agreement with total assets.

b For each of the nine numbered items above, explain your reasoning in deciding whether or not to include the items in the balance sheet and in determining the proper dollar valuation.

Business decision cases

Case 1-1
Using a balance sheet in business decisions

Sun Corporation and Terra Corporation are in the same line of business and both were recently organized, so it may be assumed that the recorded costs for assets are close to current market values. The balance sheets for the two companies are as follows at July 31, 19___ :

SUN CORPORATION
Balance Sheet
July 31, 19___

Assets		Liabilities & Stockholders' Equity		
Cash.........................	$ 18,000	Liabilities:		
Accounts receivable	26,000	Notes payable (due in		
Land........................	37,200	60 days)..................		$ 12,400
Building	38,000	Accounts payable...........		9,600
Office equipment	1,200	Total liabilities............		$ 22,000
		Stockholders' equity:		
		Capital stock	$60,000	
		Retained earnings..	38,400	98,400
Total.......................	$120,400	Total.......................		$120,400

TERRA CORPORATION

Balance Sheet

July 31, 19___

Assets		Liabilities & Stockholders' Equity		
		Liabilities:		
Cash.......................	$ 4,800	Notes payable (due in		
Accounts receivable	9,600	60 days).................		$ 22,400
Land.......................	96,000	Accounts payable...........		43,200
Building	60,000	Total liabilities............		$ 65,600
Office equipment	12,000	**Stockholders' equity:**		
		Capital stock	$72,000	
		Retained earnings..	44,800	116,800
Total.......................	$182,400	Total.......................		$182,400

Instructions

a Assume that you are a banker and that each company had applied to you for a 90-day loan of $12,000. Which would you consider to be the more favorable prospect? Explain your answer fully.

b Assume that you are an investor considering purchasing all the capital stock of one or both of the companies. For which business would you be willing to pay the higher price? Do you see any indication of a financial crisis which you might face shortly after buying either company? Explain your answer fully. (It is recognized that for either decision, additional information would be useful, but you are to reach your decision on the basis of the information available.)

Case 1-2
Preparing a
balance sheet for
a corporation;
discussion of
accounting
principles

Linda Shields and Mark Ryan own all the capital stock of Property Management Corporation. Both stockholders also work full time in the business. The company performs management services for apartment house owners, including finding tenants, collecting rents, and doing maintenance and repair work.

When the business was organized early this year, Shields and Ryan invested a total of $50,000 to acquire the capital stock. At December 31, a partial list of the corporation's balance sheet items included cash of $15,700, office equipment of $6,100, accounts payable of $16,100, and income taxes payable of $2,900. Additional information on financial position and operations appears in the following six numbered paragraphs. Some of this information should be included in the balance sheet; some should not.

(1) Earlier this year the corporation purchased an office building from Shields at a price of $42,000 for the land and $67,000 for the building. Shields had acquired the property several years ago at a cost of $25,000 for the land and $50,000 for the building. At December 31, Shields and Ryan estimated that the land was worth $47,000 and the building was worth $70,000. The corporation owes Shields a $49,000 note payable in connection with the purchase of the property.

(2) While working, Shields drives her own automobile, which cost $12,600. Ryan uses a car owned by the corporation, which cost $10,200.

(3) One of the apartment houses managed by the company is owned by Ryan. Ryan's cost was $100,000 for the land and $190,000 for the building.

(4) Company records show a $1,900 account receivable from Ryan and $23,400 accounts receivable from other clients.

(5) Shields has a $20,000 bank account in the same bank used by the corporation.

Chapter 2
Recording changes in financial position

CHAPTER PREVIEW

In this chapter we illustrate the accounting cycle — the procedures used by a business to record, classify, and summarize the effects of business transactions in its accounting records. The activities of Greenhill Real Estate, which were described in Chapter 1, are now recorded in the company's general journal and posted to the general ledger accounts. The preparation of a trial balance also is illustrated, and the uses and limitations of the trial balance are discussed. The chapter concludes by comparing the accounting procedures applied in manual accounting systems with those in computer-based systems.

After studying this chapter you should be able to meet these Learning Objectives:

1 Describe a ledger account and a ledger.
2 State the rules of debit and credit for balance sheet accounts.
3 Explain the double-entry system of accounting.
4 Explain the purpose of a journal and its relationship to the ledger.
5 Prepare journal entries to record common business transactions.
6 Post information from the journal to ledger accounts.
7 Prepare a trial balance and explain its uses and limitations.
8 Describe the basic steps of the accounting cycle in both manual and computer-based accounting systems.

The role of accounting records

Many business concerns have several hundred or even several thousand business transactions each day. It would not be practicable to prepare a balance sheet after each transaction and it is quite unnecessary to do so. Instead, the many individual transactions are recorded in the accounting records, and, at the end of the month or other accounting period, a balance sheet is prepared from these records. In this chapter, we shall see how business transactions are analyzed, entered in the accounting records, and classified for use in preparing a balance sheet. In later chapters, we shall also see that the accounting records contain the data necessary to prepare an income statement, income tax returns, and other financial reports.

THE LEDGER

1 Describe a ledger account and a ledger.

An accounting system includes a separate record for each item that appears in the balance sheet. For example, a separate record is kept for the asset cash, showing all the increases and decreases in cash which result from the many transactions in which cash is received or paid. A similar record is kept for every other asset, for every liability, and for owners' equity. The form of record used to record increases and decreases in a single balance sheet item is called an *account,* or sometimes a *ledger account.* All these separate accounts are usually kept in a loose-leaf binder, and the entire group of accounts is called a *ledger.*

Many businesses use computers for maintaining accounting records, and store data on magnetic discs rather than in ledgers. However, an understanding of accounting concepts is most easily acquired by study of a manual accounting system. The knowledge gained by working with manual accounting records is readily transferable to any type of automated accounting system. For these reasons, we shall use standard written accounting records such as ledger accounts in our study of basic accounting concepts. These written records continue to be used by a great many businesses, but for our purposes they should be viewed as conceptual devices rather than as physical components of an accounting system.

The use of ledger accounts

A ledger account is a means of accumulating in one place all the information about changes in a specific asset, a liability, or owners' equity. For example, a ledger account for the asset cash provides a record of the amount of cash receipts, cash payments, and the current cash balance. By maintaining a Cash account, management can keep track of the amount of cash available for meeting payrolls and for making current purchases of assets or services. This record of cash is also useful in planning future operations and in advance planning of applications for bank loans.

In its simplest form, an account has only three elements: (1) a title, consisting of the name of the particular asset, liability, or owners' equity; (2) a left side, which is called the *debit* side; and (3) a right side, which is called the *credit* side. This form of account, illustrated below, is called a *T account* because of its resemblance to the letter T. More complete forms of accounts will be illustrated later.

T-account: a ledger account in simplified form

Title of Account	
Left or debit side	Right or credit side

Debit and credit entries

An amount recorded on the left or debit side of an account is called a **debit,** or a **debit entry;** an amount entered on the right or credit side is called a **credit,** or a **credit entry.** Accountants also use the words debit and credit as verbs. The act of recording a debit in an account is called **debiting** the account; the recording of a credit is called **crediting** the account.

Students beginning a course in accounting often have erroneous notions about the meanings of the terms debit and credit. For example, to some people unacquainted with accounting, the word credit may carry a more favorable connotation than does the word debit. Such connotations have no validity in the field of accounting. Accountants use **debit** to mean an entry on the left-hand side of an account, and **credit** to mean an entry on the right-hand side. Thus, debit and credit simply mean left and right, without any hidden or subtle implications.

To illustrate the recording of debits and credits in an account, let us go back to the cash transactions of Greenhill Real Estate as illustrated in Chapter 1. When these cash transactions are recorded in an account, the receipts are listed in vertical order on the debit side of the account and the payments are listed on the credit side. The dates of the transactions may also be listed, as shown in the following illustration:

Cash

Cash transactions entered in ledger account	9/1		180,000	9/3		141,000
	9/20	*22,500*	1,500	9/5		15,000
			181,500	9/30		3,000
						159,000

Note that the total of the cash receipts, $181,500, is in small-size, handwritten figures so that it will not be mistaken for a debit entry. The total of the cash payments (credits), amounting to $159,000, is also in small-size, handwritten figures to distinguish it from the credit entries. These **footings,** or memorandum totals, are merely a convenient step in determining the amount of cash on hand at the end of the month. The difference in dollars between the total debits and the total credits in an account is called the **balance.** If the debits exceed the credits the account has a **debit balance;** if the credits exceed the debits the account has a **credit balance.** In the illustrated Cash account, the debit total of $181,500 is larger than the credit total of $159,000; therefore, the account has a debit balance. By subtracting the credits from the debits ($181,500 − $159,000), we determine that the balance of the Cash account is $22,500. This debit balance is noted on the debit (left) side of the account. The balance of the Cash account represents the amount of cash owned by the business on September 30; in a balance sheet prepared at this date, Cash in the amount of $22,500 would be listed as an asset.

2 State the rules of debit and credit for balance sheet accounts.

Debit balances in asset accounts. In the preceding illustration of a cash account, increases were recorded on the left or debit side of the account and decreases were recorded on the right or credit side. The increases were greater than the decreases and the result was a debit balance in the account.

All asset accounts normally have debit balances; in fact, the ownership of cash, land, or any other asset indicates that the increases (debits) to that asset have been greater than the decreases (credits). It is hard to imagine an account for an asset such as land having a credit balance, as this would indicate that the business had disposed of more land than it had acquired and had reached the impossible position of having a negative amount of land.

The fact that assets are located on the left side of the balance sheet is a convenient means of remembering the rule that an increase in an asset is recorded on the *left* (debit) side of the account, and also that an asset account normally has a debit *(left-hand)* balance.

	Any Asset Account	
Asset accounts normally have debit balances	(Debit) Increase	(Credit) Decrease

Credit balances in liability and owners' equity accounts. Increases in liability and owners' equity accounts are recorded by credit entries and decreases in these accounts are recorded by debits. The relationship between entries in these accounts and their position on the balance sheet may be summed up as follows: (1) liabilities and owners' equity belong on the *right* side of the balance sheet; (2) an increase in a liability or an owners' equity account is recorded on the *right* (credit) side of the account; and (3) liability and owners' equity accounts normally have credit *(right-hand)* balances.

	Any Liability Account or Owners' Equity Account	
Liability and owners' equity accounts normally have credit balances	(Debit) Decrease	(Credit) Increase

The diagram on page 46 emphasizes again the relationship between the position of an account in the balance sheet and the method of recording an increase or decrease in the account. The accounts used are those previously shown in the balance sheet prepared for Greenhill Real Estate (page 25).

Concise statement of the rules of debit and credit. The rules of debit and credit, which have been explained and illustrated in the preceding sections, may be concisely summarized as follows:

	Asset Accounts	Liability & Owners' Equity Accounts
Mechanics of debit and credit	Increases are recorded by debits Decreases are recorded by credits	Increases are recorded by credits Decreases are recorded by debits

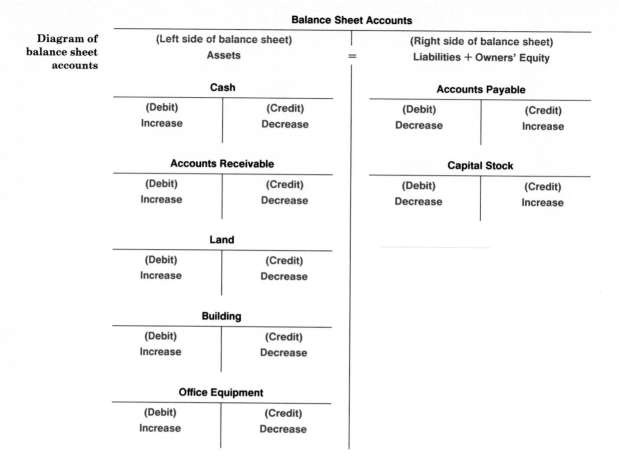

Diagram of balance sheet accounts

Balance Sheet Accounts

(Left side of balance sheet)			(Right side of balance sheet)	
Assets		**=**	**Liabilities + Owners' Equity**	

Cash

(Debit)	(Credit)
Increase	Decrease

Accounts Payable

(Debit)	(Credit)
Decrease	Increase

Accounts Receivable

(Debit)	(Credit)
Increase	Decrease

Capital Stock

(Debit)	(Credit)
Decrease	Increase

Land

(Debit)	(Credit)
Increase	Decrease

Building

(Debit)	(Credit)
Increase	Decrease

Office Equipment

(Debit)	(Credit)
Increase	Decrease

3 Explain the double-entry system of accounting.

Double-entry accounting: the equality of debits and credits. The rules of debit and credit are designed so that *equal amounts of debit and credit entries are needed to record every business transaction.* Assume, for example, that a company purchases land for $50,000. If the land were purchased for cash, the Land account would be debited for $50,000, and the Cash account would be credited for the same amount. If the land were purchased by issuing a note payable, the Land account would be debited and the liability account, Notes Payable, would be credited. If the land were purchased by paying $10,000 cash and issuing a note payable for the remaining $40,000, the transaction would be recorded as follows: debit Land, $50,000; credit Cash, $10,000; credit Notes Payable, $40,000. Notice that in each case, *equal dollar amounts* of debit and credit entries are needed to record the transaction.

The need for equal amounts of debit and credit entries to record every business transaction is called the *double-entry* system of accounting. The double-entry system is used by virtually every business organization, regardless of whether the company's accounting records are maintained manually or by computer.

Since every transaction is recorded by equal amounts of debits and credits, it follows that the total of all debit entries in the ledger is equal to the total of all credit entries. Later in this chapter, we shall see that this equality of debits and credits enables us to locate many types of errors which might be made while maintaining accounting records.

Recording transactions in ledger accounts: illustration

The procedure for recording transactions in ledger accounts will be illustrated by using the September transactions of Greenhill Real Estate. Each transaction will first be analyzed in terms of increases and decreases in assets, liabilities, and owners' equity. Then we shall follow the rules of debit and credit in entering these increases and decreases in T accounts. Asset accounts will be shown on the left side of the page; liability and owners' equity accounts on the right side. For convenience in following the transactions into the ledger accounts, the letter used to identify a given transaction will also appear opposite the debit and credit entries for that transaction. This use of identifying letters is for illustrative purposes only and is not used in actual accounting practice.

Transaction (a). The sum of $180,000 cash was invested in the business on September 1, and 18,000 shares of $10 par value capital stock were issued.

	Analysis	Rule	Entry
Recording an investment in the business	The asset Cash was increased	Increases in assets are recorded by debits	Debit: Cash, $180,000
	The stockholders' equity was increased	Increases in stockholders' equity are recorded by credits	Credit: Capital Stock, $180,000

Cash		Capital Stock	
9/1 (a) 180,000			9/1 (a) 180,000

Transaction (b). On September 3, Greenhill Real Estate purchased land for cash in the amount of $141,000.

	Analysis	Rule	Entry
Purchase of land for cash	The asset Land was increased	Increases in assets are recorded by debits	Debit: Land, $141,000
	The asset Cash was decreased	Decreases in assets are recorded by credits	Credit: Cash, $141,000

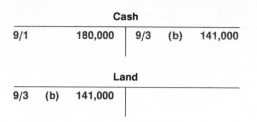

Transaction (c). On September 5, Greenhill Real Estate purchased a building from Kent Company at a total price of $36,000. The terms of the purchase required a cash payment of $15,000 with the remainder of $21,000 payable within 90 days.

	Analysis	Rule	Entry
Purchase of an asset, with partial payment	A new asset, Building, was acquired	Increases in assets are recorded by debits	Debit: Building, $36,000
	The asset Cash was decreased	Decreases in assets are recorded by credits	Credit: Cash, $15,000
	A new liability, Accounts Payable, was incurred	Increases in liabilities are recorded by credits	Credit: Accounts Payable, $21,000

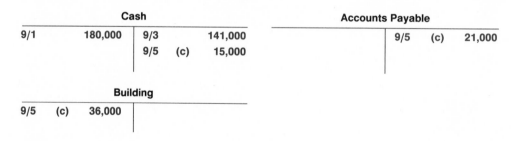

Transaction (d). On September 10, Greenhill Real Estate sold a portion of its land on credit to Carter's Drugstore for a price of $11,000. The land was sold at its cost, so there was no gain or loss on the transaction.

	Analysis	Rule	Entry
Sale of land on credit	A new asset, Accounts Receivable, was acquired	Increases in assets are recorded by debits	Debit: Accounts Receivable, $11,000
	The asset Land was decreased	Decreases in assets are recorded by credits	Credit: Land, $11,000

Accounts Receivable

9/10	(d)	11,000		

Land

9/3	141,000	9/10	(d)	11,000

Transaction (e). On September 14, Greenhill Real Estate purchased office equipment on credit from General Equipment, Inc., in the amount of $5,400.

<table>
<tr><td></td><td>Analysis</td><td>Rule</td><td>Entry</td></tr>
<tr><td rowspan="2">Purchase of an asset on credit</td><td>A new asset, Office Equipment, was acquired</td><td>Increases in assets are recorded by debits</td><td>Debit: Office Equipment, $5,400</td></tr>
<tr><td>A new liability, Accounts Payable, was incurred</td><td>Increases in liabilities are recorded by credits</td><td>Credit: Accounts Payable, $5,400</td></tr>
</table>

Office Equipment

9/14	(e)	5,400

Accounts Payable

	9/5		21,000
	9/14	(e)	5,400

Transaction (f). On September 20, cash of $1,500 was received as partial collection of the account receivable from Carter's Drugstore.

<table>
<tr><td></td><td>Analysis</td><td>Rule</td><td>Entry</td></tr>
<tr><td rowspan="2">Collection of an account receivable</td><td>The asset Cash was increased</td><td>Increases in assets are recorded by debits</td><td>Debit: Cash, $1,500</td></tr>
<tr><td>The asset Accounts Receivable was decreased</td><td>Decreases in assets are recorded by credits</td><td>Credit: Accounts Receivable, $1,500</td></tr>
</table>

Cash

9/1		180,000	9/3		141,000
9/20	(f)	1,500	9/5		15,000

Accounts Receivable

9/10	11,000	9/20 (f)	1,500

Transaction (g). A cash payment of $3,000 was made on September 30 in partial settlement of the amount owing to General Equipment, Inc.

Payment of a liability

Analysis	Rule	Entry
The liability Accounts Payable was decreased	Decreases in liabilities are recorded by debits	Debit: Accounts Payable, $3,000
The asset Cash was decreased	Decreases in assets are recorded by credits	Credit: Cash, $3,000

Cash					Accounts Payable				
9/1	180,000	9/3		141,000	9/30	(g)	3,000	9/5	21,000
9/20	1,500	9/5		15,000				9/14	5,400
		9/30	(g)	3,000					

Running balance form of ledger account

The T form of account used thus far is very convenient for illustrative purposes. Details are avoided and we can concentrate on basic ideas. T accounts are also often used in advanced accounting courses and by professional accountants for preliminary analysis of a transaction. In other words, the simplicity of the T account provides a concise conceptual picture of the elements of a business transaction. In formal accounting records, however, more information is needed, and the T account is replaced in many manual accounting systems by a ledger account with special rulings, such as the following illustration of the Cash account for Greenhill Real Estate:

Ledger account with a balance column

Cash					Account No. 1
Date	Explanation	Ref	Debit	Credit	Balance
19—					
Sept 1			1 80 0 0 0 00		1 80 0 0 0 00
3				1 41 0 0 0 00	39 0 0 0 00
5				1 5 0 0 0 00	24 0 0 0 00
20			1 5 0 0 00		25 5 0 0 00
30				3 0 0 0 00	22 5 0 0 00

The **Date** column shows the date of the transaction — which is not necessarily the same as the date the entry is made in the account. The **Explanation** column is needed only for unusual items, and in many companies it is seldom used. The **Ref** (Reference) column is used to list the page number of the journal in which the transaction is recorded, thus making it possible to trace ledger entries back to their source (a journal). The use of a *journal* is explained later in this chapter. In the *Balance* column of the account, the new balance is entered each time the account is debited or credited. Thus the current balance of the account can always be observed at a glance.

Although we shall make extensive use of this three-column running balance form of account in later chapters, there also will be many situations in which we shall continue to use T accounts to achieve simplicity in illustrating accounting principles and procedures.

The normal balance of an account

The running balance form of ledger account does not indicate specifically whether the balance of the account is a debit or credit balance. However, this causes no difficulty because we know that asset accounts normally have debit balances and that accounts for liabilities and owners' equity normally have credit balances.

The balance of any account normally results from recording more increases than decreases. In asset accounts, increases are recorded as debits, so asset accounts normally have debit balances. In liability and owners' equity accounts, increases are recorded as credits, so these accounts normally have credit balances.

Occasionally an asset account may temporarily acquire a credit balance, either as the result of an accounting error or because of an unusual transaction. For example, an account receivable may acquire a credit balance because a customer overpays his account. However, a credit balance in the Building account could be created only by an accounting error.

Sequence and numbering of ledger accounts

Accounts are usually arranged in the ledger in *financial statement order;* that is, assets first, followed by liabilities, owners' equity, revenue, and expenses. The number of accounts needed by a business will depend upon its size, the nature of its operations, and the extent to which management and regulatory agencies want detailed classification of information. An identification number is assigned to each account. A *chart of accounts* is a listing of the account titles and account numbers being used by a given business.

In the following list of accounts, certain numbers have not been assigned; these numbers are held in reserve so that additional accounts can be inserted in the ledger in proper sequence whenever such accounts become necessary. In this illustration, the numbers from 1 to 29 are used exclusively for asset accounts; numbers from 30 to 49 are used for liabilities; numbers in the 50s signify owners' equity accounts; numbers in the 60s represent revenue accounts; and numbers from 70 to 99 designate expense accounts. Revenue and expense accounts are discussed in Chapter 3. The balance sheet accounts with which we are concerned in this chapter are numbered as shown in the following brief chart of accounts.

	Account Title	Account Number
System for numbering ledger accounts	**Assets:**	
	Cash..	1
	Accounts Receivable...	4
	Land..	20
	Building..	22
	Office Equipment	25
	Liabilities:	
	Accounts Payable	32
	Stockholders' Equity:	
	Capital Stock	50
	Retained Earnings	51

In large businesses with many more accounts, a more elaborate numbering system would be needed. Some companies use an eight- or ten-digit number for each account; each of these digits carries a special significance as to the classification of the account.

Sequence of asset accounts. At this point we need to give further attention to the sequence of accounts within the asset group. As shown in all the balance sheets illustrated thus far, cash is always listed first. It is followed by notes receivable, accounts receivable, and supplies. Next come the relatively permanent assets used in the business (often called *plant assets*). Of this group, land is listed first and followed by buildings. After these two items, any order is acceptable for other assets used in the business, such as automobiles, furniture and fixtures, computers, lighting equipment, store equipment, etc.

THE JOURNAL

4 Explain the purpose of a journal and its relationship to the ledger.

In our preceding discussion, we recorded business transactions directly in the company's ledger accounts. We did this in order to stress the effects of business transactions upon the individual asset, liability, and owners' equity accounts appearing in the company's balance sheet. In an actual accounting system, however, the information about each business transaction is initially recorded in an accounting record called the *journal.* After the transaction has been recorded in the journal, the debit and credit changes in the individual accounts are entered in the ledger. Since the journal is the accounting record in which transactions are *first recorded,* it is sometimes called the *book of original entry.*

The journal is a chronological (day-by-day) record of business transactions. The information to be recorded about each transaction is the date of the transaction, the debit and credit changes in specific ledger accounts, and a brief explanation of the transaction. At convenient intervals, the debit and credit amounts recorded in the journal are transferred to the accounts in the ledger. The updated ledger accounts, in turn, serve as the basis for preparing the balance sheet and other financial statements.

Why use a journal?

Since it is technically possible to record transactions directly in the ledger, why bother to maintain a journal? The answer is that the unit of organization for the journal is the *transaction,* whereas the unit of organization for the ledger is the *account.* By having both a journal and a ledger, we achieve several advantages which would not be possible if transactions were recorded directly in ledger accounts:

1 *The journal shows all information about a transaction in one place and also provides an explanation of the transaction.* In a journal entry, the debits and credits for a given transaction are recorded together, but when the transaction is recorded in the ledger, the debits and credits are entered in different accounts. Since a ledger may contain hundreds of accounts, it would be very difficult to locate all the facts about a particular transaction by looking in the ledger. The journal is the record which shows the complete story of a transaction in one entry.

2 *The journal provides a chronological record of all the events in the life of a business.* If we want to look up the facts about a transaction of some months or years back, all we need is the date of the transaction in order to locate it in the journal.

3 *The use of a journal helps to prevent errors.* If transactions were recorded directly in the ledger, it would be very easy to make errors such as omitting the debit or the credit, or entering the debit twice or the credit twice. Such errors are not likely to be made in the journal, since the offsetting debits and credits appear together for each transaction.

The general journal: illustration of entries

5 Prepare journal entries to record common business transactions. Many businesses maintain several types of journals. The nature of operations and the volume of transactions in the particular business determine the number and type of journals needed. The simplest type of journal is called a *general journal* and is shown on page 54. It has only two money columns, one for debits and the other for credits; it may be used for all types of transactions.

The process of recording a transaction in a journal is called journalizing the transaction. To illustrate the use of the general journal, we shall now journalize the September transactions of Greenhill Real Estate which have been discussed previously.

Efficient use of a general journal requires two things: (1) ability to analyze the effect of a transaction upon assets, liabilities, and owners' equity; and (2) familiarity with the standard form and arrangement of journal entries. Our primary interest is in the analytical phase of journalizing; the procedural steps can be learned quickly by observing the following points in the illustration of journal entries:

		General Journal					Page /	
Date		**Account Titles and Explanation**	**LP**	**Debit**			**Credit**	
19–								
Sept	1	Cash	1	180000				
		Capital Stock	50				180000	
		Issued 18,000 shares of $10 par value stock						
	3	Land	20	141000				
		Cash	1				141000	
		Purchased land for office site.						
	5	Building	22	36000				
		Cash	1				15000	
		Accounts Payable	32				21000	
		Purchased building to be moved to our lot. Paid part cash; balance payable within 90 days to Kent Company.						
	10	Accounts Receivable	4	11000				
		Land	20				11000	
		Sold the unused part of our lot at cost to Carter's Drugstore. Due within 3 months.						
	14	Office Equipment	25	5400				
		Accounts Payable	32				5400	
		Purchased equipment on credit from General Equipment, Inc.						
	20	Cash	1	1500				
		Accounts Receivable	4				1500	
		Collected part of receivable from Carter's Drugstore.						
	30	Accounts Payable	32	3000				
		Cash	1				3000	
		Made partial payment of the liability to General Equipment, Inc.						

1 The year, month, and day of the first entry on the page are written in the date column. The year and month need not be repeated for subsequent entries until a new page or a new month is begun.

2 The name of the account to be debited is written on the first line of the entry and is customarily placed at the extreme left next to the date column. The amount of the debit is entered on the same line in the *left-hand* money column.

3 The name of the account to be credited is entered on the line below the debit entry and is *indented,* that is, placed about 1 inch to the right of the date column. The amount credited is entered on the same line in the *right-hand* money column.

4 A brief explanation of the transaction is begun on the line immediately below the last account credited. The explanation is not indented.

5 A blank line should be left after each entry. This spacing causes each journal entry to stand out clearly as a separate unit and makes the journal easier to read.

6 An entry which includes more than one debit or more than one credit (such as the entry on September 5) is called a *compound journal entry.* Regardless of how many debits or credits are contained in a compound journal entry, *all the debits* are entered *before any credits* are listed.

7 The LP (ledger page) column just to the left of the debit money column is left blank at the time of making the journal entry. When the debits and credits are later transferred to ledger accounts, the numbers of the ledger accounts will be listed in this column to provide a convenient cross reference with the ledger.

In journalizing transactions, remember that the *exact title* of the ledger accounts to be debited and credited should be used. For example, in recording the purchase of office equipment for cash, *do not* make a journal entry debiting "Office Equipment Purchased" and crediting "Cash Paid Out." There are no ledger accounts with such titles. The proper journal entry would consist of a debit to *Office Equipment* and a credit to *Cash.*

A familiarity with the general journal form of describing transactions is just as essential to the study of accounting as a familiarity with plus and minus signs is to the study of mathematics. The journal entry is a *tool* for *analyzing* and *describing* the impact of various transactions upon a business entity. The ability to describe a transaction in journal entry form requires an understanding of the nature of the transaction and its effects upon the financial position of the business.

Posting

6 Post information from the journal to ledger accounts.

The process of transferring the debits and credits from the general journal to the proper ledger accounts is called *posting.* Each amount listed in the debit column of the journal is posted by entering it on the debt side of an account in the ledger, and each amount listed in the credit column of the journal is posted to the credit side of a ledger account.

The mechanics of posting may vary somewhat with the preferences of the individual. The following sequence is commonly used:

1 Locate in the ledger the first account named in the journal entry.
2 Enter in the debit column of the ledger account the amount of the debit as shown in the journal.
3 Enter the date of the transaction in the ledger account.
4 Enter in the reference column of the ledger account the number of the journal page from which the entry is being posted.
5 The recording of the debit in the ledger account is now complete; as evidence of this fact, return to the journal and enter in the LP (ledger page) column the number of the ledger account or page to which the debit was posted.
6 Repeat the posting process described in the preceding five steps for the credit side of the journal entry.

Illustration of posting. To illustrate the posting process, the journal entry for the first transaction of Greenhill Real Estate is repeated below, along with the two ledger accounts affected by this entry.

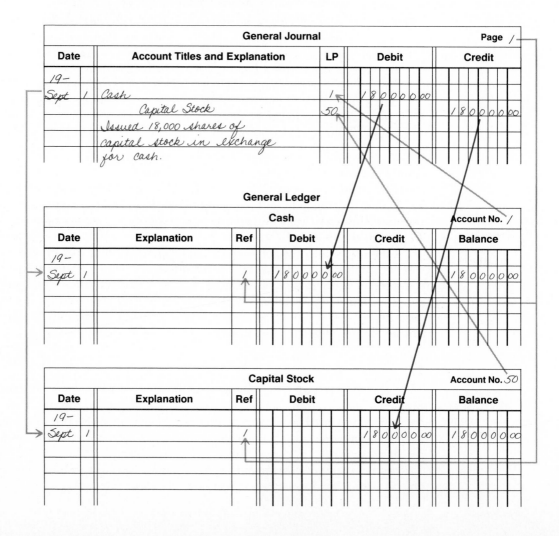

Note that the Ref (Reference) column of each of the two ledger accounts illustrated contains the number 1, indicating that the posting was made from page 1 of the general journal. Entering the journal page number in the ledger account and listing the ledger page in the journal provide a cross reference between these two records. The audit of accounting records always requires looking up some journal entries to obtain more information about the amounts listed in ledger accounts. A cross reference between the ledger and journal is therefore essential to efficient audit of the records. Another advantage gained from entering in the journal the number of the account to which a posting has been made is to provide evidence throughout the posting work as to which items have been posted. Otherwise, any interruption in the posting might leave some doubt as to what had been posted.

Journalizing and posting by hand is a useful method for the study of accounting, both for problem assignments and for examinations. The manual approach is also followed in many small businesses. One shortcoming is the opportunity for error that exists whenever information is being copied from one record to another. In businesses having a large volume of transactions, the posting of ledger accounts is performed by a computer, which speeds up the work and reduces errors.

Ledger accounts after posting

After all the September transactions have been posted, the ledger of Greenhill Real Estate appears as follows. The accounts are arranged in the ledger in balance sheet order, that is, assets first, followed by liabilities and stockholders' equity.

To conserve space in this illustration, several ledger accounts appear on a single page. In actual practice, each account occupies a separate page in the ledger.

Ledger showing September transactions

	Cash					Account No. 1
Date	Explanation	Ref	Debit	Credit	Balance	
19—						
Sept 1		1	18 000 00		18 000 00	
3		1		14 100 00	3 900 00	
5		1		1 500 00	2 400 00	
20		1	1 500 00		25 500 00	
30		1		3 000 00	22 500 00	

	Accounts Receivable					Account No. 4
Date	Explanation	Ref	Debit	Credit	Balance	
19—						
Sept 10		1	11 000 00		11 000 00	
20		1		1 500 00	9 500 00	

Land				Debit		Credit		Balance	Account No. 20
Date		**Explanation**	**Ref**	**Debit**		**Credit**		**Balance**	
19—									
Sept	3		1	1 41 000 00				1 41 000 00	
	10		1			11 000 00		1 30 000 00	

Building				Debit		Credit		Balance	Account No. 22
Date		**Explanation**	**Ref**	**Debit**		**Credit**		**Balance**	
19—									
Sept	5		1	36 000 00				36 000 00	

Office Equipment				Debit		Credit		Balance	Account No. 25
Date		**Explanation**	**Ref**	**Debit**		**Credit**		**Balance**	
19—									
Sept	14		1	5 400 00				5 400 00	

Accounts Payable				Debit		Credit		Balance	Account No. 32
Date		**Explanation**	**Ref**	**Debit**		**Credit**		**Balance**	
19—									
Sept	5		1			21 000 00		21 000 00	
	14		1			5 400 00		26 400 00	
	30		1	3 000 00				23 400 00	

Capital Stock				Debit		Credit		Balance	Account No. 50
Date		**Explanation**	**Ref**	**Debit**		**Credit**		**Balance**	
19—									
Sept	1		1			1 80 000 00		1 80 000 00	

THE TRIAL BALANCE

Since equal dollar amounts of debits and credits are entered in the accounts for every transaction recorded, the sum of all the debits in the ledger must be equal to the sum of all the credits. If the computation of account balances has been accurate, it follows that the total of the accounts with debit balances must be equal to the total of the accounts with credit balances.

7 Prepare a trial balance and . . .

Before using the account balances to prepare a balance sheet, it is desirable to **prove** that the total of accounts with debit balances is in fact equal to the total of accounts with credit balances. This proof of the equality of debit and credit balances is called a **trial balance.** A trial balance is a two-column schedule listing the names and balances of all the accounts **in the order in which they appear in the ledger;** the debit balances are listed in the left-hand column and the credit balances in the right-hand column. The totals of the two columns should agree. A trial balance taken from the ledger of Greenhill Real Estate follows:

GREENHILL REAL ESTATE, INC.
Trial Balance
September 30, 19__

Trial balance at month-end proves ledger is in balance

Cash	$ 22,500	
Accounts receivable	9,500	
Land	130,000	
Building	36,000	
Office equipment	5,400	
Accounts payable		$ 23,400
Capital stock		180,000
	$203,400	$203,400

Uses and limitations of the trial balance

. . . explain its uses and limitations.

The trial balance provides proof that the ledger is in balance. The agreement of the debit and credit totals of the trial balance gives assurance that:

1 Equal debits and credits have been recorded for all transactions.
2 The debit or credit balance of each account has been correctly computed.
3 The addition of the account balances in the trial balance has been correctly performed.

Suppose that the debit and credit totals of the trial balance do not agree. This situation indicates that one or more errors have been made. Typical of such errors are (1) the posting of a debit as a credit, or vice versa; (2) arithmetic mistakes in balancing accounts; (3) clerical errors in copying account balances into the trial balance; (4) listing a debit balance in the credit column of the trial balance, or vice versa; and (5) errors in addition of the trial balance.

The preparation of a trial balance does not prove that transactions have been correctly analyzed and recorded in the proper accounts. If, for example, a receipt of cash were erroneously recorded by debiting the Land account instead of the Cash account, the trial balance would still balance. Also, if a transaction were completely omitted from the ledger, the error would not be disclosed by the trial balance. In brief, ***the trial balance proves only one aspect of the ledger, and that is the equality of debits and credits.***

Despite these limitations, the trial balance is a useful device. It not only provides assurance that the ledger is in balance, but it also serves as a convenient stepping-stone for the preparation of financial statements. As explained in Chapter 1, the balance sheet is a formal statement showing the financial position of the business, intended for distribution to managers, owners, bankers, and various outsiders. The trial balance, on the other hand, is merely a working paper, useful to the accountant but not intended for distribution to others. The balance sheet and other financial statements can be prepared more conveniently from the trial balance than directly from the ledger, especially if there are a great many ledger accounts.

Locating errors

In the illustration given, the trial balance was in balance. Every accounting student soon discovers in working problems, however, that errors are easily made which prevent trial balances from balancing. The lack of balance may be the result of a single error or a combination of several errors. An error may have been made in adding the trial balance columns or in copying the balances from the ledger accounts. If the preparation of the trial balance has been accurate, then the error may lie in the accounting records, either in the journal or in the ledger accounts. What is the most efficient approach to locating the error or errors? There is no single technique which will give the best results every time, but the following procedures, done in sequence, will often save considerable time and effort in locating errors.

1 Prove the addition of the trial balance columns by adding these columns in the opposite direction from that previously followed.
2 If the error does not lie in addition, next determine the exact amount by which the schedule is out of balance. The amount of the discrepancy is often a clue to the source of the error. If the discrepancy is ***divisible by 9,*** this suggests either a ***transposition*** error or a ***slide.*** For example, assume that the Cash account has a balance of $2,175, but in copying the balance into the trial balance the figures are ***transposed*** and written as $2,157. The resulting error is $18, and like all transposition errors is divisible by 9. Another common error is the slide, or incorrect placement of the decimal point, as when $2,175.00 is copied as $21.75. The resulting discrepancy in the trial balance will also be an amount divisible by 9.

To illustrate another method of using the amount of a discrepancy as a clue to locating the error, assume that the Office Equipment account has a ***debit*** balance of $420, but that it is erroneously listed in the ***credit*** column of the trial balance. This will cause a discrepancy of two times $420, or $840, in the trial balance totals. Since such errors as recording a debit in a credit column are not uncommon, it is advisable, after determining the discrepancy in the trial balance totals, to scan the columns for an amount equal to exactly **one-half** of the discrepancy. It is also advisable to look over the transactions for an item of the exact amount of the discrepancy. An error may have been made by recording the debit side of the transaction and forgetting to enter the credit side.

3 Compare the amounts in the trial balance with the balances in the ledger. Make sure that each ledger account balance has been included in the correct column of the trial balance.

4 Recompute the balance of each ledger account.

5 Trace all postings from the journal to the ledger accounts. As this is done, place a check mark in the journal and in the ledger after each figure verified. When the operation is completed, look through the journal and the ledger for unchecked amounts. In tracing postings, be alert not only for errors in amount but also for debits entered as credits, or vice versa.

Dollar signs

Dollar signs are not used in journals or ledgers. Some accountants use dollar signs in trial balances; some do not. In this book, dollar signs are used in trial balances. Dollar signs should always be used in the balance sheet, the income statement, and other formal financial reports. In the balance sheet, for example, a dollar sign is placed by the first amount in each column and also by the final amount or total. Many accountants also place a dollar sign by each subtotal or other amount listed below an underlining. In the published financial statements of large corporations, such as those listed in the appendix of this book, the use of dollar signs is often limited to the first and last figures in a column.

When dollar amounts are being entered in the columnar paper used in journals and ledgers, commas and decimal points are not needed. On unruled paper, commas and decimal points should be used. Most of the problems and illustrations in this book are in even dollar amounts. In such cases the cents column can be left blank or, if desired, zeros or dashes may be used.

THE ACCOUNTING CYCLE: AN INTRODUCTION

8 Describe the basic steps of the accounting cycle in both manual and computer-based accounting systems.

The sequence of accounting procedures used to record, classify, and summarize accounting information is often termed the ***accounting cycle.*** The accounting cycle begins with the initial recording of business transactions and concludes with the preparation of formal financial statements summarizing the effects of these transactions upon the assets, liabilities, and owners' equity of the business. The term "cycle" indicates that these procedures must be repeated continuously to enable the business to prepare new, up-to-date financial statements at reasonable intervals.

At this point, we have illustrated a complete accounting cycle as it relates to the preparation of a balance sheet for a service type business with a manual accounting system. The accounting procedures discussed to this point may be summarized as follows:

1 ***Record transactions in the journal.*** As each business transaction occurs, it is entered in the journal, thus creating a chronological record of events. This procedure completes the recording step in the accounting cycle.

2 ***Post to ledger accounts.*** The debit and credit changes in account balances are posted from the journal to the ledger. This procedure classifies the effects of the business transactions in terms of specific asset, liability, and owners' equity accounts.

3 ***Prepare a trial balance.*** A trial balance proves the equality of the debit and credit entries in the ledger. The purpose of this procedure is to verify the accuracy of the posting process and the computation of ledger account balances.

4 ***Prepare financial statements.*** At this point, we have discussed only one financial statement — the balance sheet. This statement shows the financial position of the business at a specific date. The preparation of financial statements summarizes the effects of business transactions occurring through the date of the statements and completes the accounting cycle.

In the next section of this chapter, and throughout this textbook, we shall extend our discussion to include computer-based accounting systems. In Chapters 3 and 4, we shall expand the accounting cycle to include the measurement of business income and the preparation of an income statement.

Manual and computer-based systems: a comparison

In our preceding discussion, we have assumed the use of a manual accounting system, in which all the accounting procedures are performed manually by the company's accounting personnel. The reader may wonder about the relevance of such a discussion in an era when even many small businesses use computer-based accounting systems. However, the concepts and procedures involved in the operation of manual and computer-based accounting systems are ***essentially the same.*** The differences are largely a question of whether specific procedures require human attention, or whether they can be performed automatically by machine.

Computers can be programmed to perform mechanical tasks with great speed and accuracy. For example, they can be programmed to read data, to perform mathematical computations, and to rearrange data into any desired format. However, computers cannot think. Therefore, they are not able to ***analyze*** business transactions. Without human guidance, computers cannot determine which events should be recorded in the accounting records, or which accounts should be debited and credited to properly record an event. With these abilities and limitations in mind, we will explore the effects of computer-based systems upon the basic accounting cycle.

Recording business transactions. The recording of transactions requires two steps. First, the transaction must be ***analyzed*** to determine whether it should be recorded in the accounting records and, if so, which accounts should be debited and credited and for what dollar amounts. Second, the transaction must be ***physically***

entered (recorded) in the accounting system. As computers do not know which transactions should be recorded, or how to record them properly, these two functions must be performed by accounting personnel in both manual and computerized systems.

Differences do exist, however, in the manner in which data are physically entered into manual and computer-based systems. In manual systems, the data are entered in the form of handwritten journal entries. In a computer-based system, the data will be entered through a keyboard, an optical scanner, or other input device. Also, data entered into a computer-based system need *not* be arranged in the format of a journal entry. The data usually are entered into a *data base,* instead of a journal.

What is a data base? A data base is a warehouse of information stored within a computer system. The purpose of the data base is to allow information that will be used for several different purposes to be entered into the computer system *only once.* Data are originally entered into the data base. Then, as data are needed, the computer refers to the data base, selects the appropriate data, and arranges them in the desired format.

The information that must be entered into the data base is the same as that contained in a journal entry — the date, the accounts to be debited and credited, the dollar amounts, and an explanation of the transaction. However, this information need not be arranged in the format of a journal entry. For example, in a data base, accounts usually are identified by number, rather than by title. Also, abbreviations such as "D" or "C" are used to indicate whether an account should be debited or credited. Once information has been entered in the data base, the computer can arrange this information into any desired format, such as journal entries, ledger accounts, and financial statements.

Posting to ledger accounts. Posting merely transfers existing information from one accounting record to another — a function which can be easily performed by a computer. In a computer-based system, data posted to the ledger accounts come directly from the data base, rather than from the journal.

Preparation of a trial balance. Preparation of a trial balance involves three steps: (1) determining the balances of ledger accounts, (2) arranging the account balances in the format of a trial balance, and (3) adding up the trial balance columns and comparing the column totals. All these functions involve information already contained in the data base and can be performed by the computer.

Preparation of financial statements. The preparation of a balance sheet is similar to the preparation of a trial balance and can be readily performed by the computer. The preparation of an income statement involves additional procedures which will be discussed in Chapter 3.

Summary. Computers can eliminate the need for copying and rearranging information which already has been entered into the system. They also can perform mathematical computations. In short, computers eliminate most of the "paper work" involved in the operation of an accounting system. However, they **do not** eliminate the need for accounting personnel who can analyze business transactions and explain these events in conformity with generally accepted accounting principles.

The differences in manual and computer-based systems with respect to the accounting procedures discussed in this chapter are summarized graphically in the flowcharts below. Functions which are performed by accounting personnel are shown in color; tasks which can be performed automatically by the computer are shown in black.

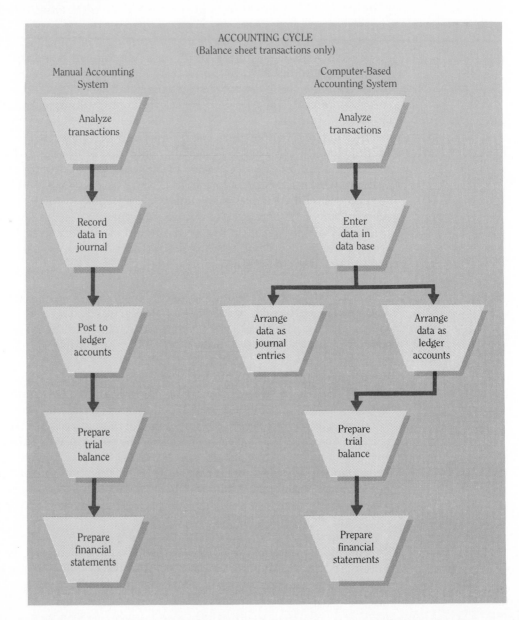

ACCOUNTING CYCLE
(Balance sheet transactions only)

Manual Accounting System

Analyze transactions

Record data in journal

Post to ledger accounts

Prepare trial balance

Prepare financial statements

Computer-Based Accounting System

Analyze transactions

Enter data in data base

Arrange data as journal entries

Arrange data as ledger accounts

Prepare trial balance

Prepare financial statements

END-OF-CHAPTER REVIEW

Summary of chapter learning objectives

1 Describe a ledger account and a ledger.

A ledger account is a device for recording the increases or decreases in one financial statement item, such as a particular asset, a type of liability, or owners' equity. The ledger is an accounting record which includes all the ledger accounts — that is, a separate account for each item included in the company's financial statements.

2 State the rules of debit and credit for balance sheet accounts.

Increases in assets are recorded by debits and decreases are recorded by credits. Increases in liabilities and in owners' equity are recorded by credits and decreases are recorded by debits. Notice that the debit and credit rules are related to an account's *location in the balance sheet.* If the account appears on the *left-hand side* of the balance sheet (asset accounts), increases in the account balance are recorded by *left-side entries* (debits). If the account appears on the **right-hand side** of the balance sheet (liability and owners' equity accounts), increases are recorded by *right-side entries* (credits).

3 Explain the double-entry system of accounting.

The double-entry system of accounting takes its name from the fact that every business transaction is recorded by *two sets of entries:* (1) debit entries to one or more accounts, and (2) credit entries to one or more accounts. In recording any transaction, the total dollar amount of the debit entries must equal the total dollar amount of the credit entries.

4 Explain the purpose of a journal and its relationship to the ledger.

The journal, or book of original entry, is the accounting record in which business transactions are initially recorded. The entry in the journal shows which ledger accounts have increased as a result of the transaction, and which have decreased. After the effects of the transaction have been recorded in the journal, the changes in the individual ledger accounts are then posted to the ledger.

5 Prepare journal entries to record common business transactions.

The effects of business transactions upon the assets, liabilities, or owners' equity of a business are recorded in the journal. Each journal entry includes the date of the transaction, the names of the ledger accounts affected, the dollar amounts of the changes in these accounts, and a brief explanation of the transaction.

6 Post information from the journal to ledger accounts.

The posting process transfers the information concerning changes in specific account balances from the journal into the ledger.

7 Prepare a trial balance and explain its uses and limitations.

In a trial balance, separate debit and credit columns are used to list the balances of the individual ledger accounts. The two columns are then totaled to prove the equality of the debit and credit balances. This process provides assurance that (1) the total of the debits posted to the ledger was equal to the total of the credits, and (2) the balances of the individual ledger accounts were correctly computed. While a trial balance proves the equality of debit and credit entries in the ledger, it does *not* detect such errors as failure to record a business transaction, improper analysis of the accounts affected by the transaction, or the posting of debit or credit entries to the wrong accounts.

8 Describe the basic steps of the accounting cycle in both manual and computer-based accounting systems.

At this stage of our study, the steps in any accounting system are: (1) record transactions in a journal, (2) post the information to the ledger accounts, (3) prepare a trial balance, and (4) prepare financial statements. In a manual accounting system, all four steps are performed by accounting personnel. In a computer-based system, steps (2), (3), and (4) are performed automatically by the computer.

Key terms introduced or emphasized in chapter 2

Account. A record used to summarize all increases and decreases in a particular asset, such as Cash, or any other type of asset, liability, owners' equity, revenue, or expense.

Accounting cycle. The sequence of accounting procedures applied in recording, classifying, and summarizing accounting information. The cycle begins with the occurrence of business transactions and concludes with the preparation of financial statements. This concept will be expanded in later chapters.

Credit. An amount entered on the right-hand side of an account. A credit is used to record a decrease in an asset and an increase in a liability or owners' equity.

Credit balance. The balance of an account in which the total amount of credits exceeds the total amount of debits.

Data base. A storage center of information within a computer-based accounting system. The idea behind a data base is that data intended for a variety of uses may be entered into the computer system only once, at which time the information is stored in the data base. Then, as the information is needed, the computer can retrieve it from the data base and arrange it in the desired format.

Debit. An amount entered on the left-hand side of an account. A debit is used to record an increase in an asset and a decrease in a liability or in owners' equity.

Debit balance. The balance of an account in which the total amount of debits exceeds the total amount of credits.

Double-entry method. In recording transactions, the total dollar amount of debits must equal the total dollar amount of credits.

Financial statement order. The usual sequence of accounts in a ledger; that is, assets first, followed by liabilities, owners' equity, revenue, and expenses.

Footing. The total of amounts in a column.

Journal. A chronological record of transactions, showing for each transaction the debits and credits to be entered in specific ledger accounts. The simplest type of journal is called a general journal.

Journalizing. The process of recording a transaction in a journal. To journalize means to prepare an entry in a journal.

Ledger. A loose-leaf book, file, or other record containing all the separate accounts of a business.

Posting. The process of transferring information from the journal to individual accounts in the ledger.

Trial balance. A two-column schedule listing the names and the debit or credit balances of all accounts in the ledger.

Demonstration problem for your review

Stadium Parking, Inc., was organized on July 1 to operate a parking lot near a new sports arena. The following transactions occurred during July prior to the company beginning its regular business operations.

July 1 Issued 4,500 shares of $10 par value capital stock to the owners of the corporation in exchange for their investment of $45,000 cash.

July 2 Purchased land to be used as the parking lot for a total price of $140,000. A cash down payment of $28,000 was and a note payable was issued for the balance of the purchase price.

July 5 Purchased a small portable building for $4,000 cash. The purchase price included installation of the building on the parking lot.

July 12 Purchased office equipment on credit from Suzuki & Co. for $3,000.

July 28 Paid $2,000 of the amount owed to Suzuki & Co.

The account titles and account numbers used by Auto Parks, Inc., to record these transactions are

Cash...............................	1	Notes payable........................	30
Land...............................	20	Accounts payable.....................	32
Building	22	Capital stock........................	50
Office equipment....................	25		

Instructions

a Prepare journal entries for the month of July.
b Post to ledger accounts of the three-column running balance form.
c Prepare a trial balance at July 31.

Solution to demonstration problem

a

		General Journal			Page 1
Date		**Account Titles and Explanations**	**LP**	**Debit**	**Credit**
19__					
July	1	Cash.......................................	1	45,000	
		Capital stock	50		45,000
		Issued 4,500 shares of $10 par value capital stock.			
	2	Land.......................................	20	140,000	
		Cash	1		28,000
		Notes Payable	30		112,000
		Purchased land. Paid part cash and issued a note payable for the balance.			
	5	Building	22	4,000	
		Cash	1		4,000
		Purchased a small portable building for cash.			
	12	Office Equipment	25	3,000	
		Accounts Payable	32		3,000
		Purchased office equipment on credit from Suzuki & Co.			
	28	Accounts Payable...........................	32	2,000	
		Cash	1		2,000
		Paid part of account payable to Suzuki & Co.			

b

		Cash			Account No. *1*
Date	**Explanation**	**Ref**	**Debit**	**Credit**	**Balance**
19—					
July 1		*1*	450 00		450 00
2		*1*		280 00	170 00
5		*1*		40 00	130 00
28		*1*		20 00	110 00

		Land			Account No. *20*
Date	**Explanation**	**Ref**	**Debit**	**Credit**	**Balance**
19—					
July 2		*1*	1 400 00		1 400 00

		Building			Account No. *22*
Date	**Explanation**	**Ref**	**Debit**	**Credit**	**Balance**
19—					
July 5		*1*	40 00		40 00

		Office Equipment			Account No. *25*
Date	**Explanation**	**Ref**	**Debit**	**Credit**	**Balance**
19—					
July 12		*1*	30 00		30 00

Notes Payable					Account No. *30*
Date	Explanation	Ref	Debit	Credit	Balance
19—					
July 2		*1*		*112000*	*112000*

Accounts Payable					Account No. *32*
Date	Explanation	Ref	Debit	Credit	Balance
19—					
July 12		*1*		*3000*	*3000*
28		*1*	*2000*		*1000*

Capital Stock					Account No. *50*
Date	Explanation	Ref	Debit	Credit	Balance
19—					
July 1				*45000*	*45000*

c

STADIUM PARKING, INC.
Trial Balance
July 31, 19___

	Debit	Credit
Cash	$ 11,000	
Land	140,000	
Building.	4,000	
Office equipment	3,000	
Notes payable		$112,000
Accounts payable		1,000
Capital stock		45,000
	$158,000	$158,000

ASSIGNMENT MATERIAL

Review questions

1 In its simplest form, an account has only three elements or basic parts. What are these three elements?

2 What relationship exists between the position of an account on the balance sheet and the rules for recording increases in that account?

3 State briefly the rules of debit and credit as applied to asset accounts. As applied to liability and owners' equity accounts.

4 Is it true that favorable events are recorded by credits and unfavorable events by debits? Explain.

5 Does the term *debit* mean increase and the term *credit* mean decrease? Explain.

6 What requirement is imposed by the double-entry system in the recording of any business transaction?

7 Explain precisely what is meant by each of the phrases listed below. Whenever appropriate, indicate whether the left or right side of an account is affected and whether an increase or decrease is indicated.
   a A debit of $200 to the Cash account
   b Credit balance
   c Credit side of an account
   d A debit of $600 to Accounts Payable
   e Debit balance
   f A credit of $50 to Accounts Receivable
   g A debit to the Land account

8 For each of the following transactions, indicate whether the account in parentheses should be debited or credited, and give the reason for your answer.
   a Purchased a copying machine on credit, promising to make payment in full within 30 days. (Accounts Payable)
   b Purchased land for cash. (Cash)
   c Sold an old, unneeded typewriter on 30-day credit. (Office Equipment)
   d Obtained a loan of $30,000 from a bank. (Cash)

9 For each of the following accounts, state whether it is an asset, a liability, or owners' equity; also state whether it would normally have a debit or a credit balance: (a) Office Equipment, (b) Capital Stock, (c) Accounts Receivable, (d) Accounts Payable, (e) Cash, (f) Notes Payable, (g) Land.

10 List the following four items in a logical sequence to illustrate the flow of accounting information through a manual accounting system:
   a Information entered in journal
   b Financial statements prepared from ledger
   c Occurrence of a business transaction
   d Debits and credits posted from journal to ledger

11 Why is a journal sometimes called the *book of original entry?*

12 Compare and contrast a *journal* and a *ledger.*

13 Which step in the recording of transactions requires greater understanding of accounting principles: (a) the entering of transactions in the journal, or (b) the posting of entries to ledger accounts?

14 What is a *compound journal entry?*

15 What purposes are served by a trial balance?

16 In preparing a trial balance, an accounting student listed the balance of the Office

Equipment account in the credit column. This account had a balance of $2,450. What would be the amount of the discrepancy in the trial balance totals? Explain.

17 Are dollar signs used in journal entries? In ledger accounts? In trial balances? In financial statements?

18 A student beginning the study of accounting prepared a trial balance in which two unusual features appeared. The Buildings account showed a credit balance of $20,000, and the Accounts Payable account a debit balance of $100. Considering each of these two abnormal balances separately, state whether the condition was the result of an error in the records or could have resulted from proper recording of an unusual transaction.

19 Since it is possible to record the effects of business transactions directly in ledger accounts, why is it desirable for a business to maintain a journal?

20 List the procedures in the *accounting cycle* as described in this chapter.

21 What is a *data base?* How does a data base relate to the preparation of journal entries and ledger accounts in a computer-based system?

Exercises

Exercise 2-1
Accounting terminology

Listed below are nine technical accounting terms introduced in this chapter:

Account	Debit	Ledger
Credit	Double-entry	Posting
Data base	Journal	Trial balance

Each of the following statements may (or may not) describe one of these technical terms. For each statement, indicate the accounting term described, or answer "none" if the statement does not correctly describe any of the terms.

a An entry on the right-hand side of a ledger account.
b The accounting record in which transactions are initially recorded in a manual accounting system.
c Information stored in a computer-based accounting system which can be arranged into any desired format.
d A device which will detect the failure to record a business transaction in the accounting records.
e The accounting record from which a trial balance is prepared.
f The system of accounting in which every business transaction is recorded by an equal dollar amount of debit and credit entries.

Exercise 2-2
Analysis of transactions; double-entry accounting

Analyze separately each of the following transactions using the format illustrated at the end of the exercise. In each situation, explain the debit portion of the transaction before the credit portion.

a On May 1, Linda McKaig organized McKaig Software Corporation. The corporation issued 9,000 shares of $10 par value capital stock to McKaig in exchange for her investment of $90,000 cash in the business.
b On May 3, land was acquired for $55,000 cash.
c On May 5, a prefabricated building was purchased at a cost of $45,000 from Custom Company. A cash down payment of $20,000 was made and it was agreed that the balance should be paid in full within 30 days.
d On May 8, office equipment was purchased on credit from Taylor Office Supply Co. at a price of $8,500. The account payable was to be paid within 60 days.
e On May 31, a partial payment of $3,500 was made on the liability to Taylor Office Supply Co.

Note: The type of analysis to be made is shown by the following illustration, using transaction (a) as an example.

a (1) The asset Cash was increased. Increases in assets are recorded by debits. Debit Cash, $90,000.
  (2) The owners' equity was increased. Increases in owners' equity are recorded by credits. Credit Capital Stock, $90,000.

Exercise 2-3
Using ledger
accounts

Enter the following transactions in T accounts drawn on ordinary notebook paper. Enter the dates and amounts and label each debit and credit with the letter identifying the transaction. Prepare a trial balance at June 30.

a On June 10, Dan King organized Fence Corporation. The corporation issued 15,000 shares of $5 par value capital stock in exchange for $75,000 cash.
b On June 13, purchased land and an office building at a total price of $160,000, of which $120,000 was applicable to the land and $40,000 to the building. A cash payment of $50,000 was made and a note payable was issued for the balance.
c On June 20, office equipment was purchased at a cost of $8,400. A cash down payment of $2,800 was made, and it was agreed that the balance should be paid within 30 days.
d On June 30, paid $2,800 of the $5,600 liability arising from the purchase of office equipment on June 20.

Exercise 2-4
Effects of debits
and credits on
ledger account
balances

The first six transactions of a newly organized company appear in the following T accounts. The company is a single proprietorship.

Cash					
(1)	57,500	(2)	42,500		
		(4)	2,500		
		(5)	6,250		

Office Equipment	
(3) 11,250	

Accounts Payable			
(5)	6,250	(3)	11,250

Land	
(2) 30,000	

Delivery Truck	
(4) 10,000	

Bob Love, Capital		
	(1)	57,500

Building	
(2) 45,000	

Notes Payable		
	(2)	32,500
	(4)	7,500

For each of the six transactions in turn, indicate the type of accounts affected (asset, liability, or owner's equity) and whether the account was increased or decreased. Arrange your answers in the form illustrated for transaction (1), shown here as an example.

	Account(s) Debited		Account(s) Credited	
Transaction	Type of Account(s)	Increase or Decrease	Type of Account(s)	Increase or Decrease
(1)	Asset	Increase	Owner's equity	Increase

Exercise 2-5
Recording transactions in a journal

Enter the following transactions in the two-column journal of Cameron Sporting Goods. Include a brief explanation of the transaction as part of each journal entry.

Nov. 3 Purchased an adjacent vacant lot for use as parking space. The price was $98,800, of which $28,800 was paid in cash; a note payable was issued for the balance.
Nov. 12 Collected an account receivable of $4,800 from a customer, Gene Krieger.
Nov. 17 Acquired office equipment from Tower Company for $7,600 cash.
Nov. 21 Issued a check for $864 in full payment of an account payable to Hampton Supply Co.
Nov. 28 Borrowed $35,000 cash from the bank by signing a 90-day note payable.

Exercise 2-6
Relationship between journal entries and ledger accounts

Transactions are recorded first in a journal and then posted to ledger accounts. In this exercise, however, your understanding of the relationship between journal and ledger is tested by asking you to study some ledger accounts and determine the journal entries which were probably made by the company's accountant to produce these ledger entries. The following accounts show the first six transactions of the South Pacific Travel Agency, Inc. Prepare a journal entry (include written explanation) for each transaction.

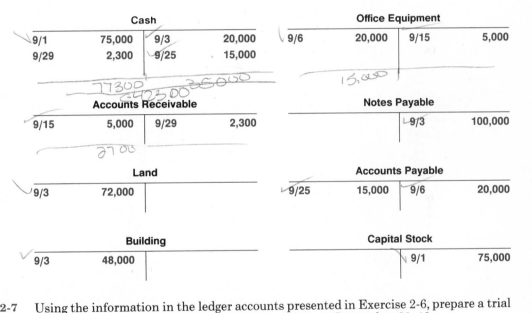

Cash					Office Equipment		
9/1	75,000	9/3	20,000	9/6	20,000	9/15	5,000
9/29	2,300	9/25	15,000				

Accounts Receivable					Notes Payable		
9/15	5,000	9/29	2,300			9/3	100,000

Land					Accounts Payable		
9/3	72,000			9/25	15,000	9/6	20,000

Building					Capital Stock		
9/3	48,000					9/1	75,000

Exercise 2-7
Preparing a trial balance

Using the information in the ledger accounts presented in Exercise 2-6, prepare a trial balance for the South Pacific Travel Agency, Inc., at September 30, 19__ .

Exercise 2-8
Effects of errors upon a trial balance

The trial balance prepared by Field Company at September 30 was not in balance. In searching for the error, an employee discovered that a transaction for the purchase of a typewriter on credit for $610 had been recorded by a ***debit*** of $610 to the Office Equipment account and a ***debit*** of $610 to Accounts Payable. The credit column of the incorrect trial balance had a total of $92,600.

In answering each of the following five questions, explain briefly the reasons underlying your answer and state the dollar amount of the error if any.

a Was the Office Equipment account overstated, understated, or correctly stated in the trial balance?

b Was the total of the debit column of the trial balance overstated, understated, or correctly stated?

c Was the Accounts Payable account overstated, understated, or correctly stated in the trial balance?

d Was the total of the credit column of the trial balance overstated, understated, or correctly stated?

e How much was the total of the debit column of the trial balance before correction of the error?

Exercise 2-9
Uses and limitations of a trial balance

Some of the following errors would cause the debit and credit columns of the trial balance to have unequal totals. For each of the four paragraphs, write a statement explaining with reasons whether the error would cause unequal totals in the trial balance. Each paragraph is to be considered independently of the others.

a A $540 payment for a new typewriter was recorded by a debit to Office Equipment of $54 and a credit to Cash of $54.

b A payment of $400 to a creditor was recorded by a debit to Accounts Payable of $400 and a credit to Cash of $40.

c An account receivable in the amount of $800 was collected in full. The collection was recorded by a debit to Cash for $800 and a debit to Accounts Payable for $800.

d An account payable was paid by issuing a check for $350. The payment was recorded by debiting Accounts Payable $350 and crediting Accounts Receivable $350.

Exercise 2-10
Steps in the accounting cycle; computerized accounting systems

Various steps and decisions involved in the accounting cycle are described in the seven lettered statements below. Indicate which of these procedures are mechanical functions that can be performed by machine in a computerized accounting system, and which require the judgment of people familiar with accounting principles and concepts.

(a) Decide whether or not events should be recorded in the accounting records.

(b) Determine which ledger accounts should be debited and credited to describe specific business transactions.

(c) Arrange recorded data in the format of journal entries.

(d) Arrange recorded data in the format of ledger accounts.

(e) Prepare a trial balance.

(f) Prepare financial statements (a balance sheet).

(g) Evaluate the debt-paying ability of one company relative to another.

Problems

Problem 2-1
Analyzing transactions and preparing journal entries

Yoko Toyoda is the founder and only stockholder in Perfect Portraits, Inc., a photography studio. A few of the company's business transactions occurring during July are described below:

(1) On July 2, collected cash of $700 from accounts receivable.

(2) On July 7, purchased photographic equipment for $2,175, paying $500 in cash and charging the remainder on the company's 30-day account at Camera Supply Co.

(3) On July 9, returned to Camera Supply Co. $200 of photographic equipment which did not work properly. The return of this equipment reduced by $200 the amount owed to Camera Supply Co.

(4) On July 25, Perfect Portraits issued an additional 5,000 shares of its $1 par value capital stock to Toyoda in exchange for $5,000 cash.

(5) On July 31, paid the remaining $1,475 owed to Camera Supply Co.

Instructions

a Prepare an analysis of each of the above transactions. The form of analysis to be used is as follows, using transaction (1) as an example.

1(a) The asset Cash was increased. Increases in assets are recorded by debits. Debit Cash, $700.

(b) The asset Accounts Receivable was decreased. Decreases in assets are recorded by credits. Credit Accounts Receivable, $700.

b Prepare journal entries, including explanations, for the above transactions.

**Problem 2-2
Preparation of a
trial balance**

Fine-Line Blueprints, Inc., provides fast production and distribution of blueprints and other drawings and documents to customers throughout the city. At September 30, the ledger accounts appear as follows:

Cash			Notes Payable	
4,280	3,000		3,000	35,000
3,270	720			
2,930	570			
5,380	5,050			
	4,000			

Accounts Receivable			Accounts Payable	
11,200	3,270		570	640
7,820	2,930			210
				1,060

Office Supplies			Capital Stock	
680	510			30,000
930				

Office Equipment			Retained Earnings	
38,400			4,000	8,270
				6,580

Delivery Equipment	
19,350	

Instructions. Determine the account balances and prepare a trial balance as of September 30, 19__.

Problem 2-3
Recording
transactions in a
journal

Susan Cole, a certified public accountant, resigned from her position with a large CPA firm in order to begin her own public accounting practice. The practice was organized as a corporation, called Susan Cole, An Accountancy Corporation. The business transactions during September while the new corporation was being organized are listed below.

Sept. 1 The corporation issued 15,000 shares of $2 par value capital stock to Cole in exchange for her investment of $30,000 in cash.

Sept. 10 Purchased a small office building located on a large lot for a total price of $91,200, of which $48,000 was applicable to the land and $43,200 to the building. A cash payment of $18,240 was made and a note payable was issued for the balance of the purchase price.

Sept. 15 Purchased a micro-computer system from Computer Stores, Inc., for $4,680 cash.

Sept. 19 Purchased office furniture, filing cabinets, and a typewriter from Davidson Office Supply Co. at a cost of $3,960. A cash down payment of $720 was made, the balance to be paid in three equal installments due September 28, October 28, and November 28. The purchase was on open account and did not require signing of a promissory note.

Sept. 26 A $140 monitor in the micro-computer system purchased on September 15 stopped working. The monitor was returned to Computer Stores, Inc., which promised to refund the $140 within five days.

Sept. 28 Paid Davidson Office Supply Co. $1,080 cash as the first installment due on the account payable for office equipment.

Sept. 30 Received $140 cash from Computer Stores, Inc., in full settlement of the account receivable created on September 26.

Instructions. Prepare journal entries to record the above transactions. Select the appropriate account titles from the following chart of accounts:

Cash	Office Equipment
Accounts Receivable	Notes Payable
Land	Accounts Payable
Building	Capital Stock

Problem 2-4
Posting to ledger
accounts;
preparing a trial
balance and a
balance sheet

Tom Morgan is a veterinarian. In January, he began organizing his own animal hospital, to be known as Animal Care Center. Morgan has prepared the following journal entries to record all January business transactions. He has not posted these entries to ledger accounts.

The account titles and account numbers to be used are

Cash	1	Medical equipment	27
Office supplies	10	Notes payable	30
Land	20	Accounts payable	31
Building	25	Capital stock	50

Instructions

a Post the journal entries to ledger accounts of the three-column running balance form.

b Prepare a trial balance at January 31 from the ledger accounts completed in part a.

c Prepare a balance sheet at January 31, 19___ .

		General Journal			Page 1
Jan	2	Cash	50	60,000	
		Capital Stock..........................			60,000
		Issued 6,000 shares of $10 par value capital stock in exchange for cash.			
	4	Land		45,000	
		Building......................................		115,000	
		Cash......................................			40,000
		Notes Payable.........................			120,000
		Purchased land and building.			
	7	Medical Equipment		7,480	
		Accounts Payable......................			7,480
		Bought equipment on credit from Medco, Inc.			
	8	Office Supplies.............................		590	
		Accounts Payable......................			590
		Bought supplies from Miller Supply.			
	13	Accounts Payable		1,400	
		Medical Equipment.....................			1,400
		Returned defective medical equipment to Medco, Inc., for credit on account.			
	18	Accounts Payable		590	
		Cash......................................			590
		Made payment of liability to Miller Supply.			

Problem 2-5
Preparing journal entries, posting, and preparing a trial balance

Ryan Land Company is a corporation organized on October 2 by Ann Ryan. Ryan is a licensed real estate broker, and the business will operate as a real estate brokerage. The following events occurred during October:

Oct. 1 The corporation issued 2,500 shares of capital stock to its owner, Ann Ryan, in exchange for her investing $25,000 cash in the business.

Oct. 6 Purchased land and a small office building at a total price of $97,500 of which $64,000 was applicable to land and $33,500 to the building. The terms of the purchase required a cash payment of $19,500 and the issuance of a note payable for $78,000.

Oct. 15 Sold one quarter of the land at its cost of $16,000 to a neighboring business, Village Medical Clinic, which wanted to expand its parking lot. No down payment was required; Village Medical Clinic issued a note promising payment of the $16,000 in a series of five monthly installments of $3,200 each, beginning October 30 (ignore interest). As the land was sold at the same price per square foot as Ryan Land Company had paid to acquire it, no gain or loss results on this transaction.

Oct. 20 Purchased office equipment on credit from Buffington Company in the amount of $5,280.

Oct. 30 Paid $3,440 as partial settlement of the liability to Buffington Company.

Oct. 31 Received the first $3,200 monthly installment on the note receivable from Village Medical Clinic.

The account titles and account numbers to be used are:

Cash	1	Office equipment	26
Notes receivable	5	Notes payable	30
Land.................................	21	Accounts payable	32
Building.............................	23	Capital stock.........................	50

Instructions

a Prepare journal entries for the month of October.

b Post to ledger accounts of the three-column running balance form.

c Prepare a trial balance at October 31, 19__ .

Problem 2-6
Preparing journal entries, posting, and preparing a trial balance

After playing several seasons of professional football, George Harris had saved enough money to start a business, to be called Number One Auto Rentals, Inc. The transactions during March while the new business was being organized are listed below:

Mar. 1 George Harris invested $150,000 cash in the business, in exchange for which the corporation issued 30,000 shares of its $5 par value capital stock.

Mar. 3 The new company purchased land and a building at a cost of $120,000, of which $72,000 was regarded as applicable to the land and $48,000 to the building. The transaction involved a cash payment of $41,500 and the issuance of a note payable for $78,500.

Mar. 5 Purchased 20 new automobiles at $8,600 each from Fleet Sales Company. Paid $40,000 cash, and agreed to pay $32,000 by March 31 and the remaining balance by April 15. The liability is viewed as an account payable.

Mar. 7 Sold an automobile at cost to Harris' father-in-law, Howard Facey, who paid $2,400 in cash and agreed to pay the balance within 30 days.

Mar. 8 One of the automobiles was found to be defective and was returned to Fleet Sales Company. The amount payable to this creditor was thereby reduced by $8,600.

Mar. 20 Purchased office equipment at a cost of $4,000 cash.

Mar. 31 Issued a check for $32,000 in partial payment of the liability to Fleet Sales Company.

The account titles and the account numbers used by the company are as follows:

Cash	10	Automobiles	22
Accounts receivable	11	Notes payable	31
Land.................................	16	Accounts payable	32
Buildings............................	17	Capital stock.........................	50
Office equipment	20		

Instructions

a Journalize the March transactions.

b Post to ledger accounts. Use the running balance form of ledger account.

c Prepare a trial balance at March 31.

Problem 2-7
Preparing
journal entries,
posting, prepar-
ing a trial
balance, and a
balance sheet

Educational TV, Inc., was organized in February 19__ , to operate as a local television station. The account titles and numbers used by the corporation are listed below:

Cash	1	Telecasting equipment	24
Accounts receivable	5	Film library	25
Supplies	9	Notes payable	31
Land	21	Accounts payable	32
Building	22	Capital stock	51
Transmitter	23		

The transactions for February 19__ , were as follows:

Feb. 1   A charter was granted to Paul and Alice Marshal for the organization of Educational TV, Inc. The Marshals invested $300,000 cash and received 30,000 shares of stock in exchange.

Feb. 2   Educational TV purchased the land, buildings, and telecasting equipment previously used by a local television station which had gone bankrupt. The total purchase price was $250,000, of which $100,000 was attributable to the land, $80,000 to the building, and the remainder to the telecasting equipment. The terms of the purchase required a cash payment of $160,000 and the issuance of a note payable for the balance.

Feb. 5   Purchased a transmitter at a cost of $200,000 from AC Mfg. Co., making a cash down payment of $56,000. The balance, in the form of a note payable, was to be paid in monthly installments of $12,000, beginning February 15. (Interest expense is to be ignored.)

Feb. 9   Purchased a film library at a cost of $32,000 from Modern Film Productions, making a down payment of $15,000 cash, with the balance on account payable in 30 days.

Feb. 12   Bought supplies costing $3,000, paying cash.

Feb. 15   Paid $12,000 to AC Mfg. Co. as the first monthly payment on the note payable created on February 5. (Interest expense is to be ignored.)

Feb. 25   Sold part of the film library to City College; cost was $7,000 and the selling price also was $7,000. City College agreed to pay the full amount in 30 days.

Instructions

a Prepare journal entries for the month of February.
b Post to ledger accounts of the three-column running balance form.
c Prepare a trial balance at February 28, 19__ .
d Prepare a balance sheet at February 28, 19__ .

Business decision cases

Case 2-1
Computer-based
accounting
systems

Bill Gates is planning to create a computer-based accounting system for small businesses. His system will be developed from a data base program and will be suitable for use on personal computers.

The idea underlying data base software is that data needed for a variety of uses is entered into the data base only once. The computer is programmed to arrange this data into any number of desired formats. In the case of Gates' accounting system, the company's accounting personnel must enter the relevant information about each business transaction into the data base. The program which Gates plans to write will then enable the computer operator to have the information arranged by the computer into the formats of (1) journal entries (with written explanations), (2) three-column running balance form ledger accounts, (3) a trial balance, and (4) a balance sheet.

Instructions

a Identify the ***relevant information*** about each business transaction that the company's accounting personnel must enter into the data base to enable Gates' program to prepare the four types of accounting records and statements described above.

b As described in this chapter, the accounting cycle includes the steps of (1) analyzing and recording business transactions, (2) posting the debit and credit amounts to ledger accounts, (3) preparing a trial balance, and (4) preparing financial statements (at this stage, only a balance sheet). Indicate which of these functions can be performed automatically by Gates' computer program and which must still be performed by the company's accounting personnel.

Case 2-2
Preparing
balance sheets
and an introduc-
tion to measuring
income

David Ray, a college student with several summers' experience as a guide on canoe camping trips, decided to go into business for himself. On June 1, Ray organized Birchbark Canoe Trails by depositing $1,800 of personal savings in a bank account in the name of the business. This business is organized as a ***single proprietorship.*** Also on June 1, the business borrowed an additional $3,000 cash from John Ray (David's father) by issuing a three-year note payable. To help the business get started, John Ray agreed that no interest would be charged on the loan. The following transactions were also carried out by the business on June 1:

(1) Bought a number of canoes at a total cost of $5,100; paid $2,000 cash and agreed to pay the balance within 60 days.
(2) Bought camping equipment at a cost of $4,400 payable in 60 days.
(3) Bought supplies for cash, $700.

After the close of the season on September 10, Ray asked another student, Sharon Lee, who had taken a course in accounting, to help determine the financial position of the business.

The only record Ray had maintained was a checkbook with memorandum notes written on the check stubs. From this source Lee discovered that Ray had invested an additional $1,400 of savings in the business on July 1, and also that the accounts payable arising from the purchase of the canoes and camping equipment had been paid in full. A bank statement received from the bank on September 10 showed a balance on deposit of $2,910.

Ray informed Lee that all cash received by the business had been deposited in the bank and all bills had been paid by check immediately upon receipt; consequently, as of September 10 all bills for the season had been paid. However, nothing had been paid on the note payable.

The canoes and camping equipment were all in excellent condition at the end of the season and Ray planned to resume operations the following summer. In fact he had already accepted reservations from many customers who wished to return.

Lee felt that some consideration should be given to the wear and tear on the canoes and equipment but she agreed with Ray that for the present purpose the canoes and equipment should be listed in the balance sheet at the original cost. The supplies remaining on hand had cost $80 and Ray felt that these supplies could be used next summer.

Lee suggested that two balance sheets be prepared, one to show the condition of the business on June 1 and the other showing the condition on September 10. She also recommended to Ray that a complete set of accounting records be established.

Instructions

a Use the information in the first paragraph (including the three numbered transactions) as a basis for preparing a balance sheet dated June 1.

b Prepare a balance sheet at September 10. Remember, this business is a single proprietorship; for guidance in preparing the owner's equity section of the balance sheet, see page 19. Total cash belonging to the business is the $2,910 appearing in the September 10 bank statement.

c By comparing the two balance sheets, compute the change in owner's equity. Explain the sources of this change in owner's equity and state whether you consider the business to be successful. Also comment on the cash position at the beginning and end of the season. Has the cash position improved significantly?

Explain.

Chapter 3
Measuring
business
income

CHAPTER PREVIEW

In Chapter 3 our coverage of the accounting cycle is expanded to include the measurement of business income. Attention is focused on the accounting concepts of revenue, expense, net income, dividends, and retained earnings. Two important accounting principles are introduced—the realization principle and the matching principle. The continuing example of Greenhill Real Estate is then used to show how a business records revenue and expense transactions and prepares an income statement and statement of retained earnings. As Greenhill Real Estate owns depreciable assets, the concept of depreciation is introduced, and the recording of depreciation expense is illustrated. The procedures for closing the revenue and expense accounts at the end of the accounting period also are illustrated and explained. In summary, this chapter introduces and illustrates the basic concepts of accrual accounting.

After studying this chapter you should be able to meet these Learning Objectives:

1 Explain the nature of retained earnings, net income, revenue, and expenses.
2 Relate the time-period principle to the need for frequent financial statements.
3 Relate the realization principle and the matching principle to the recording of revenue and expenses.
4 Apply the rules of debit and credit to revenue and expense transactions.
5 Define and record depreciation expense.
6 Prepare an income statement and a statement of retained earnings. Explain how these statements provide a link between two successive balance sheets.
7 Prepare closing entries.
8 Describe the sequence of procedures in the accounting cycle.
9 Distinguish between the accrual basis and the cash basis of accounting.

In this chapter you will be introduced to the challenge of measuring income. Some people mistakenly assume that measuring income is a matter of simple arithmetic. In fact, no topic in accounting is more complex and controversial than measuring the net income of a specific business for a specific year. We will be concerned with one aspect or another of measuring and reporting income throughout this book.

The earning of **net income,** or profits, is a major goal of almost every business enterprise, large or small. Profit is the **increase in the owners' equity resulting from operation of the business.** This increase usually is accompanied by an increase in total assets. The opposite of profit, a decrease in owners' equity resulting from operation of the business, is termed a **net loss.** If you were to organize a small business of your own, you would do so with the hope and expectation that the business would operate at a profit, thereby increasing your ownership equity. Individuals who invest in the capital stock of large corporations also expect the business to earn a profit which will increase the value of their investment.

The resources generated by profitable operation may be retained in the business to finance expansion, or they may be distributed as dividends to the stockholders. Some of the largest corporations have become large by retaining their profits in the business and using these profits to finance growth. If profits are retained in the business, a company may be in a better position to acquire new plant and equipment, to carry on research leading to new and better products, and to extend sales operations into new territories.

Retained earnings

1 Explain the nature of retained earnings, net income, revenue, and expenses.

The increase in owners' equity resulting from profitable operations is credited to an account called **Retained Earnings,** which appears in the stockholders' equity section of the balance sheet. If a business has sufficient cash, a distribution of profits may be made to the stockholders. Distributions of this nature are termed **dividends** and decrease both total assets and total stockholders' equity. The decrease in stockholders' equity is reflected by a decrease in the Retained Earnings account. Thus, the balance of the Retained Earnings account represents only the earnings which have **not** been distributed as dividends.

Some people mistakenly believe that retained earnings represent a fund of cash available to a corporation. **Retained earnings is not an asset; it is an element of stockholders' equity.** Although the amount of retained earnings indicates the portion of total assets which were **financed** by earning and retaining net income, it does **not** indicate the **form** in which these resources are currently held. The resources generated by retaining profits may have been invested in land, buildings, equipment, or any other kind of asset. The total amount of cash owned by a corporation is shown by the balance of the Cash account, which appears in the asset section of the balance sheet.

Net income

Since the drive for profits underlies the very existence of business organizations, it follows that a most important function of an accounting system is to provide information about the profitability of a business. Before we can measure the profits of a business, we need to establish a sharp, clear meaning for *profits.* Economists often define profits as the amount by which an entity becomes *better off* during a period of time. Unfortunately, how much "better off" an entity has become is largely a matter of personal opinion and cannot be measured *objectively* enough to provide a useful definition for accountants.

For this reason, accountants usually look to actual business transactions to provide objective evidence that a business has been profitable or unprofitable. For example, if an item which cost a business $60 is sold for $100 cash, we have objective evidence that the business has earned a profit of $40. Since business managers and economists use the word *profits* in somewhat different senses, accountants prefer to use the alternative term *net income,* and to define this term very carefully. *Net income is the excess of the price of goods sold and services rendered over the cost of goods and services used up during a given time period.* At this point, we shall adopt the technical accounting term *net income* in preference to the less precise term *profits.*

To determine net income, it is necessary to measure for a given time period (1) the price of goods sold and services rendered and (2) the cost of goods and services used up. The technical accounting terms for these elements of net income are *revenue* and *expenses.* Therefore, we may state that *net income equals revenue minus expenses,* as shown in the following income statement:

GREENHILL REAL ESTATE
Income Statement
For the Month Ended October 31, 19__

Income statement for October		
Revenue:		
Sales commissions earned		$10,640
Expenses:		
Advertising expense..	$ 630	
Salaries expense..	7,100	
Telephone expense..	144	
Depreciation expense: building..	150	
Depreciation expense: office equipment	45	8,069
Net income		$ 2,571

We will show how this income statement is developed from Greenhill's accounting records late in this chapter. For the moment, however, this illustration will assist us in discussing some of the basic concepts involved in measuring business income.

Income must be related to a specified period of time. Notice that Greenhill's income statement covers a *period* of time—namely, the month of October. A balance sheet shows the financial position of a business at a *particular date.* An income statement, on the other hand, shows the results of business operations over a span of time. We cannot evaluate net income unless it is associated with a specific time period. For example, if an executive says, "My business earns a net income of $10,000," the profitability of the business is unclear. Does it earn $10,000 per week, per month, or per year?

● **CASE IN POINT** ● The late J. Paul Getty, one of the world's first billionaires, was once interviewed by a group of business students. One of the students asked Getty to estimate the amount of his income. As the student had not specified a time period, Getty decided to have some fun with his audience and responded, "About $11,000 . . ." He paused long enough to allow the group to express surprise over this seemingly low amount, and then completed his sentence, ". . . per hour." Incidentally, $11,000 per hour amounts to about $100 million per year.

Every business prepares an annual income statement, and most businesses prepare quarterly and monthly income statements as well. The period of time covered by an income statement is termed the company's *accounting period.* This period may be a month, a quarter of a year, a year, or any other specified period of time.

A 12-month accounting period used by an entity is called its *fiscal year.* The fiscal year used by most companies coincides with the calendar year and ends on December 31. However, some businesses elect to use a fiscal year which ends on some other date. It may be convenient for the business to end its fiscal year during a slack season rather than during a time of peak business activity. The fiscal year of the federal government, for example, begins on October 1 and ends 12 months later on September 30.

The time-period principle

2 Relate the time-period principle to the need for frequent financial statements.

The activities of a business entity may go on for many years without interruption. Some transactions such as the acquisition of a new building or the development of a new product make sense only because they hold the promise of benefits to be derived over a long term of years. However, the measuring of net income over the entire life of a business does not meet the needs of management, stockholders, or government agencies (such as the IRS). These groups demand annual financial statements. As previously mentioned, most businesses go a step further and prepare quarterly and monthly financial statements. Accountants, therefore, must measure net income for short periods of time.

The time-period principle is one of the generally accepted accounting principles that guide the interpretation of financial events and the preparation of financial statements. It tells us that the life of a business entity must be divided for accounting purposes into time periods of equal length, so that decision-makers will be informed on current trends within the business. If net income for the first quarter of this year is, say, 5% below the net income of the first quarter of last year, the users of financial statements need this information promptly as a basis for today's decisions.

Let us now explore the meaning of the accounting terms *revenue* and *expenses.*

Revenue

Revenue is the price of goods sold and services rendered during a given accounting period. When a business renders services to its customers or delivers merchandise to them, it either receives immediate payment in cash or acquires an account receivable which will be collected and thereby become cash within a short time. The revenue for any given period is equal to the inflow of cash and receivables from sales made in that period. For any single transaction, the amount of revenue is a measurement of the asset values received from the customer.

Revenue causes an increase in owners' equity. The inflow of cash and receivables from customers increases the total assets of the company; on the other side of the accounting equation, the liabilities do not change, but owners' equity is increased to match the increase in total assets. Thus, revenue is the gross increase in owners' equity resulting from business activities.

Various terms are used to describe different types of revenue; for example, the revenue earned by a real estate broker might be called ***Sales Commissions Earned,*** or alternatively, ***Commissions Revenue.*** In the professional practice of lawyers, physicians, dentists, and CPAs, the revenue is called ***Fees Earned.*** A business which sells merchandise rather than services (General Motors, for example) will use the term ***Sales*** to describe the revenue earned. Another type of revenue is ***Interest Earned,*** which means the amount received as interest on notes receivable, bank deposits, government bonds, or other securities.

3 Relate the realization principle and the matching principle to the recording of revenue and expenses.

When to record revenue: the realization principle. When is revenue recorded in the accounting records? For example, assume that on May 24, a real estate company signs a contract to represent a client in selling the client's personal residence. The contract entitles the real estate company to a commission equal to 5% of the selling price, due 30 days after the date of sale. On June 10, the real estate company sells the house at a price of $120,000, thereby earning a $6,000 commission ($120,000 × 5%), to be received on July 10. When should the company record this $6,000 commission revenue—in May, June, or July?

The company should record this revenue on June 10—the day it ***rendered the service*** of selling the client's house. As the company will not collect this commission until July, it must also record an account receivable on June 10. In July, when this receivable is collected, the company must not record revenue a second time. Collecting an account receivable increases one asset, Cash, and decreases another asset, Accounts Receivable. Thus, collecting an account receivable ***does not increase owners' equity*** and does not represent revenue.

Our answer illustrates a generally accepted accounting principle called the ***realization principle.*** The realization principle states that a business should record revenue at the time ***services are rendered to customers*** or ***goods sold are delivered to customers.*** In short, revenue is recorded when it is ***earned,*** without regard as to when the cash is received.

Expenses

Expenses are the cost of the goods and services used up in the process of earning revenue. Examples include the cost of employees' salaries, advertising, rent, utilities, and the gradual wearing-out (depreciation) of such assets as buildings, automobiles, and office equipment. All these costs are necessary to attract and service customers and thereby earn revenue. Expenses are often called the "costs of doing business," that is, the cost of the various activities necessary to carry on a business.

An expense always causes a decrease in owners' equity. The related changes in the accounting equation can be either (1) a decrease in assets, or (2) an increase in liabilities. An expense reduces assets if payment occurs at the time that the expense is recorded. If the expense will not be paid until later, as, for example, the purchase of advertising services on account, the recording of the expense will be accompanied by an increase in liabilities.

When to record expenses: the matching principle. A significant relationship exists between revenue and expenses. Expenses are incurred for the ***purpose of producing revenue.*** In measuring net income for a period, revenue should be offset by ***all the expenses incurred in producing that revenue.*** This concept of offsetting expenses against revenue on a basis of "cause and effect" is called the ***matching principle.***

Timing is an important factor in matching (offsetting) revenue with the related expenses. For example, in preparing monthly income statements, it is important to offset this month's expenses against this month's revenue. We should not offset this month's expenses against last month's revenue, because there is no cause and effect relationship between the two.

To illustrate the matching principle, assume that the salaries earned by sales personnel waiting on customers during July are not paid until early August. In which month should these salaries be regarded as an expense? The answer is July, because this is the month in which the sales personnel's services ***helped to produce revenue.***

We previously explained that revenue and cash receipts are not one and the same thing. Similarly, expenses and cash payments are not identical. The cash payment for an expense may occur before, after, or in the same period that an expense helps to produce revenue. In deciding when to record an expense, the critical question is ***"In what period will this expenditure help to produce revenue?"*** not "When will the cash payment occur?"

Expenditures benefiting more than one accounting period. Many expenditures made by a business benefit two or more accounting periods. Fire insurance policies, for example, usually cover a period of 12 months. If a company prepares monthly income statements, a portion of the cost of such a policy should be allocated to insurance expense each month that the policy is in force. In this case, apportionment of the cost of the policy by months is an easy matter. If the 12-

month policy costs $960, for example, the insurance expense for each month amounts to $80 ($960 cost ÷ 12 months).

Not all transactions can be so precisely divided by accounting periods. The purchase of a building, furniture and fixtures, machinery, a typewriter, or an automobile provides benefits to the business over all the years in which such an asset is used. No one can determine in advance exactly how many years of service will be received from such long-lived assets. Nevertheless, in measuring the net income of a business for a period of one year or less, the accountant must *estimate* what portion of the cost of the building and other long-lived assets is applicable to the current year. Since the allocations of these costs are estimates rather than precise measurements, it follows that income statements should be regarded as useful *approximations* of net income rather than as exact measurements.

For some expenditures, such as those for advertising or employee training programs, it is not possible to estimate objectively the number of accounting periods over which revenue is likely to be produced. In such cases, generally accepted accounting principles require that the expenditure be charged *immediately to expense.* This treatment is based upon the accounting principles of *objectivity* and *conservatism.* Accountants require *objective evidence* that an expenditure will produce revenue in future periods before they will view the expenditure as creating an asset. When this objective evidence does not exist, they follow the conservative practice of recording the expenditure as an expense. *Conservatism,* in this context, means applying the accounting treatment which results in the lowest (most conservative) estimate of net income for the current period.

Dividends

A dividend is a distribution of assets (usually cash) by a corporation to its stockholders. In some respects, dividends are similar to expenses — they reduce both the assets and the owners' equity in the business. However, *dividends are not an expense, and they are not deducted from revenue in the income statement.* The reason that dividends are not viewed as an expense is that these payments do not serve to generate revenue. Rather, they are a *distribution of profits* to the owners of the business.

Since the declaration of a dividend reduces the stockholders' equity, the dividend could be recorded by debiting the Retained Earnings account. However, a clearer record is created if a separate *Dividends* account is debited for all amounts distributed as dividends to stockholders. The disposition of the Dividends account when financial statements are prepared will be illustrated later in this chapter.

Debit and credit rules for revenue and expense

4 Apply the rules of debit and credit to revenue and expense transactions.

We have stressed that revenue increases owners' equity and that expenses decrease owners' equity. The debit and credit rules for recording revenue and expenses in the ledger accounts are a natural extension of the rules for recording changes in owners' equity. The rules previously stated for recording increases and decreases in owners' equity were as follows:

Increases in owners' equity are recorded by *credits.*
Decreases in owners' equity are recorded by *debits.*

This rule is now extended to cover revenue and expense accounts:

Revenue increases owners' equity; therefore revenue is recorded by a *credit.*
Expenses decrease owners' equity; therefore expenses are recorded by *debits.*

Ledger accounts for revenue and expenses. During the course of an accounting period, a great many revenue and expense transactions occur in the average business. To classify and summarize these numerous transactions, a separate ledger account is maintained for each major type of revenue and expense. For example, almost every business maintains accounts for Advertising Expense, Telephone Expense, and Salaries Expense. At the end of the period, all the advertising expenses appear as debits in the Advertising Expense account. The debit balance of this account represents the total advertising expense of the period and is listed as one of the expense items in the income statement.

Revenue accounts are usually much less numerous than expense accounts. A small business such as Greenhill Real Estate in our continuing illustration may have only one or two types of revenue, such as commissions earned from arranging sales of real estate and fees earned from managing properties in behalf of clients. In a business of this type, the revenue accounts might be called Sales Commissions Earned and Management Fees Earned.

Recording revenue and expense transactions: an illustration

The organization of Greenhill Real Estate during September has already been described in Chapters 1 and 2. The illustration is now continued for October, during which month the company earned commissions by selling several residences for its clients. Bear in mind that the company does not own any residential property; it merely acts as a broker or agent for clients wishing to sell their houses. A commission of 6% of the selling price of the house is charged for this service. During October the company not only earned commissions but incurred a number of expenses.

Note that each illustrated transaction which affects an income statement account also affects a balance sheet account. This pattern is consistent with our previous discussion of revenue and expenses. In recording revenue transactions, we debit the assets received and credit a revenue account. In recording expense transactions, we debit an expense account and credit the asset Cash, or a liability account if payment is to be made later. The transactions of Greenhill Real Estate for October were as follows:

Oct. 1 Paid $360 for publication of newspaper advertising describing various houses offered for sale.

	Analysis	Rule	Entry
Advertising expense incurred and paid	The cost of advertising is an expense	Expenses decrease the owners' equity and are recorded by debits	Debit: Advertising Expense, $360
	The asset Cash was decreased	Decreases in assets are recorded by credits	Credit: Cash, $360

Oct. 6 Earned and collected a commission of $2,250 by selling a residence previously listed by a client.

	Analysis	Rule	Entry
Revenue earned and collected	The asset Cash was increased	Increases in assets are recorded by debits	Debit: Cash, $2,250
	Revenue was earned	Revenue increases the owners' equity and is recorded by a credit	Credit: Sales Commissions Earned, $2,250

Oct. 16 Newspaper advertising for October was ordered at a price of $270, payment to be made within 30 days.

	Analysis	Rule	Entry
Advertising expense incurred but not paid	The cost of advertising is an expense	Expenses decrease the owners' equity and are recorded by debits	Debit: Advertising Expense, $270
	An account payable, a liability, was incurred	Increases in liabilities are recorded by credits	Credit: Accounts Payable, $270

Oct. 20 A commission of $8,390 was earned by selling a client's residence. The sales agreement provided that the commission would be paid in 60 days.

	Analysis	Rule	Entry
Revenue earned, to be collected later	An asset in the form of an account receivable was acquired	Increases in assets are recorded by debits	Debit: Accounts Receivable, $8,390
	Revenue was earned	Revenue increases the owners' equity and is recorded by a credit	Credit: Sales Commissions Earned, $8,390

Oct. 30 Paid salaries of $7,100 to employees for services rendered during October.

	Analysis	Rule	Entry
Salaries expense incurred and paid	Salaries of employees are an expense	Expenses decrease the owners' equity and are recorded by debits	Debit: Salaries Expense, $7,100
	The asset Cash was decreased	Decreases in assets are recorded by credits	Credit: Cash, $7,100

Oct. 30 A telephone bill for October amounting to $144 was received. Payment was required by November 10.

	Analysis	Rule	Entry
Telephone expense incurred, to be paid later	The cost of telephone service is an expense	Expenses decrease the owners' equity and are recorded by debits	Debit: Telephone Expense, $144
	An account payable, a liability, was incurred	Increases in liabilities are recorded by credits	Credit: Accounts Payable, $144

Oct. 30 A dividend was declared and paid to the owners of the 18,000 shares of capital stock. The amount of the dividend was 10 cents per share, or a total of $1,800. (As explained on page 88, a dividend is not an expense.)

	Analysis	Rule	Entry
Payment of a dividend	Payment of a dividend decreases the owners' equity	Decreases in owners' equity are recorded by debits	Debit: Dividends, $1,800
	The asset Cash was decreased	Decreases in assets are recorded by credits	Credit: Cash, $1,800

The journal

The journal entries to record the October transactions are as follows:

General Journal   **Page 2**

October journal
entries for
Greenhill Real
Estate Company

Date		Account Titles and Explanation	LP	Debit	Credit
19__ Oct.	1	Advertising Expense.............................	70	360	
		Cash......................................	1		360
		Paid for newspaper advertising.			
	6	Cash	1	2,250	
		Sales Commissions Earned	60		2,250
		Earned and collected commission by selling residence for client.			
	16	Advertising Expense.............................	70	270	
		Accounts Payable........................	32		270
		Purchased newspaper advertising; payable in 30 days.			
	20	Accounts Receivable	4	8,390	
		Sales Commissions Earned	60		8,390
		Earned commission by selling residence for client; commission to be received in 60 days.			
	30	Salaries Expense...............................	72	7,100	
		Cash......................................	1		7,100
		Paid salaries for October.			
	30	Telephone Expense	74	144	
		Accounts Payable........................	32		144
		To record liability for October telephone service.			
	30	Dividends	52	1,800	
		Cash......................................	1		1,800
		Paid dividend to stockholders (18,000 shares at 10 cents per share).			

The column headings at the top of the illustrated journal page (***Date, Account Titles and Explanation, LP, Debit,*** and ***Credit***) are seldom used in practice. They are included here as an instructional guide but will be omitted from some of the later illustrations of journal entries.

The ledger

The ledger of Greenhill Real Estate after the October transactions have been posted is now illustrated. The accounts appear in the ledger in financial statement order, as illustrated.

Cash — Account No. 1

Date		Explanation	Ref	Debit	Credit	Balance
Sept	1		1	1 80 000 00		1 80 000 00
	3		1		1 41 000 00	39 000 00
	5		1		15 000 00	24 000 00
	20		1	1 500 00		25 500 00
	30		1		3 000 00	22 500 00
Oct	1		2		360 00	22 140 00
	6		2	2 250 00		24 390 00
	30		2		7 100 00	17 290 00
	30		2		1 800 00	15 490 00

Accounts Receivable — Account No. 4

Date		Explanation	Ref	Debit	Credit	Balance
Sept	10		1	11 000 00		11 000 00
	20		1		1 500 00	9 500 00
Oct	20		2	8 390 00		17 890 00

Land — Account No. 20

Date		Explanation	Ref	Debit	Credit	Balance
Sept	3		1	1 41 000 00		1 41 000 00
	10		1		11 000 00	1 30 000 00

Building — Account No. 22

Date		Explanation	Ref	Debit	Credit	Balance
Sept	5		1	36 000 00		36 000 00

Office Equipment — Account No. 25

Date		Explanation	Ref	Debit	Credit	Balance
Sept	14		1	5 400 00		5 400 00

Accounts Payable — Account No. 32

Date		Explanation	Ref	Debit	Credit	Balance
Sept	5		1		2 1 0 0 00	2 1 0 0 00
	14		1		5 4 0 00	2 6 4 0 00
	30		1	3 0 0 00		2 3 4 0 00
Oct	16		2		2 7 00	2 3 6 7 00
	30		2		1 4 4 00	2 3 8 1 4 00

Capital Stock — Account No. 50

Date		Explanation	Ref	Debit	Credit	Balance
Sept	1		1		1 8 0 0 0 00	1 8 0 0 0 00

Dividends — Account No. 52

Date		Explanation	Ref	Debit	Credit	Balance
Oct	30		2	1 8 0 0 00		1 8 0 0 00

Sales Commissions Earned — Account No. 60

Date		Explanation	Ref	Debit	Credit	Balance
Oct	6		2		2 2 5 0 00	2 2 5 0 00
	20		2		8 3 9 0 00	1 0 6 4 0 00

Advertising Expense — Account No. 70

Date		Explanation	Ref	Debit	Credit	Balance
Oct	1		2	3 6 0 00		3 6 0 00
	16		2	2 7 0 00		6 3 0 00

		Salaries Expense			Account No. 72
Date	**Explanation**	**Ref**	**Debit**	**Credit**	**Balance**
Oct 30		2	7 1 0 0 00		7 1 0 0 00

		Telephone Expense			Account No. 75
Date	**Explanation**	**Ref**	**Debit**	**Credit**	**Balance**
Oct 30		2	1 4 4 00		1 4 4 00

Sequence of accounts in the ledger. Accounts are located in the ledger in financial statement order; that is, the balance sheet accounts first (assets, liabilities, and stockholders' equity) followed by the income statement accounts (revenue and expenses). The usual sequence of accounts within these five groups is shown by the following list.

Balance Sheet Accounts	**Income Statement Accounts**
Assets:	Revenue:
01 Cash	61 Commissions earned
02 Marketable securities	Expenses (No standard sequence of listing
03 Notes receivable	exists for individual expense accounts.)
04 Accounts receivable	70 Advertising
08 Inventory (discussed in Chapter 5)	72 Salaries
10 Office supplies	74 Rent
20 Land	75 Telephone
22 Buildings	76 Depreciation expense: buildings
23 Accumulated depreciation: buildings	78 Depreciation expense: equipment
25 Equipment	79–99 Various other expenses
26 Accumulated depreciation: equipment	
Liabilities:	
30 Notes payable	
32 Accounts payable	
34 Salaries payable	
Stockholders' equity:	
50 Capital stock	
51 Retained earnings	
52 Dividends	
53 Income summary	

Why are ledger accounts arranged in financial statement order? Remember that a trial balance is prepared by listing the ledger account balances shown in the ledger, working from the first ledger page to the last. Therefore, if the accounts are located in the ledger in *financial statement order,* the same sequence will naturally be followed in the trial balance, and this arrangement will make it easier to prepare the balance sheet and income statement from the trial balance. Also, this standard arrangement of accounts will make it easier to locate any account in the ledger.

Notice that an account number has been assigned to each account. The number assigned to a particular account depends upon the account's location in the ledger and will not be the same from one company to the next. In a manual accounting system, these account numbers are entered in the *LP* column of the journal to show that an entry has been posted. In a computer-based system, accounts often are identified only by number, thus eliminating the need for the computer operator to enter the entire account title. In addition, the account numbers enable the computer to determine in which financial statement an account should be listed.

The trial balance

A trial balance prepared from Greenhill's ledger accounts is shown below:

GREENHILL REAL ESTATE
Trial Balance
October 31, 19__

Proving the equality of debits and credits		
Cash	$ 15,490	
Accounts receivable	17,890	
Land	130,000	
Building...	36,000	
Office equipment...	5,400	
Accounts payable		$ 23,814
Capital stock		180,000
Dividends...	1,800	
Sales commissions earned		10,640
Advertising expense...	630	
Salaries expense...	7,100	
Telephone expense	144	
	$214,454	$214,454

This trial balance proves the equality of the debit and credit entries in the company's ledger. Note that the trial balance contains income statement accounts as well as balance sheet accounts.

Adjusting entry for depreciation expense

The trial balance includes all the expenses arising from the October business transactions, but it does not include any *depreciation expense.* Our definition of expense is *the cost of goods and services used up in the process of obtaining revenue.* Some of the goods used up are purchased in advance and used up gradually over a long period of time. Buildings and office equipment, for example, are used up over a period of years. Each year, a portion of these assets *expires,* and a portion of their total cost should be recognized as *depreciation expense.* The term *depreciation* means the *systematic allocation of the cost of an asset to expense over the accounting periods making up the asset's useful life.*

Depreciation expense does not require monthly cash outlays; in effect, it is paid in advance when the related asset is originally acquired. Nevertheless, depreciation is an inevitable and continuing expense. Failure to record depreciation would result in *understating* total expenses of the period and consequently *overstating* the net income.

Building. The office building purchased by Greenhill Real Estate at a cost of $36,000 is estimated to have a useful life of 20 years. The purpose of the $36,000 expenditure was to provide a place in which to carry on the business and thereby to obtain revenue. After 20 years of use the building is expected to be worthless and the original cost of $36,000 will have been entirely consumed. In effect, the company has purchased 20 years of "housing services" at a total cost of $36,000. A portion of this cost expires during each year of use of the building. If we assume that each year's operations should bear an equal share of the total cost (straight-line depreciation), the annual depreciation expense will amount to $\frac{1}{20}$ of $36,000, or $1,800. On a monthly basis, depreciation expense is $150 ($36,000 cost ÷ 240 months). There are alternative methods of spreading the cost of a depreciable asset over its useful life, some of which will be considered in Chapter 9.

The journal entry to record depreciation of the building during October follows:

General Journal

Date		Account Titles and Explanation	LP	Debit	Credit
19__					
Oct.	31	Depreciation Expense: Building....................	76	150	
		Accumulated Depreciation: Building..........	23		150
		To record depreciation for October. Cost of $36,000 ÷			
		240 months = $150 a month.			

Recording depreciation of the building

The depreciation expense account will appear in the income statement for October along with the other expenses of salaries, advertising, and telephone expense. The Accumulated Depreciation: Building account will appear in the balance sheet as a deduction from the Building account, as shown by the following illustration of a *partial* balance sheet:

GREENHILL REAL ESTATE
Partial Balance Sheet
October 31, 19__

Building (at cost).. $36,000
Less: Accumulated depreciation...................................... 150 $35,850

The end result of crediting the Accumulated Depreciation: Building account is much the same as if the credit had been made to the Building account; that is, the net amount shown on the balance sheet for the building is reduced from $36,000 to $35,850. Although the credit side of a depreciation entry *could* be made directly to the asset account, it is customary and more efficient to record such credits in a separate account entitled Accumulated Depreciation. The original cost of the asset and the total amount of depreciation recorded over the years can more easily be determined from the ledger when separate accounts are maintained for the asset and for the accumulated depreciation.

Accumulated Depreciation: Building is an example of a *contra-asset account,* because it has a credit balance and is offset against an asset account (Building) to produce the proper balance sheet amount for the asset.

Office equipment. Depreciation on the office equipment of Greenhill Real Estate must also be recorded at the end of October. This equipment cost $5,400 and is assumed to have a useful life of 10 years. Monthly depreciation expense on the straight-line basis is, therefore, $45, computed by dividing the cost of $5,400 by the useful life of 120 months. The journal entry is as follows:

General Journal   Page 2

	Date		Account Titles and Explanation	LP	Debit	Credit
Recording depreciation of office equipment	19__ Oct.	31	Depreciation Expense: Office Equipment............	78	45	
			Accumulated Depreciation: Office Equipment...	26		45
			To record depreciation for October. Cost of $5,400 ÷			
			120 months = $45 a month.			

No depreciation was recorded on the building and office equipment for September, the month in which these assets were acquired, because regular operations did not begin until October. Generally, depreciation is not recognized until the business begins active operation and the assets are placed in use. Accountants often use the expression *matching costs and revenue* to convey the idea of writing off the cost of an asset to expense during the time periods in which the business uses the asset to generate revenue.

The journal entry by which depreciation is recorded at the end of the month is called an *adjusting entry.* The adjustment of certain accounts is a necessary step at the end of each accounting period so that the information presented in the financial statements will be as accurate and complete as possible. In the next chapter, adjusting entries will be shown for some other items in addition to depreciation.

The adjusted trial balance

After all the necessary adjusting entries have been journalized and posted, an **adjusted trial balance** is prepared to prove that the ledger is still in balance. It also provides a complete listing of the account balances to be used in preparing the financial statements. The following adjusted trial balance differs from the trial balance shown on page 96 because it includes accounts for depreciation expense and accumulated depreciation.

GREENHILL REAL ESTATE
Adjusted Trial Balance
October 31, 19__

Adjusting trial balance

Cash	$ 15,490	
Accounts receivable	17,890	
Land	130,000	
Building	36,000	
Accumulated depreciation: building		$ 150
Office equipment	5,400	
Accumulated depreciation: office equipment		45
Accounts payable		23,814
Capital stock		180,000
Dividends	1,800	
Sales commissions earned		10,640
Advertising expense	630	
Salaries expense	7,100	
Telephone expense	144	
Depreciation expense: building	150	
Depreciation expense: office equipment	45	
	$214,649	$214,649

FINANCIAL STATEMENTS

Now that Greenhill Real Estate has been operating for a month, managers and outside parties will want to know more about the company than just its financial position. They will want to know the results of operations—whether the company's activities have been profitable or unprofitable. To provide this additional information, we will prepare a more complete set of financial statements, including an income statement, a statement of retained earnings, and a balance sheet.[1]

---

[1] A complete set of financial statements also includes a statement of cash flows, which will be discussed in Chapter 14.

The income statement

When we measure the net income earned by a business we are measuring its economic performance — its success or failure as a business enterprise. Stock-holders, prospective investors, managers, bankers, and other creditors are anxious to see the latest available income statement and thereby to judge how well the company is doing. The October income statement for Greenhill Real Estate appears below.

GREENHILL REAL ESTATE
Income Statement
For the Month Ended October 31, 19__

Revenue:		
Sales commissions earned		$10,640
Expenses:		
Advertising expense	$ 630	
Salaries expense	7,100	
Telephone expense	144	
Depreciation expense: building	150	
Depreciation expense: office equipment	45	8,069
Net income		$ 2,571

Income statement for October

6 Prepare an income statement and a statement of retained earnings. Explain how these statements provide a link between two successive balance sheets.

This income statement consists of the last six accounts in the adjusted trial balance shown above. It shows that the revenue during October exceeded the expenses of the month, thus producing a net income of $2,571. Bear in mind, however, that our measurement of net income is not absolutely accurate or precise, because of the assumptions and estimates involved in the accounting process.

An income statement has certain limitations. Remember that the amounts shown for depreciation expense are based upon estimates of the useful lives of the company's buildings and office equipment. Also, the income statement includes only those events which have been evidenced by business transactions. Perhaps during October, Greenhill Real Estate has made contact with many people who are right on the verge of buying or selling homes. Good business contacts are an important step toward profitable operations. However, such contacts are not reflected in the income statement because their value cannot be objectively measured until actual transactions take place. Despite these limitations, the income statement is of vital importance and indicates that the new business has been profitable during its first month of operation.

At this point we are purposely ignoring income taxes on corporations. Corporate income taxes will be introduced in Chapter 5 and considered more fully in Chapter 16.

Alternative titles for the income statement include **earnings statement, statement of operations,** and **profit and loss statement.** However, **income statement** is by far the most popular term for this important financial statement. In brief, we can say that an income statement is used to summarize the **operating** *results* of a business by matching the revenue earned during a given time period with the expenses incurred in obtaining that revenue.

Statement of retained earnings

Retained earnings is that portion of the stockholders' equity created by earning and retaining net income. The **statement of retained earnings,** which covers the same time period as the related income statement, shows the increases and decreases in retained earnings for the period.

GREENHILL REAL ESTATE
Statement of Retained Earnings
For the Month Ended October 31, 19__

<table>
<tr><td>Retained earnings, Sept. 30, 19__</td><td>$ -0-</td></tr>
<tr><td>Net income for October</td><td>2,571</td></tr>
<tr><td>   Subtotal</td><td>$2,571</td></tr>
<tr><td>Less: Dividends</td><td>1,800</td></tr>
<tr><td>Retained earnings, Oct. 31, 19__</td><td>$ 771</td></tr>
</table>

Statement of retained earnings for October

The ending amount of retained earnings, $771, will appear in Greenhill's October 31 balance sheet. In this example the company had no retained earnings at the beginning of the period. The statement for the following month (November) will show beginning retained earnings of $771.

The balance sheet

In preparing a balance sheet for Greenhill Real Estate at October 31, we can obtain the balances of the asset, liability, and capital stock accounts from the adjusted trial balance on page 99. The amount of retained earnings at October 31 does not appear in the adjusted trial balance, but has been determined in the statement of retained earnings.

Previous illustrations of balance sheets have been arranged in the **account form,** that is, with the assets on the left side of the page and the liabilities and stockholders' equity on the right side. The balance sheet on the next page is presented in **report form,** that is, with the liabilities and stockholders' equity sections listed below rather than to the right of the asset section. Both the account form and the report form are widely used.

If we compare the October 31 balance sheet to the one prepared at September 30 (page 25), we see that the stockholders' original investment of $180,000 appears unchanged under the caption of Capital Stock. The amount of retained earnings, however, has changed between the two balance sheet dates. The Retained Earnings account had a zero balance at September 30, but as explained in the statement of retained earnings, it was increased by the $2,571 net income earned during October and decreased by the $1,800 dividend paid, leaving a balance of $771 at October 31. Thus, the amount of retained earnings shown in the October 31 balance sheet is taken from the statement of retained earnings, not from the adjusted trial balance.

GREENHILL REAL ESTATE
Balance Sheet
October 31, 19__

Assets

Balance sheet at
October 31:
report form

Cash..		$ 15,490
Accounts receivable		17,890
Land..		130,000
Building	$ 36,000	
Less: Accumulated depreciation.....................................	150	35,850
Office equipment...	$ 5,400	
Less: Accumulated depreciation....................................	45	5,355
Total assets		$204,585

Liabilities & Stockholders' Equity

Liabilities:		
Accounts payable...		$ 23,814
Stockholders' equity:		
Capital stock	$180,000	
Retained earnings...	771	180,771
Total liabilities & stockholders' equity..		$204,585

The amount of retained earnings at any balance sheet date represents the total earnings of the corporation since it started in business, minus all dividends distributed to its stockholders. One reason for maintaining a distinction between capital stock and retained earnings is that a corporation usually cannot legally pay dividends greater than the amount of retained earnings. The separation of these two elements of ownership also may be informative because it shows how much of the total stockholders' equity resulted from the investment of funds by stockholders and how much was derived from earning and retaining net income.

In the Greenhill Real Estate illustration, we have shown the two common ways in which the stockholders' equity may be increased: (1) investment of cash or other assets by the owners and (2) operating the business at a profit. There are also two common ways in which the stockholders' equity may be decreased: (1) payment of dividends and (2) operating the business at a loss.

Income statement and retained earnings statement: a link between two balance sheets

A set of financial statements becomes easier to understand if we recognize that the balance sheet, income statement, and statement of retained earnings are all *related to one another.* The balance sheet prepared at the end of the previous accounting period and the one prepared at the end of the current period each show the amount of retained earnings at the respective balance sheet dates. The statement of retained earnings summarizes the factors (net income and dividends) which have caused the amount of retained earnings to change between these two balance sheet dates. The income statement explains in greater detail the change in retained earnings resulting from profitable operation of the business. Thus, the income statement and the retained earnings statement provide an informative link between successive balance sheets.

CLOSING THE ACCOUNTS

7 Prepare closing entries.   The accounts for revenue, expenses, and dividends are *temporary owners' equity accounts* used during the accounting period to classify certain changes affecting the owners' equity. At the end of the period, we must update the balance of the Retained Earnings account for those changes in owners' equity that were temporarily recorded in the revenue, expense, and dividends accounts. We also want to reduce the balances of the temporary owners' equity accounts to *zero,* so that these accounts will again be ready for use in accumulating information during the next accounting period. These objectives are accomplished by the use of *closing entries.*

Revenue and expense accounts are *closed* at the end of each accounting period by *transferring their balances* to a summary account called *Income Summary.* When the credit balances of the revenue accounts and the debit balances of the expense accounts have been transferred into one summary account, the balance of this Income Summary will be the *net income* or *net loss* for the period. If the revenue (credit balances) exceeds the expenses (debit balances), the Income Summary account will have a credit balance representing net income. Conversely, if expenses exceed revenue, the Income Summary will have a debit balance representing net loss. This is consistent with the rule that increases in owners' equity are recorded by credits and decreases are recorded by debits.

As previously explained, all debits and credits in the ledger are posted from the journal; therefore, the closing of revenue and expense accounts requires the making of journal entries and the posting of these journal entries to ledger accounts. A journal entry made for the purpose of closing a revenue or expense account by transferring its balance to the Income Summary account is called a closing entry. This term is also applied to the journal entries (to be explained later) used in closing the Income Summary account and the Dividends account into the Retained Earnings account.

A principal purpose of the year-end process of closing the revenue and expense accounts is to reduce their balances to zero. Since the revenue and expense accounts provide information for the income statement of *a given accounting period,* it is essential that these accounts have *zero balances* at the beginning of each new period. The closing of the accounts has the effect of "wiping the slate clean" and preparing the accounts for the recording of revenue and expenses during the succeeding accounting period.

It is common practice to close the accounts only once a year, but for illustration, we shall now demonstrate the closing of the accounts of Greenhill Real Estate at October 31 after one month's operation.

Closing entries for revenue accounts. Revenue accounts have credit balances. Therefore, closing a revenue account means transferring its credit balance to the Income Summary account. This transfer is accomplished by a journal entry debiting the revenue account in an amount equal to its credit balance, with an offsetting credit to the Income Summary account. The debit portion of this closing entry returns the balance of the revenue account to zero; the credit portion transfers the former balance of the revenue account into the Income Summary account.

The only revenue account of Greenhill Real Estate is Sales Commissions Earned, which had a credit balance of $10,640 at October 31. The journal entry necessary to close this account is as follows:

General Journal   Page 3

	Date		Account Titles and Explanation	LP	Debit	Credit
Closing a revenue account	19__ Oct.	31	Sales Commissions Earned	61	10,640	
			Income Summary.........................	53		10,640
			To close the Sales Commissions Earned account.			

After this closing entry has been posted, the two accounts affected will appear as shown below. A directional arrow has been added to show the transfer of the $10,640 balance of the revenue account into the Income Summary account.

Sales Commissions Earned   61   Income Summary   53

Date		Exp.	Ref	Debit	Credit	Balance	Date		Exp.	Ref	Debit	Credit	Balance
Oct.	6		2		2,250	2,250	Oct.	31		3		10,640	10,640
	20		2		8,390	10,640							
	31	To close	3	10,640		-0-							

Closing entries for expense accounts. There are five expense accounts in the ledger of Greenhill Real Estate. Five separate journal entries could be made to close these five expense accounts, but the use of one *compound journal entry* is an easier, timesaving method of closing all five expense accounts. A compound journal entry is an entry that includes debits to more than one account or credits to more than one account.

General Journal						Page 3
Date		Accounts Titles and Explanation	LP	Debit		Credit
19__ Oct.	31	Income Summary..................................	53	8,069		
		Advertising Expense	70			630
		Salaries Expense	72			7,100
		Telephone Expense	75			144
		Depreciation Expense: Building	76			150
		Depreciation Expense: Office Equipment	78			45
		To close the expense accounts.				

Closing the various expense accounts by use of a compound journal entry

After this closing entry has been posted, the Income Summary account has a credit balance of $2,571, and the five expense accounts have zero balances, as shown on the next page.

Closing the Income Summary account. The five expense accounts have now been closed and the total amount of $8,069 formerly contained in these accounts appears in the debit column of the Income Summary account. The commissions of $10,640 earned during October appear in the credit column of the Income Summary account. Since the credit entry of $10,640 representing October revenue is larger than the debit of $8,069 representing October expenses, the account has a credit balance of $2,571 — the net income for October.

The net income of $2,571 earned during October causes the owners' equity to increase. The *credit* balance of the Income Summary account is, therefore, transferred to the Retained Earnings account by the following closing entry:

General Journal						Page 3
Date		Account Titles and Explanation	LP	Debit		Credit
19__ Oct.	31	Income Summary..................................	53	2,571		
		Retained Earnings	51			2,571
		To close the Income Summary account for October by transferring the net income to the Retained Earnings account.				

Net income earned increases the owners' equity

After this closing entry has been posted, the Income Summary account has a zero balance, and the net income for October will appear as an increase or credit entry in the Retained Earnings account, as shown on page 107.

**Expense accounts
have zero
balances after
closing entries
have been posted**

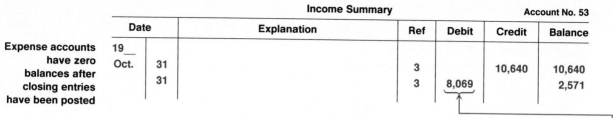

Income Summary   Account No. 53

Date		Explanation	Ref	Debit	Credit	Balance
19__						
Oct.	31		3		10,640	10,640
	31		3	8,069		2,571

Advertising Expense   Account No. 70

Date		Explanation	Ref	Debit	Credit	Balance
19__						
Oct.	2		2	360		360
	16		2	270		630
	31	To close	3		630	-0-

Salaries Expense   Account No. 72

Date		Explanation	Ref	Debit	Credit	Balance
19__						
Oct.	30		2	7,100		7,100
	31	To close	3		7,100	-0-

Telephone Expense   Account No. 75

Date		Explanation	Ref	Debit	Credit	Balance
19__						
Oct.	30		2	144		144
	31	To close	3		144	-0-

Depreciation Expense: Building   Account No. 76

Date		Explanation	Ref	Debit	Credit	Balance
19__						
Oct.	31		2	150		150
	31	To close	3		150	-0-

Depreciation Expense: Office Equipment   Account No. 78

Date		Explanation	Ref	Debit	Credit	Balance
19__						
Oct.	31		2	45		45
	31	To close	3		45	-0-

Income Summary						Account No. 53	
19__						10,640	10,640
Oct.	31	Revenue	3				2,571
	31	Expenses	3	8,069			-0-
	31	To close	3	2,571			

Retained Earnings						Account No. 51	
19__						2,571	2,571
Oct.	31	Net Income for October	3				

In our illustration the business has operated profitably with revenue in excess of expenses. Not every business is so fortunate. If the expenses of a business are larger than its revenue, the Income Summary account will have a debit balance, representing a **net loss** for the accounting period. In this case, the closing of the Income Summary account requires a debit to the Retained Earnings account and an offsetting credit to the Income Summary account. A debit balance in the Retained Earnings account is referred to as a ***deficit;*** it is shown as a deduction from Capital Stock in the balance sheet.

Note that the Income Summary account is used only at the end of the period when the accounts are being closed. The Income Summary account has no entries and no balance except during the process of closing the accounts at the end of the accounting period.

Closing the Dividends account. As explained earlier in the chapter, the payment of dividends to the owners is not considered as an expense of the business and, therefore, is not taken into account in determining the net income for the period. Since dividends do not constitute an expense, the Dividends account is **not** closed into the Income Summary account. Instead, it is closed directly to the Retained Earnings account, as shown by the following entry:

	General Journal				Page 3
Date	**Account Titles and Explanation**		**LP**	**Debit**	**Credit**
19__					
Oct.	31	Retained Earnings.	51	1,800	
		Dividends.	52		1,800
		To close the Dividends account.			

Dividends account is closed to Retained Earnings

After this closing entry has been posted, the Dividends account will have a zero balance, and the dividends distributed during October will appear as a deduction or debit entry in the Retained Earnings account, as follows:

		Dividends					**Account No. 52**
19__							
Oct.	30	Declaration and payment	2	1,800			1,800
	31	To close	3		1,800		-0-

		Retained Earnings					**Account No. 51**
19__							
Oct.	31	Net Income for October	3			2,571	2,571
	31	Dividends	3	1,800			771

The closing process — in summary. The closing of the accounts may be illustrated graphically by the use of T accounts as shown below:

Diagram showing closing of the accounts

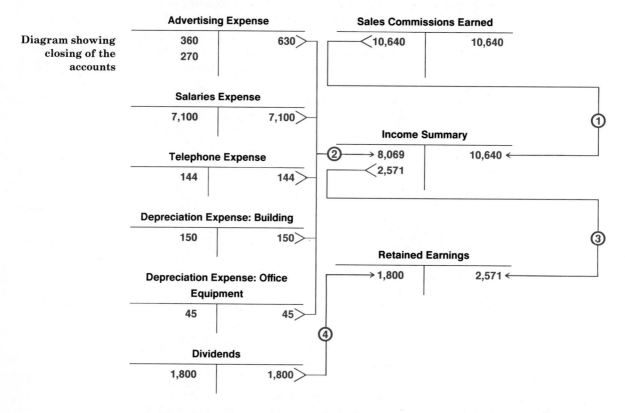

As illustrated in the preceding diagram, the closing process consists of four steps:

1 Close the various revenue accounts by transferring their balances into the Income Summary account.
2 Close the various expense accounts by transferring their balances into the Income Summary account.

3 Close the Income Summary account by transferring its balance into the Retained Earnings account.

4 Close the Dividends account by transferring its balance into the Retained Earnings account.

After-closing trial balance

After the revenue and expense accounts have been closed, it is desirable to prepare an *after-closing trial balance,* which of course will consist solely of balance sheet accounts. There is always the possibility that an error in posting the closing entries may have upset the equality of debits and credits in the ledger. The after-closing trial balance, or *post-closing trial balance* as it is often called, is prepared from the ledger. It gives assurance that the accounts are in balance and ready for the recording of the transactions of the new accounting period. The after-closing trial balance of Greenhill Real Estate follows:

GREENHILL REAL ESTATE
After-Closing Trial Balance
October 31, 19__

Only the balance sheet accounts remain open

Cash	$ 15,490	
Accounts receivable	17,890	
Land	130,000	
Building	36,000	
Accumulated depreciation: building		$ 150
Office equipment	5,400	
Accumulated depeciation: office equipment		45
Accounts payable		23,814
Capital stock		180,000
Retained earnings, Oct. 31		771
	$204,780	$204,780

Sequence of procedures in the accounting cycle

The accounting procedures described to this point may be summarized in eight steps, as follows:

8 Describe the sequence of procedures in the accounting cycle.

1 *Journalize transactions.* Enter all transactions in the journal, thus creating a chronological record of events.

2 *Post to ledger accounts.* Post debits and credits from the journal to the proper ledger accounts, thus creating a record classified by accounts.

3 *Prepare a trial balance.* Prove the equality of debits and credits in the ledger.

4 *Prepare end-of-period adjustments.* Enter adjusting entries in the general journal, and post to ledger accounts.

5 *Prepare an adjusted trial balance.* Prove again the equality of debits and credits in the ledger.

6 *Prepare financial statements.* An income statement shows the results of operation for the period. A statement of retained earnings shows the changes in retained earnings during the period and the closing balance. A balance sheet shows the financial position of the business at the end of the period.

7 *Journalize and post the closing entries.* The closing entries clear the revenue, expense, and dividends accounts, making them ready for recording the events of the next accounting period, and also bring the Retained Earnings account up-to-date.

8 *Prepare an after-closing trial balance.* This step ensures that the ledger remains in balance after posting of the closing entries.

Accounting procedures in a computer-based system

The sequence of procedures performed in computer-based systems is essentially the same as in manual systems. Of course, the computer is programmed to perform a number of these steps automatically. In the preceding list, procedures 1 and 4 both involve the analysis of business transactions and judgmental decisions as to accounts to be debited and credited and the dollar amounts. These two steps in the accounting cycle require human judgment, regardless of whether the data is processed manually or by computer. As mentioned in Chapter 2, a computer-based system may call for recording transactions first in a data base, rather than in a journal. The computer then arranges the data into the format of journal entries, ledger accounts, trial balances, and financial statements.

Procedures such as posting and the preparation of trial balances and financial statements involve the rearrangement of recorded data and may easily be performed by computer. The preparation of closing entries also is a mechanical task, involving the transfer of recorded data from one ledger account to another. Thus, closing entries may be performed automatically in a computer-based system.

Dividends — declaration and payment

Earlier in this chapter the declaration and the payment of a cash dividend were treated as a single event recorded by one journal entry. A small corporation with only a few stockholders may choose to declare and pay a dividend on the same day. In large corporations with thousands of stockholders and constant transfers of shares, an interval of a month or more will separate the date of declaration from the later date of payment.

Assume for example that on April 1 the board of directors of Universal Corporation declares the regular quarterly dividend of $1 per share on the 1 million shares of outstanding capital stock. The board's resolution specifies that the dividend will be payable on May 10 to stockholders of record on April 25. To be eligible to receive the dividend, an individual must be listed on the corporation's records as a stockholder on April 25, the date of record. Two entries are required: one on April 1 for the declaration of the dividend and one on May 10 for its payment, as shown below.

Dividends declared and . . .	Apr. 1	Dividends..	1,000,000	
		Dividends payable..............................		1,000,000
		Declared dividend of $1 per share payable May 10 to stock-		
		holders of record Apr. 25.		

. . . Dividends paid	May 10	Dividends Payable...................................	1,000,000	
		Cash..		1,000,000
		Paid the $1 per share dividend declared on Apr. 1.		

The Dividends Payable account is a liability which comes into existence when the dividend is declared and is discharged when the dividend is paid.

The procedures of formally declaring and distributing dividends are performed only in businesses organized as corporations. In unincorporated businesses (single proprietorships and partnerships) the owners may withdraw cash or other assets from the business without any formal declaration.

Accrual basis of accounting versus cash basis of accounting

9 Distinguish between the accrual basis and the cash basis of accounting.

A business which recognizes revenue in the period in which it is earned and which deducts in the same period the expenses incurred in generating this revenue is using the *accrual basis of accounting.*

The alternative to the accrual basis of accounting is the *cash basis.* Under cash basis accounting, revenue is not recorded until received in cash; expenses are assigned to the period in which cash payment is made. Most business concerns use the accrual basis of accounting, but individuals, professionals (such as physicians and lawyers), and many small service-type companies, usually maintain their accounting records on a cash basis.

The cash basis of accounting does not give a good picture of profitability. For example, it ignores uncollected revenue which has been earned and expenses which have been incurred but not paid. However, the cash basis does offer several advantages in the preparation of income tax returns. Throughout this book we shall be working with the accrual basis of accounting, except for that portion of Chapter 16 dealing with the income tax returns of individuals.

END-OF-CHAPTER REVIEW

Summary of chapter learning objectives

1 **Explain the nature of retained earnings, net income, revenue, and expenses.**

Retained earnings is an element of stockholders' equity. It represents the earnings of a corporation since its beginning, minus any losses incurred and any dividends declared. Net income is the increase in stockholders' equity that results from the profitable operation of a business during an accounting period. The net income of an accounting period is also equal to revenue minus expenses. Revenue is the price of goods sold or services rendered during the accounting period. Expenses are the cost of goods or services used up in the process of earning revenue.

2 Relate the time-period principle to the need for frequent financial statements.

The time-period principle requires that the life of a business be divided for accounting purposes into time periods of equal length. Thus, every business prepares yearly financial statements, and most companies prepare quarterly and monthly statements as well.

3 Relate the realization principle and the matching principle to the recording of revenue and expenses.

Revenue should be recorded in the accounting records when it is realized. In this context, "realized" means "earned." In short, revenue is recognized when goods are sold or when services are rendered to customers. The matching principle indicates that expenses should be offset against revenue on a basis of cause and effect. That is, an expense should be recorded in the accounting records when the related good or service is consumed in the process of earning revenue.

4 Apply the rules of debit and credit to revenue and expense transactions.

Revenue increases owners' equity; therefore, revenue is recorded by a credit. Expenses decrease owners' equity; therefore, expenses are recorded by debits.

5 Define and record depreciation expense.

The term *depreciation* refers to the systematic allocation of the cost of a long-lived asset (such as equipment or a building) to expense over the asset's useful life. Depreciation is recorded by an entry debiting *Depreciation Expense* and crediting the contra-asset account, *Accumulated Depreciation.*

6 Prepare an income statement and a statement of retained earnings. Explain how these statements provide a link between two successive balance sheets.

An income statement shows the revenue and expenses of a business during a specified accounting period. Expenses are offset (matched) against revenue to measure net income for the period. Net income is then listed in the statement of retained earnings as an addition to the beginning balance of retained earnings. Dividends are shown as a deduction. Thus, the statement of retained earnings shows the increases and decreases in retained earnings during the period from one balance sheet date to the next.

7 Prepare closing entries.

Closing entries serve two basic purposes. The first is to return the balances of the temporary owners' equity accounts (revenue, expenses, and dividends) to zero so that these accounts may be used to measure the activities of the next accounting period. The second purpose of closing entries is to update the balance of the Retained Earnings account. Four closing entries generally are needed: (1) close the revenue accounts into the Income Summary account, (2) close the expense accounts into the Income Summary account, (3) close the balance of the Income Summary account (representing net income or net loss) into the Retained Earnings account, and (4) close the Dividends account into the Retained Earnings account.

8 Describe the sequence of procedures in the accounting cycle.

The accounting procedures in the accounting cycle may be summarized as follows: (1) journalize transactions, (2) post to ledger accounts, (3) prepare a trial balance, (4) make end-of-period adjustments, (5) prepare an adjusted trial balance, (6) prepare financial statements, (7) journalize and post closing entries, and (8) prepare an after-closing trial balance.

9 Distinguish between the accrual basis and the cash basis of accounting.
Under accrual accounting, revenue is recognized when it is earned and expenses are recognized in the period in which they are incurred in the effort to generate revenue. Under the cash basis, on the other hand, revenue is recognized when cash is received and expenses are recognized when cash payments are made. The accrual basis gives a better measurement of profitability than does the cash basis, because the accrual basis associates the determination of income with the underlying earning process.

Key terms introduced or emphasized in chapter 3

Accounting period. The span of time covered by an income statement. One year is the accounting period for much financial reporting, but financial statements are also prepared by companies for each quarter of the year and also for each month.

Accrual basis of accounting. Calls for recording revenue in the period in which it is earned and recording expenses in the period in which they are incurred. The effect of events on the business is recognized as services are rendered or consumed rather than when cash is received or paid.

Accumulated depreciation. A contra-asset account shown as a deduction from the related asset account in the balance sheet. Depreciation taken throughout the useful life of an asset is accumulated in this account.

Adjusted trial balance. A listing of all ledger account balances after the amounts have been changed to include the adjusting entries made at the end of the period.

Adjusting entries. Entries required at the end of the period to update the accounts before financial statements are prepared. Adjusting entries serve to apportion transactions properly between the accounting periods affected and to record any revenue earned or expenses incurred which have not been recorded prior to the end of the period.

After-closing trial balance. A trial balance prepared after all closing entries have been made. Consists only of accounts for assets, liabilities, and owners' equity.

Cash basis of accounting. Revenue is recorded when received in cash and expenses are recorded in the period in which cash payment is made. Fails to match revenue with related expenses and therefore does not lead to a logical measurement of income. Use is limited mostly to individual income tax returns and to accounting records of physicians and other professional firms.

Closing entries. Journal entries made at the end of the period for the purpose of closing temporary accounts (revenue, expense, and dividends accounts) and bringing the Retained Earnings account up-to-date.

Conservatism. The traditional accounting practice of resolving uncertainty by choosing the solution which leads to the lower (more conservative) amount of income being recognized in the current accounting period. This concept is designed to avoid overstatement of financial strength or earnings.

Contra-asset account. An account with a credit balance which is offset against or deducted from an asset account to produce the proper balance sheet valuation for the asset.

Depreciation. The systematic allocation to expense of the cost of an asset (such as a building) during the periods of its useful life.

Dividend. A distribution of cash by a corporation to its stockholders.

Expenses. The cost of the goods and services used up in the process of obtaining revenue.

Financial statement order. Sequence of accounts in the ledger; balance sheet accounts first (assets, liabilities, and owners' equity), followed by income statement accounts (revenue and expenses).

Fiscal year. Any 12-month accounting period adopted by a business.

Income statement. A financial statement showing the results of operations for a business by matching revenue and related expenses for a particular accounting period. Shows the net income or net loss.

Income Summary account. The summary account in the ledger to which revenue and expense accounts are closed at the end of the period. The balance (credit balance for a net income, debit balance for a net loss) is transferred to the Retained Earnings account.

Matching principle. In the measurement of net income, revenue earned during the accounting period is offset with all expenses incurred in generating that revenue whether or not these expenses were paid during the accounting period.

Net income. The excess of revenue earned over the related expenses for a given period.

Realization principle. The generally accepted accounting principle that determines when revenue should be recorded in the accounting records. Revenue is realized when services are rendered to customers or when goods are sold and delivered to customers.

Retained earnings. That portion of stockholders' equity resulting from profits earned and retained in the business.

Revenue. The price of goods sold and services rendered by a business. Equal to the inflow of cash and receivables in exchange for services rendered or goods delivered during the period.

Statement of retained earnings. A financial statement showing the changes in the amount of retained earnings over the accounting period.

Demonstration problem for your review

Key Insurance Agency was organized on September 1, 19__. Assume that the accounts are closed and financial statements prepared each month. The company occupies rented office space but owns office equipment estimated to have a useful life of 10 years from date of acquisition, September 1. The trial balance for Key Insurance Agency at November 30 is shown below.

Cash	$ 3,750	
Accounts receivable	1,210	
Office equipment	4,800	
Accumulated depreciation: office equipment		$ 80
Accounts payable		1,640
Capital stock		6,000
Retained earnings		1,490
Dividends	500	
Commissions earned		6,220
Advertising expense	800	
Salaries expense	3,600	
Rent expense	770	
	$15,430	$15,430

Instructions

a Prepare the adjusting journal entry to record depreciation of the office equipment for the month of November.

b Prepare an adjusted trial balance at November 30, 19__.

c Prepare an income statement and a statement of retained earnings for the month ended November 30, 19__, and a balance sheet in report form at November 30, 19__.

Solution to demonstration problem

a Adjusting journal entry:

Depreciation Expense: Office Equipment   40
        Accumulated Depreciation: Office Equipment   40
To record depreciation for November ($4,800 ÷ 120 months).

b
KEY INSURANCE AGENCY
Adjusted Trial Balance
November 30, 19__

Cash	$ 3,750	
Accounts receivable	1,210	
Office equipment	4,800	
Accumulated depreciation: office equipment		$ 120
Accounts payable		1,640
Capital stock		6,000
Retained earnings		1,490
Dividends	500	
Commissions earned		6,220
Advertising expense	800	
Salaries expense	3,600	
Rent expense	770	
Depreciation expense: office equipment	40	
Totals	$15,470	$15,470

c
KEY INSURANCE AGENCY
Income Statement
For the Month Ended November 30, 19__

Commissions earned		$6,220
Expenses:		
Advertising expense	$ 800	
Salaries expense	3,600	
Rent expense	770	
Depreciation expense: office equipment	40	5,210
Net income		$1,010

KEY INSURANCE AGENCY
Statement of Retained Earnings
For the Month Ended November 30, 19__

Retained earnings, Oct. 31, 19__	$1,490
Net income for the month	1,010
Subtotal	$2,500
Dividends	500
Retained earnings, Nov. 30, 19__	$2,000

KEY INSURANCE AGENCY
Balance Sheet
November 30, 19__

Assets

Cash...		$3,750
Accounts receivable...		1,210
Office equipment..	$4,800	
Less: Accumulated depreciation..................................	120	4,680
Total assets..		$9,640

Liabilities & Stockholders' Equity

Liabilities		
Accounts payable...		$1,640
Stockholders' equity:		
Capital stock	$6,000	
Retained earnings...	2,000	8,000
Total liabilities & stockholders' equity.........................		$9,640

ASSIGNMENT MATERIAL

Review questions

1 What is the meaning of the term ***revenue?*** Does the receipt of cash by a business indicate that revenue has been earned? Explain.

2 What is the meaning of the term ***expenses?*** Does the payment of cash by a business indicate that an expense has been incurred? Explain.

3 Explain the effect of operating profitably upon the balance sheet of a business entity.

4 Does the Retained Earnings account represent a supply of cash which could be distributed to stockholders? Explain.

5 Does a well-prepared income statement provide an exact and precise measurement of net income for the period or does it represent merely an approximation of net income? Explain.

6 For each of the following financial statements, indicate whether the statement relates to a single date or to a period of time:
a Balance sheet
b Income statement
c Statement of retained earnings

7 Explain the rules of debit and credit with respect to transactions recorded in revenue and expense accounts.

8 Supply the appropriate term (debit or credit) to complete the following statements.
a The Capital Stock account, Retained Earnings account, and revenue accounts are increased by _____ entries.
b Asset accounts and expense accounts are increased by _____ entries.
c Liability accounts and owners' equity accounts are decreased by _____ entries.

9 Supply the appropriate term (debit or credit) to complete the following statements.

   a When a business is operating profitably, the journal entry to close the Income Summary account will consist of a _____ to that account and a _____ to Retained Earnings.

   b When a business is operating at a loss, the journal entry to close the Income Summary account will consist of a _____ to that account and a _____ to Retained Earnings.

   c The journal entry to close the Dividends account consists of a _____ to that account and a _____ to Retained Earnings.

10 How does depreciation expense differ from other operating expenses?

11 Assume that a business acquires a delivery truck at a cost of $9,600. Estimated life of the truck is four years. State the amount of depreciation expense per year and per month. Give the adjusting entry to record depreciation on the truck at the end of the first month, and explain where the accounts involved would appear in the financial statements.

12 All ledger accounts belong in one of the following five groups: asset, liability, owners' equity, revenue, and expense. For each of the following accounts, state the group in which it belongs. Also indicate whether the normal balance would be a debit or a credit.

   a Fees Earned   e Building
   b Notes Payable   f Depreciation Expense
   c Telephone Expense   g Accumulated Depreciation: Building
   d Retained Earnings

13 A service enterprise performs services in the amount of $500 for a customer in May and receives payment in June. In which month is the $500 of revenue recognized? What is the journal entry to be made in May and the entry to be made in June?

14 Which of the following accounts should be closed by a debit to Income Summary and a credit to the account listed?

   Dividends   Salaries Expense
   Fees Earned   Accounts Payable
   Advertising Expense   Depreciation Expense
   Accounts Receivable   Accumulated Depreciation

15 Supply the appropriate terms to complete the following statements. _____ and _____ accounts are closed at the end of each accounting period by transferring their balances to a summary account called _____ _____. A _____ balance in this summary account represents net income for the period; a _____ balance represents a net loss for the period.

16 Which of the ten accounts listed below are affected by closing entries at the end of the accounting period?

   Cash   Capital Stock
   Fees Earned   Dividends
   Income Summary   Accumulated Depreciation
   Accounts Payable   Accounts Receivable
   Telephone Expense   Depreciation Expense

17 How does the accrual basis of accounting differ from the cash basis of accounting? Which gives a more accurate picture of the profitability of a business? Explain.

18 Remington Corporation pays dividends regularly. Should these dividends be considered an expense of the business? Explain.

Exercises

Listed below are twelve technical accounting terms introduced in this chapter:

Accounting period	Depreciation	Net income
Accrual basis of accounting	Expenses	Realization
Cash basis of accounting	Income statement	Revenue
Closing entries	Matching	Dividends

Each of the following statements may (or may not) describe one of these technical terms. For each statement, indicate the accounting term described, or answer "None" if the statement does not correctly describe any of the terms.

a The generally accepted accounting principle used in determining when to recognize revenue.
b Recognizing revenue when it is earned and expenses when the related goods or services are used in the effort to obtain revenue.
c The systematic allocation of the cost of a long-lived asset, such as a building or equipment, to expense over the useful life of the asset.
d The procedures for transferring the balances of the revenue, expense, Income Summary, and Dividends accounts into the Retained Earnings account.
e The cost of goods and services used up in the process of earning revenue.
f The span of time covered by an income statement.
g An increase in owners' equity as a result of earning revenue and incurring expenses.
h A decrease in owners' equity not reported in the income statement.
i The generally accepted accounting principle used in determining when expenses should be offset against revenue.

On October 12, 1990 the accountant for Sunray Appliance Corporation prepared an income statement for the fiscal year ended September 30, 1990. The accountant used the following heading on this financial statement:

SUNRAY CO.
Profit and Loss Statement
October 12, 1990

Instructions

a Identify any errors in this heading.
b Prepare a corrected heading.

The following transactions were carried out during the month of June by K. Davis and Company, a firm of real estate brokers. For each of the five transactions, you are to state whether the transaction represented revenue to the firm during the month of June. Give reasons for your decision in each case.

a Collected cash of $2,400 from an account receivable. The receivable originated in May from services rendered to a client.
b Arranged a sale of an apartment building owned by a client. The commission for making the sale was $14,400, but this amount will not be received until August 20.
c K. Davis and Company received $25,000 cash by issuing additional shares of capital stock.

d Borrowed $12,800 from Century Bank to be repaid in three months.
e Earned $63 interest on a company bank account during the month of June. No withdrawals were made from this account in June.

**Exercise 3-4
When are expenses incurred?**

During May the Columbus Company carried out the following transactions. Which of these transactions represented expenses in May? Explain.

a Purchased a copying machine for $2,750 cash.
b Paid $192 for gasoline purchases for a delivery truck during May.
c Paid $1,280 salary to an employee for time worked during May.
d Paid an attorney $560 for legal services rendered in April.
e Declared and paid an $1,800 dividend to shareholders.

**Exercise 3-5
Relationship between net income and owners' equity**

Total assets and total liabilities of Mannix Corporation as shown by the balance sheets at the beginning and end of the year were as follows:

	Beginning of Year	End of Year
Assets..	$280,000	$390,000
Liabilities	110,000	160,000

Compute the net income or net loss from operations for the year in each of the following independent cases:

a No dividends were declared or paid during the year and no additional capital stock was issued.
b No dividends were declared or paid during the year, but additional capital stock was issued at par in the amount of $50,000.
c Dividends of $20,000 were declared and paid during the year. No change occurred in capital stock.
d Dividends of $10,000 were declared and paid during the year, and additional capital stock was issued at par in the amount of $25,000.

**Exercise 3-6
Relationship between net income and stockholders' equity**

Supply the missing figure in the following five independent cases:

a	Retained earnings at beginning of year....................................	$130,000
	Net income for the year...	-?-
	Dividends for the year..	32,000
	Retained earnings at end of year..	145,500

b	Retained earnings at beginning of year....................................	$ 91,200
	Net income for the year...	28,500
	Dividends for the year..	-?-
	Retained earnings at end of year..	99,700

c	Retained earnings at beginning of year....................................	-?-
	Net income for the year...	$189,400
	Dividends for the year..	106,000
	Retained earnings at end of year..	532,900

d   Total stockholders' equity at beginning of year . . . . $ 74,000

Additional issuance of capital stock during year   10,000

Net income for the year   17,500

Dividends for the year   12,000

Total stockholders' equity at end of year . . . .   -?-

e   Total stockholders' equity at beginning of year $362,500

Additional issuance of capital stock during year   85,000

Net income for the year . . . .   -?-

Dividends for the year   30,000

Total stockholders' equity at end of year   469,100

Exercise 3-7
Preparing journal entries for revenue, expenses, and dividends

Shown below are selected transactions of the law firm of Emmons & Associates, Inc. You are to prepare journal entries to record the transactions in the firm's accounting records. The firm closes its accounts at the end of each calendar year.

Mar. 19   Drafted a prenuptial agreement for C. J. McCall. Sent McCall an invoice for $750, requesting payment within 30 days. (The appropriate revenue account is entitled Legal Fees Earned.)

May 15   Declared a dividend of $60,000, payable on June 30 to stockholders of record on June 10.

May 31   Received a bill from Lawyers' Delivery Service for process service during the month of May, $1,150. Payment due by June 10. (The appropriate expense account is entitled Process Service Expense.)

June 30   Paid the dividend declared on May 15.

Dec. 31   Made a year-end adjusting entry to record depreciation expense on the firm's law library, $2,700.

Exercise 3-8
Prepare an income statement and statement of retained earnings

From the following account balances, prepare first an income statement and then a statement of retained earnings for Chambers Painting Contractors for the year ended December 31, 19___. Include the proper headings on both financial statements.

Retained earnings, Jan. 1, 19___ . .	$ 27,200	Salaries Expense	$66,800
Dividends	18,000	Rent Expense	9,600
Painting Fees Earned	140,000	Advertising Expense	3,200
Paint & Supplies Expense	27,500	Depreciation Expense: Painting	
		Equipment	1,200

Exercise 3-9
Preparing closing entries

During the absence of the regular accountant of Sunbelt Center, a new employee, Ralph Jones, prepared the closing entries from the ledger accounts for the year 19___. Jones has very little understanding of accounting and the closing entries he prepared were not satisfactory in several respects. The entries by Jones were:

Entry 1

Sales Commissions Earned	136,800	
Accumulated Depreciation: Building	12,800	
Accounts Payable	43,200	
Income Summary		192,800

To close accounts with credit balances.

Entry 2

Income Summary..	130,800	
Salaries Expense		103,200
Dividends		18,000
Advertising Expense		6,400
Depreciation Expense: Building		3,200

To close accounts with debit balances.

Entry 3

Capital Stock	62,000	
Income Summary		62,000

To close Income Summary account.

Instructions

a For each entry, identify any errors which Jones made.

b Prepare four correct closing entries, following the pattern illustrated on pages 104–109.

Problems

Problem 3-1
Preparing
journal entries

WhirlyBird Corporation provides transportation by helicopter for skiers, backpackers, and others to remote mountainous areas. Among the ledger accounts used by the company are the following:

Cash	Fuel expense
Accounts payable	Rent expense
Dividends payable	Repair & maintenance expense
Passenger fare revenue	Salaries expense
Advertising expense	

Some of the January transactions of WhirlyBird are listed below.

Jan. 3 Paid $1,600 rent for the building for January.

Jan. 4 Placed advertising in local newspapers for publication during January. The agreed price of $520 was payable within 10 days after the end of the month.

Jan. 15 Cash receipts from passengers for the first half of January amounted to $9,470.

Jan. 15 Paid a $7,500 cash dividend declared in December of the preceding year. This dividend was properly recorded as a liability at the declaration date.

Jan. 16 Paid salaries to employees for services rendered in first half of January, $5,265.

Jan. 29 Received a bill for fuel used from Western Oil Co., amounting to $1,930, and payable by February 10.

Jan. 31 Paid $1,642 to Stevens Aircraft for repair and maintenance work during January.

Instructions. Prepare a journal entry (including an explanation) for each of the above transactions.

Problem 3-2
Analyzing transactions and preparing journal entries

Garwood Marine is a boat repair yard. During August its transactions included the following:

(1) On August 1, paid rent for the month of August, $4,000.
(2) On August 3, at request of St. Francis Insurance, Inc., made repairs on boat of Tom Blackaller. Sent bill for $680 for services rendered to St. Francis Insurance, Inc. (Credit Repair Service Revenue.)
(3) On August 9, made repairs to boat of Dennis Conner and collected in full the charge of $575.
(4) On August 14, placed advertisement in *Wooden Boat News* to be published in issue of August 20 at cost of $95, payment to be made within 30 days.
(5) On August 25, received a check for $680 from St. Francis Insurance, Inc., representing collection of the receivable of August 3.
(6) On August 31, declared a cash dividend of $3,500, payable on September 30.

Instructions

a Write an analysis of each transaction. An example of the type of analysis desired is as follows:

(1)(a) Rent is an operating expense. Expenses are recorded by debits. Debit Rent Expense, $4,000.
  (b) The asset Cash was decreased. Decreases in assets are recorded by credits. Credit Cash, $4,000.

b Prepare a journal entry (including explanation) for each of the above transactions.

Problem 3-3
Recording transactions: a comprehensive problem

Metro Parking Systems, Inc., was organized on March 1 for the purpose of operating an automobile parking lot. Included in the company's ledger are the following ledger accounts and their identification numbers.

Cash............................	11	Dividends.........................	46
Land.............................	21	Parking fees earned..................	51
Notes payable......................	31	Advertising expense	61
Accounts payable...................	32	Utilities expense.....................	63
Dividends payable	35	Salaries expense	65
Capital stock.......................	41		

The business was organized and operations were begun during the month of March. Transactions during March were as follows:

Mar. 1 The corporation issued 5,000 shares of $10 par value capital stock in exchange for $50,000 cash.

Mar. 5 Purchased land for $160,000, of which $40,000 was paid in cash. A short-term note payable was issued for the balance of $120,000.

Mar. 6 An arrangement was made with the Century Club to provide parking privileges for its customers. Century Club agreed to pay $1,200 monthly, payable in advance. Cash was collected for the month of March.

Mar. 7 Arranged with Times Printing company for a regular advertisement in the *Times* at a monthly cost of $390. Paid for advertising during March by check, $390.

Mar. 15 Parking receipts for the first half of the month were $1,836, exclusive of the monthly fee from Century Club.

Mar. 31 Received bill for light and power from Pacific Power Company in the amount of $78, to be paid by April 10.

Mar. 31 Paid $2,720 to employees for services rendered during the month. (Payroll taxes are to be ignored.)

Mar. 31 Parking receipts for the second half of the month amounted to $5,338.

Mar. 31 Declared a $2,000 dividend, payable on June 15.

Mar. 31 Paid $5,000 cash on the note payable incurred with the purchase of land. (You are to ignore any interest on the note.)

Instructions

a Journalize the March transactions.

b Post to ledger accounts. Enter ledger account numbers in the LP column of the journal as the posting work is done.

c Prepare a trial balance at March 31.

Problem 3-4
Preparing closing entries

Family Fun Park is a miniature golf course, operating on land rented within a city park. At year-end, the company prepared the following adjusted trial balance:

FAMILY FUN PARK
Adjusted Trial Balance
December 31, 19__

Cash	$ 13,500	
Accounts receivable	2,800	
Buildings	60,000	
Accumulated depreciation: buildings		$ 18,000
Golf course structures	30,000	
Accumulated depreciation: golf course structures		10,000
Capital stock		50,000
Retained earnings, November 30, 19__		22,000
Dividends	25,000	
Admissions revenue		182,000
Advertising expense	15,000	
Rent expense	36,000	
Repairs expense	5,200	
Salaries expense	79,000	
Light & power expense	4,500	
Depreciation expense: buildings	6,000	
Depreciation expense: golf course structures	5,000	
	$282,000	$282,000

Instructions

a Prepare journal entries to close the accounts. Use four entries: (1) to close the revenue account, (2) to close the expense accounts, (3) to close the Income Summary account, and (4) to close the Dividends account.

b Assume that in the following year, Family Fun Park again had $182,000 of admissions revenue, but that expenses increased to **$197,000.** Assuming that the revenue account and all the expense accounts had been closed into the Income Summary account at December 31, prepare a journal entry to close the Income Summary account.

Problem 3-5
Preparing
financial state-
ments and closing
entries

Celebrity Caterers closes its accounts and prepares financial statements at the end of each calendar year. The following adjusted trial balance was prepared at December 31 of the most recent year.

CELEBRITY CATERERS
Adjusted Trial Balance
December 31, 19__

Cash	$ 7,900	
Accounts receivable	14,740	
Land	67,000	
Building.	126,000	
Accumulated depreciation: building		$ 15,120
Catering equipment.	16,800	
Accumulated depreciation: catering equipment		10,080
Notes payable		120,000
Accounts payable		2,100
Capital stock		30,000
Retained earnings, January 1, 19__		34,000
Dividends	20,500	
Catering service revenue.		285,000
Advertising expense.	4,000	
Depreciation expense: building.	5,040	
Depreciation expense: catering equipment	3,360	
Food and beverage expense.	98,640	
Interest expense	14,400	
Salaries and wages expense.	117,920	
	$496,300	$496,300

Instructions

a Prepare journal entries to close the accounts at December 31. Use four entries: (1) to close the revenue account, (2) to close the expense accounts, (3) to close the Income Summary account, and (4) to close the Dividends account.

b Prepare financial statements for the year ended December 31, 19__ (income statement, statement of retained earnings, and a balance sheet in report form).

c What were the estimated lives of the building and equipment as assumed by the company in setting the depreciation rates?

Problem 3-6
End-of-period
adjusting and
closing proce-
dures; preparing
financial
statements

Home Repair is a new business which began operations on July 1. The company follows a policy of closing its accounts and preparing financial statements at the end of each month. A trial balance at September 30 appears on the next page.

HOME REPAIR
Trial Balance
September 30, 19__

Cash	$ 2,500	
Accounts receivable	1,500	
Land	27,520	
Building...	50,400	
Accumulated depreciation: building		$ 336
Repair equipment	7,500	
Accumulated depreciation: repair equipment		250
Notes payable		28,000
Accounts payable		1,594
Capital stock		50,000
Retained earnings, August 31, 19__		7,800
Dividends	2,000	
Repair service revenue...................................		11,520
Advertising expense......................................	150	
Repair parts expense	1,700	
Utilities expense	170	
Wages expense...	5,780	
Interest expense	280	
	$99,500	$99,500

Note that the trial balance includes two assets subject to depreciation: the building and the repair equipment. The accumulated depreciation accounts in the trial balance show the total depreciation for July and August; depreciation has not yet been recorded for September.

Instructions

a Prepare adjusting entries at September 30 to record depreciation. Use one entry to record depreciation on the building and a second entry to record depreciation on the repair equipment. The amounts of depreciation for September are $168 on the building and $125 on the repair equipment.

b Prepare an *adjusted* trial balance at September 30. (This will differ from the trial balance only by inclusion of the depreciation recorded in part a.)

c Prepare an income statement and a statement of retained earnings for the month of September, and a balance sheet as of September 30.

d Prepare journal entries to close the accounts. Use four entries: (1) to close the revenue account, (2) to close the expense accounts, (3) to close the Income Summary account, and (4) to close the Dividends account.

e Prepare an after-closing trial balance.

Problem 3-7
Complete
accounting cycle

After completing her medical education, April Stein established her own medical practice. The practice was organized as a corporation, named April Stein, M.D., Incorporated. The following transactions occurred during the corporation's first month of operations:

May 1 Issued 6,000 shares of $2 par value capital stock to April Stein, M.D., in exchange for $12,000 cash.

May 1 Paid office rent for May, $1,700.

May 2 Purchased office equipment for cash, $7,200.

May 3 Purchased medical instruments from Niles Instruments, Inc., at a cost of $9,000. A cash down payment of $1,000 was made and a note payable was issued for the remaining $8,000. The note is due in 60 days and does not bear interest.

May 4 Retained by Brandon Construction to be on call for emergency service at a monthly fee of $400. The fee for May was collected in cash.

May 15 Excluding the retainer of May 4, fees earned during the first 15 days of the month amounted to $1,600, of which $600 was in cash and $1,000 was in accounts receivable.

May 15 Paid Mary Hester, R.N., her salary for the first half of May, $1,000.

May 16 Dr. Stein wanted to establish a policy of paying dividends at the end of every calendar quarter. Therefore, the corporation declared a $1,200 dividend payable on June 30.

May 19 Treated Michael Tracy for minor injuries received in an accident during employment at Brandon Construction. No charge was made as these services were covered by Brandon's payment on May 4.

May 27 Treated Cynthia Knight, who paid $25 cash for an office visit and who agreed to pay $35 on June 1 for laboratory medical tests completed May 27.

May 31 Excluding the treatment of Cynthia Knight on May 27, fees earned during the last half of month amounted to $5,000, of which $2,100 was in cash and $2,900 was in accounts receivable.

May 31 Paid Mary Hester, R.N., $1,000 salary for the second half of month.

May 31 Received a bill from McGraw Medical Supplies in the amount of $640 representing the amount of medical supplies used during May.

May 31 Paid utilities for the month, $300.

Other information. Dr. Stein estimated the useful life of medical instruments at 3 years and of office equipment at 5 years. The account titles to be used and the account numbers are as follows:

Cash	10		Retained earnings	45
Accounts receivable	13		Dividends	47
Medical instruments	20		Income summary	49
Accumulated depreciation:			Fees earned	50
medical instruments	21		Medical supplies expense	60
Office equipment	22		Rent expense	61
Accumulated depreciation:			Salaries expense	62
office equipment	23		Utilities expense	63
Notes payable	30		Depreciation expense:	
Accounts payable	31		medical instruments	64
Dividends payable	35		Depreciation expense:	
Capital stock	40		office equipment	65

Instructions

a Journalize the above transactions. (Number journal pages to permit cross-reference to ledger.)

b Post to ledger accounts. (Use running balance form of ledger account. Number ledger accounts to permit cross reference to journal.)

c Prepare a trial balance at May 31, 19___.

d Prepare adjusting entries to record depreciation for the month of May and post to ledger accounts. (For medical instruments, cost $9,000 ÷ 3 years × $\frac{1}{12}$. For office equipment, cost $7,200 ÷ 5 × $\frac{1}{12}$.)

e Prepare an adjusted trial balance.
f Prepare an income statement and a statement of retained earnings for May, and a balance sheet as of May 31, 19__ , in report form.
g Prepare closing entries and post to ledger accounts.
h Prepare an after-closing trial balance.

Business decision cases

**Case 3-1
Accrual account-
ing; relationship
of depreciation
expense to cash
outlays**

The Dark Room is a business that develops film within one hour, using a large and expensive developing machine. The business is organized as a single proprietorship and operates in rented quarters in a large shopping center. Sharon Douglas, owner of The Dark Room, plans to retire and has offered the business for sale. A typical monthly income statement for The Dark Room appears below:

Revenue:		
Fees earned..		$8,900
Operating expenses:		
Wages...	$1,600	
Rent..	1,850	
Supplies	920	
Depreciation: developing machine................................	1,510	
Miscellaneous..	460	6,340
Net income..		$2,560

Revenue is received in cash at the time that film is developed. The wages, rent, supplies, and miscellaneous expenses are all paid in cash on a monthly basis. Douglas explains that the developing machine, which is 12 months old and is fully paid for, is being depreciated over a period of five years. She is using this estimated useful life because she believes that faster and more efficient machines will probably be available at that time. However, if the business does not purchase a new machine, the existing machine should last for 10 years or more.

Dave Berg, a friend of yours, is negotiating with Douglas to buy The Dark Room. Berg does not have enough money to pay the entire purchase price in cash. However, Douglas has offered to accept a note payable from Berg for a substantial portion of the purchase price. The note would call for 18 monthly payments in the amount of $2,500, which would pay off the remainder of the purchase price as well as the interest charges on the note. Douglas points out that these monthly payments can be made "out of the monthly earnings of the business."

Berg comes to you for advice. He feels that the sales price asked by Douglas is very reasonable, and that the owner-financing makes this an excellent opportunity. However, he is worried about turning over $2,500 of the business's earnings to Douglas each month. Berg states, "This arrangement will only leave me with about $60 each month. I figure that my family and I need to take about $1,200 out of this business each month just to meet our living expenses." Also, Berg is concerned about the depreciation expense. He does not understand when or to whom the depreciation expense must be paid, or how long this expense will continue.

Instructions

a Explain to Berg the nature of depreciation expense, including when this expense is paid and what effect, if any, it has upon monthly cash expenditures.
b Advise Berg as to how much cash the business will generate each month. Will

this amount enable Berg to pay $2,500 per month to the former owner and still withdraw $1,200 per month to meet his personal living expenses?

c Caution Berg about the need to replace the developing machine. Briefly discuss when this expenditure might occur and how much control, if any, Berg has over the timing and dollar amount of this expenditure.

**Case 3-2
Accrual accounting; relationship of revenue to cash receipts**

Nancy Jo Hoover, owner of a small business called Imports from India, has accepted a salaried position overseas and is trying to interest you in buying the business. Hoover describes the operating results of the business as follows: "The business has been in existence for only 18 months, but the growth trend is very impressive. Just look at these figures."

	Cash Collections from Customers
First six-month period.	$120,000
Second six-month period	160,000
Third six-month period	180,000

"I think you'll agree those figures show real growth," Hoover concluded.

You then asked Hoover whether sales were made only for cash or on both a cash and credit basis. She replied as follows:

"At first we sold both for cash and on open account. In the first six months we made total sales of $200,000 and 70% of those sales were made on credit. We had $80,000 of accounts receivable at the end of the first six-month period.

"During the second six-month period, we tried to discourage selling on credit because of the extra paper work involved and the time required to follow up on slow-paying customers. Our sales on credit in that second six-month period amounted to $70,000, and our total accounts receivable were down to $60,000 at the end of that period.

"During the third six-month period we made sales only for cash. Although we prefer to operate on a cash basis only, we did very well at collecting receivables. We collected in full from every customer to whom we ever sold on credit and we don't have a single dollar of accounts receivable at this time."

Instructions

a To assist you in evaluating the performance of Imports from India, prepare a schedule comparing cash collections and sales data for each of the three 6-month periods under review. Use the following column headings:

	(1) Sales on Credit	(2) Collections on Accounts Receivable	(3) Ending Balance of Accounts Receivable	(4) Total Cash Collections from Customers	(5) Sales for Cash (4) − (2)	(6) Total Sales (1) + (5)
First six months	$140,000		$80,000	$120,000		
Second six months	70,000		60,000	160,000		
Third six months.	-0-		-0-	180,000		

b Based upon your analysis in part a, do you consider Hoover's explanation of the "growth trend" of cash collections to be a well-founded portrayal of the progress of the business? Explain fully any criticism you may have of Hoover's line of reasoning.

Chapter 4
Completion of the accounting cycle

CHAPTER PREVIEW

In Chapter 4 we complete our coverage of the accounting cycle for a service-type business. Emphasis is placed upon steps performed at the end of the cycle, including adjusting entries, preparation of a work sheet, and reversing entries. The continuing example of Greenhill Real Estate is used to illustrate and explain the four basic types of adjusting entries and the preparation of a work sheet. The discussion of reversing entries emphasizes the optional nature of this final step in the accounting cycle. As in our earlier chapters on the accounting cycle, the procedures employed in computer-based accounting systems are compared with those in manual systems.

After studying this chapter you should be able to meet these Learning Objectives:

1 **Explain how accounting periods of equal length are useful in evaluating the income of a business.**
2 **State the purpose of adjusting entries and explain how these entries are related to the concepts of accrual accounting.**
3 **Describe the four basic types of adjusting entries.**
4 **Prepare a work sheet and discuss its usefulness.**
5 **Describe the steps in the accounting cycle.**
6 **Explain when and why reversing entries may be used.**

Accounting periods and financial statements

1 Explain how accounting periods of equal length are useful in evaluating the income of a business.

For the purpose of measuring income and preparing financial statements, the life of a business is divided into accounting periods of equal length. Because accounting periods are equal in length, we can compare the income of the current period with that of prior periods to see if our operating results are improving or declining.

As explained in Chapter 3, the *accounting period* means the span of time covered by an income statement. The usual accounting period for which complete

129

financial statements are prepared and distributed to investors, bankers, and governmental agencies is one year. However, most businesses also prepare quarterly and monthly financial statements in more condensed form so that management will be currently informed on the profitability of the business from month to month.

Transactions affecting more than one accounting period

Dividing the life of a business into relatively short accounting periods requires the use of *adjusting entries* at the end of each period. Adjusting entries are required for those transactions which affect the revenue or the expenses of *more than one accounting period.* For example, assume that a company which prepares monthly financial statements purchases a one-year insurance policy at a cost of $1,200. Clearly, the entire $1,200 does not represent the insurance expense of the current month. Rather, it is the insurance expense for 12 months; only $\frac{1}{12}$ of this cost, or $100, should be recognized as expense in each month covered by the policy. The allocation of this cost to expense in 12 separate accounting periods is accomplished by making an adjusting entry at the end of each period.

Some transactions affect the revenue or expense of only one period. An example is the payment of a monthly salary to an employee on the last day of each month. Adjusting entries are not required for transactions of this type.

ADJUSTING ENTRIES: A CLOSER LOOK

The *realization principle,* as explained in Chapter 3, requires that revenue be recognized and recorded in the period it is earned. The *matching principle* stresses that expenses are incurred in order to produce revenue. To measure net income for an accounting period, we must "match" or compare the revenue earned during the period with the expenses incurred to produce that revenue. At the end of an accounting period, adjusting entries are needed so that all revenue *earned* is reflected in the accounts regardless of whether it has been collected. Adjusting entries are also needed for expenses to assure that all expenses *incurred* are matched against the revenue of the current period regardless of when cash payment of the expense occurs.

2 State the purpose of adjusting entries and explain how these entries are related to the concepts of accrual accounting.

Thus, adjusting entries help in achieving the goals of accrual accounting—recording revenue when it is *earned* and recording expenses when the related goods and services are *used.* The realization principle and the matching principle are key elements of accrual accounting. Adjusting entries are a technique of applying these principles to transactions which affect two or more accounting periods.

In Chapter 3, the concept of adjusting entries was introduced when Greenhill Real Estate recorded depreciation for the month of October. Adjusting entries are necessary to record depreciation expense, because buildings and equipment are purchased in a single accounting period but are used over many periods. Some portion of the cost of these assets should be allocated to expense in each period of the asset's estimated life. In this chapter, we will see that the use of adjusting entries is not limited to recording depreciation expense. Adjusting entries are needed *whenever transactions affect the revenue or expense of more than one accounting period.*

Types of adjusting entries

A business may need to make a dozen or more adjusting entries at the end of each accounting period. The exact number of adjustments will depend upon the nature of the company's business activities. However, all adjusting entries fall into one of four general categories:

3 Describe the four basic types of adjusting entries.

1 *Entries to apportion recorded costs.* A cost that will benefit more than one accounting period usually is recorded by debiting an asset account. In each period that benefits from the use of this asset, an adjusting entry is made to allocate a portion of the asset's cost to expense.

2 *Entries to apportion unearned revenue.* A business may collect in advance for services to be rendered to customers in future accounting periods. In the period in which these services are actually rendered, an adjusting entry is made to record the portion of the revenue earned during the period.

3 *Entries to record unrecorded expenses.* An expense may be incurred in the current accounting period even though no bill has yet been received and payment will not occur until a future period. Such unrecorded expenses are recorded by an adjusting entry made at the end of the accounting period.

4 *Entries to record unrecorded revenue.* Revenue may be earned during the current period, but not yet billed to customers or recorded in the accounting records. Such unrecorded revenue is recorded by making an adjusting entry at the end of the period.

Characteristics of adjusting entries

It will be helpful to keep in mind two important characteristics of all adjusting entries. First, every adjusting entry *involves the recognition of either revenue or expense.* Revenue and expenses represent changes in owners' equity. However, owners' equity cannot change by itself; there also must be a corresponding change in either assets or liabilities. *Thus, every adjusting entry affects both an income statement account* (revenue or expense) *and a balance sheet account* (asset or liability).

Second, adjusting entries are based upon the concepts of accrual accounting, *not upon monthly bills or month-end transactions.* No one sends us a bill saying, "Depreciation expense on your building amounts to $500 this month." Yet, we must be aware of the need to estimate and record depreciation expense if we are to measure net income properly for the period. Making adjusting entries requires a greater understanding of accrual accounting concepts than does the recording of routine business transactions. In many businesses, the adjusting entries are made by the company's controller or by a professional accountant, rather than by the regular accounting staff.

To demonstrate the various types of adjusting entries, the illustration of Green-hill Real Estate will be continued for November. We shall consider in detail only those November transactions which require adjusting entries at the end of the month.

Apportioning recorded costs

When a business makes an expenditure that will benefit more than one accounting period, the amount usually is debited to an asset account. At the end of each period benefiting from this expenditure, an adjusting entry is made to transfer an appropriate portion of the cost from the asset account to an expense account. This adjusting entry reflects the fact that part of the asset has been used up — or become expense — during the current accounting period.

An adjusting entry to apportion a recorded cost consists of a debit to an expense account and a credit to an asset account (or a contra-asset account). Examples of these adjustments include the entries to record depreciation expense and to apportion the costs of *prepaid expenses.*

Prepaid expenses. Payments in advance are often made for such items as insurance, rent, and office supplies. If the advance payment (or prepayment) will benefit more than just the current accounting period, the cost *represents an asset* rather than an expense. The cost of this asset will be allocated to expense in the accounting periods in which the services or the supplies are used. In summary, *prepaid expenses are assets;* they become expenses only as the goods or services are used up.

Insurance. To illustrate these concepts, assume that on November 1, Greenhill Real Estate paid $600 for a one-year fire insurance policy covering the building. This expenditure was debited to an asset account by the following journal entry:

Expenditure for insurance policy recorded as asset

Unexpired Insurance	600	
Cash		600
Purchased a one-year fire insurance policy.		

Since this expenditure of $600 will protect the company against fire loss for one year, the insurance expense applicable to each month's operations is $\frac{1}{12}$ of the annual expense, or $50. In order that the accounting records for November show insurance expense of $50, the following *adjusting entry* is required at November 30:

Adjusting entry. Portion of asset expires (becomes expense)

Insurance Expense	50	
Unexpired Insurance		50
To record insurance expense for November.		

This adjusting entry serves two purposes: (1) it apportions the proper amount of insurance expense to November operations and (2) it reduces the asset account to

$550 so that the correct amount of unexpired insurance will appear in the balance sheet at November 30.

What would be the effect on the income statement for November if the above adjustment were not made? The expenses would be understated by $50 and consequently the net income would be overstated by $50. The balance sheet also would be affected by failure to make the adjustment: the assets would be overstated by $50 and so would the owners' equity. The overstatement of the owners' equity would result from the overstated amount of net income transferred to the Retained Earnings account when the accounts were closed at November 30.

Office supplies. On November 2, Greenhill Real Estate purchased enough stationery and other office supplies to last for several months. The cost of the supplies was $720, and this amount was debited to an asset account by the following journal entry:

Expenditure for office supplies recorded as asset	Office Supplies 720	
	Cash	720
	Purchased office supplies.	

No entries were made during November to record the day-to-day usage of office supplies, but on November 30 a count was made of the supplies still on hand. This physical count showed unused supplies with a cost of $500. Thus, supplies costing $220 were used during November. On the basis of the November 30 count, an adjusting entry is made debiting an expense account $220 (the cost of supplies consumed during November), and reducing the asset account by $220. The *adjusting entry* follows:

Adjusting entry. Portion of supplies used represents expense	Office Supplies Expense 220	
	Office Supplies	220
	To record consumption of office supplies in November.	

After this entry is posted, the asset account, Office Supplies, will have a balance of $500, representing the cost of office supplies on hand at November 30. The Office Supplies account will appear in the balance sheet as an asset; the Office Supplies Expense account will be shown in the income statement.

How would failure to make this adjustment affect the financial statements? In the income statement for November, the expenses would be understated by $220 and the net income overstated by the same amount. Since the overstated amount for net income in November would be transferred into the Retained Earnings account in the process of closing the accounts, the owners' equity section of the balance sheet would be overstated by $220. Assets also would be overstated because Office Supplies would be listed at $220 too much.

Recording prepayments directly in the expense accounts. In our illustration, payments for insurance and office supplies which are expected to provide benefits for more than one accounting period are recorded by debiting an asset account, such as Unexpired Insurance or Office Supplies. However, some companies follow an alternative practice of debiting these prepayments directly to an expense account such as Insurance Expense. At the end of the period, the adjusting entry would then consist of a debit to Unexpired Insurance and a credit to Insurance Expense for the portion of the insurance cost *which has not yet expired.*

This alternative method leads to the same results in the balance sheet and income statement as does the method used in our Greenhill illustration. Under both procedures, the cost of benefits consumed in the current period is treated as an expense, and the cost of benefits applicable to future periods is carried forward in the balance sheet as an asset.

In this text and in the end-of-chapter problem material, we will follow Greenhill's practice of recording prepayments in asset accounts and then making adjusting entries to transfer these costs to expense accounts as the assets expire.

Depreciation of building. The recording of depreciation expense at the end of an accounting period provides another example of an adjusting entry which *apportions a recorded cost.* The November 30 adjusting entry to record depreciation of the building used by Greenhill Real Estate is exactly the same as the October 31 *adjusting entry* explained in Chapter 3.

Adjusting entry. **Cost of building** **is gradually** **converted to ex-** **pense**	Depreciation Expense: Building . . . . 150 Accumulated Depreciation: Building. . . . . 150 To record depreciation for November.	

This allocation of depreciation expense to November operations is based on the following facts: the building cost $36,000 and is estimated to have a useful life of 20 years (240 months). Using the straight-line method of depreciation, the portion of the original cost which expires each month is $\frac{1}{240}$ of $36,000, or $150.

The Accumulated Depreciation: Building account now has a credit balance of $300 as a result of the October and November credits of $150 each. The book value of the building is $35,700, that is, the original cost of $36,000 minus the accumulated depreciation of $300. The term *book value* means the net amount at which an asset is shown in the accounting records, as distinguished from its market value. *Carrying value* is an alternative term, with the same meaning as book value.

Depreciation of office equipment. The November 30 adjusting entry to record depreciation of the office equipment is the same as the *adjusting entry* for depreciation a month earlier, as shown in Chapter 3.

Adjusting entry. **Cost of office** **equipment** **gradually con-** **verted to expense**	Depreciation Expense: Office Equipment . . . . 45 Accumulated Depreciation: Office Equipment. . . . . 45 To record depreciation for November.	

The original cost of the office equipment was $5,400, and the estimated useful life was 10 years (120 months). Depreciation each month under the straight-line method is therefore $\frac{1}{120}$ of $5,400, or $45.

What is the book value of the office equipment at this point? The original cost of $5,400, minus accumulated depreciation of $90 for two months, leaves a book value of $5,310.

Apportioning unearned revenue

In some instances, customers may **pay in advance** for services to be rendered in later accounting periods. For example, a football team collects much of its revenue in advance through the sale of season tickets. Health clubs collect in advance by selling long-term membership contracts. Airlines sell many of their tickets well in advance of a scheduled flight.

For accounting purposes, amounts collected in advance **do not represent revenue,** because these amounts have **not yet been earned.** Amounts collected from customers in advance are recorded by debiting the Cash account and crediting an **unearned revenue** account. Unearned revenue also may be called **deferred revenue.**

When a company collects money in advance from its customers, it has an **obligation** to render services in the future. Therefore, the balance of an unearned revenue account is considered to be a liability; **it appears in the liability section of the balance sheet, not in the income statement.** Unearned revenue differs from other liabilities because it usually will be settled by rendering services, rather than by making payment in cash. In short, it will be **worked off** rather than **paid off.** Of course if the business is unable to render the service, it must discharge this liability by refunding money to its customers.

● **CASE IN POINT** ● One of the largest liabilities in the balance sheet of UAL, Inc., (United Air Lines) is "Advance ticket sales and customer deposits." This account, with a balance of approximately $500 million, represents unearned revenue resulting from the sale of tickets for future flights. Most of this unearned revenue will be earned as the future flights occur. Some customers, however, will change their plans and will return their tickets to United Airlines for a cash refund.

When the company renders the services for which customers have paid in advance, it is working off its liability to these customers and is earning the revenue. At the end of the accounting period in which the revenue is earned, an **adjusting entry** is made to transfer an appropriate amount from the unearned revenue account to a revenue account. This adjusting entry consists of a debit to a liability account (unearned revenue) and a credit to a revenue account.

To illustrate these concepts, assume that on November 1, Greenhill Real Estate agreed to act as manager of some rental properties for a monthly fee of $300. The owner of the properties, Frank Day, was leaving the country on an extended trip and therefore paid the company for six months' service in advance. The journal entry to record the transaction on November 1 was:

Management fee collected but not yet earned

```
Cash .................................................................  1,800
     Unearned Management Fees .......................................         1,800
Collected in advance six months' fees for management of properties owned by
Frank Day.
```

Remember that Unearned Management Fees is a *liability* account, not a revenue account. This management fee will be earned gradually over a period of six months as Greenhill performs the required services. At the end of each monthly accounting period, Greenhill will make an adjusting entry transferring $\frac{1}{6}$ of this management fee, or $300, from the unearned revenue account to a revenue account. The first in this series of monthly transfers will be made on November 30 by the following *adjusting entry:*

Adjusting entry to recognize earning of a part of management fee

```
Unearned Management Fees ..............................................  300
     Management Fees Earned............................................        300
Fee earned by managing Frank Day property during November.
```

After this entry has been posted, the Unearned Management Fees account will have a $1,500 credit balance. This balance represents Greenhill's obligation to render $1,500 worth of services over the next five months and will appear in the liability section of the company's balance sheet. The Management Fees Earned account will be shown as revenue in the November income statement.

Recording advance collections directly in the revenue accounts. We have stressed that amounts collected from customers in advance represent liabilities, not revenue. However, some companies follow an accounting policy of crediting these advance collections directly to revenue accounts. The adjusting entry then should consist of a debit to the revenue account and a credit to the unearned revenue account for the portion of the advance payments *not yet earned.* This alternative accounting practice leads to the same results as does the method used in our Greenhill Real Estate illustration.

In this text, we will follow the originally described practice of crediting advance payments from customers to an unearned revenue account.

Recording unrecorded expenses

This type of adjusting entry recognizes expenses that will be paid in future transactions; therefore, no cost has yet been recorded in the accounting records. Salaries of employees and interest on borrowed money are common examples of expenses which accumulate from day to day, but which usually are not recorded until they are paid. These expenses are said to *accrue* over time, that is, to grow or to accumulate. At the end of the accounting period, an adjusting entry should be made to record any expenses which have accrued, but which have not yet been recorded. Since these expenses will be paid at a future date, the adjusting entry consists of a debit to an expense account and a credit to a liability account. We shall now use the example of Greenhill Real Estate to illustrate this type of adjusting entry.

Accrual of interest. On November 1, Greenhill Real Estate borrowed the sum of $3,000 from a bank. Banks require every borrower to sign a ***promissory note,*** that is, a formal, written promise to repay the amount borrowed plus interest at an agreed future date. (Various forms of notes in common use and the accounting problems involved will be discussed more fully in Chapter 10.) The note signed by John Green, with certain details omitted, is shown below.

Note payable issued to bank

$3,000   Los Angeles, California   November 1, 19___

Three months .... after date ...... Greenhill Real Estate ...... promises to pay

to the order of ...... American National Bank ......

---Three thousand and no/100--- ...... dollars

for value received, with interest at ...... 12 percent per year ......

       Greenhill Real Estate ......

By ...... *John Green* ......
       President

The note payable is a liability of Greenhill Real Estate, similar to an account payable but different in that a formal written promise to pay is required and interest is charged on the amount borrowed. A Notes Payable account is credited when the note is issued; the Notes Payable account will be debited three months later when the note is paid. Interest accrues throughout the life of the note, but it is not payable until the note matures on February 1.

The journal entry made on November 1 to record the borrowing of $3,000 from the bank was as follows:

Entry when bank loan is obtained

Cash 3,000
    Notes Payable... 3,000
Obtained from bank three-month loan with interest at 12% a year.

Three months later, Greenhill Real Estate must pay the bank $3,090, representing payment of the $3,000 note payable plus $90 interest ($3,000 $\times$ .12 $\times \frac{3}{12}$). The $90 is the total interest expense for the three months. Although no payment will be made for three months, one-third of the interest expense ($30) is ***incurred*** each month, as shown on the next page..

Accrual of interest

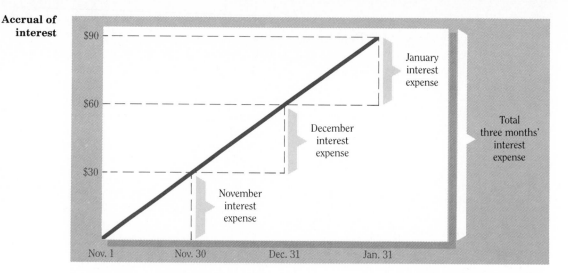

The following ***adjusting entry*** is made at November 30 to charge November operations with one month's interest expense and also to record the amount of interest owed to the bank at the end of November.

Adjusting entry for interest expense incurred in November

Interest Expense	30	
Interest Payable		30
To record interest expense applicable to November ($3,000 × .12 × $\frac{1}{12}$).		

The debit balance in the Interest Expense account will appear in the November income statement; the credit balances in the Interest Payable and Notes Payable accounts will be shown in the balance sheet as liabilities. These two liability accounts will remain in the records until the maturity date of the loan, at which time a cash payment to the bank will wipe out both the Notes Payable account and the Interest Payable account.

Accrual of salary. On November 20, Greenhill hired Carl Nelson as a part-time salesperson whose duties were to work evenings calling on property owners to secure listings of property for sale or rent. The agreed salary was $225 for a five-evening week, payable each Friday; payment for the first week was made on Friday, November 24. Personal income taxes and other taxes relating to payroll are ignored in this illustration.

Assume that the last day of the accounting period, November 30, fell on Thursday. Nelson had worked four evenings since being paid the preceding Friday and therefore had earned $180 ($\frac{4}{5}$ × $225). In order that this $180 of November salary expense be reflected in the accounts before the financial statements are prepared, an ***adjusting entry*** is necessary at November 30.

Salaries Expense   180

     Salaries Payable   180

**To record salary expense and related liability to salesperson for last four evenings'
work in November.**

The debit balance in the Salaries Expense account will appear as an expense in the November income statement; the credit balance of $180 in the Salaries Payable account is the amount owing to the salesperson for work performed during the last four days of November and will appear among the liabilities in the balance sheet at November 30.

The next regular payday for Nelson will be Friday, December 1, which is the first day of the new accounting period. Since the accounts were adjusted and closed on November 30, all the revenue and expense accounts have zero balances at the beginning of business on December 1. The payment of a week's salary to Nelson will be recorded by the following entry on December 1:

Salaries Payable   180

Salaries Expense   45

     Cash   225

Paid weekly salary to salesperson.

Note that the net result of the November 30 accrual entry has been to split the weekly salary expense between November and December. Four days of the work week fell in November, so four days' pay, or $180, was recognized as November expense. One day of the work week fell in December so $45 was recorded as December expense.

No accrual entry is necessary for other salaries in Greenhill Real Estate because everyone except Nelson is paid regularly on the last working day of the month.

Recording unrecorded revenue

A business may earn revenue during the current accounting period but not bill the customer until a future accounting period. This situation is likely to occur if additional services are being performed for the same customer, in which case the bill might not be prepared until all services are completed. Any revenue which has been ***earned but not recorded*** during the current accounting period should be recorded at the end of the period by means of an adjusting entry. This adjusting entry consists of a debit to an account receivable and a credit to the appropriate revenue account. The term ***accrued revenue*** often is used to describe revenue which has been earned during the period but which has not been recorded prior to the closing date.

To illustrate this type of adjusting entry, assume that on November 16, Greenhill Real Estate entered into a management agreement with Angela Clayton, the owner of two small office buildings. The company agreed to manage the Clayton properties for a fee of $240 a month, payable on the fifteenth of each month. No entry is made in the accounting records at the time of signing a contract, because no services have yet been rendered and no change has occurred in assets or liabilities. The managerial duties are to begin immediately, but the first monthly fee will not be received until December 15. The following **adjusting entry** is therefore necessary at November 30:

Adjusting entry for fees earned but uncollected	**Management Fees Receivable**... **120**	
	Management Fees Earned...	**120**
	To record accrued revenue from services rendered to Angela Clayton during November.	

The debit balance in the Management Fees Receivable account will be shown in the balance sheet as an asset. The credit balance of the Management Fees Earned account, including earnings from both the Day and Clayton contracts, will appear in the November income statement.

The collection of the first monthly fee from Clayton will occur in the next accounting period (December 15, to be exact). Of this $240 cash receipt, half represents collection of the asset account, Management Fees Receivable, created at November 30 by the adjusting entry. The other half of the $240 cash receipt represents revenue earned during December; this should be credited to the December revenue account for Management Fees Earned. The entry on December 15 is as follows:

Management fee applicable to two accounting periods	**Cash** **240**	
	Management Fees Receivable	**120**
	Management Fees Earned...	**120**
	Collected commission for month ended December 15.	

The net result of the November 30 accrual entry has been to divide the revenue from managing the Clayton properties between November and December in accordance with the timing of the services rendered.

Adjusting entries and the accrual basis of accounting

Adjusting entries help make accrual basis accounting work successfully. By preparing adjusting entries, we can recognize revenue in the accounting period in which it is **earned** and also recognize expenses which helped to **produce that revenue.** For example, the adjusting entry to record revenue which has been earned but not yet recorded helps achieve our goal of including in the income statement all the revenue **realized** during the accounting period. The adjusting entries which recognize expenses help to achieve the **matching principle**—that is, offsetting revenues with all the expenses incurred in generating that revenue.

THE WORK SHEET

4 Prepare a work sheet and discuss its usefulness.

The work necessary at the end of an accounting period includes construction of a trial balance, journalizing and posting of adjusting entries, preparation of financial statements, and journalizing and posting of closing entries. So many details are involved in these end-of-period procedures that it is easy to make errors. If these errors are recorded in the journal and in the ledger accounts, considerable time and effort can be wasted in correcting them. Both the journal and the ledger are formal, permanent records. They may be prepared manually in ink or printed by a computer. One way of avoiding errors in the permanent accounting records and also of simplifying the work to be done at the end of the period is to use a **_work sheet._**

In a manual accounting system, a work sheet is a large columnar sheet of paper, especially designed to arrange in a convenient systematic form all the accounting data required at the end of the period. The work sheet is not a part of the permanent accounting records; it is prepared in pencil by accountants for their own convenience. (The use of a computer to prepare a work sheet is discussed later in this chapter.) If an error is made on the work sheet, it may be erased and corrected much more easily than an error in the formal accounting records. Furthermore, the work sheet is designed to reduce errors by automatically bringing to light many types of discrepancies which otherwise might be entered in the journal and posted to the ledger accounts. Dollar signs, decimal points, and commas are not used with the amounts entered on work sheets, although commas are shown in this example. A work sheet for Greenhill Real Estate appears on page 142.

The work sheet may be thought of as a testing ground on which the ledger accounts are adjusted, balanced, and arranged in the general form of financial statements. The satisfactory completion of a work sheet provides considerable assurance that all the details of the end-of-period accounting procedures have been properly brought together. After this point has been established, the work sheet then serves as the source from which the formal financial statements are prepared and the adjusting and closing entries are made in the journal.

Preparing the work sheet

Note that the heading of the work sheet illustrated for Greenhill Real Estate consists of three parts: (1) the name of the business, (2) the title **Work Sheet,** and (3) the period of time covered. The body of the work sheet contains five pairs of money columns, each pair consisting of a debit and a credit column. The procedures to be followed in preparing a work sheet will now be illustrated in five simple steps.

1 Enter the ledger account balances in the Trial Balance columns. The titles and balances of the ledger accounts at November 30 are copied into the Trial Balance columns of the work sheet. In practice these amounts may be taken directly from the ledger. It would be a duplication of work to prepare a trial balance as a separate schedule and then to copy this information into the work sheet. As soon as the account balances have been listed on the work sheet, these two columns should be added and the totals entered.

GREENHILL REAL ESTATE
Work Sheet
For the Month Ended November 30, 19___

Enter ledger account balances before adjustments in Trial Balance columns on work sheet

	Trial Balance		Adjustments		Adjusted Trial Balance		Income Statement		Balance Sheet	
	Dr	Cr	Dr	Cr	Dr	Cr	Dr	Cr	Dr	Cr
Cash	21,740									
Accounts receivable	16,990									
Unexpired insurance	600									
Office supplies	720									
Land	130,000									
Building	36,000									
Accumulated depreciation: building		150								
Office equipment	5,400									
Accumulated depreciation: office equipment		45								
Notes payable		3,000								
Accounts payable		23,595								
Unearned management fees		1,800								
Capital stock		180,000								
Retained earnings, Oct. 31, 19___		771								
Dividends	1,500									
Sales commissions earned		15,484								
Advertising expense	1,275									
Salaries expense	9,425									
Telephone expense	1,195									
	224,845	224,845								

2 Enter the adjustments in the Adjustments columns. The required adjustments for Greenhill Real Estate were explained earlier in this chapter; these same adjustments are now entered in the Adjustments columns of the work sheet. (See page 144.)

As a cross reference, the debit and credit parts of each adjustment are keyed together by placing a key letter to the left of each amount. For example, the adjustment debiting Insurance Expense and crediting Unexpired Insurance is identified by the key letter (a). The use of the key letters makes it easy to match a debit entry in the Adjustments columns with its related credit. The identifying letters also key the debit and credit entries in the Adjustments columns to the brief explanations which appear at the bottom of the work sheet.

The titles of any accounts debited or credited in the adjusting entries but not listed in the trial balance should be written on the work sheet below the trial balance. For example, Insurance Expense does not appear in the trial balance; therefore it should be written on the first available line below the trial balance totals. After all the adjustment debits and credits have been entered in the Adjustments columns, this pair of columns must be totaled. Proving the equality of debit and credit totals helps to detect any arithmetical errors and to prevent them from being carried over into other columns of the work sheet.

3 Enter the account balances as adjusted in the Adjusted Trial Balance columns. The work sheet as it appears after completion of the Adjusted Trial Balance columns is illustrated on page 145. Each account balance in the first pair of columns is combined with the adjustment, if any, in the second pair of columns, and the combined amount is entered in the Adjusted Trial Balance columns. This process of combining the items on each line throughout the first four columns of the work sheet requires horizontal addition or subtraction. It is called *cross footing,* in contrast to the addition of items in a vertical column, which is called *footing* the column.

For example, the Office Supplies account has a debit balance of $720 in the Trial Balance columns. This $720 debit amount is combined with the $220 credit appearing on the same line in the Adjustments column; the combination of a $720 debit with a $220 credit produces an adjusted debit amount of $500 in the Adjusted Trial Balance debit column. As another example, consider the Office Supplies Expense account. This account had no balance in the Trial Balance columns but shows a $220 debit in the Adjustments debit column. The combination of a zero starting balance and $220 debit adjustment produces a $220 debit amount in the Adjusted Trial Balance.

Many of the accounts in the trial balance are not affected by the adjustments made at the end of the month; the balances of these accounts (such as Cash, Land, Building, or Notes Payable in the illustrated work sheet) are entered in the Adjusted Trial Balance columns in exactly the same amounts as shown in the Trial Balance columns. After all the accounts have been extended into the Adjusted Trial Balance columns, this pair of columns is totaled to prove that no arithmetical errors have been made up to this point.

4 Extend each amount in the Adjusted Trial Balance columns into the Income Statement columns or into the Balance Sheet columns. Assets and

GREENHILL REAL ESTATE
Work Sheet
For the Month Ended November 30, 19____

	Trial Balance Dr	Cr	Adjustments Dr	Cr	Adjusted Trial Balance Dr	Cr	Income Statement Dr	Cr	Balance Sheet Dr	Cr
Cash	21,740									
Accounts receivable	16,990									
Unexpired insurance	600			(a) 50						
Office supplies	720			(b) 220						
Land	130,000									
Building	36,000									
Accumulated depreciation: building		150		(c) 150						
Office equipment	5,400									
Accumulated depreciation: office equipment		45		(d) 45						
Notes payable		3,000								
Accounts payable		23,595								
Unearned management fees		1,800	(e) 300							
Capital stock		180,000								
Retained earnings, Oct. 31, 19___		771								
Dividends	1,500									
Sales commissions earned		15,484								
Advertising expense	1,275									
Salaries expense	9,425		(g) 180							
Telephone expense	1,195									
Totals	224,845	224,845								
Insurance expense			(a) 50							
Office supplies expense			(b) 220							
Depreciation expense: building			(c) 150							
Depreciation expense: office equipment			(d) 45							
Management fees earned				(e) 300						
				(h) 120						
Interest expense			(f) 30							
Interest payable				(f) 30						
Salaries payable				(g) 180						
Management fees receivable			(h) 120							
			1,095	1,095						

Explanatory footnotes keyed to adjustments

* Adjustments:
(a) Portion of insurance cost which expired during November
(b) Office supplies used during November
(c) Depreciation of building during November
(d) Depreciation of office equipment during November
(e) Earned one-sixth of the commission collected in advance on the Day properties
(f) Interest expense accrued during November on note payable
(g) Salesperson's salary for last four days of November
(h) Rental commission accrued on Clayton contract in November

GREENHILL REAL ESTATE
Work Sheet
For the Month Ended November 30, 19___

Enter the adjusted amounts in columns 5 and 6 of work sheet

	Trial Balance Dr	Trial Balance Cr	Adjustments Dr	Adjustments Cr	Adjusted Trial Balance Dr	Adjusted Trial Balance Cr	Income Statement Dr	Income Statement Cr	Balance Sheet Dr	Balance Sheet Cr
Cash	21,740				21,740					
Accounts receivable	16,990				16,990					
Unexpired insurance	600			(a) 50	550					
Office supplies	720			(b) 220	500					
Land	130,000				130,000					
Building	36,000				36,000					
Accumulated depreciation: building		150		(c) 150		300				
Office equipment	5,400				5,400					
Accumulated depreciation: office equipment		45		(d) 45		90				
Notes payable		3,000				3,000				
Accounts payable		23,595				23,595				
Unearned management fees		1,800	(e) 300			1,500				
Capital stock		180,000				180,000				
Retained earnings, Oct. 31, 19		771				771				
Dividends	1,500				1,500					
Sales commissions earned		15,484				15,484				
Advertising expense	1,275				1,275					
Salaries expense	9,425		(g) 180		9,605					
Telephone expense	1,195				1,195					
Totals	224,845	224,845								
Insurance expense			(a) 50		50					
Office supplies expense			(b) 220		220					
Depreciation expense: building			(c) 150		150					
Depreciation expense: office equipment			(d) 45		45					
Management fees earned				(e) 300 (h) 120		420				
Interest expense			(f) 30		30					
Interest payable				(f) 30		30				
Salaries payable				(g) 180		180				
Management fees receivable			(h) 120		120					
			1,095	1,095	225,370	225,370				

* Explanatory notes relating to adjustments are the same as on page 144.

GREENHILL REAL ESTATE
Work Sheet
For the Month Ended November 30, 19___

	Trial Balance		Adjustments*		Adjusted Trial Balance		Income Statement		Balance Sheet	
	Dr	Cr	Dr	Cr	Dr	Cr	Dr	Cr	Dr	Cr
Cash	21,740				21,740				21,740	
Accounts receivable	16,990				16,990				16,990	
Unexpired insurance	600			(a) 50	550				550	
Office supplies	720			(b) 220	500				500	
Land	130,000				130,000				130,000	
Building	36,000				36,000				36,000	
Accumulated depreciation: building		150		(c) 150		300				300
Office equipment	5,400				5,400				5,400	
Accumulated depreciation: office equipment		45		(d) 45		90				90
Notes payable		3,000				3,000				3,000
Accounts payable		23,595				23,595				23,595
Unearned management fees		1,800	(e) 300			1,500				1,500
Capital stock		180,000				180,000				180,000
Retained earnings, Oct. 31, 19		771				771				771
Dividends	1,500				1,500				1,500	
Sales commissions earned		15,484				15,484		15,484		
Advertising expense	1,275				1,275		1,275			
Salaries expense	9,425		(g) 180		9,605		9,605			
Telephone expense	1,195				1,195		1,195			
Totals	224,845	224,845								
Insurance expense			(a) 50		50		50			
Office supplies expense			(b) 220		220		220			
Depreciation expense: building			(c) 150		150		150			
Depreciation expense: office equipment			(d) 45		45		45			
Management fees earned				(e) 300 (h) 120		420		420		
Interest expense			(f) 30		30		30			
Interest payable				(f) 30		30				30
Salaries payable				(g) 180		180				180
Management fees receivable			(h) 120		120				120	
			1,095	1,095	225,370	225,370				

Extend each adjusted amount to columns for income statement or balance sheet

146

* Explanatory notes relating to adjustments are the same as on page 144.

liabilities are entered in the Balance Sheet columns. The owners' equity accounts (Capital Stock, Retained Earnings, and Dividends) are also entered in the Balance Sheet columns. The revenue and expense accounts are entered in the Income Statement columns.

The process of extending amounts horizontally across the work sheet should begin with the account at the top of the work sheet, which is usually Cash. The cash figure is extended to the Balance Sheet debit column. Then the accountant goes down the work sheet line by line, extending each account balance to the appropriate column. The work sheet as it appears after completion of this sorting process is illustrated on page 146. Note that each amount in the Adjusted Trial Balance columns is extended to one *and only one* of the four remaining columns.

5 Total the Income Statement columns and the Balance Sheet columns. Enter the net income or net loss as a balancing figure in both pairs of columns, and again compute column totals. The work sheet as it appears after this final step is shown on page 148.

The net income or net loss for the period is determined by computing the difference between the totals of the two Income Statement columns. In the illustrated work sheet, the credit column total is the larger and the excess represents net income:

Income Statement credit column total (revenue)	$15,904
Income Statement debit column total (expenses)	12,570
Difference: net income for period...	$ 3,334

Note that the net income of $3,334 is entered in the Income Statement *debit* column as a balancing figure and also on the same line as a balancing figure in the Balance Sheet *credit* column. The caption Net Income is written in the space for account titles to identify and explain this item. New totals are then computed for both the Income Statement columns and the Balance Sheet columns. Each pair of columns is now in balance.

The reason for entering the net income of $3,334 in the Balance Sheet *credit column* is that the net income accumulated during the period in the revenue and expense accounts causes an increase in the owners' equity. If the balance sheet columns did not have equal totals after the net income had been recorded in the credit column, the lack of agreement would indicate that an error had been made in the work sheet.

Let us assume for a moment that the month's operations had produced a loss rather than a profit. In that case the Income Statement debit column would exceed the credit column. The excess of the debits (expenses) over the credits (revenue) would have to be entered in the *credit column* in order to bring the two Income Statement columns into balance. The incurring of a loss would decrease the owners' equity; therefore, the loss would be entered as a balancing figure in the Balance Sheet *debit column.* The Balance Sheet columns would then have equal totals.

Self-balancing nature of the work sheet. Why does the entering of the net income or net loss in one of the Balance Sheet columns bring this pair of columns

Completed work sheet

GREENHILL REAL ESTATE
Work Sheet
For the Month Ended November 30, 19___

	Trial Balance		Adjustments*		Adjusted Trial Balance		Income Statement		Balance Sheet	
	Dr	Cr	Dr	Cr	Dr	Cr	Dr	Cr	Dr	Cr
Cash	21,740				21,740				21,740	
Accounts receivable	16,990				16,990				16,990	
Unexpired insurance	600			(a) 50	550				550	
Office supplies	720			(b) 220	500				500	
Land	130,000				130,000				130,000	
Building	36,000				36,000				36,000	
Accumulated depreciation: building		150		(c) 150		300				300
Office equipment	5,400				5,400				5,400	
Accumulated depreciation: office equipment		45		(d) 45		90				90
Notes payable		3,000				3,000				3,000
Accounts payable		23,595				23,595				23,595
Unearned management fees		1,800	(e) 300			1,500				1,500
Capital stock		180,000				180,000				180,000
Retained earnings, Oct. 31, 19___		771				771				771
Dividends	1,500				1,500				1,500	
Sales commissions earned		15,484				15,484		15,484		
Advertising expense	1,275				1,275		1,275			
Salaries expense	9,425		(g) 180		9,605		9,605			
Telephone expense	1,195				1,195		1,195			
Totals	224,845	224,845								
Insurance expense			(a) 50		50		50			
Office supplies expense			(b) 220		220		220			
Depreciation expense: building			(c) 150		150		150			
Depreciation expense: office equipment			(d) 45		45		45			
Management fees earned				(e) 300 (h) 120		420		420		
Interest expense			(f) 30		30		30			
Interest payable				(f) 30		30				30
Salaries payable				(g) 180		180				180
Management fees receivable			(h) 120		120				120	
Totals			1,095	1,095	225,370	225,370	12,570	15,904	212,800	209,466
Net income							3,334			3,334
Totals							15,904	15,904	212,800	212,800

* Explanatory notes relating to adjustments are the same as on page 144.

148

into balance? The answer is short and simple. All the accounts in the Balance Sheet columns have November 30 balances with the exception of the Retained Earnings account, which still shows the October 31 balance of $771. By bringing in the current month's net income of $3,334 and the Dividends of $1,500, the total owners' equity is brought up to date as of November 30. The Balance Sheet columns now prove the familiar proposition that assets are equal to the total of liabilities and owners' equity.

Uses for the work sheet

Preparing financial statements. Preparing the formal financial statements from the work sheet is an easy step. All the information needed for both the income statement and the balance sheet has already been sorted and arranged in convenient form in the work sheet. For example, compare the amounts on the following income statement with the amounts listed in the Income Statement columns of the completed work sheet.

GREENHILL REAL ESTATE
Income Statement
For the Month Ended November 30, 19__

Data taken from Income Statement columns of work sheet		
Revenue:		
Sales commissions earned..		$15,484
Management fees earned..		420
Total revenue...		$15,904
Expenses:		
Advertising	$1,275	
Office supplies	220	
Salaries	9,605	
Telephone	1,195	
Insurance..	50	
Depreciation: building...	150	
Depreciation: office equipment	45	
Interest...	30	
Total expenses...		12,570
Net income		$ 3,334

As noted in Chapter 3, we are purposely ignoring income taxes on corporations at this stage of our study. Corporate income taxes are introduced in Chapter 5 and considered more fully in Chapter 16.

The amounts used in the statement of retained earnings to compute the ending balance of retained earnings can be taken directly from the work sheet. Compare the following statement of retained earnings with amounts shown on the completed work sheet for November. The October 31 balance of $771 in retained earnings, the $3,334 of net income earned in November, and the $1,500 of dividends all appear in the balance sheet columns of the work sheet. Together, these amounts comprise the new ending balance of the Retained Earnings account, $2,605, as shown below:

GREENHILL REAL ESTATE
Statement of Retained Earnings
For the Month Ended November 30, 19__

Net income
exceeded
dividends

Retained earnings, Oct. 31, 19__	$ 771
Net income for November	3,334
Subtotal	$4,105
Less: Dividends	1,500
Retained earnings, Nov. 30, 19__	$2,605

Finally, the Greenhill balance sheet illustrated for the month of November contains the amounts for assets, liabilities, and capital stock listed in the Balance Sheet columns of the work sheet, along with the new balance of retained earnings.

GREENHILL REAL ESTATE
Balance Sheet
November 30, 19__

Assets

Compare these
amounts with fig-
ures in Balance
Sheet columns of
work sheet

Cash		$ 21,740
Accounts receivable		16,990
Management fees receivable............................		120
Unexpired insurance.....................................		550
Office supplies...		500
Land		130,000
Building	$ 36,000	
Less: Accumulated depreciation	300	35,700
Office equipment	$ 5,400	
Less: Accumulated depreciation	90	5,310
Total assets		$210,910

Liabilities & Stockholders' Equity

Liabilities:		
Notes payable		$ 3,000
Accounts payable		23,595
Interest payable......................................		30
Salaries payable		180
Unearned management fees		1,500
Total liabilities.......................................		$ 28,305
Stockholders' equity:		
Capital stock...	$180,000	
Retained earnings	2,605	182,605
Total liabilities & stockholders' equity		$210,910

Recording adjusting entries in the accounting records. After the financial statements have been compiled from the work sheet at the end of the period, adjusting journal entries are prepared to bring the ledger accounts into agreement with the financial statements. This is an easy step because the adjustments have already been computed on the work sheet. The amounts appearing in the Adjustments columns of the work sheet and the related explanations at the bottom of the work sheet provide all the necessary information for the adjusting entries, as shown in the journal illustration below. These adjusting entries are first entered in the journal and then posted to the ledger accounts.

			General Journal			Page 5
	Date		Account Titles and Explanation	LP	Debit	Credit
Adjustments on work sheet are entered in general journal	19__ Nov.	30	Insurance Expense .... Unexpired Insurance .... Insurance expense for November.		50	50
		30	Office Supplies Expense........................... Office Supplies .... Office supplies used during November.		220	220
		30	Depreciation Expense: Building..................... Accumulated Depreciation: Building............ Depreciation for November ($36,000 ÷ 240 = $150).		150	150
		30	Depreciation Expense: Office Equipment .... Accumulated Depreciation: Office Equipment..... Depreciation for November ($5,400 ÷ 120 = $45).		45	45
		30	Unearned Management Fees .... Management Fees Earned..................... Earned one-sixth of fee collected in advance for management of the properties owned by John Day.		300	300
		30	Interest Expense .... Interest Payable .... Interest expense accrued during November on note payable ($3,000 × 12% × $\frac{1}{12}$).		30	30
		30	Salaries Expense.................................. Salaries Payable............................ To record expense and related liability to salesperson for last four evenings' work in November.		180	180
		30	Management Fees Receivable....................... Management Fees Earned..................... To record the receivable and related revenue earned for managing properties owned by Angela Clayton.		120	120

Recording closing entries. When the financial statements have been prepared, the revenue and expense accounts have served their purpose for the current period and should be closed. These accounts then will have zero balances and will be ready for the recording of revenue and expenses during the next fiscal period. The completed work sheet provides in convenient form all the information needed to make the closing entries. The preparation of closing entries from the work sheet may be summarized as follows:

1 To close the accounts listed in the Income Statement credit column, debit the revenue accounts and credit Income Summary.
2 To close the accounts listed in the Income Statement debit column, debit Income Summary and credit the expense accounts.
3 To close the Income Summary account, transfer the balancing figure in the Income Statement columns of the work sheet ($3,334 in the illustration) to the Retained Earnings account. A profit is transferred by debiting Income Summary and crediting the Retained Earnings account; a loss is transferred by debiting the Retained Earnings account and crediting Income Summary.
4 To close the Dividends account, debit the Retained Earnings account and credit the Dividends account.

The entries to close the revenue and expense accounts, as well as the Dividends account, at November 30 are shown below:

General Journal   Page 6

Date		Account Titles and Explanation	LP	Debit	Credit
19__					
Nov.	30	Sales Commissions Earned.........................		15,484	
		Management Fees Earned..........................		420	
		Income Summary.............................			15,904
		To close the revenue accounts.			
	30	Income Summary..................................		12,570	
		Advertising Expense.........................			1,275
		Salaries Expense............................			9,605
		Telephone Expense..........................			1,195
		Insurance Expense			50
		Office Supplies Expense.....................			220
		Depreciation Expense: Building..............			150
		Depreciation Expense: Office Equipment			45
		Interest Expense			30
		To close the expense accounts.			
	30	Income Summary..................................		3,334	
		Retained Earnings			3,334
		To close the Income Summary account.			
	30	Retained Earnings................................		1,500	
		Dividends			1,500
		To close the Dividends account.			

Closing entries derived from work sheet

Work sheets in computer-based systems

The "work sheet" in a computer-based accounting system usually consists of a display on the monitor screen rather than a sheet of columnar paper. Spreadsheet programs, such as Lotus 1-2-3 or VP Planner, are ideally suited to preparing a work sheet in a computerized accounting system.

Most of the steps involved in preparing a work sheet are mechanical and can be performed automatically in a computer-based system. Thus, the work sheet can be prepared faster and more easily than in a manual system. A trial balance, for example, is merely a listing of the ledger account balances, and can be prepared instantly by computer. Entering the adjustments, on the other hand, requires human judgment and analysis. Someone familiar with generally accepted accounting principles and with the unrecorded business activities of the company must decide what adjustments are necessary and must enter the adjustment data. Once the adjustments have been entered, the computer can instantly complete the work sheet. When the accountant is satisfied that the adjustments shown in the work sheet are correct, the adjusting and closing entries can be entered in the formal accounting records with the touch of a button.

The accounting cycle

5 Describe the steps in the accounting cycle.

As stated at the beginning of this chapter, the life of a business is divided into accounting periods of equal length. In each period we repeat a standard sequence of accounting procedures beginning with the journalizing of transactions and concluding with an after-closing trial balance.

Because the work sheet includes the trial balance, the adjusting entries in preliminary form, and an adjusted trial balance, the use of a work sheet will modify the sequence of procedures given in Chapter 3, as follows:

1 Journalize transactions. Analyze business transactions as they occur and record them promptly in the journal.

2 Post to ledger accounts. Transfer debits and credits from journal entries to ledger accounts.

3 Prepare a work sheet. Begin with a trial balance of the ledger, enter all necessary adjustments, compute the adjusted account balances, sort the adjusted balances between income statement accounts and balance sheet accounts, and determine the net income or net loss.

4 Prepare financial statements. Utilize the information in the work sheet to prepare an income statement, a statement of retained earnings, and a balance sheet.

5 Adjust and close the accounts. Using the information in the work sheet as a guide, enter the adjusting entries in the journal. Post these entries to ledger accounts. Prepare and post journal entries to close the revenue and expense accounts into the Income Summary account and to transfer the net income or net loss to the Retained Earnings account. Also prepare and post a journal entry to close the Dividends accounts into the Retained Earnings account.

6 Prepare an after-closing trial balance. Prove that equality of debit and credit balances in the ledger has not been upset by the adjusting and closing procedures.

The above sequence of accounting procedures constitutes a complete accounting process. The regular repetition of this standardized set of procedures in each accounting period is often referred to as the ***accounting cycle.*** The procedures of a complete accounting cycle are illustrated on page 155. The white symbols indicate the accounting procedures; the shaded gray symbols represent accounting records, schedules, and statements.

Note that the preparing of financial statements (Step 4) comes before entering adjusting and closing entries in the journal and posting these entries to the ledger (Step 5). This sequence reflects the fact that ***management wants the financial statements as soon as possible.*** Once the work sheet is complete, all information required for the financial statements is available. Top priority then goes to preparation of the financial statements.

In most business concerns the accounts are closed only once a year; for these companies the accounting cycle is one year in length. For purposes of illustration in a textbook, however, it is often convenient to assume that the entire accounting cycle is performed within the time period of one month. The completion of the accounting cycle is the occasion for preparing financial statements and closing the revenue and expense accounts.

Preparing monthly financial statements without closing the accounts

Many companies which close their accounts only once a year nevertheless prepare ***monthly*** financial statements for managerial use. These monthly statements are prepared from work sheets, but the adjustments indicated on the work sheets are not entered in the accounting records and no closing entries are made. Under this plan, the time-consuming operation of journalizing and posting adjustments and closing entries is performed only at the end of the fiscal year, but the company has the advantage of monthly financial statements. Monthly and quarterly financial statements are often referred to as ***interim statements,*** because they are in between the year-end statements. The annual or year-end statements are usually audited by a firm of certified public accountants; interim statements are usually unaudited.

Reversing entries

6 Explain when and why reversing entries may be used. Reversing entries are an optional procedure which may be carried out at year-end to simplify the recording of certain routine cash receipts and cash payments in the following period. As the name suggests, a ***reversing entry*** is the exact reverse of

ILLUSTRATION OF THE ACCOUNTING CYCLE

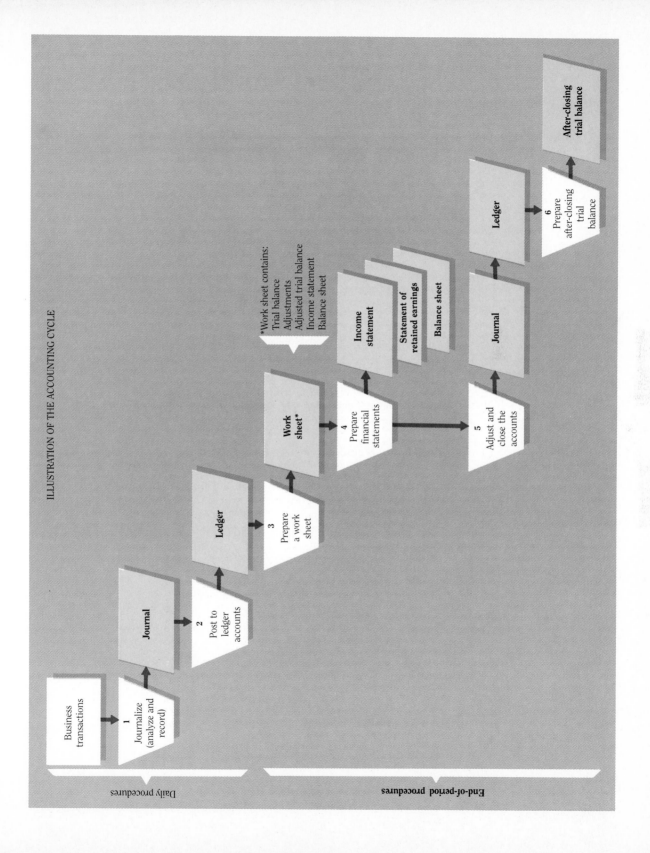

an adjusting entry. It contains the same account titles and dollar amounts as the related adjusting entry, but the debits and credits are the reverse of those in the adjusting entry and the date is the first day of the next accounting period.

Let us use as an example a small company on a five-day work week which pays its employees each Friday. Assume that the payroll is $600 a day or $3,000 for a five-day week. Throughout the year, a company employee makes a journal entry each Friday as follows:

Regular weekly entry for payroll

Salaries Expense..	3,000	
Cash..		3,000

To record payment of salaries for the week.

Next, let us assume that December 31, the last working day of Year 1, falls on Wednesday. All expenses of Year 1 must be recorded before the accounts are closed and financial statements prepared at December 31. Therefore, an adjusting entry must be made to record the salaries expense and the related liability to employees for the three days they have worked since the last payday. The adjusting entry for $1,800 (computed as 3 × $600 daily salary expense) is shown below:

Adjusting entry at end of year

Dec. 31	Salaries Expense	1,800	
	Salaries Payable		1,800

To record salaries expense and the related liability to employees for last three days worked in December.

The closing of the accounts on December 31 will reduce the Salaries Expense account to zero, but the liability account, Salaries Payable, will remain open with its $1,800 credit balance at the beginning of the new year. On the next regular payday, Friday, January 2, an employee can record the $3,000 payroll by a debit of $1,800 to Salaries Payable, a debit of $1,200 to Salaries Expense, and a credit of $3,000 to Cash. However, splitting the debit side of the entry in this manner ($1,800 to the liability account and $1,200 to expense) requires more understanding and alertness from company personnel than if the entry were identical with the other 51 payroll entries made during the year.

By making a reversing entry as of the first day of the new accounting period, we can simplify the recording of routine transactions and avoid the need for employees to refer to prior adjusting entries for guidance. The reversing entry for the $1,800 year-end accrual of salaries would be dated January 1, Year 2, and would probably be made under the direction of the accountant responsible for the year-end closing of the accounts and preparation of financial statements. The entry would be as follows:

Reversing entry makes possible . . .

Jan. 1	Salaries payable	1,800	
	Salaries Expense		1,800

To reverse the accrual of salaries made on Dec. 31, Year 1.

This reversing entry closes the Salaries Payable account by transferring the $1,800 liability to the credit side of the Salaries Expense account. Thus, the Salaries

Expense account begins the new year with an abnormal credit balance of $1,800. On Friday, January 2, the normal payroll entry for $3,000 will be made to the same accounts as on every other Friday during the year.

. . . regular
payroll entry for
first payday of
new year

Jan. 2 Salaries Expense... 3,000

Cash.. 3,000

Paid salaries for week ended Jan. 2, Year 2.

After this January 2 entry has been posted, the ledger account for Salaries Expense will show a debit balance of $1,200, the result of this $3,000 debit and the $1,800 credit from the reversing entry on January 1. The amount of $1,200 is the correct expense for the two workdays of the new year at $600 a day. The results, of course, are *exactly the same* as if no reversing entry had been used and the company's accounting personnel had split the debit side of the January 2 payroll entry between Salaries Payable and Salaries Expense.

Salaries Expense			Debit	Credit	Balance
Various	(51 weekly entries of $3,000)				1 5 3 0 0 0
Dec 31	Adjusting entry (3 days @ $600)		1 8 0 0		1 5 4 8 0 0
31	To close at year-end			1 5 4 8 0 0	- 0 -
Year 2					
Jan 1	Reversing entry			1 8 0 0	1 8 0 0 cr
2	Weekly payroll		3 0 0 0		1 2 0 0

Salaries Payable			Debit	Credit	Balance
Dec 31	Adjusting entry (3 days @ $600)			1 8 0 0	1 8 0 0
Year 2					
Jan 1	Reversing entry		1 8 0 0		- 0 -

Which adjusting entries should be reversed? Even when a company follows a policy of making reversing entries, *not all adjusting entries should be reversed.* Only those adjustments which *create an account receivable or a short-term liability* should be reversed. These adjustments will be followed by cash receipts or cash payments within the near future. Reversing these adjusting entries will enable the company's personnel to record the upcoming cash transactions in a routine manner.

An adjusting entry which apportions an amount recorded in the past *should not be reversed.* Thus we do *not* reverse the adjusting entries which apportion recorded costs (such as depreciation), or which record the earning of revenue collected in advance.

In summary, reversing entries may be made for those adjusting entries which record *unrecorded expenses* or *unrecorded revenue.* Reversing entries are *not* made for adjustments which apportion recorded costs or recorded revenue.

Reversing entries in a computer-based system. Reversing entries do not require any analysis of transactions. Rather, they merely involve reversing the debit and credit amounts of specific adjusting entries. The adjusting entries to be reversed can be identified by a simple rule — namely, reverse those adjustments which increase accounts receivable or short-term liabilities. Thus, a computer may be programmed to prepare reversing entries automatically.

Finally, remember that reversing entries are *optional.* They are intended to simplify the accounting process, but they are *not essential* in the application of generally accepted accounting principles or in the preparation of financial statements.

END-OF-CHAPTER REVIEW

Summary of chapter learning objectives

1 Explain how accounting periods of equal length are useful in evaluating the income of a business.

The net income of a business is measured for a specified period of time, termed the accounting period. When accounting periods are of equal length, we can compare the income of the current period with that of prior periods to see if operating results are improving or declining.

2 State the purpose of adjusting entries and explain how these entries are related to the concepts of accrual accounting.

The purpose of adjusting entries is to record certain revenue and expenses that are not properly measured in the course of recording daily business transactions. Adjusting entries help to achieve the basic goals of accrual accounting — recognizing revenue when it is earned, and recognizing expenses when the goods or services are used.

3 Describe the four basic types of adjusting entries.

The four basic types of adjusting entries are entries to: (1) apportion recorded costs, (2) apportion unearned revenue, (3) record unrecorded expenses, and (4) record unrecorded revenue.

4 Prepare a work sheet and discuss its usefulness.

A work sheet is a "testing ground" on which the ledger accounts are adjusted, balanced, and arranged in the format of financial statements. A work sheet consists of a trial balance, the end-of-period adjusting entries, an adjusted trial balance, and columns showing the ledger accounts arranged as an income statement and balance sheet. The completed work sheet is used as the basis for preparing financial statements and for recording adjusting and closing entries in the formal accounting records.

5 Describe the steps in the accounting cycle.

When a work sheet is prepared, the steps in the accounting cycle may be summarized as follows: (1) journalize transactions, (2) post to ledger accounts, (3) prepare a work sheet, (4) prepare financial statements, (5) adjust and close the accounts, and (6) prepare an after-closing trial balance.

6 Explain when and why reversing entries may be used.

Reversing entries are an optional procedure which may be applied at the end of the accounting period to simplify the recording of routine cash receipts and payments in the following accounting period. When reversing entries are used, they should be made for any adjusting entry that creates an account receivable or a short-term liability. In short, for any adjusting entry that accrues either revenue or expense.

Key terms introduced or emphasized in chapter 4

Accounting cycle. The sequence of accounting procedures performed during an accounting period. The procedures include journalizing transactions, posting, preparation of a work sheet and financial statements, adjusting and closing the accounts, and preparation of an after-closing trial balance.

Accrued expenses. Expenses such as salaries of employees and interest on notes payable which have been accumulating day-by-day, but are unrecorded and unpaid at the end of the period. Also called *unrecorded expenses.*

Accrued revenue. Revenue which has been earned during the accounting period but has not been recorded or collected prior to the closing date. Also called *unrecorded revenue.*

Book value. The net amount at which an asset is shown in accounting records. For depreciable assets, book value equals cost minus accumulated depreciation. Also called *carrying value.*

Carrying value. See book value.

Deferred revenue. See unearned revenue.

Interim statements. Financial statements prepared at intervals of less than one year. Usually quarterly and monthly statements.

Prepaid expenses. Advance payments for such expenses as rent and insurance. The portion which has not been used up at the end of the accounting period is included in the balance sheet as an asset.

Promissory note. A formal written promise to repay an amount borrowed plus interest at a future date.

Reversing entries. An optional year-end technique consisting of the reversal on the first day of the new accounting period of those year-end adjusting entries which accrue expenses or revenue and thus will be followed by later cash payments or receipts. Purpose is to permit company personnel to record routine transactions in a standard manner without referring to prior adjusting entries.

Unearned revenue. An obligation to render services or deliver goods in the future because of receipt of advance payment.

Unrecorded expenses. See accrued expenses.

Unrecorded revenue. See accrued revenue.

Work sheet. A large columnar sheet designed to arrange in convenient form all the accounting data required at the end of the period. Facilitates preparation of financial statements and the work of adjusting and closing the accounts.

Demonstration problem for your review

Reed Geophysical Company adjusts and closes its accounts at the end of the calendar year. At December 31, 19__, the following trial balance was prepared from the ledger:

REED GEOPHYSICAL COMPANY
Trial Balance
December 31, 19__

Cash	$ 12,540	
Prepaid office rent	3,300	
Prepaid dues and subscriptions	960	
Supplies	1,300	
Equipment	40,000	
Accumulated depreciation: equipment		$ 1,200
Notes payable		5,000
Unearned consulting fees		35,650
Capital stock		6,000
Retained earnings		11,040
Dividends	7,000	
Consulting fees earned		90,860
Salaries expense	66,900	
Telephone expense	2,550	
Rent expense	11,000	
Miscellaneous expenses	4,200	
	$149,750	$149,750

Other data

(a) For the first 11 months of the year, office rent had been charged to the Rent Expense account at a rate of $1,000 per month. On December 1, however, the company signed a new rental agreement and paid three months' rent in advance at a rate of $1,100 per month. This advance payment was debited to the Prepaid Rent account.

(b) Dues and subscriptions expired during the year in the total amount of $710.

(c) A count of supplies on hand was made at December 31; the cost of the unused supplies was $450.

(d) The useful life of the equipment has been estimated at 20 years from date of acquisition.

(e) Accrued interest on notes payable amounted to $100 at year-end. Set up accounts for Interest Expense and for Interest Payable.

(f) Consulting services valued at $32,550 were rendered during the year for clients who had made payment in advance.

(g) It is the custom of the firm to bill clients only when consulting work is completed or, in the case of prolonged engagements, at six-month intervals. At December 31, engineering services valued at $3,000 had been rendered to clients but not yet billed. No advance payments had been received from these clients.

(h) Salaries earned by employees but not yet paid amounted to $2,200 at December 31.

Instructions. Prepare a work sheet for the year ended December 31, 19__.

Solution to demonstration problem

REED GEOPHYSICAL COMPANY
Work Sheet
For the Year Ended December 31, 19___

	Trial Balance Dr	Trial Balance Cr	Adjustments Dr	Adjustments Cr	Adjusted Trial Balance Dr	Adjusted Trial Balance Cr	Income Statement Dr	Income Statement Cr	Balance Sheet Dr	Balance Sheet Cr
Cash	12,540				12,540				12,540	
Prepaid office rent	3,300			(a) 1,100	2,200				2,200	
Prepaid dues and subscriptions	960			(b) 710	250				250	
Supplies	1,300			(c) 850	450				450	
Equipment	40,000				40,000				40,000	
Accumulated depreciation: equipment		1,200		(d) 2,000		3,200				3,200
Notes payable		5,000				5,000				5,000
Unearned consulting fees		35,650	(f) 32,550			3,100				3,100
Capital stock		6,000				6,000				6,000
Retained earnings		11,040				11,040				11,040
Dividends	7,000				7,000				7,000	
Consulting fees earned		90,860		(f) 32,550 (g) 3,000		126,410		126,410		
	149,750	149,750								
Salaries expense	66,900		(h) 2,200		69,100		69,100			
Telephone expense	2,550				2,550		2,550			
Rent expense	11,000		(a) 1,100		12,100		12,100			
Miscellaneous expense	4,200				4,200		4,200			
Dues and subscriptions expense			(b) 710		710		710			
Supplies expense			(c) 850		850		850			
Depreciation expense: equipment			(d) 2,000		2,000		2,000			
Interest expense			(e) 100		100		100			
Interest payable				(e) 100		100				100
Consulting fees receivable			(g) 3,000		3,000				3,000	
Salaries payable				(h) 2,200		2,200				2,200
			42,510	42,510	157,050	157,050	91,610	126,410	65,440	30,640
Net income							34,800			34,800
							126,410	126,410	65,440	65,440

* Adjustments:
(a) Rent expense for December.
(b) Dues and subscriptions expense for year.
(c) Supplies used for year ($1,300 − $450 = $850).
(d) Depreciation expense for year.

(e) Accrued interest on notes payable.
(f) Consulting services performed for clients who paid in advance.
(g) Services rendered but not billed.
(h) Salaries earned but not paid.

161

ASSIGNMENT MATERIAL

Review questions

1 What is the purpose of making adjusting entries? Your answer should relate adjusting entries to the goals of accrual accounting.

2 Do all transactions involving revenue or expenses require adjusting entries at the end of the accounting period? If not, what is the distinguishing characteristic of those transactions which do require adjusting entries?

3 Do adjusting entries affect income statement accounts, balance sheet accounts, or both? Explain.

4 Why does the recording of adjusting entries require a better understanding of the concepts of accrual accounting than does the recording of routine revenue and expense transactions occurring throughout the period?

5 Why does the purchase of a one-year insurance policy four months ago give rise to insurance expense in the current month?

6 If services have been rendered to customers during the current accounting period but no revenue has been recorded and no bill has been sent to the customers, why is an adjusting entry needed? What types of accounts should be debited and credited by this entry?

7 What is meant by the term *unearned revenue?* Where should an unearned revenue account appear in the financial statements? As the work is done, what happens to the balance of an unearned revenue account?

8 At the end of the current year, the adjusted trial balance of the Midas Company showed the following account balances, among others:

Building, $126,400

Depreciation Expense: Building, $6,320

Accumulated Depreciation: Building, $37,920

Assuming that straight-line depreciation has been used, what length of time do these facts suggest that the Midas Company has owned the building?

9 The weekly payroll for employees of Ryan Company, which works a five-day week, amounts to $5,000. All employees are paid up-to-date at the close of business each Friday. If December 31 falls on Tuesday, what year-end adjusting entry is needed?

10 The Marvin Company purchased a one-year fire insurance policy on August 1 and debited the entire cost of $3,600 to Unexpired Insurance. The accounts were not adjusted or closed until the end of the year. Give the adjusting entry at December 31.

11 Office supplies on hand in the Melville Company amounted to $642 at the beginning of the year. During the year additional office supplies were purchased at a cost of $1,561 and charged to the asset account. At the end of the year a physical count showed that supplies on hand amounted to $812. Give the adjusting entry needed at December 31.

12 At year-end the adjusting entry to reduce the Unexpired Insurance account by the amount of insurance premium applicable to the current period was accidentally omitted. Which items in the income statement will be in error? Will these items be overstated or understated? Which items in the balance sheet will be in error? Will they be overstated or understated?

13 What is the purpose of a work sheet?

14 In performing the regular end-of-period accounting procedures, does the preparation of the work sheet precede or follow the posting of adjusting entries to ledger accounts? Why?

15 Assume that when the Income Statement columns of a work sheet are first totaled, the total of the debit column exceeds the total of the credit column by $60,000. Explain how the amount of net income (or net loss) should be entered in the work sheet columns.

16 Does the ending balance of retained earnings appear in the work sheet? Explain.

17 Can each step in the preparation of a work sheet be performed automatically in a computer-based accounting system? Explain.

18 List in order the procedures comprising the accounting cycle when a work sheet is used.

19 Is a work sheet ever prepared when there is no intention of closing the accounts?

20 The weekly payroll of Stevens Company, which has a five-day work week, amounts to $15,000 and employees are paid up to date every Friday. On January 1 of the current year, the Salaries Expense account showed a credit balance of $9,000. Explain the nature of the accounting entry or entries which probably led to this balance.

21 Four general types of adjusting entries were discussed in this chapter. If reversing entries are made, which of these types of adjusting entries should be reversed? Why?

Exercises

Exercise 4-1
Accounting terminology

Listed below are nine technical accounting terms introduced in this chapter:

Accrued expense	Interim statements	Statement of retained earnings
Accrued revenue	Prepaid expense	Unearned revenue
Adjusting entries	Reversing entries	Work sheet

Each of the following statements may (or may not) describe one of these technical terms. For each statement, indicate the accounting term described, or answer "None" if the statement does not correctly describe any of the terms.

a Entries made during the accounting period to correct errors found in the accounting records.

b Interest expense which has been incurred, but has not yet been paid or recorded.

c A liability to customers who have made advance payments for services to be rendered in a future accounting period.

d An optional year-end procedure designed to simplify the recording of routine cash transactions in the upcoming accounting period.

e A device for working out the end-of-period accounting procedures before adjusting and closing entries are entered into the formal accounting records.

f Entries needed to achieve the goals of accrual accounting when transactions affect the revenue or expenses of more than one accounting period.

Exercise 4-2
Effects of adjusting entries

Design Services, Inc., uses a one-month accounting period. On November 30, adjusting entries are prepared to record:

a Interest expense that has accrued during November.

b Depreciation expense for November.

c The portion of the company's prepaid insurance which has expired during November.

d Earning a portion of the amount collected in advance from a customer, Harbor Restaurant.

e Salaries payable to company employees which have accrued since the last payday in November.

f Revenue earned during November which has not yet been billed to customers.

Indicate the effect of each of these adjusting entries upon the major elements of the company's financial statements — that is, upon revenue, expenses, net income, assets, liabilities, and owners' equity. Organize your answer in tabular form, using the column headings shown below and the symbols + for increase, — for decrease, and NE for no effect. The answer for adjusting entry (a) is provided as an example.

| Adjusting Entry | Income Statement | | | Balance Sheet | | |
	Revenue	Expenses	Net Income	Assets	Liabilities	Owners' Equity
a	NE	+	—	NE	+	—

Exercise 4-3
Preparing adjusting entries for recorded costs and recorded revenue

The Outlaws, a professional football team, prepare financial statements on a monthly basis. Football season begins in August, but in July the team engaged in the following transactions:

a Paid $1,050,000 to Dodge City as advance rent for use of Dodge City Stadium for the five-month period from August 1 through December 31. This payment was debited to the asset account, Prepaid Rent.

b Collected $2,080,000 cash from sales of season tickets for the team's eight home games. This amount was credited to Unearned Ticket Revenue.

During the month of August, The Outlaws played one home game and two games on the road. Their record was two wins, one loss.

Instructions. Prepare the two adjusting entries required at August 31 to apportion this recorded cost and recorded revenue.

Exercise 4-4
Preparing adjusting entries for unrecorded revenue and expenses

The law firm of Barlow & Cloud prepares its financial statements on an annual basis at December 31. Among the situations requiring year-end adjusting entries were the following:

a Salaries to staff attorneys are paid on the fifteenth day of each month. Salaries accrued since December 15 amount to $14,300 and have not yet been recorded.

b The firm is defending R. H. Dominelli in a civil lawsuit. The agreed upon legal fees are $2,000 per day while the trial is in progress. The trial has been in progress for nine days during December and is not expected to end until late January. No legal fees have yet been billed to Dominelli. (Legal fees are recorded in an account entitled Legal Fees Earned.)

Instructions. Prepare the two adjusting entries required at December 31 to record the accrued salaries expense and the accrued legal fees revenue.

Exercise 4-5
Adjusting entry and subsequent business transaction

On Friday of each week, Relic Company pays its sales personnel weekly salaries amounting to $75,000 for a five-day work week.

a Draft the necessary adjusting entry at year-end, assuming that December 31 falls on Wednesday.

b Also draft the journal entry for the payment by Relic Company of a week's salaries to its sales personnel on Friday, January 2, the first payday of the new year. (Assume that the company does not use reversing entries.)

Exercise 4-6
Preparing
various adjusting
entries

Hill Corporation adjusts and closes its accounts at the end of the calendar year. Prepare the adjusting entries required at December 31 based on the following information. (Not all of these items may require adjusting entries.)

a A bank loan had been obtained on September 1. Accrued interest on the loan at December 31 amounts to $4,800. No interest expense has yet been recorded.
b Depreciation of office equipment is based on an estimated life of five years. The balance in the Office Equipment account is $25,000; no change has occurred in the account during the year.
c Interest receivable on United States government bonds owned at December 31 amounts to $2,300. This accrued interest revenue has not been recorded.
d On December 31, an agreement was signed to lease a truck for 12 months beginning January 1 at a rate of 35 cents a mile. Usage is expected to be 2,000 miles per month and the contract specifies a minimum payment equivalent to 18,000 miles a year.
e The company's policy is to pay all employees up-to-date each Friday. Since December 31 fell on Monday, there was a liability to employees at December 31 for one day's pay amounting to $2,800.

Exercise 4-7
Relationship of
adjusting entries
to business
transactions

Among the ledger accounts used by Glenwood Speedway are the following: Prepaid Rent, Rent Expense, Unearned Admissions Revenue, Admissions Revenue, Prepaid Printing, Printing Expense, Concessions Receivable, and Concessions Revenue. For each of the following items, write first the journal entry (if one is needed) to record the external transaction and second the adjusting entry, if any, required on May 31, the end of the fiscal year.

a On May 1, borrowed $200,000 cash from National Bank by issuing a 12% note payable due in three months.
b On May 1, paid rent for six months beginning May 1 at $25,000 per month.
c On May 2, sold season tickets for a total of $700,000 cash. The season includes 70 racing days: 20 in May, 25 in June, and 25 in July.
d On May 4, an agreement was reached with Snack-Bars, Inc., allowing that company to sell refreshments at the track in return for 10% of the gross receipts from refreshment sales.
e On May 6, schedules for the 20 racing days in May and the first 10 racing days in June were printed and paid for at a cost of $9,000.
f On May 31, Snack-Bars, Inc., reported that the gross receipts from refreshment sales in May had been $145,000 and that the 10% owed to Glenwood Speedway would be remitted on June 10.

Exercise 4-8
Preparing closing
entries from a
work sheet

Using the information contained in the work sheet illustrated on page 161, prepare the four year-end closing entries for Reed Geophysical Company.

Exercise 4-9
Preparing
reversing entries

Milo Company closes its accounts at the end of each calendar year. The company operates on a five-day work week and pays its employees up to date each Friday. The weekly payroll is regularly $5,000. On Wednesday, December 31, 1990, an adjusting entry was made to accrue $3,000 salaries expense for the three days worked since the last payday. The company *did not* make a reversing entry. On Friday, January 2, 1991, the regular weekly payroll of $5,000 was paid and recorded by the usual entry debiting Salaries Expense $5,000 and crediting Cash $5,000.

Were Milo Company's accounting records correct for 1990? For 1991? Explain two alternatives the company might have followed with respect to payroll at year-end. One of the alternatives should include a reversing entry.

Problems

Problem 4-1
Preparing
adjusting entries

East Beach Motel adjusts and closes its accounts once a year on December 31. Most guests of the motel pay at the time they check out, and the amounts collected are credited to Rental Revenue. A few guests pay in advance for rooms and these amounts are credited to Unearned Rental Revenue at the time of receipt. The following information is available as a source for preparing adjusting entries at December 31:

(a) A one-year bank loan in the amount of $80,000 had been obtained on November 1. No interest has been paid and no interest expense has been recorded. The interest accrued at December 31 is $1,600.

(b) On December 16, a suite of rooms was rented to a corporation for six months at a monthly rental of $3,200. The entire six months' rent of $19,200 was collected in advance and credited to Unearned Rental Revenue. At December 31, the amount of $1,600, representing one-half month's rent, was considered to be earned and the remainder of $17,600 was considered to be unearned.

(c) As of December 31 the motel has earned $18,090 rental revenue from current guests who will not be billed until they are ready to check out. (Debit Rent Receivable.)

(d) Salaries earned by employees at December 31 but not yet paid amount to $11,640.

(e) Depreciation on the motel for the year ended December 31 was $51,250.

(f) Depreciation on a station wagon owned by the motel was based on a four-year life. The station wagon had been purchased new on September 1 of the current year at a cost of $12,600. Depreciation for four months should be recorded at December 31.

(g) On December 31, East Beach Motel entered into an agreement to host the National Building Suppliers Convention in June of next year. The motel expects to earn rental revenue of at least $30,000 from the convention.

Instructions. For each of the above numbered paragraphs, draft a separate adjusting journal entry (including explanation), if the information indicates that an adjusting entry is needed. One or more of the above paragraphs may not require any adjusting entry.

Problem 4-2
Preparing
adjusting entries
from a trial
balance

On January 1, 19__, Dale Cole organized Executive Valet, Inc., to operate a valet parking service in the garage of a large office building. The business rents the garage from the owner of the building. The company makes adjusting and closing entries at the end of each month. Shown below is a trial balance and other information needed in making adjusting entries at January 31.

EXECUTIVE VALET, INC.
Trial Balance
January 31, 19__

Cash	$11,280	
Unexpired insurance	12,600	
Office supplies	400	
Equipment	10,500	
Notes payable		$ 9,000
Unearned parking fees		14,740
Capital stock		10,000
Parking fees earned		18,750
Rent expense	12,000	
Utilities expense	890	
Salaries expense	4,820	
	$52,490	$52,490

Other data

(a) The monthly insurance expense amounted to $2,100.

(b) The amount of office supplies on hand, based on a physical count on January 31, was $150.

(c) No interest had as yet been paid or recorded on the note payable; as of January 31 accrued interest amounted to $90.

(d) The useful life of the equipment used in the business was estimated at five years (60 months).

(e) Many businesses in the office building had made advance payments to cover several months' parking privileges for their executives and employees. These advance payments had been credited to the Unearned Parking Fees account. At January 31, it was determined that $3,210 of these advance payments had been earned.

(f) Security Bank, one of the tenants in the building, agreed to pay $2,000 per month for the use of 10 ground floor parking spaces for bank customers. The $2,000 fee for January is due on February 10 and has not yet been recorded.

(g) Salaries earned by employees but not paid amounted to $1,240 at January 31.

Instructions. You are to use the above trial balance and other information as a basis for preparing the adjusting entries (with explanations) needed at January 31.

Problem 4-3
Preparing adjusting entries, an adjusted trial balance, and financial statements

Action Investigations, Inc., is a private detective agency owned and operated by Bret Rockford. Some clients are required to pay in advance for the services, while others are billed after the services have been rendered. Advance payments are credited to an account entitled Unearned Retainer Fees, which represents unearned revenue. Action Investigations adjusts and closes its accounts each month. At May 31, the trial balance appears as follows:

ACTION INVESTIGATIONS, INC.
Trial Balance
May 31, 19__

Cash	$14,900	
Prepaid rent	3,000	
Office supplies...	1,100	
Office equipment	10,800	
Accumulated depreciation: office equipment...........................		$ 3,960
Automobiles..	36,000	
Accumulated depreciation: automobiles		8,250
Accounts payable		2,000
Unearned retainer fees...		19,000
Dividends payable..		5,000
Capital stock		15,000
Retained earnings, Apr. 30, 19__		16,890
Dividends	5,000	
Fees earned..		14,000
Telephone expense...	800	
Travel expense	1,000	
Salaries expense...	11,500	
	$84,100	$84,100

Other data

(a) The monthly rent is $600.
(b) Office supplies on hand May 31 amount to $900.
(c) The office equipment is being depreciated over a period of five years (60 months).
(d) The automobiles are being depreciated over a period of four years (48 months).
(e) Fees of $4,000 were earned during the month by performing services for clients who had paid in advance. (Debit Unearned Retainer Fees.)
(f) Investigative services rendered during the month but not yet collected or billed to clients amount to $1,200. (Debit Professional Fees Receivable.)
(g) Salaries earned by employees during the month, but not yet paid, amount to $1,300.

Instructions

a Prepare adjusting entries.
b Prepare an adjusted trial balance. Accounts not appearing in the trial balance but used in the adjusting entries should be listed in the proper sequence in the adjusted trial balance. For example, Professional Fees Receivable should be listed among the assets, and Rent Expense should be listed among the expense accounts.
c Prepare an income statement, a statement of retained earnings, and a balance sheet in report form. Follow the format illustrated on pages 149 and 150.

<table>
<tr><td>Problem 4-4
A puzzle—
analysis of ad-
justed data</td><td>Gulf Water Taxi was organized to transport tourists to a nearby resort island. The company adjusts and closes its accounts at the end of each month. Selected account balances appearing on the June 30 **adjusted** trial balance are as follows:</td></tr>
</table>

Prepaid rent	$ 2,700
Unexpired insurance	720
Boats...	28,800
Accumulated depreciation: boats	$2,100
Unearned passenger revenue	750

Other data

(1) Four months' rent had been prepaid on June 1.

(2) The unexpired insurance is a 36-month fire insurance policy purchased on January 1.

(3) The boats are being depreciated over an eight-year estimated useful life, with no residual value.

(4) The unearned passenger revenue represents tickets good for future rides sold to a resort hotel for $6 per ticket on June 1. During June, 175 of the tickets were used by guests of the hotel in exchange for water taxi rides.

Instructions

a Determine:

  (1) The monthly rent expense

  (2) The original cost of the 36-month fire insurance policy

  (3) The age in months of the boats

  (4) How many $6 tickets for future rides originally were sold to the resort hotel on June 1

b Prepare the adjusting entries which were made on June 30.

<table>
<tr><td>Problem 4-5
Format of a work
sheet</td><td>Rolling Hills Golf Course obtains revenue from greens fees and also from a contract with a concessionaire who sells refreshments on the premises. The books are closed at the end of each calendar year; at December 31 the data for adjustments were compiled and a work sheet was prepared. The first four columns of the work sheet contained the account balances and adjustments shown below:</td></tr>
</table>

	Trial Balance		Adjustments*	
	Dr	Cr	Dr	Cr
Cash	9,100			
Unexpired insurance	2,100			(a) 700
Prepaid advertising	1,000			(b) 300
Land	375,000			
Equipment	48,000			
Accumulated depreciation:				
equipment......................		8,000		(f) 4,000
Notes payable		110,000		
Unearned revenue from concessions ..		7,500	(d) 5,000	
Capital stock		200,000		
Retained earnings		68,000		
Dividends	15,000			
Revenue from greens fees...........		174,500		
Advertising expense	5,500		(b) 300	
Water expense....................	10,400			
Salaries expense..................	78,900		(e) 1,100	
Repairs and maintenance expense....	17,500			
Miscellaneous expense	5,500			
	568,000	568,000		
Insurance expense			(a) 700	
Interest expense			(c) 400	
Interest payable...................				(c) 400
Revenue from concessions				(d) 5,000
Salaries payable				(e) 1,100
Depreciation expense: equipment.....			(f) 4,000	
			11,500	11,500

* Adjustments:
(a) $700 insurance expired during year.
(b) $300 prepaid advertising expired at end of year.
(c) $400 accrued interest expense on notes payable.
(d) $5,000 concession revenue earned during year.
(e) $1,100 of salaries earned but unpaid at Dec. 31, 19__.
(f) $4,000 depreciation expense for year.

Instructions. Prepare a 10-column work sheet utilizing the trial balance and adjusting data provided. Include at the bottom of the work sheet a brief explanation keyed to each adjusting entry.

Problem 4-6
Preparing a work sheet

Oceanside Cinema closes its accounts each month. At July 31, the trial balance and other information given below were available for adjusting and closing the accounts.

OCEANSIDE CINEMA
Trial Balance
July 31, 19__

Cash	$ 17,000	
Prepaid film rental	31,200	
Land	80,000	
Building	168,000	
Accumulated depreciation: building		$ 10,500
Projection equipment	36,000	
Accumulated depreciation: projection equipment		3,000
Notes payable		190,000
Accounts payable		4,400
Unearned admissions revenue (YMCA)		1,000
Capital stock		60,000
Retained earnings, June 30, 19__		47,350
Dividends	7,500	
Admissions revenue		33,950
Salaries expense	8,700	
Light and power	1,800	
	$350,200	$350,200

Other data

(a) Film rental expense for July amounts to $21,050. However, the film rental expense for several months has been paid in advance.
(b) The building is being depreciated over a period of 20 years (240 months).
(c) The projection equipment is being depreciated over five years (60 months).
(d) At July 31, accrued interest payable on the note payable amounts to $1,650. No entry has yet been made to record interest expense for the month of July.
(e) Oceanside Cinema allows the local YMCA to bring children attending summer camp to the movies on any weekday afternoon for a fixed fee of $500 per month. On May 28, the YMCA made a $1,500 advance payment covering the months of June, July, and August.
(f) Oceanside Cinema receives a percentage of the revenue earned by Tastie Corp., the concessionaire operating the snack bar. For snack bar sales in July, Tastie Corp. owes Oceanside Cinema $2,250, payable on August 10. No entry has yet been made to record this revenue. (Credit Concessions Revenue.)
(g) Salaries earned by employees, but unpaid as of July 31, amount to $1,500. No entry has yet been made to record this liability and expense.

Instructions. Prepare a 10-column work sheet utilizing the trial balance and adjusting data provided. Include at the bottom of the work sheet a brief explanation keyed to each adjusting entry.

Problem 4-7
Preparing a work
sheet, financial
statements, and
adjusting and
closing entries

Island Hopper Airlines provides passenger and freight service among some Pacific islands. The accounts are adjusted and closed each month. At June 30 the trial balance shown below was prepared from the ledger.

ISLAND HOPPER AIRLINES
Trial Balance
June 30, 19__

Cash..	$ 38,000	
Accounts receivable.................................	7,200	
Prepaid rent..	9,600	
Unexpired insurance.................................	21,000	
Prepaid maintenance service	22,500	
Spare parts	57,000	
Airplanes	1,200,000	
Accumulated depreciation: airplanes.................		$ 320,000
Notes payable		400,000
Unearned passenger revenue..........................		60,000
Capital stock		450,000
Retained earnings...................................		120,250
Dividends...	12,000	
Passenger revenue earned		102,950
Fuel expense..	13,800	
Salaries expense	66,700	
Advertising expense.................................	5,400	
	$1,453,200	$1,453,200

Other data

(a) Monthly rent amounted to $3,200, reducing the Prepaid Rent account to $6,400.

(b) Insurance expense for June was $2,400. Reduce the Unexpired Insurance account.

(c) All necessary maintenance work was provided by Ryan Air Service at a fixed charge of $7,500 a month. Service for three months had been paid for in advance on June 1. (Debit Maintenance Expense.)

(d) Spare parts used in connection with maintenance work amounted to $3,750 during the month. (Debit Maintenance Expense. Use two lines on work sheet for this expense account.)

(e) Depreciation of the airplanes for the month of June was $10,000.

(f) The amount shown as unearned passenger revenue represents tickets sold to customers in advance of the scheduled flights. During June, $38,650 of this unearned revenue was earned by the airlines.

(g) Guests of Paradise Hotel are allowed to charge flights on Island Hopper to their hotel bills. The hotel pays Island Hopper for these flights on the fifteenth day of the following month. No entry has yet been made to record $4,600 in revenue earned in June from guests of the Paradise Hotel.

(h) Salaries earned by employees but not paid amounted to $3,300 at June 30.

(i) Interest accrued on notes payable at June 30 amounted to $7,000.

Instructions

  a Prepare a work sheet for the month ended June 30, 19__.

  b Prepare an income statement, a statement of retained earnings, and a balance sheet. Follow the format illustrated on pages 149 and 150.

  c Prepare adjusting and closing journal entries.

Problem 4-8
Use of reversing
entries

Financial Press maintains its accounts on the basis of a fiscal year ending June 30. The company works a five-day week and pays its employees up-to-date each Friday. Weekly salaries have been averaging $15,000. At the fiscal year-end, the following events occurred relating to salaries:

June 26 (Friday) Paid regular weekly salaries of $15,000.
June 30 (Tuesday) Prepared an adjusting entry for accrued salaries of $6,000.
July 1 (Wednesday) Prepared a reversing entry for accrued salaries.
July 3 (Friday) Paid regular weekly salaries of $15,000.

Instructions

  a Prepare journal entries (with explanations) for the four above events relating to salaries.

  b How much of the $15,000 in salaries paid on July 3 represents a July expense? Explain.

  c Assume that no reversing entry had been made by Financial Press; prepare the journal entry for payment of salaries on July 3.

Business decision cases

Case 4-1
Computer-based
accounting
systems

In Case 2-1, Bill Gates used data base software to design a simple accounting system for use on personal computers. Gates' first system prepared only a balance sheet; he is now ready to design an enhanced system which will perform all of the steps in the accounting cycle and will produce a complete set of financial statements. This enhanced system also will utilize data base software.

The idea underlying data base software is that data intended for a variety of different uses must be entered into the data base only once. The computer can then arrange these data into any number of desired formats. It can also combine data and perform mathematical computations using data in the data base.

In Gates' new accounting system, the computer will arrange the data into the following formats: (1) journal entries (with explanations) for all transactions, (2) three-column running balance ledger accounts, (3) a 10-column work sheet, (4) a complete set of financial statements, (5) journal entries for all adjusting and closing entries, (6) an after-closing trial balance, and (7) reversing entries. As each of these records and statements is prepared, any totals or subtotals in the record are included automatically in the data base. For example, when ledger accounts are updated, the new account balances become part of the data base.

Instructions. In Chapter 4, the steps of the accounting cycle were described as follows: (a) journalize transactions, (b) post to ledger accounts, (c) prepare a work sheet, (d) prepare financial statements, (e) adjust and close the accounts, (f) prepare an after-closing trial balance, and (g) prepare reversing entries. For each step in this cycle, briefly describe the types of data used in performing the step. Indicate whether this data is already contained in the data base, or whether the computer operator must enter data to enable the computer to perform the step.

Sam Reed is interested in buying Foxie's, an aerobic dance studio. He has come to you for help in interpreting the company's financial statements and to seek your advice about purchasing the business.

Foxie's has been in operation for one year. The business is a single proprietorship owned by Pam Austin. Foxie's rents the building in which it operates, as well as all of its exercise equipment. As virtually all of the company's business transactions involve cash receipts or cash payments, Austin has maintained the accounting records on a **cash basis.** She has prepared the following "income statement" and "balance sheet" from these cash basis records at year-end:

Income Statement

Revenue:

Membership sales	$150,000	
Membership dues	30,000	$180,000
Expenses:		
Rent	$ 18,000	
Wages	52,000	
Advertising	20,000	
Miscellaneous	15,000	105,000
Net income		$ 75,000

Balance Sheet
Assets

Cash	$ 25,000

Liabilities & Owner's Equity

Pam Austin, Capital	$ 25,000

Austin is offering to sell Foxie's for the balance of her capital account — $25,000. Reed is very enthusiastic and states, "How can I go wrong? I'll be paying $25,000 to buy $25,000 cash, and I'll be getting a very profitable business which generates large amounts of cash in the deal."

In a meeting with you and Reed, Austin makes the following statement: "This business has been very good to me. In the first year of operations, I've been able to withdraw $50,000 in cash. Yet the business is still quite solvent — it has lots of cash and no debts."

You ask Austin to explain the difference between membership sales and membership dues. She responds, "Foxie's is an exclusive club. We cater only to members. This year, we sold 500 five-year memberships. Each membership requires the customer to pay $300 cash in advance and to pay dues of $10 per month for five years. I credited the advance payments to the Membership Sales account and credited the $10 monthly payments to Membership Dues. Thus, all the revenue is hard cash — no 'paper profits' like you see in so many businesses."

You then inquire as to when these five-year memberships were sold. Austin responds, "On the average, these memberships are only six months old. No members have dropped out, so Foxie's should continue receiving dues from these people for another four and one-half years, thus assuring future profitability. Another beneficial factor is that the company hasn't sold any new memberships in the last several months. Therefore, I think that the company could discontinue its advertising and further increase future profitability."

Instructions

a The financial statements of Foxie's were prepared on the cash basis of accounting, not the accrual basis. Prepare a revised income statement and balance sheet applying the concepts of accrual accounting. Remember that only $\frac{1}{10}$ (or $\frac{6}{60}$) of the customers' advance payments for memberships has been **_earned_** as of year-end.

b Assume that none of the 500 members drop out of Foxie's during the next year, and that the business sells no new memberships. What would be the amount of the company's expected cash receipts? Assuming that advertising expense is discontinued but that other expenses remain the same, what would be the expected amount of cash payments for the coming year?

c Use the information in your analysis in parts a and b to draft a letter to Reed advising him on the wisdom of purchasing Foxie's for $25,000. Specifically address the issues of whether the business (1) is profitable, (2) has no debts, and (3) is likely to generate sufficient cash to enable the owner to make large cash withdrawals during the coming year.

Part One: Comprehensive Problem
Friend With A Truck, Inc.

A short practice set, based upon a service business.

On September 1, Anthony and Christine Ferrara formed a corporation called Friend With A Truck, Inc., for the purpose of operating an equipment rental yard. The new corporation was able to begin operations immediately by purchasing the assets and taking over the location of Rent-It, an equipment rental company that was going out of business.

Friend With A Truck, Inc., uses the following chart of accounts:

Cash...............................	1	Capital Stock.........................	30
Accounts Receivable.................	4	Retained Earnings	35
Prepaid Rent........................	6	Dividends...........................	38
Office Supplies	8	Income Summary	40
Rental Equipment....................	10	Rental Fees Earned	50
Accumulated Depreciation:		Salaries Expense	60
Rental Equipment...................	12	Maintenance Expense	61
Notes Payable.......................	20	Utilities Expense......................	62
Accounts Payable....................	22	Rent Expense	63
Interest Payable	25	Office Supplies Expense	64
Salaries Payable.....................	26	Depreciation Expense	65
Dividends Payable	28	Interest Expense	66
Unearned Rental Fees................	29		

The corporation closes its accounts and prepares financial statements at the end of each month. During September, the corporation entered into the following transactions:

Sept. 1   Issued to Anthony and Christine Ferrara 20,000 shares of $5 par value capital stock in exchange for $100,000 cash.

Sept. 1   Paid $9,000 to Shapiro Realty as three months' advance rent on the rental yard and office formerly occupied by Rent-It.

Sept. 1   Purchased for $180,000 all of the equipment formerly owned by Rent-It. Paid $70,000 cash and issued a one-year note payable for $110,000, plus interest at the annual rate of 9%.

176

Sept. 4	Purchased office supplies on account from Modern Office Co., $1,630. Payment due in 30 days. (These supplies are expected to last for several months; debit the Office Supplies asset account.)
Sept. 8	Received $10,000 cash as advance payment on equipment rental from McBryan Construction Co. (Credit Unearned Rental Fees.)
Sept. 12	Paid salaries for the first two weeks in September, $3,600.
Sept. 15	Excluding the McBryan advance, equipment rental fees earned during the first 15 days of September amounted to $6,100, of which $5,300 was received in cash and $800 was an account receivable.
Sept. 17	Purchased on account from Earth Movers, Inc., $340 in parts needed to repair a rental tractor. (Debit an expense account.) Payment is due in 10 days.
Sept. 23	Collected $210 of the accounts receivable recorded on September 15.
Sept. 25	Rented a backhoe to Mission Landscaping at a price of $100 per day, to be paid when the backhoe is returned. Mission Landscaping expects to keep the backhoe for about two or three weeks.
Sept. 26	Paid biweekly salaries, $3,600.
Sept. 27	Paid the account payable to Earth Movers, Inc., $340.
Sept. 28	Declared a dividend of 10 cents per share, payable on October 15.
Sept. 30	Received a bill from Universal Utilities for the month of September, $270. Payment is due in 30 days.
Sept. 30	Cash received from equipment rental during the second half of September, $6,450.

Data for adjusting entries

(a) The advance payment of rent on September 1 covered a period of three months.

(b) Interest accrued on the note payable to Rent-It amounted to $825 at September 30.

(c) The rental equipment is being depreciated over a period of 10 years.

(d) Office supplies on hand at September 30 are estimated at $1,100.

(e) During September, the company earned $4,840 of the rental fees paid in advance by McBryan Construction Co. on September 8.

(f) As of September 30, Friend With A Truck has earned five days' rent on the backhoe rented to Mission Landscaping on September 25.

(g) Salaries earned by employees since the last payroll date (September 26) amounted to $900 at month-end.

Instructions

a Journalize the above transactions.

b Post to ledger accounts. (Use running balance form of ledger accounts. Enter numbers of journal pages and ledger accounts to complete the cross-referencing between the journal and ledger.)

c Prepare a 10-column work sheet for the month ended September 30, 19__.

d Prepare an income statement and a statement of retained earnings for the month of September, and a balance sheet (in report form) as of September 30.

e Prepare adjusting and closing entries and post to ledger accounts.

f Prepare an after-closing trial balance as of September 30.

g Prepare appropriate reversing entries (dated October 1) and post to ledger accounts.

Part Two	**Merchandising concerns, internal control, and accounting systems**
Chapter 5	Accounting for purchases and sales of merchandise
Chapter 6	Internal control and accounting systems

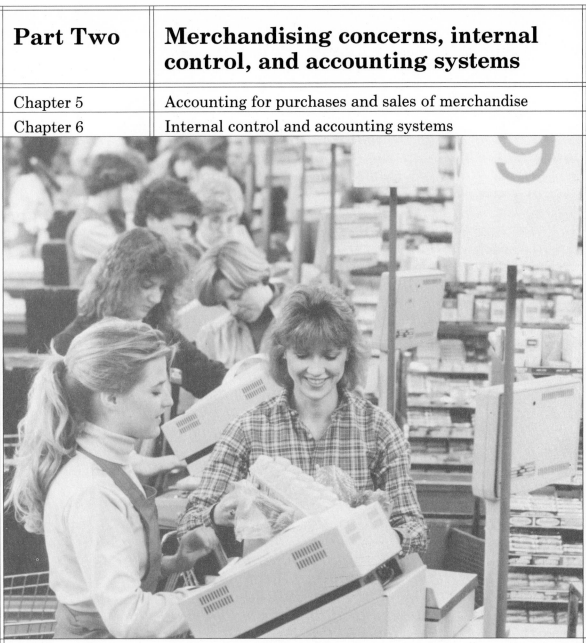

This part consists of two chapters. In the first, we explain the accounting concepts relating to merchandising activities. In the second chapter, we explore means of achieving internal control and of modifying an accounting system to handle efficiently a large volume of transactions.

Chapter 5
Accounting for purchases
and sales of merchandise

CHAPTER PREVIEW

In this chapter our discussion of the accounting cycle is expanded to include merchandising concerns — those businesses that sell goods rather than services. We illustrate and explain various types of merchandising transactions, the computation of net sales and the cost of goods sold, and a work sheet and closing entries for a merchandising company. Both the perpetual and periodic inventory systems are described. In addition, this chapter introduces classified financial statements and two important measures of debt-paying ability — working capital and the current ratio.

After studying
this chapter
you should be
able to meet
these Learning
Objectives:

1 **Account for sales, sales returns, and sales discounts.**
2 **Determine the cost of goods sold using the periodic inventory system.**
3 **Account for purchases of merchandise.**
4 **Prepare a work sheet for a merchandising company.**
5 **Prepare closing entries for a merchandising company.**
6 **Distinguish between the periodic and the perpetual inventory systems.**
7 **Prepare a classified balance sheet and either a single-step or a multiple-step income statement.**
8 **Explain the purpose of the current ratio and the meaning of working capital.**

MERCHANDISING COMPANIES

The preceding four chapters have illustrated step by step the complete accounting cycle for businesses rendering personal services. Service-type companies represent an important part of our economy. They include, for example, airlines, railroads, hotels, insurance companies, ski resorts, hospitals, and professional sports teams. These enterprises earn revenue by rendering services to their customers. The net income of a service-type business is equal to the excess of revenue over the operating expenses incurred.

In contrast to service-type businesses, merchandising companies — both wholesalers and retailers — earn revenue by selling goods or merchandise. The term *merchandise* refers to goods held for resale to customers. The accounting principles and methods we have studied for service-type businesses also apply to merchandising companies. However, some additional accounts and techniques are needed to account for purchases and sales of merchandise.

Selling merchandise introduces a new and major cost of doing business — the cost to the company of the merchandise being resold to customers. This cost is termed the *cost of goods sold* and is so important that it is shown separately from operating expenses in the income statement of a merchandising concern. Thus, the income statement of a merchandising company has *three main sections:* (1) the revenue section, (2) the cost of goods sold section, and (3) the operating expenses section.

A highly condensed income statement for a merchandising business is shown below. In comparison with the income statement of a service-type business, the new features of this statement are the inclusion of the cost of goods sold and a subtotal called *gross profit.*

OFFICE PRODUCTS
Income Statement
For the Year Ended December 31, 19___

Revenue from sales	$1,000,000
Less: Cost of goods sold..	550,000
Gross profit on sales	$ 450,000
Less: Operating expenses...	400,000
Net income..	$ 50,000

Revenue from sales represents the selling price of merchandise sold during the period. The cost of goods sold, on the other hand, represents the cost to the merchandising concern of buying these goods. The difference between revenue from sales and the cost of goods sold is called *gross profit.* (Gross profit also may be called *gross margin.*)

If a merchandising business is to operate profitably, its gross profit must exceed its operating expenses. Thus, the net income of a merchandising company is the excess of revenue over the *sum* of (1) the cost of goods sold and (2) the operating expenses of the business.

Revenue from sales

1 Account for sales, sales returns, and sales discounts. Revenue earned by selling merchandise is credited to a revenue account entitled *Sales.* The figure shown in our illustrated income statement, however, is the *net sales* for the accounting period. The term net sales means total sales revenue *minus* sales returns and allowances, and sales discounts. To illustrate this concept, let us now illustrate the revenue section of Office Products' income statement in greater detail:

OFFICE PRODUCTS
Partial Income Statement
For the Year Ended December 31, 19__

Revenue from sales:

Sales...		$1,012,000
Less: Sales returns and allowances	$8,000	
Sales discounts	4,000	12,000
Net sales..		$1,000,000

The $1,012,000 figure labeled "sales" in the partial income statement is sometimes called **gross sales.** This amount represents the total of both cash and credit sales made during the year. When a business sells merchandise to its customers, it either receives immediate payment in cash or acquires an account receivable to be collected at a later date. Cash sales are rung up on cash registers as the transactions occur. At the end of the day, the total shown on all the company's cash registers represents total cash sales for the day and is recorded by a journal entry, as follows:

Journal entry for cash sales

Cash	900
Sales..	900
To record the sale of merchandise for cash.	

For a sale of merchandise on credit, a typical journal entry would be

Journal entry for sale on credit

Accounts Receivable..	500
Sales..	500
Sold merchandise on credit to Kay's Gift Shop; payment due within 30 days.	

Sales revenue is earned in the period in which the merchandise is **delivered to the customer,** even though payment may not be received for a month or more after the sale. Consequently, the revenue earned in a given accounting period may differ considerably from the cash receipts of that period.

Sales returns and allowances

Most merchandising companies allow customers to obtain a refund by returning merchandise which is found to be unsatisfactory. When customers find that merchandise purchased has minor defects, they may agree to keep such merchandise if an allowance is made on the sales price. Refunds and allowances have the effect of nullifying previously recorded sales and reducing the amount of revenue earned by the business. The journal entry to record sales returns and allowances is shown on the next page.

Journal entry for sales returns and allowances

Sales Returns and Allowances... 100	
Cash (or Accounts Receivable)...	100
Made refund for merchandise returned by customer.	

Sales Returns and Allowances is a **_contra-revenue_** account — that is, it appears in the income statement as a deduction from gross sales revenue.

Why use a separate Sales Returns and Allowances account rather than recording refunds by directly debiting the Sales account? The answer is that using a separate contra-revenue account enables management to see both the total amount of sales and the amount of sales returns. The relationship between these two amounts gives management an indication of customer satisfaction with the merchandise.

Sales discounts

When merchandise is sold on account, the payment terms may vary greatly from one seller to another. Some retail businesses, for example, allow customers to buy merchandise on "installment plans," payable over a period of perhaps 12 or 18 months. Manufacturers and wholesalers, on the other hand, usually require full payment within 30 or 60 days. Often these companies also offer the buyer a discount for paying earlier.

Perhaps the most common credit terms offered by manufacturers and wholesalers are "2/10, net/30." This expression is read "2, 10, net 30," and means that full payment is due in 30 days, but that the buyer may take a 2% discount if payment is made within 10 days. The 10-day period during which the discount is available is called the **_discount period._** Because a sales discount provides an incentive to the customer to make an early cash payment, it is often referred to as a **_cash discount._**

For example, assume that on November 3 Office Products sells merchandise for $1,000 on credit to Zipco, Inc., terms 2/10, n/30. At the time of the sale, the seller does not know if the buyer will take advantage of the discount by paying within the discount period; therefore, Office Products records the sale at the full price by the following entry:

Nov. 3	Accounts Receivable 1,000	
	Sales	1,000
	To record sale to Zipco, Inc., terms 2/10, n/30.	

The customer now has a choice between saving $20 by paying within the discount period, or waiting a full 30 days and paying the full price. If Zipco mails its check on or before November 13, it is entitled to deduct 2% of $1,000 or $20, and settle the obligation for $980. If Zipco decides to forgo the discount, it may postpone payment an additional 20 days until December 3 but must then pay $1,000.

Assuming that payment is made by Zipco on November 13, the last day of the discount period, the entry by Office Products to record collection of the receivable is

Nov. 13	Cash	980	
	Sales Discount	20	
	Accounts Receivable		1,000

Collected from Zipco, Inc., for our sale of Nov. 3, less 2% cash discount.

If a customer returns a portion of the merchandise before making payment, the discount applies only to the portion of the goods kept by the customer. In the above example, if Zipco had returned $300 worth of goods out of the $1,000 purchase, the discount would have been applicable only to the $700 portion of the order which the customer kept.

Sales Discounts is a contra-revenue account. In the income statement, sales discounts are deducted from gross sales revenue along with any sales returns and allowances. This treatment was illustrated in the partial income statement on page 183.

Cost of goods sold

Merchandising companies continuously buy and sell merchandise. The cost of merchandise sold during the year appears in the income statement as a deduction from the net sales revenue. The cost of merchandise still on hand at year-end appears in the balance sheet as an asset called ***inventory.***

The cost of the inventory at year-end can be determined relatively easily. These goods are actually on hand, so they may be counted and their unit costs may be determined from the accounting records. Determining the cost of goods ***sold*** is a more challenging task, because the goods are no longer on hand. Two approaches may be used to measure the cost of goods sold: (1) the ***periodic inventory system*** or (2) the ***perpetual inventory system.*** We shall begin our discussion with the periodic inventory system. The perpetual inventory system will be discussed later in the chapter.

The periodic inventory system

2 Determine the cost of goods sold using the periodic inventory system. The foundation of the periodic inventory system is a ***physical count*** of the goods on hand at the end of the period. This procedure, called taking a physical inventory, is both inconvenient and costly. Therefore, a physical inventory usually is taken only at year-end. Thus, the periodic inventory system is well suited to the preparation of annual financial statements, but not to preparing statements for shorter accounting periods, such as months or quarters.[1]

To determine the cost of goods sold by the periodic inventory system, the accounting records must show: (1) the costs of the inventories at the beginning and at the end of the year, and (2) the cost of merchandise purchased throughout the year.

---

[1] In Chapter 8 we discuss several estimating techniques that may be used in preparing monthly or quarterly financial statements.

Using this information, the cost of goods sold during the year may be computed as follows:

Inventory, beginning of the year.	$180,000
Purchases	570,000
Cost of goods available for sale.	$750,000
Less: Inventory, end of the year.	200,000
Cost of goods sold.	$550,000

In this example, the business had $180,000 of merchandise on hand at the beginning of the year. During the year, it purchased an additional $570,000 of merchandise. Thus, the total cost of goods offered for sale to customers during the year was $750,000. At year-end, only $200,000 of these goods remained on hand. Consequently, the cost of goods sold during the year must have been $550,000.

In summary, the periodic inventory system works as follows:

1   Physical inventories are taken at the end of each year to determine the ***ending inventory.*** These physical counts also determine the ***beginning inventory,*** as the ending inventory from the prior year is the beginning inventory of the current year.
2   ***Purchases*** of merchandise during the year are recorded in the accounting records.
3   The beginning inventory is added to net purchases in order to determine the ***cost of goods available for sale*** during the period.
4   The cost of the ***ending inventory*** is ***subtracted*** from the ***cost of goods available for sale.*** The resulting figure represents the ***cost of goods sold*** during the period.

Computation of the cost of goods sold is an important concept that requires careful attention. To gain a thorough understanding of this concept, we need to consider the nature of the accounts and accounting procedures used in determining the cost of goods sold.

Beginning inventory and ending inventory

The goods on hand at the beginning of an accounting period are called ***beginning inventory;*** the goods on hand at the end of the period are called ***ending inventory.*** Since a new accounting period begins as soon as the old one ends, the ending inventory of one accounting period becomes the beginning inventory of the next period.

A business using the periodic inventory system takes a physical inventory at the end of each period to determine the goods on hand. Taking inventory involves three basic steps:

1   All merchandise on hand is counted.
2   The quantity counted for each item is multiplied by the cost per unit shown in the accounting records.

3 The costs of the various kinds of merchandise are added together to determine the total cost of inventory on hand.

The resulting ending inventory appears as an asset in the balance sheet and also is used in computing the cost of goods sold for the period.

At the end of each accounting period, entries are made in the Inventory account to remove the cost of the beginning inventory and to enter the cost of the ending inventory, as determined by the physical count. (These entries are made during the closing process, and will be discussed later.) Notice that throughout the year, the Inventory account shows only the amount of the *beginning inventory.* The balance of this account *does not change* until the new ending inventory is recorded at year-end. Thus, *no entries are made in the Inventory account to record the costs of merchandise bought and sold during the period.*

Purchases of merchandise

3 Account for purchases of merchandise.

Under the periodic inventory system, the cost of merchandise purchased for resale is recorded by debiting an account called Purchases, as shown below:

Nov. 3	Purchases	10,000	
	Accounts Payable		10,000
	Purchased merchandise from ABC Supply Co. Credit terms 2/10, n/30.		

The Purchases account *is used only for merchandise acquired for resale;* assets acquired for use in the business (such as a delivery truck, a typewriter, or office supplies) are recorded by debiting the appropriate asset account, not the Purchases account. The Purchases account does not indicate whether the purchased goods have been sold or are still on hand.

At the end of the period, the balance in the Purchases account represents the cost of all goods purchased during the period. This amount is added to the beginning inventory to determine the *cost of goods available for sale*—an important step in computing the cost of goods sold.

Other accounts included in the cost of goods sold. In our illustration on page 186, we used only three items in computing the cost of goods sold: beginning inventory, purchases, and ending inventory. In most cases, however, some additional accounts are involved in this computation. These include accounts for Purchase Returns and Allowances, Purchase Discounts, and Transportation-in.

Purchase returns and allowances. When merchandise purchased from suppliers is found to be unsatisfactory, the goods may be returned, or a request may be made for an allowance on the price. A return of goods to the supplier is recorded as follows:

Journal entry for
return of goods to
supplier

| Accounts Payable | 1,200 | |
| Purchase Returns and Allowances. | | 1,200 |

To reduce liability to Jet Supply Co. by the cost of goods returned for credit.

It is preferable to credit Purchase Returns and Allowances when merchandise is returned to a supplier rather than crediting the Purchases account directly. The accounts then show both the total amount of purchases and the amount of purchases which required adjustment or return. Management is interested in the percentage relationship between goods purchased and goods returned, because the returning of merchandise for credit is an expensive, time-consuming process. Excessive returns suggest inefficiency in the operation of the purchasing department and a need to find more dependable suppliers.

Purchase discounts. As explained earlier, manufacturers and wholesalers frequently grant a cash discount to customers who will pay promptly for goods purchased on credit. The selling company regards a cash discount as a *sales discount;* the buying company calls the discount a *purchase discount.*

If the $10,000 purchase of November 3 shown on page 187 is paid for on or before November 13, the last day of the discount period, the purchasing company will save 2% of the price of the merchandise, or $200, as shown by the following entry:

Nov. 13	Accounts Payable	10,000	
	Purchase Discounts		200
	Cash.		9,800

Paid ABC Supply Co. for purchase of Nov. 3, less 2% cash discount.

The effect of the discount was to reduce the cost of the merchandise to the buying company. The credit balance of the Purchase Discounts account should therefore be deducted in the income statement from the debit balance of the Purchases account.

Do companies usually take advantage of available cash discounts? The answer is *yes.* The terms 2/10, n/30 offer the buyer a 2% discount for sending payment 20 days before it is otherwise due. Saving 2% by paying 20 days early is equivalent to earning an annual return of over 36% ($2\% \times \frac{365}{20} = 36.5\%$). Thus, taking cash discounts represents an excellent investment opportunity. Most companies take these discounts even if they must borrow from a bank in order to have the necessary cash available.

Transportation-in. The cost of merchandise acquired for resale logically includes any transportation charges necessary to bring the goods to the purchaser's place of business. A separate ledger account is used to accumulate transportation charges on merchandise purchased. The journal entry to record transportation charges on inbound shipments of merchandise is as follows:

Journalizing
transportation
charges on
purchases of
merchandise

| Transportation-in | 125 | |
| Cash (or Accounts Payable) | | 125 |

Air freight charges on merchandise purchased from Miller Brothers, Kansas City.

Since transportation charges are part of the **delivered cost** of merchandise purchased, the Transportation-in account is combined with the Purchases account in the income statement to determine the cost of goods available for sale.

Transportation charges on inbound shipments of merchandise must not be confused with transportation charges on **outbound** shipments of goods to customers. Freight charges and other expenses incurred in making deliveries to customers are regarded as selling expenses; these outlays are debited to a separate account entitled Delivery Expense and are **not included** in the cost of goods sold.

Shoplifting and inventory "shrinkage" losses

Under the periodic inventory system, it is assumed that all goods available for sale during the year are either sold or are on hand at year-end for the ending inventory. As a result of this assumption, the cost of merchandise lost because of shoplifting, employee theft, breakage, and spoilage will be included automatically in cost of goods sold. For example, assume that a store has goods available for sale which cost $600,000. Assume that shoplifters steal $10,000 worth of goods and that the ending inventory is $100,000. (If the thefts had not occurred, the ending inventory would have been $10,000 larger.) The cost of goods sold is computed at $500,000 by subtracting the $100,000 ending inventory from the $600,000 cost of goods available for sale. In reality, the cost of goods **sold** was $490,000, and the cost of goods **stolen** was $10,000.

Income statement for a merchandising company

To pull together the various concepts discussed thus far in the chapter, we need to look at a detailed income statement for a merchandising business. The income statement of Olympic Sporting Goods is shown on the next page.

Notice that the income statement is divided into three major sections: revenue, the cost of goods sold, and operating expenses. We have already discussed the various accounts appearing in the first two sections. The operating expenses in the third section of the income statement are classified either as selling expenses or general and administrative expenses. **Selling expenses** include all expenses of storing and marketing merchandise, including advertising, sales salaries, and delivery expense. **General and administrative expenses** include those expenses relating to other business operations, such as expenses of the corporate headquarters, and of the accounting, finance, and personnel departments.

In many companies certain expenses, such as depreciation of the building, need to be divided, part to selling expense and part to general and administrative expenses. Olympic Sporting Goods divided its $8,000 of depreciation expense by allocating $6,000 to selling expenses and $2,000 to general and administrative expenses. This allocation can conveniently be made when the income statement is prepared from the work sheet; thus no additional ledger accounts are required. The account for utilities expense, $2,100, was not divided because management did not consider the amount large enough to warrant such treatment.

OLYMPIC SPORTING GOODS
Income Statement
For the Year Ending December 31, 19__

Revenue:			
Sales			$617,000
Less: Sales returns and allowances................................		$ 12,000	
Sales discounts...		5,000	17,000
Net sales			$600,000
Cost of goods sold:			
Inventory, Jan. 1		$ 60,000	
Purchases..	$367,000		
Less: Purchase returns and			
allowances	$6,700		
Purchase discounts	3,300	10,000	
Net purchases	$357,000		
Add: Transportation-in	13,000		
Delivered cost of purchases		370,000	
Cost of goods available for sale		$430,000	
Less: Inventory, Dec. 31......................................		70,000	
Cost of goods sold			360,000
Gross profit on sales			$240,000
Operating expenses:			
Selling expenses:			
Sales salaries......................................		$ 74,000	
Advertising		29,000	
Delivery service		10,900	
Depreciation		6,000	
Total selling expenses		$119,900	
General & administrative expenses:			
Office salaries.....................................		$ 57,000	
Utilities...		2,100	
Depreciation		2,000	
Total general & administrative expenses.......................		61,100	
Total operating expenses			181,000
Income from operations..			$ 59,000
Income taxes expense			9,000
Net income			$ 50,000

This income statement consists of three major sections

Income taxes often are shown separately from other expenses

Note that the final deduction on the income statement is for income taxes expense. A corporation is a legal entity subject to corporation income tax; consequently, the ledger of a corporation must contain accounts for recording income taxes. No such accounts are needed for a business organized as a single proprietorship or partnership. Income taxes are based on a corporation's earnings and are recorded by an adjusting entry such as the following:

Income Taxes Expense...	9,000	
Income Taxes Payable..		9,000

To record income taxes payable.

The account debited in this entry, Income Taxes Expense, is shown as the last deduction on the income statement to arrive at the "bottom line" figure for net income. The account for Income Taxes Payable is a current liability.

Analyzing the income statement

Perhaps the most important figure in an income statement is net income. The amount and the trend of net income are important to managers, investors, and others interested in the progress of a company. However, for merchandising companies, the trends in net sales and in gross profit are also of special importance.

A rising volume of sales is evidence of growth and suggests the probability of an increase in earnings. A declining trend in sales, on the other hand, is often the first signal of reduced earnings and of financial difficulties ahead. The amount of sales for each year is compared with the sales of the preceding year. The sales of each month may be compared with the sales of the preceding month and also with the corresponding month of the preceding year. These comparisons bring to light significant trends in the volume of sales.

Gross profit rate: a key statistic. A useful step in evaluating the performance of a merchandising company is to express the gross profit as a *percentage* of net sales. For Olympic Sporting Goods, the gross profit amounts to 40% of net sales (gross profit, $240,000, divided by net sales, $600,000, equals 40%). This percentage is called the *gross profit rate.*

By computing the gross profit rate of a business for several years in a row, the user of financial statements gains insight into whether business is improving or declining. A rising gross profit rate is a sign of financial strength, indicating strong demand for the company's products. A falling gross profit rate, on the other hand, may indicate that the business is having to cut prices in order to sell its products, or that it is unable to pass cost increases on to its customers.

Of course, the gross profit rate will vary among different companies and different industries. Users of financial statements may compare the gross profit rate of one business to that of other companies in the same industry, or to the gross profit rate of the same company in prior years. In most merchandising companies, the rate of gross profit usually varies between 30% and 50% of net sales.

Accountants, investors, bankers, and business managers have the habit of mentally computing percentage relationships when they look at financial statements. Formation of this habit will be helpful throughout the study of accounting, as well as in many business situations. In analyzing an income statement, the amount of net sales is regarded as 100%, and every other item or subtotal in the statement is expressed as a percentage of net sales.

Work sheet for a merchandising business

4 Prepare a work sheet for a merchandising company.

A merchandising company, like the service business discussed in Chapter 4, uses a work sheet at the end of the period to organize the information needed to prepare financial statements and to adjust and close the accounts. The new elements in the work sheet for Olympic Sporting Goods on the following page are the beginning inventory, the ending inventory, and the other merchandising accounts. The inventory accounts are shown in black to help focus your attention on their treatment.

Trial Balance columns. The Trial Balance columns were prepared by listing the ledger account balances at December 31. Notice that the Inventory account in the Trial Balance debit column shows a balance of $60,000, the cost of merchandise on hand at the end of the prior year. No entries were made in the Inventory account during the current year despite the various purchases and sales of merchandise. The significance of the Inventory account in the trial balance is that it shows the amount of merchandise Olympic Sporting Goods owned on January 1 of the current year.

Adjustment columns and Adjusted Trial Balance columns. The merchandising accounts usually do not require adjustment. Their balances are carried directly from the Trial Balance columns to the Adjusted Trial Balance columns.

In our illustration, only two adjustments were necessary at December 31: one to record depreciation of the building and the other to record the income taxes expense for the year. (The amount of income taxes is given as $9,000. We are not concerned at this point with the procedures for computing income taxes expense.) After these two adjustments were recorded, the Adjustments columns were then totaled to prove the equality of the adjustment debits and credits.

Income Statement columns. The accounts which will appear in a company's income statement are the ones to be carried from the Adjusted Trial Balance columns to the Income Statement columns of the work sheet. These are the revenue accounts, cost of goods sold accounts, and expense accounts.

Recording the ending inventory on the work sheet. The key point to be observed in this work sheet is the method of recording the ***ending inventory***. On December 31, the manager and staff of Olympic Sporting Goods took a physical inventory of all merchandise on hand. The entire inventory, priced at cost, amounted to $70,000. This ending inventory, dated December 31, does not appear in the trial balance; it is therefore written on the first available line below the trial balance totals. The amount of $70,000 is listed in the Income Statement credit column and also in the Balance Sheet debit column.

By entering the ending inventory in the Income Statement ***credit*** column, we are in effect ***deducting*** it from the total of the beginning inventory, the purchases, and the transportation-in, all of which are extended from the trial balance to the Income Statement ***debit*** column.

OLYMPIC SPORTING GOODS
Work Sheet
For the Year Ended December 31, 19 __

	Trial Balance DR	Trial Balance CR	Adjustments* DR	Adjustments* CR	Adjusted Trial Balance DR	Adjusted Trial Balance CR	Income Statement DR	Income Statement CR	Balance Sheet DR	Balance Sheet CR
Cash	14,500				14,500				14,500	
Accounts receivable	43,500				43,500				43,500	
Inventory, Jan. 1	60,000				60,000		60,000			
Land	52,000				52,000				52,000	
Building	160,000				160,000				160,000	
Accumulated depreciation: building		56,000		(a) 8,000		64,000				64,000
Accounts payable		55,000				55,000				55,000
Capital stock		50,000				50,000				50,000
Retained earnings, Jan. 1		138,000				138,000				138,000
Dividends	26,000				26,000				26,000	
Sales		617,000				617,000		617,000		
Sales returns and allowances	12,000				12,000		12,000			
Sales discounts	5,000				5,000		5,000			
Purchases	367,000				367,000		367,000			
Purchase returns and allowances		6,700				6,700		6,700		
Purchase discounts		3,300				3,300		3,300		
Transportation-in	13,000				13,000		13,000			
Sales salaries	74,000				74,000		74,000			
Advertising expense	29,000				29,000		29,000			
Delivery service expense	10,900				10,900		10,900			
Office salaries	57,000				57,000		57,000			
Utilities expense	2,100				2,100		2,100			
	926,000	926,000								
Depreciation expense: building			(a) 8,000		8,000		8,000			
Income taxes expense			(b) 9,000		9,000		9,000			
Income taxes payable				(b) 9,000		9,000				9,000
			17,000	17,000	943,000	943,000				
Inventory, Dec. 31								70,000	70,000	
							647,000	697,000	366,000	316,000
Net income							50,000			50,000
Totals							697,000	697,000	366,000	366,000

Note the treatment of the beginning inventory . . .

. . . and of the ending inventory

* Adjustment: (a) Depreciation of building during the year.
(b) To accrue income taxes.

193

One of the functions of the Income Statement columns is to bring together all the accounts involved in determining the cost of goods sold. The accounts with debit balances are the beginning Inventory, Purchases, and Transportation-in; these accounts total $440,000. Against this total the three credit items of Purchase Returns and Allowances, $6,700, Purchase Discounts, $3,300, and ending Inventory, $70,000, are offset. The three accounts with debit balances exceed in total the three credit balances by an amount of $360,000; this amount is the cost of goods sold, as shown in the income statement on page 190.

The ending inventory is also entered in the Balance Sheet debit column of the work sheet, because this inventory of merchandise on December 31 will appear as an asset in the year-end balance sheet.

Completing the work sheet. When all the accounts on the work sheet have been extended into the Income Statement or Balance Sheet columns, the final four columns are totaled. The net income is computed, and the work sheet completed in the same manner as illustrated in Chapter 4 for a service business.

Financial statements

The work to be done at the end of the period is much the same for a merchandising business as for a service-type firm. First, the work sheet is completed; then, financial statements are prepared from the data in the work sheet; next, the adjusting and closing entries are entered in the journal and posted to the ledger accounts; and finally, an after-closing trial balance is prepared. This completes the accounting cycle.

Income statement. The income statement on page 190 was prepared from the Olympic Sporting Goods work sheet. Note particularly the arrangement of items in the cost of goods sold section of the income statement; this portion of the income statement shows in summary form most of the essential accounting concepts covered in this chapter.

Statement of retained earnings. The statement of retained earnings shows the increase in retained earnings resulting from the year's net income and the decrease resulting from dividends declared during the year. Note that the final amount in the statement of retained earnings also appears in the stockholders' equity section of the balance sheet as the new amount of retained earnings.

OLYMPIC SPORTING GOODS
Statement of Retained Earnings
For the Year Ended December 31, 19__

Retained earnings, Jan. 1, 19__	$138,000
Net income	50,000
Subtotal	$188,000
Less: Dividends	26,000
Retained earnings, Dec. 31, 19__	$162,000

Balance sheet. In studying the following balance sheet, note that all items are taken from the Balance Sheet columns of the work sheet, except for the amount of retained earnings. Retained earnings is shown at $162,000, the ending balance computed in the preceding statement of retained earnings.

OLYMPIC SPORTING GOODS
Balance Sheet
December 31, 19__

Assets

Cash.		$ 14,500
Accounts receivable		43,500
Inventory		70,000
Land.		52,000
Building	$160,000	
Less: Accumulated depreciation.	64,000	96,000
Total assets		$276,000

Liabilities & Stockholders' Equity

Liabilities:		
Accounts payable.		$ 55,000
Income taxes payable		9,000
Total liabilities.		$ 64,000
Stockholders' equity:		
Capital stock	$ 50,000	
Retained earnings.	162,000	212,000
Total liabilities & stockholders' equity.		$276,000

Closing entries

5 Prepare closing entries for a merchandising company.

The entries used in closing revenue and expense accounts have been explained in preceding chapters. The important new elements in this illustration of closing entries for a trading business are the entries showing the *elimination* of the beginning inventory and the *recording* of the ending inventory. The beginning inventory is cleared out of the inventory account by a debit to Income Summary and a credit to Inventory. A separate entry could be made for this purpose, but we can save time by making one compound entry which will debit the Income Summary account with the amount of the beginning inventory and with the amounts of all temporary owners' equity accounts having debit balances.

The *temporary owners' equity accounts* are those which appear in the income statement. As the name suggests, the temporary owners' equity accounts are used during the period to accumulate temporarily the increases and decreases in the owners' equity resulting from operation of the business. The entry to close out the beginning inventory and temporary owners' equity accounts with debit balances is illustrated below. (For emphasis, the accounts unique to a merchandising business are shown in black.)

<table>
<tr><td>Closing tempo-
rary owners'
equity accounts
with debit
balances</td><td>Dec. 31</td><td>Income Summary ....</td><td>647,000</td><td></td></tr>
</table>

Closing tempo-rary owners' equity accounts with debit balances

Dec. 31 Income Summary 647,000

      Inventory (Jan. 1)................................... 60,000

      Sales Returns and Allowances........................ 12,000

      Sales Discounts 5,000

      Purchases.. 367,000

      Transportation-in 13,000

      Sales Salaries 74,000

      Advertising Expense................................. 29,000

      Delivery Service.................................... 10,900

      Office Salaries 57,000

      Utilities Expense 2,100

      Depreciation Expense............................... 8,000

      Income Taxes Expense.............................. 9,000

To close out the beginning inventory and the temporary owners' equity accounts with debit balances.

The preceding closing entry closes the operating expense accounts and Income Taxes Expense, as well as the accounts used to accumulate the cost of goods sold. It also closes the accounts for Sales Returns and Allowances and for Sales Discounts. After this first closing entry is posted, the Inventory account has a zero balance. Therefore, it is time to record in this account the new inventory of $70,000 determined by the physical count at December 31.

To bring the ending inventory into the accounting records after the physical inventory on December 31, we could make a separate entry debiting Inventory and crediting the Income Summary account. It is more convenient, however, to combine this step with the closing of the Sales account and any other temporary owners' equity accounts having credit balances, as illustrated in the following closing entry:

Closing tempo-rary proprietor-ship accounts with credit balances

Dec. 31 Inventory (Dec. 31)..................................... 70,000

      Sales... 617,000

      Purchase Returns and Allowances........................ 6,700

      Purchase Discounts 3,300

          Income Summary.................................. 697,000

To record the ending inventory and to close all temporary owners' equity accounts with credit balances.

The remaining closing entries serve to transfer the balance of the Income Summary account to the Retained Earnings account and to close the Dividends account, as follows:

Closing Income Summary account and Dividends account

Dec. 31 Income Summary 50,000

      Retained Earnings................................... 50,000

To close the Income Summary account.

    31 Retained Earnings 26,000

      Dividends 26,000

To close the Dividends account.

After the preceding four closing entries have been posted to the ledger, the only accounts left with dollar balances will be balance sheet accounts. An after-closing trial balance should be prepared to prove that the ledger is in balance after the year-end entries to adjust and close the accounts.

Summary of merchandising transactions and related accounting entries

The transactions regularly encountered in merchandising operations and the related accounting entries may be concisely summarized as follows:

	Accounting Entries	
Transactions	**Debit**	**Credit**
Sell merchandise to customers	Cash (or Accounts Receivable)	Sales
Permit customers to return merchandise, or grant them a reduction from original price	Sales Returns & Allowances	Cash (or Accounts Receivable)
Collect account receivable within discount period	Cash; Sales Discounts	Accounts Receivable
Purchase merchandise for resale	Purchases	Cash (or Accounts Payable)
Incur transportation charges on merchandise purchased for resale	Transportation-in	Cash (or Accounts Payable)
Return unsatisfactory merchandise to supplier, or obtain a reduction from original price	Cash (or Accounts Payable)	Purchase Returns and Allowances
Pay for merchandise within discount period	Accounts Payable	Cash; Purchase Discounts
Inventory Procedures at End of Period		
Transfer the balance of the beginning inventory to the Income Summary account	Income Summary	Inventory
Take a physical inventory of goods on hand at the end of the period, and price these goods at cost	Inventory	Income Summary

Sales taxes

Sales taxes are levied by many states and cities on retail sales. Sales taxes actually are imposed upon the consumer, not upon the seller. However, the seller must collect the tax, file tax returns at times specified by law, and remit the taxes collected on all reported sales.

For cash sales, sales tax is collected from the customer at the time of the sales transaction. For credit sales, the sales tax is included in the amount charged to the customer's account. The liability to the governmental unit for sales taxes may be recorded at the time the sale is made as shown in the following journal entry:

Sales tax recorded at time of sale

Accounts Receivable (or Cash) 1,050		
Sales Tax Payable		50
Sales		1,000

To record sales of $1,000 subject to 5% sales tax.

This approach requires a separate credit entry to the Sales Tax Payable account for each sale. At first glance, this may seem to require an excessive amount of bookkeeping. However, today's electronic cash registers can be programmed to record automatically the sales tax liability at the time of each sale.

An alternative approach to sales taxes. Instead of recording the sales tax liability at the time of sale, some businesses prefer to credit the Sales account with the entire amount collected, including the sales tax, and to make an adjustment at the end of each period to reflect sales tax payable. For example, suppose that the total recorded sales for the period under this method were $315,000. Since the Sales account includes both the sales price and the sales tax (say, 5%), it is apparent that $315,000 is *105*% of the actual sales figure. Actual sales are $300,000 (computed $315,000 ÷ 1.05) and the amount of sales tax due is $15,000. (Proof: 5% of $300,000 = $15,000). The entry to record the liability for sales taxes would be

Sales tax recorded as adjustment of Sales account

Sales.. 15,000		
Sales Tax Payable		15,000

To remove sales taxes of 5% on $300,000 of sales from the Sales account, and reflect as a liability.

This second approach is widely used in businesses which do not use electronic devices for recording each sales transaction.

If some of the products being sold are not subject to sales tax (such as food), the business must keep separate records of taxable and nontaxable sales.

Perpetual inventory systems

6 Distinguish between the periodic and the perpetual inventory systems. In this chapter, we have emphasized the *periodic inventory system* as a means of valuing inventories and determining the cost of goods sold. Under this system, the amount of inventory is determined at the end of each accounting period by a physical count, and the cost of goods sold is determined by a computation. This system is in widespread use, especially by businesses that sell products of relatively low unit cost.

The *perpetual inventory system* provides a sharp contrast to the periodic inventory system. Under the perpetual inventory system, the Inventory account is kept continuously up-to-date; hence the name, *perpetual* inventory system. Under this system, a ledger account also is maintained showing the cost of goods sold during the period. The Inventory account is debited whenever merchandise is purchased. When merchandise is sold, two entries are made. The first entry records the sales revenue (debit Cash or Accounts Receivable, credit Sales). The second entry reduces the balance of the Inventory account *and records the cost of goods sold* (debit the Cost of Goods Sold account, credit Inventory).

Traditionally, the perpetual inventory system has been used by companies selling items of **high unit value,** such as automobiles, computers, or furniture. These businesses have relatively few sales transactions each day; thus, recording the cost of each sale is an easy matter.

In a business that sells large quantities of low cost merchandise, recording the cost of each sales transaction is not feasible without a computerized system. Therefore, businesses such as grocery stores, department stores, and most small retailers traditionally use the periodic inventory system. Today, however, "point-of-sale" computer terminals make it possible for almost every merchandising company to maintain a perpetual inventory system.

● **CASE IN POINT** ● A large supermarket may sell between 5,000 and 10,000 items per hour, each with a relatively low unit cost. Clearly, it would be impossible for clerks to look up and record the cost of each item sold. Thus, grocery stores traditionally have used the periodic inventory system. Now, however, electronic cash registers are able to read "product codes" (a pattern of thick and thin vertical bars) printed on each product. These product codes enable a computer to identify each item being sold, to record the sale, and to update perpetual inventory records and the cost of goods sold.

In summary, a perpetual inventory system is suited for use by businesses that (1) have a relatively low number of daily sales transactions, or (2) use point-of-sale computer terminals to determine and record the cost of each sale. Perpetual inventory systems are discussed further in Chapter 8.

CLASSIFIED FINANCIAL STATEMENTS

7 Prepare a classified balance sheet and either a single-step or a multiple-step income statement.

The financial statements illustrated up to this point have been rather short and simple because of the limited number of accounts used in these introductory chapters. Now let us look briefly at a more comprehensive balance sheet for a merchandising business.

In the balance sheet of Graham Corporation illustrated on the next page, the assets are classified into three groups: (1) current assets, (2) plant and equipment, and (3) other assets. The liabilities are classified into two types: (1) current liabilities and (2) long-term liabilities. This classification of assets and liabilities is virtually a standard one throughout American business.

The purpose of balance sheet classification

The purpose underlying a standard classification of assets and liabilities is to aid management, stockholders, creditors, and other interested persons in understanding the financial position of the business. Standard practices as to the order and arrangement of a balance sheet are a means of saving the time of the reader and of giving a clearer picture of the company's financial position.

GRAHAM CORPORATION
Balance Sheet
December 31, 19__

Assets

Current assets:

Cash..		$ 25,000
Marketable securities..		13,000
Notes receivable...		30,000
Accounts receivable..		70,000
Inventory		100,000
Prepaid expenses..		12,000
Total current assets		$250,000

Plant and equipment:

Land		$ 60,000	
Building..	$140,000		
Less: Accumulated depreciation	56,000	84,000	
Store equipment..	$ 24,000		
Less: Accumulated depreciation	18,000	6,000	
Delivery equipment	$ 19,000		
Less: Accumulated depreciation	10,000	9,000	
Total plant and equipment..			159,000

Other assets:

Land (future building site)..	125,000
Total assets	$534,000

Liabilities & Stockholders' Equity

Current liabilities:

Notes payable (due in 6 months)		$ 15,000
Accounts payable...		59,900
Income taxes payable		6,100
Accrued expenses payable..		8,000
Unearned revenue		11,000
Total current liabilities		$100,000

Long-term liabilities:

Mortgage payable (due in 10 years)		181,000
Total liabilities..		$281,000

Stockholders' equity:

Capital stock	$100,000	
Retained earnings..	153,000	253,000
Total liabilities & stockholders' equity..................................		$534,000

Current assets. Current assets include cash, government bonds and other marketable securities, receivables, inventories, and prepaid expenses. To qualify for inclusion in the current asset category, an asset must be capable of being converted into cash within a relatively short period without interfering with the normal operation of the business. The period is usually one year, but it may be longer for businesses having an operating cycle in excess of one year.

The term **operating cycle** means the average time period between the purchase of merchandise and the conversion of this merchandise back into cash. The series of transactions comprising a complete cycle often runs as follows: (1) purchase of merchandise, (2) sale of the merchandise on credit, (3) collection of the account receivable from the customer. The word **cycle** suggests the circular flow of capital from cash to inventory to receivables and back into cash again. This cycle of transactions in a merchandising business is portrayed in the following diagram:

The operating cycle repeats continuously

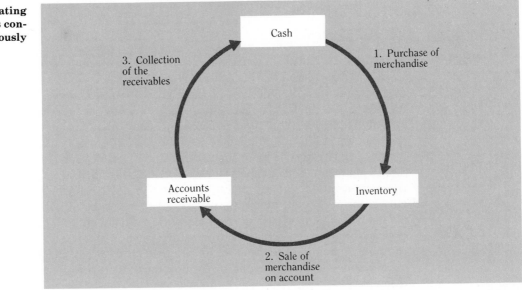

In a business handling fast-moving merchandise (a supermarket, for example) the operating cycle may be completed in a few weeks; for most merchandising businesses the operating cycle requires several months but less than a year.

Curret assets are listed in order of liquidity; the closer an asset is to becoming cash the higher is its liquidity. The total amount of a company's current assets and the relative amount of each type give some indication of the company's short-run, debt-paying ability.

Current liabilities. Liabilities that must be paid within one year or the operating cycle (whichever is longer) are called **current liabilities.** Among the more common types of current liabilities are notes payable, accounts payable, taxes payable, salaries payable, interest payable, and unearned revenue. Notes payable are usually listed first, followed by accounts payable; any sequence of listing is acceptable for other current liabilities.

Settlement of most types of current liabilities requires writing a check to the creditor; in other words, use of the current asset cash. A somewhat different procedure for settlement is followed for the current liability of unearned revenue. As explained in Chapter 4, unearned revenue is a liability which arises when money is received from customers in advance for goods or services to be delivered in the future. To meet such obligations usually will require using up current assets either through delivering merchandise to the customer or making payments to employees or others to provide the agreed services.

The key point to recognize is the relationship between current liabilities and current assets. Current liabilities must be paid in the near future and current assets must be available to make these payments. Comparison of the amount of current liabilities with the amount of current assets is an important step in evaluating the ability of a company to pay its debts in the near future.

Current ratio

8 Explain the purpose of the current ratio and the meaning of working capital.

Many bankers and other users of financial statements believe that for a business to qualify as a good credit risk, the total current assets should be about twice as large as the total current liabilities. In studying a balance sheet, a banker or other creditor will compute the *current ratio* by dividing total current assets by total current liabilities. The current ratio is a convenient measure of the short-run debt-paying ability of a business.

In the illustrated balance sheet of Graham Corporation, the current assets of $250,000 are two and one-half times as great as the current liabilities of $100,000; the current ratio is therefore $2\frac{1}{2}$ to 1, which would generally be regarded as a strong current position. The current assets could shrink substantially and still be sufficient for payment of the current liabilities. Although a strong current ratio is desirable, an extremely high current ratio (such as 4 to 1 or more) may signify that a company is holding too much of its resources in cash, marketable securities, and other current assets and is not pursuing opportunities for growth as aggressively as it might.

Working capital

The excess of current assets over current liabilities is called *working capital;* the relative amount of working capital is another indication of short-term financial strength. In the illustrated balance sheet of Graham Corporation, working capital is $150,000, computed by subtracting the current liabilities of $100,000 from the current assets of $250,000. The importance of *solvency* (ability to meet debts as they fall due) was emphasized in Chapter 1. Ample working capital permits a company to meet its short-term obligations, to qualify for favorable credit terms, and to take advantage of opportunities quickly. Many companies have been forced to suspend business because of inadequate working capital, even though total assets were much larger than total liabilities.

Classification and format of income statements

There are two common forms of income statements: the **multiple-step income statement** and the **single-step income statement.** The multiple-step statement is more convenient in illustrating accounting principles and has been used consistently in our illustrations thus far. The income statement for Olympic Sporting Goods on page 190 is in multiple-step form. It is also a **classified** income statement because the various items of expense are classified into significant groups. The single-step form of income statement is illustrated on page 204.

Multiple-step income statements

The multiple-step income statement is so named because of the **series of steps** in which costs and expenses are deducted from revenue. As a first step, the cost of goods sold is subtracted from net sales to produce an amount for **gross profit** on sales. As a second step, operating expenses are deducted to obtain a subtotal called **income from operations** (or **operating income**). As a final step, income taxes expense is subtracted to determine net income. The multiple-step income statement is noted for its numerous sections and significant subtotals. It is widely used by small businesses.

The operating expenses of Olympic Sporting Goods were classified into two categories: selling expenses and general and administrative expenses. These classifications aid management in controlling expenses by emphasizing that certain expenses are the responsibility of sales executives and that other expenses relate to the business as a whole. Of course, many small companies are not organized into departments; consequently they do not subdivide operating expenses on the income statement.

Income taxes are **not** included among operating expenses because income taxes **do not help to produce operating revenue** (sales). Other examples of **nonoperating** expenses include interest expense and losses on sales of investments. Nonoperating expenses appear in a final section of the income statement after the figure showing **income from operations.** Any **nonoperating revenue,** such as interest earned and gains on sales of investments, also should be listed in this final section of the income statement.

Single-step income statements

The income statements prepared by large corporations for distribution to thousands of stockholders often are greatly condensed because the public presumably is more interested in a concise report than in the details of operations. The **single-step** form of income statement takes its name from the fact that the total of all expenses (including the cost of goods sold) is deducted from total revenue in a single step. All types of revenue, such as sales, interest earned, and rent revenue, are added together to show the total revenue. Then all expenses are grouped together and deducted in one step without the use of subtotals. A condensed income statement in single-step form is shown below for National Corporation, a large merchandising company.

NATIONAL CORPORATION

Income Statement

For the Year Ended December 31, 19__

Condensed single-step income statement

Revenue:		
Net sales		$90,000,000
Interest earned		1,800,000
Total revenue..		$91,800,000
Expenses:		
Cost of goods sold	$60,000,000	
Selling expenses.......................................	14,400,000	
General & administrative expenses	9,750,000	
Income taxes expense...................................	3,150,000	
Total expenses		87,300,000
Net income..		$ 4,500,000

END-OF-CHAPTER REVIEW

Summary of chapter learning objectives

1 Account for sales, sales returns, and sales discounts.

When merchandise is sold, the revenue is recorded by crediting the Sales account. Sales returns & allowances and sales discounts are recorded by debit entries to contra-revenue accounts. In the income statement, the balances of these contra-revenue accounts are deducted from the balance of the Sales account to determine the net sales for the period.

2 Determine the cost of goods sold using the periodic inventory system.

Under the periodic inventory system, the cost of goods sold is equal to the beginning inventory, plus net purchases (including transportation-in), minus the ending inventory.

3 Account for purchases of merchandise.

Under the periodic inventory system, purchases of merchandise are debited to the Purchases account. Purchase returns & allowances and purchase discounts are credited to accounts that are deducted from the balance of the Purchases account to determine the net purchases for the period. Net purchases is an important element of the cost of goods sold.

4 Prepare a work sheet for a merchandising company.

A work sheet for a merchandising business is much like the work sheet for a service-type business. The basic difference is the addition of beginning and ending inventories. The beginning inventory appears in the Trial Balance debit column and is extended into the Income Statement debit column. The ending inventory is entered in the Income Statement credit column and in the Balance Sheet debit column.

5 Prepare closing entries for a merchandising company.

In addition to closing the revenue and expense accounts, a merchandising company also must close into the Income Summary the contra-revenue accounts and accounts used in computing the cost of goods sold.

The entry closing temporary equity accounts with ***debit balances*** closes the expense accounts, beginning inventory, Purchases, Transportation-in, Sales Returns & Allowances, and Sales discount. The entry closing temporary equity accounts with *credit balances* closes the revenue accounts, Purchase Returns & Allowances, and Purchase Discounts. In addition, this entry records the ending inventory by debiting Inventory and crediting Income Summary.

The entries to close the Income Summary and Dividends accounts are similar to those illustrated in Chapter 4 for a service-type business.

6 Distinguish between the periodic and the perpetual inventory systems.

Under the periodic system, the beginning and ending inventory are determined by a physical count. Purchases of merchandise are recorded in a Purchases account, and *no entries are made to record the cost of individual sales transactions.* Rather, the cost of goods sold is determined by a computation at the end of the period. No entries are made in the Inventory account until (1) the account is closed and (2) the ending inventory is recorded.

Under the perpetual inventory system, ledger accounts are maintained both for Inventory and for Cost of Goods Sold. These accounts are kept *perpetually up to date* — hence the name *perpetual* inventory system. The Inventory account is debited whenever goods are purchased. When sales occur, Cost of Goods Sold is debited and Inventory is credited for the cost of the merchandise sold.

7 Prepare a classified balance sheet and either a single-step or a multiple-step income statement.

In a classified balance sheet, assets are subdivided into the categories of *current assets, plant and equipment,* and *other assets.* Liabilities are classified as *current liabilities* (those due within one year or an operating cycle), or *long-term liabilities.*

In a multiple-step income statement, the cost of goods sold is deducted from net sales to provide the subtotal, gross profit. Operating expenses then are deducted to arrive at income from operations. As a final step, nonoperating items are added or subtracted to arrive at net income. In a single-step income statement all revenue items are combined, and then all expenses are combined and deducted from total revenue in a single step.

8 Explain the purpose of the current ratio and the meaning of working capital.

The purpose of the current ratio (current assets divided by current liabilities) is to provide the users of financial statements with a quick indication of the solvency of a business.

Working capital is the excess of current assets over current liabilities. This measurement indicates the amount of uncommitted liquid resources on hand.

Key terms introduced or emphasized in chapter 5

Cost of goods sold. A computation appearing as a separate section of an income statement showing the cost of goods sold during the period. Computed by adding net delivered cost of merchandise purchases to beginning inventory to obtain cost of goods available for sale, and then deducting from this total the amount of the ending inventory.

Current assets. Cash and other assets that can be converted into cash within one year or the operating cycle (whichever is longer) without interfering with the normal operation of the business.

Current ratio. Current assets divided by current liabilities. A measure of short-run debt-paying ability.

Gross profit on sales. Revenue from sales minus cost of goods sold.

Gross profit rate. Gross profit expressed as a percentage of net sales. Usually between 30% and 50% of net sales.

Inventory shrinkage. The loss of merchandise through such causes as shoplifting, employee theft, breakage, and spoilage. Under the periodic inventory system, losses from inventory shrinkage automatically are included in the cost of goods sold.

Multiple-step income statement. An income statement in which cost of goods sold and expenses are subtracted from revenue in a series of steps, thus producing significant subtotals prior to net income.

Net sales. Gross sales revenue minus sales returns and allowances and minus sales discounts.

Operating cycle. The average time period from the purchase of merchandise to its sale and conversion back into cash.

Periodic inventory system. A system of accounting for merchandise in which inventory at the balance sheet date is determined by counting and pricing the goods on hand. Cost of goods sold is computed by subtracting the ending inventory from the cost of goods available for sale.

Perpetual inventory system. A system of accounting for merchandise that provides a continuous record showing the quantity and cost of all goods on hand.

Single-step income statement. An income statement in which the cost of goods sold and all expenses are combined and deducted from total revenue in a single step to determine net income.

Working capital. Current assets minus current liabilities. A measure of short-run debt-paying ability.

Demonstration problem for your review

Ski America sells a wide variety of products and uses the periodic inventory method. During October, the company engaged in the following merchandising transactions. Terms of 2/10, n/30 are offered on all credit sales.

Oct. 3 Sold merchandise left over from last season to Freight Liquidators for $32,880 cash.

Oct. 9 Sold merchandise on account to Matterhorn Lodge, $24,820.

Oct. 12 Matterhorn Lodge returned $420 of the merchandise purchased on Nov. 7. Full credit was given to Matterhorn for this return.

Oct. 16 Purchased merchandise on account from Sports Fashions for $18,900; terms, 2/10, n/30.

Oct. 17 Paid freight charges on shipment received from Sports Fashions, $126.

Oct. 19 Received a check for $23,912 from Matterhorn Lodge in full settlement of the Oct. 9 sale, less the return on Oct. 12 and the allowable sales discount.

Oct. 22 Purchased merchandise on account from Outdoor Products, $17,100; terms, 5/10, n/60.

Oct. 24 Returned defective goods costing $900 to Outdoor Products. Received full credit on our account.

Oct. 26 Paid Sports Fashions for the purchase on Nov. 16, less 2%.

Instructions

a Prepare journal entries to record these transactions.

b Prepare a partial income statement for October, showing the accounts included in computing net sales, the cost of goods sold, and gross profit. Assume that inventory was $31,400 on September 30, and $33,920 on October 31.

Solution to demonstration problem

a   General Journal

Oct.	3	Cash..	32,880	
		Sales..		32,880
		To record the sale of merchandise for cash.		
	9	Accounts Receivable....................................	24,820	
		Sales..		24,820
		To record sale to Matterhorn Lodge.		
	12	Sales Returns & Allowances............................	420	
		Accounts Receivable		420
		Gave credit to Matterhorn Lodge for merchandise returned.		
	16	Purchases..	18,900	
		Accounts Payable................................		18,900
		To record purchase from Sports Fashions, terms 2/10, n/30.		
	17	Transportation-in	126	
		Cash..		126
		Paid transportation charges on goods purchased from Sports Fashions.		
	19	Cash..	23,912	
		Sales Discount	488	
		Accounts Receivable		24,400
		Collected from Matterhorn Lodge for our Oct. 9 sale, $24,820— return of $420 and 2% discount on balance of $24,400.		
	22	Purchases..	17,100	
		Accounts Payable................................		17,100
		To record purchase from Outdoor Products, less 1% cash discount available, terms 5/10, n/60		
	24	Accounts Payable	900	
		Purchase Returns & Allowances.....................		900
		Returned portion of Oct. 22 purchase from Outdoor Products because goods were defective.		
	26	Accounts Payable	18,900	
		Purchase Discount		378
		Cash..		18,522
		Paid Oct. 16 purchase invoice from Sports Fashions, less 2% discount.		

b

SKI AMERICA
Partial Income Statement
For the Month Ended October 31, 19__

Revenue:

Sales		$57,700
Less: Sales returns and allowances	$ 420	
Sales discounts	488	908
Net sales		$56,792

Cost of goods sold:

Inventory, Sept. 30		$31,400	
Purchases	$36,000		
Less: Purchase returns and allowances	$900		
Purchase discounts	378	1,278	
Net purchases	$34,722		
Add: Transportation-in	126		
Delivered cost of purchases		34,848	
Cost of goods available for sale		$66,248	
Less: Inventory, Oct. 31		33,920	
Cost of goods sold			32,328
Gross profit on sales			$24,464

ASSIGNMENT MATERIAL

Review questions

1 During the current year, Green Bay Company made all sales of merchandise at prices in excess of cost. Will the business necessarily report a net income for the year? Explain.

2 The income statement for Color Sound showed gross profit on sales of $144,000, operating expenses of $130,000, and cost of goods sold of $216,000. What was the amount of net sales?

3 Valley Mart during its first year of operations had cost of goods sold of $480,000 and a gross profit equal to 40% of sales. What was the dollar amount of net sales for the year?

4 Is the normal balance of the Sales Returns and Allowances account a debit or a credit? Is the normal balance of the Purchase Returns and Allowances account a debit or a credit?

5 Supply the proper terms to complete the following statements:
a Net sales − cost of goods sold = ?
b Beginning inventory + purchases − purchase returns and allowances − purchase discounts + transportation-in = ?
c Cost of goods sold + ending inventory = ?
d Cost of goods sold + gross profit on sales = ?
e Net income + operating expenses = ?

6 During the current year, Davis Corporation purchased merchandise costing $200,000. State the cost of goods sold under each of the following alternative assumptions:

a No beginning inventory; ending inventory $40,000
b Beginning inventory $60,000; no ending inventory
c Beginning inventory $58,000; ending inventory $78,000
d Beginning inventory $90,000; ending inventory $67,000

7 Reed Labs purchased merchandise on account from Health Products for $13,500, on terms of 2/10, n/30. Within the discount period, Reed Labs returned some of the merchandise and paid $9,800 in full settlement of the account. What was the cost of the merchandise returned by Reed Labs? Explain your reasoning.

8 Zenith Company uses the periodic inventory system and maintains its accounting records on a calendar-year basis. Does the beginning or the ending inventory figure appear in the trial balance prepared from the ledger on December 31?

9 Compute the amount of cost of goods sold, given the following account balances: beginning inventory $40,000, purchases $84,000, purchase returns and allowances $4,500, purchase discounts $1,500, transportation-in $1,000, and ending inventory $36,000.

10 In which columns of the work sheet for a merchandising company does the ending inventory appear?

11 State briefly the difference between the *perpetual* inventory system and the *periodic* inventory system.

12 When the periodic inventory method is in use, how is the amount of inventory determined at the end of the period?

13 What is the purpose of a closing entry consisting of a debit to the Income Summary account and a credit to the Inventory account?

14 Tireco is a retail store in a state that imposes a 5% sales tax. Would you expect to find an account entitled Sales Tax Expense and another account entitled Sales Tax Payable in Tireco's ledger? Explain your answer.

15 Explain the terms *current assets, current liabilities,* and *current ratio.*

16 Madison Corporation has current assets of $540,000 and current liabilities of $300,000. Compute the current ratio and the amount of working capital.

17 Barnes Imports has a current ratio of 3 to 1 and working capital of $60,000. What are the amounts of current assets and current liabilities?

18 Three items appearing in the annual income statement of Fashion House are: total operating expenses, $300,000; gross profit, $470,000; and income taxes expense, $50,000. Did Fashion House prepare a single-step or multiple-step income statement? Explain.
   Now assume that Fashion House had prepared the *other type* of income statement. What would have been the amount of net income shown in the statement?

Exercises

Exercise 5-1
Accounting
terminology

Listed below are nine technical accounting terms emphasized in this chapter:

Cost of goods available for sale	Periodic inventory system	Perpetual inventory system
Cost of goods sold	Gross profit	Working capital
Purchase discount	Inventory	Current ratio

Each of the following statements may (or may not) describe one of these technical terms. For each statement, indicate the accounting term described, or answer "None" if the statement does not correctly describe any of the terms.

a Goods acquired and held for sale to customers.
b Current assets minus current liabilities.
c A reduction in revenue resulting from allowing a reduction in sales price to a customer whose purchases received slight damage during delivery.
d Accounting procedures which involve taking a physical inventory in order to determine the amount of inventory and the cost of goods sold.
e Net sales minus the cost of goods sold.
f Beginning inventory plus the delivered cost of net purchases.
g Beginning inventory minus gross profit.

Exercise 5-2
Accounting for purchases and sales of merchandise

Delta Traders sold merchandise to Denver Suppliers for $84,000 terms 2/10, n/30. Denver Suppliers paid for the merchandise within the discount period.

a Give the journal entries by Delta Traders to record the sale and the subsequent collection.
b Give the journal entries by Denver Suppliers to record the purchase and the subsequent payment.

Exercise 5-3
Relationships among merchandising accounts

Some of the items in the income statement of Traders' Market are listed below.

Net sales	$400,000
Gross profit on sales	160,000
Beginning inventory	30,000
Purchase discounts	1,000
Purchase returns & allowances	4,000
Transportation-in	6,000
Operating expenses	80,000
Purchases	250,000

Use the appropriate items from this list as a basis for computing (a) the cost of goods sold, (b) the cost of goods available for sale, and (c) the ending inventory.

Exercise 5-4
Income statement relationships in a merchandising business

This exercise stresses the sequence and relationship of items in a multiple-step income statement for a merchandising business. Each of the five horizontal lines in the table represents a separate set of income statement items. You are to copy the table and fill in the missing amounts. A net loss in the right-hand column is to be indicated by placing brackets before and after the amount, as for example, in line e (25,000).

	Net Sales	Beginning Inventory	Net Purchases	Ending Inventory	Cost of Goods Sold	Gross Profit	Expenses	Net Income or (Loss)
a	200,000	54,000	130,000	44,000	?	60,000	70,000	?
b	500,000	60,000	340,000	?	330,000	?	?	25,000
c	600,000	120,000	?	85,000	390,000	210,000	165,000	?
d	800,000	?	500,000	150,000	?	260,000	205,000	?
e	?	230,000	?	255,000	660,000	240,000	?	(25,000)

Exercise 5-5
Preparing closing
entries from a
worksheet

The accountant for Village Ski Shop prepared a work sheet for the year ended December 31, 19__. Shown below are the Income Statement columns from that work sheet. Dividends declared by the company during the year amounted to $22,000. Using this information, prepare four separate journal entries to close the accounts at December 31. Use the sequence of closing entries illustrated in this chapter.

	Income Statement	
	Debit	Credit
Inventory, Jan. 1	30,000	
Sales...		520,350
Sales returns & allowances	8,700	
Sales discounts	2,650	
Purchases...	325,000	
Purchase returns & allowances.............................		3,200
Purchase discounts..		5,100
Transportation-in	4,300	
Selling expenses..	48,000	
General and administrative expenses	36,000	
Income taxes expense	17,000	
Inventory, Dec. 31		31,000
	471,650	559,650
Net income	88,000	
	559,650	559,650

Exercise 5-6
Multiple-step and
single-step
income state-
ments

Use the data from the Village Ski Shop work sheet in Exercise 5-5 to prepare:

a A multiple-step income statement in as much detail as the work sheet data will allow.

b A single-step income statement in condensed form. "Condensed form" means that net sales and the cost of goods sold will each be shown as a single amount, without showing the individual account balances which are used to compute these subtotals.

Exercise 5-7
Accounting for
sales taxes

Christine's Shoe Store operates in an area in which a 5% sales tax is levied on all products handled by the store. On cash sales, the salesclerks include the sales tax in the amount collected from the customer and ring up the entire amount on the cash register without recording separately the tax liability. On credit sales, the customer is charged for the list price of the merchandise plus 5%, and the entire amount is debited to Accounts Receivable and credited to the Sales account. On sales of less than one dollar, the tax collected is rounded to the nearest cent.

Sales tax must be remitted to the government quarterly. At March 31 the Sales account showed a balance of $214,830 for the three-month period ended March 31.

a What amount of sales tax is owed at March 31?

b Give the journal entry to record the sales tax liability in the accounts.

The balance sheet of Hunt Company contained the following items, among others:

Cash.	$ 39,600
Accounts receivable	158,000
Accounts payable.	142,400
Retained earnings	152,000
Accumulated depreciation	28,800
Mortgage payable (due in three years).	48,000
Notes payable (due in 10 days)	19,200
Inventory	206,400
Capital stock.	100,000
Equipment.	165,000

Instructions

a From the above information compute the amount of current assets and the amount of current liabilities.

b How much working capital does Hunt Company have?

c Compute the current ratio.

Problems

Runners' World deals in a wide variety of low-priced merchandise and uses the periodic inventory system. Shown below is a partial list of the transactions occurring during May.

May 2 Purchased merchandise (running shoes) on credit from MinuteMan Shoes, $9,600. Terms, 2/10, n/30.

May 3 Paid freight charges of $45 on the shipment of merchandise purchased from MinuteMan Shoes.

May 4 Upon unpacking the shipment from MinuteMan, discovered that some of the shoes were the wrong style. Returned these shoes, which cost $400, to MinuteMan and received full credit.

May 9 Sold merchandise on account to Desert Spa Hotel, $4,100. Terms, 2/10, n/30.

May 11 Paid $22 freight charges on the outbound shipment to Desert Spa Hotel.

May 12 Paid MinuteMan Shoes within the discount period the remaining amount owed for the May 2 purchase, after allowing for the purchase return on May 4.

May 16 Sold merchandise on account to Holiday Sportswear, $2,755. Terms, 2/10, n/30.

May 19 Received check from Desert Spa Hotel within the discount period in full settlement of the May 9 sale.

May 21 Holiday Sportswear returned $650 of the merchandise it had purchased on May 16. Runners' World has a policy of accepting all merchandise returns within 30 days of the date of sale without question. Full credit was given to Holiday for the returned merchandise.

31 Colect from May 16

Instructions. Prepare journal entries to record each of these transactions in the accounting records of Runners' World. Include a written explanation for each journal entry.

Problem 5-2
Journalizing
merchandising
transactions;
alternate to
Problem 5-1

Design Center sells furnishings for office interiors and uses the periodic inventory system. Shown below is a partial list of the transactions occurring during June.

June 1 Sold merchandise for cash in the amount of $1,700.

June 2 Purchased merchandise on credit from Original Interiors, $18,000. Terms, 2/10, n/30.

June 4 Paid inbound transportation charges on merchandise purchased from Original Interiors, $600.

June 9 Sold merchandise on account to Law Offices of Sherri Mason, $3,960. Terms, 2/10, n/30.

June 10 Paid transportation charges on shipment to customer Law Offices of Sherri Mason, $80.

June 12 Paid Original Interiors within discount period for purchase made on June 2. Issued check for $17,640.

June 12 Purchased merchandise for cash, $324.

June 16 Sold merchandise on account to S. W. Hardy, $6,100. Terms 2/10, n/30.

June 17 Granted a $100 allowance to S. W. Hardy on merchandise delivered on June 16, because of minor defects discovered in the merchandise.

June 26 Received check from S. W. Hardy within discount period in settlement of transaction of June 16. Customer took discount applicable to remaining balance after $100 allowance on June 17.

Instructions. Prepare a separate journal entry (including an explanation) for each of the above transactions.

Problem 5-3
Preparing an in-
come statement
and closing
entries

The following accounts relate to the income of Leather Bandit for the three-month period ended March 31, 19__:

Sales	$500,000	Transportation-in	$ 900
Sales returns & allowances.......	15,000	Inventory, Jan. 1, 19__..........	170,000
Sales discounts	7,800	Inventory, Mar. 31, 19__	164,100
Purchases....................	310,000	Operating expenses.............	121,400
Purchase returns & allowances ...	4,500	Income taxes expense...........	7,400
Purchase discounts	6,200		

Instructions

a Compute the amount of net sales for the three-month period.

b Compute the cost of goods sold.

c Prepare a **condensed** multiple-step income statement. Show both net sales and the cost of goods sold as "one-line items," without showing the accounts used to compute these amounts. Income taxes expense should be shown after determining income from operations.

d Prepare closing entries for the three-month period ended March 31. Only three closing entries are required, as the company did not declare any dividends during the period.

Problem 5-4
Preparing a work
sheet and
adjusting and
closing entries

A four-column schedule consisting of the first four columns of a 10-column work sheet for Foreign Auto Parts, Inc., appears below.

FOREIGN AUTO PARTS, INC.
Work Sheet
For the Year Ended December 31, 19__

	Trial Balance		Adjustments	
	Debit	Credit	Debit	Credit
Cash...................................	18,500			
Accounts receivable......................	59,500			
Inventory, Jan. 1........................	75,000			
Equipment...............................	25,000			
Accumulated depreciation: equipment		7,500		(a) 2,500
Accounts payable........................		65,000		
Capital stock............................		40,000		
Retained earnings, Jan. 1..................		35,900		
Dividends...............................	20,000			
Sales		640,000		
Sales returns & allowances................	27,000			
Sales discounts..........................	8,000			
Purchases	384,000			
Purchase returns & allowances		12,600		
Purchase discounts		6,000		
Transportation-in	12,000			
Advertising expense	48,000			
Rent expense	36,000			
Salaries expense	94,000			
	807,000	807,000		
Depreciation expense: equipment			(a) 2,500	
Income taxes expense.....................			(b) 7,300	
Income taxes payable				(b) 7,300
			9,800	9,800

The company uses the periodic inventory system and maintains its accounting records on a calendar-year basis. The completed Adjustments columns have been included in the work sheet to minimize the detail work involved. These adjustments were derived from the following information available at December 31:

(a) Depreciation expense for the year on equipment, $2,500.
(b) Income taxes owed for the year, $7,300.

A physical inventory taken at December 31 showed the ending inventory to be $69,100.

Instructions

a Prepare a 10-column work sheet following the format illustrated on page 193. Include at the bottom of the work sheet a legend consisting of a brief explanation keyed to each adjusting entry.

b Prepare the two journal entries to adjust the accounts at December 31.

c Prepare the necessary journal entries to close the accounts on December 31.

Problem 5-5
Preparing a work
sheet, financial
statements, and
closing entries

The trial balance below was prepared from the ledger of Jessop's Boots & Saddles at December 31. The company maintains its accounts on a calendar-year basis and closes the accounts only once a year. The periodic inventory system is in use.

JESSOP'S BOOTS & SADDLES
Trial Balance
December 31, 19__

Cash	$ 20,000	
Accounts receivable	76,000	
Inventory, Jan. 1	160,000	
Unexpired insurance	4,000	
Office supplies	1,800	
Land	35,000	
Buildings	100,000	
Accumulated depreciation: buildings		$ 20,000
Notes payable		80,000
Accounts payable		60,000
Capital stock		100,000
Retained earnings		94,800
Dividends	26,000	
Sales		658,000
Sales returns and allowances	42,000	
Sales discounts	16,000	
Purchases	431,000	
Purchase returns and allowances		23,000
Purchase discounts		8,000
Transportation-in	10,000	
Advertising expense	5,000	
Salaries expense	110,000	
Utilities expense	7,000	
Totals	$1,043,800	$1,043,800

Other data

(a) The depreciation on the building is based on a 25-year life.
(b) Unexpired insurance at the end of the year was determined to be $1,500.
(c) Office supplies unused and on hand at year-end amounted to $800, indicating that supplies costing $1,000 had been consumed.
(d) Income taxes expense for the year was determined to be $7,500.
(e) A physical inventory of merchandise at December 31, showed goods on hand of $140,000.

Instructions

a Prepare a 10-column work sheet at December 31. Use the format illustrated on page 193.
b Prepare a multiple-step income statement for the year. Operating expenses are not to be subdivided between selling expenses and general and administrative expenses. Show income taxes expense after determining income from operations.
c Prepare a statement of retained earnings for the year.
d Prepare a classified balance sheet as of December 31.
e Prepare adjusting and closing entries at December 31.

Problem 5-6
Computing cur-
rent ratio and
working capital;
evaluating
solvency

Some of the accounts appearing in the year-end financial statements of Diet Frozen Dinners appear below. This list includes all of the company's current assets and current liabilities.

Sales..	$1,980,000
Accumulated depreciation: equipment...	370,000
Notes payable (due in 90 days).................................	70,000
Retained earnings..	221,320
Cash..	47,600
Capital stock	150,000
Marketable securities..	175,040
Accounts payable	125,430
Mortgage payable (due in 15 years)..	320,000
Salaries payable	7,570
Dividends..	25,000
Income taxes payable..	14,600
Accounts receivable..	230,540
Inventory (ending)..	179,600
Unearned revenue..	10,000
Unexpired insurance..	4,500
Purchases	1,150,200

Instructions

a Prepare a partial balance sheet for Diet Frozen Dinners consisting of the current asset section and the current liability section *only*. Select the appropriate items from the above list.

b Compute the current ratio and the amount of working capital. Explain how each of these measurements is computed. State with reasons whether you consider the company to be in a strong or weak current position.

Business decision cases

Village Hardware is a retail store selling hardware, small appliances, and sporting goods. The business follows a policy of selling all merchandise at exactly twice the amount of its delivered cost to the store.

At year-end, the following information is taken from the accounting records:

Net sales	$500,000
Inventory, January 1..	70,000
Delivered cost of purchases	255,000

A physical count indicates merchandise costing $64,000 on hand at December 31.

Instructions

a Prepare a partial income statement showing computation of the gross profit for the year.

b Upon seeing your income statement, the owner of the store makes the following comment. "Inventory shrinkage losses are really costing me. If it weren't for shrinkage losses, the store's gross profit would be 50% of net sales. I'm going to hire a security guard and put an end to shoplifting once and for all."

Determine the amount of loss from inventory "shrinkage" stated (1) at cost, and (2) at retail sales value. (Hint: Without any shrinkage losses, the cost of goods sold and the amount of gross profit would each amount to 50% of net sales.)

c Assume that Village Hardware could virtually eliminate shoplifting by hiring a security guard at a cost of $1,500 per month. Would this strategy be profitable? Explain your reasoning.

Case 5-2
Using a balance
sheet to evaluate
solvency

Megan DeLong, an experienced engineer, is considering buying Eastern Engineering Company at year-end from its current owner, Jack Peterson. Eastern Engineering Company, a single proprietorship, has been a profitable business, earning about $70,000 to $75,000 each year. DeLong is certain she could operate the business just as profitably. The principal activity of the business has been the performance of engineering studies for government agencies interested in the development of air and water pollution control programs.

Peterson has agreed to sell the business for "what he has in it"—namely, $200,000. DeLong comes to you with the balance sheet of Eastern Engineering Company shown below and asks your advice about buying the business.

EASTERN ENGINEERING COMPANY
Balance Sheet
December 31, 19__

Assets

Cash...	$ 40,500
U.S. government contract receivable..	110,000
Other contracts receivable	21,500
Equipment (net of accumulated depreciation)	76,000
Patents...	38,000
Total assets..	$286,000

Liabilities & Owner's Equity

Liabilities:	
Notes payable	$ 60,000
Accounts payable..	20,600
Wages payable	5,400
Total liabilities	$ 86,000
Owner's equity:	
J. Peterson, capital...	200,000
Total liabilities & owner's equity..	$286,000

DeLong immediately points out, as evidence of the firm's solvency, that the current ratio for Eastern Engineering is 2 to 1. In discussing the specific items on the balance sheet, you find that the patents were recently purchased by Eastern, and DeLong believes them to be worth their $38,000 cost. The notes payable liability consists of one note to the manufacturer of the equipment owned by Eastern, which Peterson had incurred five years ago to finance the purchase of the equipment. The note becomes payable, however, in February of the coming year. The accounts payable all will become due within 30 to 60 days.

Since DeLong does not have enough cash to buy Peterson's equity in the business, she is considering the following terms of purchase: (1) Peterson will withdraw all the cash from the business, thus reducing his equity to $159,500, (2) Peterson will also keep the $110,000 receivable from the U.S. government, leaving his equity in the business at $49,500, and (3) by borrowing heavily, DeLong thinks she can raise $49,500 in cash, which she will pay to Peterson for his remaining equity. DeLong will assume the existing liabilities of the business.

Instructions

a Prepare a classified balance sheet for Eastern Engineering Company as it would appear immediately after DeLong acquired the business, assuming that the purchase is carried out immediately on the proposed terms.

b Compute the current ratio and the working capital position of Eastern Engineering Company after DeLong's purchase of the business.

c Write a memorandum to DeLong explaining what problems she might encounter if she purchases the business as planned.

Chapter 6
Internal control and accounting systems

CHAPTER PREVIEW

In the first part of Chapter 6, we explore the topic of internal control, and explain its relationship to accounting. We then discuss several methods of achieving strong internal control, including the subdivision of duties, the use of various business documents, and the "net-price method" of recording merchandise purchases. In the second section of the chapter, we address the problem of streamlining an accounting system to process efficiently a large volume of transactions. Special journals are illustrated and explained, along with subsidiary ledgers and controlling accounts. This discussion covers both manual and computer-based accounting systems.

After studying this chapter you should be able to meet these Learning Objectives:

1 **Explain the purpose of a system of internal control.**
2 **Identify several specific measures useful in achieving strong internal control.**
3 **Explain the role of purchase orders and receiving reports in verifying a purchase invoice.**
4 **Describe the advantage of recording purchase invoices by the net-price method.**
5 **Explain the nature of special journals and the reasons for their use.**
6 **Use special journals to record credit sales, credit purchases, and cash transactions.**
7 **Explain the usefulness of a subsidiary ledger and its relationship to a controlling account in the general ledger.**
8 **Describe several advantages of a computer-based accounting system.**

THE SYSTEM OF INTERNAL CONTROL

1 Explain the purpose of a system of internal control.

As defined in Chapter 1, a system of internal control includes all measures taken by an organization for the purposes of (1) protecting its resources against waste, fraud, or inefficient use, (2) ensuring the accuracy and reliability of accounting records,

(3) securing compliance with management's policies, and (4) evaluating the performance of individual departments. In short, the system of internal control includes all measures and procedures designed to cause the organization to operate in accordance with management's plans and policies.

Accounting controls and administrative controls

Internal control procedures fall into two broad categories: accounting controls and administrative controls. **Accounting controls** are those measures that relate directly to the protection of assets or to the reliability of accounting information. One example is the use of cash registers to create an immediate record of cash receipts. Another example is the policy of making an annual physical count of inventory even when a perpetual inventory system is in use.

Administrative controls are measures designed to increase operational efficiency, but that have **no direct bearing** upon the reliability of the accounting records. An example of an administrative control is a requirement that traveling salespeople submit reports showing the names of customers called upon each day. Another example is the requirement that airline pilots have annual medical examinations.

In this textbook, we will emphasize **internal accounting controls** — those controls that have a **direct bearing** upon the reliability of accounting records and accounting reports. Bear in mind, however, that sound administrative controls also play a vital role in the successful operation of a business.

Relationship between the accounting system and the system of internal control

The primary objective of an accounting system is to provide useful financial information. The objective of the system of internal control is to keep the business "on track," operating in accordance with the policies and plans of management. These two systems are closely related; in fact, each depends greatly upon the other.

The accounting system depends upon internal control procedures to ensure the **reliability** of accounting data. Many internal control procedures, on the other hand, make use of accounting data in keeping track of assets and monitoring the performance of departments. The need for adequate internal control explains the nature and the very existence of many accounting records, reports, documents, and procedures. Thus, the topic of internal control and the study of accounting go hand-in-hand.

Guidelines to achieving strong internal control

2 Identify several specific measures useful in achieving internal control.

Lines of responsibility. Every organization should indicate clearly the persons or departments responsible for such functions as sales, purchasing, receiving and inspecting incoming shipments, paying bills, and maintaining accounting records. The lines of authority and responsibility can be shown in an **organization chart.** (A partial organization chart is illustrated on the next page.) The organization

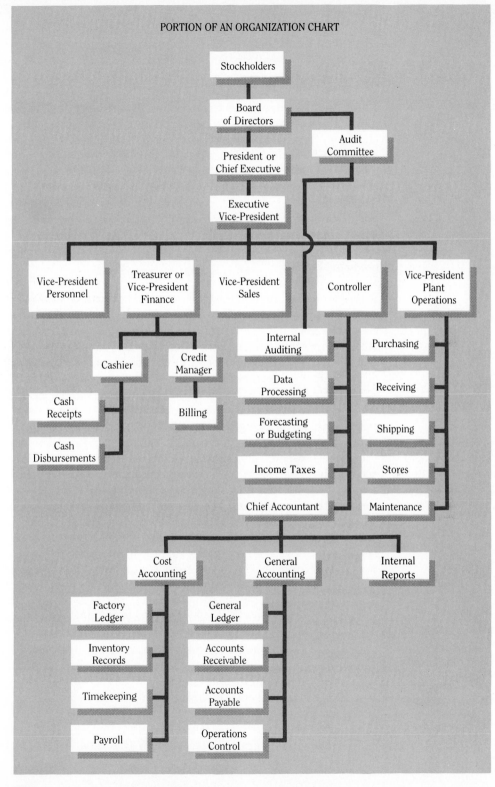

PORTION OF AN ORGANIZATION CHART

chart should be supported by written job descriptions and by procedures manuals that explain in detail the authority and responsibilities of each person or department appearing in the chart.

Established procedures for processing each type of transaction. If management is to direct the activities of a business according to plan, every transaction should go through four separate steps: it should be ***authorized, approved, executed,*** and ***recorded.*** For example, consider the sale of merchandise on credit. Top management has the authority and responsibility to ***authorize*** credit sales to categories of customers who meet certain standards. The manager of the credit department is responsible for ***approving*** a credit sale of a given dollar amount to a particular customer. The transaction is ***executed*** by the shipping department, which ships or delivers the merchandise to the customer. Finally, the transaction is ***recorded*** in the accounting department by debiting Accounts Receivable and crediting Sales.

Subdivision of duties. Perhaps the most important concept in achieving internal control is an appropriate subdivision — or separation — of duties. Responsibilities should be assigned so that ***no one person or department handles a transaction completely from beginning to end.*** When duties are divided in this manner, the work of one employee serves to verify that of another and any errors which occur tend to be detected promptly.

To illustrate this concept, let us review the typical procedures applied by a wholesaler in processing a credit sale. The sales department of the company is responsible for securing the order from the customer; the credit department must approve the customer's credit before the order is filled; the stock room assembles the goods ordered; the shipping department packs and ships the goods; and the accounting department records the transaction. Each department receives written evidence of the action of the other departments and reviews the documents describing the transaction to see that the actions taken correspond in all details. The shipping department, for instance, does not release the merchandise until after the credit department has approved the customer as a good credit risk. The accounting department does not record the sale until it has received documentary evidence that (1) an order was received from a customer, (2) the extension of credit was approved, and (3) the merchandise was shipped to the customer.

Accounting function separate from custody of assets. Perhaps the most basic separation of duties is the idea that an employee who has custody of an asset (or access to an asset) should ***not*** maintain the accounting record for that asset. If one person has custody of assets and also maintains the accounting records, there is both opportunity and incentive to falsify the records to conceal a shortage. However, the person with custody of the asset will not be inclined to waste it, steal it, or give it away if he or she is aware that another employee is maintaining a record of the asset.

The following diagram illustrates how this separation of duties contributes to strong internal control.

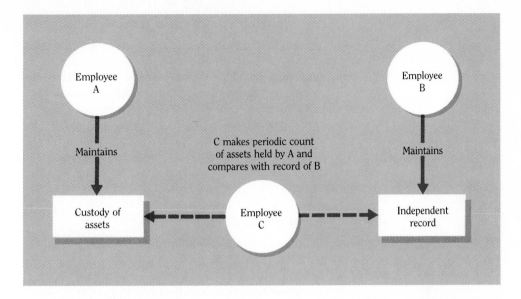

In this diagram Employee A has custody of assets and Employee B maintains an accounting record of the assets. Employee C periodically counts the assets and compares the count with the record maintained by B. This comparison should reveal any errors made by either A or B unless the two have collaborated to conceal an error or irregularity.

Prevention of fraud. If one employee is permitted to handle all aspects of a transaction, the danger of fraud is increased. Studies of fraud cases suggest that many individuals may be tempted into dishonest acts if given complete control of company property. Most of these persons, however, would not engage in fraud if doing so required collaboration with another employee. Losses through employee dishonesty occur in a variety of ways: merchandise may be stolen; payments by customers may be withheld; suppliers may be overpaid with a view to kickbacks to employees; and lower prices may be allowed to favored customers. The opportunities for fraud are almost endless if all aspects of a sale or purchase transaction are concentrated in the hands of one employee.

Other steps toward achieving internal control. Other important internal control measures include the following:

1 *Internal auditing.* Virtually every large organization has an internal auditing staff. The objectives of the internal auditors are to monitor and improve the system of internal control. Internal auditors test and evaluate both accounting controls and administrative controls in all areas of the organization and prepare reports to top management on their findings and recommendations.

2 *Financial forecasts.* A plan of operations is prepared each year setting goals for each division of the business, as, for example, the expected volume of sales,

amounts of expenses, and future cash balances. ***Actual*** results are compared with ***forecast*** amounts month by month. This comparison strengthens control because variations from planned results are investigated promptly.

3 ***Serially numbered documents.*** Documents such as checks, purchase orders, and sales invoices should be serially numbered. If a document is misplaced or concealed, the break in the sequence of numbers will call attention to the missing item.

4 ***Competent personnel.*** Even the best-designed system of internal control will not work well unless the people using it are competent. Competence and integrity of employees are in part developed through training programs, but they also are related to the policies for selection of personnel, and the adequacy of supervision.

The role of business documents

3 Explain the role of purchase orders and receiving reports in verifying a purchase invoice.

We have made the point that strong internal control requires subdivision of duties among the departments of the business. How does each department know that the other departments have fulfilled their responsibilities? The answer lies in the use of carefully designed ***business documents.*** Some of the more important business documents used in controlling purchases of merchandise are summarized below:

Business Document	Initiated by	Sent to
Purchase requisition		
Issued when quantity of goods on hand falls below established reorder point	Departmental sales managers or stores department	Original to purchasing department, copy to accounting department
Purchase order		
Issued when order is placed. Indicates type, quantities, and prices of merchandise ordered.	Purchasing department	Original to selling company (vendor, supplier), copies to department requisitioning goods and the accounting department
Invoice		
Confirms that goods have been shipped and requests payment	Seller (supplier)	Accounting department of buying company
Receiving report		
Based on count and inspection of goods received	Receiving department of buying company	Original to accounting department, copies to purchasing department and to department requisitioning goods
Invoice approval form		
Based upon the documents listed above; authorizes payment of the purchase invoice	Accounting department of buying company	Finance department, to support issuance of check. Returned to accounting department with a copy of the check

Purchase requisition. A purchase requisition is a request from the sales department or stores department (warehousing) for the purchasing department to order merchandise. Thus, the purchasing department is not authorized to order goods *unless it has first received a purchase requisition.* A copy of the purchase requisition is sent to the accounting department.

Purchase orders. Once a purchase requisition has been received, the purchasing department determines the lowest-cost supplier of the merchandise and places an order. This order is documented in a *purchase order.* A purchase order issued by Fairway Pro Shop to Adams Manufacturing Company is illustrated below:

A serially numbered purchase order

PURCHASE ORDER   Order No. 999

FAIRWAY PRO SHOP
10 Fairway Avenue, San Francisco, California

To: Adams Manufacturing Company   Date Nov. 10, 19—

    19 Union Street   Ship via Jones Truck Co.

    Kansas City, Missouri   Terms: 2/10, n/30

Please enter our order for the following:

Quantity	Description	Price	Total
15 sets	Model S irons	$120.00	$1,800.00
50 dozen	X3Y Shur-Par golf balls	14.00	700.00
			$2,500.00

Fairway Pro Shop

By *D. D. McCarthy*

Several copies of a purchase order are usually prepared. The original is sent to the supplier; it constitutes an authorization to deliver the merchandise and to submit a bill based on the prices listed. A second copy is sent to the department that initiated the purchase requisition to show that the requisition has been acted upon. Another copy is sent to the accounting department of the buying company.

The issuance of a purchase order does not call for any entries in the accounting records of either the prospective buyer or seller. The company which receives an order does not consider that a sale has been made *until the merchandise is delivered.* At that point ownership of the goods changes, and both buyer and seller should make accounting entries to record the transaction.

Invoices. When a manufacturer or wholesaler receives an order for its products, it takes two actions. One is to ship the goods to the customer and the other is to send the customer an invoice. By the act of shipping the merchandise, the seller is giving up ownership of one type of asset, inventory; by issuing the invoice the seller is recording ownership of another form of asset, an account receivable.

An invoice contains a description of the goods being sold, the quantities, prices, credit terms, and method of shipment. The illustration below shows an invoice issued by Adams Manufacturing Company in response to the previously illustrated purchase order from Fairway Pro Shop.

INVOICE

ADAMS MANUFACTURING COMPANY   Invoice no. 782
19 Union Street
Kansas City, Missouri

Sold to: Fairway Pro Shop   Invoice date Nov. 15, 19___

         10 Fairway Avenue   Your order no. 999

         San Francisco, Calif.   Date shipped Nov. 15, 19___

Shipped to Same   Shipped via Jones Truck Co.

Terms 2/10, n/30

Quantity	Description	Price	Amount
15 sets	Model S irons	$120.00	$1,800.00
50 dozen	X3Y Shur-Par golf balls	14.00	700.00
			$2,500.00

From the viewpoint of the seller, an invoice is a **sales invoice;** from the buyer's viewpoint it is a **purchase invoice.** The invoice is the basis for an entry in the accounting records of **both** the seller and the buyer because it evidences the **transfer of ownership of goods.** At the time of issuing the invoice, the selling company makes an entry debiting Accounts Receivable and crediting Sales. The buying company however, does not record the invoice as a liability until the invoice has been approved for payment.

Receiving report. Evidence that the merchandise has been received in good condition must be obtained from the receiving department. It is the function of the receiving department to receive all incoming goods, to inspect them as to quality and condition, and to determine the quantities received by counting, measuring, or weighing. The receiving department should prepare a serially numbered report for each shipment received; one copy of this ***receiving report*** is sent to the accounting department for use in approving the invoice for payment.

Invoice approval form. The approval of the invoice in the accounting department is accomplished by comparing the purchase requisition, purchase order, the invoice, and the receiving report. Comparison of these documents establishes that the merchandise described in the invoice was actually ordered, has been received in good condition, and was billed at the prices specified in the purchase order.

The person who performs these comparisons then records the liability (debit Purchases, credit Accounts Payable) and signs an ***invoice approval form*** authorizing payment of the invoice by the finance department. One type of invoice approval form, called a ***voucher,*** is illustrated in the following chapter.

Debit and credit memoranda (debit memos, credit memos). If merchandise purchased on account is unsatisfactory and is to be returned to the supplier (or if a price reduction is agreed upon), a ***debit memorandum*** may be prepared by the purchasing company and sent to the supplier. The debit memorandum informs the supplier that his or her account is being debited (reduced) by the buyer and explains the circumstances.

Upon being informed of the return of damaged merchandise (or having agreed to a reduction in price), the seller will send the buyer a ***credit memorandum*** indicating that the account receivable from the buyer has been credited (reduced).

Notice that issuing a credit memorandum has the same effect upon a customer's account as does receiving payment from the customer — that is, the account receivable is credited (reduced). Thus, an employee with authority to issue credit memoranda ***should not be allowed to handle cash receipts from customers.*** If both of these duties were assigned to the same employee, that person could abstract some of the cash collected from customers and conceal this theft by issuing credit memoranda.

Recording purchase invoices at net price

4 Describe the advantage of recording purchase invoices by the net-price method.

Most well-managed companies have a policy of taking all purchase discounts offered. The recording of purchase invoices at their gross amount and making payment of a reduced amount within the discount period was described in Chapter 5. Some companies which regularly take advantage of all available purchase discounts prefer the alternative method of recording purchase invoices at the ***net amount*** after discount rather than at the gross amount. If the amount which the buyer intends to pay is the invoice amount ***minus a purchase discount,*** why not record this net amount as the liability at the time the invoice is received? For example, if Fairway Pro Shop receives a $10,000 purchase invoice from Gator Sportswear bearing terms of 2/10, n/30, the entry could be

Entry for purchase: net-price method

Nov.	3	Purchases 9,800	
		Accounts Payable	9,800
		To record purchase invoice from Gator Sportswear less 2% cash discount available.	

Assuming that the invoice is paid within 10 days, the entry for the payment is as follows:

Nov. 13 Accounts Payable... 9,800
    Cash   9,800
   **To record payment of $10,000 invoice from Gator Sportswear less 2%
   cash discount.**

Through oversight or carelessness, the purchasing company occasionally may fail to make payment of an invoice within the 10-day discount period. If such a delay occurred in paying the invoice from Gator Sportswear, the full amount of the invoice would have to be paid rather than the recorded liability of $9,800. The journal entry to record the late payment on, say, December 3, is as follows:

Dec. 3 Accounts Payable... 9,800
   Purchase Discounts Lost.. 200
    Cash   10,000
   **To record payment of invoice and loss of discount by delaying
   payment beyond the discount period.**

Under this method the cost of goods purchased is properly recorded at $9,800, and the additional payment of $200 caused by failure to pay the invoice promptly is placed in a special expense account designed to attract the attention of management. The gross-price method of recording invoices described in Chapter 5 shows the amount of purchase discounts **taken** each period; the **net-price method** now under discussion shows the amount of purchase discounts **lost** each period. The net-price method has the advantage of drawing the attention of management to a breakdown in internal control. The fact that purchase discounts have been taken does not require attention by management, but discounts lost because of inefficiency in processing accounts payable do call for managerial investigation.

Under the net-price method, inefficiency and delay in paying invoices is not concealed by including the lost discount in the cost of merchandise purchased. The purchases are stated at the net price available if all discounts had been taken; any purchase discounts lost are shown separately in the income statement as an operating expense.

Limitations and cost of internal control

Although internal control is highly effective in increasing the reliability of accounting data and in protecting assets, no system of internal control is foolproof. Controls based upon a subdivision of duties may be defeated — at least temporarily by collusion among two or more dishonest employees. Carelessness by employees and misunderstanding of instructions can cause a breakdown in controls. Finally, the question of cost of controls cannot be ignored. Too elaborate a system of internal control may entail greater expense than is justified by the protection gained. For this reason, a system of internal control must be tailored to meet the needs of an individual business.

TAILORING AN ACCOUNTING SYSTEM TO THE NEEDS OF A LARGER BUSINESS

An accounting system consists of the business documents, journals, ledgers, procedures, and internal controls needed to produce reliable financial statements and other accounting reports. Accounting systems in common use range from simple systems in which accounting records are maintained by hand to sophisticated systems in which accounting records are maintained on magnetic discs. The accounting system used in any given company should be tailored to the size and to the information needs of the company.

In the early chapters of an introductory accounting book, basic accounting principles can be discussed most conveniently in terms of a small business with only a few customers and suppliers. This simplified model of a business has been used in preceding chapters to demonstrate the analysis and recording of the more common types of business transactions.

The recording procedures illustrated thus far call for recording each transaction by an entry in the general journal, and then posting each debit and credit from the general journal to the proper account in the ledger. We must now face the practical problem of streamlining and speeding up this basic accounting system so that the accounting department can keep pace with the rapid flow of transactions in a sizable business.

Two devices used in tailoring an accounting system to the needs of a business are *special journals* and *subsidiary ledgers.* These specialized accounting records are most easily illustrated in the context of a manual accounting system. However, special journals and subsidiary ledgers may be used to even greater advantage in computer-based accounting systems.

Special journals

5 Explain the nature of special journals and the reasons for their use.

We have seen that any type of business transaction may be recorded in a general journal. A *special journal,* however, is an accounting record designed to handle the recording of *only one type* of business transaction. In order to record *all* types of business transactions, a business usually needs several special journals, as well as a general journal.

Why use a separate special journal to record a particular type of business transaction? The answer is that transactions may be recorded *much more quickly* in a journal that is specially designed for recording that particular type of transaction. Also, the amount of time spent posting transaction data may be greatly reduced. Finally, the use of special journals permits the work of recording transactions to be divided among several employees. Each special journal may be maintained by a different person.

The savings of time and effort are greatest when a separate special journal is designed to record each type of business transaction which **occurs frequently.** In most businesses, the great majority of transactions (perhaps 90 to 95%) fall into four types. These four types of transactions and the four corresponding special journals are listed below:

Type of Transaction	Name of Special Journal
Sales of merchandise on account	Sales journal
Purchases of merchandise on account	Purchases journal
Receipts of cash	Cash receipts journal
Payments of cash	Cash payments journal

In addition to these special journals, a general journal still must be used to record those transactions which **do not fit** into any of the special journals. The general journal has been illustrated in preceding chapters. The adjective **"general"** is used to distinguish this multipurpose journal from the special journals. We will now discuss the four special journals mentioned above, along with the related concept of subsidiary ledgers.

Sales journal

6 Use special journals to record credit sales, credit purchases, and cash transactions.

Shown below is a **sales journal** containing entries for **all sales on account** made during November by the Seaside Company. Whenever merchandise is sold on credit, several copies of a sales invoice are prepared. The information listed on a sales invoice usually includes the date of the sale, the serial number of the invoice, the customer's name, the amount of the sale, and the credit terms. One copy of the sales invoice is used as the basis for entry in the sales journal.

Sales Journal

Page 1

Date		Account Debited	Invoice No.	✓	Amount
19__					
Nov	2	Jill Adams	301	✓	450
	4	Harold Black	302	✓	1,000
	5	Robert Cross	303	✓	975
	11	H. R. Davis	304	✓	620
	18	C. D. Early	305	✓	900
	23	Mary Frost	306	✓	400
	29	D. H. Gray	307	✓	11,850
					16,195
					(5)(41)

Notice that the illustrated sales journal contains special columns for recording each of these aspects of the sales transaction, except the credit terms. If the business offers different credit terms to different customers, a column is inserted in the sales journal to show the terms of sale. Seaside Company, however, makes all credit sales on terms of 2/10, n/30; consequently, there is no need to write the credit terms as part of each entry.

Only sales on credit are entered in the sales journal. When merchandise is sold for cash, the transaction is recorded in a *cash receipts* journal, which is illustrated later in this chapter.

Advantages of the sales journal. Note that each of the seven sales transactions is recorded on a single line. Each entry consists of a debit to a customer's account; the offsetting credit to the Sales account is understood without being written, because sales on account are the only transactions recorded in this special journal.

An entry in a sales journal *need not include an explanation;* if more information about the transaction is desired it can be obtained by referring to the file copy of the sales invoice. The invoice number is listed in the sales journal as part of each entry. The one-line entry in the sales journal requires much less writing than would be necessary to record a sales transaction in the general journal. Since there may be several hundred or several thousand sales transactions each month, the time saved in recording transactions in this streamlined manner becomes quite important.

Another advantage of the special journal for sales is the great saving of time in posting credits to the Sales account. Remember that every amount entered in the sales journal represents a credit to Sales. In the illustrated sales journal on page 230, there are seven transactions (and in practice there might be 700). Instead of posting a separate credit to the Sales account for each sales transaction, we can wait until the end of the month and make *one posting* to the Sales account for the *total* of the amounts recorded in the sales journal.

In the illustrated sales journal for November, the sales on account totaled $16,195. On November 30 this amount is posted as a credit to the Sales account, and the ledger account number for Sales, (41), is entered under the total figure in the sales journal to show that the posting operation has been performed. The total sales figure is also posted as a debit to ledger account no. 5, Accounts Receivable.

Notice the check marks (✓) in the column just to the left of the dollar amounts. These check marks indicate that the amount of the sale has been posted to the customer's account in the accounts receivable *subsidiary ledger.*

Controlling accounts and subsidiary ledgers

7 Explain the usefulness of a subsidiary ledger and its relationship to a controlling account in the general ledger.

In preceding chapters all transactions involving accounts receivable from customers have been posted to a single account entitled Accounts Receivable. Under this procedure, however, it is not easy to look up the amount receivable from a given customer. In practice, businesses which sell goods on credit *maintain a separate account receivable for each customer.* If there are 4,000 customers, this would require a ledger with 4,000 accounts receivable, in addition to the accounts for other assets, and for liabilities, owners' equity, revenue, and expenses. Such a ledger would be bulky and unwieldy. Also, the trial balance prepared from such a large ledger would be a very long one. If the trial balance showed the ledger to be out of balance, the task of locating the error or errors would be most difficult. All these factors indicate that it is not desirable to have too many accounts in one ledger. Fortunately, a simple solution is available; this solution is to **divide the ledger into several separate ledgers.**

In a business which has a large number of customers and a large number of creditors, it is customary to divide the ledger into three separate ledgers. All the accounts with **customers** are placed in alphabetical order in a separate ledger, called the **accounts receivable ledger.** All the accounts with **creditors** are arranged alphabetically in another ledger called the **accounts payable ledger.** Both of these ledgers are known as **subsidiary ledgers,** because they support and are controlled by the general ledger.

After placing the accounts receivable from customers in one subsidiary ledger and the accounts payable to creditors in a second subsidiary ledger, we have left in the original ledger all the revenue and expense accounts and also all the balance sheet accounts except those with individual customers and individual creditors. This ledger is called the **general ledger,** to distinguish it from the subsidiary ledgers.

When the numerous individual accounts receivable from customers are placed in a subsidiary ledger, an account entitled Accounts Receivable continues to be maintained in the general ledger. This account shows the **total amount due from all customers;** in other words, this single **controlling account** in the general ledger represents the numerous customers' accounts which make up the subsidiary ledger. The general ledger is still in balance because the controlling account, Accounts Receivable, has a balance equal to the total of the individual customers' accounts.

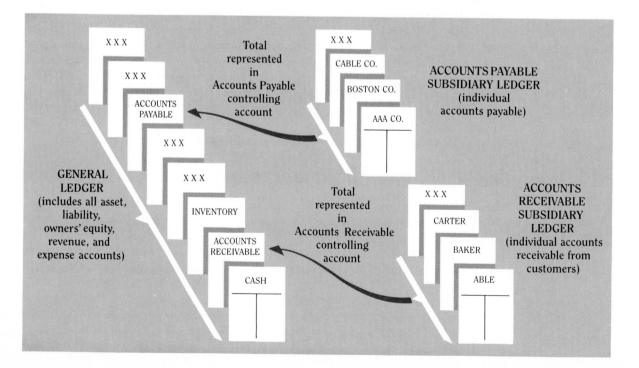

Agreement of the controlling account with the sum of the accounts receivable in the subsidiary ledger also provides assurance of accuracy in the subsidiary ledger.

A controlling account entitled Accounts Payable is also kept in the general ledger in place of the numerous accounts with creditors which form the accounts payable subsidiary ledger. Because the two controlling accounts represent the total amounts receivable from customers and payable to creditors, a trial balance can be prepared from the general ledger alone. The following illustration shows the relationship of the subsidiary ledgers to the controlling accounts in the general ledger.

Posting to subsidiary ledgers and to controlling accounts. To illustrate the posting of subsidiary ledgers and of controlling accounts, let us refer again to the sales journal illustrated on page 230. Each debit to a customer's account is posted currently during the month from the sales journal to the customer's account in the accounts receivable ledger. The accounts in this subsidiary ledger are usually kept in alphabetical order and are not numbered. When a posting is made to a customer's account, a check mark (✓) is placed in the sales journal as evidence that the posting has been made to the subsidiary ledger.

At month-end the sales journal is totaled. The total amount of sales for the month, **$16,195,** is posted as a credit to the Sales account and also as a debit to the controlling account, Accounts Receivable, in the general ledger. The controlling account will, therefore, equal the total of all the customers' accounts in the subsidiary ledger.

The diagram on page 234 shows the day-to-day posting of individual entries from the sales journal to the subsidiary ledger. The diagram also shows the month-end posting of the total of the sales journal to the two general ledger accounts affected, Accounts Receivable and Sales. Note that the amount of the monthly debit to the controlling account is equal to the *sum of the debits* posted to the subsidiary ledger.

Other subsidiary ledgers. In this chapter, we discuss only two subsidiary ledgers — accounts receivable and accounts payable. However, subsidiary ledgers are used for any account in which detailed information is needed about the *individual items that comprise the account balance.* The following schedule lists some of the general ledger accounts often supported by subsidiary ledgers and also indicates the unit of organization used within these subsidiary ledgers.

Controlling Account in the General Ledger	Unit of Organization within the Subsidiary Ledger
Cash	Each bank account
Notes receivable	Copy of each note receivable
Inventory	Each type of merchandise
Plant assets	Each asset (or category of assets)
Notes payable	Copy of each note payable
Capital stock	Individual stockholders (shows number of shares owned)
Any revenue or expense	The revenue or expense on a departmental basis

These other subsidiary ledgers will be discussed in later chapters.

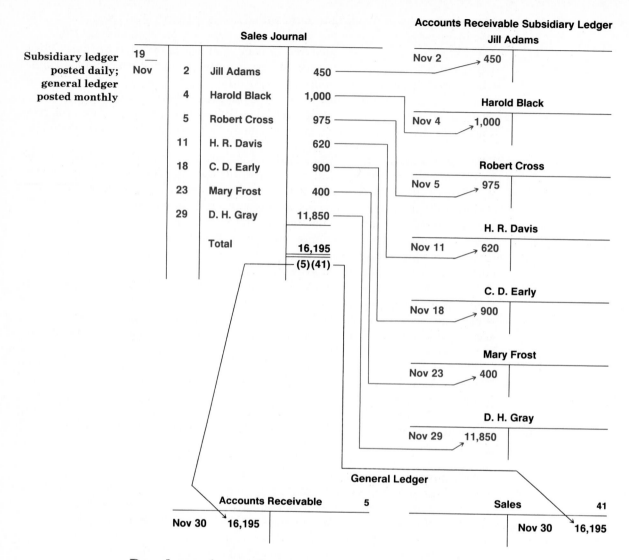

Subsidiary ledger posted daily; general ledger posted monthly

Purchases journal

The handling of purchase transactions when a purchases journal is used follows a pattern quite similar to the one described for the sales journal.

The purchases journal shown on the following page includes **all purchases of merchandise on credit** during the month by the Seaside Company. The date of each purchase invoice is shown in a separate column, because the cash discount period begins on this date. Seaside Company follows a policy of recording purchase invoices at their **gross amount.** The five entries for purchases are posted as they occur during the month as credits to the creditors' accounts in the subsidiary ledger for accounts payable. As each posting is completed a check mark (✓) is placed in the purchases journal.

At the end of each month, the Amount column in the purchases journal is totaled. The total amount of purchases for the month, $7,250, is posted in the general ledger as a debit to the Purchases account and also as a credit to the Accounts Payable controlling account. The account numbers for Purchases (50) and for Accounts Payable (21) are then placed in parentheses below the column total of the purchases journal to show that the postings have been made, as shown below.

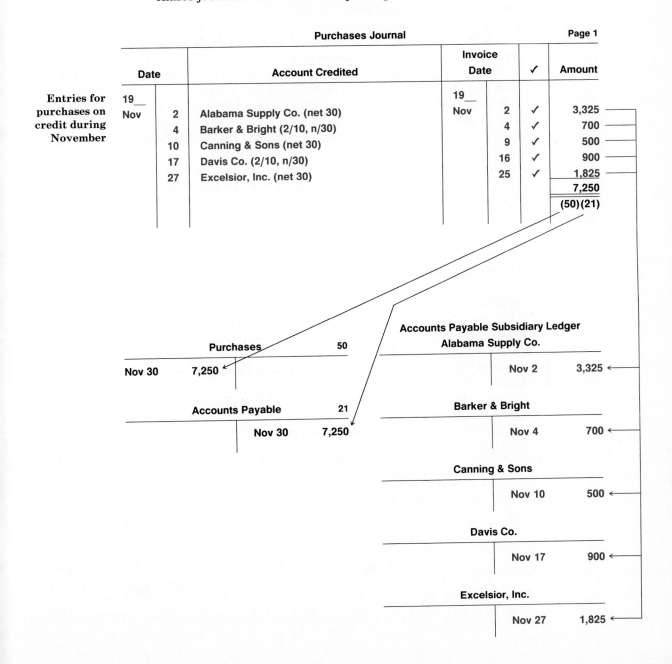

Purchases Journal   Page 1

Date		Account Credited	Invoice Date		✓	Amount
19__			19__			
Nov	2	Alabama Supply Co. (net 30)	Nov	2	✓	3,325
	4	Barker & Bright (2/10, n/30)		4	✓	700
	10	Canning & Sons (net 30)		9	✓	500
	17	Davis Co. (2/10, n/30)		16	✓	900
	27	Excelsior, Inc. (net 30)		25	✓	1,825
						7,250
						(50)(21)

Entries for purchases on credit during November

Purchases   50

Nov 30   7,250

Accounts Payable   21

                Nov 30   7,250

Accounts Payable Subsidiary Ledger
Alabama Supply Co.

                Nov 2   3,325

Barker & Bright

                Nov 4   700

Canning & Sons

                Nov 10   500

Davis Co.

                Nov 17   900

Excelsior, Inc.

                Nov 27   1,825

The preceding diagram shows the day-to-day posting of individual entries from the purchases journal to the accounts with creditors in the subsidiary ledger for accounts payable. The diagram also shows how the column total of the purchases journal is posted at the end of the month to the general ledger accounts, Purchases and Accounts Payable. One objective of this diagram is to emphasize that the amount of the monthly credit to the controlling account is equal to the *sum of the credits* posted to the subsidiary ledger.

Under the particular system being described, the only transactions recorded in the purchases journal are *purchases of merchandise on credit.* The term *merchandise* means goods acquired for resale to customers. If merchandise is purchased for cash rather than on credit, the transaction should be recorded in the *cash payments journal,* not in the purchases journal.

When assets *other than merchandise* are being acquired, the journal to be used depends upon whether a cash payment is made. If assets of this type are purchased for cash, the transaction is entered in the *cash payments journal;* if the transaction is on credit, the *general journal* is used. The purchases journal is *not* used to record the acquisition of these assets because the total of this journal is posted to the Purchases account, which is used in determining the cost of goods sold.

Cash receipts journal

All transactions involving the receipt of cash are recorded in the cash receipts journal. One common example is the sale of merchandise for cash. As each cash sale is made, it is rung up on a cash register. At the end of the day the total of the cash sales is computed by striking the total key on the register. This total is entered in the cash receipts journal, which therefore contains one entry for the total cash sales of the day. For other types of cash receipts, such as the collection of accounts receivable from customers, a separate journal entry may be made for each transaction.

The cash receipts journal illustrated on the following page contains entries for all of the November transactions of Seaside Company which involved the receipt of cash. These transactions are listed below:

Nov. 1 Issued an additional 7,500 shares of $10 par value capital stock in exchange for $75,000 cash.

Nov. 4 Sold merchandise for cash, $300.

Nov. 5 Sold merchandise for cash, $400.

Nov. 8 Collected from Jill Adams for sales invoice of Nov. 2, $450 less 2% cash discount.

Nov. 10 Sold a small portion of land not needed in business for a total price of $17,000, consisting of cash of $7,000 and a note receivable for $10,000. The cost of the land sold was $14,000; thus, a $3,000 gain was realized on the sale.

Nov. 12 Collected from Harold Black for sales invoice of Nov. 4, $1,000 less 2% cash discount.

Includes all transactions involving receipt of cash

Cash Receipts Journal

		Debits						Credits				
				Other Accounts				Accounts Receivable			Other Accounts	
Date	Explanation	Cash	Sales Discounts	Name	LP	Amount	Account Credited	✓	Amount	Sales	LP	Amount
19 Nov 1	Issued capital stock	75,000					Capital Stock				30	75,000
4	Cash sales	300								300		
5	Cash sales	400								400		
8	Invoice Nov. 2, less 2%	441	9				Jill Adams	✓	450			
10	Sale of land	7,000		Notes Receivable	3	10,000	Land				11	15,000
							Gain on Sale of Land				40	2,000
12	Invoice Nov. 4, less 2%	980	20				Harold Black	✓	1,000			
20	Invoice Nov. 18, less 2%	882	18				C. D. Early	✓	900			
27	Cash sales	125								125		
30	Obtained bank loan	4,000				10,000	Notes Payable				20	4,000
		89,128	47						2,350	825		96,000
		(1)	(43)			(X)			(5)	(41)		(X)

237

Nov. 20   Collected from C. D. Early for sales invoice of Nov. 18, $900 less 2% cash discount.

Nov. 27   Sold merchandise for cash, $125.

Nov. 30   Obtained $4,000 loan from bank. Issued a note payable in that amount.

Note that the cash receipts journal has three debit columns and three credit columns as follows:

Debits:

1 *Cash.* This column is used for every entry, because only those transactions which include the receipt of cash are entered in this special journal.

2 *Sales discounts.* This column is used to accumulate the sales discounts allowed during the month. Only one line of the cash receipts book is required to record a collection from a customer who takes advantage of a cash discount.

3 *Other accounts.* This third debit column is used for debits to any and all accounts other than cash and sales discounts, and space is provided for writing in the name of the account. For example, the entry of November 10 in the illustrated cash receipts journal shows that cash and a note receivable were obtained when land was sold. The amount of cash received, $7,000, is entered in the Cash debit column; the account title Notes Receivable is written in the Other Accounts debit column along with the amount of the debit to this account, $10,000. These two debits are offset by credit entries to Land, $15,000, and to Gain on Sale of Land, $2,000, in the Other Accounts credit column.

Credits:

1 *Accounts receivable.* This column is used to list the credits to customers' accounts as receivables are collected. The name of the customer is written in the space entitled Account Credited to the left of the Accounts Receivable column.

2 *Sales.* The existence of this column will save posting by permitting the accumulation of all sales for cash during the month and the posting of the column total at the end of the month as a credit to the Sales account.

3 *Other accounts.* This column is used for credits to any and all accounts other than Accounts Receivable and Sales. In some instances, a transaction may require credits to two accounts. Such cases are handled by using two lines of the special journal, as illustrated by the transaction of November 10, which required credits to both the Land account and to Gain on Sale of Land.

Posting the cash receipts journal. It is convenient to think of the posting of a cash receipts journal as being divided into two phases. The first phase consists of the daily posting of individual amounts throughout the month; the second phase consists of the posting of column totals at the end of the month.

Posting during the month. Daily posting of the Accounts Receivable credit column is desirable. Each amount is posted to an individual customer's account in the accounts receivable subsidiary ledger. A check mark (✓) is placed in the cash receipts journal alongside each item posted to a customer's account to show that the posting operation has been performed. When debits and credits to customers' accounts are posted daily, the current status of each customer's account is available for use in making decisions as to further granting of credit and as a guide to collection efforts on past-due accounts.

The debits and credits in the Other Accounts sections of the cash receipts journal may be posted daily or at convenient intervals during the month. If this portion of the posting work is done on a current basis, less detailed work will be left for the busy period at the end of the month. As the postings of individual items are made, the number of the ledger account debited or credited is entered in the LP (ledger page) column of the cash receipts journal opposite the item posted. Evidence is thus provided in the special journal as to which items have been posted.

Posting column totals at month-end. At the end of the month, the cash receipts journal is ruled as shown above. Before posting any of the column totals, it is first important to prove that *the sum of the debit column totals is equal to the sum of the credit column totals.*

After the totals of the cash receipts journal have been crossfooted, the following column totals are posted:

1 Cash debit column. Posted as a debit to the Cash account.
2 Sales Discounts debit column. Posted as a debit to the Sales Discounts account.
3 Accounts Receivable credit column. Posted as a credit to the controlling account, Accounts Receivable.
4 Sales credit column. Posted as a credit to the Sales account.

As each column total is posted to the appropriate account in the general ledger, the ledger account number is entered in parentheses just below the column total in the special journal. This notation shows that the column total has been posted and also indicates the account to which the posting was made. The totals of the Other Accounts columns in both the debit and credit sections of the special journal are not posted, because the amounts listed in the column affect various general ledger accounts and have already been posted as individual items. The symbol (**X**) is placed below the totals of these two columns to indicate that no posting is made.

Cash payments journal

Another widely used special journal is the cash payments journal, sometimes called the cash disbursements journal, in which *all payments of cash* are recorded. Among the more common of these transactions are payments of accounts payable to creditors, payment of operating expenses, and cash purchases of merchandise.

The cash payments journal illustrated on the following page contains entries for all November transactions of the Seaside Company which required the payment of cash. These transactions are listed on page 241.

Includes all transactions involving payment of cash

Cash Payments Journal

Date	Check No.	Payee	Credits: Cash	Credits: Purchase Discounts	Credits: Other Accounts Name	LP	Amount	Account Debited	Debits: Accounts Payable ✓	Amount	Purchases	LP	Debits: Other Accounts Amount
19— Nov 1	420	Westgate Mall	800					Store Rent Expense				54	800
2	421	Novelty Products	500								500		
8	422	Barker & Bright	686	14				Barker & Bright	✓	700			
9	423	Admiralty Escrow Co.	70,000		Notes Payable	20	30,000	Land				11	65,000
								Building				12	35,000
17	424	Payroll Services, Inc.	3,600					Salaries Expense				53	3,600
26	425	Davis Co.	882	18				Davis Co.	✓	900			
27	426	Coast Distributors, Inc.	400								400		
28	427	PaperWorld	650								650		
29	428	Daily Tribune	50					Advertising Expense				55	50
29	429	National Insurance Co.	720					Unexpired Insurance				6	720
			78,288	32			30,000			1,600	1,550		105,170
			(1)	(52)			(X)			(21)	(50)		(X)

Nov. 1 Paid to Westgate Mall rent on store building for November, $800.

Nov. 2 Purchased merchandise from Novelty Products for cash, $500.

Nov. 8 Paid Barker & Bright for invoice of Nov. 4, $700 less 2%.

Nov. 9 Bought land, $65,000, and building, $35,000, for future use in business. Paid cash of $70,000 and signed a promissory note for the balance of $30,000. (Land and building were acquired in a single transaction.)

Nov. 17 Paid salaries, $3,600. (Issued one check for entire payroll to Payroll Services, Inc.)

Nov. 26 Paid Davis Co. for invoice of Nov. 16, $900 less 2%.

Nov. 27 Purchased merchandise from Coast Distributors, Inc., for cash, $400.

Nov. 28 Purchased merchandise from PaperWorld for cash, $650.

Nov. 29 Paid for newspaper advertising, in the Daily Tribune, $50.

Nov. 29 Paid National Insurance Co. for one-year insurance policy, $720.

Note in the illustrated cash payments journal that the three credit columns are located to the left of the three debit columns; any sequence of columns is satisfactory in a special journal as long as the column headings clearly distinguish debits from credits. The Cash column is often placed first in both the cash receipts journal and the cash payments journal because it is the column used in every transaction.

Good internal control over cash disbursements requires that all payments be made by check. The checks are serially numbered and as each transaction is entered in the cash payments journal, the check number is listed in a special column provided just to the right of the date column. An unbroken sequence of check numbers in this column gives assurance that every check issued has been recorded in the accounting records.

Posting the cash payments journal. The posting of the cash payments journal falls into the same two phases already described for the cash receipts journal. The first phase consists of the daily posting of entries in the Accounts Payable debit column to the individual accounts of creditors in the accounts payable subsidiary ledger. Check marks (✓) are entered opposite these items to show that the posting has been made. If a creditor telephones to inquire about any aspect of its account, information on all purchases and payments made to date is readily available in the accounts payable subsidiary ledger.

The individual debit and credit entries in the Other Accounts columns of the cash payment journal may be posted daily or at convenient intervals during the month. As the posting of these individual items are made, the number of the ledger account debited or credited is entered in the LP (ledger page) column of the cash payments journal opposite the item posted.

The second phase of posting the cash payments journal is performed at the end of the month. When all the transactions of the month have been journalized, the cash payments journal is ruled as shown in our illustration, and the six money columns are totaled. The equality of debits and credits is then proved before posting.

After the totals of the cash payments journal have been proved to be in balance, the totals of the columns for Cash, Purchase Discounts, Accounts Payable, and Purchases are posted to the corresponding accounts in the general ledger. The numbers of the accounts to which these postings are made are listed in parentheses just below the respective column totals in the cash payments journal. The totals of the Other Accounts columns in both the debit and credit section of this special journal are not to be posted, and the symbol **(X)** is placed below the totals of these two columns to indicate that no posting is required.

The general journal

When all transactions involving cash or the purchase and sale of merchandise are recorded in special journals, only a few types of transactions remain to be entered in the general journal. Examples include the declaration of dividends, the purchase or sale of plant and equipment on credit, the return of merchandise for credit to a supplier, and the return of merchandise by customers for credit to their accounts. The general journal is also used for adjusting and closing entries at the end of the accounting period.

The following transactions of the Seaside Company during November could not conveniently be handled in any of the four special journals and were therefore entered in the general journal.

Nov. 25   A customer, Mary Frost, returned for credit $50 worth of merchandise that had been sold to her on Nov. 23.

Nov. 28   The Seaside Company returned to a supplier, Excelsior, Inc., for credit $300 worth of the merchandise purchased on Nov. 27.

Nov. 29   Purchased for use in the business office equipment costing $1,225. Agreed to make payment within 30 days to XYZ Equipment Co.

General Journal   Page 1

Date		Account Titles and Explanation	LP	DR	CR
19__					
Nov	25	Sales Returns and Allowances	42	50	
		Accounts Receivable, Mary Frost	5/✓		50
		Allowed credit to customer for return of merchandise from sale of Nov. 23.			
	28	Accounts Payable, Excelsior, Inc..	21/✓	300	
		Purchase Returns and Allowances	51		300
		Returned to supplier for credit a portion of merchandise purchased on Nov. 27.			
	28	Office Equipment	14	1,225	
		Accounts Payable, XYZ Equipment Co.	21/✓		1,225
		Purchased office equipment on 30-day credit.			

Transactions which do not "fit" in any of the special journals

Each of the preceding three entries includes a debit or credit to a controlling account (Accounts Receivable or Accounts Payable) and also identifies by name a particular creditor or customer. When a ***controlling account*** is debited or credited by a general journal entry, the debit or credit must be posted **twice:** one posting to the controlling account in the **general ledger** and another posting to a customer's account or a creditor's account in a **subsidiary ledger.** This double posting is necessary to keep the controlling account in agreement with the subsidiary ledger.

For example, in the illustrated entry of November 25 for the return of merchandise by a customer, the credit part of the entry is posted twice:

1 To the Accounts Receivable controlling account in the general ledger; this posting is evidence by listing the account number (5) in the LP column of the general ledger.
2 To the account of Mary Frost in the subsidiary ledger for accounts receivable; this posting is indicated by the check mark (✓) placed in the LP (ledger page) column of the general journal.

Showing the source of postings in ledger accounts

When a general journal and several special journals are in use, the ledger accounts should indicate the book of original entry from which each debit and credit was posted. An identifying symbol is placed opposite each entry in the reference column of the account. The symbols used in this text are as follows:

S1	meaning page 1 of the Sales Journal
P1	meaning page 1 of the Purchases Journal
CR1	meaning page 1 of the Cash Receipts Journal
CP1	meaning page 1 of the Cash Payments Journal
J1	meaning page 1 of the General Journal

The following illustration shows a typical customer's account in a subsidiary ledger for accounts receivable:

			Aaron, Henry			Credit limit $2,000
Date			**Ref**	**Debit**	**Credit**	**Balance**
19__						
July	1		S2	400		400
	20		S3	200		600
Aug	4		CR2		400	200
	15		S6	120		320

Notice that the Reference column shows the source of each debit and credit entry. Similar references are entered in general ledger accounts.

Reconciling subsidiary ledgers with controlling accounts

We have made the point that the balance in a controlling account should be equal to the sum of the balances of the related subsidiary ledger accounts. Proving the equality is termed **reconciling** the subsidiary ledger with its controlling account.

This process may bring to light errors in either the subsidiary ledger or in the controlling account.

The first step in reconciling a subsidiary ledger is to prepare a schedule of the balances of the subsidiary ledger accounts. For example, the balances in Seaside Company's accounts receivable subsidiary ledger at November 30 are shown below. The total of this schedule should agree with the balance in the controlling account in the general ledger.

Schedule of Accounts Receivable
November 30, 19__

Robert Cross..	$ 975
H. R. Davis...	620
Mary Frost...	350
D. H. Gray	11,850
Total (should equal balance of the controlling account)	$13,795

Reconciling subsidiary ledgers with their controlling accounts is an important internal control procedure and should be performed at least once a month. This procedure may disclose such errors in the subsidiary ledger as failure to post transactions, transposition or slide errors, or mathematical errors in determining the balances of specific accounts receivable or accounts payable. However, this procedure will *not* disclose an entry which was posted to the wrong account within the subsidiary ledger.

If the subsidiary ledger and controlling account are *not* in agreement, the error may be difficult to find. The disagreement may be caused by an incorrect posting or by an error in the computation of an account balance. Thus, we may need to verify postings and recompute account balances until the error is found. Fortunately, most businesses use computer programs to maintain accounts receivable records. These programs have built-in internal control procedures that effectively prevent differences between amounts posted to the subsidiary ledger and to the related controlling account.

Variations in special journals

The number of columns to be included in each special journal and the number of special journals to be used will depend upon the nature of the particular business and especially upon the volume of the various kinds of transactions. For example, the desirability of including a Sales Discounts column in the cash receipts journal depends upon whether a business offers discounts to its customers for prompt payment.

A retail store may find that customers frequently return merchandise for credit. To record efficiently this large volume of sales returns, the store may establish a special sales returns and allowances journal. A special purchase returns and allowances journal may also be desirable if returns of goods to suppliers occur frequently.

Special journals should be regarded as laborsaving devices which may be designed with any number of columns appropriate to the needs of the particular business. A business will usually benefit by establishing a special journal for any type of transaction that *occurs quite frequently.*

COMPUTER-BASED ACCOUNTING SYSTEMS

The concepts of special journals and subsidiary ledgers apply to computer-based accounting systems as well as manual systems. In fact, special journals and subsidiary ledgers are far easier to maintain in computerized systems. We have stressed that two purposes of special journals are to reduce the amount of time involved in writing journal entries and posting to ledger accounts. In a computer-based system, the accountant need only enter the data needed for the computer to prepare journal entries. All the writing and all the posting to general ledger and subsidiary ledger accounts is then handled by machine with no further human effort.

Recording retail sales — computers reduce the work

The *point-of-sale terminals* now prominent in many retail establishments greatly reduce the work involved in accounting for sales transactions. Many of these terminals use an optical scanner or other electronic device to "read" magnetically coded labels attached to the merchandise. As the merchandise is passed over the optical scanner, the code is sent instantaneously to the computer. From the code number, the computer is able to identify the item being sold, record the amount of the sale, and transfer the cost of the item from the Inventory account to the Cost of Goods Sold account. If the transaction is a credit sale, the salesclerk enters the customer's credit card number in the electronic register. This number enables the computer to update instantly the customer's account in the subsidiary ledger.

Note that all of the accounting is done automatically as the salesclerk rings up the sale. Thus any number of transactions can be recorded and posted with virtually no manual work. At the end of each day, the computer prints a complete sales journal along with up-to-date balances for the general ledger and subsidiary ledger accounts relating to sales transactions.

Advantages of computer-based systems

8 Describe several advantages of a computer-based accounting system.

The primary advantage of the computer is its incredible speed. The time needed for a computer to post a transaction or determine an account balance is but a few millionths of a second. This speed creates several advantages over manual accounting systems, including the following:

1 *Large amounts of data can be processed quickly and efficiently.* Large businesses may engage in tens of thousands of transactions per day. In processing such a large volume of data, computers can save vast amounts of time in each step of the accounting process, including the recording of transactions, posting to ledger accounts, and preparing of accounting records, schedules, and reports.

2 ***Account balances may be kept up-to-date.*** The speed with which data may be processed by a computer enables businesses to keep subsidiary ledger accounts, perpetual inventory records, and most general ledger accounts continually up-to-date.

3 ***Additional information may be developed at virtually no additional cost.*** On page 230 we illustrated the type of sales journal that might be prepared in a manual accounting system. A similar journal can be maintained in a computerized system. However, the computer can also rearrange this information to show daily sales totals for each sales department, for each salesperson, and for specific products. Time and cost considerations often make the preparation of such supplementary information impractical in a manual accounting system.

4 ***Instant feedback may be available as transactions are taking place.*** In ***online, real-time (OLRT)*** computer systems, the employee executing a transaction may have a terminal which is in direct communication with the computer. Thus, the employee has immediate access to accounting information useful in executing the current transaction.

● **CASE IN POINT** ● The electronic cash registers now found in many department stores are point-of-sale terminals in direct communication with the store's computer system. When a salesperson makes a credit sale to a customer who is using a store credit card, the salesperson enters the credit card number into the terminal. The computer compares this number to a list of cancelled or stolen credit cards and also determines whether the current sales transaction would cause the customer's account balance to exceed a predetermined credit limit. If any of these procedures indicate that credit should not be extended to the customer, the computer notifies the salesperson not to make the credit sale.

---

5 ***Additional internal control procedures may be possible in a computer-based system.*** Approval of each credit sale, described in the preceding ***Case in point,*** is but one example of an internal control procedure that makes use of the unique capabilities of the computer. Such a control procedure may not be practical in a manual system, especially if the accounts receivable subsidiary ledger is not kept continually up-to-date.

END-OF-CHAPTER REVIEW

Summary of chapter learning objectives

1 Explain the purpose of a system of internal control.

A system of internal control includes all measures to (1) protect assets from waste, fraud, or inefficient use, (2) ensure the reliability of accounting data, (3) obtain compliance with company policies, and (4) evaluate performance. In short, the system of internal control attempts to keep the entire business organization operating in accordance with management's plans and policies.

2 Identify several specific measures used in achieving strong internal control.

Among the internal control measures emphasized in this chapter were: establishing clear lines of responsibility, establishing routine procedures for processing each type of transaction, appropriate subdivision of duties, separation of the accounting function from custody of assets, the use of business documents, and the use of the "net-price" method of recording purchase invoices.

Other internal control measures discussed, but given less emphasis, include internal auditing, the use of financial forecasts, serially numbered documents, the need for competent personnel, separating responsibility for handling cash from authority to issue credit memoranda, and reconciling subsidiary ledgers to the controlling accounts.

3 Explain the role of purchase orders and receiving reports in verifying a purchase invoice.

A purchase invoice is a bill for purchased merchandise. The purchase order is prepared by the buyer's purchasing department when the order is placed, and the receiving report is prepared by the receiving department when the goods are received. The buyer's accounting department compares these documents before recording the purchase or approving payment of the invoice.

Comparing the purchase invoice to the purchase order verifies (a) the type and quantity of goods ordered, and (b) the prices that the buyer had agreed to pay. Comparing the invoice to the receiving report indicates that the merchandise was received in good condition.

4 Describe the advantage of recording purchase invoices by the net-price method.

When purchases are recorded at the net amount, purchase discounts *lost* are recorded in a separate account and are promptly brought to management's attention. When purchases are recorded at the gross amount, only those discounts *taken* are recorded in the accounting records. Thus, discounts passed up are concealed in the cost of purchases, rather than being highlighted.

5 Explain the nature of special journals and the reasons for their use.

Special journals are accounting records specially designed for efficiently journalizing a particular type of business transaction. The reasons for using special journals are (1) to divide the task of recording business transactions among several different employees, and (2) to minimize the amount of work involved in recording and posting business transactions which occur frequently.

6 Use special journals to record credit sales, credit purchases, and cash transactions.

All sales on credit are recorded in the sales journal, and all purchases of merchandise on account are recorded in the purchases journal. Both of these types of transactions affect only two ledger accounts. All transactions involving the receipt of cash are recorded in the cash receipts journal, and all transactions requiring cash payments are recorded in the cash payments journal.

7 Explain the usefulness of a subsidiary ledger and its relationship to a controlling account in the general ledger.

A subsidiary ledger provides detailed information about the individual items which comprise the balance of a general ledger account. Consider, for example, the general ledger account entitled Accounts Receivable. This account shows the total amount of a company's accounts receivables from all its customers. While this total figure is useful in preparing financial statements, it does not show the amounts owed by specific individuals. Thus, it does not provide the information needed to send monthly statements to individual customers. The accounts receivable subsidiary ledger, on the other hand, includes a separate account showing the amount receivable from each customer. A subsidiary ledger also is maintained for accounts payable, so that the business will have a record of the amount owed to each individual creditor.

The sum of the account balances in a subsidiary ledger is equal to the balance of the related controlling account in the general ledger.

8 Describe several advantages of a computer-based accounting system.

The incredible speed with which information is processed in a computer-based accounting system offers numerous advantages, including (1) processing large amounts of data quickly and efficiently, (2) keeping account balances up-to-date, (3) developing additional data at virtually no additional cost, (4) providing instant "feedback" as transactions are taking place, and (5) allowing the application of many internal control procedures that might not be practical in a manual accounting system.

Key terms introduced or emphasized in chapter 6

Accounting control. An internal control procedure that **relates directly** to the protection of assets or to the reliability of accounting records.

Accounts payable ledger. A subsidiary ledger containing an account with each supplier or vendor. The total of the ledger agrees with the general ledger controlling account, Accounts Payable.

Accounts receivable ledger. A subsidiary ledger containing an account with each credit customer. The total of the ledger agrees with the general ledger controlling account, Accounts Receivable.

Administrative control. An internal control procedure that has **no direct bearing** upon the reliability of the accounting records.

Cash payments journal. A special journal used to record all payments of cash.

Controlling account. A general ledger account which is supported by detailed information in a subsidiary ledger.

Credit memorandum. A document issued by the seller to the buyer indicating the seller's willingness to reduce (credit) its account receivable from the buyer as the result of a sales return or allowance.

Debit memorandum. A document issued by the buyer to the seller indicating that the buyer intends to reduce (debit) its account payable to the seller in connection with a purchase return or allowance.

Internal auditors. Professional accountants employed by an organization to continually test and evaluate the system of internal control and to report their findings and recommendations to top management.

Internal control. All measures used by a business to guard against errors, waste, or fraud and to assure the reliability of accounting data. Designed to aid in the efficient operation of a business and to encourage compliance with company policies.

Invoice. An itemized statement of goods being bought or sold. Shows quantities, prices, and credit terms. Serves as the basis for an entry in the accounting records of both seller and buyer because it evidences the transfer of ownership of goods.

Invoice approval form. A business document prepared by a purchasing company's accounting department prior to recording or approving payment of a purchase invoice. Preliminary steps include comparing the purchase order and receiving report with the purchase invoice.

Net-price method. A policy of recording purchase invoices at amounts net of (reduced by) allowable cash discounts.

Point-of-sale terminal. Electronic cash registers used for computer-based processing of sales transactions. Widely used in large retail stores.

Purchase order. A serially numbered document sent by the purchasing department of a business to a supplier or vendor for the purpose of ordering materials or services.

Receiving report. An internal form prepared by the receiving department for each incoming shipment showing the quantity and condition of goods received.

Sales journal. A special journal used exclusively to record sales of merchandise on credit.

Security controls. Internal control procedures designed to protect computer programs, records, and equipment against theft, damage, and unauthorized use.

Subsidiary ledger. A supplementary record used to provide detailed information for a control account in the general ledger. The total of accounts in a subsidiary ledger equals the balance of the related control account in the general ledger.

Demonstration problem for your review

The Signal Corporation began operations on November 1, 19__. The chart of accounts used by the company included the following accounts, among others:

Cash	10	Purchase returns & allowances	62
Office supplies	18	Purchase discounts	64
Notes payable	30	Salaries expense	70
Accounts payable	32	Utilities expense	71
Purchases	60		

November transactions relating to the purchase of merchandise and to accounts payable are listed below, along with selected other transactions.

Nov. 1 Purchased merchandise from Moss Co. for $3,000. Invoice dated today; terms 2/10, n/30.

Nov. 3 Received shipment of merchandise from Wilmer Co. and invoice dated November 2 for $7,600; terms 2/10, n/30.

Nov. 6 Purchased merchandise from Archer Company at cost of $5,600. Invoice dated November 5; terms 2/10, n/30.

Nov. 10 Issued check no. 841 to Moss Co. in the amount of $2,940 in settlement of the invoice dated November 1, less 2% discount.

Nov. 12 Received shipment of merchandise from Cory Corporation and an invoice dated November 11 in the amount of $7,100; terms, due in 30 days.

Nov. 14 Issued check no. 842 to Archer Company for $5,488 in settlement of invoice dated November 5, less 2% discount.

Nov. 16 Issued check no. 843 to Willis Stationary for office supplies, $110.

Nov. 17 Issued check no. 844 for $950 to purchase merchandise from Ward Products.

Nov. 19 Purchased merchandise from Klein Co. for $11,500. Invoice dated November 18; terms 2/10, n/30.

Nov. 21 Purchased merchandise from Belmont Company for $8,400. Invoice dated November 20; terms 1/10, n/30.

Nov. 24 Purchased merchandise for cash from Paper Tiger, Inc., $375. Check no. 845.

Nov. 26 Purchased merchandise from Brooker Co. for $6,500. Invoice dated today; terms 2/10, n/30.

Nov. 28 Paid utility bill to City Electric Co., $150. Check no. 846.

Nov. 30   Issued check no. 847 to Payroll Service Co. for November salaries expense, $5,700. (Payroll Service Co. handles the distribution of this payroll to employees.)

Nov. 30   Issued check no. 848 to Wilmer Co. for $2,600 and also issued a 12%, 90-day note payable for $5,000 in settlement of the $7,600 invoice dated November 2.

Instructions

a Record the transactions in the appropriate journals. Use a single-column purchases journal and a six-column cash payments journal.

b Indicate how postings would be made by placing ledger account numbers and check marks in the appropriate columns of the journals.

c Prepare a schedule of accounts payable at November 30 to prove that the subsidiary ledgers is in balance with the controlling account.

Solution to demonstration problem

a & b   Purchases Journal   Page 1

Date		Account Credited		Invoice Date		✓	Amount
19__				19__			
Nov	1	Moss Co.	(terms 2/10, n/30)	Nov	1	✓	3,000
	3	Wilmer Co.	(terms 2/10, n/30)		2	✓	7,600
	6	Archer Company	(terms 2/10, n/30)		5	✓	5,600
	12	Cory Corporation	(terms net 30)		11	✓	7,100
	19	Klein Co.	(terms 2/10, n/30)		18	✓	11,500
	21	Belmont Company	(terms 1/10, n/30)		20	✓	8,400
	26	Brooker Co.	(terms 2/10, n/30)		26	✓	6,500
							49,700
							(60)(32)

c

SIGNAL CORPORATION
Schedule of Accounts Payable
November 30, 19__

Belmont Company	$ 8,400
Brooker Co.	6,500
Cory Corporation	7,100
Klein Co.	11,500
Total (per general ledger controlling account)	$33,500

Cash Payments Journal

Date	Check No.	Payee	Credits Cash	Credits Purchase Discounts	Credits Other Accounts Name	LP	Amount	Account Debited	Debits Accounts Payable ✓	Amount	Debits Purchases	LP	Debits Other Accounts Amount
19__ Nov 10	841	Moss Co.	2,940	60				Moss Co.	✓	3,000			
14	842	Archer Company	5,488	112				Archer Company	✓	5,600			
16	843	Willis Stationary	110					Office Supplies				18	110
17	844	Ward Products	950								950		
24	845	Paper Tiger, Inc.	375								375		
28	846	City Electric Co.	150					Utilities Expense				71	150
30	847	Payroll Service Co.	5,700					Salaries Expense				70	5,700
30	848	Wilmer Co.	2,600		Notes Payable	30	5,000	Wilmer Co.	✓	7,600			
			18,313	172			5,000			16,200	1,325		5,960
			(10)	(64)			(X)			(32)	(60)		(X)

251

ASSIGNMENT MATERIAL

Review questions

1 List four specific objectives of a system of internal control.

2 A system of internal control includes ***accounting controls*** and ***administrative*** controls. Describe each group and give an example of each.

3 Criticize the following statement: "In our company we get things done by requiring that a person who initiates a transaction follow it through in all particulars. For example, an employee who issues a purchase order is held responsible for inspecting the merchandise upon arrival, approving the invoice, and preparing the check in payment of the purchase. If any error is made, we know definitely whom to blame."

4 Suggest a control device to protect against the loss or nondelivery of invoices and other documents which are routed from one department to another.

5 Explain why the operations and custodianship functions should be separate from the accounting function.

6 Name three documents (business papers) which are needed by the accounting department to verify that a purchase of merchandise has occurred and that payment of the related liability should be made.

7 A company which has received a shipment of merchandise and a related invoice from the supplier sometimes finds it necessary to issue a debit memorandum. Describe a situation that would justify such action by the purchasing company.

8 Company A sells merchandise to Company B on credit and two days later agrees that B can return a portion of the merchandise. B does so. Should Company A issue a debit memorandum or a credit memorandum? Explain.

9 Briefly explain why a person who handles cash collections from customers should not also have authority to issue credit memoranda for sales returns and allowances.

10 Lap-Top Computer has a policy of taking all available purchase discounts. Explain how recording purchase invoices by the net-price method may assist management in enforcing this policy of taking all available purchase discounts.

11 What advantages are offered by the use of special journals?

12 Arrow Company uses a general journal and four special journals described in this chapter. Which journal should the company use to record (a) cash sales, (b) depreciation, and (c) credit sales? Explain.

13 The column total of one of the four special journals described in this chapter is posted at month-end to two general ledger accounts. One of these two accounts is Accounts Payable. What is the name of the special journal? What account is debited and what account is credited with this total?

14 Pine Hill General Store makes about 500 sales on account each month, using only a two-column general journal to record these transactions. What would be the extent of the work saved by using a sales journal?

15 When accounts receivable and accounts payable are kept in subsidiary ledgers, will the general ledger be self-balancing with equal debits and credits? Explain.

16 Explain how, why, and when the cash receipts journal and cash payments journal are crossfooted.

17 July sales on credit by Jayco amounted to $41,625, but a $1,000 error was made in totaling the sales journal. When and how will the error be discovered?

18 For a large modern department store, such as a Sears or J.C. Penney, is it necessary to maintain a manual single-column sales journal? Explain.

19 Briefly describe some of the advantages of processing accounting information by computer rather than manually.

Exercises

Exercise 6-1
Accounting terminology

Listed below are nine technical accounting terms emphasized in this chapter:

Internal auditing	Net-price method	System of internal control
Special journal	Reconciling	Debit memorandum
Subsidiary ledger	Accounting system	Credit memorandum

Each of the following statements may (or may not) describe one of these technical terms. For each statement, indicate the accounting term described, or answer "None" if the statement does not correctly describe any of the terms.

a The activity of conducting an investigation for the purpose of rendering an independent opinion upon the fairness of a company's financial statements.
b Responsibility for issuing this document should not be assigned to an employee who handles cash collections from customers.
c Measures intended to make all aspects of a business operate in accordance with management's plans and policies.
d A policy of originally recording purchase invoices at the amount that will be paid if payment is made within the discount period.
e A business document indicating the quantity of goods received and that the goods were in satisfactory condition.
f An accounting record used to record in an efficient manner a type of business transaction that occurs frequently.
g The activity of testing and evaluating internal controls throughout the organization and reporting the findings to top management.

Exercise 6-2
Subdivision of duties

Robert Hale, owner of Hale Equipment, a merchandising business, explains to you how duties have been assigned to employees. Hale states: "In order to have clearly defined responsibility for each phase of our operations, I have made one employee responsible for the purchasing, receiving, and storage of merchandise. Another employee has been charged with responsibility for maintaining the accounting records and for making all collections from customers. I have assigned to a third employee responsibility for maintaining personnel records for all our employees and for timekeeping, preparation of payroll records, and distribution of payroll checks. My goal in setting up this organization plan is to have a strong system of internal control."

You are to evaluate Hale's plan of organization and explain fully the reasoning underlying any criticism you may have.

Exercise 6-3
Business documents

Jet Auto Supply Store received from a manufacturer a shipment of 200 gasoline cans. Harold Abbott, who handles all purchasing activities, telephoned the manufacturer and explained that only 100 cans were ordered. The manufacturer replied that two separate purchase orders for 100 cans each had recently been received from Jet Auto Supply Store. Harold Abbott is sure that the manufacturer is in error and is merely trying to justify an excess shipment, but he can find no means of proving the point. What is the missing element in internal control over purchases by Jet Auto Supply Store?

Exercise 6-4
Using credit
memoranda

James Company sold merchandise to Bay Company on credit. On the next day, James Company received a telephone call from Bay Company stating that one of the items delivered was defective. James Company immediately issued credit memorandum no. 163 for $100 to Bay Company.

a Give the accounting entry required in James Company's records to record the issuance of the credit memorandum.

b Give the accounting entry required on Bay Company's accounting records when the credit memorandum is received. (Assume that Bay Company had previously recorded the purchase at the full amount of the seller's invoice and had not issued a debit memorandum.)

Exercise 6-5
Recording
purchases by the
net method

Taft Company received purchase invoices during July totaling $44,000, all of which carried credit terms of 2/10, n/30. It was the company's regular policy to take advantage of all available cash discounts, but because of employee vacations during July, there was confusion and delay in making payments to suppliers, and none of the July invoices was paid within the discount period.

a What was the amount of the additional cost incurred by Taft Company as a result of the company's failure to take the available purchase discounts?

b Explain briefly two alternative ways in which Taft Company's amount of purchases might be presented in the July income statement.

c What method of recording purchase invoices can you suggest that would call to the attention of the Taft Company management the inefficiency of operations in July?

Exercise 6-6
Recording
transactions in
special journals

Medical Supply Co. uses a cash receipts journal, a cash payments journal, a sales journal, a purchases journal, and a general journal. Indicate which journal should be used to record each of the following transactions.

a Payment of property taxes
b Purchase of office equipment on credit
c Sale of merchandise on credit
d Sale of merchandise for cash
e Cash refund to a customer who returned merchandise
f Return of merchandise to a supplier for credit
g Adjusting entry to record depreciation
h Purchase of delivery truck for cash
i Purchase of merchandise on account
j Return of merchandise by a customer company for credit to its account.

Exercise 6-7
Using subsidiary
ledgers

Pacific Products uses a sales journal to record all sales of merchandise on credit. During July the transactions in this journal were as follows:

Sales Journal

Date		Account Debited	Invoice No.	Amount
July	6	Robert Baker	437	3,600
	15	Minden Company	438	8,610
	17	Pell & Warden	439	1,029
	26	Stonewall Corporation	440	17,500
	27	Robert Baker	441	3,000
				33,739

Entries in the general journal during July include one for the return of merchandise by a customer, as follows:

July	18	Sales Returns and Allowances..................		500	
		Accounts Receivable, Minden Company			500
		Allowed credit to customer for return of merchandise from sale of July 15.			

a Prepare a subsidiary ledger for accounts receivable by opening a T account for each of the four customers listed above. Post the entries in the sales journal to these individual customers' accounts. From the general journal, post the credit to the account of Minden Company.

b Prepare a general ledger account in T form as follows: a controlling account for Accounts Receivable, a Sales account, and a Sales Returns and Allowances account. Post to these accounts the appropriate entries from the sales journal and general journal.

c Prepare a schedule of accounts receivable at July 31 to prove that this subsidiary ledger is in agreement with its controlling account.

Exercise 6-8
Posting from special journals

The accounting system used by Adams Company includes a general journal and also four special journals for cash receipts, cash payments, sales, and purchases of merchandise. On January 31, after all January posting had been completed, the Accounts Receivable controlling account in the general ledger had a debit balance of $160,000, and the Accounts Payable controlling account had a credit balance of $48,000.

The February transactions recorded in the four special journals can be summarized as follows:

Sales journal............................	Total transactions, $96,000
Purchases journal........................	Total transactions, $56,000
Cash receipts journal.....................	Accounts Receivable column total, $76,800 (credit)
Cash payments journal	Accounts Payable column total, $67,200 (debit)

a What posting would be made of the $76,800 total of the Accounts Receivable column in the cash receipts journal at February 28?

b What posting would be made of the $96,000 total of the sales journal at February 28?

c What posting would be made of the $56,000 total of the purchases journal at February 28?

d What posting would be made of the $67,200 total of the Accounts Payable column in the cash payments journal at February 28?

e Based on the above information, state the balances of the Accounts Receivable controlling account and the Accounts Payable controlling account in the general ledger after completion of posting at February 28?

Exercise 6-9
Locating errors in special journals and subsidiary ledgers

Keystone Company maintains a manual accounting system with the four special journals and general journal described in this chapter. During September, the following errors were made. For each of the errors you are to explain how and when the error will be brought to light.

a Incorrectly added the debit entries in a customer's account in the accounts receivable subsidiary ledger and listed the total as $950 when it should have been $550.

b A purchase of merchandise on credit from Rex Company in the amount of $1,000 was erroneously entered in the purchases journal as a $100 purchase.

c Recorded correctly in the sales journal a $400 sale of merchandise on credit but posted the transaction to the customer's account in the subsidiary ledger as a $40 sale.

Exercise 6-10
Internal control in a computer-based system

Mission Stores uses electronic registers to record its sales transactions. All merchandise bears a magnetic code number which can be read by an optical scanner. When merchandise is sold, the sales clerk passes each item over the scanner. The computer reads the code number, determines the price of the item from a master price list, and displays the price on a screen for the customer to see. After each item has been passed over the scanner, the computer displays the total amount of the sale and records the transaction in the company's accounting records.

If the transaction is a credit sale, the sales clerk enters the customer's credit card number into the register. The computer checks the customer's credit status and updates the accounts receivable susidiary ledger.

Paragraphs **a** through **d** describe problems which may arise in a retailing business which uses manual cash registers and accounting records. Explain how the electronic registers used by Mission Stores will help reduce or eliminate these problems. If the electronic registers will not help to eliminate the problems, explain why not.

a A sales clerk is unaware of a recent change in the price of a particular item.

b Merchandise is stolen by a shoplifter.

c A sales clerk fails to record a cash sale and keeps the cash received from the customer.

d A customer buys merchandise on account using a stolen Mission Stores credit card.

Problems

Problem 6-1
Internal control measures

Shown below are eight possible errors or problems which might occur in a merchandising business. List the letter (**a** through **h**) designating each of these errors or problems. Beside each letter, place the number indicating the internal control measure that would prevent this type of problem from occurring. If none of the specified control measures would effectively prevent the problem, place "0" after the letter.

Possible Errors or Problems

a The cashier conceals the embezzlement of cash by reducing the balance of the Cash account.

b Management is unaware that the company often fails to pay its bills in time to take advantage of the cash discounts offered by its suppliers.

c Paid a supplier for goods that were never received.

d The purchasing department ordered goods from one supplier when a better price could have been obtained by ordering from another supplier.

e Paid an invoice in which the supplier had accidentally doubled the price of the merchandise.

f Paid a supplier for goods that were delivered, but that were never ordered.

g Purchased merchandise which turned out not to be popular with customers.

h Several sales invoices were misplaced and the accounts receivable department is therefore unaware of the unrecorded credit sales.

Internal Control Measures

1 Use of serially numbered documents
2 Comparison of purchase invoice with the receiving report
3 Comparison of purchase invoice with the purchase order
4 Separation of the accounting function from custody of assets
5 Separation of the responsibilities for approving and recording transactions
6 Use of the net price method of recording purchases
0 None of the above control procedures can effectively prevent this error from occurring

**Problem 6-2
Internal control
measures—
emphasis upon
computer-based
systems**
The lettered paragraphs below describe eight possible errors or problems which might occur in a retail business. Also listed are seven internal control measures. List the letter (*a* through *h*) designating the errors or problems. Beside each letter, place the number indicating the internal control measure that should prevent this type of problem from occurring. If none of the specified internal control measures would effectively prevent the problem, place a "0" opposite the letter. Unless stated otherwise, assume that a computer-based accounting system is in use.

Possible Errors or Problems

a A salesclerk unknowingly makes a credit sale to a customer whose account has already reached the customer's prearranged credit limit.
b The cashier of a business conceals a theft of cash by adjusting the balance of the Cash account in the company's computer-based accounting records.
c Certain merchandise proves to be so unpopular with customers that it cannot be sold except at a price well below its original cost.
d A salesclerk rings up a sale at an incorrect price.
e A salesclerk uses a point-of-sale terminal to improperly reduce the balance of a friend's account in the company's accounts receivable records.
f One of the salesclerks is quite lazy and leaves most of the work of serving customers to the other salesclerks in the department.
g A customer is never billed because through oversight the credit sale was never posted from the sales journal to the accounts receivable subsidiary ledger. (Assume that a manual accounting system is in use.)
h A shoplifter steals merchandise while the salesclerk is busy with another customer.

Internal Control Measures

1 Limiting the types of transactions which can be processed from point-of-sale terminals to cash sales and credit sales.
2 All merchandise has a magnetically coded label which can be read automatically by a device attached to the electronic cash register. This code identifies to the computer the merchandise being sold.
3 Credit cards issued by the store have magnetic codes which can be read automatically by a device attached to the electronic cash register. Credit approval and posting to customers accounts are handled by the computer.
4 Subsidiary ledger accounts are periodically reconciled to the balance of the controlling account in the general ledger.
5 The computer prepares a report with separate daily sales totals for each sales person.
6 Employees with custody of assets do not have access to accounting records.
0 None of the above control measures effectively prevent this type of error from occurring.

Problem 6-3
Internal control:
a short case study

At the Uptown Theater, the cashier is located in a box office at the front of the building. The cashier receives cash from customers and operates a ticket machine which ejects serially numbered tickets. The serial number appears on each end of the ticket. The tickets come from the printer in large rolls which fit into the ticket machine and are removed at the end of each cashier's working period.

After purchasing a ticket from the cashier, in order to be admitted to the theater a customer must hand the ticket to a doorman stationed some 50 feet from the box office at the entrance to the theater lobby. The doorman tears the ticket in half, opens the door for the customer, and returns the ticket stub to the customer. The other half of the ticket is dropped by the doorman into a locked box.

Instructions

a Describe the internal controls present in Uptown Theater's method of handling cash receipts.

b What steps should be taken regularly by the theater manager or other supervisor to make these internal controls work most effectively?

c Assume that the cashier and the doorman decided to collaborate in an effort to abstract cash receipts. What action might they take?

d On the assumption made in *c* of collaboration between the cashier and the doorman, what features of the control procedures would be most likely to disclose the embezzlement?

Problem 6-4
Recording
purchases by the
net price method

The following transactions were completed by Data Tech during November, the first month of operation. The company uses the periodic inventory method and records purchase invoices at the ***net amount.***

Nov. 1   Purchased merchandise from Hayes Company, $9,000; terms 2/10, n/30.

Nov. 7   Purchased merchandise from Joseph Corporation, $12,000; terms 2/10, n/30.

Nov. 8   Merchandise having a list price of $1,200, purchased from Hayes Company, was found to be defective. It was returned to the seller, accompanied by debit memorandum no. 382. (Note: This purchase return must be recorded at the ***net*** purchase price.)

Nov. 17   Paid Joseph Corporation's invoice of November 7, less cash discount.

Nov. 24   Purchased merchandise from Joseph Corporation, $7,600; terms 2/10, n/30.

Nov. 30   Paid Hayes Company's invoice of November 1, taking into consideration the return of goods on November 8. (Notice that this payment occurred ***after*** expiration of the discount period.)

Assume that the merchandise inventory on November 1 was $31,980; on November 30, $40,000.

Instructions

a Journalize the above transactions, recording invoices at the ***net amount.***

b Prepare the cost of goods sold section of the income statement.

c Based upon these November transactions, what is the amount of accounts payable at the end of November? What would the amount of accounts payable be at the end of November if Data Tech followed the policy of recording purchase invoices at the gross amount?

Problem 6-5
Relationship be-
tween subsidiary
ledgers and
controlling
accounts

Tyrolian Products sells skis and ski clothing. The company uses journals and ledgers similar to those illustrated in Chapter 6. At November 30, the subsidiary ledger for accounts receivable included accounts with individual customers as shown on the next page. Note that these accounts include postings from three different journals.

The purpose of this problem is to show the relationship between a controlling account and a subsidiary ledger. By studying the four subsidiary ledger accounts, you can determine what amounts should appear in the controlling account. (In actual practice, of course, both the controlling account and the subsidiary ledger would be completed by posting amounts from the various journals.)

NORDIC SPORTSWEAR

Date		Explanation	Ref	Debit	Credit	Balance
19—						
Oct.	31	Balance				124 00
Nov.	10		J1		6 30	117 70
	11		54	80 00		197 70
	30		CR2		117 70	80 00

OLLIE'S SKI SHOP

Date		Explanation	Ref	Debit	Credit	Balance
19—						
Nov.	4		54	281 60		281 60
	29		54	76 80		358 40
	29		CR2		281 60	76 80

PACIFIC SPORTS CENTER

Date		Explanation	Ref	Debit	Credit	Balance
19—						
Nov.	3		S4	22 40		22 40
	9		54	41 60		64 00
	27		CR2		22 40	41 60

QUALITY STORES, INC.

Date		Explanation	Ref	Debit	Credit	Balance
19—						
Oct.	31	Balance				207 36
Nov.	8		CR1		128 00	79 36
	8		J1		25 60	53 76
	28		CR2		53 76	-0-

Instructions. You are to make the necessary entries in the general ledger controlling account, Accounts Receivable, for the month of November. Use a three-column, running balance form of ledger account. (Remember that a controlling account is posted on a daily basis for transactions recorded in the general journal, but is posted only at the end of the month for the **monthly totals** of special journals such as the sales journal and the cash receipts journal.)

Include in the controlling account the balance at October 31, the transactions from the general journal during November in chronological order, and the running balance of the account after each entry. Finally, make one posting for all sales on credit during November and one posting for all cash collections from credit customers during November. For each amount entered in the Accounts Receivable controlling account, the date and source (name of journal and journal page) should be listed. Use the symbols shown on page 243 to identify the various journals.

Problem 6-6
Special journals;
sales and cash
receipts

The accounting records of Video Games, a wholesale distributor of packaged software for computer games, include a general journal, four special journals, a general ledger, and two subsidiary ledgers. The chart of accounts includes the following accounts, among others.

Cash............................	10	Sales	50
Notes receivable....................	15	Sales returns & allowances............	52
Accounts receivable.................	17	Sales discounts	54
Notes payable......................	30	Purchase returns & allowances	62
Accounts payable...................	32		

Transactions in June involving the sale of merchandise and the receipt of cash are shown below.

June 1 Sold merchandise to The Game Store for cash, $472.

June 4 Sold merchandise to Bravo Company, $8,500. Invoice no. 618; terms 2/10, n/30.

June 5 Received cash refund of $1,088 for merchandise returned to a supplier.

June 8 Sold merchandise to Micro Stores for $4,320. Invoice no. 619; terms 2/10, n/30.

June 11 Received $2,310 cash as partial collection of a $6,310 account receivable from Olympus Corporation. Also received a note receivable for the $4,000 remaining balance due.

June 13 Received check from Bravo Company in settlement of invoice dated June 4, less discount.

June 16 Sold merchandise to Books, Etc. for $4,040. Invoice no. 620; terms 2/10, n/30.

June 16 Returned $960 of merchandise to supplier, Software Co., for reduction of account payable.

June 20 Sold merchandise to Graphics, Inc., for $7,000. Invoice no. 621; terms 2/10, n/30.

June 21 Books, Etc. returned for credit $640 of merchandise purchased on June 16.

June 23 Borrowed $24,000 cash from a local bank, signing a six-month note payable.

June 25 Received $3,332 from Books, Etc., in full settlement of invoice dated June 16, less return on June 21 and 2% discount.

June 30 Collected from Graphics, Inc., amount of invoice dated June 20, less 2% discount.

June 30 Received a 60-day note receivable for $4,320 from Micro Stores in settlement of invoice dated June 8.

Instructions. Record the above transactions in the appropriate journals. Use a single-column sales journal, a six-column cash receipts journal, and a two-column general journal. Foot and rule the special journals and indicate how postings would be made by placing ledger account numbers and check marks in the appropriate columns of the journals.

Problem 6-7
Special journals;
purchases and
cash payments

Among the ledger accounts used by Poison Creek Drug Store are the following:

Cash	10	Accounts payable	30
Office supplies	18	Purchases	50
Land	20	Purchase returns & allowances	52
Building	22	Purchase discounts	53
Notes payable	28	Salaries expense	60

The August transactions relating to the purchase of merchandise for resale and to accounts payable are listed below along with selected other transactions. It is Poison Creek Drug's policy to record purchase invoices at their gross amount.

Aug. 1 Purchased merchandise from Medco Labs at a cost of $8,470. Invoice dated today; terms 2/10, n/30.

Aug. 4 Purchased merchandise from American Products for $19,300. Invoice dated August 3; terms 2/10, n/30.

Aug. 5 Returned for credit to Medco Labs defective merchandise having a list price of $1,220.

Aug. 6 Received shipment of merchandise from Tricor Corporation and their invoice dated August 5 in amount of $14,560. Terms net 30 days.

Aug. 8 Purchased merchandise from Vita-Life, Inc., $24,480. Invoice dated today with terms 1/10, n/60.

Aug. 10 Purchased merchandise from King Corporation, $30,000. Invoice dated August 9; terms 2/10, n/30.

Aug. 10 Issued check no. 631 for $7,105 to Medco Labs in settlement of balance resulting from purchase of August 1 and purchase return of August 5.

Aug. 11 Issued check no. 632 for $18,914 to American Products in payment of August 3 invoice, less 2%.

Aug. 18 Issued check no. 633 for $29,400 to King Corporation in settlement of invoice dated August 9, less 2% discount.

Aug. 20 Purchased merchandise for cash, $1,080. Issued check no. 634 to Candy Corp.

Aug. 21 Bought land and building for $208,800. Land was worth $64,800 and building, $144,000. Paid cash of $36,000 and signed a promissory note for the balance of $172,800. Check no. 635, in the amount of $36,000, was issued to Security Escrow Co.

Aug. 23 Purchased merchandise from Novelty Products for cash, $900. Issued check no. 636.

Aug. 26 Purchased merchandise from Ralston Company for $32,400. Invoice dated August 26, terms 2/10, n/30.

Aug. 28 Paid cash for office supplies, $270. Issued check no. 637 to Super Office, Inc.

Aug. 29 Purchased merchandise from Candy Corp. for cash, $1,890. Issued check no. 638.

Aug. 31 Paid salaries for August, $17,920. Issued check no. 639 to National Bank, which handles the distribution of the payroll to employees.

Instructions

a Record the transactions in the appropriate journals. Use a single-column purchases journal, a six-column cash payments journal, and a two-column general journal. Foot and rule the special journals. Make all postings to the proper general ledger accounts and to the accounts payable subsidiary ledger.

b Prepare a schedule of accounts payable at August 31 to prove that the subsidiary ledger is in balance with the controlling account for accounts payable.

Problem 6-8
Cash journals

Marshal Ross, Inc., wholesales designer sportswear to boutiques and other retail outlets. The company uses multicolumn cash receipts and cash payments journals similar to those illustrated in this chapter. The cash activities for May are listed below:

May 1 Issued additional shares of capital stock in exchange for $45,000 cash.

May 2 Issued check no. 418 to Gaslamp Center in payment of store rent for May, $3,600.

May 4 Purchased store fixtures for $10,500 from Themes & Things, making a cash down payment of $1,500 (check no. 419) and issuing a 12%, 120-day note payable for the $9,000 balance. (Debit Fixtures.)

May 5 Sold merchandise for cash to Surprise Store, $12,300.

May 9 Received $2,100 as a partial collection of a $6,300 account receivable from Graffiti, Inc. Also received a $4,200 note receivable for the uncollected balance.

May 12 Paid Dallas at Night invoice of $9,000, less 2% discount. Check no. 420, in the amount of $8,820.

May 15 Received $3,822 from LA Stores in settlement of our $3,900 sales invoice, less allowable discount of 2%.

May 19 Purchased merchandise from Fashion World for cash, $7,200. Issued check no. 421.

May 25 Cash sales of merchandise, $8,045.

May 26 Paid Post Co. invoice, $9,900 less 2%. Check no. 422 for $9,702.

May 28 Purchased merchandise for cash from Albertson Corp., $6,450. Issued check no. 423.

May 30 Received check of $7,644 in full settlement of $7,800 sales invoice to Mix 'N Match dated May 21, less 2% discount for prompt payment.

May 31 Paid monthly salaries, $28,034. Issued one check, no. 424, to Third Street Bank. The bank issues the individual payroll checks to employees.

May 31 Paid Third Street Bank installment due today on a note payable. Issued check no. 425 in the amount of $1,440, representing interest expense of $702 and a reduction in the note payable of the remaining $738.

Instructions. Enter the above transactions in a six-column journal for cash receipts and a six-column journal for cash payments. Compute column totals and rule the journals. Determine the equality of debits and credits in column totals.

Business decision cases

Case 6-1
The Baker Street
Diversion

Printing Made Easy sells a variety of printers for use with personal computers. Last April, Arthur Doyle, the company's purchasing agent, discovered a weakness in internal control and engaged in a scheme to steal printers. Doyle issued a purchase order for 20 printers to one of the company's regular suppliers, but included a typewritten note requesting that the printers be delivered to 221B Baker Street, Doyle's home address.

The supplier shipped the printers to Baker Street and sent a sales invoice to Printing Made Easy. When the invoice arrived, an accounting clerk carefully complied with company policy and compared the invoice with a copy of the purchase order. After noting agreement between these documents as to quantities, prices, and model numbers, the clerk recorded the transaction in the accounting records and authorized payment of the invoice.

Instructions. What is the weakness in internal control discovered by the purchasing agent to enable him to commit this theft? What changes would you recommend in the company's internal documentation and invoice approval procedures to prevent such problems in the future?

Case 6-2
Designing a
special journal
and explaining its
use

Leisure Clothing is a mail-order company which sells clothes to the public at discount prices. Recently Leisure Clothing initiated a new policy allowing a 10-day free trial on all clothes bought from the company. At the end of the 10-day period, the customer may either pay cash for the purchase or return the goods to Leisure Clothing. The new policy caused such a large boost in sales that, even after considering the many sales returns, the policy appeared quite profitable.

The accounting system of Leisure Clothing includes a sales journal, purchases journal, cash receipts journal, cash payments journal, and a general journal. As an internal control procedure, an officer of the company reviews and initials every entry in the general journal before the amounts are posted to the ledger accounts. Since the 10-day free trial policy has been in effect, hundreds of entries recording sales returns have been entered in the general journal each week. Each of these entries has been reviewed and initialed by an officer of the firm, and the amounts have been posted to Sales Returns & Allowances and to the Accounts Receivable controlling account in the general ledger, and also to the customer's account in the accounts receivable subsidiary ledger.

Since these sales return entries are so numerous, it has been suggested that a special journal be designed to handle them. This could not only save time in journalizing and posting the entries, but also eliminate the time-consuming individual review of each of these repetitive entries by an officer of the company.

Instructions

a How many amounts are entered in the general journal to describe a single sales return transaction? Are these amounts the same?

b Explain why these sales return transactions are suited to the use of a special journal. Explain in detail how many money columns the special journal should have, and what postings would have to be done either at the time of the transaction or at the end of the period.

c Assume that there were 3,000 sales returns during the month. How many postings would have to be made during the month if these transactions were entered in the general journal? How many postings would have to be made if the special journal you designed in b were used? (Assume a one-month accounting period.)

Part Two: Comprehensive Problem
Crestline Lumber Co.

The use of special journals and subsidiary ledgers.

A partial chart of accounts for Crestline Lumber Co. is shown below:

Cash................................	1	Dividends............................	53
Notes Receivable....................	2	Sales	60
Accounts Receivable.................	4	Sales Returns and Allowances.........	62
Supplies............................	6	Sales Discounts	64
Unexpired Insurance	8	Purchases............................	70
Land................................	20	Purchase Returns and Allowances......	72
Equipment...........................	26	Purchase Discounts	74
Notes Payable.......................	30	Transportation-in	76
Accounts Payable....................	32	Salaries Expense....................	80
Dividends Payable	34		

The schedules of accounts receivable and accounts payable for the company at October 31, 19__, are shown below:

Schedule of Accounts Receivable October 31, 19__		Schedule of Accounts Payable October 31, 19__	
Ace Contractors	$20,800	Northwest Mills	$30,000
Reliable Builders, Inc.............	18,750		
Total	$39,550		

The accounting records of Crestline Lumber Co. include a general ledger and two subsidiary ledgers, one for accounts receivable and one for accounts payable. The company uses the four special journals illustrated in Chapter 6 as well as the customary two-column general journal. Crestline Lumber Co. uses the periodic inventory system and records purchase invoices at their gross amount. All credit sales are made on terms of 2/10, n/30.

The November transactions of the corporation are as follows:

Nov. 2 Purchased merchandise on account from Northwest Mills, $28,000. Invoice was dated today with terms of 2/10, n/30.

Nov. 3   Sold merchandise to Ace Contractors, $16,000. Invoice no. 428; terms, 2/10, n/30.

Nov. 4   Issued check no. 920 to Northwest Mills for $29,400, in full payment of balance at October 31, less 2% purchase discount.

Nov. 5   Sold merchandise for cash, $5,600.

Nov. 6   Collected $18,375 from Reliable Builders, Inc., representing the account receivable at October 31, less 2% cash discount.

Nov. 9   Purchased supplies for cash, $875. Issued check no. 921 to Aero Supply Co.

Nov. 10   Purchased merchandise from Tri-State Gypsum, $12,500. Invoice dated November 9, terms 2/10, n/30.

Nov. 11   Sold merchandise to Mountain Homes, $21,750. Invoice no. 429; terms 2/10, n/30.

Nov. 12   Received $36,480 from Ace Contractors, representing collection of the October 31 balance receivable, upon which the discount has lapsed, and invoice no. 428 (see Nov. 3), less 2% cash discount.

Nov. 13   Paid transportation charges of $510 on goods purchased November 10 from Tri-State Gypsum. Issued check no. 922 to Cannonball Trucking.

Nov. 16   Sold a parcel of land not needed in the business at its cost of $25,000. Received $10,000 cash and a note receivable for $15,000.

Nov. 17   Issued credit memo. no. 78 in recognition of a $1,750 sales return by Mountain Homes of some of the merchandise purchased on November 11.

Nov. 17   Sold merchandise for cash, $4,675.

Nov. 18   Issued check no. 923 to Empire Insurance, $1,425, in full payment of a one-year fire insurance policy. (Debit Unexpired Insurance.)

Nov. 19   Purchased merchandise for cash from Modern Tool Co., $2,625. Issued check no. 924.

Nov. 19   Issued check no. 925 for $12,250 to Tri-State Gypsum in payment of the purchase on November 10, less 2% cash discount.

Nov. 20   Received $19,600 from Mountain Homes in settlement of invoice no. 429 (Nov. 11), less sales return on Nov. 17, and less 2%.

Nov. 20   Sold merchandise on account to Ace Contractors, $13,650, invoice no. 430.

Nov. 23   Purchased merchandise from Specialty Moldings for cash, $4,050, check no. 926.

Nov. 24   Sold merchandise on account to Lake Development Co., $39,950. Invoice no. 431.

Nov. 25   Declared a cash dividend of $17,500 on the capital stock, payable December 20.

Nov. 26   Purchased merchandise from Timber Products, $26,500. Invoice dated November 24, terms 2/10, n/30.

Nov. 27   Returned to Timber Products merchandise costing $2,125. Issued debit memo. no. 42.

Nov. 30   Purchased equipment for $60,000. Issued check no. 927 to Electro-Lift of $10,000 as a cash down payment and issued a note payable for the $50,000 balance.

Nov. 30   Paid monthly salaries of $14,800. Issued one check (no. 928) to Payroll Service Co. in the amount of the entire payroll. Payroll Service Co. handles the preparation and distribution of paychecks to individual employees.

Instructions

a Record the November transactions in the appropriate journals and make all individual postings to the general ledger and subsidiary ledgers. Individual postings include:

(1) All entries in the general journal.

(2) Entries in the Other Accounts columns of the cash receipts journal and the cash payments journal.

(3) All entries in any journal which affect subsidiary ledger accounts.
In the journals, use check marks (✓) and ledger account numbers to indicate which amounts have been posted. In the ledger accounts, use the Ref column to indicate the source of each posting. (Assume that you are using page 7 of each journal.)

b Foot and rule the special journals and post the appropriate column totals to the general ledger. Make all appropriate posting cross-references.

c Prepare a schedule of the individual accounts receivable at November 30 and a separate schedule of the individual accounts payable. Determine that these schedules are in agreement with the related controlling accounts in the general ledger.

Part Three	Accounting for assets

Chapter 7	Cash and accounts receivable
Chapter 8	Inventories
Chapter 9	Plant and equipment, depreciation, and intangible assets

The manner in which a business records and values its assets affects both the balance sheet and the income statement. By studying the accounting principles involved in asset valuation, we will learn much about the content and limitations of financial statements.

Chapter 7
Cash and accounts receivable

CHAPTER PREVIEW

In this chapter we discuss two of the most liquid types of current assets — cash and receivables. In our discussion of cash, we emphasize that adequate internal control requires that each day's cash receipts be deposited intact in the bank and that all disbursements be made by check. We also illustrate and explain the use of regular bank reconciliations and the operation of a petty cash fund. In the area of accounts receivable, we explore methods of measuring the expense of uncollectible accounts and of reflecting this expense in the financial statements. We also consider notes receivable, including the accrual of interest, and the discounting of notes to banks.

After studying this chapter you should be able to meet these Learning Objectives:

1 **State the major steps in achieving internal control over cash transactions.**
2 **Describe the operation of a petty cash fund.**
3 **Prepare a bank reconciliation and explain its purpose.**
4 **Record estimates of uncollectible accounts receivable, write-offs of uncollectible accounts, and any later recoveries.**
5 **Apply the balance sheet approach and the income statement approach to estimating uncollectible accounts.**
6 **Compare the allowance method and the direct charge-off method of accounting for uncollectible accounts.**
7 **Account for sales to customers using national credit cards.**
8 **Account for the receipt of notes, accrual of interest, collection or default, and the discounting of notes receivable.**

CASH

Accountants define cash as money on deposit in banks and any items that banks will accept for immediate deposit. These items include not only coins and paper money, but also checks, bank drafts, and money orders. Savings accounts are classified as cash too.

Some short-term investments are so liquid that they are called *cash equivalents.* Examples include money market funds, U.S. Treasury bills, and commercial paper. Cash equivalents convert into cash so quickly that they are combined with cash in the balance sheet.[1]

Cash is listed first among current assets, because it is the most liquid of all assets. A company that has several bank accounts will maintain a separate ledger account for each bank account. Separate ledger accounts also are maintained for cash equivalents. In the balance sheet, however, all the cash and cash equivalents owned by the company are shown as a single amount.

Some bank accounts may be restricted as to their use. For example, a bond sinking fund consists of cash held for the specific purpose of paying off long-term debt and is not available for any other use. Restricted cash is *not regarded as a current asset* because it is not available for use in paying current liabilities. Therefore, cash subject to such restrictions is listed in the balance sheet just below the current assets section, under the caption *long-term investments.*

The need for internal control

1 State the major steps in achieving internal control over cash transactions.

Many of our accounting policies and procedures relating to cash stem from the special need for internal control over this asset. Cash is more susceptible to theft than any other asset and, therefore, requires physical protection. Also, cash transactions affect every classification within the financial statements — assets, liabilities, owners' equity, revenue, and expenses. If financial statements are to be reliable, it is *absolutely essential* that cash transactions be properly recorded.

The major steps in achieving internal control over cash transactions include:

1 Separate the function of handling cash from the maintenance of accounting records. Employees who handle cash *should not have access to the accounting records,* and accounting personnel should not have access to cash.

2 Prepare a *control listing* of cash receipts at the time and place the money is received. For cash sales, this listing may be a cash register tape, created by ringing up each sale on a cash register. For checks received through the mail, a control listing of incoming checks should be prepared by the employee assigned to open the mail.

3 Require that all cash receipts be deposited daily in the bank.

4 Make all payments by check. The only exception should be for small payments to be made in cash from a petty cash fund.

5 Require that every expenditure be verified, approved, and recorded before a check is issued in payment.

6 Separate the function of approving expenditures from the function of signing checks.

---

[1] A statement of cash flows is a financial statement summarizing the cash receipts and cash payments of the accounting period. In this statement, "cash" is defined as including cash equivalents. The FASB has taken the position that the same definition should be used in the balance sheet. The statement of cash flows is discussed in Chapter 14.

The application of these principles in building an adequate system of internal control over cash can best be illustrated by considering separately the topics of cash receipts and cash disbursements. A company may supplement its system of internal control by obtaining a **fidelity bond** from an insurance company. Under a fidelity bond, the insurance company agrees to reimburse an employer for **proven** losses resulting from fraud or embezzlement by bonded employees.

Cash receipts

Cash receipts consist primarily of two types: cash received through the mail as collections of accounts receivable, and cash received over the counter from cash sales.

Cash received through the mail. Cash received through the mail should be in the form of checks made payable to the company. When the mail is first opened, an employee should stamp the back of each check with a restrictive endorsement stamp, indicating that the check is **"For Deposit Only"** into the company's bank account. This **restrictive endorsement** prevents anyone else from being able to cash the check or deposit it into another bank account.

Next, the employee should prepare a **control listing** of the checks received each day. This list shows each customer's name (or account number) and the amount received. One copy of this list is sent with the customers' checks to the cashier, who deposits the money in the bank. Another copy is sent to the accounting department, to be recorded in the cash receipts journal. Daily comparisons of this control listing with the amounts deposited by the cashier and with the receipts recorded by the accounting department should bring to light any cash shortages or recording errors.

Cash received over the counter. Cash sales should be rung up on a cash register located so that the customer can see the amount recorded. The register has a locked-in tape, which serves as a control listing for cash sales. When the salesperson ends a workday, he or she will count the cash in the register and turn it over to the cashier. A representative of the accounting department will remove the tape from the cash register, compare the total shown on the tape with the amount turned in to the cashier, and record the cash sales in the cash receipts journal. In many larger stores, every cash register is linked directly to a computer, and each cash sale transaction immediately becomes part of the accounting records.

● **CASE IN POINT** ● Many large supermarkets have achieved faster checkout lines and stronger internal control by using electronic scanning equipment to read and record the price of all groceries passing the checkout counters. (The electronic scanning equipment replaces the traditional cash register.) All 12,000 or so grocery items on the shelves bear a product code, consisting of a pattern of thick and thin vertical bars. At the checkout counter, the code on each item is read by a scanning laser. The code is sent instantaneously to a computer which locates the price and description of the item and flashes that information on a display panel in view of the customer and the checkout clerk. After all of the items have been passed through the scanner, the display panel shows the total amount of the sale. The clerk then enters the amount of cash received from the customer, and the display panel shows the amount of change that the customer should receive.

This system has many advantages. Not only is an immediate record made of all cash receipts, but the risk of errors in pricing merchandise or in making change is greatly reduced. This system also improves inventory control by giving management continuous information on what is being sold moment by moment, classified by product and by manufacturer.

Recording cash over and short. In handling over-the-counter cash receipts, a few errors in making change will inevitably occur. These errors will cause a cash shortage or overage at the end of the day, when the cash is counted and compared with the reading on the cash register.

For example, assume that the total cash sales for the day amount to $1,500 as recorded by the cash register, but that the cash in the drawer when counted amounts to only $1,490. The following entry would be made to record the day's sales and the cash shortage of $10.

Recording a small cash shortage

Cash	1,490	
Cash Over and Short	10	
Sales		1,500

To record cash sales for the day and a $10 cash shortage.

The account entitled Cash Over and Short is debited with shortages and credited with overages. If the cash shortages during an entire accounting period are in excess of the cash overages, the Cash Over and Short account will have a debit balance and will be shown as miscellaneous **expense** in the income statement. On the other hand, if the overages exceed the shortages, the Cash Over and Short account will show a credit balance at the end of the period and should be treated as an item of miscellaneous **revenue.**

Subdivision of duties. Employees who handle cash receipts should **not have access to the accounting records.** This combination of duties might enable the employee to alter the accounting records and thereby conceal a cash shortage.

Employees who handle cash receipts also should **not have authority to issue credit memoranda for sales returns.** This combination of duties might enable the employee to conceal cash shortages by issuing fictitious credit memoranda. Assume, for example, that an employee with these responsibilities collects $100 cash from a customer as payment of the customer's account. The employee might remove this cash and issue a $100 credit memorandum, indicating that the customer had returned the merchandise instead of paying off the account. The credit memoranda would cause the customer's account to be credited. However, the offsetting debit would be to the Sales Returns & Allowances account, not to the Cash account. Thus, the books would remain in balance, the customer would receive credit for the abstracted payment, and there would be no record of cash having been received.

Cash disbursements

To achieve adequate internal control over cash disbursements, all payments (except from petty cash) should be *made by check.* The use of checks automatically provides a written record of each cash payment. In addition, adequate internal control requires that every transaction requiring a cash payment be *verified,* *approved,* and *recorded* before a check is issued. Responsibility for approving cash disbursements should be *clearly separated* from the responsibility for signing checks.

The voucher system. One widely used method of establishing internal control over cash disbursements is a voucher system. In a typical voucher system, the accounting department is responsible for approving cash payments and for recording the transactions. In approving an expenditure, the accounting department will examine such supporting documents as the supplier's invoice, the purchase order, and the receiving report. Once payment has been approved, the accounting department signs a *voucher* authorizing payment and records the transaction in the accounting records.[2]

The voucher and supporting documents then are sent to the treasurer or other official in the finance department. This official reviews the voucher and supporting documents before issuing a check. When the check is signed, the voucher and supporting documents are perforated or stamped "Paid" to eliminate any possibility of their being presented later in support of another check.

Notice that neither the personnel in the accounting department nor in the finance department are in a position to make unapproved cash disbursements. Accounting personnel, who verify and approve disbursements, are not authorized to sign checks. Finance department personnel, who issue and sign checks, are not authorized to issue a check unless they have first received an authorization voucher from the accounting department.

Petty cash

2 Describe the operation of a petty cash fund.

As previously emphasized, adequate internal control over cash requires that all receipts be deposited in the bank and all disbursements be made by check. However, every business finds it convenient to have a small amount of cash on hand with which to make some minor expenditures. Examples include payments for small purchases of office supplies, postage stamps, and taxi fares. Internal control over these small cash payments can best be achieved through a petty cash fund.

Establishing the petty cash fund. To create a petty cash fund, a check is written for a round amount such as $100 or $200, which will cover the small expenditures to be paid in cash for a period of two or three weeks. This check is cashed and the money kept on hand in a petty cash box or drawer in the office.

---

[2] Other names for a *"voucher"* include *"invoice approval form"* and *"check authorization."*

The entry for the issuance of the check is

Petty Cash 200
　　Cash.. 　　 200
To establish a petty cash fund.

Making disbursements from the petty cash fund. As cash payments are made out of the petty cash box, the custodian of the fund is required to fill out a *petty cash voucher* for each expenditure. A petty cash voucher shows the amount paid, the purpose of the expenditure, the date, and the signature of the person receiving the money. A petty cash voucher should be prepared for every payment made from the fund. The petty cash box should, therefore, always contain cash/or vouchers totaling the exact amount of the fund.

The petty cash custodian should be informed that occasional surprise counts of the fund will be made and that he or she is personally responsible for the fund being intact at all times. Careless handling of petty cash has often been a first step toward large thefts; consequently, misuse of petty cash funds should not be tolerated.

Replenishing the petty cash fund. Assume that a petty cash fund of $200 was established on June 1 and that payments totaling $174.95 were made from the fund during the next two weeks. Since the $200 originally placed in the fund is nearly exhausted, the fund should be replenished. To replenish a petty cash fund means to replace the amount of money that has been spent, thus restoring the fund to its original amount. A check is drawn payable to Petty Cash for the exact amount of the expenditures, $174.95. This check is cashed and the money placed in the petty cash box. The vouchers totaling that amount are perforated to prevent their reuse and filed in support of the replenishment check. The journal entry to record the issuance of the check will debit the expense accounts indicated by inspection of the vouchers, as follows:

Office Supplies Expense 80.60
Freight-in 16.00
Postage Expense 45.25
Miscellaneous Expense 33.10
　　Cash.. 　　 174.95
To replenish the petty cash fund.

Note that *expense accounts* are debited each time the fund is replenished. The Petty Cash account is debited only when the fund is first established. There ordinarily will be no further entries in the Petty Cash account after the fund is established, unless the fund is discontinued or a decision is made to change its size from the original $200 amount.

The petty cash fund is usually replenished at the end of an accounting period, even though the fund is not running low, so that all vouchers in the fund are charged to expense accounts before these accounts are closed and financial statements prepared.

Bank statements

Each month the bank will provide the depositor with a statement of the depositor's account, accompanied by the checks paid and charged to the account during the month.[3] As illustrated below, a bank statement shows the balance on deposit at the beginning of the month, the deposits, the checks paid, any other debits and credits

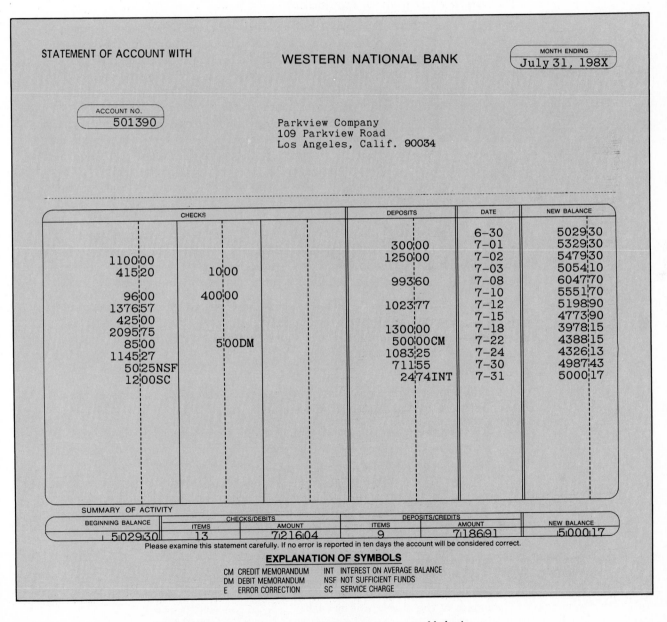

STATEMENT OF ACCOUNT WITH

WESTERN NATIONAL BANK

MONTH ENDING
July 31, 198X

ACCOUNT NO.
501390

Parkview Company
109 Parkview Road
Los Angeles, Calif. 90034

CHECKS		DEPOSITS	DATE	NEW BALANCE
			6-30	5029.30
		300.00	7-01	5329.30
1100.00		1250.00	7-02	5479.30
415.20	10.00		7-03	5054.10
		993.60	7-08	6047.70
96.00	400.00		7-10	5551.70
1376.57		1023.77	7-12	5198.90
425.00			7-15	4773.90
2095.75		1300.00	7-18	3978.15
85.00	5.00DM	500.00CM	7-22	4388.15
1145.27		1083.25	7-24	4326.13
50.25NSF		711.55	7-30	4987.43
12.00SC		24.74INT	7-31	5000.17

SUMMARY OF ACTIVITY

BEGINNING BALANCE	CHECKS/DEBITS		DEPOSITS/CREDITS		NEW BALANCE
	ITEMS	AMOUNT	ITEMS	AMOUNT	
5029.30	13	7216.04	9	7186.91	5000.17

Please examine this statement carefully. If no error is reported in ten days the account will be considered correct.

EXPLANATION OF SYMBOLS

CM CREDIT MEMORANDUM   INT INTEREST ON AVERAGE BALANCE
DM DEBIT MEMORANDUM   NSF NOT SUFFICIENT FUNDS
E   ERROR CORRECTION   SC SERVICE CHARGE

[3] Large businesses may receive bank statements on a weekly basis.

during the month, and the new balance at the end of the month. (To keep the illustration short, we have shown a limited number of deposits rather than one for each business day in the month.)

Reconciling the bank statement

3 Prepare a bank
reconciliation
and explain its
purpose.

A *bank reconciliation* is a schedule *explaining any differences* between the balance shown in the bank statement and the balance shown in the depositor's accounting records. Remember that both the bank and the depositor are maintaining independent records of the deposits, the checks, and the current balance of the bank account. Each month, the depositor should prepare a bank reconciliation to verify that these independent sets of records are in agreement. This reconciliation may disclose internal control failures, such as unauthorized cash disbursements or failures to deposit cash receipts, as well as errors in either bank statement or the depositor's accounting records. In addition, the reconciliation helps to determine the "actual" amount of cash on deposit.

For strong internal control, the employee who reconciles the bank statement should not have any other responsibilities for cash.

Normal differences between bank records and accounting records. The balance shown in a monthly bank statement seldom equals the balance appearing in the depositor's accounting records. Certain transactions recorded by the depositor may not have been recorded by the bank. The most common examples are:

1 *Outstanding checks.* Checks issued and recorded by the company, but not yet presented to the bank for payment.
2 *Deposits in transit.* Cash receipts recorded by the depositor, but which reached the bank too late to be included in the bank statement for the current month.

In addition, certain transactions appearing in the bank statement may not have been recorded by the depositor. For example:

1 *Service charges.* Banks often charge a fee for handling small accounts. The amount of this charge usually depends upon both the average balance of the account and the number of checks paid during the month.
2 *Charges for depositing NSF checks. NSF* stands for "Not Sufficient Funds." When checks are deposited in an account, the bank generally gives the depositor immediate credit. On occasion, one of these checks may prove to be uncollectible, because the maker of the check does not have sufficient funds in his or her account. In such cases, the bank will reduce the depositor's account by the amount of this uncollectible item and return the check to the depositor marked "NSF."

The depositor should view an NSF check as an account receivable from the maker of the check, not as cash.

3 *Credits for interest earned.*[4] The checking accounts of unincorporated businesses often earn interest. At month-end, this interest is credited to the depositor's account and reported in the bank statement. (Current law prohibits interest on corporate checking accounts.)

4 *Miscellaneous bank charges and credits.* Banks charge for services — such as printing checks, handling collections of notes receivable, and processing NSF checks. The bank *deducts* these charges from the depositor's account and notifies the depositor by including a *debit memorandum* in the monthly bank statement.[4] If the bank collects a note receivable on behalf of the depositor, it adds the money to the depositor's account and issues a *credit memorandum.*

In a bank reconciliation, the balances shown in the bank statement and in the accounting records both are *adjusted for any unrecorded transactions.* Additional adjustment may be required to correct any errors discovered in the bank statement or in the accounting records.

Steps in preparing a bank reconciliation. The specific steps in preparing a bank reconciliation are:

1 Compare deposits listed on the bank statement with the deposits shown in the accounting records. Any deposits not yet recorded by the bank are deposits in transit and should be added to the balance shown in the bank statement.

2 Arrange paid checks in sequence by serial numbers and compare each check with the corresponding entry in the cash payments journal. Any checks issued but not yet paid by the bank should be listed as outstanding checks to be deducted from the balance reported in the bank statement.

3 Add to the balance per the depositor's accounting records any credit memoranda issued by the bank which have not been recorded by the depositor.

4 Deduct from the balance per the depositor's records any debit memoranda issued by the bank which have not been recorded by the depositor.

5 Make appropriate adjustments to correct any errors in either the bank statement or the depositor's accounting records.

6 Determine that the adjusted balance of the bank statement is equal to the adjusted balance in the depositor's records.

7 Prepare journal entries to record any items in the bank reconciliation listed as adjustments to the balance per depositor's records.

Illustration of a bank reconciliation. The July bank statement sent by the bank to Parkview Company was illustrated on page 275. This statement shows a balance of cash on deposit at July 31 of $5,000.17. Assume that on July 31, Park-

---

[4] Banks view each depositor's account as a liability. Debit memoranda are issued for transactions that reduce this liability, such as bank service charges. Credit memoranda are issued to recognize an increase in this liability, as results, for example, from interest earned by the depositor.

view's ledger shows a bank balance of $4,262.83. The employee preparing the bank reconciliation has identified the following reconciling items:

1 A deposit of $410.90 made after banking hours on July 31 does not appear in the bank statement.
2 Four checks issued in July have not yet been paid by the bank. These checks are:

Check No.	Date	Amount
801	June 15	$100.00
888	July 24	10.25
890	July 27	402.50
891	July 30	205.00

3 Two credit memoranda were included in the bank statement:

Date	Amount	Explanation
July 22	$500.00	Proceeds from collection of a non-interest-bearing note receivable from J. David. Parkview Company had left this note with the bank's collection department.
July 31	24.74	Interest earned on average account balance during July.

4 Three debit memoranda accompanied the bank statement:

Date	Amount	Explanation
July 22	$ 5.00	Fee charged by bank for handling collection of note receivable.
July 30	50.25	Check from customer J. B. Ball deposited by Parkview Company charged back as NSF.
July 31	12.00	Service charge by bank for the month of July.

5 Check no. 875 was issued July 20 in the amount of $85 but was erroneously recorded in the cash payments journal as $58. The check, in payment of telephone expense, was paid by the bank and correctly listed at $85 in the bank statement. In Parkview's ledger, the Cash account is **overstated** by $27 because of this error ($85 − $58 = $27).

The July 31 bank reconciliation for Parkview Company is shown on the next page. (The numbered arrows coincide both with the steps in preparing a bank reconciliation listed on page 277 and with the reconciling items listed above.)

Updating the accounting records. The last step in reconciling a bank statement is to update the depositor's accounting records for any unrecorded cash transactions brought to light. In the bank reconciliation, every adjustment to the **balance per depositor's records** is a cash receipt or a cash payment that has not been recorded in the depositor's accounts. Therefore, **each of these items should be recorded.**

PARKVIEW COMPANY
Bank Reconciliation
July 31, 19__

Balance per bank statement, July 31, 19__		$5,000.17
①———→Add: Deposit of July 31 not recorded by bank................................		410.90
		$5,411.07
②———→Deduct: Outstanding checks:		
No. 801	$100.00	
No. 888	10.25	
No. 890	402.50	
No. 891	205.00	717.75
Adjusted cash balance (as above)		**$4,693.32**
Balance per depositor's records, July 31, 19__		$4,262.83
③———→Add: Note receivable collected for us by bank........................	$500.00	
Interest earned during July	24.74	524.74
		$4,787.57
④———→Deduct: Collection fee..	$ 5.00	
NSF check of J. B. Ball	50.25	
Service charge...	12.00	
⑤———→Error on check stub no. 875	27.00	94.25
Adjusted cash balance...		**$4,693.32**

⑥

In this illustration and in our assignment material, we will follow a policy of making one journal entry to record the unrecorded cash receipts, and another to record the unrecorded cash reductions. (Acceptable alternatives would be to make separate journal entries for each item or to make one compound entry for all items.) Based on our recording policy, the entries to update the accounting records of Parkview Company are:

Per bank credit memoranda . . .	Cash	524.74	
	Notes Receivable..		500.00
	Interest Revenue		24.74
	To record collection of note receivable from J. David collected by bank and interest earned on bank account in July.		
. . . per bank debit memoranda (and correction of an error)	Bank Service Charges	17.00	
	Accounts Receivable, J. B. Ball......................................	50.25	
	Telephone Expense	27.00	
	Cash..		94.25
	To record bank charges (service charge, $12; collection fee, $5), to reclassify NSF check from customer J. B. Ball as an account receivable, and to correct understatement of cash payment for telephone expense.		

ACCOUNTS RECEIVABLE

One of the key factors underlying the growth of the American economy is the trend toward selling goods and services on credit. Accounts receivable are very liquid assets, usually being converted into cash within a period of 30 to 60 days. Therefore, accounts receivable from customers are classified as current assets, appearing in the balance sheet immediately after cash and marketable securities.

Sometimes companies sell merchandise on longer-term installment plans, requiring 12, 24, or even 48 months to collect the entire amount receivable from the customer. By definition, the normal period of time required to collect accounts receivable is part of a company's **operating cycle.** Therefore, accounts receivable arising from "normal" sales transactions usually are classified as current assets, even if the credit terms extend beyond one year.[5]

Uncollectible accounts

No business wants to sell on credit to a customer who will prove unable or unwilling to pay his or her account. Therefore, most businesses have a credit department that investigates the credit worthiness of each prospective customer. This investigation usually includes obtaining a credit report from a national credit-rating agency such as **Dun & Bradstreet, Inc.** If the prospective customer is a business concern, its financial statements will be obtained and analyzed to determine its financial strength and the trend of its operating results.

A business that sells its goods or services on credit will inevitably find that some of its accounts receivable are uncollectible. Regardless of how thoroughly the credit department investigates prospective customers, some uncollectible accounts will arise as a result of errors in judgment or because of unexpected developments. In fact, a limited amount of uncollectible accounts is evidence of a sound credit policy. If the credit department should become too cautious and conservative in rating customers, it might avoid all credit losses but, in so doing, lose profitable business by rejecting many acceptable customers.

4 Record estimates of uncollectible accounts receivable, write-offs of uncollectible accounts, and any later recoveries.

Reflecting uncollectible accounts in the financial statements. An account receivable that has been determined to be uncollectible is no longer an asset. The loss of this asset represents an **expense,** termed uncollectible accounts expense.

In measuring business income, one of the most fundamental principles of accounting is that revenue should be **matched** with (offset by) the expenses incurred in generating that revenue. Uncollectible accounts expense is **caused by selling goods** on credit to customers who fail to pay their bills. Therefore, this expense is incurred in the month in which the **related sales** are made, even though specific accounts receivable may not be determined to be uncollectible until a later accounting period. Thus, an account receivable that originates from a sale on credit in January and is determined to be uncollectible in August represents an expense in

[5] As explained in Chapter 5, the period used to define current assets and current liabilities is one year or the company's operating cycle, whichever is longer. The **operating cycle** is the period of time needed to convert cash into inventory, the inventory into accounts receivable, and the accounts receivable back into cash.

January. Unless each month's uncollectible accounts expense is ***estimated*** and reflected in the month-end income statement and balance sheet, these financial statements may show overstated earnings and overvalued assets.

To illustrate, assume that World Famous Toy Co. begins business on January 1 and makes most of its sales on account. At January 31, accounts receivable amount to $250,000. On this date, the credit manager reviews the accounts receivable and estimates that approximately $10,000 of these accounts will prove to be uncollectible. The following adjusting entry should be made at January 31:

Provision for uncollectible accounts

Uncollectible Accounts Expense... 10,000	
Allowance for Doubtful Accounts....................................	10,000
To record the portion of total accounts receivable estimated to be uncollectible.	

The ***Uncollectible Accounts Expense*** account created by the debit part of this entry is closed into the Income Summary account in the same manner as any other expense account. The ***Allowance for Doubtful Accounts*** which was credited in the above journal entry will appear in the balance sheet as a deduction from the face amount of the accounts receivable. It serves to reduce the accounts receivable to their ***net realizable value*** in the balance sheet, as shown by the following illustration:

WORLD FAMOUS TOY CO.
Partial Balance Sheet
January 31, 19___

How much is the estimated net realizable value of the accounts receivable?

Current assets:		
Cash..		$ 75,000
Marketable securities......................................		25,000
Accounts receivable	$250,000	
Less: Allowance for doubtful accounts....................	10,000	240,000
Inventory		300,000
Total current assets		$640,000

The Allowance for Doubtful Accounts

There is no way of telling in advance ***which*** accounts receivable will prove to be uncollectible. It is therefore not possible to credit the accounts of specific customers for our estimate of probable uncollectible accounts. Neither should we credit the Accounts Receivable controlling account in the general ledger. If the Accounts Receivable controlling account were to be credited with the estimated amount of doubtful accounts, this controlling account would no longer be in balance with the total of the numerous customers' accounts in the subsidiary ledger. The only practical alternative, therefore, is to credit a separate account called ***Allowance for Doubtful Accounts*** with the amount estimated to be uncollectible.

The Allowance for Doubtful Accounts often is described as a ***contra-asset*** account or a ***valuation*** account. Both of these terms indicate that the Allowance for Doubtful Accounts has a credit balance, which is offset against the asset Accounts Receivable to produce the proper balance sheet value for this asset.

Estimating the amount of uncollectible accounts. The estimate of accounts receivable likely to prove uncollectible is based upon the company's past experience, modified by current economic conditions. For instance, losses from uncollectible receivables tend to be greater during periods of recession than in periods of growth and prosperity. Because the allowance for doubtful accounts is necessarily an estimate and not a precise calculation, the factor of personal judgment plays a considerable part in determining the size of this valuation account.

Conservatism as a factor in valuing accounts receivable. The larger the allowance established for doubtful accounts, the lower the net valuation of accounts receivable will be. Some accountants and some business executives tend to favor the most conservative valuation of assets that logically can be supported. *Conservatism* in the preparation of a balance sheet implies a tendency to resolve uncertainties in the valuation of assets by reporting assets at the lower end of the range of reasonable values rather than by establishing values in a purely objective manner.

The valuation of assets at conservative amounts is a long-standing tradition in accounting, stemming from the days when creditors were the major users of financial statements. From the viewpoint of bankers and others who use financial statements as a basis for granting loans, conservatism in valuing assets has long been regarded as a desirable policy.

In considering the argument for balance sheet conservatism, it is important to recognize that the income statement also is affected by the estimate made of uncollectible accounts. The act of providing a relatively large allowance for doubtful accounts involves a correspondingly heavy charge to expense. Minimizing the valuation of assets in the balance sheet has the related effect of minimizing the amount of net income reported in the current period.

Monthly adjustments of the allowance account. In the adjusting entry made by World Famous Toy Co. at January 31, the amount of the adjustment ($10,000) was equal to the estimated amount of uncollectible accounts. This is true only because January was the first month of operations and this was the company's first estimate of its uncollectible accounts. In future months, the amount of the adjusting entry will depend upon two factors: (1) the estimate of uncollectible accounts, and (2) the *current balance* in the Allowance for Doubtful Accounts. Before we illustrate the adjusting entry for a future month, let us first see why the balance in the allowance account may change during the accounting period.

Writing off an uncollectible account receivable

Whenever an account receivable from a specific customer is determined to be uncollectible, it no longer qualifies as an asset and should be written off. To *write off* an account receivable is to reduce the balance of the customer's account to zero. The journal entry to accomplish this consists of a credit to the Accounts Receivable controlling account in the general ledger (and to the customer's account in the subsidiary ledger), and an offsetting debit to the *Allowance for Doubtful Accounts.*

To illustrate, assume that early in February World Famous Toy Co. learns that

Discount Stores has gone out of business and that the $4,000 account receivable from this customer is now worthless. The entry to write off this uncollectible account receivable is:

Writing off a receivable "against the allowance"

Allowance for Doubtful Accounts   4,000
    Accounts Receivable, Discount Stores   4,000
To write off the receivable from Discount Stores as uncollectible.

The important thing to note in this entry is that the debit is made to the **_Allowance for Doubtful Accounts_** and **_not_** to the Uncollectible Accounts Expense account. The estimated expense of credit losses is charged to the Uncollectible Accounts Expense account at the end of each accounting period. When a particular account receivable is later determined to be worthless and is written off, this action does not represent an additional expense but merely confirms our previous estimate of the expense. If the Uncollectible Accounts Expense account were first charged with **_estimated_** credit losses and then later charged with **_proven_** credit losses, we would be double counting the actual uncollectible accounts expense.

Notice also that the entry to write off an uncollectible account receivable reduces both the asset account and the contra-asset account by the same amount. Thus, writing off an uncollectible account **_does not change_** the net realizable value of accounts receivable in the balance sheet. The following illustration shows the net realizable value of World Famous Toy Co.'s accounts receivable before and after the write-off of the account receivable from Discount Stores:

What happens to net realizable value?

Before the Write-Off		After the Write-Off	
Accounts receivable	$250,000	Accounts receivable	$246,000
Less: Allowance for doubtful		Less: Allowance for doubtful	
accounts	10,000	accounts	6,000
Net realizable value	$240,000	Net realizable value	$240,000

Why is the net realizable value of accounts receivable **_unchanged_** by the write-off of the $4,000 account? The answer is that the company has **_already provided for uncollectible accounts of up to $10,000._** The net realizable value of accounts receivable will not be affected unless the accounts actually proving to be uncollectible **_exceed_** the balance in the Allowance for Doubtful Accounts.

Recovery of an account previously written off

Occasionally a receivable that has been written off as worthless will later be collected in full or in part. Such collections often are referred to as **_recoveries_** of bad debts. Collection of an account receivable previously written off is evidence that the write-off was an error; therefore, the receivable should be reinstated as an asset.

Assume, for example, that in February World Famous Toy Co. makes the following entry to write off a past-due account receivable from L. B. Brown:

Writing off the account . . .

Allowance for Doubtful Accounts   200
    Accounts Receivable, L. B. Brown   200
To write off the receivable from L. B. Brown as uncollectible.

Later in February, full payment of this account is received unexpectedly from L. B. Brown. The entry to restore Brown's account receivable is:

<table>
<tr><td style="width:20%">. . . and reinstating the account</td><td>Accounts Receivable, L. B. Brown . . . .</td><td>200</td><td></td></tr>
<tr><td></td><td>   Allowance for Doubtful Accounts . . . .</td><td></td><td>200</td></tr>
<tr><td></td><td>To reinstate as an asset an account receivable previously written off.</td><td></td><td></td></tr>
</table>

Notice that this entry is **exactly the opposite** of the entry made when the account was written off as uncollectible. A separate entry will be made in the cash receipts journal to record the receipt of cash from L. B. Brown.

Monthly estimates of credit losses

At the end of each month, management should again estimate the probable amount of uncollectible accounts **and adjust the Allowance for Doubtful Accounts to this new estimate.**

To illustrate, assume that at the end of February the credit manager of World Famous Toy Co. analyzes the accounts receivable and estimates that approximately **$11,000** of these accounts will prove uncollectible. Currently, the Allowance for Doubtful Accounts has a credit balance of only **$6,000** determined as follows:

<table>
<tr><td style="width:20%">Current balance in the allowance account</td><td>Balance at January 31 (credit) . . . .</td><td></td><td>$10,000</td></tr>
<tr><td></td><td>Less: Write offs of accounts determined to be uncollectible:</td><td></td><td></td></tr>
<tr><td></td><td>   Discount Stores . . . .</td><td>$4,000</td><td></td></tr>
<tr><td></td><td>   L. B. Brown . . . .</td><td>200</td><td>4,200</td></tr>
<tr><td></td><td>Subtotal . . . .</td><td></td><td>$ 5,800</td></tr>
<tr><td></td><td>Add: Recoveries of accounts previously written off:</td><td></td><td></td></tr>
<tr><td></td><td>   L. B. Brown . . . .</td><td></td><td>200</td></tr>
<tr><td></td><td>Balance at end of February (prior to adjusting entry) . . . .</td><td></td><td>$ 6,000</td></tr>
</table>

To increase the balance in the allowance account to $11,000 at February 27, the month-end adjusting entry must **add $5,000** to the allowance. The entry will be:

<table>
<tr><td style="width:20%">Increasing the allowance for doubtful accounts</td><td>Uncollectible Accounts Expense . . . .</td><td>5,000</td><td></td></tr>
<tr><td></td><td>   Allowance for Uncollectible Accounts . . . .</td><td></td><td>5,000</td></tr>
<tr><td></td><td>To increase the Allowance for Uncollectible Accounts to $11,000, computed as follows:</td><td></td><td></td></tr>
<tr><td></td><td>   Required allowance at Feb. 27 . . . .</td><td>$11,000</td><td></td></tr>
<tr><td></td><td>   Credit balance prior to adjustment . . . .</td><td>6,000</td><td></td></tr>
<tr><td></td><td>   Required adjustment . . . .</td><td>$ 5,000</td><td></td></tr>
</table>

5 Apply the balance sheet approach and the income statement approach to estimating uncollectible accounts. **Estimating credit losses — the "balance sheet" approach.** The most widely used method of estimating the probable amount of uncollectible accounts is based upon an **aging** of the accounts receivable. This method is sometimes called the **balance sheet** approach, because the method emphasizes the proper balance sheet valuation of accounts receivable.

"Aging" accounts receivable means classifying each receivable according to its age. An ***aging schedule*** for the accounts receivable of Valley Ranch Supply is illustrated below:

Analysis of Accounts Receivable by Age
December 31, 19___

	Total	Not Yet Due	1–30 Days Past Due	31–60 Days Past Due	61–90 Days Past Due	Over 90 Days Past Due
Animal Care Center	$ 9,000	$ 9,000				
Butterfield, John D.	2,400			$ 2,400		
Citrus Groves, Inc.	4,000	3,000	$ 1,000			
Dairy Fresh Farms	1,600				$ 600	$1,000
Eastlake Stables	13,000	7,000	6,000			
(Other customers)	70,000	32,000	22,000	9,600	2,400	4,000
Totals	$100,000	$51,000	$29,000	$12,000	$3,000	$5,000

An aging schedule is useful to management in reviewing the status of individual accounts receivable and in evaluating the overall effectiveness of credit and collection policies. In addition, the schedule is used as the basis for estimating the amount of uncollectible accounts.

The longer an account is past due, the greater the likelihood that it will not be collected in full. Based upon past experience, the credit manager estimates the percentage of credit losses likely to occur in each age group of accounts receivable. This percentage, when applied to the total dollar amount in the age group, gives the estimated uncollectible portion for that group. By adding together the estimated uncollectible portions for all age groups, the ***required balance*** in the Allowance for Doubtful Accounts is determined. The following schedule lists the group totals from the aging schedule and shows how the estimated total amount of uncollectible accounts is computed:

Estimated Uncollectible Accounts Receivable
December 31, 19___

	Age Group Total	Percentage Considered Uncollectible*	Estimated Uncollectible Accounts
Not yet due.......................................	$ 51,000	1	$ 510
1–30 days past due	29,000	3	870
31–60 days past due	12,000	10	1,200
61–90 days past due	3,000	20	600
Over 90 days past due	5,000	50	2,500
Totals.......................................	$100,000		$5,680

* These percentages are estimated each month by the credit manager, based upon recent experience and current economic conditions.

At December 31, Valley Ranch Supply has total accounts receivable of $100,000, of which $5,680 are estimated to be uncollectible. Thus, an adjusting entry is needed to increase the Allowance for Doubtful Accounts from its present level to $5,680. If the allowance account currently has a credit balance of, say, $4,000, the month-end adjusting entry should be in the amount of *$1,680.*[6]

An alternative approach to estimating credit losses. The procedures above describe the *balance sheet* approach to estimating and recording credit losses. This approach is based upon an aging schedule, and the Allowance for Doubtful Accounts is *adjusted to a required balance.* An alternative method, called the *income statement* approach, focuses upon estimating the uncollectible accounts *expense* for the period. Based upon past experience, the uncollectible accounts expense is estimated at some percentage of net credit sales. The adjusting entry is made in the *full amount of the estimated expense,* without regard for the current balance in the Allowance for Doubtful Accounts.

To illustrate, assume that a company's past experience indicates that about 2 percent of its credit sales prove to be uncollectible. If credit sales for September amount to $150,000, the month-end adjusting entry to record uncollectible accounts expense is:

<table>
<tr><td>The "income statement" approach</td><td>Uncollectible Accounts Expense...</td><td>3,000</td><td></td></tr>
<tr><td></td><td>   Allowance for Doubtful Accounts....................................</td><td></td><td>3,000</td></tr>
<tr><td></td><td colspan="3">To record uncollectible accounts expense, estimated at 2% of credit sales
($150,000 × 2% = $3,000).</td></tr>
</table>

This approach is fast and simple — no aging schedule is required and no consideration is given to the existing balance in the Allowance for Doubtful Accounts. The aging of accounts receivable, however, provides a more reliable estimate of uncollectible accounts because of the consideration given to the age and collectibility of specific accounts receivable at the balance sheet date.

In past years, many small companies used the income statement approach as a shortcut in preparing monthly financial statements but used the balance sheet method in preparing annual financial statements. Today, however, most businesses have computer software that quickly and easily prepares monthly aging

---

[6] If accounts receivable written off during the period *exceed* the Allowance for Doubtful Accounts at the last adjustment date, the allowance account temporarily acquires a *debit balance.* This situation seldom occurs if the allowance is adjusted each month, but often occurs if adjusting entries are made only at year-end.

If Valley Ranch Supply makes only an annual adjustment for uncollectible accounts, the allowance account might have a debit balance of, say, $10,000. In this case, the year-end adjusting entry should be for *$15,680* in order to bring the allowance to the required credit balance of $5,680.

Regardless of how often adjusting entries are made, the balance in the allowance account of Valley Ranch Supply should be *$5,680 at year-end.* Uncollectible accounts expense will be the same for the year regardless of whether adjusting entries are made annually or monthly. The only difference is in whether this expense is recognized in one annual adjusting entry or in 12 monthly adjusting entries, each for a smaller amount.

schedules of accounts receivable. Thus, most businesses today use the **balance sheet approach** in their monthly as well as annual financial statements.

Direct charge-off method

6 Compare the allowance method and the direct charge-off method of accounting for uncollectible accounts.

Some companies do not use any valuation allowance for accounts receivable. Instead of making period adjusting entries to record uncollectible accounts expense on the basis of estimates, these companies recognize no uncollectible accounts expense until specific receivables are determined to be worthless. This method makes no attempt to match revenue and related expenses. Uncollectible accounts expense is recorded in the period in which individual accounts receivable are determined to be worthless rather than in the period in which the sales were made.

When a particular customer's account is determined to be uncollectible, it is written off directly to Uncollectible Accounts Expense, as follows:

Uncollectible Accounts Expense	250	
Accounts Receivable, Bell Products		250
To write off the receivable from Bell Products as uncollectible.		

When the direct charge-off method is in use, the accounts receivable will be listed in the balance sheet at their gross amount, and **no valuation allowance** will be used. The receivables, therefore, are not stated at estimated net realizable value.

In some situations, use of the direct charge-off method is appropriate. If a company makes most of its sales for cash, the amount of its accounts receivable will be small in relation to other assets. The expense from uncollectible accounts should also be small. Consequently, the direct charge-off method is acceptable because its use does not have a **material** effect on the reported net income. Another situation in which the direct charge-off method works satisfactorily is in a company which sells all or most of its output to a few large companies which are financially strong. In this setting there may be no basis for making advance estimates of any credit losses.

For many years, income tax rules permitted the use of either the direct charge-off method or the allowance method of measuring uncollectible accounts expense. However, the Tax Reform Act of 1986 made the direct charge-off method the **only** acceptable means of determining taxable income. From the standpoint of accounting theory, the allowance method is better, for it enables expenses to be **matched with the related revenue** and thus aids in making a logical measurement of net income.

Credit card sales

7 Account for sales to customers using national credit cards.

Many retailing businesses avoid the risk of uncollectible accounts by making credit sales to customers who use well-known credit cards, such as American Express, Visa, and MasterCard. A customer who makes a purchase using one of these cards must sign a multiple-copy form, which includes a **credit card draft.** A credit card draft is similar to a check which is drawn upon the funds of the credit card company rather than upon the personal bank account of the customer. The credit card company promptly pays cash to the merchant to redeem these drafts. At the end of each month, the credit card company bills the credit card holder for all the drafts it has redeemed during the month. If the credit card holder fails to pay the amount owed, it is the credit card company which sustains the loss.

By making sales through credit card companies, merchants receive cash more quickly from credit sales and avoid uncollectible accounts expense. Also, the merchant avoids the expenses of investigating customers' credit, maintaining an accounts receivable subsidiary ledger, and making collections from customers.

Bank credit cards. Some widely used credit cards (such as Visa and MasterCard) are issued by banks. When the credit card company is a bank, the retailing business may deposit the signed credit card drafts directly in its bank account, along with the currency and personal checks received from customers. Since banks accept these credit card drafts for immediate deposit, sales to customers using bank credit cards are recorded as cash sales.

In exchange for handling the credit card drafts, the bank makes a monthly service charge which usually runs between $1\frac{1}{4}$ and $3\frac{1}{2}\%$ of the amount of the drafts deposited by the merchant during the month. This monthly service charge is automatically deducted from the merchant's bank account and appears with other bank service charges in the merchant's monthly bank statement.

Other credit cards. When customers use nonbank credit cards (such as American Express, Diners' Club, and Carte Blanche), the retailing business cannot deposit the credit card drafts directly in its bank account. Instead of debiting Cash, the merchant records an account receivable from the credit card company. Periodically, the credit card drafts are mailed to the credit card company, which then sends a check to the merchant. Credit card companies, however, do not redeem the drafts at the full sales price. The agreement between the credit card company and the merchant usually allows the credit card company to take a discount of between $3\frac{1}{2}$ and 5% when redeeming the drafts.

To illustrate the procedures in accounting for these credit card sales, assume that Bradshaw Camera Shop sells a camera for $200 to a customer who uses a Quick Charge credit card. The entry would be

Receivable is from the credit card company

Accounts Receivable, Quick Charge Co.	200	
Sales		200

To record sale to customer using Quick Credit card.

At the end of the week, Bradshaw Camera Shop mails credit card drafts totaling $1,200 to Quick Charge Co., which redeems the drafts less a 5% discount. When payment is received, the entry is

Cash	1,140	
Credit Card Discount Expense	60	
Accounts Receivable, Quick Charge Co.		1,200

To record collection of account receivable from Quick Charge Co., less 5% discount.

The expense account, Credit Card Discount Expense, should be included among the selling expenses in the income statement of Bradshaw Camera Shop.

Analysis of accounts receivable

What dollar amount of accounts receivable would be reasonable for a business making annual credit sales of $1,200,000? Comparison of the average amount of accounts receivable with the sales made on credit during the period indicates how long it takes to convert receivables into cash. For example, if annual credit sales of $1,200,000 are made at a uniform rate throughout the year and the accounts receivable at year-end amount to $200,000, we can see at a glance that the receivables represent one-sixth of the year's sales, or about 60 days of uncollected sales. Management naturally wants to make efficient use of the available capital in the business, and therefore is interested in a rapid "turnover" of accounts receivable. If the credit terms offered by the business in this example were, say, 30 days net, the existence of receivables equal to 60 days' sales would indicate difficulty in making collections and would warrant investigation. The analysis of receivables is considered more fully in Chapter 15.

Internal controls for receivables

One of the most important principles of internal control is that employees who have custody of cash or other negotiable assets must not maintain accounting records. In a small business, unfortunately, it is not uncommon to find that one employee has responsibility for handling cash receipts from customers, maintaining the accounts receivable records, issuing credit memos for goods returned by customers, and writing off receivables judged to be uncollectible. Such a combination of duties is a virtual invitation to fraud. The employee in this situation is able to remove the cash collected from a customer without making any record of the collection. The next step is to dispose of the balance in the customer's account. This can be done by issuing a credit memo indicating that the customer has returned merchandise, or by writing off the customer's account as uncollectible. Thus, the employee has the cash, the customer's account shows a zero amount, and the books are in balance.

To avoid fraud in the handling of receivables, some of the most important rules are that employees who maintain the accounts receivable subsidiary ledger must **not have access** to cash receipts, and employees who handle cash receipts must not have access to the records of receivables. Furthermore, **neither** the employees who maintain records of receivables **nor** those who handle cash receipts should have authority to issue credit memoranda or to authorize the write-off of receivables as uncollectible. These are classic examples of incompatible duties.

NOTES RECEIVABLE

A promissory note is an unconditional promise in writing to pay on demand or at a future date a definite sum of money.

The person who signs the note and thereby promises to pay is called the **maker** of the note. The person to whom payment is to be made is called the **payee** of the note. In the illustration below, G. L. Smith is the maker of the note and A. B. Davis is the payee.

$1,000	Los Angeles, California	July 10, 19__

One month .... after date .... I .... promise to pay

to the order of .... A. B. Davis ....

-----One thousand and no/100----- .... dollars

payable at .... First National Bank of Los Angeles ....

for value received, with interest at .... 12% per annum. ....

G. L. Smith

From the viewpoint of the maker, G. L. Smith, the illustrated note is a liability and is recorded by crediting the Notes Payable account. However, from the viewpoint of the payee, A. B. Davis, this same note is an asset and is recorded by debiting the Notes Receivable account. The maker of a note expects to pay cash at the maturity date; the payee expects to receive cash at that date.

Nature of interest

Interest is a charge made for the use of money. A borrower incurs interest expense. A lender earns interest revenue. When you encounter notes payable in a company's financial statements, you know that the company is borrowing and you should expect to find interest expense. When you encounter notes receivable, you should expect interest revenue.

Computing interest. A formula used in computing interest is as follows:

Principal $\times$ Rate of Interest $\times$ Time = Interest

(Often expressed as $P \times R \times T = I$.)

Interest rates are usually stated on an annual basis. For example, the interest on a $1,000, one-year, 12% note is computed as follows:

$$\$1,000 \times 0.12 \times 1 = \$120$$

If the term of the note were only four months instead of a year, the interest charge would be $40, computed as follows:

$$\$1,000 \times 0.12 \times \tfrac{4}{12} = \$40$$

If the term of the note is expressed in days, the exact number of days must be used in computing the interest. ***The day on which a note is dated is not included; the day on which a note falls due is included.*** Thus, a note dated today and maturing tomorrow involves only one day's interest. To simplify the computation of interest, we shall assume that a year contains 360 days rather than 365.[7] This assumption applies to illustrations and problems throughout this book. Suppose, for example, that a 60-day, 12% note for $1,000 is drawn on June 10. The interest charge could be computed as follows:

$$\$1,000 \times 0.12 \times \tfrac{60}{360} = \$20$$

The principal of the note ($1,000) plus the interest ($20) equals $1,020, and this amount (the ***maturity value***) will be payable on August 9. The computation of days to maturity is as follows:

Days remaining in June (30 − 10; date of origin is not included)	20
Days in July	31
Days in August to maturity date (date of payment is included)	9
Total days called for by note	60

Accounting for notes receivable

8 Account for the receipt of notes, accrual of interest, collection or default, and the discounting of notes receivable.

In some lines of business, notes receivable are seldom encountered; in other fields they occur frequently and may constitute an important part of total assets. Business concerns that sell high-priced durable goods such as automobiles and farm machinery often accept notes receivable from their customers. Many companies obtain notes receivable in settlement of past-due accounts receivable.

All notes receivable are usually posted to a single account in the general ledger. A subsidiary ledger is not essential because the notes themselves, when filed by due dates, are the equivalent of a subsidiary ledger and provide any necessary information as to maturity, interest rates, collateral pledged, and other details. The amount debited to Notes Receivable is always the ***face amount*** of the note, regardless of whether or not the note bears interest. When an interest-bearing note is collected, the amount of cash received will be larger than the face amount of the note. The interest collected is credited to an Interest Revenue account, and only the face amount of the note is credited to the Notes Receivable account.

---

[7] In calculating interest, banks and other businesses traditionally assumed that a year contained 360 days rather than 365. Consequently, one day's interest was treated as 1/360 of a year, rather than 1/365. This assumption causes the interest amount for a short-term note to be slightly higher, but makes interest computations much simpler. In recent years, however, most banks have changed to the use of a 365-day year for interest calculations.

Illustrative entries. Assume that on December 1 a 12%, 90-day note receivable is acquired from a customer, Marvin White, in settlement of an existing account receivable of $30,000. The entry for acquisition of the note is as follows:

Note received to replace account receivable

Notes Receivable 30,000
    Accounts Receivable, Marvin White 30,000
Accepted 12%, 90-day note in settlement of account receivable.

At December 31, the end of the company's fiscal year, the interest earned to date on notes receivable should be accrued by an adjusting entry as follows:

Adjusting entry for interest revenue earned in December

Interest Receivable... 300
    Interest Revenue 300
To accrue interest for the month of December on Marvin White note ($30,000 × 12% × $\frac{1}{12}$ = $300).

On March 1 (90 days after the date of the note), the note matures. The entry to record collection of the note will be:

Collection of principal and interest

Cash 30,900
    Notes Receivable... 30,000
    Interest Receivable 300
    Interest Revenue 600
Collected 12%, 90-day note from Marvin White ($30,000 × 12% × $\frac{3}{12}$ = $900 interest of which $600 was earned in current year).

The preceding three entries show that interest is being earned throughout the life of the note and that the interest should be apportioned between years on a time basis. The revenue of each year will then include the interest actually earned in that year.

If the maker of a note defaults. A note receivable which cannot be collected at maturity is said to have been **_defaulted_** by the maker. Immediately after the default of a note, an entry should be made by the holder to transfer the amount due from the Notes Receivable account to an account receivable from the debtor.

To illustrate, assume that on March 1 Marvin White had defaulted on the note used in our preceding example. In this case, the entry on March 1 would have been:

Accounts Receivable, Marvin White 30,900
    Notes Receivable... 30,000
    Interest Receivable 300
    Interest Revenue 600
To record default by Marvin White on 12%, 90-day note.

Notice that the interest earned on the note is recorded through the maturity date and is included in the account receivable from the maker. The interest receivable on a defaulted note is just as valid a claim against the maker as is the principal amount of the note.

If the account receivable from White cannot be collected, it ultimately will be written off against the Allowance for Doubtful Accounts. Therefore, the balance in the Allowance for Doubtful Accounts should provide for estimated uncollectible *notes* receivable as well as uncollectible *accounts* receivable.

● **CASE IN POINT** ● For many companies, the provision for doubtful accounts is small and does not have a material affect upon net income for the period. Notes receivable, however, are the largest and most important asset for nearly every bank. Interest on these notes is a bank's largest and most important type of revenue. Thus, the collectibility of notes owned by a bank is a key factor in determining the success or failure of that bank.

Citicorp, the nation's largest bank, recently added a staggering $3 billion to its allowance for doubtful loans to developing countries. The related debit to expense caused Citicorp to report one of the largest net losses for a single quarter (three-month period) in the history of American business. Citicorp is not alone in having problems with uncollectible loans. In recent years, uncollectible loans have been the largest expense in the income statements of many American banks.

Discounting notes receivable

Many business concerns which obtain notes receivable from their customers prefer to sell the notes to a bank for cash rather than to hold them until maturity. Selling a note receivable to a bank or finance company is often called *discounting* a note receivable. The holder of the note endorses the back of the note (as in endorsing a check) and delivers the note to the bank. The bank expects to collect the *maturity value* (principal plus interest) from the maker of the note at the maturity date, but if the maker fails to pay, the bank can demand payment from the endorser.

When a business endorses a note and turns it over to a bank for cash, it is promising to pay the note if the maker fails to do so. The endorser is therefore contingently liable to the bank. A *contingent liability* may be regarded as a potential liability which either will develop into a full-fledged liability or will be eliminated entirely by a future event. The future event in the case of a discounted note receivable is the payment (or default) of the note by the maker. If the maker pays, the contingent liability of the endorser is thereby ended. If the maker fails to pay, the endorser must pay in his stead. In either case the period of contingent liability ends at the maturity date of the note.

The amount of cash obtained from the bank by discounting a note receivable is called the *proceeds* from discounting the note. The proceeds are always less than the maturity value of the note; the difference represents the return that the bank expects to earn on the transaction. The company discounting the note recognizes any difference between the proceeds and the carrying value of the note as *interest revenue* or *interest expense*.

To illustrate, assume that Retail Sales Co. receives a 60-day, 12% note for $10,000 from Chris Kelly. Several days later, Retail Sales Co. discounts this note to its bank, receiving cash of $9,970. The entry to record discounting this note is:

```
Cash ...................................................................  9,970
Interest Expense ......................................................     30
     Note Receivable ..................................................           10,000
To record discounting the Chris Kelly note receivable to Security Bank.
```

In this illustration, the proceeds of $9,970 were less than the $10,000 face amount of the note. The proceeds received from discounting a note may be *either* more or less than the face amount of the note, depending upon interest rates and the amount of time left until the note matures. If the proceeds are less than the face amount, the difference is debited to Interest Expense. However, if the proceeds exceed the face amount of the note, the difference is credited to interest revenue.

Discounted note receivable paid by its maker. Before the maturity date of the discounted note, the bank will notify the maker, Chris Kelly, that it now holds the note. Kelly will therefore make payment directly to the bank. Kelly's payment of the note will require no entries in the accounting records of Retail Sales Co.

Discounted note receivable defaulted by its maker. Now let us assume that when the note matures, Kelly is unable to pay the bank. Retail Sales Co. would then be obligated to "make the note good" — that is, to immediately pay the bank the full $10,200 maturity value of the note.[8] Thus, the company's contingent liability becomes a real liability. The entry to record payment of this note in the event of Kelly's default is shown below:

```
Accounts Receivable, Chris Kelly ......................................  10,200
     Cash .............................................................           10,200
To record payment to bank of maturity value of discounted Kelly note,
defaulted by maker.
```

Disclosure of contingent liabilities. Since contingent liabilities are potential liabilities rather than full-fledged liabilities, they are not included in the liability section of the balance sheet. However, these potential liabilities may affect the financial position of the business if future events cause them to become real liabilities. Therefore, contingent liabilities should be *disclosed in footnotes to the*

---

[8] The maturity value of the note includes both the principal amount of the note plus any interest due at the maturity date. The maturity value of the 12%, 60-day note receivable from Chris Kelly may be computed as follows:

```
Principal amount......................................................  $10,000
Interest ($10,000 × 12% × 2/12) ......................................      200
Maturity value .......................................................  $10,200
```

financial statements. The contingent liability arising from the discounting of notes receivable could be disclosed by the following footnote:

Note 6: Contingencies and commitments

At December 31, 19___, the Company was contingently liable for notes receivable discounted with maturity values in the amount of $250,000.

END-OF-CHAPTER REVIEW

Summary of chapter learning objectives

1 State the major steps in achieving internal control over cash transactions.

The major steps in achieving internal control over cash transactions are: (1) to separate cash handling from the accounting function, (2) to prepare a control listing of all cash received through the mail and from over-the-counter cash sales, (3) to deposit all cash receipts in the bank daily, (4) to make all payments by check, (5) to verify every expenditure before issuing a check in payment, and (6) to separate the function of approving payments from the function of signing checks.

2 Describe the operation of a petty cash fund.

A petty cash fund represents an exception to the general rule of making all payments by check. A few small payments, such as postage due and taxi fares, can be made more conveniently through a petty cash fund than by the time-consuming and expensive process of issuing a check. The petty cash fund is established by writing and cashing a check payable to Petty Cash. For each cash payment from the fund, a petty cash voucher is placed in the fund. When the cash in the fund runs low, it is replenished by a check for the amount of vouchers in the fund. The debits are to expense accounts and the credit is to cash.

3 Prepare a bank reconciliation and explain its purpose.

The balance of cash shown on the month-end bank statement usually will differ from the amount of cash shown in the depositor's ledger. The difference is caused by items which have been recorded by either the depositor or the bank, but not recorded by both. Examples are outstanding checks and deposits in transit. The bank reconciliation adjusts the cash balance per the books and the cash balance per the bank statement for any unrecorded items, and thus produces the correct amount of cash to be shown in the balance sheet at the end of the month.

The purpose of a bank reconciliation is to achieve the control inherent in the maintenance of two independent records of cash transactions; one record maintained by the depositor and the other by the bank. When these two records are reconciled (brought into agreement), we gain assurance of a correct accounting for cash transactions.

4 Record estimates of uncollectible accounts receivable, write-offs of uncollectible accounts, and any later recoveries.

To accomplish the objective of matching revenue with all related expenses, the portion of each period's credit sales that will prove to be uncollectible must be estimated. This estimated amount is recorded by a debit to Uncollectible Accounts Expense and a credit to the contra-asset account, Allowance for Doubtful Accounts. When specific accounts are determined to be uncollectible, they are written off by debiting Allowance for Doubtful Accounts and crediting Accounts Receivable.

Occasionally a receivable which has been written off as worthless will later be collected. Such collections are called recoveries of bad debts. Two accounting entries are needed: (1) to reinstate the receivable by debiting Accounts Receivable and crediting the Allowance for Doubtful Accounts, and (2) to record the collection by debiting Cash and crediting Accounts Receivable.

5 Apply the balance sheet approach and the income statement approach to estimating uncollectible accounts.

Under the balance sheet approach, we arrange the year-end accounts receivable into age groups and estimate the uncollectible portion. Then, we adjust the allowance account to equal this estimate.

Under the income statement approach, we compute the amount of the adjusting entry for uncollectible accounts as a percentage of the year's net sales. This approach leaves out of consideration any existing balance in the allowance account.

6 Compare the allowance method and the direct charge-off method of accounting for uncollectible accounts.

The allowance method is theoretically preferable because it applies the matching principle to revenue and to the expenses incurred in producing that revenue. Thus, bad debts associated with the year's sales are recognized as expenses of the period in which the sales were made. However, some companies (for which bad debts are not material) use the direct charge-off method. Under this method, no uncollectible accounts expense is recognized until specific receivables are determined to be worthless.

7 Account for sales to customers using national credit cards.

Many retail businesses avoid the risk of uncollectible accounts by making credit sales to customers who present well-known bank credit cards, such as Visa and MasterCard. The credit card drafts received by a merchant are deposited at the bank for immediate credit, hence are the equivalent of cash sales. For nonbank credit cards, such as American Express and Diners' Club, the merchant collects directly from the credit card company, which deducts a service charge.

8 Account for the receipt of notes, accrual of interest, collection or default, and the discounting of notes receivable.

Notes receivable are recorded at their face amount. Interest revenue is recognized as earned at the end of the accounting period and at the maturity of the note. If the maker defaults, the principal of the note and the interest earned are transferred to an account receivable pending collection or write-off. Notes receivable are often discounted or sold to a bank for cash. The amount received (proceeds) is equal to the maturity value of the note minus the discount charged by the bank. A contingent liability to the bank exists until the note matures, which means that the person discounting the note must pay the bank if the maker of the note should default.

Key terms introduced or emphasized in chapter 7

Aging the accounts receivable. The process of classifying accounts receivable by age groups such as current, past due 1–30 days, past due 31–60 days, etc. A step in estimating the uncollectible portion of the accounts receivable.

Allowance for doubtful accounts. A valuation account or contra account relating to accounts receivable and showing the portion of the receivables estimated to be uncollectible.

Bank reconciliation. An analysis that explains the difference between the balance of cash shown on the bank statement and the balance of cash shown on the depositor's records.

Cash over and short. A ledger account used to accumulate the cash overages and shortages resulting from errors in making change.

Conservatism. A traditional practice of resolving uncertainties by choosing an asset valuation at the lower point of the range of reasonableness. Also refers to the policy of postponing recognition of revenue to a later date when a range of reasonable choice exists. Designed to avoid overstatement of financial strength and earnings.

Contingent liability. A potential liability which either will develop into a full-fledged liability or will be eliminated entirely by a future event.

Contra-asset account. A ledger account which is deducted from or offset against a related account in the financial statements, for example, Allowance for Doubtful Accounts and Discount on Notes Receivable.

Default. Failure to pay interest or principal of a promissory note at the due date.

Direct charge-off method. A method of accounting for uncollectible receivables in which no expense is recognized until individual accounts are determined to be worthless. At that point the account receivable is written off with an offsetting debit to uncollectible accounts expense. The method used for income tax purposes.

Discounting notes receivable. Selling a note receivable prior to its maturity date.

Maker (of a note). A person or entity who issues a promissory note.

Maturity date. The date on which a note becomes due and payable.

Maturity value. The value of a note at its maturity date, consisting of principal plus interest.

NSF check. A customer's check which was deposited but returned because of a lack of funds (Not Sufficient Funds) in the account on which the check was drawn.

Outstanding checks. Checks issued by a business to suppliers, employees, or other payees but not yet presented to the bank for payment.

Payee. The person named in a promissory note to whom payment is to be made (the creditor).

Petty cash fund. A small amount of cash set aside for making minor cash payments for which writing of checks is not practicable.

Proceeds. The amount received from selling a note receivable prior to its maturity. Maturity value minus discount equals proceeds.

Voucher. A written authorization used in approving a transaction for recording and payment.

Voucher system. An accounting system designed to provide strong internal control over cash disbursements. Requires that every transaction which will result in a cash payment be verified, approved, and recorded before a check is prepared.

Demonstration problem for your review

Shown below are selected transactions of Jamestown Corporation during the month of June:

June 10   An account receivable from S. Willis in the amount of $700 is determined to be uncollectible and is written off against the Allowance for Doubtful Accounts.

June 15   Received a 12%, 90-day note for $10,000 from Target Co. in settlement of an account receivable due today.

June 22   Unexpectedly received $200 from F. Hill in full payment of her account. The $200 account receivable from Hill had previously been written off as uncollectible.

June 25   Discounted the Target Co. note at First Texas Bank, receiving proceeds of $10,025.

June 30   Replenished the petty cash fund. Petty cash vouchers indicated office supplies expense, $44; miscellaneous expense, $32.

June 30   The month-end bank reconciliation includes the following reconciling items: outstanding checks, $4,240; deposit in transit, $3,150; check from customer T. Jones returned by bank as "NSF," $128; non-interest-bearing note receivable collected by bank on the company's behalf, $3,500; service charge by bank for handling collection of note receivable, $10.

Data for adjusting entries:

(1) An aging of accounts receivable indicates probable uncollectible accounts totaling $9,000. Prior to the month-end adjustment, the Allowance for Doubtful Accounts has a credit balance of $5,210.

(2) Notes receivable totaling $22,000 were held by the company throughout the month of June. All these notes bear interest at an annual rate of 12%.

Instructions

a   Prepare entries in general journal entry form for the June transactions. In adjusting the accounting records from the bank reconciliation, make one entry to record any increases in the Cash account and a separate entry to record any decreases.

b   Prepare the month-end adjustments indicated by the two numbered paragraphs.

c   Draft the footnote for the June 30 balance sheet disclosing the contingent liability for the note receivable discounted on June 25.

Solution to demonstration problem

a
General Journal

June 10 Allowance for Doubtful Accounts..............................	700	
Accounts Receivable, S. Willis		700
To write off receivable from S. Willis as uncollectible.		
15 Notes Receivable...	10,000	
Accounts Receivable, Target Co.........................		10,000
Received 12%, 90-day note from Target Co. in settlement of account receivable.		
22 Accounts Receivable, F. Hill...................................	200	
Allowance for Doubtful Accounts		200
To reinstate account receivable previously written off as uncollectible.		
22 Cash	200	
Accounts Receivable, F. Hill		200
To record collection of account receivable.		
25 Cash	10,025	
Notes Receivable		10,000
Interest Revenue..		25
To record discounting Target Co. note at First Texas Bank.		

30	Office Supplies Expense...	44	
	Miscellaneous Expense	32	
	Cash..		76
	To replenish petty cash fund.		

30	Cash	3,500	
	Notes Receivable		3,500
	To record collection of note by bank.		

30	Account Receivable, T. Jones	128	
	Bank Service Charges..	10	
	Cash..		138
	To record bank service charge and to reclassify NSF check from T. Jones as an account receivable.		

b

Adjusting Entries

June 30	Uncollectible Accounts Expense	3,790	
	Allowance for Doubtful Accounts		3,790
	To increase Allowance for Doubtful Accounts to $9,000 ($9,000 − $5,210 = $3,790).		
30	Interest Receivable	220	
	Interest Revenue.......................................		220
	To accrue interest on notes receivable for June ($22,000 × 12% × $\frac{1}{12}$ = $220).		

c Note: Contingent liabilities

At June 30, 19__, the company was contingently liable for a note receivable discounted at a bank. The maturity value of this note is $10,300.

ASSIGNMENT MATERIAL

Review questions

1 If a company has checking accounts in three banks, should it maintain a separate ledger account for each? Should the company's balance sheet show the amount on deposit in each of the three checking accounts as a separate item? Explain.

2 Mention some principles to be observed by a business in establishing strong internal control over cash receipts.

3 Explain how internal control over cash transactions is strengthened by compliance with the following rule: "Deposit each day's cash receipts intact in the bank, and make all disbursements by check."

4 Ringo Store sells only for cash and records all sales on cash registers before delivering merchandise to the customers. On a given day the cash count at the close of business indicated $10.25 less cash than was shown by the totals on the cash register tapes. In what account would this cash shortage be recorded? Would the account be debited or credited?

5 Name three internal control practices relating to cash which would be practicable even in a small business having little opportunity for division of duties.

6 What information usually appears on a bank statement?

7 Pico Stationery Shop has for years maintained a petty cash fund of $75, which is replenished twice a month.

   a How many debit entries would you expect to find in the Petty Cash account each year?

   b When would expenditures from the petty cash fund be entered in the ledger accounts?

8 List two items often encountered in reconciling a bank account which may cause cash per the bank statement to be larger than the balance of cash shown in the accounts.

9 In the reconciliation of a bank account, what reconciling items necessitate a journal entry in the depositor's accounting records?

10 A check for $455 issued in payment of an account payable was erroneously listed in the cash payments journal as $545. The error was discovered early in the following month when the paid check was returned by the bank. What corrective action is needed?

11 It is standard accounting practice to treat as cash all checks received from customers. When a customer's check is received, recorded, and deposited, but later returned by the bank marked NSF, what accounting entry or entries would be appropriate?

12 Explain the relationship between the *matching principle* and the need to estimate uncollectible accounts receivable.

13 Company A and Company B are virtually identical in size and nature of operations, but Company A is more conservative in valuing accounts receivable. Will this greater emphasis on conservatism cause A to report higher or lower net income than Company B? Assume that you are a banker considering identical loan applications from A and B and you know of the more conservative policy followed by A. In which set of financial statements would you feel more confidence? Explain.

14 Adams Company determines at year-end that its Allowance for Doubtful Accounts should be increased by $6,500. Give the adjusting entry to carry out this decision.

15 Mill Company, which has accounts receivable of $309,600 and an allowance for doubtful accounts of $3,600 decides to write off as worthless a past-due account receivable for $1,500 from J. D. North. What effect will the write-off have upon total current assets? Upon net income for the period? Explain.

16 Bell Company, which uses the allowance method of accounting for uncollectible accounts, wrote off as uncollectible a $1,200 receivable from Dailey Company. Several months later, Dailey Company obtained new long-term financing and promptly paid all its old debts in full. Give the journal entry or entries (in general journal form) which Bell Company should make to record this recovery of $1,200.

17 Describe a procedure by which management could be informed each month of the status of collections and the overall quality of the accounts receivable on hand.

18 In making the annual adjusting entry for uncollectible accounts, a company may utilize a *balance sheet approach* to make the estimate or it may use an *income statement approach.* Explain these two alternative approaches.

19 What is the direct charge-off method of handling credit losses as opposed to the allowance method? What is its principal shortcoming?

20 Morgan Corporation has decided to write off its account receivable from Brill Company because the latter has entered bankruptcy. What general ledger accounts should be debited and credited, assuming that the allowance method is in use? What general ledger accounts should be debited and credited if the direct charge-off method is in use?

21 What are the advantages to a retailer of making credit sales only to customers who use nationally recognized credit cards?

22 Alta Mine Co., a restaurant that had always made cash sales only, adopted a new policy of honoring several nationally known credit cards. Sales did not increase, but many of Alta Mine Co.'s regular customers began charging dinner bills on the credit cards. Has the new policy been beneficial to Alta Mine Co.? Explain.

23 Determine the maturity date of the following notes:
a A three-month note dated March 10
b A 30-day note dated August 15
c A 90-day note dated July 2

24 X Company acquires a 9%, 60-day note receivable from a customer, Robert Waters, in settlement of an existing account receivable of $4,000. Give the journal entry to record acquisition of the note and the journal entry to record its collection at maturity.

25 Explain the nature of a ***contingent liability***. What is the contingent liability that arises when notes receivable are discounted with a bank?

26 Does a contingent liability appear on a balance sheet? If so, in what part of the balance sheet?

Exercises

Exercise 7-1
Accounting
terminology

Listed below are nine technical accounting terms emphasized in this chapter:

Default	**Aging schedule**	**Direct charge-off method**
Conservatism	**Petty cash fund**	**Contingent liability**
NSF checks	**Voucher system**	**Bank reconciliation**

Each of the following statements may (or may not) describe one of these technical terms. For each statement, indicate the accounting term described, or answer "None" if the statement does not correctly describe any of the terms.

a A system used for making small cash disbursements which do not justify the procedures involved in issuing a check.
b Checks issued by a business which have not yet been presented for payment.
c Resolving uncertainties in the valuation of assets by reporting assets at the lower end of the range of reasonable values rather than establishing values in a purely objective manner.
d Recognition of credit losses only when specific accounts receivable are determined to be worthless.
e A sequence of procedures for assuring that every potential expenditure has been reviewed and approved before a check is issued.
f Failure to make payment of principal or interest per the terms of a promissory note.
g The obligation of the endorser of a discounted note receivable to make payment if the maker fails to pay at the due date.
h A control procedure that should bring to light any unrecorded cash disbursements.

Exercise 7-2
Internal control: identifying strength and weakness

Some of the following practices are suggestive of strength in internal controls; others are suggestive of weakness. Identify each of the eight practices with the term Strength or Weakness. Give reasons for your answers.

a Accounting department personnel are not authorized to prepare bank reconciliations. This procedure is performed in the finance department and the accounting department is notified of any required adjustments to the accounts.

b Checks received through the mail are recorded daily by the person maintaining accounts receivable records.

c All cash receipts are deposited daily.

d Any difference between a day's over-the-counter cash receipts and the day's total shown by the cash register is added to or removed from petty cash.

e After the monthly bank reconciliation has been prepared, any difference between the adjusted balance per the depositor's records and the adjusted balance per the bank statement is entered in the Cash Over and Short account.

f Employees who handle cash receipts are not authorized to issue credit memoranda or to write off accounts receivable as uncollectible.

g Vouchers and all supporting documents are perforated with a "PAID" stamp before being sent to the finance department for review and signing of checks.

h Personnel in the accounting department are not authorized to handle cash receipts. Therefore, accounts receivable records are maintained by the credit manager, who handles all collections from customers.

Exercise 7-3
Subdivision of duties

Certain subdivisions of duties are highly desirable for the purpose of achieving a reasonable degree of internal control. For each of the following six responsibilities, explain whether or not assigning the duty to an employee who also handles cash receipts would represent a significant weakness in internal control. Briefly explain your reasoning.

a Responsibility for issuing credit memoranda for sales returns.

b Responsibility for preparing a control listing of all cash collections.

c Responsibility for preparing monthly bank statements.

d Responsibility for executing both cash and credit sales transactions.

e Responsibility for maintaining the general ledger.

f Responsibility for maintaining the accounts receivable subsidiary ledger.

Exercise 7-4
Short bank reconciliation

The following information relating to the bank checking account is available for Data Center at July 31:

Balance per depositor's records at July 31	$8,671.25
Balance per bank statement at July 31	9,893.15
Outstanding checks	2,102.50
Deposit in transit	872.60
Service charge by bank	8.00

Prepare a bank reconciliation for Data Center at July 31.

Exercise 7-5
Bank reconciliation and adjusting entries

The information shown below relates to the cash position of Whipstock, Inc., at September 30.

(1) At September 30, cash per the accounting records was $5,815; cash per the bank statement was $5,327.

(2) Cash receipts of $1,451 on September 30 were not deposited until October 1.

(3) The following memoranda accompanied the bank statement:
(a) A debit memo for service charges for the month of September, $8.
(b) A debit memo attached to a $200 check drawn by Susan Scott, marked NSF.

(4) The following checks had been issued but were not included among the paid checks returned by the bank: no. 921 for $326, no. 924 for $684, and no. 925 for $161.

Instructions

a Prepare a bank reconciliation as of September 30.
b Prepare the necessary adjusting journal entry (include both adjustments in one entry).

Exercise 7-6
Petty cash

Three-Par, Inc., established a petty cash fund of $200 on December 1. At December 31, the end of the company's fiscal year, the fund contained the following:

Currency and coins	$ 78.82
Expense vouchers:	
Taxi fares (debit Travel Expense)	34.90
Office supplies expense	46.28
Contributions to Boy Scouts and others	40.00
Total..	$200.00

Prepare journal entries in general journal form to record the establishment of the petty cash fund on December 1 and its replenishment on December 31.

Exercise 7-7
Uncollectible accounts expense

The credit manager of Road Warrior Tires has gathered the following information about the company's accounts receivable and credit losses during the current year:

Net credit sales for the year		$2,000,000
Accounts receivable at year-end		240,000
Uncollectible accounts receivable:		
Actually written off during the year	$29,100	
Estimated portion of year-end receivables expected to prove		
uncollectible (per aging schedule)................................	12,000	41,100

Prepare one journal entry summarizing the recognition of uncollectible accounts expense for the entire year under each of the following independent assumptions:

(1) Uncollectible accounts expense is estimated at an amount equal to $1\frac{1}{2}\%$ of net credit sales.
(2) Uncollectible accounts expense is recognized by adjusting the balance in the Allowance for Doubtful Accounts to the amount indicated in the year-end aging schedule. The balance in the allowance account at the beginning of the current year was $10,000. (Consider the effect of the write-offs during the year upon the balance in the Allowance for Doubtful Accounts.)
(3) The company uses the direct charge-off method of accounting for uncollectible accounts.

Exercise 7-8
Write-offs and recoveries

The balance sheet of Barco, Inc., at September 30 includes the following items:

Notes receivable from customers	$ 36,000
Accrued interest on notes receivable	720
Accounts receivable	151,200
Less: Allowance for doubtful accounts	3,600

Using general journal entries, you are to record the following events occurring in October:

a Accounts receivable of $3,456 are written off as uncollectible.

b A customer's note for $990 on which interest of $54 has been accrued in the accounts is deemed uncollectible, and both balances are written off against the Allowance for Doubtful Accounts.

c An account receivable for $468 previously written off is collected.

d Aging of accounts receivable at October 31 indicates a need for a $5,400 allowance to cover possible failure to collect accounts currently outstanding. (Consider the effect of entries for a, b, and c on the amount of the Allowance for Doubtful Accounts.)

Exercise 7-9
Notes and interest

On November 1, a 12%, 90-day note receivable is acquired from Sharon Rogers, a customer, in settlement of her $10,000 account receivable. Prepare journal entries to record (a) the receipt of the note on November 1, (b) the adjustment to record 60 days' interest revenue on December 31, and (c) collection of the principal and interest on January 30.

Exercise 7-10
Discounting notes receivable

Morgan Company received a 9%, 6-month note receivable from John Ross in the face amount of $20,000. Soon thereafter, Morgan Company discounted this note at National Bank.

Instructions

a Prepare the journal entry to record the discounting of this note under each of the following assumptions:
(1) The proceeds amounted to $19,915.
(2) The proceeds amounted to $20,210.

b Draft a footnote to Morgan Company's financial statement to disclose the contingent liability from discounting this note.

c Prepare the journal entry that would be made at the maturity date if John Ross defaults and Morgan Company must pay off the note.

Problems

Problem 7-1
Internal control procedures

Listed below are nine errors or problems which might occur in the processing of cash transactions. Also shown is a list of internal control procedures.

Possible Errors or Problems

a An employee steals the cash collected from a customer for an account receivable and conceals this theft by issuing a credit memorandum indicating that the customer returned the merchandise.

b The same voucher was circulated through the system twice, causing the supplier to be paid twice for the same invoice.

c Without fear of detection, the cashier sometimes abstracts cash forwarded to him from the mailroom or the sales department instead of depositing these receipts in the company's bank account.

d The custodian of the petty cash fund often "borrows" money from the fund, but replaces it before the fund is replenished.

e A salesclerk often rings up a sale at less than the actual sales price and then removes the additional cash collected from the customer.

f The cashier conceals a shortage of cash by making an entry in the general ledger debiting Miscellaneous Expense and crediting Cash.

g A salesclerk occasionally makes an error in the amount of change given to a customer.

h The employee designated to sign checks is able to steal blank checks and issue them for unauthorized purposes without fear of detection.

i All cash received during the last four days is lost in a burglary on Thursday night.

Internal Control Procedures

1 Monthly reconciliation of bank statements to accounting records.

2 Use of a Cash Over and Short account.

3 Adequate subdivision of duties.

4 Require that all cash disbursements material in dollar amount be made by check.

5 Deposit each day's cash receipts intact in the bank.

6 Use of electronic cash registers equipped with optical scanners to read magnetically coded labels on merchandise.

7 Immediate preparation of a control listing when cash is received, and the comparison of this listing to bank deposits.

8 Cancellation of paid vouchers.

9 Occasional surprise counts of the petty cash.

0 None of the above control procedures can effectively prevent this type of error from occurring.

Instructions. List the letters (a through i) designating each possible error or problem. Beside this letter, place the number indicating the internal control procedure that should prevent this type of error or problem from occurring. If none of the specified internal control procedures would effectively prevent the error, place a "0" opposite the letter.

**Problem 7-2
Operating a petty
cash fund**

In order to handle small cash disbursements in an efficient manner, Whitehall Company established a petty cash fund on July 10. The company does not use a voucher system. The following events relating to petty cash occurred in July.

July 10   A check for $300 drawn payable to Petty Cash was issued and cashed to establish the fund.

July 31   At month-end a count of the fund disclosed the following:

Office supplies expense	$50.40
Postage expense	69.00
Travel expense	49.38
Miscellaneous expense	50.62
Currency and coin remaining in the fund	80.60

July 31   A check was issued to replenish the petty cash fund.

Instructions

a Prepare an entry in general journal form to record the establishment of the petty cash fund on July 10.

b Prepare an entry to record the replenishment of the petty cash fund on July 31.

c Net income for Whitehall Company in July was $6,785.20. What amount of net income would have appeared in the July income statement if the company had not replenished the petty cash fund on July 31?

Problem 7-3
Preparing a bank
reconciliation

At November 30, West Coast Imports has available the following data concerning its bank checking account:

(1) At November 30, cash per the accounting records was $42,500; per bank statement, $37,758.
(2) The cash receipts of $6,244 on November 30 were deposited on December 1.
(3) Included on the bank statement was a credit for $167 interest earned on this checking account during November.
(4) Two checks were outstanding at November 30: no. 921 for $964 and no. 925 for $1,085.
(5) Enclosed with the bank statement were two debit memoranda for the following items:
(a) Service charge for November, $14.
(b) A $700 check of customer Frank Miller, marked NSF.

Instructions

a Prepare a bank reconciliation at November 30.
b Prepare two journal entries for any items in the bank statement which have not yet been recorded in the depositor's accounting records. In the first entry, record increases in cash; in the second entry, record decreases.

Problem 7-4
Another bank
reconciliation

The information needed to prepare a bank reconciliation and the related adjusting entries for Wicked Pony at March 31 is listed below.

(1) Cash balance per the accounting records of Wicked Pony, $18,100.
(2) The bank statement showed a balance of $21,873.98 at March 31.
(3) Accompanying the bank statement was a debit memorandum relating to a check for $186 from a customer, D. Jones. The check was returned by the bank and stamped NSF.
(4) Checks outstanding as of March 31 were as follows: no. 84 for $1,841.02; no. 88 for $1,323.00; no. 89 for $16.26.
(5) Also accompanying the bank statement was a debit memorandum for $44.80 for safe deposit box rent; the bank had erroneously charged this item to the account of Wicked Pony.
(6) On March 29, the bank collected a non-interest-bearing note for Wicked Pony. The note was for $2,700.00, the bank charged a collection fee of $5.00.
(7) A deposit of $2,008.50 was in transit; it had been mailed to the bank on March 31.
(8) In recording a $160 check received on account from a customer, Ross Company, the accountant for Wicked Pony erroneously listed the collection in the cash receipts journal as $16. The check appeared correctly among the deposits on the March bank statement.
(9) The bank service charge for March amounted to $6.00; a debit memo in this amount was returned with the bank statement.

Instructions

a Prepare a bank reconciliation at March 31.
b Prepare the necessary journal entries.
c What amount of cash should appear on the company's March 31 balance sheet?

**Problem 7-5
Aging accounts
receivable;
write-offs**

Best Products uses the balance sheet approach to estimate uncollectible accounts expense. At year-end an aging of the accounts receivable produced the following classification:

Not yet due	$ 74,000
1–30 days past due	26,000
31–60 days past due	13,000
61–90 days past due	8,000
Over 90 days past due	4,000
Total	$125,000

On the basis of past experience, the company estimated the percentages probably uncollectible for the above five age groups to be as follows: Group 1, 1%; Group 2, 3%; Group 3, 10%; Group 4, 20%; and Group 5, 50%.

The Allowance for Doubtful Accounts before adjustment at December 31 showed a credit balance of $1,800.

Instructions

a Compute the estimated amount of uncollectible accounts based on the above classification by age groups.

b Prepare the adjusting entry needed to bring the Allowance for Doubtful Accounts to the proper amount.

c Assume that on January 10 of the following year, Best Products learned that an account receivable which had originated on September 1 in the amount of $1,900 was worthless because of the bankruptcy of the customer, Mesa Company. Prepare the journal entry required on January 10 to write off this account.

**Problem 7-6
Estimating bad
debts: income
statement
approach and
balance sheet ap-
proach**

Snowwhite, Inc., owned by Linda Snow, had for the past three years been engaged in selling paper novelty goods to retail stores. Sales are made on credit and each month the company has estimated its uncollectible accounts expense as a percentage of net sales. The percentage used has been $\frac{1}{2}$ of 1% of net sales. However, it appears that this provision has been inadequate because the Allowance for Doubtful Accounts has a debit balance of $2,700 at May 31 prior to making the monthly provision. Snow has therefore decided to change the method of estimating uncollectible accounts expense and to rely upon an analysis of the age and character of the accounts receivable at the end of each month.

At May 31, the end of the company's fiscal year, the accounts receivable totaled $180,000. This total amount included past-due accounts in the amount of $38,000. None of these past-due accounts was considered hopeless; all accounts regarded as worthless had been written off as rapidly as they were determined to be uncollectible. After careful investigation of the past-due accounts at May 31, Linda Snow decided that the probable loss contained therein was 10%, and that in addition she should anticipate a loss of 1% of the current accounts receivable.

Instructions

a Compute the probable uncollectible accounts expense applicable to the accounts receivable at May 31, based on the analysis by the owner.

b Prepare the journal entry necessary to carry out the change in company policy with respect to providing for uncollectible accounts expense.

Problem 7-7
Accounts
receivable: a
comprehensive
problem

Specialty Products has 250 accounts receivable in its subsidiary ledger. All accounts are due in 30 days. On June 30, an aging schedule was prepared. The results are summarized below:

Customer	Total	Not Yet Due	1–30 Days Past Due	31–60 Days Past Due	61–90 Days Past Due	Over 90 Days Past Due
(248 names)						
Subtotals	$345,250	$183,590	$94,680	$43,340	$9,000	$14,640

Two accounts receivable were accidentally omitted from this schedule. The following data is available regarding these accounts:

(1) R. Jones owes $4,250 from two invoices; invoice no. 218, dated March 14, in the amount of $2,980; and invoice no. 568, dated May 9, in the amount of $1,270.
(2) F. Smith owes $3,760 from two invoices; invoice no. 574, dated May 19, in the amount of $1,350; and invoice no. 641, dated June 5, in the amount of $2,410.

Instructions

a Complete the aging schedule as of June 30 by adding to the column subtotals an aging of the accounts of Jones and Smith.
b Prepare a schedule to compute the estimated portion of each age group that will prove uncollectible and the required balance in the Allowance for Doubtful Accounts. Arrange your schedule in the format illustrated on page 285. The following percentages of each age group are estimated to be uncollectible: Not yet due, 1%; 1–30 days, 4%; 31–60 days, 10%; 61–90 days, 30%; over 90 days, 50%.
c Prepare the journal entry to bring the Allowance for Doubtful Accounts up to its required balance at June 30, 19__. Prior to making this adjustment, the account has a credit balance of $13,800.
d Show how accounts receivable would appear in the company's balance sheet at June 30, 19__.
e On July 7, the credit manager of Specialty Products learns that the $4,250 account receivable from R. Jones is uncollectible because Jones has declared bankruptcy. Prepare the journal entry to write off this account.

Problem 7-8
Note receivable:
entries for
collection and for
default

Hanover Mills sells merchandise to retail stores on 30-day credit, but insists that any customer who fails to pay an invoice when due must replace it with an interest-bearing note. The company adjusts and closes its accounts at December 31. Among the transactions relating to notes receivable were the following.

Nov. 1   Received from a customer (Jones Brothers) a 12%, 6-month note for $10,000 in settlement of an account receivable due today.
May 1   Collected in full the 12%, 6-month note receivable from Jones Brothers, including interest.

Instructions

a Prepare journal entries (in general journal form) to record: (1) the receipt of the note on November 1; (2) the adjustment for interest on December 31; and (3) collection of principal and interest on May 1. Assume that the company does not use reversing entries.
b Assume that instead of paying the note on May 1, the customer (Jones Brothers) had defaulted. Give the journal entry by Hanover Mills to record the default. Assume that Jones Brothers has sufficient resources that the note will eventually be collected.

Problem 7-9
Notes receivable
—including
discounting

Union Square, a wholesaler, sells merchandise on 30-day open account, but requires customers who fail to pay invoices within 30 days to substitute promissory notes for their past-due accounts. No sales discount is offered. Among recent transactions were the following:

Mar. 17 Sold merchandise to S. R. Davis on account, $72,000, terms n/30.

Apr. 16 Received a 60-day, 10% note from Davis dated today in settlement of the open account of $72,000.

May 26 Discounted the Davis note at the bank, receiving proceeds of $72,712. The bank discount rate was 12% applied to the maturity value of the note for the 20 days remaining to maturity.

June 15 Received notice from the bank that the Davis note due today was in default. Paid the bank the maturity value of the note. Since Davis has extensive business interests, the management of Union Square is confident that no loss will be incurred on the defaulted note.

June 25 Made a $48,000 loan to John Raymond on a 30-day, 15% note.

Instructions

a Prepare in general journal form the entries necessary to record the above transactions. (In making interest calculations, assume a 360-day year.)

b Prepare the adjusting journal entry needed at June 30, the end of the company's fiscal year, to record interest accrued on the two notes receivable. [Accrue interest at 10% per annum from date of default (June 15) on the maturity value of the Davis note.]

Business decision cases

Case 7-1
Internal control
—a short case
study

P. K. Panther, a trusted employee of Bluestem Products, found himself in personal financial difficulties and decided to "borrow" (steal) $3,000 from the company and to conceal his theft.

As a first step, Panther removed $3,000 in currency from the cash register. This amount represented the bulk of the cash received in over-the-counter sales during the three business days since the last bank deposit. Panther then removed a $3,000 check from the day's incoming mail; this check had been mailed in by a customer, Michael Adams, in full payment of his account. Panther made no entry in the cash receipts journal for the $3,000 collection from Adams but deposited the check in Bluestem Products' bank account in place of the $3,000 over-the-counter cash receipts he had stolen.

In order to keep Adams from protesting when his month-end statement reached him, Panther made a general journal entry debiting Sales Returns and Allowances and crediting Accounts Receivable — Michael Adams. Panther posted this entry to the two general ledger accounts affected and also to Adams's account in the subsidiary ledger for accounts receivable.

Instructions

a Did these actions by Panther cause the general ledger to be out of balance or the subsidiary ledger to disagree with the controlling account? Explain.

b Assume that Bluestem Products prepares financial statements at the end of the month without discovering the theft. Would any items in the balance sheet or the income statement be in error? Explain.

c Several weaknesses in internal control apparently exist in Bluestem Products. Indicate three specific changes needed to strengthen internal control over cash receipts.

Allan Carter was a long-time employee in the accounting department of Marston Company. Carter's responsibilities included the following:

(1) Maintain the accounts receivable subsidiary ledger.
(2) Prepare vouchers for cash disbursements. The voucher and supporting documents were forwarded to John Marston, owner of the company.
(3) Compute depreciation on all plant assets.
(4) Authorize all sales returns and allowances given to credit customers and prepare the related credit memoranda. The credit memoranda were forwarded to Howard Smith, who maintains the company's journals and general ledger.

John Marston personally performs the following procedures in an effort to achieve strong internal control:

(1) Prepare monthly bank reconciliations.
(2) Prepare monthly trial balances from the general ledger and reconcile the accounts receivable controlling account with the subsidiary ledger.
(3) Prepare from the subsidiary ledger all monthly bills sent to customers and investigate any complaints from customers about inaccuracies in these bills.
(4) Review all vouchers and supporting documents before signing checks for cash disbursements.

Carter became terminally ill and retired. Shortly thereafter, he died. However, he left a letter confessing that over a period of years he had embezzled over $300,000 from Marston Company. As part of his scheme, he had managed to obtain both a bank account and a post office box in the name of Marston Company. He had then contacted customers whose accounts were overdue and offered them a 20% discount if they would make payment within five days. He instructed them to send their payments to the post office box. When the payments arrived, he deposited them in his "Marston Company" bank account. Carter stated in his letter that he had acted alone, and that no other company employees knew of his dishonest actions.

Marston cannot believe that Carter committed this theft without the knowledge and assistance of Howard Smith, who maintained the journals and the general ledger. Marston reasoned that Carter must have credited the customers' accounts in the accounts receivable subsidiary ledger, because no customers had complained about not receiving credit for their payments. Smith must also have recorded these credits in the general ledger, or Marston would have discovered the problem by reconciling the subsidiary ledger with the controlling account. Finally, Smith must have debited some other account in the general ledger to keep the ledger in balance. Thus, Marston is about to bring criminal charges against Smith.

Instructions

a Explain how Carter might have committed this theft without Smith's knowledge and without being detected by Marston's control procedures. (Assume that Carter had no personal access to the journals or general ledger.)

b Which of the duties assigned to Carter should not have been assigned to an employee responsible for maintaining accounts receivable? Would internal control be strengthened if this duty were assigned to the company's cashier? Explain.

Chapter 8
Inventories

CHAPTER PREVIEW

Our first goal in Chapter 8 is to show that determining the valuation of inventory also establishes the cost of goods sold. Thus, the validity of both the balance sheet and the income statement rest on accuracy in the valuation of inventory. A second goal is to stress that inventory is valued at cost, but that several alternative methods are available to measure cost. Four methods are illustrated and evaluated: specific identification; average cost; first-in, first-out (FIFO); and last-in, first-out (LIFO). Both the gross profit method and the retail method are introduced as examples of techniques for estimating inventory. The chapter concludes by emphasizing the importance of internal control over inventories and the advantages of using the perpetual inventory system whenever feasible.

After studying this chapter you should be able to meet these Learning Objectives:

1 Define inventory and explain how the valuation of inventory relates to the measurement of income.

2 Describe the effects of an inventory error on the income statement of the current year and of the following year.

3 Determine the cost of inventory by using (a) specific identification; (b) average cost; (c) first-in, first out (FIFO); and (d) last-in, first-out (LIFO). Discuss the merits and shortcomings of these methods.

4 Define inventory profits and explain why some accountants consider these profits fictitious.

5 Explain the lower-of-cost-or-market rule.

6 Estimate ending inventory by the gross profit method and by the retail method.

7 Explain how a perpetual inventory system operates.

Inventory defined

1 Define inventory and explain how the valuation of inventory relates to the measurement of income.

One of the largest assets in a retail store or in a wholesale business is the inventory of merchandise, and the sale of this merchandise is the major source of revenue. For a merchandising company, *the inventory consists of all goods owned and held for sale in the regular course of business.* Merchandise held for sale will normally be converted into cash within less than a year's time and is therefore regarded as a current asset. In the balance sheet, inventory is listed immediately after accounts receivable, because it is just one step further removed from conversion into cash than are the accounts receivable.

In manufacturing businesses there are three major types of inventories: *raw materials, goods in process of manufacture,* and *finished goods.* All three classes of inventories are included in the current asset section of the balance sheet.

To expand our definition of inventory to fit manufacturing companies as well as merchandising companies, we can say that inventory means "the aggregate of those items of tangible personal property which (1) are held for sale in the ordinary course of business, (2) are in process of production for such sale, or (3) are to be currently consumed in the production of goods or services to be available for sale." [1]

Periodic inventory system versus perpetual inventory system

The distinction between a periodic inventory system and a perpetual inventory system was explained earlier in Chapter 5. To summarize briefly, a periodic system of inventory accounting requires that acquisitions of merchandise be recorded by debits to a Purchases account. When merchandise is sold to a customer, the only accounting entry is a debit to Cash or Accounts Receivable and a credit to Sales for the sales price of the goods sold. No entry is made to reduce the inventory by the *cost* of the goods sold. Under the periodic inventory system, the Inventory account remains *unchanged* until the end of the accounting period. At year-end, all the goods on hand are counted and priced at cost; the total cost figure is then entered in the accounts as the amount of the year-end inventory.

The periodic inventory system is likely to be used by a business that sells a variety of merchandise with low unit prices, such as a hardware store or a drugstore. To maintain perpetual inventory records in such a business may be considered too time-consuming and expensive. However, the growing use of computers and electronic price tags is enabling some businesses with merchandise of low unit cost to adopt perpetual inventory systems.

Companies that sell products of high unit value such as automobiles and television sets usually maintain a perpetual inventory system that shows at all times the amount of inventory on hand. As merchandise is acquired, its cost is added to an inventory account; as goods are sold, their cost is transferred out of inventory and into a cost of goods sold account. This continuous updating of the inventory account explains the name *perpetual* inventory system.

In the early part of this chapter we will use the periodic inventory system as a point of reference; in the latter part we will emphasize perpetual inventories.

[1] AICPA, *Accounting Research and Terminology Bulletins,* Final Edition (New York: 1961), p. 27.

The matching principle as applied to inventories

The matching principle, as explained in Chapter 3, is fundamental to the measurement of net income for an accounting period. **Matching** revenue and related expenses means that the revenue for the period must be offset by all the expenses incurred in producing that revenue. In a merchandising business, the cost of goods sold is the largest single deduction from revenue. The huge size of this deduction makes accuracy in its measurement of special importance in producing a reliable income statement.

The American Institute of Certified Public Accountants has summarized the relationship between inventory valuation and the measurement of income in the following words: "A major objective of accounting for inventories is the proper determination of income through the process of matching appropriate costs against revenues." [2] The expression "matching costs against revenues" means determining what portion of the cost of goods available for sale should be deducted from the revenue of the current period and what portion should be carried forward (as inventory) to be matched against the revenue of the following period. The above quotation from the AICPA indicates that in accounting for inventories the proper determination of income takes precedence over other goals. As explained later in this chapter, an inventory valuation method which leads to a realistic value for the cost of goods sold may not produce the most realistic balance sheet valuation for inventories.

Inventory valuation and the measurement of income

In measuring the gross profit on sales earned during an accounting period, we subtract the **cost of goods sold** from the total **sales** of the period. The figure for sales is easily accumulated from the daily record of sales transactions, but in many businesses no day-to-day record is maintained showing the cost of goods sold.[3] The figure representing the cost of goods sold during an entire accounting period is computed at the end of the period by separating the **cost of goods available for sale** into two elements:

1 The cost of the goods sold
2 The cost of the goods not sold, which therefore comprise the ending inventory

This idea, with which you are already quite familiar, may be concisely stated in the form of an equation as follows:

Finding cost of goods sold

$$\begin{array}{c}\text{Cost of Goods}\\\text{Available for Sale}\end{array} - \begin{array}{c}\text{Ending}\\\text{Inventory}\end{array} = \begin{array}{c}\text{Cost of}\\\text{Goods Sold}\end{array}$$

Determining the amount of ending inventory is the key step in establishing the cost of goods sold. In separating the **cost of goods available for sale** into its

---

[2] AICPA, Accounting Research and Terminology Bulletins, Final Edition (New York: 1961), p. 28.

[3] As explained in Chap. 5, a company that maintains perpetual inventory records will have a day-to-day record of the cost of goods sold and of goods in inventory. Our present discussion, however, is based on the assumption that the periodic system of inventory is being used.

components of **goods sold** and **goods not sold,** we are as much or more interested in establishing the proper amount for cost of goods sold as in determining a proper figure for inventory. Throughout this chapter you should bear in mind that the procedures for determining the amount of the ending inventory are also the means for determining the cost of goods sold. The valuation of inventory and the determination of the cost of goods sold are in effect the two sides of a single coin.

Importance of an accurate valuation of inventory

The most important current assets in the balance sheets of most companies are cash, accounts receivable, and inventory. Of these three, the inventory of merchandise is usually by far the largest. Because of the relatively large size of the inventory, an error in the valuation of this asset may not be readily apparent. However, a large error in inventory can cause a material misstatement of financial position and of net income. An error of 20% in valuing the inventory may have as much effect on the financial statements as would the complete omission of the asset cash.

An error in inventory will of course lead to other erroneous figures in the balance sheet, such as the total current assets, total assets, owners' equity, and the total of liabilities and owners' equity. The error will also affect key figures in the income statement, such as the cost of goods sold, the gross profit on sales, and the net income for the period. Finally, it is important to recognize that *the ending inventory of one year is also the beginning inventory of the following year.* Consequently, the income statement of the second year will also be in error by the full amount of the original error in inventory valuation.

2 Describe the effects of an inventory error on the income statement of the current year and of the following year.

Effects of an error in valuing inventory: illustration. Assume that on December 31, 1989, the inventory of the Hillside Company is actually $100,000 but, through an accidental error, it is recorded as $90,000. The effects of this $10,000 error on the income statement for 1989 are indicated in the first illustration shown below, showing two income statements side by side. The left-hand set of figures shows the inventory of December 31 at the *proper value of $100,000* and represents a correct income statement. The right-hand set of figures represents an incorrect income statement, because the ending inventory is *erroneously listed as $90,000.* For emphasis, amounts affected by this error are shown in black. Note the differences between the two income statements with respect to net income, gross profit on sales, and cost of goods sold. Income taxes have purposely been omitted in this illustration.

This illustration shows that an understatement of $10,000 in the ending inventory caused an understatement of $10,000 in the net income for 1989. Next, consider the effect of this error on the income statement of the following year. The ending inventory of 1989 is, of course, the beginning inventory of 1990. The preceding illustration is now continued to show side by side a correct income statement and an incorrect statement for 1990. Amounts affected by this error are shown in black. The *ending* inventory of $120,000 for 1990 is the same in both statements and is to be considered correct. Note that the $10,000 error in the beginning

HILLSIDE COMPANY
Income Statement
For the Year Ended December 31, 1989

		With Correct Ending Inventory		With Incorrect Ending Inventory
Sales			$240,000	$240,000
Cost of goods sold:				
Beginning inventory, Jan. 1, 1989	$ 75,000			$ 75,000
Purchases	210,000			210,000
Cost of goods available for sale	$285,000			$285,000
Less: Ending inventory, Dec. 31, 1989	100,000			90,000
Cost of goods sold		185,000		195,000
Gross profit on sales		$ 55,000		$ 45,000
Operating expenses................................		30,000		30,000
Net income		$ 25,000		$ 15,000

Effects of error in inventory

inventory of the right-hand statement causes an error in the cost of goods sold, in gross profit, and in net income for 1990.

Counterbalancing errors. The illustrated income statements for 1989 and 1990 show that an understatement of the ending inventory in 1989 caused an understatement of net income in that year and an offsetting overstatement of net income for 1990. Over a period of two years the effects of an inventory error on net income will *counterbalance,* and the total net income for the two years together will be the same as if the error had not occurred. Since the error in reported net income for the first year is exactly offset by the error in reported net income for the second

HILLSIDE COMPANY
Income Statement
For the Year Ended December 31, 1990

		With Correct Beginning Inventory		With Incorrect Beginning Inventory
Sales			$265,000	$265,000
Cost of goods sold:				
Beginning inventory, Jan. 1, 1990	$100,000			$ 90,000
Purchases	230,000			230,000
Cost of goods available for sale	$330,000			$320,000
Less: Ending inventory, Dec. 31, 1990	120,000			120,000
Cost of goods sold		210,000		200,000
Gross profit on sales		$ 55,000		$ 65,000
Operating expenses................................		33,000		33,000
Net income		$ 22,000		$ 32,000

Effects on succeeding year

year, it might be argued that an inventory error has no serious consequences. Such an argument is not sound, for it disregards the fact that accurate yearly figures for net income are a primary objective of the accounting process. Moreover, many actions by management and many decisions by creditors and owners are based upon *trends* indicated in the financial statements for two or more years. Note that the inventory error has made the 1990 net income appear to be more than twice as large as the 1989 net income, when in fact *less* net income was earned in 1990 than in 1989. Anyone relying on the erroneous financial statements would be greatly misled as to the trend of Hillside Company's earnings.

Relation of inventory errors to net income. The effects of errors in inventory upon net income may be summarized as follows:

1 When the *ending* inventory is understated, the net income for the period will be understated.
2 When the *ending* inventory is overstated, the net income for the period will be overstated.
3 When the *beginning* inventory is understated, the net income for the period will be overstated.
4 When the *beginning* inventory is overstated, the net income for the period will be understated.

A few companies (usually small and unaudited) intentionally understate their ending inventory year after year for the purpose of evading income taxes. This type of fraud is discussed further at a later point in this chapter.

Taking a physical inventory

To establish a dollar value for the ending inventory, a business conducts a count of all merchandise owned. This count includes all goods on shelves and sales counters, and in storerooms and warehouses. The quantity counted of each item is multiplied by its unit cost; then the costs for all the various kinds of merchandise are added together to arrive at the total value for the ending inventory.

The physical inventory is usually taken at the end of the fiscal year. Often a business selects a fiscal year ending in a season of low activity. Thus, many department stores have a fiscal year ending in January or February. It is common practice to take inventory after regular business hours. By taking inventory while business operations are suspended, a more accurate count is possible than if goods were being sold or received while the count was in process.

Planning the physical inventory. Unless the taking of a physical inventory is carefully planned and supervised, serious errors are likely to occur which will invalidate the results of the count. The goal is to prevent such errors as the double counting of items, the omission of goods from the count, the inclusion of damaged goods, and other quantitative errors. If the business is audited each year by a CPA firm, the independent auditors will review the plans for the physical count and will be on hand during the taking of the inventory to perform test counts and to determine that the count is performed in accordance with the written plans developed in advance.

The first step in carrying out an accurate physical inventory is to designate one person to be responsible for all aspects of planning and controlling the count. Written instructions should be distributed to all supervisors and employees who are to participate, and meetings should be conducted to ensure that every supervisor and employee understands his or her role in carrying out the year-end inventory.

There are various methods of counting merchandise. One of the simplest procedures is carried out by the use of two-member teams. One member of the team counts and calls the description and quantity of each item. The other person lists the descriptions and quantities on an inventory sheet. (In some situations a tape recorder is useful in recording quantities counted.) When all goods have been counted and listed, the items on the inventory sheets are priced at cost, and the unit cost prices are multiplied by the quantities to determine the valuation of the inventory.

The year-end cutoff of transactions

A proper **cutoff** of transactions at year-end is essential to the preparation of accurate financial statements. Our goal is to prepare financial statements that reflect all transactions occurring through the last day of the period and none that occur thereafter.

The term **cutoff** as applied to inventory means that all purchases of merchandise through the last day of the period are included in the ending inventory and all goods sold on or before the last day of the period are excluded from ending inventory. A sale of merchandise occurs **when title to the goods passes from the seller to the buyer.** Title passes when the goods are delivered.

Passage of title to merchandise

A sale of merchandise is recorded by the seller as a debit to Accounts Receivable and an offsetting credit to the Sales account. This entry should be made when title to the goods passes to the customer. Obviously it would be improper for the seller to set up an account receivable and at the same time to include the goods in question in inventory. Great care is necessary at year-end to ensure that all last-minute shipments to customers are recorded as sales of the current year and, on the other hand, that no customer's order is recorded as a sale until the date the goods are shipped. Sometimes, in an effort to meet sales quotas, companies have recorded sales on the last day of the accounting period, when in fact the merchandise was not shipped until early in the next period. Such practices lead to an overstatement of the year's earnings and are not in accordance with generally accepted principles of accounting.

Merchandise in inventory is valued at **cost,** whereas accounts receivable are stated at the **sales price** of the merchandise sold. Consequently, the recording of a sale prior to delivery of the goods results in an unjustified increase in the total assets of the company. The increase will equal the difference between the cost and the selling price of the goods in question. The amount of the increase will also be reflected in the income statement, where it will show up as additional earnings. An unscrupulous company, which wanted to make its financial statements present a more favorable picture than actually existed, might do so by treating year-end orders from customers as sales even though the goods were not yet shipped.

Goods in transit. Do goods in transit belong in the inventory of the seller or of the buyer? If the selling company makes delivery of the merchandise in its own trucks, the merchandise remains its property while in transit. If the goods are shipped by rail, air, or other public carrier, the question of ownership of the goods while in transit depends upon whether the public carrier is acting as the agent of the seller or of the buyer. If the terms of the shipment are *F.O.B.* (free on board) *shipping point,* title passes at the point of shipment and the goods are the property of the buyer while in transit. If the terms of the shipment are *F.O.B. destination,* title does not pass until the shipment reaches the destination, and the goods belong to the seller while in transit. In deciding whether goods in transit at year-end should be included in inventory, it is therefore necessary to refer to the terms of the agreement with vendors (suppliers) and customers.

Pricing the inventory

One of the most interesting and widely discussed issues in accounting is the pricing of inventory. Even those business executives who have little knowledge of accounting are usually interested in the various methods of pricing inventory, because inventory valuation may have a significant effect upon reported net income.

Accounting for inventories involves determination of cost and of current fair value or replacement cost. An understanding of the meaning of the term *cost* as applied to inventories is a first essential in dealing with the question of inventory valuation.

Cost basis of inventory valuation

In the words of the AICPA's Committee on Accounting Procedure, "The primary basis of accounting for inventory is cost, which has been defined generally as the price paid or consideration given to acquire an asset. As applied to inventories, cost means in principle the sum of the applicable expenditures and charges directly or indirectly incurred in bringing an article to its existing condition and location."[4] A number of interesting questions arise in determining the *cost* of inventory. For example, should any expenditures other than the invoice price of purchased goods be considered as part of inventory cost? Another provocative question — if identical items of merchandise are purchased at different prices during the year, which of these purchase prices represent the cost of the items remaining in inventory at year-end? We will now address these and other questions involved in determining the cost of inventory.

Inclusion of additional incidental costs in inventory — a question of materiality. From a theoretical point of view, the cost of an item of inventory includes the invoice price, minus any discount, plus all expenditures necessary to place the

[4] AICPA, *Accounting Research and Terminology Bulletins,* Final Edition (New York: 1961), p. 28.

article in the proper location and condition for sale. Among these additional incidental costs are import duties, transportation-in, storage, insurance of goods being shipped or stored, and costs of receiving and inspecting the goods.

In determining the cost of the ending inventory, some companies add to the net invoice price of the goods a reasonable share of the charges for transportation-in incurred during the year. However, in other lines of business, it is customary and logical to price the year-end inventory **without** adding transportation-in or any other incidental costs because these charges **are not material in amount.** Although this practice results in a slight understatement of inventory cost, the understatement is so small that it does not affect the usefulness or reliability of the financial statements. Thus, the omission of transportation and other incidental charges from the cost of inventory often may be justified by the factors of convenience and economy. Accounting textbooks stress theoretical concepts of cost and income determination. The student of accounting should be aware, however, that in many business situations a close **approximation** of cost will serve the purpose at hand. The extra work involved in developing more precise accounting data must be weighed against the benefits that will result.

To sum up, we can say that in theory a portion of all the incidental costs of acquiring goods should be assigned to each item in the year-end inventory. However, the expense of computing cost in such a precise manner would usually outweigh the benefits to be derived. Consequently, these incidental costs relating to the acquisition of merchandise are usually treated as expense of the period in which incurred, rather than being carried forward to another accounting period by inclusion in the balance sheet amount for inventory. Thus, the accounting principle of **materiality** may at times take priority over the principle of **matching costs and revenue.**

Inventory valuation methods

3 Determine the cost of inventory by using (a) specific identification, (b) average cost, (c) FIFO, and (d) LIFO. Discuss the merits and shortcomings of these methods.

The prices of many kinds of merchandise are subject to frequent change. When **identical** lots of merchandise are purchased at various dates during the year, each lot may be acquired at a different cost price.

To illustrate the several alternative methods in common use for determining which purchase prices apply to the identical units remaining in inventory at the end of the period, assume the data shown below.

	Number of Units	Cost per Unit	Total Cost
Beginning inventory..	100	$ 80	$ 8,000
First purchase (Mar. 1)	50	90	4,500
Second purchase (July 1).....................................	50	100	5,000
Third purchase (Oct. 1)......................................	50	120	6,000
Fourth purchase (Dec. 1)	50	130	6,500
Available for sale..	300		$30,000
Units sold	180		
Units in ending inventory	120		

This schedule shows that 180 units were sold during the year and that 120 identical units are on hand at year-end to make up the ending inventory. In order to establish a dollar amount for cost of goods sold and for the ending inventory, we must make an assumption as to which units were sold and which units remain on hand at the end of the year. There are several acceptable assumptions on this point; four of the most common will be considered. Each assumption made as to the cost of the units in the ending inventory leads to a different method of pricing inventory and to different amounts in the financial statements. The four assumptions (and inventory valuation methods) to be considered are known as (1) specific identification, (2) average cost, (3) first-in, first-out, and (4) last-in, first-out.

Although each of these four methods will produce a different answer as to the cost of goods sold and the cost of the ending inventory, the valuation of inventory in each case is said to be at "cost." In other words, *these methods represent alternative definitions of inventory cost.*

Specific identification method. The specific identification method is best suited to inventories of high-priced, low-volume items. If each item in inventory is different from all others, as in the case of valuable paintings, custom jewelry, estate homes, and most other types of real estate, the specific identification method is clearly the logical choice. This type of inventory presents quite different problems from an inventory composed of large quantities of identical items.

If the units in the ending inventory can be identified as coming from specific purchases, they *may* be priced at the amounts listed on the purchase invoices. Continuing the example already presented, if the ending inventory of 120 units can be identified as, say, 50 units from the purchase of March 1, 40 units from the purchase of July 1, and 30 units from the purchase of December 1, the cost of the ending inventory may be computed as follows:

Specific identification method and . . . 50 units from the purchase of Mar. 1 @ $90	$ 4,500
40 units from the purchase of July 1 @ $100	4,000
30 units from the purchase of Dec. 1 @ $130	3,900
Ending inventory (specific identification)	$12,400

The cost of goods sold during the period is determined by subtracting the ending inventory from the cost of goods available for sale.

. . . cost of goods sold computation Cost of goods available for sale	$30,000
Less: Ending inventory	12,400
Cost of goods sold (specific identification method)	$17,600

The specific identification method has an intuitive appeal because it assigns actual purchase costs to the specific units purchased. For decision-making purposes, however, this approach does not always provide the most useful accounting information for a company handling a large volume of identical units.

As a simple example, assume that a coal dealer purchased 100 tons of coal at $60 a ton and a short time later made a second purchase of 100 tons of the same grade of coal at $80 a ton. The two purchases are in separate piles and it is a matter of indifference as to which pile is used in making sales to customers. Assume that the dealer makes a retail sale of one ton of coal at a price of $100. In measuring the gross profit on the sale, which cost figure should be used, $60 or $80? To insist that the cost depended on which of the two identical piles of coal was used in filling the delivery truck is an argument of questionable logic.

A situation in which the specific identification method is more likely to give meaningful results is in the purchase and sale of such high-priced articles as boats, automobiles, and jewelry.

Average-cost method. Average cost is computed by dividing the total cost of goods available for sale by the number of units available for sale. This computation gives a ***weighted-average unit cost,*** which is then applied to the units in the ending inventory.

<table>
<tr><td>*Average-cost*</td><td>Cost of goods available for sale</td><td>$30,000</td></tr>
<tr><td>*method and . . .*</td><td>Number of units available for sale</td><td>300</td></tr>
<tr><td></td><td>Average unit cost</td><td>$ 100</td></tr>
<tr><td></td><td>Ending inventory (at average cost, 120 units @ $100)</td><td>$12,000</td></tr>
</table>

Note that this method, when compared with the specific identification method, leads to a different amount for cost of goods sold as well as a different amount for the ending inventory.

<table>
<tr><td>*. . . cost of goods*</td><td>Cost of goods available for sale</td><td>$30,000</td></tr>
<tr><td>*sold computation*</td><td>Less: Ending inventory</td><td>12,000</td></tr>
<tr><td></td><td>Cost of goods sold (average-cost method)</td><td>$18,000</td></tr>
</table>

When the average-cost method is used, the cost figure of $12,000 determined for the ending inventory is influenced by all the various prices paid during the year. The price paid early in the year may carry as much weight in pricing the ending inventory as a price paid at the end of the year. A common criticism of the average-cost method of pricing inventory is that it attaches no more significance to current prices than to prices which prevailed several months earlier.

First-in, first-out method. The first-in, first-out method, which is often referred to as ***FIFO,*** is based on the assumption that the first merchandise acquired is the first merchandise sold. In other words, each sale is made out of the ***oldest*** goods in stock; ***the ending inventory therefore consists of the most recently acquired goods.*** The FIFO method of determining inventory cost may be adopted by any business, regardless of whether or not the physical flow of merchandise actually corresponds to this assumption of selling the oldest units in stock. Using the same data as in the preceding illustrations, the 120 units in the ending inventory would be regarded as consisting of the most recently acquired goods as follows:

First-in, first-out method and . . .	50 units from the Dec. 1 purchase @ $130	$ 6,500
	50 units from the Oct. 1 purchase @ $120	6,000
	20 units from the July 1 purchase @ $100	2,000
	Ending inventory, 120 units (at FIFO cost)	$14,500

During a period of *rising prices* the first-in, first-out method will result in a larger amount ($14,500) being assigned as the cost of the ending inventory than would be assigned under the average-cost method. When a relatively large amount is allocated as cost of the ending inventory, a relatively small amount will remain as cost of goods sold, as indicated by the following calculation:

. . . cost of goods sold computation	Cost of goods available for sale	$30,000
	Less: Ending inventory	14,500
	Cost of goods sold (first-in, first out method)	$15,500

It may be argued in support of the first-in, first-out method that the inventory valuation reflects recent costs and is therefore a realistic value in the light of conditions prevailing at the balance sheet date.

Last-in, first-out method. The last-in, first-out method, commonly known as *LIFO,* is one of the most interesting methods of pricing inventories. The title of this method suggests that the most recently acquired goods are sold first, and that *the ending inventory consists of "old" goods acquired in the earliest purchases.* Although this assumption is not in accord with the physical movement of merchandise in most businesses, there is a strong logical argument to support the LIFO method.

For the purpose of measuring income, the *flow of costs* may be more significant than the physical flow of merchandise. Supporters of the LIFO method contend that the measurement of income should be based upon *current* market conditions. Therefore, current sales revenue should be offset by the *current* cost of the merchandise sold. Under the LIFO method, the costs assigned to the cost of goods sold are relatively current, because they stem from the most recent purchases. Under the FIFO method, on the other hand, the cost of goods sold is based on "older" costs.

Using the same data as in the preceding illustrations, the 120 units in the ending inventory would be priced as if they were the oldest goods available for sale during the period, as follows:

Last-in, first-out method and . . .	100 units from the beginning inventory @ $80	$8,000
	20 units from the purchase of Mar. 1 @ $90	1,800
	Ending inventory, 120 units (at LIFO cost)	$9,800

Note that the LIFO cost of the ending inventory ($9,800) is very much lower than the FIFO cost ($14,500) of ending inventory in the preceding example. Since a relatively small part of the cost of goods available for sale is assigned to ending inventory, it follows that a relatively large portion must have been assigned to cost of goods sold, as shown by the following computation:

... cost of goods
sold computation

Cost of goods available for sale.	$30,000
Less: Ending inventory	9,800
Cost of goods sold (last-in, first-out method)	$20,200

Comparison of the alternative methods of pricing inventory. We have now illustrated four common methods of pricing inventory at cost: specific identification; average-cost; first-in, first-out; and last-in, first-out. By way of contrasting the results obtained from the four methods illustrated, especially during a period of rapid price increases, let us summarize the amounts computed for ending inventory, cost of goods sold, and gross profit on sales under each of the four methods. Assume that sales for the period amounted to $27,500.

Four methods of
determining
inventory cost
compared

	Specific Identification	Average-Cost	First-In, First-Out	Last-In, First-Out
Sales	$27,500	$27,500	$27,500	$27,500
Cost of goods sold:				
Beginning Inventory	$ 8,000	$ 8,000	$ 8,000	$ 8,000
Purchases	22,000	22,000	22,000	22,000
Cost of goods available for sale	$30,000	$30,000	$30,000	$30,000
Less: Ending inventory	12,400	12,000	14,500	9,800
Cost of goods sold	$17,600	$18,000	$15,500	$20,200
Gross profit on sales	$ 9,900	$ 9,500	$12,000	$ 7,300

This comparison of the four methods makes it apparent that during periods of *rising prices,* the use of LIFO will result in lower reported profits and lower income taxes than would be the case under the other methods of inventory valuation. Perhaps for this reason, many businesses have adopted LIFO. Current income tax regulations permit virtually any business to use the last-in, first-out method in determining taxable income.[5]

Which method of inventory valuation is best? All four of the inventory methods described are regarded as acceptable accounting practice and all four are acceptable in determining taxable income. In the selection of a method, consideration should be given to the probable effect on the income statement, upon the balance sheet, upon the amount of taxable income, and upon such business decisions as the establishment of selling prices for merchandise.

The specific identification method has the advantage of portraying the actual physical flow of merchandise. However, this method permits manipulation of in-

[5] Income tax laws require the use of lifo for financial reporting if it is used for tax purposes.

come by selecting which items to deliver in filling a sales order. Also, the specific identification method may lead to faulty pricing decisions by implying that identical items of merchandise have different economic values. On balance, there is little to support the specific identification method in a business which has an inventory composed of large quantities of identical items.

Identical items will have the same accounting values only under the average-cost method. Assume for example that a hardware store sells a given size nail for 65 cents per pound. The hardware store buys the nails in 100-pound quantities at different times at prices ranging from 40 to 50 cents per pound. Several hundred pounds of nails are always on hand, stored in a large bin. The average-cost method properly recognizes that when a customer buys a pound of nails it is not necessary to know exactly which nails the customer happened to select from the bin in order to measure the gross profit on the sale.

A shortcoming in the average-cost method is that changes in current replacement costs of inventory are concealed because these costs are averaged with older costs. As a result of this averaging, the reported gross profit may not reflect current market conditions.

The principal criticism of the FIFO method is that it tends to overstate income under conditions of inflation. The FIFO method will lead to a balance sheet valuation of inventory in line with current replacement costs, but this is achieved only by understating the cost of goods sold.

As explained early in this chapter, the proper determination of income should take precedence over other objectives in accounting for inventories. When this concept is applied to the choice of a method of inventory valuation, the preferred method in most cases will be last-in, first-out. Sales revenue reflects current prices; therefore, the cost of goods sold should reflect the current costs of merchandise. The LIFO method comes closest to this objective by assigning to cost of goods sold the prices paid for the most recent purchases of merchandise.

Inflation has been a major economic force in the United States for the last 40 years or more. In many other countries, inflation has been much more severe. This inflationary environment is a strong argument for the use of the LIFO method, because LIFO comes closer than the other methods to measuring income in the light of current selling prices and current replacement costs.

Some business concerns which adopted LIFO more than 40 years ago now show a balance sheet figure for inventory which is less than half the present replacement cost of the goods in stock. An inventory valuation method which gives significant figures for the income statement thus may produce unrealistic amounts for the balance sheet, whereas a method which produces a realistic figure for inventory on the balance sheet may provide less realistic data for the income statement.

The search for the "best" method of inventory valuation is rendered difficult because the inventory figure is used in both the balance sheet and the income statement, and these two financial statements are intended for different purposes. In the income statement, the function of the inventory figure is to permit a matching of costs and revenue. In the balance sheet the inventory and the other current assets are regarded as a measure of the company's ability to meet its current debts. To compensate in some degree for an unrealistically low balance sheet amount for inventory when LIFO is in use, it may be desirable to disclose in a parenthetical note the current replacement cost of the inventory.

Consistency in the valuation of inventory

The **principle of consistency** is one of the basic concepts underlying reliable financial statements. This principle means that once a company has adopted a particular accounting method, the company should follow that method consistently rather than switch methods from one year to the next. Consider the consequences if we were to ignore the principle of consistency in accounting for inventories. A company could cause its net income for any given year to increase or decrease merely by changing its method of inventory valuation. The principle of consistency does not mean that every company in an industry must use the same accounting method; it does mean that a given company should not switch year after year from one accounting method to another.

Bear in mind that a company has considerable latitude in selecting a method of inventory valuation best suited to its needs. The principle of consistency comes into play after a given method has been selected. We have already illustrated in the example on page 323 how different methods can produce differences in reported income. Consequently, a change from one inventory method to another will usually cause reported income to change significantly in the year in which the change is made. Frequent switching of methods would make the income statements undependable as a means of portraying trends in operating results. Because of the principle of consistency, the user of financial statements is able to assume that the company has followed the same accounting methods it used in the preceding year. Thus, the value of financial statements is increased because they enable the user to make reliable comparisons of the results achieved from year to year.

The principle of consistency does not mean that a business can **never** change its method of inventory valuation. However, when a change is made, the effects of the change upon reported net income should be **disclosed fully** in the footnotes accompanying the financial statements.[6] **Adequate disclosure** of all information necessary for the proper interpretation of financial statements is another basic principle of accounting. Even when the same method of inventory pricing is being followed consistently, the financial statements should include a disclosure of the pricing method in use.

The environment of inflation

We have previously discussed the relationship between the valuation of assets in the balance sheet and the recognition of costs and expenses in the income statement. As assets are sold or used up, their cost is removed from the balance sheet and recognized in the income statement as a cost or expense. In the case of inventory, the cost of units sold is transferred from the balance sheet to the income statement

---

[6] A change in the method of inventory valuation also requires the approval of the Internal Revenue Service.

as cost of goods sold. In the case of depreciable assets, such as a building, the cost is gradually transferred to the income statement as depreciation expense. This flow of costs is illustrated in the chart below.

Historical costs appear in both balance sheet and income statement

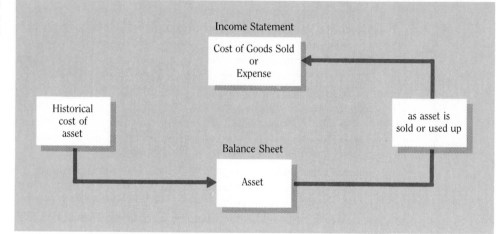

A period of sustained inflation causes some distortion in financial statements which are based upon historical costs. Rising price levels may cause assets to be valued in the balance sheets at amounts substantially below their current replacement cost. Similarly, the cost assigned to the income statement as these assets are sold or used up tends to understate the cost to the business of replacing these assets.

Inflationary policies and high income tax rates have stimulated the interest of business management in the choice of inventory methods. Although the rate of inflation slowed significantly in the 1980s, most business executives and government officials expect the trend of rising prices to continue. In other words, an environment of inflation has come to be considered as normal. The **LIFO** method of inventory valuation causes reported net income to reflect the increasing cost of replacing the merchandise sold during the year and also tends to avoid basing income tax payments on an exaggerated measurement of taxable income. Therefore, the existence of inflation is an argument for the lifo method of inventory valuation.

Inventory profits

4 Define inventory profits and explain why some accountants consider these profits fictitious.

Many accountants believe that the use of **FIFO** or of average cost during a period of inflation results in the reporting of overstated profits and consequently in the payment of excessive income taxes. Profits are overstated under both the FIFO and average-cost methods because the gross profit is computed by subtracting "old" inventory costs rather than current replacement costs from sales revenue. These old costs are relatively low, resulting in a high reported gross profit. However, the company must pay the higher current cost in order to replenish its inventory.

To illustrate this concept, assume that TV Sales Shop has an inventory of 20 television sets which were acquired at an average cost of $270. During the current month, 10 television sets are sold for cash at a sales price of $350 each. Using the average-cost method to value inventory, the company will report the following gross profit for the month:

Sales (10 × $350)	$3,500
Cost of goods sold (10 × $270)	2,700
Gross profit on sales	$ 800

However, TV Sales Shop must replace its inventory of television sets to continue in business. Because of inflation, TV Sales Shop can no longer buy 10 television sets for $2,700. Let us assume that the current replacement cost of television sets is $325 each; TV Sales Shop must pay $3,250 to replenish its inventory. Thus, TV Sales Shop is able to keep only $250 ($3,500 − $3,250) of the reported $800 gross profit; the remaining $550 has to be **reinvested in inventory** because of the increasing cost of television sets. This $550 would be considered a fictitious profit, or an **inventory profit,** by many accountants and business executives.

The inventory profit included in the reported net income of a business may be computed by deducting the cost of goods as shown in the income statement from the **replacement cost** (computed at the date of sale) of these goods.

In periods of rapid inflation, a significant portion of the reported net income of companies using FIFO or average cost actually may be inventory profits. The net income of companies using LIFO will include much less inventory profit because LIFO causes more current costs to be included in the cost of goods sold.

The lower-of-cost-or-market rule (LCM)

5 Explain the lower-of-cost-or-market rule.

Although cost is the primary basis for valuation of inventories, circumstances may arise under which inventory may properly be valued at less than its cost. If the **utility** of the inventory has fallen below cost because of a decline in the price level, a loss has occurred. This loss may appropriately be recognized as a loss of the current period by reducing the accounting value of the inventory from cost to a lower level designated as **market.** The word **market** as used in this context means **current replacement cost.** For a merchandising company, **market** is the amount which the concern would have to pay at the present time for the goods in question, purchased in the customary quantities through the usual sources of supply and including transportation-in. To avoid misunderstanding, the rule might better read "lower of actual cost or replacement cost."

A restriction of the lower-of-cost-or-market rule is that inventory should never be carried at an amount greater than **net realizable value,** which may be defined as prospective selling price minus anticipated selling expenses. Assume, for example, that because of unstable market conditions, it is believed that goods acquired at a cost of $5,000 and having a current replacement cost of $4,500 will probably have to be sold for no more than $5,200 and that the selling expenses involved will amount to $1,200. The inventory should then be reduced to a carrying value (net realizable value) of $4,000, which is less than current replacement cost.

Application of the lower-of-cost-or-market rule. The lower of cost or market for inventory is often computed by determining the cost and the market figures for each item in inventory and using the lower of the two amounts in every case. If, for example, item A cost $100 and replacement cost is $90, the item should be priced at $90. If item B cost $200 and replacement cost is $225, this item should be priced at $200. The total cost of the two items is $300 and total replacement cost is $315, but the total inventory value determined by applying the lower-of-cost-or-market rule to each item in inventory is only $290. This application of the lower-of-cost-or-market rule is illustrated by the tabulation shown below:

Application of Lower-of-Cost-or-Market Rule, Item-by-Item Method

			Unit Cost		Total Cost		Lower of Cost or Market
Item	Quantity	Cost	Market	Cost	Market		
A	10	$100	$ 90	$ 1,000	$ 900	$ 900
B	8	200	225	1,600	1,800	1,600
C	50	50	60	2,500	3,000	2,500
D	80	90	70	7,200	5,600	5,600
Totals............................				$12,300	$11,300	$10,600

Pricing inventory at lower of cost or market

If the lower-of-cost-or-market rule is applied item by item, the carrying value of the above inventory would be $10,600. However, an alternative and less rigorous version of the lower-of-cost-or-market rule calls for applying it to the total of the entire inventory rather than to the individual items. Under this approach, the balance sheet amount for inventory is determined merely by comparing the total cost of $12,300 with the total replacement cost of $11,300 and using the lower of the two figures. Still another alternative method of using the lower-of-cost-or-market concept is to apply it to categories of the inventory rather than item by item. Each of these alternative methods of applying the lower-of-cost-or-market rule is acceptable in current accounting practice, although once a method has been selected it should be followed consistently from year to year.

Other writedowns of inventory. Big writedowns of inventory are more likely to arise because merchandise has become obsolete or has been damaged by water, smoke, heat, or other factors. Inventory which becomes unsalable because it is damaged or obsolete should be written down to zero, or to scrap value, if any. Writedowns of this type are not an application of the lower-of-cost-or-market rule, because the inventory is being written off as unsalable rather than being reduced to a current replacement cost for salable merchandise.

● **CASE IN POINT** ● An automobile dealership operating as a partnership retained a CPA firm to make a first audit of the business. During the audit the

CPAs observed the taking of a physical inventory of repair parts. They noticed a large number of new fenders of a design and shape not used in current model automobiles. Investigation revealed that the fenders (with a total inventory valuation of many thousands of dollars) were for a model of automobile discontinued seven years earlier. The records showed that only one of these fenders had been sold during recent years. The partners explained to the CPAs that these fenders had been included in the parts inventory when they purchased the business and they had no idea why such a large supply had originally been acquired. The partners agreed that few, if any, of this model of fender would ever be sold. It had not occurred to the partners to write down the carrying value of these obsolete parts, but they agreed with the CPA firm's suggestion that the fenders, being virtually unsalable, should be reduced to scrap value.

Estimating ending inventory and cost of goods sold

6 Estimate ending inventory by the gross profit method and by the retail method. A physical inventory taken at the end of the year provides the inventory amount needed for the preparation of annual financial statements. Many business managers, however, also want monthly and quarterly financial statements. To take a physical inventory every month would be very expensive and time-consuming. Consequently, it is common practice to use an estimated amount for inventory in preparing monthly or quarterly financial statements. One method of *estimating* inventories is the *gross profit method;* another method used by retail stores is called the *retail inventory method.*

The gross profit method of estimating ending inventory

The gross profit method is a quick, simple technique for estimating inventories, and can be used in almost all types and sizes of business. In using this method, it is assumed that the rate of gross profit earned in the preceding year will remain the same for the current year. When we know the rate of gross profit, we can divide the dollar amount of net sales into two elements: (1) the gross profit and (2) the cost of goods sold. We view net sales as 100%. If gross profit, for example, is 40%, the cost of goods sold must be 60%. In other words, the cost of goods sold percentage (cost percentage) is determined by deducting the gross profit percentage from 100%.

When the gross profit percentage is known, the ending inventory can be estimated by the following procedures:

1 Determine the *cost of goods available for sale* from the general ledger records of beginning inventory and net purchases.
2 Estimate the *cost of goods sold* by multiplying the net sales by the cost percentage.
3 Deduct the *cost of goods sold* from the *cost of goods available for sale* to find the estimated ending inventory.

To illustrate, assume that Metro Hardware has a beginning inventory of $50,000 on January 1. During the month of January, net purchases amount to $20,000 and net sales total $30,000. Assume that the company's normal gross profit rate is 40% of net sales; it follows that the cost percentage is 60%. Using these facts, the inventory on January 31 may be estimated as follows:

	Goods available for sale:		
	Beginning inventory, Jan. 1..		$50,000
	Net purchases		20,000
Step 1 . . .	Cost of goods available for sale...		$70,000
	Deduct: Estimated cost of goods sold:		
	Net sales	$30,000	
Step 2 . . .	Cost percentage (100% − 40%)....................................	60%	
	Estimated cost of goods sold...		18,000
Step 3 . . .	Estimated ending inventory, Jan. 31.......................................		$52,000

The gross profit method of estimating inventory has several uses apart from the preparation of monthly financial statements. If an inventory is destroyed by fire, the company must determine the amount of the inventory on hand at the date of the fire in order to file an insurance claim. The most convenient way to determine this inventory amount is often the gross profit method.

The gross profit method is also used at year-end after the taking of a physical inventory to confirm the overall reasonableness of the amount determined by the counting and pricing process.

The retail method of estimating ending inventory

The retail method of inventory is widely used by department stores and other types of retail business. To use the retail inventory method, a store must maintain records showing the beginning inventory *at cost* and *at retail.* The term "at retail" means the marked selling prices of all items in the store. The records also must show the purchases during the period both *at cost* and *at retail.* The only other information needed is the net sales for the month. The amount of net sales, of course, is equal to the amount recorded in the Sales revenue account during the period minus any sales returns and sales discounts.

The records described above enable us to know the amount of goods available for sale, stated both at cost and at retail selling prices. (As you know, goods available for sale are the total of beginning inventory and net purchases.) With this information, all we need to do is to deduct the net sales for the month from the retail sales value of the goods available for sale. The result will be the ending inventory at retail selling price. A final step is to convert the ending inventory at retail selling price to a cost basis by multiplying it by the *cost percentage.* The cost percentage is the *ratio of cost to selling price for the current period.* To compute the cost percentage, divide the cost of goods available for sale by the retail sales value of these goods. The end result of these procedures is that we have an estimated cost value for inventory without going through the extensive work of taking a physical inventory.

The following illustration shows the calculation of an ending inventory of $280,000 by the retail inventory method.

	Cost Price	Retail Selling Price
Goods available for sale:		
Beginning inventory	$415,000	$ 560,000
Net purchases	285,000	440,000
Goods available for sale.................................	$700,000	$1,000,000
Cost percentage: $700,000 ÷ $1,000,000 = 70%		
Deduct: Net sales at retail		600,000
Ending inventory at retail selling price...........................		$ 400,000
Ending inventory at cost ($400,000 × 70%).......................	$280,000	

Estimating inventory for monthly financial statements

Reducing a physical inventory to cost by the retail method. A second use for the retail inventory method is to aid in the completion of the annual physical inventory. Goods on sale in retail stores have price tags attached, showing retail prices. When the annual physical inventory is taken, it is more convenient to list the retail prices from the price tags than to look up purchase invoices to find the unit cost of each item in the store. The total of the inventory at retail selling price is then reduced to cost by applying the cost percentage, that is, the ratio between cost and selling price during the current period. The following illustration shows a year-end physical inventory amounting to $170,000 at retail selling price. This amount is reduced to a cost basis of $102,000 by applying the cost percentage of 60%.

	Cost Price	Retail Selling Price
Goods available for sale:		
Beginning inventory	$ 98,000	$160,000
Net purchases..	262,000	440,000
Goods available for sale	$360,000	$600,000
Cost percentage: $360,000 ÷ $600,000 = 60%		
Ending inventory at retail selling price (per physical inventory).........		$170,000
Ending inventory at cost ($170,000 × 60%)	$102,000	

Take year-end physical inventory at retail; then reduce it to cost

In this illustration we have shown the calculation of inventory by the retail inventory method without going into the complications which would arise from markups and markdowns in the original retail selling prices. Such changes in price are considered in advanced accounting courses.

Although the inventory amount is an estimate, experience has shown this retail inventory method to be a reliable one. An inventory amount established in this manner is acceptable in audited financial statements and also in federal income tax returns.

Internal control of inventories

Inventories are usually the largest current asset of a merchandising or manufacturing business. Furthermore, the very nature of inventories makes them subject to theft and to major errors and misstatement. The large dollar amounts involved, coupled with the rapid turnover of inventory items, and the variety of alternative valuation methods make it possible for a major shortage to occur in inventories without attracting immediate attention. Thus, the accountant's approach to inventories should stress an awareness of the possibility of large intentional errors as well as major accidental errors in establishing inventory quantities and amounts. If one or more members of a company's management is determined to evade income taxes, to conceal shortages arising from irregularities, or to mislead absentee owners, inventories constitute the most likely area for such fraudulent action to take place.

To provide the strong internal control procedures needed to protect inventories, the various physical functions involved in acquiring and handling merchandise should be assigned to separate departments. These functions may include purchasing, receiving, storing, issuing, and shipping the items which comprise the inventory. Thus, the organizational structure of a company should include a purchasing department with exclusive authority to make all purchases. All merchandise received by the company should be cleared through a receiving department. This department will count the merchandise received, detect any damaged items, issue a receiving report to the accounts payable department and other departments, and transmit the merchandise to the stores department.

In addition to the protection afforded by extensive subdivision of duties, another important approach to assuring reliability in the amounts reported as inventory and cost of goods sold is an annual audit by a CPA firm. Every independent audit includes first-hand observation of the annual taking of a physical inventory. Such observation by a competent outsider provides assurance that the physical inventory is carefully counted and priced, thus leading to valid amounts for inventory and cost of goods sold in the financial statements. In addition, the independent auditors will study and test the system of internal control.

Many small companies have too few employees to permit the extensive subdivision of duties described above. Moreover, these small concerns usually are unwilling to incur the cost of an annual audit by a CPA firm. Under these circumstances, the amounts shown in the financial statements (especially inventory, cost of goods sold, gross profit, and net income) should be viewed with caution by absentee owners, bankers, creditors, IRS agents, and other outsiders.

● **CASE IN POINT** ● The Internal Revenue Service (IRS) conducts audits of the income tax returns of most business organizations to see that these companies have not understated taxable income and thereby evaded income taxes. The IRS has found that a business which wants to understate its taxable income is likely to do so by understating inventory. Small businesses, in particular, which are not audited by CPA firms, may make a practice of regularly understating the ending inventory year after year in order to understate taxable income. In income tax audits, therefore, the IRS makes it standard practice to verify as fully as possible the determination of the amount of ending inventory. An ending inventory which is quite small in relation to the year's sales volume is a "red flag signal" to the tax auditor.

Perpetual inventory system

7 Explain how a perpetual inventory system operates.

Companies which deal in merchandise of high unit cost, such as automobiles, television sets, or expensive jewelry, find a perpetual inventory system worthwhile and efficient. Since inventory is often one of the largest assets in a business and has a rapid rate of turnover, strong internal control is especially important. A perpetual inventory system, if properly designed and operated, can provide the strongest possible internal control over the inventory of merchandise. The key feature of a perpetual inventory system is that the records show continuously the amount of inventory on hand and the cost of goods sold. Companies with computer-based accounting records including point-of-sale terminals are in a good position to carry on continuous updating of inventory records.

Internal control and perpetual inventory systems

A perpetual inventory system has the potential of providing excellent internal control. However, the fact that perpetual inventory records are in use does not automatically guarantee strong internal control. Such basic internal control concepts as the subdivision of duties, the control of documents by serial numbers, and separation of the accounting function from the custody of assets are essential elements with either the perpetual or periodic inventory systems.

● **CASE IN POINT** ● Par-Flite, a manufacturer of golf equipment, maintained an inventory of several thousand sets of golf clubs. The clubs were kept in a storeroom with barred windows and doors under the supervision of John Adams. Adams was also responsible for maintaining detailed perpetual inventory records of the golf clubs in the storeroom. Another employee acquired an unauthorized key to the storeroom and began stealing large numbers of clubs. Adams discovered that the quantities on hand did not agree with the perpetual records he maintained. Afraid that his records would be criticized as highly inaccurate, he made numerous changes in the records so they would agree with quantities of golf clubs on hand. The theft of clubs continued and large losses were sustained before the inventory shortage came to the attention of management.

If the person maintaining records had not also been responsible for physical custody of the merchandise, there would have been no incentive or opportunity to conceal a shortage by falsifying the records. Satisfactory internal control over inventories requires that the accounting function be separate from the custody of assets. Frequent comparison of quantities of merchandise on hand with the quantities shown by the perpetual inventory records should be made by employees who do not have responsibility either for custody of assets or for maintenance of records.

Perpetual inventory records

The information required for a perpetual system can be processed electronically or manually. In a manual system a subsidiary record card, as shown below, is used for each type of merchandise on hand. If the company has 100 different kinds of products in stock, then 100 inventory record cards will make up the subsidiary inventory record. Shown below is an inventory record card for item XL-2000.

Perpetual inventory record card

| Item | XL-2000 | | Maximum | 20 |
| Location | Storeroom 2 | | Minimum | 8 |

	PURCHASED			SOLD			BALANCE		
Date	Units	Unit Cost	Total	Units	Unit Cost	Total	Units	Unit Cost	Balance
Jan. 1							12	$50.00	$600.00
7				2	$50.00	$100.00	10	50.00	500.00
9	10	$55.00	$550.00				10	50.00	
							10	55.00	1,050.00
12				8	50.00	400.00	2	50.00	
							10	55.00	650.00
31				2	50.00	100.00			
				1	55.00	55.00	9	55.00	495.00

On this card, the quantity and cost of units received will be listed at the date of receipt; the quantity and cost of units sold will be recorded at the date of sale; and after each purchase or sales transaction, the balance remaining on hand will be shown. This running balance will be shown in number of units, cost per unit, and total dollar amount.

The information on the illustrated inventory record shows that the first-in, first-out basis of pricing the inventory is being used. After the sale of two units on January 7, the remaining inventory consisted of 10 units at a cost of $50 each. The purchase on January 9 of 10 units carried a unit cost of $55, rather than $50, hence must be accounted for separately. The balance on hand after the January 9 purchase appears on two lines: 10 units at $50 and 10 units at $55. When eight units were sold on January 12, they were treated as coming from the oldest stock on hand and therefore had a cost of $50 each. The balance remaining on hand then consisted of two units at $50 and 10 units at $55. When three units were sold on January 31, the cost consisted of two units at $50 and one unit at $55. The ending inventory of nine units consists of the most recently acquired units with a cost of $55 each.

Perpetual inventory records may also be maintained on a last-in, first-out basis or on an average-cost basis, but these systems involve some complexities which are considered in advanced accounting courses.

Control over the amount invested in inventory can be strengthened by listing on each inventory card the maximum and minimum quantities that should be kept in stock. By maintaining quantities within these limits, overstocking and out-of-stock situations can be avoided.

General ledger entries for a perpetual inventory system. The general ledger controlling account entitled *Inventory* is continuously (perpetually) updated when a perpetual inventory system is in use. This Inventory account controls the many subsidiary record cards discussed above. A continuously updated Cost of Goods Sold account is also maintained in the general ledger.

The purchase of merchandise by a company using a perpetual inventory system requires a journal entry affecting general ledger controlling accounts as follows:

Inventory 1,500
      Accounts Payable, Lake Company 1,500
To record purchase of merchandise on credit.

This purchase transaction would also be recorded in the subsidiary ledger (the perpetual inventory cards) showing the quantity of each kind of merchandise purchased. The $1,500 purchase from Lake Company might affect only one or perhaps a dozen of the subsidiary records, depending on how many types of merchandise were included in this purchase transaction.

For every sales transaction, we can determine the cost of the goods sold by referring to the appropriate perpetual inventory card record. Therefore, at the time of a sale, we can record both the amount of the selling price and the *cost* of the goods sold, as illustrated in the following pair of related entries.

Accounts Receivable, J. Williams 140
      Sales 140
To record the sale of merchandise on credit.

Cost of Goods Sold 100
      Inventory 100
To record the cost of goods sold and the related decrease in inventory.

To avoid making a large number of entries in the general journal, a special column can be entered in the sales journal to show the cost of the goods involved in each sales transaction. At the end of the month the total of this "Cost" column can be posted as a debit to Cost of Goods Sold and a credit to Inventory.

When a perpetual inventory system is in use, the Inventory account is increased by purchases of merchandise. It is decreased by the cost of goods sold, by purchase returns and allowances, and by purchase discounts. At the end of the year the dollar balances of all the subsidiary inventory record cards should be added to see that the total is in agreement with the general ledger controlling account. The only adjustment necessary at year-end will be to correct the Inventory controlling account and the subsidiary records for any discrepancies indicated by the taking of a physical inventory.

The advantages of a perpetual inventory system as indicated in the preceding discussion include:

1 Stronger internal control. By comparing the physical inventory with the perpetual records, management will be made aware of any shortages or errors and can take corrective action.
2 The accounting records provide information about the cost and quantity of goods on hand. This information is useful in avoiding overstocking and out-of-stock situations.
3 Quarterly or monthly financial statements can be prepared more readily because of the availability of dollar amounts for inventory and cost of goods sold in the accounting records.

Need for an annual physical inventory

An annual physical inventory is essential in every merchandising business even though a perpetual inventory system is in use. The perpetual inventory records show the amount of merchandise which **should be** on hand; the physical count shows the amount of merchandise which actually **is** on hand. The taking of a physical inventory usually discloses significant differences from the perpetual records. These discrepancies may be the result of errors in the accounting process, or from shrinkage of inventory because of shoplifting, employee theft, or other factors. The discrepancies should be disposed of by adjusting the perpetual inventory records to agree with the physical count.

For example, assume that the perpetual inventory records of Baxter Corporation show an inventory of $290,000 at year-end. A physical inventory taken at December 31 shows merchandise on hand of $279,100. The adjusting entry to correct the perpetual inventory records is:

Cost of Goods Sold	10,900	
Inventory...		10,900

To adjust the perpetual inventory records to the amount indicated by the year-end physical inventory.

END-OF-CHAPTER REVIEW

Summary of chapter learning objectives

1 Define inventory and explain how the valuation of inventory relates to the measurement of income.

For a merchandising company, the inventory consists of all goods owned and held for sale in the regular course of business. The first objective of accounting for inventories is the proper determination of income. In dividing the cost of goods available for sale between cost of goods sold and ending inventory, we are matching costs against revenue. Any overstatement of ending inventory will lead to an overstatement of net income, and any understatement of ending inventory will lead to an understatement of net income.

2 Describe the effects of an inventory error on the income statement of the current year and of the following year.

The ending inventory of one year is also the beginning inventory of the next year. Therefore, an error in the year-end inventory affects the income statements of two successive years. For example, an overstatement of ending inventory will cause an overstatement of net income this year and a counterbalancing understatement of net income next year.

3 Determine the cost of inventory by using (a) specific identification; (b) average cost; (c) first-in, first-out (FIFO); and (d) last-in, first-out (LIFO). Discuss the merits and shortcomings of these methods.

When identical units of merchandise are purchased at various prices during the year, one of four assumptions is made as to which units were sold and which units remain on hand at year-end. The four assumptions (and inventory valuation methods) are (a) specific identification, (b) average cost, (c) first-in, first-out (FIFO), and (d) last-in, first-out (LIFO). The *specific identification method* is suitable for high-priced items, but not for a large volume of low-priced merchandise. *Average cost* is computed by dividing total cost of goods available for sale by the number of units available for sale. This method utilizes both current costs and prices which prevailed several months earlier. The *FIFO method* assumes that the first merchandise acquired is the first merchandise sold. The ending inventory, therefore, consists of the most recently acquired goods priced at recent prices. This method gives a realistic inventory amount in the balance sheet. The *LIFO method* assumes that the most recently acquired goods are sold first. Therefore, the ending inventory consists of "old" goods acquired in the earlier purchases and priced at prices which prevailed in the past. During periods of inflation, the LIFO method results in lower reported profits and lower income taxes than the other methods.

4 Define inventory profits and explain why some accountants consider these profits fictitious.

The use of FIFO or average cost during periods of inflation results in reporting higher profits and higher income taxes than would be reported under LIFO. Some accountants believe that current replacement costs rather than "old" inventory costs should be subtracted from sales revenue in computing gross profit. These accountants believe that using FIFO or average costs during periods of inflation leads to "fictitious inventory profits," because these methods do not recognize that units sold must be replaced in inventory at today's higher prices.

5 Explain the lower-of-cost-or-market rule.

The word *market* in this context means current replacement cost. The rule indicates that if market (current replacement cost) at year-end is less than the cost of inventory, the lower value should be used.

6 Estimate ending inventory by the gross profit method and by the retail method.

Estimating inventory by the gross profit method or by the retail method is useful to corroborate year-end inventories established by physical count. These estimating methods also permit the preparation of monthly financial statements without taking monthly physical inventories. Also, these methods are useful in estimating losses of inventory from fire or theft. Under the gross profit method, the cost of goods sold is computed by deducting the estimated gross profit margin from sales. The cost of goods sold is then deducted from cost of goods available for sale to determine ending inventory. With the retail method, the inventory is computed at retail price and then converted to a cost basis by multiplying it by the cost percentage. The cost percentage is the ratio of cost to selling price for the current period.

7 Explain how a perpetual inventory system operates.

Under a perpetual inventory system, the records are continuously updated as purchases and sales are made. Thus the records show at all times the amount of inventory on hand and the cost of goods sold in the current accounting period. A perpetual inventory system provides stronger internal control than does the periodic inventory system illustrated in prior chapters. However, a perpetual inventory system may not be suitable for a business having a large volume of transactions in low-price items.

Key terms introduced or emphasized in chapter 8

Average-cost method. A method of inventory valuation. Weighted-average unit cost is computed by dividing the total cost of goods available for sale by the number of identical units available for sale.

Consistency in inventory valuation. An accounting standard that calls for the use of the same method of inventory pricing from year to year, with full disclosure of the effects of any change in method. Intended to make financial statements comparable.

First-in, first-out (FIFO) method. A method of computing the cost of inventory and the cost of goods sold based on the assumption that the first merchandise acquired is the first merchandise sold, and that the ending inventory consists of the most recently acquired goods.

F.O.B. destination. A term meaning the seller bears the cost of shipping goods to the buyer's location. Title to the goods remains with the seller while the goods are in transit.

F.O.B. shipping point. The buyer of goods bears the cost of transportation from the seller's location to the buyer's location. Title to the goods passes at the point of shipment and the goods are the property of the buyer while in transit.

Gross profit method. A method of estimating the cost of the ending inventory based on the assumption that the rate of gross profit remains approximately the same from year to year.

Inventory profits. The amount by which the cost of replacing goods sold (computed at the date of sale) exceeds the reported cost of goods sold. Many accountants consider inventory profits to be a "fictitious" profit, because this amount usually must be reinvested in inventories and therefore is not available for distribution to stockholders.

Last-in, first-out (LIFO) method. A method of computing the cost of goods sold by use of the prices paid for the most recently acquired units. Ending inventory is valued on the basis of prices paid for the units first acquired.

Lower-of-cost-or-market method. A method of inventory pricing in which goods are valued at original cost or replacement cost (market), whichever is lower.

Net realizable value. The prospective selling price minus anticipated selling expenses. Inventory should not be carried at more than net realizable value.

Perpetual inventory system. Provides a continuous (perpetual) running record of the goods on hand. As goods are sold their cost is transferred to a Cost of Goods Sold account.

Physical inventory. A systematic count of all goods on hand, followed by the application of unit prices to the quantities counted and development of a dollar value for ending inventory.

Retail method. A method of estimating inventory in a retail store based on the assumption that the cost of goods on hand bears the same percentage relationship to retail prices as does the cost of all goods available for sale to the original retail prices. Inventory is first priced at retail and then converted to cost by application of a cost-to-retail percentage.

Specific identification method. A method of pricing inventory by identifying the units in the ending inventory as coming from specific purchases.

Demonstration problem for your review

Information relating to the inventory quantities, purchases, and sales of a certain type of capacitor by Morton Electronics during the year is shown below:

	Number of Units	Cost per Unit	Total Cost
Inventory, Jan. 1	8,000	$5.89	$ 47,120
First purchase (Mar. 15)	10,300	6.20	63,860
Second purchase (June 6)	12,400	6.60	81,840
Third purchase (Sept. 20)	9,600	6.80	65,280
Fourth purchase (Dec. 31)	7,700	7.00	53,900
Goods available for sale	48,000		$312,000
Units sold during the year	37,200		
Inventory, Dec. 31	10,800		

Instructions. Compute the cost of the December 31 inventory and the cost of goods sold for the capacitors during the year using:

   a The first-in, first-out method
   b The last-in, first-out method
   c The average-cost method

Solution to demonstration problem

   a FIFO method

Inventory:
7,700 units from the Dec. 31 purchase @ $7.00	$ 53,900
3,100 units from the Sept. 20 purchase @ $6.80	21,080
Ending inventory, 10,800 units (at FIFO cost)	$ 74,980

Cost of goods sold:
Cost of goods available for sale	$312,000
Less: Ending inventory (FIFO)	74,980
Cost of goods sold (FIFO)	$237,020

b LIFO method

Inventory:

8,000 units from beginning inventory @ $5.89	$ 47,120
2,800 units from the Mar. 15 purchase @ $6.20	17,360
Ending inventory, 10,800 units (at LIFO cost)	$ 64,480

Cost of goods sold:

Cost of goods available for sale	$312,000
Less: Ending inventory (LIFO)	64,480
Cost of goods sold (LIFO)	$247,520

c Average-cost method

Inventory:

Cost of goods available for sale	$312,000
Number of units available for sale	48,000
Average cost per unit ($312,000 ÷ 48,000 units)	$ 6.50
Ending inventory (at average cost, 10,800 units × $6.50)	$ 70,200

Cost of goods sold:

Cost of goods available for sale	$312,000
Less: Ending inventory (average cost)	70,200
Cost of goods sold (average cost)	$241,800

Alternative computation of cost of goods sold:

Cost of goods sold (37,200 units at $6.50)	$241,800

ASSIGNMENT MATERIAL

Review questions

1 Which of the seven items listed below are used in computing the **cost of goods available for sale?**

    a Ending inventory   e Transportation-in
    b Sales   f Purchase returns and allowances
    c Beginning inventory   g Delivery expense
    d Purchases

2 Through an error in counting of merchandise at December 31, 1989, the Trophy Company overstated the amount of goods on hand by $8,000. Assuming that the error was not discovered, what was the effect upon net income for 1989? Upon owners' equity at December 31, 1989? Upon net income for 1990? Upon owners' equity at December 31, 1990?

3 Is the establishment of an appropriate valuation for the merchandise inventory at the end of the year more important in producing a dependable income statement, or in producing a dependable balance sheet?

4 Explain the meaning of the term **physical inventory.**

5 Near the end of December, Hadley Company received a large order from a major customer. The work of packing the goods for shipment was begun at once but could not be completed before the close of business on December 31. Since a written order from the customer was on hand and the goods were nearly all packed and ready for shipment, Hadley felt that this merchandise should not be included in the physical inventory taken on December 31. Do you agree? What is probably the reason behind Hadley's opinion?

6 During a prolonged period of rising prices, will the FIFO or LIFO method of inventory valuation result in higher reported profits?

7 Throughout several years of strongly rising prices, Company A used the LIFO method of inventory valuation and Company B used the FIFO method. In which company would the balance sheet figure for inventory be closer to current replacement cost of the merchandise on hand? Why?

8 You are making a detailed analysis of the financial statements and accounting records of two companies in the same industry, Adams Company and Bar Company. Price levels have been rising steadily for several years. In the course of your investigation, you observe that the inventory value shown on the Adams Company balance sheet is quite close to the current replacement cost of the merchandise on hand. However, for Bar Company, the carrying value of the inventory is far below current replacement cost. What method of inventory valuation is probably used by Adams Company? By Bar Company? If we assume that the two companies are identical except for the inventory valuation method used, which company has probably been reporting higher net income in recent years?

9 Why do some accountants consider the net income reported by businesses during a period of rising prices to be overstated?

10 Assume that a business uses the first-in, first-out method of accounting for inventories during a prolonged period of inflation and that the business pays dividends equal to the amount of reported net income. Suggest a problem that may arise in continued successful operation of the business. What does this situation have to do with "inventory profits"?

11 Explain the meaning of the term *market* as used in the expression "lower of cost or market."

12 One of the items in the inventory of Grayline Stores is marked for sale at $125. The purchase invoice shows the item cost $95, but a newly issued price list from the manufacturer shows the present replacement cost to be $90. What inventory valuation should be assigned to this item if Grayline Stores follows the lower-of-cost-or-market rule?

13 Explain the usefulness of the *gross profit method* of estimating inventories.

14 A store using the *retail inventory method* takes its physical inventory by applying current retail prices as marked on the merchandise to the quantities counted. Does this procedure indicate that the inventory will appear in the financial statements at retail selling price? Explain.

15 Estimate the ending inventory by the gross profit method, given the following data: beginning inventory $40,000, net purchases $100,000, net sales $106,667, average gross profit rate 25% of net sales.

16 Summarize the difference between the *periodic system* and the *perpetual system* of accounting for inventory. Which system would usually cost more to maintain? Which system would be most practicable for a restaurant, a retail drugstore, a new car dealer?

17 Identify each of the four statements shown below as true or false. Also, give a brief explanation. In the accounting records of a company using a perpetual inventory system:

a The Inventory account will ordinarily remain unchanged until the end of an accounting period.

b The Cost of Goods Sold account is debited with the sales price of merchandise sold.

c The Inventory account and the Cost of Goods Sold account will both normally have debit balances.

d The Inventory account and the Cost of Goods Sold account will normally have equal but offsetting balances.

18 A large art gallery has in inventory several hundred paintings. No two are alike. The least expensive is priced at more than $1,000 and the higher priced items carry prices of $100,000 or more. Which of the four methods of inventory valuation discussed in this chapter would you consider to be most appropriate for this business? Give reasons for your answer.

19 Assume that during the first year of Hatton Corporation's operation, there were numerous purchases of identical items of merchandise. However, there was no change during the year in the prices paid for this merchandise. Under these special circumstances how would the financial statements be affected by the choice between the FIFO and LIFO methods of inventory valuation?

Exercises

Exercise 8-1
Accounting ter-
minology

Listed below are nine technical accounting terms introduced in this chapter:

Inventory profits	LIFO method	Average cost method
Retail method	FIFO method	Gross profit method
Lower-of-cost-or-market rule	Periodic inventory system	Perpetual inventory system

Each of the following statements may (or may not) describe one of these technical terms. For each statement, indicate the accounting term described, or answer "None" if the statement does not correctly describe any of the terms.

a Procedures which provide a continuous running record of the inventory on hand and the cost of goods sold.

b The difference between the amount reported in the income statement as the cost of goods sold and the amount which a business actually must pay to replace goods sold.

c A pricing method in which inventory appears in the balance sheet at expected sales price, rather than at cost.

d A pricing method in which the oldest goods on hand are assumed to be the first ones sold.

e The pricing method most appropriate for an inventory of unique items, such as oil paintings or custom jewelry.

f The pricing method most likely to minimize income taxes during a period of rising prices.

g A method of estimating inventory and the cost of goods sold which does not require recording purchases at two separate amounts.

Exercise 8-2
Effects of errors in inventory valuation

Norfleet Company prepared the following condensed income statements for two successive years:

	1990	1989
Sales	$1,500,000	$1,440,000
Cost of goods sold	879,600	914,400
Gross profit on sales	$ 620,400	$ 525,600
Operating expenses	460,500	447,000
Net income	$ 159,900	$ 78,600

At the end of 1989 (right-hand column above) the inventory was understated by $50,400, but the error was not discovered until after the accounts had been closed and financial statements prepared at the end of 1990. The balance sheets for the two years showed owners' equity of $214,200 at the end of 1989 and $260,400 at the end of 1990.

a Compute the corrected net income figures for 1989 and 1990.
b Compute the gross profit amounts and the gross profit percentages for each year based on corrected data.
c What correction, if any, should be made in owners' equity at the end of 1989 and at the end of 1990?

Exercise 8-3
F.O.B. shipping point and F.O.B. destination

Fraser Company had two large shipments in transit at December 31. One was a $90,000 inbound shipment of merchandise (shipped December 28, F.O.B. shipping point) which arrived at the Fraser receiving dock on January 2. The other shipment was a $55,000 outbound shipment of merchandise to a customer which was shipped and billed by Fraser on December 30 (terms F.O.B. shipping point) and reached the customer on January 3.

In taking a physical inventory on December 31, Fraser counted all goods on hand and priced the inventory on the basis of average cost. The total amount was $480,000. In developing this figure, Fraser gave no consideration to goods in transit.

What amount should appear as inventory on the company's balance sheet at December 31? Explain. If you indicate an amount other than $480,000, state what asset or liability other than inventory would also be changed in amount.

Exercise 8-4
LIFO, FIFO, and average cost

The records of Harbor, Inc., showed the beginning inventory balance of Item T12 on January 1 and the purchases of this item during the current year to be as follows:

Jan. 1 Beginning inventory	900 units @ $10.00	$ 9,000
Feb. 23 Purchase	1,200 units @ $11.00	13,200
Apr. 20 Purchase	3,000 units @ $11.20	33,600
May 4 Purchase	4,000 units @ $11.60	46,400
Nov. 30 Purchase	900 units @ $13.00	11,700
Totals	10,000 units	$113,900

At December 31 the ending inventory consisted of 1,500 units.
Determine the cost of the ending inventory, based on each of the following methods of inventory valuation:

a Average cost
b First-in, first-out
c Last-in, first-out

Exercise 8-5
LIFO, FIFO, and average cost

One of the products sold by National Plumbing Supply is a ¾ inch brass gate valve. The company purchases these valves several times during the year and sells the item daily. The inventory quantities, purchases, and sales for the year are summarized below:

	Number of Units	Cost per Unit	Total Cost
Beginning inventory (Jan. 1)	9,100	$4.00	$ 36,400
First purchase (Feb. 20)	20,000	4.10	82,000
Second purchase (May 10)	30,000	4.25	127,500
Third purchase (Aug. 24)	50,000	4.60	230,000
Fourth purchase (Nov. 30)	10,900	5.00	54,500
Goods available for sale	120,000		$530,400
Units sold during the year	105,000		
Ending inventory (Dec. 31)	15,000		

Compute the cost of the ending inventory of gate valves, using the following inventory valuation methods:

a First-in, first-out
b Last-in, first-out
c Average cost

Exercise 8-6
Discussion of inventory profits

Olympic Bicycle Shop uses the first-in, first-out method of inventory valuation. At the end of the current year the shop had exactly the same number of bicycles in stock as at the beginning of the year, and the same proportion of each model. However, the year had been one of severe inflation and the cost of the ending inventory was shown in the accounts at $36,000 whereas the cost of the beginning inventory had been only $24,000. The net income reported by the shop for the year was $27,000. Comment on the validity of the reported net income and indicate what adjustment might be reasonable to give the owner of this business a realistic picture of the results of the year's operations.

Exercise 8-7
Conservatism in inventory pricing

The concept of conservatism sometimes enters into the valuation of inventory. This concept indicates that when some doubt exists about the valuation of merchandise, the accountant should favor the accounting option which produces a lower net income for the current period and a less favorable financial position. For each of the following pairs of options, indicate which is the more conservative practice.

1 a Inventory items are priced at net invoice price plus all additional incidental costs incurred to transport, store, and insure the goods until they reach the place and condition for sale.
   b All incidental costs relating to the purchase of merchandise (such as transportation-in, import duties, storage, and insurance of goods in storage or in transit) are treated as period costs; that is, they are treated as expense of the period in which incurred.
2 a Inventory is priced by the lower-of-cost-or-market rule, applied on an item-by-item basis.
   b Inventory is priced by the lower-of-cost-or-market rule, applied to the inventory as a whole.
3 a During a long period of rising prices, inventory is priced by the average-cost method.
   b During a long period of rising prices, inventory is priced by the first-in, first-out method.

Exercise 8-8
Estimating inventory by the gross profit method

When Bob Long arrived at his store on the morning of January 29, he found empty shelves and display racks; thieves had broken in during the night and stolen the entire inventory. Long's accounting records showed that he had $84,000 inventory on January 1 (cost value). From January 1 to January 29, he had made net sales of $100,000 and net purchases of $64,800. The gross profit during the past several years had consistently averaged 30% of sales. Long wishes to file an insurance claim for the theft loss. You are to use the gross profit method to estimate the cost of his inventory at the time of the theft. Show computations.

Exercise 8-9
Estimating inventory by the retail method

Vagabond Shop wishes to determine the approximate month-end inventory using data from the accounting records without taking a physical count of merchandise on hand. From the following information, estimate the cost of the September 30 inventory by the *retail method* of inventory valuation.

	Cost Price	Selling Price
Inventory of merchandise, Aug. 31	$529,600	$800,000
Purchases (net) during September	340,800	480,000
Sales (net) during September.......................................		454,000

Exercise 8-10
Using the perpetual inventory system

Fitness Equipment Corporation uses a *perpetual inventory system.* On January 1, the Inventory account had a balance of $36,200. During the first few days of January the following transactions occurred.

Jan. 2 Purchased merchandise on credit from Bell Company for $7,400.
Jan. 3 Sold merchandise for cash, $4,500. The cost of this merchandise was $2,700.

Instructions
a Prepare entries in general journal form to record the above transactions.
b What was the balance of the Inventory account at the close of business January 3?

Problems

Problem 8-1
Inventory errors: effects on earnings

Financial Fantasy is being offered for sale as a going concern. Its income statements for the last three years include the following key figures:

	1991	1990	1989
Net sales...	$540,000	$520,000	$500,000
Cost of goods sold...................................	356,400	348,800	345,000
Gross profit on sales................................	$183,600	$171,200	$155,000
Gross profit percentage	34%	33%*	31%

* Rounded to the nearest full percentage point.

In discussions with prospective buyers, the owners are emphasizing the rising trends of gross profit and gross profit percentage as very favorable factors.

Assume that you are retained by a prospective purchaser of the business to make an investigation of the fairness and reliability of Financial Fantasy's accounting records and financial statements. You find everything in order except for the following: (1) An arithmetical error in the computation of inventory at the end of 1989 had caused a $10,000 understatement in that inventory; and (2) a duplication of figures in the computation of inventory at the end of 1991 had caused an overstatement of $27,000 in that inventory. The company uses the periodic inventory system and these errors had not been brought to light prior to your investigation.

Instructions

    a Prepare a revised three-year schedule along the lines of the one illustrated above.

    b Comment on the trend of gross profit and gross profit percentage before and after the revision.

Problem 8-2
FIFO, LIFO, and
average cost

One of the popular products carried by Outrider Corporation is an 8-inch speaker unit. The inventory quantities, purchases, and sales of this unit for the current year are summarized below.

	Number of Units	Cost per Unit	Total Cost
Inventory, Jan. 1	900	$10.00	$ 9,000
First purchase (Apr. 3)	1,180	10.20	12,036
Second purchase (July 7)	800	10.35	8,280
Third purchase (Oct. 22)	620	10.70	6,634
Fourth purchase (Dec. 15)	1,000	10.85	10,850
Goods available for sale	4,500		$46,800
Units sold during the year	3,200		
Inventory, Dec. 31	1,300		

Instructions

    a Compute the cost of the December 31 inventory and the cost of goods sold for the 8-inch speaker units in the current year using:

        (1) The first-in, first-out method

        (2) The last-in, first-out method

        (3) The average-cost method

    b Which of the three inventory pricing methods provides the most realistic balance sheet valuation of inventory in light of the current replacement cost of the speaker units? Does this same method also produce the most realistic measure of income in light of the costs being incurred by Outrider Corporation to replace the speakers when they are sold? Explain.

    c Which of the three methods of pricing inventory would be the most advantageous from an income tax standpoint during a period of rising prices? Explain.

Problem 8-3
More FIFO,
LIFO, and
average cost

Much of the revenue earned by Fluid Power, Inc., comes from the sale of a specialized type of valve. During the year, the inventory quantities, purchases, and sales of this valve were as follows:

	Number of Units	Cost per Unit	Total Cost
Inventory, Jan. 1	8,000	$5.89	$ 47,120
First purchase (Mar. 15)	10,300	6.20	63,860
Second purchase (June 6)	12,400	6.60	81,840
Third purchase (Sept. 20)	9,600	6.80	65,280
Fourth purchase (Dec. 31)	7,700	7.00	53,900
Goods available for sale	48,000		$312,000
Units sold during the year	37,200		
Inventory, Dec. 31	10,800		

Instructions

a Compute the cost of the December 31 inventory and the cost of goods sold for the valves during the year using:
   (1) The first-in, first-out method
   (2) The last-in, first-out method
   (3) The average-cost method

b Which of the three inventory pricing methods provides the most realistic balance sheet valuation of inventory in light of the current replacement cost of the valves? Does this same method also produce the most realistic measure of income in light of the costs being incurred by Fluid Power to replace the valves when they are sold? Explain.

c Which of the three methods of pricing inventory would be the *least* advantageous from an income tax standpoint during a period of rising prices? Explain.

Problem 8-4
Gross profit method

On May 1, 1990, the entire inventory of Desk Top Products was destroyed by fire. The inventory had been stored in a rented warehouse; the company's office was not damaged and the accounting records were intact. Desk Top Products did not maintain perpetual inventory records, and the last physical inventory taken had been on December 31 of the prior year.

An estimate of the inventory value at May 1, the date of the fire, must be prepared in order to file an insurance claim. The income statement for the prior year is shown below to aid you in estimating the amount of the inventory at the date of the fire. Use the gross profit method.

DESK TOP PRODUCTS
Income Statement
For the Year Ended December 31, 1989

Net sales..		$740,000
Cost of goods sold:		
Inventory, Jan. 1...	$ 92,000	
Purchases	447,000	
Cost of goods available for sale..............................	$539,000	
Less: Inventory, Dec. 31	110,000	429,000
Gross profit on sales...		$311,000
Expenses		241,000
Net income		$ 70,000

Other data. Included in the purchases figure shown in the income statement was $22,000 of office equipment which Desk Top Products had acquired late in December for its own use from a competing concern which was quitting business. The bookkeeper of Desk Top Products had not understood the nature of this transaction and had recorded it by debiting the Purchases account. The office equipment, however, was not included in the physical inventory counted at December 31.

The accounting records showed the merchandise transactions between December 31 and the date of the fire to be: sales, $306,700; sales returns and allowances, $2,700; transportation-in, $1,800; purchases, $166,200; purchase returns and allowances, $3,600.

Instructions

a Prepare a report directed to the insurance adjuster summarizing your findings. Include an estimate of the inventory value as of the date of the fire and a computation of the applicable cost of goods sold percentage. (Hint: Make the necessary correction to the 1989 income statement amounts before computing the cost percentage.)

b Explain how the gross profit method of estimating inventories may be used other than in case of the loss or destruction of the inventory.

Problem 8-5
Retail inventory
method

The inventory of Porterfield's, a retail store, consists of a wide range of articles of low unit price. The selling price of each item is plainly marked on the merchandise. At each year-end, the company has taken a physical count of goods on hand and has priced these goods at cost by looking up individual purchase invoices to determine the unit cost of each item in stock. Stevens, the store manager, is anxious to find a more economical method of assigning dollar values to the year-end inventory, explaining that it takes much more time to price the inventory than to count the merchandise on hand.

By analyzing the accounting records you are able to determine that net purchases of merchandise in the year totaled $1,330,000; the retail selling price of this merchandise was $1,750,000. At the end of the year a physical inventory showed goods on hand priced to sell at $272,000. This represented a considerable increase over the inventory of a year earlier. At December 31 a year ago, the inventory on hand had appeared in the balance sheet at cost of $170,000, although it had a retail value of $250,000.

Instructions

a Outline a plan whereby the inventory can be computed without the necessity of looking up individual purchase invoices. List step by step the procedures to be followed. Ignore the possibility of markups and markdowns in the original retail price of merchandise.

b Compute the cost of the inventory at December 31 of the current year, using the method described in a.

c Explain how the inventory method you have described can be modified for the preparation of monthly financial statements when no physical count of inventory is taken.

Problem 8-6
Entries for
perpetual inven-
tory

Halley's Space Scope sells state-of-the-art telescopes to individuals and organizations interested in the study of the solar system. At December 31, the end of the fiscal year, the company's inventory amounted to $90,000. During the first week of January, the company made only one purchase and one sale. These transactions were as follows:

Jan. 3 Sold one telescope costing $28,000 to Eastern State University for cash, $40,000.

Jan. 6 Purchased merchandise on account from Solar Optics, $18,500. Terms, net 30 days.

Instructions

a Prepare journal entries to record these transactions assuming that Halley's Space Scope uses the perpetual inventory system. Use separate entries to record the sales revenue and the cost of goods sold for the sale on January 3.

b Compute the balance of the Inventory account on January 7.

c Prepare journal entries to record the two transactions assuming that Halley's Space Scope uses the periodic inventory system.

d Compute the cost of goods sold for the first week of January assuming use of a periodic inventory system. Use your answer to part b as the ending inventory.

e Which inventory system do you believe that a company such as Halley's Space Scope would probably use. Explain your reasoning.

Problem 8-7
Perpetual
inventory
records in a small
business

Executive Suites, Inc., uses a perpetual inventory system. This system includes a perpetual inventory record card for each of the 60 types of products the company keeps in stock. The following transactions show the purchases and sales of a particular desk chair (product code DC-SB2) during September.

Sept. 1 Balance on hand, 50 units, cost $60 each.................................	$3,000
Sept. 4 Purchase, 20 units, cost $65 each	1,300
Sept. 8 Sale, 35 units, sales price $100 each....................................	3,500
Sept. 9 Purchase, 40 units, cost $65 each	2,600
Sept. 20 Sale, 60 units, sales price $100 each....................................	6,000
Sept. 25 Purchase, 40 units, cost $70 each	2,800
Sept. 30 Sale, 5 units, sales price $110 each.....................................	550

Instructions

a Record the beginning inventory, the purchases, the cost of goods sold, and the running balance on an inventory record card like the one illustrated on page 334. Use the first-in, first-out method.

b Assume that all sales were made on credit. Compute the total sales and total cost of goods sold of this product for September. Prepare an entry in general journal form to record these sales and a second entry to record the cost of goods sold for September.

c Compute the gross profit on sales of this product for the month of September.

Business decision cases

Case 8-1
Have I got a deal
for you!

You are the sales manager of Continental Motors, an automobile dealership specializing in European imports. Among the automobiles in Continental Motors' showroom are two Italian sports cars, which are identical in every respect except for color; one is red and the other white. The red car had been ordered last February, at a cost of $13,300 American dollars. The white car had been ordered early last March, but because of a revaluation of the Italian lira relative to the dollar, the white car had cost only $12,000 American dollars. Both cars arrived in the United States on the same boat and had just been delivered to your showroom. Since the cars were identical except for color and both colors were equally popular, you had listed both cars at the same suggested retail price, $18,000.

Smiley Miles, one of your best salesmen, comes into your office with a proposal. He has a customer in the showroom who wants to buy the red car for $18,000. However, when Miles pulled the inventory card on the red car to see what options were included, he happened to notice the inventory card of the white car. Continental Motors, like most automobile dealerships, uses the specific identification method to value inventory. Consequently, Miles noticed that the red car had cost $13,300, while the white one had cost Continental Motors only $12,000. This gave Miles the idea for the following proposal.

"Have I got a deal for you! If I sell the red car for $18,000, Continental Motors makes a gross profit of $4,700. But if you'll let me discount that white car $500, I think I can get my customer to buy that one instead. If I sell the white car for $17,500, the gross profit will be $5,500, so Continental Motors is $800 better off than if I sell the red car for $18,000. Since I came up with this plan, I feel I should get part of the benefit, so Continental Motors should split the extra $800 with me. That way, I'll get an extra $400 commission, and the company still makes $400 more than if I sell the red car."

Instructions

   a Prepare a schedule which shows the total revenue, cost of goods sold, and gross profit to Continental Motors if **both** cars are sold for $18,000 each.

   b Prepare a schedule showing the revenue, cost of goods sold, and gross profit to Continental Motors if both cars are sold but Miles' plan is adopted and the white car is sold for $17,500. Assume the red car is still sold for $18,000. To simplify comparison of this schedule to the one prepared in part a, include the extra $400 commission to Miles in the cost of goods sold of the part b schedule.

   c Write out your decision whether or not to accept Miles' proposal, and explain to Miles why the proposal either would or would not be to the advantage of Continental Motors. (Hint: Refer to your schedules prepared in parts a and b in your explanation.)

Case 8-2
Hello. I'm from
the IRS . . .

Carla Wilson is an auditor with the Internal Revenue Service. She has been assigned to audit the income tax return of The French Connection, a corporation engaged in selling imported bicycles by mail order. Selected figures from the company's income tax return are shown below.

Sales.	$1,200,000
Beginning inventory.	30,000
Purchases.	885,000
Ending inventory	15,000
Cost of goods sold	900,000
Gross profit.	300,000

As Wilson examined these figures, she began to suspect that the income reported by The French Connection had been understated. She sent a letter to the company to arrange a date for performing the tax audit. As part of her preliminary investigation, Wilson then telephoned The French Connection. Pretending to be a customer, she asked what types of bicycles the company had available for immediate delivery. The salesclerk told her that The French Connection had in stock three makes of French bicycles and three lines of Italian bicycles.

Wilson's letter about the tax audit was received by Greg Thomas, the president and owner of The French Connection. The letter made Thomas quite nervous, because over the last five years he had understated the income reported in the company's income tax returns by a total of $100,000. Thomas hurriedly began making his own preparations for the tax audit. These preparations included renting an empty building a few blocks from The French Connection.

When Wilson arrived at The French Connection, she was met by Thomas. Wilson introduced herself and asked to see the company's accounting records. As Thomas was showing her to the company's accounting office, they passed through the bicycle warehouse. Much of the large warehouse was empty, but along one wall were about 50 bicycles. Each had the name "LeMond" written on the frame in bright red letters.

Thomas explained, "Milo LeMond is the finest bicycle maker in all of France. We have the largest selection of his bicycles in the United States."

Wilson asked if the company had more bicycles at another location.

Thomas replied, "No. This is our entire inventory. We stock about 50 bikes. After all, these bikes cost us about $300 each. One of the secrets of success in the mail-order business is not tying up a lot of money in a big inventory. We've cut way back on our inventory over the years — helps keep our costs down."

Wilson's suspicions had been confirmed. She now knew that The French Connection had substantially understated its income. Of course, she would still have to find out by just how much. She felt a little sorry for Thomas. Not only would his company have to face additional taxes and a stiff penalty, but he might be in for a jail sentence. Wilson was sure that the company's understatement of income was no accident — it was a deliberate act of tax evasion, which Thomas was now trying desperately to conceal.

Instructions

a What was it about the figures in The French Connection's income tax return that originally made Wilson suspicious that the company might have understated its income?

b What happened to confirm Wilson's suspicions? Why does she believe that the understatement of income was a deliberate act which Thomas is now attempting to conceal?

c Assume that The French Connection correctly reported all its revenue in its income tax returns. How do you think that Thomas caused the company's income to be understated year after year?

d What do you think Thomas has in the building he rented? Be as specific as possible.

Chapter 9
Plant and equipment, depreciation, and intangible assets

CHAPTER PREVIEW

In the first part of Chapter 9, our goal is to define plant and equipment and to explain the principles for determining its cost. Once cost has been recorded, the next step is to allocate this cost of plant and equipment over the years of its use by means of a depreciation program. Various methods of depreciation are then evaluated, as, for example, straight-line, units-of-output, double-declining-balance, and sum-of-the-years'-digits method. The final part of the chapter deals with the accounting treatment of natural resources and intangible assets.

After studying this chapter you should be able to meet these Learning Objectives:

1 Determine the cost of plant assets.
2 Distinguish between capital expenditures and revenue expenditures.
3 Explain the relationship between depreciation and the matching principle.
4 Compute depreciation by the straight-line, units-of-output, declining-balance, and sum-of-the-years'-digits methods.
5 Explain why depreciation based upon historical costs may cause an overstatement of profits.
6 Record the sale, trade-in, or scrapping of a plant asset.
7 Account for the depletion of natural resources.
8 Explain the nature of goodwill and indicate when this asset should appear in the accounting records.

PLANT AND EQUIPMENT

The term *plant and equipment* is used to describe long-lived assets acquired for use in the operation of the business and not intended for resale to customers. Among the more common examples are land, buildings, machinery, furniture and fixtures, office equipment, and automobiles. A delivery truck in the showroom of an automobile dealer is inventory; when this same truck is sold to a drugstore for use in making deliveries to customers, it becomes a unit of plant and equipment.

The term *fixed assets* has long been used in accounting literature to describe all types of plant and equipment. This term, however, has virtually disappeared from the published financial statements of large corporations. *Plant and equipment* appears to be a more descriptive term. Another alternative title used on many corporation balance sheets is *property, plant, and equipment.*

Plant and equipment — a stream of services

It is convenient to think of a plant asset as a stream of services to be received by the owner over a period of years. Ownership of a delivery truck, for example, may provide about 100,000 miles of transportation. The cost of the delivery truck is customarily entered in a plant and equipment account entitled Delivery Truck, which in essence represents payment in advance for many years of transportation service. Similarly, a building may be regarded as payment in advance for many years' supply of housing services. As the years go by, these services are utilized by the business and the cost of the plant asset gradually is transferred into depreciation expense.

An awareness of the similarity between plant assets and prepaid expenses is essential to an understanding of the accounting process by which the cost of plant assets is allocated to the accounting periods in which the benefits of ownership are received.

Major categories of plant and equipment

Plant and equipment items are often classified into the following groups:

1 Tangible plant assets. The term *tangible* denotes physical substance, as exemplified by land, a building, or a machine. This category may be subdivided into two distinct classifications:
   a Plant property subject to depreciation; included are plant assets of limited useful life such as buildings and office equipment.
   b Land. The only plant asset not subject to depreciation is land, which has an unlimited term of existence.
2 Intangible assets. The term *intangible assets* is used to describe assets which are used in the operation of the business but have no physical substance, and are noncurrent. Examples include patents, copyrights, trademarks, franchises, and goodwill. Current assets such as accounts receivable or prepaid rent are not included in the intangible classification, even though they are lacking in physical substance.

Determining the cost of plant and equipment

1 Determine the cost of plant assets.

The cost of plant and equipment includes all expenditures reasonable and necessary in acquiring the asset and placing it in a position and condition for use in the operations of the business. Only **reasonable** and **necessary** expenditures should be included. For example, if the company's truck driver receives a traffic ticket while hauling a new machine to the plant, the traffic fine is **not** part of the cost of the new machine. If the machine is dropped and damaged while being unloaded, the cost of repairing the damage should be recognized as expense in the current period and should **not** be added to the cost of the machine.

Cost is most easily determined when an asset is purchased for cash. The cost of the asset is then equal to the cash outlay necessary in acquiring the asset plus any expenditures for freight, insurance while in transit, installation, trial runs, and any other costs necessary to make **the asset ready for use.** If plant assets are **purchased** on the installment plan or by issuance of notes payable, the interest element or carrying charge should be recorded as interest expense and **not** as part of the cost of the plant assets. However, if a company **constructs** a plant asset for its own use, interest costs incurred **during the construction period** are viewed as part of the cost of the asset.[1]

This principle of including in the cost of a plant asset all the incidental charges necessary to put the asset in use is illustrated by the following example. A factory in Minneapolis orders a machine from a San Francisco tool manufacturer at a list price of $10,000, with terms of 2/10, n/30. Sales tax of $588 must be paid, also freight charges of $1,250. Transportation from the railroad station to the factory costs $150, and installation labor amounts to $400. The cost of the machine to be entered in the Machinery account is computed as follows:

Items included in cost of machine

List price of machine	$10,000
Less: Cash discount (2% × $10,000)	200
Net cash price	$ 9,800
Sales tax	588
Freight	1,250
Transportation from railroad station to factory	150
Installation labor	400
Cost of machine	$12,188

Why should all the incidental charges relating to the acquisition of a machine be included in its cost? Why not treat these incidental charges as expenses of the period in which the machine is acquired?

The answer is to be found in the basic accounting principle of **matching costs and revenue.** The benefits of owning the machine will be received over a span of years, 10 years, for example. During those 10 years the operation of the machine will contribute to revenue. Consequently, the total costs of the machine should be recorded in the accounts as an asset and allocated against the revenue of the 10 years. All costs incurred in acquiring the machine are costs of the services to be received from using the machine.

[1] *FASB Statement No. 34,* "Capitalization of Interest Costs" (Stamford, Conn.: 1979).

Land. When land is purchased, various incidental costs are generally incurred, in addition to the purchase price. These additional costs may include commissions to real estate brokers, escrow fees, legal fees for examining and insuring the title, delinquent taxes paid by the purchaser, and fees for surveying, draining, clearing, and grading the property. All these expenditures become part of the cost of the land.

Apportionment of a lump-sum purchase. Separate ledger accounts are necessary for land and buildings, because buildings are subject to depreciation and land is not. The treatment of land as a nondepreciable asset is based on the premise that land used as a building site has an unlimited life. When land and building are purchased for a lump sum, the purchase price must be apportioned between the land and the building. An appraisal may be necessary for this purpose. Assume, for example, that land and a building are purchased for a bargain price of $400,000. The apportionment of this cost on the basis of an appraisal may be made as follows:

	Value per Appraisal	Percentage of Total	Apportionment of Cost
Land	$200,000	40%	$160,000
Building	300,000	60%	240,000
Total	$500,000	100%	$400,000

Apportioning cost between land and building

Sometimes a tract of land purchased as a building site has on it an old building which is not suitable for the buyer's use. The Land account should be charged with the entire purchase price ***plus any costs incurred in tearing down or removing the building.*** Proceeds received from sale of the materials salvaged from the old building are recorded as a credit in the Land account.

Land improvements. Improvements to real estate such as driveways, fences, parking lots, and sprinkler systems have a limited life and are therefore subject to depreciation. For this reason they should be recorded not in the Land account but in a separate account entitled Land Improvements.

Buildings. Old buildings are sometimes purchased with the intention of repairing them prior to placing them in use. Repairs made under these circumstances are charged to the Buildings account. After the building has been placed in use, ordinary repairs are considered as maintenance expense when incurred.

Capital expenditures and revenue expenditures

2 Distinguish between capital expenditures and revenue expenditures

Expenditures for the purchase or expansion of plant assets are called ***capital expenditures*** and are recorded in asset accounts. Expenditures for ordinary repairs, maintenance, fuel, and other items necessary to the ownership and use of plant and equipment are called ***revenue expenditures*** and are recorded by debits to expense accounts. The charge to an expense account is based on the assumption that the benefits from the expenditure will be used up in the current period, and the cost should therefore be deducted from the revenue of the current period in determining the net income.

A business may purchase many small items which will benefit several accounting periods, but which have a relatively low cost. Examples of such items include auto batteries, wastebaskets, and pencil sharpeners. Such items are theoretically capital expenditures, but if they are recorded as assets in the accounting records it will be necessary to compute and record the related depreciation expense in future periods. We have previously mentioned the idea that the extra work involved in developing more precise accounting information should be weighed against the benefits that result. Thus, for reasons of convenience and economy, expenditures which are *not material* in dollar amount are treated in the accounting records as expenses of the current period. In brief, *any material expenditure that will benefit several accounting periods is considered a capital expenditure. Any expenditure that will benefit only the current period or that is not material in amount is treated as a revenue expenditure.*

Many companies develop formal policy statements defining capital and revenue expenditures as a guide toward consistent accounting practice from year to year. These policy statements often set a minimum dollar limit for a capital expenditure (such as $100 or $200).

Effect of errors in distinguishing between capital and revenue expenditures. Because a capital expenditure is recorded by debiting an asset account, the transaction has no immediate effect upon net income. However, the depreciation of the amount entered in the asset account will be reflected as an expense in future periods. A revenue expenditure, on the other hand, is recorded by debiting an expense account and therefore represents an immediate deduction from earnings in the current period.

Assume that the cost of a new delivery truck is erroneously debited to the Repairs Expense account. The result will be to overstate repairs expense, thereby understating the current year's net income. If the error is not corrected, the net income of subsequent years will be overstated because no depreciation expense will be recognized during the years in which the truck is used.

On the other hand, assume that ordinary truck repairs are erroneously debited to the asset account, Delivery Truck. The result will be to understate repairs expense, thereby overstating the current year's net income. If the error is not corrected, the net income of future years will be understated because of excessive depreciation charges based upon the inflated balance of the Delivery Truck account.

These examples indicate that a careful distinction between capital and revenue expenditures is essential to attainment of one of the most fundamental objectives of accounting—the determination of net income for each year of operation of a business.

● **CASE IN POINT** ● During an annual audit of Bowden Company, a CPA firm was reviewing entries in the general journal. An entry that caught the attention of Carol Jones, CPA, consisted of a debit to Office Furniture and a credit to Notes

Payable for $52,000. Upon investigation, Jones learned that the transaction involved a hand-carved clock acquired from James Burns, the former president of Bowden Company. Burns's hobby for many years had been the building of hand-carved clocks. At a retirement banquet honoring Burns, Bowden Company had awarded him a $52,000 bonus, represented by the company's short-term note payable. At the same banquet, Burns had presented Bowden Company with one of his clocks.

Further investigation by Jones indicated that the commercial value of the clock was about $400. Jones therefore advised the company to transfer the $52,000 expenditure out of the Office Furniture account and into Executive Compensation Expense.

DEPRECIATION

Allocating the cost of plant and equipment over the years of use

3 Explain the relationship between depreciation and the matching principle.

Plant assets, with the exception of land, are of use to a company for only a limited number of years, and the cost of each plant asset is allocated as expense among the years in which it is used. Accountants use the term *depreciation* to describe this gradual conversion of the cost of a plant asset into expense. Depreciation, as the term is used in accounting, does not mean the decrease in market value of a plant asset over a period of time. *Depreciation means the allocation of the cost of a plant asset to expense in the periods in which services are received from the asset.*

When a delivery truck is purchased, its cost is first recorded as an asset. This cost becomes expense over a period of years through the accounting process of depreciation. On the other hand, when gasoline is purchased for the truck, the price paid for each tankful is immediately recorded as expense. In theory, both outlays (for the truck and for a tank of gas) represent the acquisition of assets. However, since it is reasonable to assume that a tankful of gasoline will be consumed in the accounting period in which it is purchased, we record the outlay for gasoline as an expense immediately. It is important to recognize, however, that *both the outlay for the truck and the payment for the gasoline become expense in the period or periods in which each renders services.*

Depreciation differs from most expenses in that it does not require a cash payment at or near the time it is recorded. The entry to record depreciation (a debit to Depreciation Expense and a credit to Accumulated Depreciation) has no effect on current assets or current liabilities. However, when depreciable assets wear out, a large cash payment may be required in order to replace them.

A separate Depreciation Expense account and a separate Accumulated Depreciation account are generally maintained for each group of depreciable assets such as factory buildings, delivery equipment, and office equipment so that a proper allocation of depreciation expense can be made between functional areas of activity such as sales and manufacturing.

Depreciation not a process of valuation

Accounting records do not purport to show the constantly fluctuating market values of plant and equipment. Occasionally the market value of a building may rise substantially over a period of years because of a change in the price level, or for other reasons. Depreciation is continued, however, regardless of the increase in market value. The accountant recognizes that the building will render useful services for only a limited number of years, and that its full cost must be allocated as expense of those years regardless of fluctuations in market value.

The ***book value*** or ***carrying value*** of a plant asset is its cost minus the related accumulated depreciation. Plant assets are shown in the balance sheet at their book values, representing the portion of their cost which will be allocated to expense in future periods. Accumulated depreciation represents the portion of the assets' cost which has already been recognized as expense.

Accumulated depreciation does not consist of cash

Some readers of financial statements who have not studied accounting mistakenly believe that accumulated depreciation accounts represent money accumulated for the purpose of buying new equipment when the present equipment wears out. Perhaps the best way to combat such mistaken notions is to emphasize that a credit balance in an accumulated depreciation account represents the ***expired cost*** of assets acquired in the past. The amounts credited to the accumulated depreciation account could, as an alternative, have been credited directly to the plant and equipment account. An accumulated depreciation account has a ***credit*** balance; it does not represent an asset; and it cannot be used in any way to pay for new equipment. To pay for a new plant asset requires cash; the total amount of cash owned by a company is shown by the asset account for cash.

Causes of depreciation

The two major causes of depreciation are physical deterioration and obsolescence.

Physical deterioration. Physical deterioration of a plant asset results from use, and also from exposure to sun, wind, and other climatic factors. When a plant asset has been carefully maintained, it is not uncommon for the owner to claim that the asset is as "good as new." Such statements are not literally true. Although a good repair policy may greatly lengthen the useful life of a machine, every machine eventually reaches the point at which it must be discarded. In brief, the making of repairs does not lessen the need for recognition of depreciation.

Obsolescence. The term ***obsolescence*** means the process of becoming out of date or obsolete. An airplane, for example, may become obsolete even though it is in excellent physical condition; it becomes obsolete because better planes of superior design and performance have become available.

The usefulness of plant assets may also be reduced because the rapid growth of a company renders such assets inadequate. ***Inadequacy*** of a plant asset may necessitate replacement with a larger unit even though the asset is in good physical condition. Obsolescence and inadequacy are often closely associated; both relate to the opportunity for economical and efficient use of an asset rather than to its physical condition.

Methods of computing depreciation

4 Compute depreciation by the straight-line, units-of-output, declining-balance, and sum-of-the-years'-digits methods.

There are several alternative methods of computing depreciation. A business need not use the same method of depreciation for all its various assets. For example, a company may use straight-line depreciation on some assets and a declining-balance method for other assets. Furthermore, the methods used for computing depreciation expense in financial statements ***may differ*** from the methods used in the preparation of the company's income tax return.

Straight-line method. The simplest and most widely used method of computing depreciation is the straight-line method. This method was described in Chapter 3 and has been used repeatedly in problems throughout this book. Under the straight-line method, an equal portion of the cost of the asset is allocated to each period of use; consequently, this method is most appropriate when usage of an asset is fairly uniform from year to year.

The computation of the periodic charge for depreciation is made by deducting the estimated ***residual*** or ***salvage value*** from the cost of the asset and dividing the remaining ***depreciable cost*** by the years of estimated useful life. For example, if a delivery truck has a cost of $20,000, a residual value of $2,000, and an estimated useful life of four years, the annual computation of depreciation expense will be as follows:

$$\frac{\text{Cost} - \text{Residual Value}}{\text{Years of Useful Life}} = \frac{\$20,000 - \$2,000}{4} = \$4,500$$

This same depreciation computation is shown below in tabular form.

Computing depreciation by straight-line method

Cost of the depreciable asset. $20,000
Less: Estimated residual value (amount to be realized by sale of asset when it is
   retired from use). 2,000
Total amount to be depreciated (depreciable cost). $18,000
Estimated useful life . . . . 4 years
Depreciation expense each year ($18,000 ÷ 4) . . . . $ 4,500

The following schedule summarizes the accumulation of depreciation over the useful life of the asset. The amount to be depreciated is $18,000 (cost of $20,000 minus estimated residual value of $2,000).

Depreciation Schedule: Straight-Line Method

Constant annual
depreciation
expense

Year	Computation	Depreciation Expense	Accumulated Depreciation	Book Value
				$20,000
First	($\frac{1}{4}$ × $18,000)	$ 4,500	$ 4,500	15,500
Second.......................	($\frac{1}{4}$ × $18,000)	4,500	9,000	11,000
Third........................	($\frac{1}{4}$ × $18,000)	4,500	13,500	6,500
Fourth.......................	($\frac{1}{4}$ × $18,000)	4,500	18,000	2,000
		$18,000		

Depreciation rates for various types of assets can conveniently be stated as percentages. In the above example the asset had an estimated life of four years, so the depreciation expense each year was $\frac{1}{4}$ of the depreciable amount. The fraction "$\frac{1}{4}$" is of course equivalent to an annual rate of 25%. Similarly, a 10-year life indicates a depreciation rate of $\frac{1}{10}$, or 10% and an 8-year life a depreciation rate of $\frac{1}{8}$, or $12\frac{1}{2}$%.

In the preceding illustration we assumed that the company maintained its accounts on a calendar-year basis and that the asset was acquired on January 1, the beginning of the accounting period. If the asset had been acquired sometime during the year, on October 1 for example, it would have been in use for only three months, or $\frac{3}{12}$ of a year. Consequently, the depreciation to be recorded at December 31 would be only $\frac{3}{12}$ of $4,500, or $1,125. Stated more precisely, the depreciation expense in this situation is computed as follows: 25% × $18,000 × $\frac{3}{12}$ = $1,125.

In practice, the possibility of residual value is sometimes ignored and the annual depreciation charge computed by dividing the total cost of the asset by the number of years of estimated useful life. This practice may be justified in those cases in which residual value is not material and is difficult to estimate accurately.

Units-of-output method. For certain kinds of assets, more equitable allocation of the cost can be obtained by dividing the cost (minus salvage value, if significant) by the estimated units of output rather than by the estimated years of useful life. A truck line or bus company, for example, might compute depreciation on its vehicles by a mileage basis. If we assume that the delivery truck in our example has an estimated useful life of 200,000 miles, the depreciation rate per mile of operation is 9 cents ($18,000 ÷ 200,000). This calculation of the depreciation rate may be stated as follows:

$$\frac{\textbf{Cost} - \textbf{Residual Value}}{\textbf{Estimated Units of Output (Miles)}} = \frac{\textbf{Depreciation per}}{\textbf{Unit of Output (Mile)}}$$

or

$$\frac{\textbf{\$20,000} - \textbf{\$2,000}}{\textbf{200,000 miles}} = \textbf{\$.09 depreciation per mile}$$

At the end of each year, the amount of depreciation to be recorded would be determined by multiplying the 9-cent rate by the number of miles the truck had operated during the year. This method is suitable only when the total units of output of the asset over its entire useful life can be estimated with reasonable accuracy.

Accelerated depreciation methods. The term *accelerated depreciation* means recognition of relatively large amounts of depreciation in the early years of use and reduced amounts in the later years. Many types of plant and equipment are most efficient when new and therefore provide more and better services in the early years of useful life. If we assume that the benefits derived from owning an asset are greatest in the early years when the asset is relatively new, then the amount of the asset's cost which we allocate as depreciation expense should be greatest in these same early years. This is consistent with the basic accounting concept of matching costs with related revenue. Accelerated depreciation methods have been widely used in income tax returns because they reduce the current year's tax burden by recognizing a relatively large amount of depreciation expense.

Declining-balance method. The accelerated depreciation method which allocates the largest portion of the cost of an asset to the early years of its useful life is called *double-declining balance.* This method consists of doubling the straight-line depreciation rate and applying this doubled rate to the undepreciated cost (book value) of the asset.

To illustrate, consider our example of the $20,000 delivery truck. The estimated useful life of the truck is four years; therefore, the depreciation rate under the straight-line method would be 25%. To depreciate the automobile by the double-declining-balance method, we double the straight-line rate of 25% and apply the doubled rate of 50% to the book value. Depreciation expense in the first year would then amount to $10,000. In the second year the depreciation expense would drop to $5,000, computed at 50% of the remaining book value of $10,000. In the third year depreciation would be $2,500, and in the fourth year only $1,250. The following table shows the computation of each year's depreciation expense by the declining-balance method.

Depreciation Schedule: Declining-Balance Method

	Year	Computation	Depreciation Expense	Accumulated Depreciation	Book Value
Accelerated depreciation: declining-balance					$20,000
	First	(50% × $20,000)	$10,000	$10,000	10,000
	Second.....................	(50% × $10,000)	5,000	15,000	5,000
	Third.......................	(50% × $ 5,000)	2,500	17,500	2,500
	Fourth......................	(50% × $ 2,500)	1,250	18,750	1,250

Notice that the estimated residual value of the delivery truck did not enter into the computation of depreciation expense by the declining-balance method. This is because the declining-balance method provides an "automatic" residual value. As long as each year's depreciation expense is equal to only a portion of the undepreciated cost of the asset, the asset will never be entirely written off. However, if the asset has a significant residual value, depreciation should **stop at this point.** Since our delivery truck has an estimated residual value of $2,000, the depreciation expense for the fourth year should be limited to $500 rather than the $1,250 computed in the table. By limiting the last year's depreciation expense in this manner, the book value of the truck at the end of the fourth year will be equal to its $2,000 estimated residual value.

If the asset in the above illustration had been acquired on October 1 rather than on January 1, depreciation for only three months would be recorded in the first year. The computation would be 50% × $20,000 × $\frac{3}{12}$, or $2,500. For the next calendar year the calculation would be 50% × ($20,000 − $2,500), or $8,750.

Sum-of-the-years'-digits method. This is another method of allocating a large portion of the cost of an asset to the early years of its use. The depreciation rate to be used is a fraction, of which the numerator is the remaining years of useful life (as of the beginning of the year) and the denominator is the sum of the years of useful life. Consider again the example of the delivery truck costing $20,000 having an estimated life of four years and an estimated residual value of $2,000. Since the asset has an estimated life of four years, the denominator of the fraction will be 10, computed as follows:[2] 1 + 2 + 3 + 4 = 10. For the first year, the depreciation will be $\frac{4}{10}$ × ($20,000 − $2,000), or $7,200. (Notice that we reduced the cost of the truck by the estimated residual value in determining the amount to be depreciated.) For the second year, the depreciation will be $\frac{3}{10}$ × $18,000, or $5,400; in the third year $\frac{2}{10}$ × $18,000, or $3,600; and in the fourth year, $\frac{1}{10}$ × $18,000, or $1,800. In tabular form, this depreciation program will appear as follows:

Depreciation Schedule: Sum-of-the-Years'-Digits Method

Year	Computation	Depreciation Expense	Accumulated Depreciation	Book Value
				$20,000
First	($\frac{4}{10}$ × $18,000)	$ 7,200	$ 7,200	12,800
Second	($\frac{3}{10}$ × $18,000)	5,400	12,600	7,400
Third	($\frac{2}{10}$ × $18,000)	3,600	16,200	3,800
Fourth	($\frac{1}{10}$ × $18,000)	1,800	18,000	2,000
		$18,000		

Accelerated depreciation: sum-of-the-years'-digits

Assume that the asset being depreciated by the sum-of-the-years'-digits method was acquired on October 1 and the company maintains its accounts on a calendar-

[2] Alternatively, the denominator may be computed by using the formula $n\left(\dfrac{n+1}{2}\right)$, where n is the useful life of the asset. According to this formula, the sum of the years' digits for an asset with a four-year life is computed as follows: $4\left(\dfrac{4+1}{2}\right) = 4(2.5) = 10$. Similarly, the sum of the years' digits for an asset with a 10-year life would be computed as follows: $10\left(\dfrac{10+1}{2}\right)10(5.5) = 55$.

year basis. Since the asset was in use for only three months during the first accounting period, the depreciation to be recorded in this first period will be for only $\frac{3}{12}$ of a full year, that is, $\frac{3}{12} \times \$7,200$, or $\$1,800$. For the second accounting period the depreciation computation will be:

$\frac{9}{12} \times (\frac{4}{10} \times \$18,000)$	$\$5,400$
$\frac{3}{12} \times (\frac{3}{10} \times \$18,000)$	1,350
Depreciation expense, second period	$\underline{\$6,750}$

A similar pattern of allocation will be followed for each accounting period of the asset's life.

Depreciation for fractional periods. When an asset is acquired in the middle of an accounting period, it is not necessary to compute depreciation expense to the nearest day or week. In fact, such a computation would give a misleading impression of great precision. Since depreciation is based upon an estimated useful life of many years, the depreciation applicable to any one year is only an approximation at best.

One widely used method of computing depreciation for part of a year is to round the calculation to the nearest whole month. Thus, if an asset is acquired on July 12, depreciation is computed for the six months beginning July 1. If an asset is acquired on July 16 (or any date in the latter half of July), depreciation is recorded for only five months (August through December) in the current calendar year.

Another acceptable approach, called the **half-year convention,** is to record six months' depreciation on all assets acquired during the year. This approach is based upon the assumption that the actual purchase dates will "average out" to approximately midyear. The half-year convention is widely used for assets such as office equipment, automobiles, and machinery. For buildings, however, income tax rules require that depreciation be computed for the actual number of months that the building is owned.

The half-year convention enables us to treat similar assets acquired at different dates during the year as a single group. For example, assume that an insurance company purchases hundreds of typewriters throughout the current year at a total cost of $600,000. The company depreciates typewriters by the straight-line method, assuming a five-year life and no residual value. Using the half-year convention, the depreciation expense on all of the typewriters purchased during the year may be computed as follows: $\$600,000 \div 5$ years $\times \frac{6}{12} = \$60,000$. If we did not use the half-year convention, depreciation would have to be computed separately for typewriters which had been purchased in different months.

Revision of depreciation rates

Depreciation rates are based on estimates of the useful life of assets. These estimates of useful life are seldom precise and sometimes are grossly in error. Consequently, the annual depreciation expense based on the estimated useful life may be either excessive or inadequate. What action should be taken when, after a few years of using a plant asset, it is decided that the asset actually is going to last for a considerably longer or shorter period than was originally estimated? When either of these situations arises, a revised estimate of useful life should be made and the periodic depreciation expense decreased or increased accordingly.

The procedure for correcting the depreciation program is to *spread the remaining undepreciated cost of the asset over the years of remaining useful life.* This correction affects only the amount of depreciation expense that will be recorded in the *current and future periods.* The financial statements of past periods are *not* revised to reflect changes in the estimated useful lives of depreciable assets.

To illustrate, assume that a company acquires a $10,000 asset which is estimated to have a 10-year useful life and no residual value. Under the straight-line method, the annual depreciation expense is $1,000. At the end of the sixth year, accumulated depreciation amounts to $6,000, and the asset has an undepreciated cost (or book value) of $4,000.

At the beginning of the seventh year, it is decided that the asset will last for eight more years. The revised estimate of useful life is, therefore, a total of 14 years. The depreciation expense to be recognized for the seventh year and for each of the remaining years is $500, computed as follows:

Revision of depreciation program

Undepreciated cost at end of sixth year ($10,000 − $6,000).	$4,000
Revised estimate of remaining years of useful life.	8 years
Revised amount of annual depreciation expense ($4,000 ÷ 8).	$ 500

Depreciation and income taxes

The depreciation methods used in preparing income tax returns usually differ from the methods used in preparing financial statements. Many large corporations use straight-line depreciation in their financial statements because this permits reporting higher earnings than would result from using accelerated depreciation. Reporting higher earnings is generally helpful to a publicly owned corporation: helpful in raising the market price of its stock, helpful in obtaining bank loans, helpful in increasing executive compensation, and helpful in many other ways. In preparing income tax returns, however, most companies, large and small, use accelerated depreciation.

Income tax rules are changed frequently by Congress, and the rules relating to depreciation seem especially subject to change. For assets acquired prior to 1981, taxpayers were permitted to choose among straight-line depreciation and accelerated methods, such as double-declining balance and sum-of-the-years'-digits. For assets acquired after 1981, taxpayers were required to use a special new accelerated method called Accelerated Cost Recovery System (ACRS).

An important feature of ACRS was that it replaced the traditional concept of estimated useful life with shorter arbitrary recovery periods for allocating the cost of depreciable assets. Automobiles, for example, were to be written off in only three years, and buildings in 18 years. The recovery periods established by ACRS were modified by the Tax Reform Act of 1986, and the modified accelerated cost recovery

not permit recognition of the loss, but in a company's financial statements *the loss should be recognized.* For example, assume that a company received a trade-in allowance of only $10,000 for old machinery which has a book value of $100,000. A journal entry illustrating this situation follows:

<table>
<tr><td>Machinery (new) ....</td><td>600,000</td><td></td></tr>
<tr><td>Accumulated Depreciation: Machinery (old) ....</td><td>300,000</td><td></td></tr>
<tr><td>Loss on Trade-in of Plant Assets ....</td><td>90,000</td><td></td></tr>
<tr><td>   Machinery (old)..</td><td></td><td>400,000</td></tr>
<tr><td>   Cash...</td><td></td><td>590,000</td></tr>
</table>

Notice recognition of loss on trade-in

To recognize for financial reporting purposes a material loss on trade-in of machinery. Loss not recognized in determining taxable income.

If a trade-in transaction involved only a small loss, most companies would probably follow the income tax rules and not recognize the loss. This treatment would eliminate the need for a double record of depreciable assets and depreciation expense; the departure from financial accounting rules would be permissible if the amount of the loss was not material.

NATURAL RESOURCES

Accounting for natural resources

7 Account for the depletion of natural resources.

Mining properties, oil and gas reserves, and tracts of standing timber are leading examples of natural resources or "wasting assets." The distinguishing characteristics of these assets are that they are physically consumed and converted into inventory. Theoretically, a coal mine might be regarded as an underground "inventory" of coal; however, such an "inventory" is certainly not a current asset. In the balance sheet, mining property and other natural resources are classified as property, plant, and equipment.

We have explained that plant assets such as buildings and equipment depreciate because of physical deterioration or obsolescence. A mine or an oil reserve does not "depreciate" for these reasons, but it is gradually *depleted* as the natural resource is removed from the ground. Once all of the coal has been removed from a coal mine, for example, the mine is "fully depleted" and will be abandoned or sold for its residual value.

To illustrate the depletion of a natural resource, assume that Rainbow Minerals pays $10,500,000 to acquire the Red Valley Mine, which is believed to contain 10 million tons of coal. The residual value of the mine after all of the coal is removed is estimated to be $500,000. The depletion that will occur over the life of the mine is the original cost minus the residual value, or $10,000,000. This depletion will occur at the rate of *$1 per ton* ($10,000,000 ÷ 10 million tons) as the coal is removed from the mine. If we assume that 2 million tons are mined during the first year of operations, the entry to record the depletion of the mine would be as follows:

Depletion of Coal Deposits 2,000,000		
Accumulated Depletion: Red Valley Mine....................	2,000,000	

To record depletion of the Red Valley Mine for the year; 2,000,000 tons
mined @ $1 per ton.

Accumulated Depletion is a contra-asset account similar to the Accumulated Depreciation account; it represents the portion of the mine which has been used up (depleted) to date. In Rainbow Mineral's balance sheet, the Red Valley Mine now appears as follows:

Property, Plant & Equipment:

Mining properties: Red Valley Mine	$10,500,000	
Less: Accumulated depletion	2,000,000	$8,500,000

The Depletion of Coal Deposits account may be viewed as similar to the Purchases account of a merchandising business. This account is added to any other mining costs and any beginning inventory of coal to arrive at the cost of goods (coal) available for sale. If all of the coal has been sold by year-end, these costs are deducted from revenue as the cost of goods sold. If some of the coal is still on hand at year-end, a portion of these costs should be assigned to the ending inventory of coal, which is a current asset.

Depreciation of buildings and equipment closely related to natural resources. Buildings and equipment installed at a mine or drilling site may be useful only at that particular location. Consequently, such assets should be depreciated over their normal useful lives, or over the life of the natural resource, *whichever is shorter*. Often depreciation on such assets is computed using the units-of-output method, thus relating the depreciation expense to the rate at which units of the natural resource are removed.

INTANGIBLE ASSETS

Characteristics

As the word *intangible* suggests, assets in this classification have no physical substance. Leading examples are goodwill, patents, and trademarks. Intangible assets are classified in the balance sheet as a subgroup of plant assets. However, not all assets which lack physical substance are regarded as intangible assets. An account receivable, for example, or a short-term prepayment is of nonphysical nature but is classified as a current asset and is not regarded as an intangible. In brief, *intangible assets are assets which are used in the operation of the business but which have no physical substance and are noncurrent.*

The basis of valuation for intangible assets is cost. In some companies, certain intangible assets such as trademarks may be of great importance but may have been acquired without the incurring of any cost. An intangible asset should appear in the balance sheet **only** if a cost of acquisition or development has been incurred.

Operating expenses versus intangible assets

For an expenditure to qualify as an intangible asset, there must be reasonable evidence of future benefits. Many expenditures offer some prospects of yielding benefits in subsequent years, but the existence and life-span of these benefits is so uncertain that most companies treat these expenditures as operating expenses. Examples are the expenditures for intensive advertising campaigns to introduce new products, and the expense of training employees to work with new types of machinery or office equipment. There is little doubt that some benefits from these outlays continue beyond the current period, but because of the uncertain duration of the benefits, it is almost universal practice to treat expenditures of this nature as expense of the current period.

Amortization

The term **amortization** is used to describe the write-off to expense of the cost of an intangible asset over its useful life. The usual accounting entry for amortization consists of a debit to Amortization Expense and a credit to the intangible asset account. There is no theoretical objection to crediting an accumulated amortization account rather than the intangible asset account, but this method is seldom encountered in practice.

Although it is difficult to estimate the useful life of an intangible such as a trademark, it is highly probable that such an asset will not contribute to future earnings on a permanent basis. The cost of the intangible asset should, therefore, be deducted from revenue during the years in which it may be expected to aid in producing revenue. Under the current rules of the Financial Accounting Standards Board, the maximum period for amortization of an intangible asset cannot exceed 40 years.[3] The straight-line method of amortization is generally used for intangible assets.

Depreciation, depletion, and amortization — a common goal

The processes of depreciation, depletion, and amortization which we have discussed in this chapter all have a common goal. That goal is to allocate the acquisition cost of a long-lived asset over the years in which it will contribute to revenue. By allocating the acquisition cost of long-lived assets over the years which benefit from the use of these assets, we stress again the importance of the matching principle. The determination of income requires the matching of revenue with the expenses incurred to produce that revenue.

[3] *APB Opinion No. 17,* "Intangible Assets," AICPA (New York: 1970), par. 29.

Goodwill

Business executives used the term ***goodwill*** in a variety of meanings before it became part of accounting terminology. One of the most common meanings of goodwill in a nonaccounting sense concerns the benefits derived from a favorable reputation among customers. To accountants, however, goodwill has a very specific meaning not necessarily limited to customer relations. It means the ***present value of future earnings in excess of the normal return on net identifiable assets.*** Above-average earnings may arise not only from favorable customer relations but also from such factors as superior management, manufacturing efficiency, and weak competition.

The present value of future cash flows is the amount that a knowledgeable investor would pay today for the right to receive these future cash flows. The present value concept is discussed further in later chapters and in Appendix A.

The phrase ***normal return on net identifiable assets*** requires explanation. Net assets means the owner's equity in a business, or assets minus liabilities. Goodwill, however, is not an ***identifiable*** asset. The existence of goodwill is implied by the ability of a business to earn an above-average return; however, the cause and precise dollar value of goodwill are largely matters of personal opinion. Therefore, ***net identifiable assets*** means all assets ***except goodwill,*** minus liabilities. A ***normal return*** on net identifiable assets is the rate of return which investors demand in a particular industry to justify their buying a business at the ***fair market value*** of its net identifiable assets. A business has goodwill when investors will pay a higher price because the business earns more than the normal rate of return.

Assume that two businesses in the same line of trade are offered for sale and that the normal return on the fair market value of net identifiable assets in this industry is 15% a year. The relative earning power of the two companies during the past five years is shown below.

	Company X	Company Y
Fair market value of net identifiable assets	$1,000,000	$1,000,000
Normal rate of return on net assets	15%	15%
Average net income for past five years.........................	$ 150,000	$ 190,000
Normal earnings, computed as 15% of net identifiable assets.......	150,000	150,000
Earnings in excess of normal	$ -0-	$ 40,000

An investor would be willing to pay $1,000,000 to buy Company X, because Company X earns the normal 15% return which justifies the fair market value of its net identifiable assets. Although Company Y has the same amount of net identifiable assets, an investor would be willing to pay ***more*** for Company Y than for Company X because Company Y has a record of superior earnings which will presumably continue for some time in the future. The extra amount that a buyer would pay to purchase Company Y represents the value of Company Y's goodwill.

Estimating goodwill. How much will an investor pay for goodwill? Above-average earnings in past years are of significance to prospective purchasers only if they believe that these earnings will continue after they acquire the business. Investors' appraisals of goodwill, therefore, will vary with their estimates of the future earning power of the business. Very few businesses, however, are able to maintain above-average earnings for more than a few years. Consequently, the purchaser of a business will usually limit any amount paid for goodwill to not more than four or five times the amount by which annual earnings exceed normal earnings.

Arriving at a fair value for the goodwill of a going business is a difficult and subjective process. Any estimate of goodwill is in large part a matter of personal opinion. The following are several methods which a prospective purchaser might use in estimating a value for goodwill:

1 Negotiated agreement between buyer and seller of the business may be reached on the amount of goodwill. For example, it might be agreed that the fair market value of net identifiable assets is $1,000,000 and that the total purchase price for the business will be $1,180,000, thus providing a $180,000 payment for goodwill.

2 Goodwill may be determined as a multiple of the amount by which average annual earnings exceed normal earnings. Referring to our example involving Company Y, a prospective buyer may be willing to pay four times the amount by which average earnings exceed normal earnings, indicating a value of $160,000 (4 × $40,000) for goodwill. The purchase price of the business, therefore, would be $1,160,000.

   The multiple applied to the excess annual earnings will vary widely from perhaps 1 to 10. An investor who pays four times the excess earnings for goodwill must, of course, expect these earnings to continue for at least four years.

3 Goodwill may be estimated by *capitalizing* the amount by which average earnings exceed normal earnings. Capitalizing an earnings stream means dividing those earnings by the investor's required rate of return. The result is the maximum amount which the investor could pay for the earnings and have them represent the required rate of return on the investment. To illustrate, assume that the prospective buyer decides to capitalize the $40,000 annual excess earnings of Company Y at a rate of 20%. This approach results in a $200,000 estimate ($40,000 ÷ .20 = $200,000) for the value of goodwill. (Note that $40,000 per year represents a 20% return on a $200,000 investment.)

   A weakness in the capitalization method is that *no provision is made for the recovery* of the investment. If the prospective buyer is to earn a 20% return on the $200,000 investment in goodwill, either the excess earnings must continue *forever* (an unlikely assumption) or the buyer must be able to recover the $200,000 investment at a later date by selling the business at a price above the fair market value of net identifiable assets.

Recording goodwill in the accounting records. Goodwill is recorded in the accounting records *only when it is purchased;* this situation usually occurs only when a going business is purchased in its entirety. After the fair market values of all identifiable assets have been recorded in the accounting records of the new owners, any additional amount paid for the business may properly be debited to an asset account entitled Goodwill. This intangible asset must then be amortized over a period not to exceed 40 years, although a much shorter amortization period usually is appropriate.

Many businesses have never purchased goodwill but have generated it internally through developing good customer relations, superior management, or other factors which result in above-average earnings. Because there is no objective means of determining the dollar value of goodwill unless the business is sold, internally developed goodwill is **not recorded** in the accounting records. Thus, goodwill may be a very important asset of a successful business but may not even appear in the company's balance sheet.

Patents

A patent is an exclusive right granted by the federal government for manufacture, use, and sale of a particular product. The purpose of this exclusive grant is to encourage the invention of new machines and processes. When a company acquires a patent by purchase from the inventor or other holder, the purchase price should be recorded by debiting the intangible asset account Patents.

Patents are granted for a period of 17 years, and the period of amortization must not exceed that period. However, if the patent is likely to lose its usefulness in less than 17 years, amortization should be based on the shorter period of estimated useful life. Assume that a patent is purchased from the inventor at a cost of $100,000, after five years of the legal life have expired. The remaining **legal** life is, therefore, 12 years, but if the estimated **useful** life is only four years, amortization should be based on this shorter period. The entry to be made to record the annual amortization expense would be:

Entry for amortization of patent

Amortization Expense: Patents	25,000	
Patents		25,000

To amortize cost of patent on a straight-line basis and estimated life of four years.

Trademarks and trade names

Coca-Cola's distinctive bottle was for years the classic example of a trademark known around the world. A trademark is a word, symbol, or design that identifies a product or group of products. A permanent exclusive right to the use of a trademark, brand name, or commercial symbol may be obtained by registering it with the federal government. The costs of developing a trademark or brand name often consists of advertising campaigns which should be treated as expense when incurred. If a trademark or trade name is purchased, however, the cost may be substantial. Such cost should be capitalized and amortized to expense over a period of not more than 40 years. If the use of the trademark is discontinued or its contribution to earnings becomes doubtful, any unamortized cost should be written off immediately.

Franchises

A franchise is a right granted by a company or a governmental unit to conduct a certain type of business in a specific geographical area. An example of a franchise is the right to operate a McDonald's restaurant in a specific neighborhood. The cost of franchises varies greatly and often may be quite substantial. When the cost of a franchise is small, it may be charged immediately to expense or amortized over a short period such as five years. When the cost is material, amortization should be based upon the life of the franchise (if limited); the amortization period, however, may not exceed 40 years.

Copyrights

A copyright is an exclusive right granted by the federal government to protect the production and sale of literary or artistic materials for the life of the creator plus 50 years. The cost of obtaining a copyright in some cases is minor and therefore is chargeable to expense when paid. Only when a copyright is purchased will the expenditure be material enough to warrant its being capitalized and spread over the useful life. The revenue from copyrights is usually limited to only a few years, and the purchase cost should, of course, be amortized over the years in which the revenue is expected.

Other intangibles and deferred charges

Among the other intangibles found in the published balance sheets of large corporations are moving costs, plant rearrangement costs, organization costs, formulas, processes, name lists, and film rights. Some companies group items of this type under the title of Deferred Charges, meaning expenditures that will provide benefits beyond the current year and will be written off to expense over their useful economic lives. It is also common practice to combine these items under the heading of Other Assets, which is listed at the bottom of the balance sheet.

Research and development (R&D) costs

The spending of billions of dollars a year on research and development leading to all kinds of new products is a striking characteristic of American industry. In the past, some companies treated all research and development costs as expense in the year incurred; other companies in the same industry recorded these costs as intangible assets to be amortized over future years. This diversity of practice prevented the financial statements of different companies from being comparable.

The lack of uniformity in accounting for R&D was ended when the Financial Accounting Standards Board ruled that all research and development expenditures should be charged to expense when incurred.[4] This action by the FASB had the beneficial effect of reducing the number of alternative accounting practices and helping to make financial statements of different companies more comparable.

[4] *FASB Statement No. 2,* "Accounting for Research and Development Costs" (Stamford, Conn.: 1974), par. 12.

END-OF-CHAPTER REVIEW

Summary of chapter learning objectives

1 Determine the cost of plant assets.

Plant assets are long-lived assets acquired for use in the business and not for resale to customers. The matching principle of accounting requires that we include in the plant and equipment accounts those costs which will provide services over a period of years. During these years, the use of the plant assets contributes to the earning of revenue. The cost of a plant asset includes all expenditures reasonable and necessary in acquiring the asset and placing it in a position and condition for use in the operations of the business.

2 Distinguish between capital expenditures and revenue expenditures.

Capital expenditures include any material expenditure that will benefit several accounting periods. Revenue expenditures are expenditures that benefit only the current period or that are not material in amount.

3 Explain the relationship between depreciation and the matching principle.

Depreciation is the allocation of the cost of a plant asset to expense in the periods in which services are received from the asset. Plant assets enable a business to earn revenue; therefore, the cost of the asset becomes expense over the years in which the asset generates revenue.

4 Compute depreciation by the straight-line, units-of-output, declining-balance, and sum-of-the-years'-digits.

The straight-line method is a simple and widely used method of computing depreciation. It allocates an equal portion of the cost of an asset to each period of use. Very similar is the units-of-output method under which an equal portion of the cost is allocated to each unit produced. Accelerated methods of depreciation mean recognizing relatively large amounts of depreciation in the early years of use and reduced amounts in later years. The accelerated methods are based in part upon the assumption that plant and equipment provide greater economic benefits in the early years. The declining-balance method and the sum-of-the-years'-digits method are widely used types of accelerated depreciation.

5 Explain why depreciation based upon historical costs may cause an overstatement of profits.

During sustained inflation, net income tends to be overstated if depreciation is based upon historical cost. The depreciation expense over the life of the asset is less than the cost of replacing the asset when it must be retired. Depreciation expense must be as much as replacement cost if a company is merely to "stay even" in its productive facilities.

6 Record the sale, trade-in, or scrapping of a plant asset.

When plant assets are disposed of, depreciation should be recorded to the date of disposal. The cost is then removed from the asset account and the total recorded depreciation is removed from the accumulated depreciation account. The sale of a plant asset at a price above or below book value results in a gain or loss to be reported in the income statement. For exchanges of similar assets (trade-ins), accounting principles and tax regulations are alike in not recognizing a gain. They differ for trade-ins involving a material loss because such losses are recognized for financial accounting purposes but not in determining taxable income. For income tax purposes, the cost of the new asset is equal to the book value of the old asset traded in plus the additional amount payable.

7 Account for the depletion of natural resources.

Natural resources (or wasting assets) include mines, oil fields, and standing timber. Their cost is converted into inventory as the resource is mined, pumped, or cut. This allocation of the cost of a natural resource to inventories is called depletion. The depletion rate per unit extracted equals the cost of the resource divided by the estimated number of units it contains.

8 Explain the nature of goodwill and indicate when this asset should appear in the accounting records.

Goodwill is the present value of future earnings in excess of the normal return on net identifiable assets. A business has goodwill only if it earns more than the normal rate of return for the industry. Goodwill is recorded in the accounts only when an investor buys an entire company and pays a price higher than the fair market value of the net identifiable assets.

Key terms introduced or emphasized in chapter 9

Accelerated depreciation. Methods of depreciation that call for recognition of relatively large amounts of depreciation in the early years of an asset's useful life and relatively small amounts in the later years.

Amortization. The systematic write-off to expense of the cost of an intangible asset over the periods of its economic usefulness.

Book value. The cost of a plant asset minus the total recorded depreciation, as shown by the Accumulated Depreciation account. The remaining undepreciated cost is also known as *carrying value.*

Capital expenditure. A cost incurred to acquire a long-lived asset. An expenditure that will benefit several accounting periods.

Declining-balance depreciation. An accelerated method of depreciation in which the rate is a multiple of the straight-line rate, which is applied each year to the *undepreciated cost* of the asset. Most commonly used is double the straight-line rate.

Deferred charge. An expenditure expected to yield benefits for several accounting periods and therefore capitalized and written off during the periods benefited.

Depletion. Allocating the cost of a natural resource to the units removed as the resource is mined, pumped, cut, or otherwise consumed.

Depreciation. The systematic allocation of the cost of an asset to expense over the years of its estimated useful life.

Goodwill. The present value of expected future earnings of a business in excess of the earnings normally realized in the industry. Recorded when a business entity is purchased at a price in excess of the fair value of its net identifiable assets (excluding goodwill) less liabilities.

Half-year convention. The practice of taking six months' depreciation in the year of acquisition and the year of disposition, rather than computing depreciation for partial periods to the nearest month. This method is widely used and is acceptable for both income tax reporting and financial reports, as long as it is applied to *all* assets of a particular type acquired during the year. The half-year convention generally is *not* used for buildings.

Intangible assets. Those assets which are used in the operation of a business but which have no physical substance and are noncurrent.

Natural resources. Mines, oil fields, standing timber, and similar assets which are physically consumed and converted into inventory.

Net identifiable assets. Total of all assets *except goodwill* minus liabilities.

Present value. The amount that a knowledgeable investor would pay today for the right to receive future cash flows. The present value is always less than the sum of the future cash flows because the investor requires a return on the investment.

Replacement cost. The estimated cost of replacing an asset at the current balance sheet date.

Residual (salvage) value. The portion of an asset's cost expected to be recovered through sale or trade-in of the asset at the end of its useful life.

Revenue expenditure. Any expenditure that will benefit only the current accounting period.

Straight-line depreciation. A method of depreciation which allocates the cost of an asset (minus any residual value) equally to each year of its useful life.

Sum-of-the-years'-digits depreciation. An accelerated method of depreciation. The depreciable cost is multiplied each year by a fraction of which the numerator is the remaining years of useful life (as of the beginning of the current year) and the denominator is the sum of the years of useful life.

Units-of-output depreciation. A depreciation method in which cost (minus residual value) is divided by the estimated units of lifetime output. The unit depreciation cost is multiplied by the actual units of output each year to compute the annual depreciation expense.

Demonstration problem for your review

The ledger of Cypress Company contained an account entitled Property, which had been used to record a variety of expenditures. At the end of the year, the Property account contained the following entries:

Debit entries:

1/10	Purchase for cash of building site....................................	$200,000
2/4	Cost of removing old building from site	8,000
9/30	Paid contract price for new building completed today	560,000
9/30	Insurance, inspection fees, and other costs directly related to construction	
	of new building..	18,000
	Total debits...	$786,000

Credit entries:

2/4	Proceeds from sale of salvaged material from demolition of old		
	building	$ 3,000	
12/31	Depreciation for the year computed at 4% of balance in Property		
	account ($783,000). Debit was to Depreciation Expense	31,320	
	Total credits		34,320
12/31	Balance in Property account at year-end...........................		$751,680

Instructions

a List the errors made in the application of accounting principles or practices by Cypress Company.

b Prepare a compound correcting journal entry at December 31, assuming that the estimated life of the new building is 25 years and that depreciation is to be recognized for three months of the current year using the straight-line method. The accounts have not been closed for the year.

Solution to demonstration problem

a Errors in accounting principles or practices were
   (1) Including land (a nondepreciable asset) in the same account with building (a depreciable asset)
   (2) Using the total of land and building as a base for applying the depreciation rate on building
   (3) Recording a full year's depreciation on a new building that was in use only the last three months of the year.
   (4) Crediting the depreciation for the period directly to the asset account (Property) rather than to a contra-asset account (Accumulated Depreciation: Building)

b Correcting Journal Entry

Dec. 31	Land	205,000	
	Building	578,000	
	Property		751,680
	Accumulated Depreciation: Building		5,780
	Depreciation Expense............................		25,540

To correct the accounts reflecting land, building, and depreciation in accordance with the computations shown in the following schedule:

	Land	Building
Amount paid to acquire building site..............................	$200,000	
Cost of removing old building from site	8,000	
Less: Proceeds from salvaged materials	(3,000)	
Contract price for new building		$560,000
Insurance, inspection fees, and other costs directly related to construction of new building		18,000
Totals...	$205,000	$578,000

Depreciation: $578,000 \times 4\% \times \frac{3}{12} = \underline{\underline{\$5,780}}$

Correction of depreciation expense: $31,320 - \$5,780 = \underline{\underline{\$25,540}}$

ASSIGNMENT MATERIAL

Review questions

1 Which of the following characteristics would prevent an item from being included in the classification of plant and equipment? (a) Intangible, (b) limited life, (c) unlimited life, (d) held for sale in the regular course of business, (e) not capable of rendering benefits to the business in the future.

2 The following expenditures were incurred in connection with a large new machine acquired by a metals manufacturing company. Identify those which should be included in the cost of the asset. (a) Freight charges, (b) sales tax on the machine, (c) payment to a passing motorist whose car was damaged by the equipment used in unloading the machine, (d) wages of employees for time spent in installing and testing the machine before it was placed in service, (e) wages of employees assigned

to lubrication and minor adjustments of machine one year after it was placed in service.

3 What is the distinction between a *capital expenditure* and a *revenue expenditure?*

4 If a capital expenditure is erroneously treated as a revenue expenditure, will the net income of the current year be overstated or understated? Will this error have any effect upon the net income reported in future years? Explain.

5 Which of the following statements best describes the nature of depreciation?
  a Regular reduction of asset value to correspond to the decline in market value as the asset ages.
  b A process of correlating the carrying value of an asset with its gradual decline in physical efficiency.
  c Allocation of cost in a manner that will ensure that plant and equipment items are not carried on the balance sheet at amounts in excess of net realizable value.
  d Allocation of the cost of a plant asset to the periods in which services are received from the asset.

6 Should depreciation continue to be recorded on a building when ample evidence exists that the current market value is greater than original cost and that the rising trend of market values is continuing? Explain.

7 What connection exists between the choice of a depreciation method used to depreciate expensive new machinery for income tax reporting and the amount of income taxes payable in the near future?

8 Criticize the following quotation:

"We shall have no difficulty in paying for new plant assets needed during the coming year because our estimated outlays for new equipment amount to only $80,000, and we have more than twice that amount in our accumulated depreciation account at present."

9 A factory machine acquired at a cost of $94,200 was to be depreciated by the sum-of-the-years'-digits method over an estimated life of eight years. Residual salvage value was estimated to be $15,000. State the amount of depreciation during the first year and during the eighth year.

10 After four years of using a machine acquired at a cost of $15,000, Ohio Construction Company determined that the original estimated life of 10 years had been too short and that a total useful life of 12 years was a more reasonable estimate. Explain briefly the method that should be used to revise the depreciation program, assuming that straight-line depreciation has been used. Assume that the revision is made after recording depreciation and closing the accounts at the end of four years of use of the machine.

11 a Give some reasons why a company may change its depreciation policy for financial reporting purposes from an accelerated depreciation method to the straight-line method.
   b Is it possible for a corporation to use accelerated depreciation for income tax purposes and straight-line depreciation for financial reporting purposes?

12 Explain two approaches to computing depreciation for a fractional period in the year in which an asset is purchased. (Neither of your approaches should require the computation of depreciation to the nearest day or week.)

13 "The terms ACRS and MACRS refer to accelerated cost recovery systems established by the IRS for use in computing depreciation on income tax returns. Such endorsement of a depreciation system by the IRS automatically makes it acceptable for use in the published financial statements of major corporations." Do you agree with these two statements? Explain.

14 Explain what is meant by the following quotation: "In periods of rising prices companies do not recognize adequate depreciation expense, and reported corporate profits are substantially overstated."

15 Century Company traded in its old computer on a new model. The trade-in allowance for the old computer is greater than its book value. Should Century Company recognize a gain on the exchange in computing its taxable income or in determining its net income for financial reporting? Explain.

16 Newton Products purchased for $2 million a franchise making it the exclusive distributor of Gold Creek Beer in three western states. This franchise has an unlimited legal life and may be sold by Newton Products to any buyer who meets with Gold Creek Beer's approval. The accountant at Newton Products believes that this franchise is a permanent asset, which should appear in the company's balance sheet indefinitely at $2 million, unless it is sold. Is this treatment in conformity with generally accepted accounting principles, as prescribed by the FASB?

17 Lead Hill Corporation recognizes $1 depletion for each ton of ore mined. During the current year the company mined 600,000 tons but sold only 500,000 tons, as it was attempting to build up inventories in anticipation of a possible strike by employees. How much depletion should be deducted from revenue of the current year?

18 Define **intangible assets.** Would an account receivable arising from a sale of merchandise under terms of 2/10, n/30 qualify as an intangible asset under your definition?

19 Over what period of time should the cost of various types of intangible assets be amortized by regular charges against revenue? (Your answer should be in the form of a principle or guideline rather than a specific number of years.) What method of amortization is generally used?

20 Several years ago March Metals purchased for $120,000 a well-known trademark for padlocks and other security products. After using the trademark for three years, March Metals discontinued it altogether when the company withdrew from the lock business and concentrated on the manufacture of aircraft parts. Amortization of the trademark at the rate of $3,000 a year is being continued on the basis of a 40-year life, which the owner of March Metals says is required by accounting standards. Do you agree? Explain.

21 Under what circumstances should **goodwill** be recorded in the accounts?

22 In reviewing the financial statements of Digital Products Co. with a view to investing in the company's stock, you notice that net tangible assets total $1 million, that goodwill is listed at $400,000, and that average earnings for the past five years have been $50,000 a year. How would these relationships influence your thinking about the company?

Exercises

Exercise 9-1
Accounting terminology

Listed below are nine technical accounting terms introduced in this chapter:

Amortization	Declining-balance	Intangible asset
Revenue expenditure	ACRS or MACRS	Book value
Accumulated depletion	Research & development	Goodwill

Each of the following statements may (or may not) describe one of these technical terms. For each statement, indicate the accounting term described, or answer "None" if the statement does not correctly describe any of the terms.

    a A depreciation method which often consists of doubling the straight-line rate and applying this doubled rate to the undepreciated cost of the asset.

    b A depreciation method designed for use in income tax returns but not in conformity with generally accepted accounting principles.

    c The cost of a plant asset minus the total recorded depreciation on the asset.

    d A material expenditure that will benefit several accounting periods.

    e The systematic allocation to expense of the cost of an intangible asset.

    f The portion of the cost of a natural resource which has been consumed or used up.

    g A type of asset usually found only in the financial statements of a company which has purchased another going business in its entirety.

    h Noncurrent assets lacking in physical substance.

Exercise 9-2
Identifying costs to be capitalized

New office equipment was purchased by Valley Company at a list price of $36,000; the credit terms were 2/10, n/30. Payment of the invoice was made within the discount period. The payment included 5% sales tax on the ***net price.*** Valley Company also paid transportation charges of $430 on the new equipment as well as $760 for installing the equipment in the appropriate locations. During the unloading and installation work, some of the equipment fell from a loading platform and was damaged. Repair of the damaged parts cost $2,180. After the equipment had been in use for three months, it was thoroughly cleaned and lubricated at a cost of $260. Prepare a list of the items which should be capitalized by debit to the Office Equipment account and state the total cost of the new equipment.

Exercise 9-3
Distinguishing capital expenditures from revenue expenditures

Identify the following expenditures as capital expenditures or revenue expenditures:

    a Purchased new battery at a cost of $40 for two-year-old delivery truck.

    b Installed an escalator at a cost of $12,500 in a three-story building which had previously been used for some years without elevators or escalators.

    c Purchased a pencil sharpener at a cost of $3.50.

    d Immediately after acquiring a new delivery truck at a cost of $5,500, paid $125 to have the name of the store and other advertising material painted on the truck.

    e Painted delivery truck at a cost of $175 after two years of use.

    f Original life of the delivery truck had been estimated as four years and straight-line depreciation of 25% yearly had been recognized. After three years' use, however, it was decided to recondition the truck thoroughly, including a new engine and transmission, at a cost of $4,000. By making this expenditure it was believed that the useful life of the truck would be extended from the original estimate of four years to a total of six years.

Exercise 9-4
Units-of-output method

During the current year, Western Auto Rentals purchased 50 new automobiles at a cost of $9,000 per car. After the cars have been driven 40,000 miles each in the rental business, they will be sold to a wholesale automobile dealer at an estimated $3,800 each. Western Auto Rentals computes depreciation expense on its automobiles by the units-of-output method, based upon mileage.

    a Compute the amount of depreciation to be recognized for each mile that a rental automobile is driven.

    b Assuming that the 50 rental cars are driven a total of 1,500,000 miles during the current year, compute the total amount of depreciation expense that Western Auto Rentals should recognize on the fleet of cars for the year.

Exercise 9-5
Double-declining-balance method

Merril Products acquired machinery with an estimated life of five years and a cost of $60,000. Estimated residual value of the machinery is $6,000. Compute the annual depreciation on the machinery for each of the five years using the double-declining-balance method. Limit the depreciation recognized in the fifth year to an amount that will cause the book value of the machinery to equal the estimated $6,000 residual value at year-end.

Exercise 9-6
Trade-in and cost basis

Key Corporation traded in an old machine on a similar new one. The original cost of the old machine was $45,000 and the accumulated depreciation was $36,000. The new machine carried a list price of $60,000 and the trade-in allowance was $12,000. What amount must Key Corporation pay? Compute the indicated gain or loss regardless of whether it should be recorded in the accounts. Compute the cost basis of the new machine to be used in figuring depreciation for determination of income subject to federal income tax.

Exercise 9-7
Depreciation for fractional years

Oak Company on June 7 purchased equipment at a cost of $900,000. Useful life of the equipment was estimated to be six years and the residual value $90,000. Compute the depreciation expense to be recognized in each calendar year during the life of the equipment under each of the following methods:

a Straight-line (round computations for a partial year to the nearest full month).
b Straight-line (use the half-year convention).

Exercise 9-8
Disposal of equipment by sale, trade-in, or as scrap

A tractor which cost $25,000 had an estimated useful life of five years and an estimated salvage value of $5,000. Straight-line depreciation was used. Give the entry (in general journal form) required by each of the following alternative assumptions:

a The tractor was sold for cash of $13,500 after two years' use.
b The tractor was traded in after three years on another tractor with a list price of $37,000. Trade-in allowance was $15,000. The trade-in was recorded in a manner acceptable for income tax purposes.
c The tractor was scrapped after four years' use. Since scrap dealers were unwilling to pay anything for the tractor, it was given to a scrap dealer for his services in removing it.

Exercise 9-9
Depletion: recording and reporting

King Mining Company purchased the Lost Creek Mine for $6,800,000 cash. The mine was estimated to contain 2 million tons of ore and to have a residual value of $800,000.
During the first year of mining operations at the Lost Creek Mine, 400,000 tons of ore were mined, of which 300,000 tons were sold.

a Prepare a journal entry to record depletion of the Lost Creek Mine during the year.
b Show how the mine and the accumulated depletion would appear in King Mining Company's balance sheet after the first year of operations.
c Will the entire balance of the account debited in part *a* be deducted from revenue in determining the income for the year? Explain.

Exercise 9-10
Estimating goodwill

During the past several years the annual net income of Bell Optics Company has averaged $378,000. At the present time the company is being offered for sale. Its accounting records show net assets (total assets minus all liabilities) to be $2,100,000.
An investor negotiating to buy the company offers to pay an amount equal to the book value for the net assets and to assume all liabilities. In addition, the investor is willing to pay for goodwill an amount equal to net earnings in excess of 15% on net assets, capitalized at a rate of 25%.
On the basis of this agreement, what price is the investor offering for Bell Optics Company? Show computations.

Problems

Problem 9-1
Determining cost of plant assets

West Coast Printing, a newly organized Seattle corporation, purchased printing equipment having a list price of $176,000 from a manufacturer in the New England area. Credit terms for the transaction were 2/10, n/30. Included on the seller's invoice was an additional amount of $12,074 for sales tax. West Coast Printing paid the invoice within the discount period. (The sales tax is not subject to the cash discount.) Other payments relating to the acquisition of the equipment were a freight bill of $2,600 and a labor cost for installing the equipment of $4,200. During the installation process, an accident caused damages to the equipment which was repaired at a cost of $6,300. As soon as the equipment was in place, West Coast printing obtained insurance on it for a premium of $1,800. All the items described above were charged to the Printing Equipment account. No entry for depreciation has yet been made and the accounts have not yet been closed.

Instructions

a Prepare a list of the expenditures which should have been capitalized by debiting the Printing Equipment. Show the correct total cost for this asset.

b Prepare one compound journal entry to correct the error or errors by the company in recording these transactions.

c In one sentence state the accounting principle or concept which indicates the nature of expenditures properly included in the cost of equipment. (Do not list individual types of expenditure.)

Problem 9-2
Three deprecia-
tion methods

Trident Company purchased new equipment with an estimated useful life of five years. Cost of the equipment was $200,000 and the residual salvage value was estimated to be $23,000.

Instructions. Compute the annual depreciation expense throughout the five-year life of the equipment under each of the following methods of depreciation:

a Straight-line

b Sum-of-the-years'-digits

c Double-declining-balance. Limit the depreciation expense in the fifth year to an amount that will cause the book value of the equipment at year end to equal the $23,000 estimated residual value.

Problem 9-3
Three deprecia-
tion methods; an
alternate problem

New machinery was acquired by Video Corporation at a cost of $300,000. Useful life of the machinery was estimated to be five years, with residual salvage value of $36,000.

Instructions. Compute the annual depreciation expense throughout the five-year life of the machinery under each of the following methods of depreciation:

a Straight-line

b Sum-of-the-years'-digits

c Double-declining-balance. Limit the amount of depreciation recognized in the fifth year to an amount that will cause the book value of the machinery to equal the $36,000 estimated residual value.

Problem 9-4
Disposal of plant
assets

During 19__, Festival Productions disposed of plant assets in the following transactions:

Feb. 10 Office equipment costing $14,000 was given to a scrap dealer. No proceeds were received from the scrap dealer. At the date of disposal, accumulated depreciation on the office equpment amounted to $11,900.

Apr. 1 Festival sold land and a building to MeriMar Development Co. for $630,000, receiving $200,000 in cash and a 10% five-year note receivable for $430,000. Festival's accounting records showed the following amounts: land, $120,000; building, $350,000; accumulated depreciation: building (as of April 1), $115,000.

Aug. 15 Festival traded in an old truck for a new one. The old truck had cost $11,000, and accumulated depreciation amounted to $7,000. The list price of the new truck was $17,000; Festival received a $5,000 trade-in allowance for the old truck and paid the $12,000 balance in cash. (Trucks are included in the Vehicles account.)

Oct. 1 Festival traded in its old computer system as part of the purchase of a new system. The old computer had cost $150,000 and, as of October 1, accumulated depreciation amounted to $110,000. The new computer had a list price of $90,000. Festival was granted a $10,000 trade-in allowance for the old computer system, paid $30,000 in cash, and issued a $50,000, 9%, two-year note payable to Action Computers for the balance. (Computers are included in the Office Equipment account.)

Instructions. Prepare journal entries to record each of these transactions. Assume that depreciation expense on each asset already has been recorded up to the date of disposal. Thus, you need not update the accumulated depreciation figures stated in the problem.

Problem 9-5
Trade-in of plant
assets; a compre-
hensive problem

Hartman Editorial Services has entered into the following two transactions involving trade-ins of plant assets:

(1) A truck which had cost $12,000 was traded-in on a new truck with a list price of $16,800. The trade-in allowance on the old truck was $4,500, and the remaining $12,300 was paid in cash. At the date of the trade-in, the old truck had been fully depreciated to its estimated residual value of $2,000.

(2) A word processor with a cost of $6,700 was traded-in on a new word processor with a list price of $7,900. The trade-in allowance was $500, with the remaining $7,400 cost being paid in cash. At the date of this transaction, the accumulated depreciation on the old word processor amounted to $3,200.

Instructions

a Prepare journal entries to record each of these exchange transactions. Assume all dollar amounts are material. (The asset accounts used for trucks and for word processors are entitled Vehicles and Office Equipment, respectively.)

b Compute the cost basis of each of the newly acquired assets for federal income tax purposes.

c Compute the depreciation expense that Hartman Editorial Services will recognize for financial statement purposes on each of the newly acquired assets in the year of acquisition. Assume that each asset will be depreciated over five years using the straight-line method, with an estimated residual value of $2,000, and with use of the half-year convention.

d Compute the depreciation for income tax purposes on each of the newly acquired assets in the year of acquisition. For each asset, assume use of the straight-line method, a life of five years, zero residual value, and the half-year convention.

Problem 9-6
Depletion of an
oil field

On March 7, 19X1, Wildcat Oil Company began operations at its Southfork Oil Field. The oil field had been acquired several years earlier at a cost of $11.6 million. The field is estimated to contain 4 million barrels of oil and to have a residual value of $2 million after all of the oil has been pumped out. Equipment costing $480,000 was purchased for use at the Southfork Field. This equipment will have no economic usefulness once Southfork is depleted; therefore, it is depreciated on a units-of-output basis.

Wildcat Oil also built a pipeline at a cost of $2,880,000 to serve the Southfork Field. Although this pipeline is physically capable of being used for many years, its economic usefulness is limited to the productive life of the Southfork Field and there is no residual value. Therefore, depreciation of the pipeline also is based upon the estimated number of barrels of oil to be produced.

Production at the Southfork Field amounted to 420,000 barrels in 19X1 and 510,000 barrels in 19X2.

Instructions

   a Compute the per-barrel depletion rate of the oil field and the per-barrel depreciation rates of the equipment and the pipeline.

   b Make the year-end adjusting entries required at December 31, 19X1, and December 31, 19X2, to record depletion of the oil field and the related depreciation. (Make separate entries to record depletion of the oil field, depreciation of the equipment, and depreciation of the pipeline.)

   c Show how the Southfork Field should appear in Wildcat Oil's balance sheet at the end of 19X2. (Use "Oil Reserves: Southfork Field" as the title of the asset account; show accumulated depletion, but do not include the equipment or pipeline.)

Problem 9-7
Intangible assets
or operating
expense: GAAP

During the current year, Home Products Corporation incurred the following expenditures which should be recorded either as operating expenses of the current year or as intangible assets:

   a Expenditures for the training of new employees. The average employee remains with the company for 14 years, but is retrained for a new position every three years.

   b Purchased from another company the trademark to a household product. The trademark has an unlimited legal life, and the product is expected to contribute to revenue indefinitely.

   c Incurred significant research and development costs to develop a dirt-resistant fiber. The company expects that the fiber will be patented, and that sales of the resulting products will contribute to revenue for at least 50 years. The legal life of the patent, however, will be 17 years.

   d An expenditure to acquire the patent on a popular video game. The patent has a remaining life of 14 years, but Home Products expects to produce and sell the game for only three years.

   e Spent a large amount to sponsor a television mini-series about the French Revolution. The purpose in sponsoring the program was to make television viewers more aware of the company's name and its product lines.

Instructions. Explain whether each of the above expenditures should be recorded as an operating expense or an intangible asset. If you view the expenditure as an intangible asset, indicate the number of years over which the asset should be amortized. Explain your reasoning.

Business decision cases

Case 9-1
Effects of
depreciation
methods on re-
ported earnings

Samuel Slater is interested in buying a manufacturing business and has located two similar companies being offered for sale. Both companies are single proprietorships which began operations three years ago, each with invested capital of $400,000. A considerable part of the assets in each company is represented by a building with an original cost of $100,000 and an estimated life of 40 years, and by machinery with an original cost of $200,000 and an estimated life of 20 years. Residual value is estimated at zero.

Bay Company uses straight-line depreciation and Cove Company uses declining-balance depreciation (double the straight-line rate). In all other respects the accounting policies of the two companies are quite similar. Neither company has borrowed from banks or incurred any indebtedness other than normal trade payables. The nature of products and other characteristics of operations are much the same for the two companies.

Audited financial statements for the three years show net income as follows:

Year	Bay Company	Cove Company
1st..	$ 62,000	$ 59,000
2d...	65,200	63,200
3d...	68,400	66,900
Totals...	$195,600	$189,100

Slater asks your advice as to which company to buy. They are offered for sale at approximately the same price, and Slater is inclined to choose Bay Company because of its consistently higher earnings. On the other hand, the fact that Cove Company has more cash and a stronger working capital position is impressive. The audited financial statements show that withdrawals by the two owners have been approximately equal during the three-year life of each company.

Instructions

a Compute the depreciation recorded by each company in the first three years. Round off depreciation expense for each year to the nearest dollar.

b Write a memorandum to Slater advising which company in your judgment represents the more promising purchase. Give specific reasons to support your recommendation. Include a recomputation of the earnings of Cove Company by using straight-line depreciation in order to make its income statements comparable with those of Bay Company. Compare the earnings of the two companies year by year after such revision to a uniform basis.

Case 9-2
Did I do this right?

Protein Plus is a processor and distributor of frozen foods. The company's management is anxious to report the maximum amount of net income allowable under generally accepted accounting principles, and therefore uses the longest acceptable lives in depreciating or amortizing the company's plant assets. Depreciation and amortization computations are rounded to the nearest full month.

Near year-end the company's regular accountant was in an automobile accident, so a clerk with limited accounting experience prepared the company's financial statements. The income statement prepared by the clerk indicated a net loss of $45,000. However, the clerk was unsure that he had properly accounted for the following items:

(1) On April 4, the company purchased a small food processing business at a cost $80,000 above the value of that business's net identifiable assets. The clerk classified this $80,000 as goodwill on Protein Plus's balance sheet and recorded no amortization expense because the food processor's superior earnings are expected to continue indefinitely.

(2) During the year the company spent $32,000 on a research project to develop a method of freezing avocados. The clerk classified these expenditures as an intangible asset on the company's balance sheet and recorded no amortization expense because it was not yet known whether the project would be successful.

(3) Two gains from the disposal of plant assets were included in the income statement. One gain, in the amount of $4,300, resulted from the sale of a plant asset at a price above its book value. The other gain, in the amount of $2,700 on December 31, was based on receiving a trade-in allowance higher than the book value of an old truck that was traded in on a new one.

(4) A CPA firm had determined that the company's depreciation expense for income tax purposes was $51,400, using accelerated methods such as ACRS and MACRS. The clerk used this figure as depreciation expense in the income statement, although in prior years the company had used the straight-line method of depreciation in its financial statements. Depreciation for the current year amounts to $35,600 when computed by the straight-line method.

(5) On January 4, the company paid $90,000 to purchase a 10-year franchise to become the exclusive distributor in three eastern states for a brand of Mexican frozen dinners. The clerk charged this $90,000 to expense in the current year because the entire amount had been paid in cash.

(6) During the year, the company incurred advertising costs of $22,000 to promote the newly acquired line of frozen dinners. The clerk did not know how many periods would be benefited from these expenditures, so he included the entire amount in the selling expenses of the current year.

Instructions

a For each of the numbered paragraphs, explain whether the clerk's treatment of the item is in conformity with generally accepted accounting principles.

b Prepare a schedule determining the correct net income (or net loss) for the year. Begin with "Net loss originally reported . . . $45,000," and indicate any adjustments that you consider appropriate. If you indicate adjustments for the amortization of intangible assets acquired during the year, round the amortization to the nearest month.

Part Three: Comprehensive Problem
Alpine Village and Nordic Sports

Concepts of asset valuation and effects upon net income.

Chris Scott, a former Olympic skier, wants to purchase an established ski equipment and clothing shop in Aspen, Colorado. Two such businesses currently are available for sale: Alpine Village and Nordic Sports. Both businesses are organized as corporations and have been in business for three years. Summaries of the current balance sheet data of both shops are shown below:

Assets	Alpine Village	Nordic Sports
Cash	$ 38,700	$ 32,100
Accounts receivable	187,300	174,800
Inventory.	151,400	143,700
Plant and equipment:		
Land	40,000	35,000
Building (net of accumulated depreciation)	99,900	72,900
Equipment (net of accumulated depreciation).	7,600	8,200
Goodwill	18,500	
Total assets	$543,400	$466,700

Liabilities & Stockholders' Equity		
Total liabilities	$199,900	$206,300
Stockholders' equity.	343,500	260,400
Total liabilities & stockholders' equity	$543,400	$466,700

Income statements for the last three years show that Alpine Village has reported total net income of **$238,500** since the business was started. The income statements of Nordic Sports show total net income of **$199,400** for the same three-year period.

With the permission of the owners of the two businesses, Scott arranges for a certified public accountant to review the accounting records of both companies. This investigation discloses the following information:

Accounts receivable. Alpine Village uses the direct charge-off method of recording uncollectible accounts expense. The accountant believes that the $187,300 of accounts receivable appearing in the company's balance sheet includes about $15,000 in uncollectible accounts. Nordic Sports makes monthly estimates of its uncollectible accounts and shows accounts receivable in its balance sheet at estimated net realizable value.

Inventories. Alpine Village uses the first-in, first-out *(FIFO)* method of pricing its inventory. Had the company used the last-in, first-out method *(LIFO),* the balance sheet valuation of inventory would be about $10,000 lower. Nordic Sports uses the LIFO method to value inventory; if it had used FIFO, the balance sheet valuation of inventory would be about $9,000 greater.

Buildings. Alpine Village depreciates its building over an estimated life of 40 years using the straight-line method. Nordic Sports depreciates its building over 20 years using the double-declining balance method. Nordic has owned its building for three years, and the accumulated depreciation on the building now amounts to $27,100.

Goodwill. Three years ago, each business provided $20,000 in prize money for ski races held in the area. Alpine Village charged this expenditure to goodwill, which it is amortizing over a period of 40 years. Nordic Sports charged its $20,000 prize money expenditure directly to advertising expense.

Instructions

a Prepare a revised summary of the balance sheet data in a manner that makes the information about the two companies more comparable. You will adjust the asset values of one company or the other so that the balance sheet data for both companies meet the following standards:

   (1) Accounts receivable are valued at estimated net realizable value.
   (2) Inventories are valued by the method that will minimize income taxes during a period of rising prices.
   (3) Depreciation on the buildings is based upon the straight-line method and an estimated useful life of 40 years.
   (4) The cost of the $20,000 payment of prize money is treated in the manner required by generally accepted accounting principles.

   After making the indicated adjustments to the valuation of certain assets, show "stockholders' equity" at the amount needed to bring total liabilities & stockholders' equity into agreement with total assets.

   When you revalue an asset of either company, show supporting computations.

b Revise the cumulative amount of net income reported by each company during the last three years, taking into consideration the changes in accounting methods and policies called for in part a.

c Assume that Scott is willing to buy either company at a price equal to the revised amount of stockholders' equity as determined in part a, plus an amount for goodwill. For goodwill, Scott is willing to pay three times the amount by which average annual net income exceeds a 20% return on this revised stockholders' equity.

   Determine the price that Scott is willing to pay for each of the two companies. Base your computations on the revised data about stockholders' equity and net income that you developed in parts a and b. (Hint: Remember that the cumulative net income in part b was earned over a three-year period. To find average *annual* net income, divide this amount by 3.)

Part Four	Accounting for liabilities and owners' equity
Chapter 10	Current liabilities and payroll accounting
Chapter 11	Bonds payable, leases, and other liabilities
Chapter 12	Ownership equity: single proprietorships, partnerships, and corporations
Chapter 13	Corporations: a closer look

In the following section of this text, we examine alternative means of financing business operations and also discuss the nature of "ownership" in different forms of business organizations. Corporate securities—stocks and bonds—are considered both from the viewpoint of the issuing corporation and of the investor. This section completes our discussion of balance sheet and income statement topics.

Chapter 10
Current liabilities
and payroll
accounting

CHAPTER PREVIEW

In this chapter we concentrate on current liabilities, with special attention to notes payable. An important element of current liabilities arises from the payroll accounting system; consequently, the basic concepts of payroll accounting are discussed in the final section of this chapter. Long-term liabilities will be considered in Chapter 11.

After studying
this chapter
you should be
able to meet
these Learning
Objectives:

1 Explain how the prompt recognition of liabilities relates to the matching principle of accounting.
2 Define current liabilities and explain how this classification is used in interpreting a balance sheet.
3 Account for the issuance of notes payable, the accrual of interest, and the payment of a note at maturity.
4 Explain the accounting treatment of notes payable which have interest included in the face amount.
5 Define loss contingencies and explain how they are presented in financial statements.
6 Describe the basic separation of duties in a payroll system and explain how this plan contributes to strong internal control.
7 Account for a payroll, including computation of amounts to be withheld, and payroll taxes on the employer.

The nature of liabilities

Liabilities are obligations arising from past transactions and requiring the future payment of assets or future performance of services. We determine the dollar amount of a liability from the *cost principle.* In other words, we value the liability at the cost of the asset or service we receive in exchange for assuming the liability.

For example, assume that we make a $10,000 credit purchase of merchandise for our inventory, terms net 30 days. We should immediately record a $10,000 liability, an amount equal to the cost of the asset acquired.

Examples of transactions calling for the future performance of services are a professional football team selling season tickets, and an airline selling tickets for travel at a future date. The organization receiving such payments in advance from customers must immediately record a liability, such as Unearned Ticket Revenue or Unearned Passenger Revenue. This liability will be discharged by rendering future services rather than by making a cash payment.

Liabilities of definite amount vs. estimated liabilities. Most liabilities are of definite dollar amount clearly stated by contract. Examples are accounts payable, notes payable, bonds payable, dividends payable, sales taxes payable, accrued liabilities such as interest payable, and revenue collected in advance such as unearned management fees. Our principal responsibility in accounting for these liabilities is to see that they are identified promptly as they come into existence and are properly recorded in the accounts.

Estimated liabilities have two key characteristics: the liability is known to exist, but the precise dollar amount cannot be determined until a later date. A common example is the liability of a manufacturer to honor a warranty on products sold. For instance, assume that a company manufactures and sells television sets which carry a two-year warranty. To achieve the objective of offsetting current revenue with all related expenses, the liability for future warranty repairs on television sets sold during the current period should be estimated and recorded at the balance sheet date. This estimate will be based upon the company's past experience.

Another common example of estimated liabilities is income tax on corporations. The income earned by a corporation is subject to tax by the federal government, as well as by most states and by some cities. Because of the complexities and frequent changes in the income tax laws, a corporation often needs several weeks or months after the year-end to determine the precise amount of the income tax liability. If disputes arise between a corporation and the tax authorities over the amount of the tax owed, the issues sometimes take years to resolve. However, income tax is a major expense of the year in which income is earned. Consequently, the tax liability must be estimated. The estimated amount is entered in the accounts and appears in the financial statements both as an expense and as a liability.

Timely recognition of liabilities

1 Explain how the prompt recognition of liabilities relates to the matching principle of accounting.

Correct timing in the recognition of liabilities is essential to producing dependable financial statements. An omission of a liability from the balance sheet is usually accompanied by the understatement of an expense in the income statement. For example, if an invoice for advertising expense is not recorded in the period it is received, liabilities will be understated and advertising expense will be understated. This understatement of expenses causes net income to be overstated along with the owner's equity. The essential rule is that *a liability must be recognized in the accounting period in which it comes into being.* For purchases of merchandise on credit, the recognition of the liability (as evidenced by the purchase order, purchase invoice, and receiving report) is a routine procedure subject to strong internal controls. However, the recognition of unrecorded liabilities, such as product warranty expense, professional fees, interest, and salaries owed at the end of the period, requires the use of adjusting entries and is more subject to errors and omissions.

The need for prompt recognition of all liabilities stems from the *matching principle* of accounting. This principle requires that we recognize in each period all the expenses incurred in producing the revenue of the period. For expenses which do not require payment until some time after they are incurred, we must record the expense when incurred and credit a liability account to show our obligation to make this later payment. In performing an audit, CPA firms are especially alert to detect any omission of a liability from the balance sheet. Frauds involving the theft of assets have often been concealed by the deliberate omission of a liability.

● **CASE IN POINT** ● King Building Supply, a small but profitable business, frequently issued notes payable to suppliers when its cash position did not permit prompt payment for purchases of materials. John Smith, office manager, usually prepared these notes payable for signature by the owner, Roy King. King relied heavily on Smith for all accounting and financial activities of the company.

Smith decided to take advantage of this situation to defraud the company through theft of inventory. He prepared a note for $100,000 payable to a regular supplier and obtained King's signature on it. He then ordered $100,000 worth of building materials to be delivered to a warehouse which he (Smith) had rented. Smith paid for the materials with the note signed by King, but made no accounting entry for the transaction. Smith felt sure that when the note matured, he could use company funds to pay it and charge the payment to the Purchases account. However, his fraud was disclosed during the year-end audit. The CPA firm discovered the existence of the unrecorded note payable by obtaining month-end statements from the company's suppliers. One of these statements showed a $100,000 sale, settled by a note received from King Building Supply, whereas the company's books showed no such purchase and no $100,000 note outstanding.

Current liabilities

2 Define current liabilities and explain how this classification is used in interpreting a balance sheet.

Current liabilities are obligations that must be paid within one year or within the operating cycle whichever is longer. Another requirement for classification as a current liability is the expectation that the debt will be paid from current assets. Occasionally, a current liability may be replaced with a new short-term liability rather than being paid in cash. For example, a company short of cash may issue a short-term note payable to settle a past-due account payable. Liabilities that do not fall due within one year or within the operating cycle are classified as long-term liabilities.

The current liability classification parallels the current asset classification. As explained in Chapter 5, the amount of working capital (current assets less current liabilities) and the current ratio (current assets divided by current liabilities) are valuable indicators of a company's ability to pay its debts in the near future. In other words, these indicators help us to judge a company's solvency.

Among the more common current liabilities are accounts payable, notes payable, dividends payable, current portion of long-term debt (such as this year's required payments on a long-term mortgage), sales taxes payable, accrued liabilities (such as interest payable), revenue collected in advance (such as unearned management fees), payroll liabilities, and estimated liabilities, including product warranty liability and corporate income taxes.

Accounts payable

Accounts payable are sometimes subdivided into trade accounts payable and other accounts payable. Trade accounts payable are short-term obligations to suppliers for purchases of merchandise. Other accounts payable include the liability for acquisition of assets such as office equipment and for any goods and services other than merchandise. We have previously discussed in Chapter 6 the guidelines for maintaining strong internal control over accounts payable. These guidelines include the locating of the purchasing function in a separate purchasing department and making payment only of liabilities which have been approved after comparison of invoice, purchase order, and receiving report. The voucher system is especially useful in providing assurance of the integrity of the system for approving and paying invoices.

NOTES PAYABLE

3 Account for the issuance of notes payable, the accrual of interest, and the payment of a note at maturity.

Notes payable are issued whenever bank loans are obtained. Other transactions which may give rise to notes payable include the purchase of real estate or costly equipment, the purchase of merchandise, and the substitution of a note for a past-due account payable.

Notes payable issued to banks

Assume that on November 1 Porter Company borrows $10,000 from its bank for a period of six months at an annual interest rate of 12%. Six months later on May 1, Porter Company will have to pay the bank the ***principal*** amount of $10,000 plus $600 interest ($10,000 $\times$ .12 $\times$ $\frac{6}{12}$.) The owners of Porter Company have authorized John Caldwell, the company's treasurer, to sign notes payable issued by the company. The note issued by Porter Company could read as shown below (omitting a few minor details).

This note is for the principal amount with interest stated separately

Miami, Florida   November 1, 19__

Six months .... after this date   Porter Company ....

promises to pay to Security National Bank the sum of $ .... 10,000 ....

with interest at the rate of ...... 12% ..... per annum.

Signed... *John Caldwell* ....

Title ...... Treasurer ....

The journal entry in Porter Company's accounting records for this borrowing is:

Face amount of note

Cash 10,000
    Notes Payable... 10,000
Borrowed $10,000 for six months at 12% interest per year.

Notice that no liability is recorded for the interest charges when the note is issued. At the date that money is borrowed, the borrower has a liability *only for the principal amount of the loan;* the liability for interest accrues day by day over the life of the loan. At December 31, two month's interest expense has been incurred, and the following year-end adjusting entry is made:

A liability for interest accrues day by day

Interest Expense 200
    Interest Payable 200
To record interest expense incurred through year-end on 12%, six-month note dated Nov. 1 ($10,000 $\times$ .12 $\times \frac{2}{12}$ = $200).

If we assume that the company does not use reversing entries, the entry on May 1 when the note is paid will be:

Payment of principal and interest

Notes Payable 10,000
Interest Payable.. 200
Interest Expense 400
    Cash... 10,600
To record payment of 12%, six-month note on maturity date and to recognize interest expense incurred since year-end ($10,000 $\times$ .12 $\times \frac{4}{12}$ = $400).

Notes payable with interest charges included in the face amount

4 Explain the
accounting
treatment of
notes payable
which have
interest included
in the face amount.

Instead of stating the interest rate separately as in the preceding illustration, the note payable issued by Porter Company could have been drawn to include the interest charge in the face amount of the note, as shown below:

**This note shows
interest included
in face amount**

```
    Miami, Florida                                    November 1, 19__

    Six months                    after this date        Porter Company

promises to pay to Security National Bank the sum of $ ............ $10,600

            Signed... John Caldwell

            Title ........... Treasurer
```

Notice that the face amount of this note ($10,600) is greater than the $10,000 amount borrowed. Porter Company's liability at November 1 is only $10,000; the other $600 included in the face amount of the note represents *future interest charges.* As interest expense is incurred over the life of the note, Porter Company's liability will grow to $10,600, just as in the preceding illustration.

The entry to record Porter Company's $10,000 borrowing from the bank at November 1 will be as follows for this type of note payable:

**Interest included
in face of note**

Cash	10,000	
Discount on Notes Payable	600	
Notes Payable...		10,600

Issued a bank a 12%, six-month note payable with interest charge included in the face amount of note.

The liability account, Notes Payable, was credited with the full face amount of the note ($10,600). It is therefore necessary to debit a *contra-liability* account, *Discount on Notes Payable,* for the future interest charges included in the face amount of the note. Discount on Notes Payable is shown in the balance sheet as a deduction from Notes Payable. In our illustration, the amounts in the balance sheet would be Notes Payable, $10,600, minus Discount on Notes Payable, $600, or a net liability of $10,000 at November 1.

Discount on Notes Payable. The balance of the account Discount on Notes Payable represents *interest charges applicable to future periods.* As this interest expense is incurred, the balance of the discount account gradually is transferred into the Interest Expense account. Thus, at the maturity date of the note, Discount on Notes Payable will have a zero balance, and the net liability will have increased to $10,600. The process of transferring the amount in the Discount on Notes Payable account into the Interest Expense account is called **amortization** of the discount.

Amortization of the discount. The discount on **short-term** notes payable usually is amortized by the straight-line method, which allocates the same amount of discount to interest expense for each month the note is outstanding.[1] Thus, the $600 discount on the Porter Company note payable will be transferred from Discount on Notes Payble into Interest Expense at the rate of $100 per month ($600 ÷ 6 months).

Adjusting entries should be made to amortize the discount at the end of the year and at the date the note matures. At December 31, Porter Company will make the following adjusting entry to recognize the two months' interest expense incurred since November 1:

Amortization of discount

Interest Expense	200	
Discount on Notes Payable		200

To record interest expense incurred to end of year on 12%, six-month note dated Nov. 1 ($600 discount × $\frac{2}{6}$).

Notice that the liability for accrued interest is recorded by crediting Discount on Notes Payable rather than Accrued Interest Payable. The credit to Discount on Notes Payable reduces the debit balance in this contra-liability account from $600 to $400, thereby increasing the **net liability** for notes payable by $200.

At December 31, Porter Company's net liability for the bank loan will appear in the balance sheet as shown below:

Liability shown net of discount

Current liabilities:

Note payable	$10,600	
Less: Discount on notes payable	400	$10,200

The net liability of $10,200 consists of the $10,000 principal amount of the debt plus the $200 interest which has accrued since November 1.

When the note matures on May 1, Porter Company will recognize the four months' interest expense incurred since year-end and will pay the bank $10,600. The entry is

Two-thirds of interest applicable to second year

Notes Payable	10,600	
Interest Expense	400	
Discount on Notes Payable		400
Cash		10,600

To record payment of six-month note due today and recognize interest expense incurred since year-end ($10,000 × 12% × $\frac{4}{12}$ = $400).

[1] When an interest charge is included in the face amount of a long-term note, the effective interest method of amortizing the discount is often used instead of the straight-line method. The effective interest method of amortization is discussed in Chapter 11.

Comparison of the two forms of notes payable

We have illustrated two alternative methods which Porter Company could use in accounting for its $10,000 bank loan, depending upon the form of the note payable. The journal entries for both methods, along with the resulting balance sheet presentations of the liability at November 1 and December 31, are summarized on the next page. Notice that both methods result in Porter Company recognizing the same amount of interest expense and the same total liability in its balance sheet. The form of the note does not change the economic substance of the transaction.

Loss contingencies

5 Define loss contingencies and explain how they are presented in financial statements.

In Chapter 7, we discussed the contingent liability which arises when a business discounts a note receivable to a bank. The business endorses the note and thereby promises to pay the note if the maker fails to do so. The contingent liability created by discounting the note is a potential liability which will become a full-fledged liability or will be eliminated altogether by a future event. Contingent liabilities are also called **loss contingencies.** Loss contingencies however, is a broader term, which includes the possible impairment of assets. Assume, for example, that an American company with operations overseas faces threats by a foreign country to seize American-owned assets in that country. The possible loss is clearly a potential impairment of assets rather than a contingent liability.

A loss contingency may be defined as a possible loss, stemming from **past events,** that will be resolved as to existence and amount by some future event. Central to the definition of a loss contingency is the element of **uncertainty —** uncertainty as to the amount of loss and, on occasion, uncertainty as to whether or not any loss actually has been incurred. A common example of a loss contingency is the risk of loss from a lawsuit pending against a company. The lawsuit is based on past events, but until the suit is resolved, uncertainty exists as to the amount of the company's liability.

Loss contingencies are recorded in the accounting records at estimated amounts only when both of the following criteria are met: (1) it is **probable** that a loss has been incurred, and (2) the amount of loss can be **reasonably estimated.**[2] An example of a loss contingency which meets these criteria and is recorded in the accounts is the estimated loss from doubtful accounts receivable. Loss contingencies which do not meet both of these criteria should be **disclosed in footnotes** to the financial statements whenever there is at least a **reasonable possibility** that a loss has been incurred. Pending lawsuits, for example, almost always are disclosed in footnotes, but the loss, if any, is not recorded in the accounting records until the lawsuit is settled.

When loss contingencies are disclosed in footnotes to the financial statements, the footnote should describe the nature of the contingency and, if possible, provide an estimate of the amount of possible loss. If a reasonable estimate of the amount of possible loss cannot be made, the footnote should include the range of possible loss

---

[2] *FASB Statement No. 5,* "Accounting for Contingencies" (Stamford, Conn.: 1975).

Comparison of the Two Forms of Notes Payable

	Note Written for $10,000 Plus 12% Interest	Note Written with Interest Included in Face Amount

Entry to Record Borrowing on Nov. 1	Cash.......... 10,000
	  Notes Payable.......... 10,000
		Cash.......... 10,000
		Discount on Notes Payable.......... 600
		  Notes Payable.......... 10,600

Partial balance sheet at Nov. 1	Current liabilities:
	  Notes payable.......... $10,000
		Current liabilities:
		  Notes payable.......... $10,600
		  Less: Discount on notes payable.......... 600 $10,000

Adjusting entry at Dec. 31	Interest Expense.......... 200
	  Interest Payable.......... 200
		Interest Expense.......... 200
		  Discount on Notes Payable.......... 200

Partial balance sheet at Dec. 31	Current liabilities:
	  Notes payable.......... $10,000
	  Interest payable.......... 200 $10,200
		Current liabilities:
		  Notes payable.......... $10,600
		  Less: Discount on notes payable.......... 400 $10,200

Entry to record payment of note on May 1	Notes Payable.......... 10,000
	Interest Payable.......... 200
	Interest Expense.......... 400
	  Cash.......... 10,600
		Notes Payable.......... 10,600
		Interest Expense.......... 400
		  Discount on Notes Payable.......... 400
		  Cash.......... 10,600

or a statement that an estimate cannot be made. The following footnote is typical of the disclosure of the loss contingency arising from pending litigation:

Footnote disclo-
sure of a loss
contingency

Note 8: Contingencies

In October of the current year, the Company was named as defendant in a lawsuit alleging patent infringement and claiming damages of $408 million. The Company denies all charges in this case and is preparing its defenses against them. The Company is advised by legal counsel that it is not possible at this time to determine the ultimate legal or financial responsibility with respect to this litigation.

Users of financial statements should pay close attention to the footnote disclosure of loss contingencies. Even though no loss has been recorded in the accounting records, some loss contingencies may be so material in amount as to threaten the continued existence of the company.

● **CASE IN POINT** ● In August 1982, Manville Corp. surprised the financial community by filing for bankruptcy. Manville Corp., with its worldwide mining and manufacturing operations, had a long record of profitability and financial strength. In fact, the corporation was one of the 30 "blue chip" companies whose stock prices are used in the computation of the famous Dow-Jones Industrial Average. As late as 1981, the dollar amounts in the company's financial statements showed Manville Corp. to be both profitable and solvent.

A clue to the company's impending problems, however, could be found in the notes accompanying the statements. Beginning in 1979, the statements included a note disclosing that the company was a defendant in "numerous legal actions alleging damage to the health of persons exposed to dust from asbestos-containing products manufactured or sold by the Company. . . ." It was these pending lawsuits, which numbered over 50,000 by August of 1982, which caused the company to file for bankruptcy.

Finally, notice that loss contingencies relate only to possible losses from *past events.* In the Manville case, the past events were exposing people to asbestos. The risk that losses might be incurred as a result of *future* events is *not* a loss contingency. The risk of *future* losses is *not* disclosed in financial statements for several reasons. For one, any disclosure of possible future losses would be sheer speculation. For another, it is not possible to foresee all the events which might give rise to future losses.

Commitments. Contracts for future transactions are called commitments. They are not liabilities, but, if material, may be disclosed by footnotes to the financial statements. For example, a professional baseball club may issue a three-year contract to a player at an annual salary of, say, $1 million. This is a commitment to pay for services to be rendered in the future. There is no obligation to make payment until the services are received. Because there is no present obligation, no liability exists. Other examples of commitments include a corporation's long-term employment contract with a key officer, a contract for construction of a new plant, and a contract to buy inventory over a period of years. The common quality of all these commitments is an intent to enter into transactions in the future. Keep in mind that the balance sheet should not be cluttered with footnotes on insignificant matters. Commitments are usually disclosed only if they are unusual in nature and material in amount, or if losses from the commitment are being incurred.

PAYROLL ACCOUNTING

Labor costs and related payroll taxes constitute a large and constantly increasing portion of the total costs of operating most business organizations. In the commercial airlines, for example, labor costs traditionally have represented 40 to 50% of total operating costs.

The task of accounting for payroll costs would be an important one simply because of the large amounts involved; however, it is further complicated by the many federal and state laws which require employers to maintain certain specific information in their payroll records not only for the business as a whole but also for each individual employee. Frequent reports of total wages and amounts withheld must be filed with government agencies. These reports are prepared by every employer and must be accompanied by payment to the government of the amounts withheld from employees and of the payroll taxes levied on the employer.

A basic rule in most business organizations is that every employee must be paid on time, and the payment must be accompanied by a detailed explanation of the computations used in determining the net amount received by the employee. The payroll system must therefore be capable of processing the input data (such as employee names, social security numbers, hours worked, pay rates, overtime, and taxes) and producing a prompt and accurate output of paychecks, payroll records, withholding statements, and reports to government agencies. In addition, the payroll system must have built-in safeguards against overpayments to employees, the issuance of duplicate paychecks, payments to fictitious employees, and the continuance on the payroll of persons who have been terminated as employees.

Internal control over payrolls

Payroll fraud has a long history. Before the era of social security records and computers, payroll records were often handwritten and incomplete. Employees were commonly paid in cash and documentary evidence was scanty. Some specific characteristics of present-day payroll accounting make payroll fraud more difficult. These helpful factors include the required frequent filing of payroll data with the government, and the universal use of employer identification numbers and employees' social security numbers. For example, "padding" a payroll with fictitious names is more difficult when social security numbers must be on file for every employee, individual earnings records must be created, and quarterly reports must be submitted to the Internal Revenue Service, showing for every employee the gross earnings, social security taxes, and income tax withheld.

However, neither automation of the accounting process nor extensive reporting of payroll data to government has caused payroll fraud to disappear. Satisfactory internal control over payrolls still requires separation and subdivision of duties. In a computer-based system, this means clear separation of the functions of systems analysts, programmers, computer operators, and control group personnel.

In most organizations the payroll activities include the functions of (1) employing workers, (2) timekeeping, (3) payroll preparation and record keeping, and (4) the distribution of pay to employees. Internal control will be strengthened if each of these functions is handled by a separate department.

Employment (personnel) department. The work of the employment or personnel department begins with interviewing and hiring job applicants. When a new employee is hired, the personnel department prepares records showing the date of employment, the authorized rate of pay, and payroll deductions. The personnel department sends a written notice to the payroll department to place the new employee on the payroll. Changes in pay rates and termination of employees will be recorded in personnel department records. When a person's employment is terminated, the personnel department should conduct an exit interview and notify the payroll department to remove the employee's name from the payroll.

Timekeeping. For employees paid by the hour, the time of arrival and departure should be punched on time cards. A new time card should be placed in the rack by the time clock at the beginning of each week or other pay period. Control procedures should exist to ensure that each employee punches his or her own time card and no other. The timekeeping function should be lodged in a separate department which will control the time cards and transmit these source documents to the payroll department.

The payroll department. The input of information to the payroll department consists of hours reported by the timekeeping department, and authorized names, pay rates, and payroll deductions received from the personnel department. The output of the payroll department includes (1) payroll checks, (2) individual employee records of earnings and deductions, and (3) regular reports to the government showing the earnings of employees and taxes withheld.

Distribution of paychecks. The paychecks prepared in the payroll department are transmitted to the *paymaster,* who distributes them to the employees. The paymaster should not have responsibility for hiring or firing employees, timekeeping, or preparation of the payroll.

Paychecks for absent employees should never be turned over to other employees or to supervisors for delivery. Instead, the absent employee should later pick up the paycheck from the paymaster after presenting proper identification and signing a receipt. The distribution of paychecks by the paymaster provides assurance that paychecks will not continue to be issued to fictitious employees or employees who have been terminated.

The operation of a typical payroll system is illustrated on the flow chart below. Notes have been made indicating the major internal control points within the system.

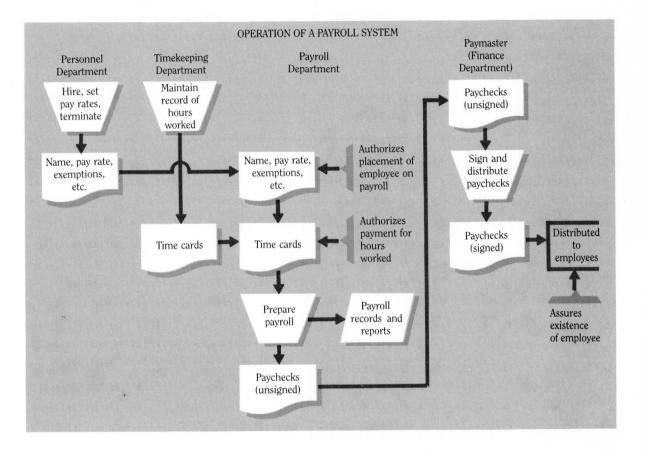

OPERATION OF A PAYROLL SYSTEM

Weaknesses in internal control. There is seldom justification for paying employees in cash. The use of paychecks provides better evidence that payments were made only to existing employees at authorized rates. Even in companies with numerous small branches, it is urgent that branch managers *not* be authorized to combine such duties as hiring and firing employees with the preparation of payrolls, or the distribution of paychecks. Much better internal control can be achieved by lodging in the headquarters office the work outlined above relating to employment, pay rates, pay changes, deductions, terminations, payroll preparation, and distribution of paychecks.

● **CASE IN POINT** ● Minox, Inc., a manufacturer with several hundred employees, permitted weaknesses in internal control that led to a large-scale payroll fraud. Supervisors in the factory had access to time cards and they also distributed

W-2 forms to employees at the end of each year. This combination of duties enabled the supervisors to maintain more than 20 fictitious names on the payroll. Paychecks for these nonexistent employees were taken by the supervisors and endorsed for their own use.

This fraud was disclosed by chance when a temporary summer employee applied for a college loan and was refused on the grounds of excessive earnings. The employee's parents wrote to the president of Minox, Inc., complaining that the company had reported to the IRS much larger earnings than he had really received. The president of the company ordered an investigation which revealed that a factory supervisor had punched the temporary employee's time card daily, thus keeping him on the payroll after his termination. The supervisor had kept and endorsed the paychecks issued in the student's name.

Deductions from earnings of employees

7 Account for a payroll including computation of amounts to be withheld and payroll taxes on the employer.

The take-home pay of most employees is much less than the gross earnings. Major factories explaining this difference between the amount earned and the amount received are social security taxes, federal income taxes withheld, and other deductions discussed in the following pages.

Social security taxes (FICA)

Under the terms of the Social Security Act, qualified workers who retire after reaching a specified age receive monthly retirement payments and Medicare benefits. Benefits are also provided for the family of a worker who dies before or after reaching this retirement age. Funds for the operation of this program are obtained through taxes levied under the Federal Insurance Contributions Act, often referred to as FICA taxes, or simply as *social security taxes.*

Employers are required by the Federal Insurance Contributions Act to withhold a portion of each employee's earnings as a contribution to the social security program. A tax at the same rate is levied against the employer. For example, assume that an employee earns $20,000 subject to FICA taxes of $7\frac{1}{2}$%. The employer will withhold $1,500 ($20,000 $\times$ .075) from the employee's earnings. The employer will then pay to the government the amount of $3,000, consisting of the $1,500 withheld from the employee plus an additional $1,500 of FICA tax on the employer.

Two factors are involved in computing the FICA tax: the **base** or amount of earnings subject to the tax; and the **rate** which is applied to the base. Both the **base** and the **rate** have been increased many times in recent years and probably will continue to be changed in future years.

● **CASE IN POINT** ● The enormous increase in social security taxes is revealed in the following table.

Year	Base (Earnings Subject to FICA Tax)	Tax Rate	Amount of Tax
1937	$ 3,000	1.0%	$ 30
1951	3,600	1.5%	54
1966	6,600	4.2%	277
1972	9,000	5.2%	468
1977	16,500	5.85%	965
1983	35,700	6.70%	2,392
1986	42,000	7.15%	3,003
1996	?	?	?

We can see from the table that individuals with earnings greater than the base were required to pay approximately 100 times as much in 1986 as they were in 1937 when the social security plan was started.

These changes in rates and in the base do not affect the accounting principles or procedures involved. For illustrative purposes in this book, we shall assume the rate of tax to be $7\frac{1}{2}\%$ on both the employee and the employer, applicable to a **base of $45,000** (the first $45,000 of wages received by each employee in each calendar year). This assumption of round amounts for both the tax and the base is a convenient one for the purpose of illustrations and for the solution of problems by the student, regardless of frequent changes in the rate and base.

An example may clarify the expression "subject to FICA tax." Assume that during a year when a $45,000 base prevails, you earn $48,000 in salary. You would have to pay the $7\frac{1}{2}\%$ FICA tax on $45,000 of your salary. You would **not** pay FICA tax on the $3,000 by which your salary exceeded the $45,000 base.

Federal income taxes

Our pay-as-you-go system of federal income tax requires employers to withhold a portion of the earnings of their employees. The amount withheld depends upon the amount of the earnings and upon the number of income tax exemptions claimed by the employee. On a federal income tax return, one exemption is allowed for oneself, one for a spouse, and one for each dependent. Each exemption causes a specified amount of yearly earnings to be exempt from income tax. An employee is required to file with the employer a Withholding Allowance Certificate (Form W-4) showing the number of exemptions claimed.

Present regulations provide a graduated system of withholding, designed to make the amount of income tax withheld approximate the individual's tax liability at the end of the year. Because persons in higher income brackets are subject to higher rates of taxation, the withholding rates are correspondingly higher for them. There is no ceiling with respect to the amount of salary subject to income tax.

Most states and cities which levy income taxes also require the employer to withhold the tax from employees' earnings. Because such situations involve a variety of rates, they will not be discussed here.

Other deductions from employees' earnings

In addition to the compulsory deductions for taxes, many other deductions are voluntarily authorized by employees. Union dues and insurance premiums already have been mentioned as examples of payroll deductions. Others include charitable contributions, retirement programs, savings bond purchases, and pension plans.

Employer's responsibility for amounts withheld

In withholding amounts from an employee's earnings for either voluntary or involuntary deductions, the employer acts merely as a collection agent. The amounts withheld are paid to the designated organization, such as a government agency or labor union. The employer is also responsible for maintaining accounting records which will enable it to file required reports and make timely payments of the amounts withheld. From the employer's viewpoint, the amounts withheld from employees' earnings represent current liabilities.

Payroll records and procedures

Although payroll records and procedures vary greatly according to the number of employees and the extent of automation in processing payroll data, there are a few fundamental steps common to payroll work in most organizations. One of these steps taken at the end of each pay period is the preparation of a **payroll register** showing for each employee the gross earnings, amounts withheld, and net pay. When the computation of the payroll register has been completed, the next step is to reflect the expense and the related liabilities in the ledger accounts. A general journal entry as shown below may be used to bring into the accounts the information summarized in the payroll register. (This entry does not include payroll taxes on the employer.)

Journal entry to record payroll

Sales Salaries Expense	4,800	
Office Salaries Expense	3,200	
FICA Tax Payable (7½% of $8,000)		600
Liability for Income Tax Withheld		1,330
Liability for Insurance Premiums Withheld		150
Accrued Payroll		5,920
To record the payroll for the period Jan. 1 – Jan. 15.		

The two debits to expense accounts indicate that the business has incurred salaries expense of $8,000; however, only $5,920 of this amount will be paid to the employees on payday. The payment will be recorded by a debit to Accrued Payroll and a credit to Cash. The remaining $2,080 (consisting of deductions for taxes and insurance premiums withheld) is lodged in liability accounts. Payment of these liabilities must be made at frequent intervals.

Wage and tax statement. By January 31 each year, employers are required to furnish every employee with a Wage and Tax Statement (Form W-2). This form shows gross earnings for the preceding calendar year and the amounts withheld for FICA tax and income taxes. The employer sends one copy of this form to the federal government, one copy to the state government, and gives three copies to the employee. When the employee files a federal income tax return, he or she must attach a copy of the withholding statement. A copy also must be attached to the state income tax return.

Payroll taxes on the employer

The discussion of payroll taxes up to this point has dealt with taxes levied on employees and withheld from their pay. From the viewpoint of the employing company, such withheld taxes are significant because they must be accounted for and remitted in a timely manner to the appropriate government agencies. However, *payroll taxes are also levied on the employer.* These taxes on the employer are expenses of the business and *are recorded by debits to expense accounts,* just as in the case of property taxes or license fees for doing business.

Social Security (FICA) tax. The employer is taxed to help finance the social security program. The tax is figured at the same rate and on the same amount of earnings used to compute FICA tax on employees. (In all problems and illustrations in this book, the tax is assumed to be $7\frac{1}{2}\%$ on the first $45,000 of gross earnings by each employee in each calendar year.)

Federal unemployment insurance tax. Unemployment insurance is another part of the national social security program designed to offer temporary relief to unemployed persons. The FUTA tax (Federal Unemployment Tax Act) is levied on *employers only* and is not deducted from the wages of employees. The rates of tax and the wage base subject to the tax are changed from time to time. For purposes of illustration in this book, we shall assume that employers are subject to federal unemployment tax at the rate of 6.2% on the first $7,000 of each employee's earnings in each calendar year. However, the employer may take a credit against this tax (not in excess of 5.4% of the first $7,000 of each employee's wages) for amounts that are paid into state unemployment funds. As a result, an employer may be subject to a *federal* tax of only .8% on wages up to $7,000 per employee.

State unemployment insurance tax. All the states participate in the federal-state unemployment insurance program. The usual rate of tax is 5.4% of the first $7,000 of earnings by each employee during the calendar year. Under this provision, the employer actually makes payment of the larger part of the FUTA tax directly to state governments which carry out the federal-state unemployment insurance program. This arrangement means that the FUTA tax is divided into two parts: the larger part, or 5.4%, of the first $7,000 of wages paid going to the state and the remainder (.8%) to the federal government.

Accounting entry for employer's payroll taxes. The entry to record the employer's payroll taxes is usually made at the same time the payroll is recorded. To illustrate, let us use again the $8,000 payroll first used on page 408 in the discussion of amounts withheld from employees. This time, however, we are illustrating taxes levied on the **employer.** (None of the employees has earned over $7,000 since this is the first pay period of the current year.)

<table>
<tr><td>Payroll Taxes Expense...</td><td>1,096</td><td></td></tr>
<tr><td>   FICA Tax Payable (7½% of $8,000) ....</td><td></td><td>600</td></tr>
<tr><td>   State Unemployment Tax Payable (5.4% of $8,000).....................</td><td></td><td>432</td></tr>
<tr><td>   Federal Unemployment Tax Payable (0.8% of $8,000)..................</td><td></td><td>64</td></tr>
<tr><td>To record payroll taxes on employer for period ended Jan. 15.</td><td></td><td></td></tr>
</table>

Journal entry to record payroll taxes on employer

Thus the total payroll expense for the employer is $9,096, which consists of wages of $8,000 and payroll taxes of $1,096.

Distinction between employees and independent contractors

Every business obtains personal services from **employees** and also from **independent contractors.** The employer-employee relationship exists when the company paying for the services has a right to direct and supervise the person rendering the services. Independent contractors, on the other hand, are retained to perform a specific task and exercise their own judgment as to the best methods for performing the work. Examples of independent contractors include CPAs engaged to perform an audit, attorneys retained to represent a company in a law suit, and a plumber called in to repair a broken pipe. The **fees** paid to independent contractors, are not included in payroll records and are not subject to withholding or payroll taxes.

END-OF-CHAPTER REVIEW

Summary of chapter learning objectives

1 Explain how the prompt recognition of liabilities relates to the matching principle of accounting.
The matching principle requires that we recognize all the expenses incurred in producing the revenue of the period. To record expenses which do not require payment until a later date, we recognize promptly our liability to make this later payment and also record the related expense.

2 Define current liabilities and explain how this classification is used in interpreting a balance sheet.
Current liabilities are debts to be paid out of current assets within one year or the operating cycle whichever is longer. By computing the current ratio and the amount of working capital, we compare the current assets with current liabilities and form an opinion as to a company's short-term debt-paying ability.

3 Account for the issuance of notes payable, the accrual of interest, and the payment of a note at maturity.

Notes payable are issued to obtain bank loans and often for the purchase of real estate and high-cost equipment. The Notes Payable account is credited with the face amount of the note at the time of issuance and debited with the face amount when the note is paid at maturity. The interest may be stated separately or included in the face amount of the note. In either case the interest accrued at the end of each fiscal period should be recognized by use of adjusting entries. Interest is also recognized at the maturity of each note.

4 Explain the accounting treatment of notes payable which have interest included in the face amount.

The face amount of a note may include the principal amount of the debt plus future interest charges for the life of the note. The entry to record a note in this form includes a debit to Discount on Notes Payable for the future interest charges and a credit to Notes Payable for the face amount of the note. The discount is amortized over the life of the note by transfer to interest expense. Amortizing the discount causes the carrying value of the liability to rise gradually over the life of the note and to reach the face amount at maturity.

5 Define loss contingencies and explain how they are presented in financial statements.

Loss contingencies are possible losses, stemming from past events, that will be resolved as to existence and amount by some future event. Central to the concept of a loss contingency is the presence of uncertainty — uncertainty as to the amount of loss and whether, in fact, any loss has occurred. Most loss contingencies are disclosed in notes to the financial statements.

6 Describe the basic separation of duties in a payroll system and explain how this plan contributes to strong internal control.

The separation of duties needed to achieve strong internal control over payrolls includes placing in separate departments the functions of (a) employment (personnel), (b) timekeeping, (c) preparation of payroll checks, records, and reports, and (d) distribution of paychecks. With this separation of duties, payroll fraud such as placing fictitious names on the payroll, overstating employees' earnings, or retaining employees' names on the payroll after their termination would be next to impossible without collusion among departments.

7 Account for a payroll, including computation of amounts to be withheld, and payroll taxes on the employer.

Accounting for a payroll includes computing the gross earnings for each employee, making the proper deductions for FICA taxes withheld, income taxes withheld, and any other deductions authorized by employees. FICA tax on the employer and FUTA tax must also be computed and recorded as expenses. The employer must maintain accounting records which will permit the filing of required reports and timely payment of both payroll taxes and amounts withheld from employees' checks.

Key terms introduced or emphasized in chapter 10

Amortization of discount. The process of systematically writing off to interest expense each period a portion of the discount on a note payable. Causes the carrying value of the liability to rise to the face value of the note by the maturity date.

Commitments. Agreements to carry out future transactions. Not a liability because the transaction has not yet been performed, but may be disclosed in footnotes to the financial statements.

Contingent liability. A potential liability which either will develop into a full-fledged liability or will be eliminated entirely by a future event.

Contra-liability account. A ledger account which is deducted from or offset against a related liability account in the balance sheet. For example, Discount on Notes Payable.

Discount on Notes Payable. A contra-liability account representing any interest charges applicable to future periods included in the face amount of a note payable. Over the life of the note, the balance of the Discount on Notes Payble account is amortized into Interest Expense.

Federal Unemployment Insurance Tax (FUTA). A tax imposed on the employer by the Federal Unemployment Tax Act based on amount of payrolls. Designed to provide temporary payments to unemployed persons.

FICA tax. Payroll tax imposed by the Federal Insurance Contribution Act on both employer and employees. Used to finance the social security program of monthly retirement payments and Medicare benefits. Benefits also are paid to the family of a worker who dies before reaching retirement age.

Gross earnings. Total amount earned by an employee before deductions such as social security taxes, federal income tax withheld, and any voluntary deductions.

Independent contractor. A person or firm providing services to a company for a fee or commission. Not controlled or supervised by the client company. Not subject to payroll taxes.

Loss contingency. A situation involving uncertainty as to whether or not a loss has occurred. The uncertainty will be resolved by a future event. An example of a loss contingency is the possible loss relating to a law suit pending against a company. Although loss contingencies are sometimes recorded in the accounts, they are more frequently disclosed only in footnotes to the financial statements.

Maturity value. The value of a note at its maturity date, consisting of principal plus any interest payable at that date.

Note payable. A liability evidenced by issuance of a formal written promise to pay a certain amount of money, usually with interest, at a future date.

Payroll. A record listing the names of employees during a given pay period, the rates of pay, time worked, gross earnings, deductions for taxes and any other amounts withheld, and net pay.

Payroll register. A form of payroll record showing for each pay period all payroll information for employees individually and in total.

Principal amount. That portion of the maturity value of a note which is attributable to the amount borrowed or to the cost of the asset acquired when the note was issued, rather than being attributable to interest charges.

State unemployment insurance tax. A tax generally levied on employers only and based on payrolls. A part of the joint federal-state program to provide payments to unemployed persons. (In a few states a tax is also levied on employees.)

Wage and Tax Statement (W-2 Form). A form furnished by the employer to every employee showing the employee's gross earnings for the calendar year and the amounts withheld for FICA taxes and income taxes.

Demonstration problem for your review

The following transactions relating to notes payable were completed by Desktop Graphics during the three months ended June 30.

Apr. 1 Bought office equipment for use in the business from Stylecraft, Inc., for $39,000, making a $5,400 cash down payment and issuing a one-year note payable for the balance. The face amount of the note was $38,976, which included a 10% interest charge. Use one compound journal entry which includes Discount on Notes Payable.

Apr. 16 Paid $15,000 cash and issued a 90-day, 8%, $27,000 note to Hall Company in settlement of open account payable in the amount of $42,000.

Apr. 25 Purchased more office equipment from ADM Company for $52,200, issuing a 60-day, 9% note payable in settlement.

May 11 Borrowed $216,000 from Manufacturers Bank, issuing a 90-day note payable as evidence of indebtedness. An interest charge computed at 17% per year was included in the face amount of the note.

June 15 Purchased merchandise on account from Phoenix Co., $54,000.

June 18 Issued a 60-day note bearing interest at 9% in settlement of the account payable to Phoenix Co.

June 24 Paid the 60-day, 9% note due to ADM Company, which matured today.

Instructions

a Prepare journal entries (in general journal form) to record the listed transactions for the three months ended June 30. (Use a 360-day year in computing interest.)

b Prepare adjusting entries to record the interest expense on notes payable through June 30. Prepare one adjusting entry to record the accrued interest payable on the two notes for which interest is stated separately (the Hall Company note and the Phoenix Co. note). The other adjusting entry should record the amortization of discount on the two notes in which interest is included in the face amount (the Stylecraft, Inc., note and the Manufacturers Bank note).

c Prepare a partial balance sheet at June 30 reflecting the above transactions. Show Notes Payable to Bank (minus the discount) as one item and Notes Payable: Other (minus the discount) as a separate liability. Also include the accrued interest payable in the current liability section of the balance sheet.

Solution to demonstration problem

a   **General Journal**

19___

Apr	1	Office Equipment	39,000	
		Discount on Notes Payable	3,360	
		Notes Payable		36,960
		Cash		5,400
		Purchased equipment from Stylecraft, Inc., paying part cash and issuing a one-year note with 10% interest charge included in the face amount.		
	16	Accounts Payable, Hall Company	42,000	
		Cash		15,000
		Notes Payable		27,000
		Paid part cash and issued a 90-day, 8% note in settlement of open account.		
	25	Office Equipment	52,200	
		Notes Payable		52,200
		Purchased office equipment from ADM Company, issuing a 60-day, 9% note in payment.		

May	11	Cash	216,000	
		Discount on Notes Payable	5,400	
		Notes Payable		221,400

Obtained loan from Manufacturers Bank; issued 90-day note with 10% interest charge ($216,000 $\times$ 10% $\times$ $\frac{90}{360}$ = $5,400) included in face amount.

| June | 15 | Purchases .... | 54,000 | |
| | | Accounts Payable, Phoenix Co. .... | | 54,000 |

Purchased merchandise on account.

| | 18 | Accounts Payable, Phoenix Co. .... | 54,000 | |
| | | Notes Payable .... | | 54,000 |

Issued 60-day, 9% note in settlement of open account.

	24	Notes Payable	52,200	
		Interest Expense	783	
		Cash		52,983

Paid 60-day, 9% note to ADM Company ($52,200 $\times$ 9% $\times$ $\frac{60}{360}$ = $783).

b   **Adjusting Entries**

| June | 30 | Interest Expense .... | 612 | |
| | | Accrued Interest Payable .... | | 612 |

To record interest expense accrued through June 30 on two notes with interest stated separately, as follows:

Hall Company ($27,000 $\times$ 8% $\times$ $\frac{75}{360}$)	$ 450
Phoenix Co. ($54,000 $\times$ 9% $\times$ $\frac{12}{360}$)	162
Total accrued interest payable	$ 612

| | 30 | Interest Expense .... | 3,840 | |
| | | Discount on Notes Payable .... | | 3,840 |

To recognize interest expense through June 30 on two notes payable with interest included in face amount, requiring amortization of discount:

Stylecraft, Inc. ($3,360 discount $\times$ $\frac{90}{360}$	$ 840
Manufacturers' Bank ($5,400 discount $\times$ $\frac{50}{90}$	3,000
Total discount amortization	$3,840

DESKTOP GRAPHICS
Partial Balance Sheet
June 30, 19___

Current liabilities:

Notes payable to bank	$221,400	
Less: Discount on notes payable (1)	2,400	$219,000
Notes payable: other (2)	$117,960	
Less: Discount on notes payable (3)	2,520	115,440
Accrued interest payable		612
Total current liabilities		$335,052

(1) $5,400 discount − $3,000 amortization through June 30 = $2,400

(2) Stylecraft, Inc. (face amount)	$ 36,960
Hall Company	27,000
Phoenix Co.	54,000
Notes payable: other	$117,960

(3) $3,360 discount on Stylecraft note, less $840 amortization
through June 30 leaves $2,520 discount.

ASSIGNMENT MATERIAL

Review questions

1 Define current liabilities, long-term liabilities, and estimated liabilities. Give an example of an estimated liability.

2 Jonas Company issues a 90-day, 12% note payable to replace an account payable to Smith Supply Company in the amount of $8,000. Draft the journal entries (in general journal form) to record the issuance of the note payable and the payment of the note at the maturity date.

3 Howard Benson applied to the City Bank for a loan of $20,000 for a period of three months. The loan was granted at an annual interest rate of 12%. Write a sentence illustrating the wording of the note signed by Benson if
a Interest is stated separately in the note.
b Interest is included in the face amount of the note.

4 With reference to Question 3 above, give the journal entry required on the books of Howard Benson for issuance of each of the two types of notes.

5 Sylmar Industries buys a substantial amount of equipment having an estimated service life of five years by issuing a two-year note payable. The note includes no mention of an interest charge. Explain the errors which will result in the future financial statements of Sylmar Industries if the equipment and related liability are recorded at the face value, rather than the present value, of the note.

6 Should commitments appear on a balance sheet? If so, in what part of the balance sheet?

7 The personnel department of Meadow Company failed to notify the payroll department that five hourly factory workers had been terminated at the end of the last pay period. Assuming a normal subdivision of duties regarding personnel, timekeeping, preparation of payroll, and distribution of paychecks, what control procedure will prevent the payroll department from preparing paychecks for these five employees in the current period?

8 That type of payroll fraud known as "padding" a payroll is a more difficult maneuver under today's payroll accounting practices than it was a generation or more ago. What present-day factors make the padding of payrolls a complex and more difficult type of fraud?

9 Name the federal taxes that most employers are required to withhold from employees. What account or accounts would be credited with the amounts withheld?

10 Explain which of the following taxes relating to an employee's wages are borne by the employee and which by the employer:
a FICA taxes
b Federal unemployment compensation taxes
c State unemployment compensation taxes
d Federal income taxes

11 Is the Salary Expense account equal to "take-home" pay or to gross earnings? Why?

12 Distinguish between an employee and an independent contractor. Why is this distinction important with respect to payroll accounting?

Exercises

Exercise 10-1
Accounting
terminology

Listed below are nine technical accounting terms introduced in this chapter:

Estimated liabilities	Payroll register	Maturity value of note
FUTA tax	Independent contractor	Contingent liabilities
Commitments	FICA tax	Discount on Notes Payable

Each of the following statements may (or may not) describe one of these technical terms. For each statement, indicate the accounting term described, or answer "None" if the statement does not correctly describe any of the terms.

a The principal amount of a promissory note plus any interest payable at the maturity date.
b A federal tax based on payrolls and imposed on employers but not on employees.
c Legal obligations which are known to exist but for which the dollar amount is presently uncertain.
d Information presented in footnotes to financial statements concerning agreements to carry out certain transactions in the future.
e Interest charges included in the face amount of a note payable.
f An employee whose compensation is based on units of output rather than an hourly wage or a monthly salary.
g A federal tax based on payrolls and imposed on both employers and employees.

Exercise 10-2
Two forms for
notes payable

Mavis Corporation on November 1 borrowed $100,000 from a local bank, and agreed to repay that amount plus 12% interest (per year) at the end of six months. (Remember that interest is stated at an annual rate.) Show two different presentations of the liability to the bank on Mavis Corporation's December 31 balance sheet, assuming that the note payable to the bank was drawn as follows:

a For $100,000, with interest stated separately and payable at maturity
b With the total interest charge included in the face amount of the note

Exercise 10-3
Interest included
in face amount of
note payable

Ram Truck Lines bought three trucks from Scott Motors on April 1 for a total price of $204,000. Under the terms of the purchase, Ram Truck Lines paid $60,000 cash and issued a promissory note due in full 18 months later. The face amount of the note was $161,280, which included interest on the note for the 18 months.

Prepare all entries (in general journal form) for Ram Truck Lines relating to the purchase of the trucks and the note for the current fiscal year ended December 31. Include the adjusting entries to record interest expense and depreciation expense to December 31. (The trucks are to be depreciated over an eight-year service life by the straight-line method. There is no estimated salvage value.)

Exercise 10-4
Internal control
over payroll

A foreman in the factory of Barton Products, a large manufacturing company, discharged an employee but did not notify the personnel department of this action. The foreman then began forging the employee's signature on time cards. When giving out paychecks, the foreman diverted to his own use the paychecks drawn payable to the discharged worker. What internal control measure would be most effective in preventing this fraudulent activity?

Exercise 10-5
FUTA tax

Windsor Milling Company had 100 employees throughout the current year. The lowest-paid employee had gross earnings of $8,000. Assume that the Federal Unemployment Tax Act specifies a rate of 6.2% on the first $7,000 of gross earnings, and that the state unemployment tax is 5.4% of the same base. The employer is permitted to take as a credit against the federal tax the 5.4% of wages paid to the state. Compute the following:

a The state unemployment tax for the year
b The federal unemployment tax for the year
c The total unemployment tax for the year

Exercise 10-6
Payroll taxes on
employer

The payroll of Fields Company may be summarized as follows:

Gross earnings of employees.. **$400,000**
Employee earnings not subject to FICA tax **48,000**
Employee earnings not subject to FUTA tax...................................... **225,000**

Assuming that the payroll is subject to a FICA tax rate of 7.5%, a 5.4% state unemployment tax rate, and a federal FUTA tax rate of .8 of 1%, compute the amount of the Fields Company's *payroll tax expense* for the year, showing separately the amount of each of the three taxes. (Note: Taxes on employees are not involved in this exercise.)

Exercise 10-7
Entries for
payroll and pay-
roll taxes

The payroll record of Miller Company for the week ended January 7 showed the following amounts for total earnings: sales employees $8,800; office employees $7,200. Amounts withheld consisted of FICA taxes at a 7.5% rate on all earnings for this period, federal income taxes $1,920, and group insurance premiums, $600.

a After computing the amount of FICA taxes withheld, prepare a general journal entry to record the payroll. Do not include taxes on the employer.
b Prepare a general journal entry to record the payroll taxes expense to Miller Company relating to this payroll. Assume that the federal unemployment tax rate is 6.2% of the first $7,000 paid each employee, and that 5.4% of this tax is payable to the state. No employee received more than $7,000 in this first pay period of the year.

Problems

Problem 10-1
Liabilities: their
valuation and
disclosure

The following six events occurred at Midway Corporation at or near the fiscal year-end of March 31.

  a On March 31, obtained a bank loan by signing a note payable promising to pay $100,000 principal, plus $9,000 interest (computed at 12% per year), all payable nine months from today.

  b On March 31, purchased a tract of land for use in the business at a price of $300,000. Signed a note payable due nine months from today in the total amount of $324,750. The note constituted full payment for the land.

  c A ledger account entitled Income Taxes Withheld had a balance of $9,000 at March 31.

  d On March 31, signed a contract with a labor union providing for annual 6% increases in wage rates for the next three years. It was estimated that the increase in the first year would amount to $2,000,000.

  e On March 31, signed a contract with a supplier of raw materials to purchase 10,000 tons a month for 12 months at a price of $70 per ton.

  f On March 31, discounted a $100,000 note receivable at a bank and received cash of $104,000. The note had a total life of one year and carried an interest rate of 12%.

Instructions. For each of the six events, you are to indicate the dollar amount, if any, which should appear in the current liability section of the March 31 balance sheet. If an event does not affect current liabilities, indicate whether it should appear in the balance sheet and the proper location and dollar amount.

Problem 10-2
Current liabili-
ties: journal
entries

During the year ended December 31, Rockport Associates had a number of transactions relating to accounts payable and notes payable. Among these transactions were the following:

Mar. 6 Purchased merchandise from A. B. Hayes on open account, $25,200.

Apr. 8 Informed A. B. Hayes that it was unable to make payment as previously agreed. Issued to Hayes a 14%, eight-month note to replace the open account payable.

Apr. 20 Borrowed $48,000 from Third National Bank today and signed a six-month, 16% note as evidence of indebtedness. The interest was added to the $48,000 amount borrowed and included in the face amount of the note.

May 15 Purchased merchandise from Birmingham, Incorporated, on 30-day open account, $19,200.

Oct. 20 Paid note (principal and interest) due today at Third National Bank.

Dec. 8 Paid note (principal and interest) due today to A. B. Hayes.

Instructions. Prepare all necessary journal entries (in general journal form) to record the above transactions in the accounts of Rockport Associates. Show all supporting computations as part of the explanations of the journal entries. Adjusting entries are not required.

Problem 10-3
Notes payable;
accruing interest

During the fiscal year ended October 31, Dunleer Corporation carried out the following transactions involving notes payable.

June 6 Borrowed $11,200 from Tom Hutchins, issuing to him a 45-day, 12% note payable.

July 13 Purchased office equipment from Harper Company. The invoice amount was $16,800 and Harper Company agreed to accept as full payment a 12%, three-month note for the invoiced amount.

July 21 Paid the Hutchins note plus accrued interest.

Sept. 1 Borrowed $235,200 from Sun National Bank at an interest rate of 12% per annum; signed a 90-day note with interest included in the face amount of the note. (Use Discount on Notes Payable account.)

Oct. 1 Purchased merchandise in the amount of $3,000 from Kramer Co. Gave in settlement a 90-day note bearing interest at 14%.

Oct. 13 The $16,800 note payable to Harper Company matured today. Paid the interest accrued and issued a new 30-day, 12% note to replace the maturing note.

Instructions

a Prepare journal entries (in general journal form) to record the above transactions. Use a 360-day year in making the interest calculations.

b Prepare the adjusting entries needed at October 31, prior to closing the accounts. Use one entry for the two notes on which interest is stated separately and a separate entry for the Sun National Bank note in which interest is included in the face amount of the note.

Problem 10-4
Notes payable: a
comprehensive
problem

During the three months ended June 30, Optics, Inc., had the following transactions relating to notes payable.

Apr. 1 Purchased office equipment for use in the business from Eastern Gear, Inc., for $13,000, making an $1,800 cash down payment and issuing a one-year note payable for the balance. The face amount of the note was $12,992, which included a 16% interest charge. (Use one compound journal entry which includes discount on Notes Payable.)

Apr. 16 Gave $5,000 cash and a 90-day, 8% note to Lees Company in settlement of open account due today in the amount of $14,000.

Apr. 25 Purchased more office equipment from ADM Company for $17,400, giving a 60-day, 9% note in settlement thereof.

May 11 Borrowed $72,000 from Manufacturers Bank, giving a 90-day note as evidence of indebtedness. An interest charge computed at 17% per annum was included in the face amount of the note.

June 15 Purchased merchandise on account from Phoenix Co., $18,000.

June 18 Issued a 60-day note bearing interest at 9% in settlement of the Phoenix Co. account.

June 24 Paid the 60-day, 9% note due to ADM Company, which matured today.

Instructions

a Prepare journal entries (in general journal form) to record the listed transactions for the three months ended June 30. (Use a 360-day year in computing interest.)

b Prepare adjusting entries to record the interest expense on notes payable through June 30. Prepare one adjusting entry to record the accrued interest payable on the two notes for which interest is stated separately (the Lees Company note and the Phoenix Co. note). The other adjusting entry should record the amortization of discount on the two notes in which interest is included in the face amount (the Eastern Gear, Inc., note and the Manufacturers Bank note).

c Prepare a partial balance sheet at June 30 reflecting the above transactions. Show Notes Payable to Bank (minus the discount) as one item and Notes Payable: Other (minus the discount) as a separate liability. Also include the accrued interest payable in the current liability section of the balance sheet.

Problem 10-5
Payroll fraud

Friendly Finance Company makes small loans through a network of more than 100 branch offices in several states. A branch manager is in charge of each office and the number of employees under the manager's supervision is usually from four to seven. Each branch manager prepares a weekly payroll sheet, including his or her own salary. All employees are paid from cash on hand. The employees sign the payroll sheet signifying receipt of their salaries. Hours worked by hourly personnel are inserted in the payroll sheet from time cards prepared by the employees and approved by the manager.

The weekly payroll sheets are sent to the home office along with other accounting statements and reports. The home office compiles employee earnings records and prepares all federal and state salary reports from the payroll sheets.

Salaries are established by home office job evaluation schedules. Salary adjustments, promotions, and transfers of full-time employees are approved by a home office salary committee based upon recommendations of branch managers and area supervisors. Branch managers advise the salary committee of new full-time employees and terminations. Part-time and temporary employees are hired without referral to the salary committee.

Instructions. You are to evaluate the company's payroll system, especially the internal control features, and then suggest five ways in which the branch managers might carry out payroll fraud.

Problem 10-6
Recording payroll and payroll taxes

The payroll records of Copper Kettle for the first week in January showed total salaries earned by employees of $12,000. This total included $7,000 of salaries to sales employees and $5,000 to office employees.

The amounts withheld from employees' pay consisted of FICA taxes computed at an assumed rate of 7.5%, federal income taxes of $1,150, and insurance premiums of $140.

Instructions

a Prepare a general journal entry to summarize the above payroll and the deductions from the earnings of employees. Payroll taxes on the employer are not to be included in this entry.

b Prepare a general journal entry to summarize the payroll taxes on the **employer** associated with the above payroll. Assumed tax rates are as follows: FICA tax of 7.5%, state unemployment tax of 5.4%, and a federal unemployment tax of .8%.

c What is the amount of the total payroll expense of Copper Kettle for the first week in January? Show computations.

Problem 10-7
Employees' earnings records: payroll taxes

The employees' earnings records thus far in the current year for Graphic Services are as follows:

Employee	Cumulative Earnings	Employee	Cumulative Earnings
Arthur, D. S.	$14,322	Hamilton, A. J.	$16,771
Barnett, S. T..	21,868	Monday, M. D.	17,328
Darwin, E. G..	2,550	Saunders, K. U.	3,930
Greer, C. K..	6,167	Taylor, M. E..	47,265

FICA taxes are assumed to be 7.5% on the first $45,000 of an employee's gross earnings. The federal unemployment tax is assumed to be 6.2% of the first $7,000 of gross earnings, but with credit to the employer for a maximum of 5.4% of gross earnings for state unemployment taxes.

Instructions

a Prepare a schedule showing for each employee the cumulative earnings, the earnings subject to unemployment compensation tax, and the earnings subject to FICA taxes for the year to date. Columnar headings for the schedule should be as follows:

		Earnings Subject to	
Employee	Cumulative Earnings	Unemployment Taxes	FICA Taxes

b Compute the total payroll taxes **deducted** from the earnings of employees as a group for the year to date.

c Compute the total payroll taxes expense of Graphic Services and the percentage of total payroll ($130,201) represented by payroll taxes expense. (Round off to the nearest tenth of a percent.)

Business decision cases

**Case 10-1
Loss contingencies?**

Discuss each of the following situations, indicating whether the situation is a loss contingency which should be recorded or disclosed in the financial statements of Aztec Airlines. If the situation is not a loss contingency, explain how (if at all) it should be reported in the company's financial statements. (Assume that all dollar amounts are material.)

a Aztec estimates that $100,000 of its accounts receivable will prove to be uncollectible.

b The company's president is in poor health and has previously suffered two heart attacks.

c As any airline, Aztec faces the risk that a future airplane crash could cause considerable loss.

d Aztec is being sued for $2 million for failing to adequately provide for passengers whose reservations were cancelled as a result of the airline overbooking certain flights. This suit will not be resolved for a year or more.

**Case 10-2
Internal control
over payrolls**

The payroll procedures of Metals, Inc., a manufacturing concern with 80 factory employees, may be summarized as follows:

1 Applicants are interviewed and hired by Carl Olson, the factory superintendent. He obtains an employee's Withholding Allowance Certificate (a W-4 form) from each new employee and writes on it the hourly rate of pay to be used. The superintendent gives this certificate to a payroll clerk as notice that a new employee has been added.

2 When hourly pay rate changes are made, the superintendent advises the payroll clerk verbally of the new rate for the employee(s) affected.

3 Blank time cards are kept in a box at the factory entrance. On Mondays each employee takes a time card, writes in his or her name, and makes pencil notations during the week of hours of arrival and departure. At the end of the week, the employee returns the card to the box.

4 The completed cards are taken from the box on Monday mornings. Two payroll clerks divide the cards alphabetically between them; compute the gross pay, deductions, and net pay; post the information to the employees' individual earnings records; and prepare and number the payroll checks.

5 The payroll checks are signed by the chief accountant and given to the superintendent, who distributes them to employees and holds those for any absent employees.

6 The payroll bank account is reconciled by the chief accountant, who also prepares the quarterly and annual payroll tax reports.

Instructions. With the objective of improving the system of internal control over the hiring practices and payroll procedures of Metals, Inc., you are to recommend any basic changes needed in organization, equipment, forms, and procedures. Then list at least six specific hiring practices and payroll procedures which you believe should be instituted.

Chapter 11
Bonds payable,
leases,
and other liabilities

CHAPTER PREVIEW

In this chapter we describe various types of long-term debt. Large corporations borrow vast amounts of money; Exxon Corporation, for example, has debts totaling more than $30 billion. Emphasis is placed upon the issuance of bonds payable—a form of borrowing which enables large corporations to raise hundreds of millions of dollars from thousands of individual investors. Both the straight-line and effective interest methods of amortizing bond discount and premium are illustrated and explained. Other long-term liabilities covered in this chapter include mortgages, lease payment obligations, and pension plans.

After studying this chapter you should be able to meet these Learning Objectives:

1 Describe the typical characteristics of corporate bonds.
2 Explain the tax advantage of raising capital by issuing bonds instead of stock.
3 Discuss the relationship between interest rates and bond prices.
4 Explain how bond discount or premium affects the cost of borrowing.
5 Amortize bond discount or premium by the straight-line and effective interest methods.
6 Explain the accounting treatment of operating leases and of capital leases.

BONDS PAYABLE

Financially sound corporations may arrange some long-term loans by issuing a note payable to a bank or an insurance company. But to finance a large project, such as building a refinery or acquiring a fleet of jumbo jets, a corporation may need more capital than any single lender can supply. When a corporation needs to raise large amounts of long-term capital—perhaps 10, 50, or 100 million dollars or more—it generally sells additional shares of capital stock or issues **bonds payable.**[1]

What is a bond issue?

1 Describe the typical characteristics of corporate bonds.

The issuance of bonds payable is a technique of splitting a large loan into a great many units, called bonds. Each bond is a long-term interest-bearing note payable, usually in the face amount of $1,000, or a multiple thereof. The bonds are sold to the investing public, thus allowing many different investors to participate in the loan. An example of a corporate bond issue is the 8% bond issue of the Singer Corporation, due January 15, 1999. With this bond issue, the Singer Corporation borrowed $100 million by issuing 100,000 bonds of $1,000 each.

Bonds payable differ from capital stock in several ways. First, bonds payable are a liability; thus, bondholders are **creditors** of the corporation, not owners. Bondholders generally do not have voting rights and do not participate in the earnings of the corporation beyond receiving contractual interest payments. Next, bond interest payments are **contractual obligations** of the corporation. Dividends, on the other hand, do not become legal obligations of the corporation until they have been formally declared by the board of directors. Finally, bonds have a specified **maturity date,** upon which the corporation must redeem the bonds at their face amount ($1,000 each). Capital stock, on the other hand, does not have a maturity date and may remain outstanding indefinitely.

Authorization of a bond issue. Formal approval of the board of directors and the stockholders is usually required before bonds can be issued. If the bonds are to be sold to the general public, approval must also be obtained from the SEC, just as for an issue of capital stock which is offered to the public.

The issuing corporation also selects a **trustee** to represent the interests of the bondholders. This trustee generally is a large bank or trust company. A contract is drawn up indicating the terms of the bond issue and the assets (if any) which are pledged as collateral for the bonds. Sometimes this contract places limitations on the payment of dividends to stockholders during the life of the bonds. For example, dividends may be permitted only when working capital is above specified amounts. If the issuing corporation defaults on any of the terms of this contract, the trustee may foreclose upon the assets which secure the bonds or may take other legal action on behalf of the bondholders.

Role of an underwriter. When bonds are issued, the corporation usually utilizes the services of an investment banking firm, called an **underwriter.** The underwriter guarantees the issuing corporation a specific price for the entire bond issue and makes a profit by selling the bonds to the investing public at a higher price. The

---

[1] Bonds payable also are issued by the federal government and by many other governmental units such as states, cities, and school districts. In this chapter, our discussion is limited to corporate bonds, although the concepts also apply to the bond issues of governmental agencies.

corporation records the issuance of the bonds at the net amount received from the underwriter. The use of an underwriter assures the corporation that the entire bond issue will be sold without delay, and the entire amount of the proceeds will be available at a specific date.

Transferability of bonds. Corporate bonds, like capital stocks, are traded daily on organized securities exchanges, such as the *New York Bond Exchange.* The holders of a 25-year bond issue need not wait 25 years to convert their investment into cash. By placing a telephone call to a broker, an investor may sell bonds within a matter of minutes at the going market price. This quality of *liquidity* is one of the most attractive features of an investment in corporate bonds.

Quoted market prices. The market price of a bond is quoted as a *percentage* of the bond's maturity value, which is usually $1,000. The *maturity value* is the amount the issuing company must pay to redeem the bond at the date it matures (becomes due). A bond quoted at *102* would therefore have a market price of $1,020 (102% of $1,000). Bond prices are quoted at the nearest one-eighth of a percentage point. The following line from the financial page of a daily newspaper summarizes the previous day's trading in bonds of Sears, Roebuck and Co.

What is the market value of this bond?

Bonds	Sales	High	Low	Close	Net Change
Sears R $7\frac{7}{8}$'07	45	$85\frac{1}{2}$	$83\frac{1}{2}$	85	+1

This line of condensed information indicates that 45 of Sears, Roebuck and Co.'s $7\frac{7}{8}$, $1,000 bonds maturing in 2007 were traded. The highest price is reported as $85\frac{1}{2}$, or $855 for a bond of $1,000 face value. The lowest price was $83\frac{1}{2}$, or $835 for a $1,000 bond. The closing price (last sale of the day) was 85, or $850. This was one point above the closing price of the previous day, an increase of $10 in the price of a $1,000 bond.

The primary factors which determine the market value of a bond are (1) the relationship of the bond's interest rate to other investment opportunities and (2) investors' confidence that the issuing company will be able to meet its obligations for future interest and principal payments. A bond selling at a market price greater than its maturity value is said to be selling at a *premium;* a bond selling at a price below its maturity value is selling at a *discount.* As a bond nears its maturity date, the market price of the bond approaches its maturity value. At the maturity date the market price of the bond should be exactly equal to its maturity value, and the issuing corporation will redeem the bond for that amount.

Types of bonds. Bonds secured by the pledge of specific assets are called *mortgage bonds.* An unsecured bond is called a *debenture bond;* its value rests upon the general credit of the corporation. A debenture bond issued by a very large and strong corporation may have a higher investment rating than a secured bond issued by a corporation in less satisfactory financial condition. For example, the $500 million of debenture bonds recently issued by IBM are rated AAA, the highest possible rating.

Some bonds have a single fixed maturity date for the entire issue. Other bond issues, called **serial bonds,** provide for varying maturity dates to lessen the problem of accumulating cash for payment. For example, serial bonds in the amount of $20 million issued in 1980 might call for $2 million of bonds to mature in 1990, and an additional $2 million to become due in each of the succeeding nine years. Almost all bonds are **callable,** which means that the corporation has the right to pay off the bonds **in advance** of the scheduled maturity date. To compensate the bondholders for being forced to give up their investments, the call price is usually somewhat higher than the face value of the bonds.

Most corporation bonds issued in recent years have been **registered bonds;** that is, the name of the owner is registered with the issuing corporation. Payment of interest is made by semiannual checks mailed to the registered owners. **Coupon bonds** were more popular some years ago and many are still outstanding. Coupon bonds have interest coupons attached; each six months during the life of the bond one of these coupons becomes due. The bondholder detaches the coupon and deposits it with a bank for collection. The names of the bondholders are not registered with the corporation.

As an additional attraction to investors, corporations sometimes include a conversion privilege in the bond indenture. A **convertible bond** is one which may be exchanged for common stock at the option of the bondholder. (Convertible securities are discussed further in Chapter 13.)

Tax advantage of bond financing

2 Explain the tax advantage of raising capital by issuing bonds instead of stock.

A principal advantage of raising money by issuing bonds instead of stock is that interest payments are **deductible** in determining income subject to corporate income taxes. Dividends paid to stockholders, however, are **not deductible** in computing taxable income.

To illustrate, assume that a corporation pays income taxes at a rate of **30%** on its taxable income. If this corporation issues $10 million of 10% bonds payable, it will incur interest expense of $1 million per year. This interest expense, however, will reduce taxable income by $1 million, thus reducing the corporation's annual income taxes by $300,000. As a result, the **after-tax** cost of borrowing the $10 million is only $700,000, as shown below:[2]

Interest expense ($10 million × 10%).	$1,000,000
Less: Income tax savings ($1,000,000 deduction × 30%).	300,000
After-tax cost of borrowing	$ 700,000

[2] A short-cut approach to computing the after-tax cost of borrowing is simply to multiply the interest expense by **one minus the company's tax rate,** as follows: **$1,000,000 × (1 − .30) = $700,000.**

Accounting entries for a bond issue

Assume that Wells Corporation on December 31, 1989 issued $1,000,000 of 20-year, 12% bonds payable. All the bonds bear the December 31, 1989 date, and interest is computed from this date. Interest on the bonds is payable semiannually, each June 30 and December 31. All the bonds were sold at par value (face value), therefore, the sale on December 31 was recorded by the following entry:

Cash..	1,000,000	
Bonds Payable..		1,000,000
To record issuance of 12%, 20-year bonds at 100 on the interest date.		

At each semiannual interest payment date, Wells Corporation must pay $60,000 to the bondholders. The computation is ($1,000,000 × .12) ÷ 2 = $60,000. Each semiannual interest payment will be recorded by an entry such as the following:

Bond Interest Expense..	60,000	
Cash..		60,000
Paid semiannual interest on 12%, 20-year bonds with face amount of $1,000,000.		

When the bonds mature 20 years later on December 31, 2009, the entry to record payment of the principal amount will be:

Bonds Payable	1,000,000	
Cash		1,000,000
Paid face amount of bonds at maturity.		

Recording the issuance of bonds between interest dates. The semiannual interest dates (such as December 31 and June 30) are printed on the bond certificates. However, bonds are often issued between the specified interest dates. The investor is then required to pay the interest accrued to date of issuance in addition to the stated price of the bond. This practice enables the corporation to pay a full six months' interest on all bonds outstanding at the semiannual interest payment date. The accrued interest collected from investors purchasing bonds between interest payment dates is thus returned to them on the next interest payment date.

To illustrate, let us modify our present example for Wells Corporation and assume that the $1,000,000 face value of 12% bonds were issued on February 28 at a price of 100 *plus two months' accrued interest.* The entry to record issuance of the bonds would be:

Bonds issued	Cash..	1,020,000	
between interest	Bonds Payable..		1,000,000
dates	Bond Interest Payable...		20,000
	Issued $1,000,000 face value of 12%, 20-year bonds at 100 plus accrued		
	interest for two months.		

Four months later on the regular semiannual interest payment date, a full six months' interest ($60 per each $1,000 bond) is paid to all bondholders, regardless of when they purchased their bonds. The entry for this semiannual interest payment is:

<table>
<tr><td></td><td>Bond Interest Payable...</td><td>20,000</td><td></td></tr>
<tr><td></td><td>Bond Interest Expense..</td><td>40,000</td><td></td></tr>
<tr><td></td><td>   Cash..</td><td></td><td>60,000</td></tr>
</table>

Notice only part of the payment is expense

Paid semiannual interest on $1,000,000 face value of 12% bonds.

Now consider these interest transactions from the standpoint of the investors. They paid for two months' accrued interest at the time of purchasing the bonds, and they received checks for six months' interest after holding the bonds for only four months. They have, therefore, been reimbursed properly for the use of their money for four months.

When bonds are subsequently sold by one investor to another, they sell at the quoted market price *plus accrued interest* since the last interest payment date. This practice enables the issuing corporation to pay all the interest for an interest period to the investor owning the bond at the interest date. Otherwise, the corporation would have to make partial payments to every investor who bought or sold the bond during the interest period.

The amount which investors will pay for bonds is the *present value* of the principal and interest payments they will receive. Before going further in our discussion of bonds payable, it will be helpful to review the concepts of present value and effective yield.

The concept of present value

The concept of present value is based upon the "time value" of money — the idea that receiving money today is preferable to receiving money at some later date. Assume, for example, that a bond will have a maturity value of $1,000 five years from today but will pay no interest in the meantime. Investors would not pay $1,000 for this bond today, because they would receive no return on their investment over the next five years. There are prices less than $1,000, however, at which investors would buy the bond. For example, if the bond could be purchased for $600, the investor could expect a return (interest) of $400 from the investment over the five-year period.

The *present value* of a future cash receipt is the amount that a knowledgeable investor will pay *today* for the right to receive that future payment. The exact amount of the present value depends upon (1) the amount of the future payment, (2) the length of time until the payment will be received, and (3) the rate of return required by the investor. However, the present value will always be *less* than the future amount. This is because money received today can be invested to earn interest and thereby becomes equivalent to a larger amount in the future.

The rate of interest which will cause a given present value to grow to a given future amount is called the discount rate or *effective interest rate.* The effective interest rate required by investors at any given time is regarded as the going *market rate* of interest. The procedures for computing the present value of a future amount are illustrated in Appendix A at the end of this textbook.

The present value concept and bond prices

3 Discuss the relationship between interest rates and bond prices.

The price at which bonds will sell is the present value to investors of the future principal and interest payments.[3] If the bonds sell at par, the effective interest rate is equal to the **contract interest rate** (or nominal rate) printed on the bonds. The higher the effective interest rate investors require, the less they will pay for bonds with a given contract rate of interest. For example, if investors insist upon a 10% return, they will pay less than $1,000 for a 9%, $1,000 bond. Thus, if investors require an effective interest rate **greater** than the contract rate of interest for the bonds, the bonds will sell at a **discount** (price less than face value). On the other hand, if investors require an effective interest rate of **less** than the contract rate, the bonds will sell at a **premium** (price above face value).

A corporation wishing to borrow money by issuing bonds must pay the going market rate of interest. Since market rates of interest are fluctuating constantly, it must be expected that the contract rate of interest may vary somewhat from the market rate at the date the bonds are issued. Thus, bonds often are issued at either a discount or a premium.

Bond prices after issuance. As stated earlier, many corporate bonds are traded daily on organized securities exchanges at quoted market prices. After bonds are issued, their market prices vary **inversely** with changes in market interest rates. As interest rates rise, investors will be willing to pay less money to own a bond that pays a given contract rate of interest. Conversely, as interest rates decline, the market prices of bonds rise.

● **CASE IN POINT** ● In October 1979, IBM sold to underwriters $500 million of $9\frac{3}{8}$% debenture bonds, due in 2004. The underwriters planned to sell the bonds to the public at a price of $99\frac{5}{8}$. Just as the bonds were offered for sale, however, a change in Federal Reserve credit policy started an upward surge in interest rates. The underwriters encountered great difficulty selling the bonds. Within one week, the market price of the bonds had fallen to $94\frac{1}{2}$. The underwriters dumped their unsold inventory at this price and sustained one of the largest underwriting losses in Wall Street history.

During the months ahead, interest rates soared to record levels. By the end of March 1980, the price of the bonds had fallen to $76\frac{3}{8}$. Thus, nearly one-fourth of the market value of these bonds evaporated in less than six months. The financial strength of IBM was never in question; this dramatic loss in market value was caused entirely by rising interest rates.

---

[3] The mechanics of determining the market price of a bond issue by using present value techniques are illustrated in Appendix A.

In addition to the current level of interest rates, the market prices of bonds are strongly influenced by the ***length of time remaining until the bonds mature*** —that is, are redeemed at their maturity value (par value) by the issuing corporation. As a bond nears its maturity date, its market price normally will move closer and closer to the maturity value.

● **CASE IN POINT** ● Exxon Corporation has outstanding two issues of $6\frac{1}{2}\%$ bonds; one issue maturing in 1989 and the other in 1998. In early 1988, the bonds maturing in 1989 were selling at a quoted market price of $97\frac{1}{2}$ whereas the bonds maturing in 1998 were selling at a price of only 82. Both bonds pay the same amount of interest, were issued by the same company, and have identical credit ratings. Thus, the difference in the market prices is caused solely by differences in the bonds' maturity dates.

Bonds sold at a discount

To illustrate the sale of bonds at a discount, assume that a corporation plans to issue $1,000,000 face value of 9%, 10-year bonds. At the issuance date, December 31, the going market rate of interest is slightly above 9% and the bonds sell at a price of only 98 ($980 for each $1,000 bond). The issuance of the bonds will be recorded by the following entry:

Issuing bonds at discount	Cash 980,000	
	Discount on Bonds Payable 20,000	
	Bonds Payable	1,000,000
	Issued $1,000,000 face value of 9%, 10-year bonds at 98.	

If a balance sheet is prepared immediately after the issuance of the bonds, the liability for bonds payable will be shown as follows:

Liability shown net of discount	Long-term liabilities:	
	9% bonds payable, due in 10 years.............................. $1,000,000	
	Less: Discount on bonds payable 20,000	$980,000

The amount of the discount is deducted from the face value of the bonds payable to show the ***carrying value*** or book value of the liability. At the date of issuance, the carrying value of bonds payable is equal to the amount for which the bonds were sold. In other words, the amount of the company's liability at the date of issuing the bonds is equal to the amount of money borrowed. Over the life of the bonds, however, we shall see that this carrying value gradually increases until it reaches the face value of the bonds at the maturity date.

4 Explain how bond discount or premium affects the cost of borrowing.

Bond discount as part of the cost of borrowing. In Chapter 10, we illustrated two ways in which interest charges can be specified in a note payable: the interest may be stated as an annual percentage rate of the face amount of the note, or it may be included in the face amount. Bonds issued at a discount include **both** types of interest charge. The $1,000,000 bond issue in our example calls for cash interest payments of $90,000 per year ($1,000,000 × 9% contract interest rate), payable semiannually. In addition to making the semiannual interest payments, the corporation must redeem the bond issue for $1 million on the maturity date. This maturity value is $20,000 greater than the $980,000 received when the bonds were issued. Thus, the $20,000 discount in the issue price may be regarded as an *interest charge included in the maturity value of the bonds.*

Although the interest charge represented by the discount will not be paid to bondholders until the bonds mature, the corporation benefits from this cost during the entire period that it has the use of the bondholders' money. Therefore, the cost represented by the discount should be allocated over the life of the bond issue. The process of allocating bond discount to interest expense is termed *amortization* of the discount.

In short, whenever bonds are issued at a discount, the total interest cost over the life of the bonds is equal to the total of the regular cash interest payments *plus the amount of the discount.* For the $1 million bond issue in our example, the total interest cost over the 10-year life of the bonds is $920,000, of which $900,000 represents the 20 semiannual cash interest payments and $20,000 represents the discount. The average annual interest expense, therefore, is $92,000 ($920,000 ÷ 10 years), consisting of $90,000 paid in cash and $2,000 amortization of the bond discount. This analysis is illustrated below:

Total cash interest payments to bondholders ($1,000,000 × 9% × 10 years)		$900,000
Add: Interest charge included in face amount of bonds:		
Maturity value of bonds...	$1,000,000	
Amount borrowed...	980,000	20,000
Total cost of borrowing over life of bond issue		$920,000
Average annual interest expense ($920,000 ÷ 10 years)		$ 92,000

Amortization of bond discount

5 Amortize bond
discount or
premium by the
straight-line and
effective interest
methods.

The simplest method of amortizing bond discount is the *straight-line method,* which allocates an equal portion of the discount to Bond Interest Expense in each period.[4] In our example, the Discount on Bonds Payable account has a beginning debit balance of $20,000; each year one-tenth of this amount, or $2,000, will be amortized into Bond Interest Expense. Assuming that the interest payment dates are June 30 and December 31, the entries to be made each six months to record bond interest expense are as follows:

Payment of bond
interest and
straight-line
amortization of
bond discount

Bond Interest Expense..	45,000	
Cash...		45,000
Paid semiannual interest on $1,000,000 of 9%, 10-year bonds.		

[4] An alternative method of amortization, called the *effective interest method,* is illustrated later in this chapter. Although the effective interest method is theoretically preferable to the straight-line method, the resulting differences generally are not material in dollar amount.

```
Bond Interest Expense.................................................  1,000
        Discount on Bonds Payable ........................................              1,000
Amortized discount for six months on 10-year bond issue ($20,000 discount × 1/20).
```

The two entries shown above to record the cash payment of bond interest and to record the amortization of bond discount can conveniently be combined into one compound entry, as follows:

```
Bond Interest Expense.................................................  46,000
        Cash.....................................................              45,000
        Discount on Bonds Payable ........................................              1,000
To record payment of semiannual interest on $1,000,000 of 9%, 10-year bonds
($1,000,000 × 9% × 1/2) and to amortize 1/20 of the discount on the 10-year bond
issue.
```

Regardless of whether the cash payment of interest and the amortization of bond discount are recorded in separate entries or combined in one entry, the amount recognized as Bond Interest Expense is the same — $46,000 each six months, or a total of $92,000 a year. An alternative accounting procedure that will produce the same results is to amortize the bond discount only at year-end rather than at each interest-payment date.

Note that the additional interest expense resulting from amortization of the discount does not require any additional cash payment. The credit portion of the entry is to the contra-liability account, Discount on Bonds Payable, rather than to the Cash account. Crediting this contra-liability account *increases the carrying value of bonds payable.* The original $20,000 discount will be completely written off by the end of the tenth year, and the net liability (carrying value) will be the full face value of the bonds.

Bonds sold at a premium

Bonds will sell above par if the contract rate of interest specified on the bonds is higher than the current market rate for bonds of this grade. Let us now change our basic illustration by assuming that the $1 million issue of 9%, 10-year bonds is sold at a price of 102 ($1,020 for each $1,000 bond). The entry is shown below:

Issuing bonds at premium

```
Cash....................................................... 1,020,000
        Bonds Payable.............................................              1,000,000
        Premium on Bonds Payable .................................              20,000
Issued $1,000,000 face value of 9%, 10-year bonds at price of 102.
```

If a balance sheet is prepared immediately following the sale of the bonds, the liability will be shown as follows:

Carrying value increased by premium

```
Long-term liabilities:
   9% bonds payable, due in 10 years ...........................  $1,000,000
   Add: Premium on bonds payable ...............................      20,000    $1,020,000
```

The amount of any unamortized premium is **added** to the maturity value of the bonds payable to show the current carrying value of the liability. Over the life of the bond issue, this carrying value will be reduced to the maturity value of $1,000,000.

Bond premium as reduction in the cost of borrowing. We have illustrated how issuing bonds at a discount increases the cost of borrowing above the amount of the regular cash interest payments. Issuing bonds at a premium, on the other hand, *reduces the cost of borrowing below the amount of the regular cash interest payments.*

The amount received from issuance of the bonds is $20,000 greater than the amount which must be repaid at maturity. This $20,000 premium is not a gain but is to be offset against the periodic interest payments in determining the net cost of borrowing. Whenever bonds are issued at a premium, the total interest cost over the life of the bonds is equal to the regular cash interest payments *minus the amount of the premium.* In our example, the total interest cost over the life of the bonds is computed as $900,000 of cash interest payments minus $20,000 of premium amortized, or a net borrowing cost of $880,000. The annual interest expense will be $88,000, consisting of $90,000 paid in cash less an offsetting $2,000 transferred from the Premium on Bonds Payable account to the credit side of the Bond Interest Expense account.

The semiannual entries on June 30 and December 31 to record the payment of bond interest and amortization of bond premium are as follows:

<table>
<tr><td rowspan="6">**Payment of bond interest and straight-line amortization of bond premium**</td><td>Bond Interest Expense...</td><td>45,000</td><td></td></tr>
<tr><td>   Cash...</td><td></td><td>45,000</td></tr>
<tr><td>Paid semiannual interest on $1,000,000 of 9%, 10-year bonds.</td><td></td><td></td></tr>
<tr><td></td><td></td><td></td></tr>
<tr><td>Premium on Bonds Payable...</td><td>1,000</td><td></td></tr>
<tr><td>   Bond Interest Expense ....</td><td></td><td>1,000</td></tr>
</table>

Amortized premium for six months on 10-year bond issue ($20,000 $\times$ $\frac{1}{20}$).

Year-end adjustments for bond interest expense

In the preceding illustration, it was assumed that one of the semiannual dates for payment of bond interest coincided with the end of the company's accounting year. In most cases, however, the semiannual interest payment dates will fall during an accounting period rather than on the last day of the year.

For purposes of illustration, assume that $1 million of 12%, 10-year bonds are issued at a price of 97 on October 1, 1989. Interest payment dates are April 1 and October 1. The total discount to be amortized amounts to $30,000, or $1,500 in each six-month interest period. The company keeps its accounts on a calendar-year basis; consequently, the adjusting entries shown below will be necessary at December 31 for the accrued interest and the amortization of discount applicable to the three-month period since the bonds were issued.

Bond Interest Expense.	30,750	
Bond Interest Payable.		30,000
Discount on Bonds Payable		750

To adjust for accrued interest on bonds and to amortize discount for period
from Oct. 1 to Dec. 31. Accrued interest: $1,000,000 \times .12 \times \frac{3}{12} = \$30,000$.
Amortization: $\$30,000 \times \frac{3}{120} = \$750$.

If the above bonds had been issued at a premium, similar entries would be made at the end of the period for any accrued interest and for amortization of premium for the fractional period from October 1 to December 31.

In the December 31 balance sheet, the $30,000 of accrued bond interest payable will appear as a current liability; the long-term liability for bonds payable will appear as follows:

Long-term liabilities:		
12% Bonds payable, due Oct. 1, 1999.	$1,000,000	
Less: Discount on bonds payable	29,250	$970,750

When the bonds were issued on October 1, the net liability for bonds payable was $970,000. Notice that the carrying value of the bonds has ***increased*** over the three months by the amount of discount amortized. When the entire discount has been amortized, the carrying value of the bonds will be $1,000,000, which is equal to their maturity value.

At April 1, 1990, it is necessary to record interest expense and discount amortization only for the three-month period since year-end. Of the semiannual $60,000 cash payment to bondholders, one-half, or $30,000, represents payment of the liability for bond interest payable recorded on December 31, 1989. The entry on April 1 is:

Bond Interest Expense.	30,750	
Bond Interest Payable.	30,000	
Discount on Bonds Payable		750
Cash.		60,000

To record bond interest expense and amortization of discount for three-month
period since year-end and to record semiannual payment to bondholders.

Straight-line amortization: a theoretical shortcoming

Although the straight-line method of amortizing bond discount or premium recognizes the full cost of borrowing over the life of a bond issue, the method has one conceptual weakness: the same dollar amount of interest expense is recognized each year. Amortizing a discount, however, causes a gradual increase in the liability for bonds payable; amortizing a premium causes a gradual decrease in the liability. If the uniform annual interest expense is expressed as a ***percentage*** of either an increasing or a decreasing liability, it appears that the borrower's cost of capital is changing over the life of the bonds.

This problem can be avoided by using the ***effective interest method*** of amortizing bond discount or premium. The effective interest method recognizes annual interest expense equal to a ***constant percentage of the carrying value of the related liability.*** This percentage is the effective rate of interest incurred by the borrower. For this reason, the effective interest method of amortization is considered theoretically preferable to the straight-line method. Whenever the two methods would produce ***materially different*** annual results, the Financial Accounting Standards Board requires the use of the effective interest method.

Over the life of the bonds, both amortization methods recognize the same total amount of interest expense. Even on an annual basis, the results produced by the two methods usually are very similar. Consequently, either method normally meets the requirements of the FASB. Because of its simplicity, the straight-line method is widely used despite the theoretical arguments favoring the effective interest method.

Effective interest method of amortization

When bonds are sold at a discount, the effective interest rate incurred by the issuing corporation is ***higher*** than the contract rate printed on the bonds. Conversely, when bonds are sold at a premium, the effective rate of interest is ***lower*** than the contract rate.

When the effective interest method is used, bond interest expense is determined by multiplying the ***carrying value of the bonds*** at the beginning of the period by the ***effective rate of interest*** for the bond issue. The amount of discount or premium to be amortized is the ***difference*** between the interest expense computed in this manner and the amount of interest paid (or payable) to bondholders for the period. The computation of effective interest expense and the amount of discount or premium amortization for the life of the bond issue is made in advance on a schedule called an ***amortization table.***

Sale of bonds at a discount. To illustrate the effective interest method, assume that on May 1 a corporation issues $1,000,000 face value, 9%, 10-year bonds with interest dates of November 1 and May 1. The bonds sell for $937,689, a price resulting in an effective interest rate of 10%.[5] An amortization table for this bond issue is shown at the top of the next page. (Amounts of interest expense have been rounded to the nearest dollar.)

This amortization table can be used to illustrate the concepts underlying the effective interest method of determining interest expense and discount amortiza-

---

[5] Computation of the exact effective interest rate involves mathematical techniques beyond the scope of this course. A very close estimate of the effective interest rate can be obtained by dividing the ***average*** annual interest expense by the ***average*** carrying value of the bonds. Computation of average annual interest expense was illustrated on page 430. The average carrying value of the bonds is found by adding the issue price and the maturity value of the bond issue and dividing this sum by 2. Applying these procedures to the bond issue in our example provides an estimated effective interest rate of 9.93%, computed [($900,000 interest + $62,311 discount) ÷ 10 years] divided by [($937,689 + $1,000,000) ÷ 2].

Amortization Table for Bonds Sold at a Discount
($1,000,000, 10-year bonds, 9% interest payable semiannually,
sold at $937,689 to yield 10% compounded semiannually)

Six-Month Interest Period	(A) Interest Paid Semiannually ($4\frac{1}{2}$% of Face Value)	(B) Effective Semiannual Interest Expense (5% of Bond Carrying Value)	(C) Discount Amortization (B − A)	(D) Bond Discount Balance	(E) Carrying Value of Bonds, End of Period ($1,000,000 − D)
Issue date				$62,311	$ 937,689
1	$45,000	$46,884	$1,884	60,427	939,573
2	45,000	46,979	1,979	58,448	941,552
3	45,000	47,078	2,078	56,370	943,630
4	45,000	47,182	2,182	54,188	945,812
5	45,000	47,291	2,291	51,897	948,103
6	45,000	47,405	2,405	49,492	950,508
7	45,000	47,525	2,525	46,967	953,033
8	45,000	47,652	2,652	44,315	955,685
9	45,000	47,784	2,784	41,531	958,469
10	45,000	47,923	2,923	38,608	961,392
11	45,000	48,070	3,070	35,538	964,462
12	45,000	48,223	3,223	32,315	967,685
13	45,000	48,384	3,384	28,931	971,069
14	45,000	48,553	3,553	25,378	974,622
15	45,000	48,731	3,731	21,647	978,353
16	45,000	48,918	3,918	17,729	982,271
17	45,000	49,114	4,114	13,615	986,385
18	45,000	49,319	4,319	9,296	990,704
19	45,000	49,535	4,535	4,761	995,239
20	45,000	49,761*	4,761	-0-	1,000,000

* In the last period, interest expense is equal to interest paid to bondholders plus the remaining balance on the bond discount. This compensates for the accumulated effects of rounding amounts.

tion. Note that the "interest periods" in the table are the **semiannual** (six-month) interest periods. Thus, the interest payments (column A), interest expense (column B), and discount amortization (column C) are for six-month periods. Similarly, the balance of the Discount on Bonds Payable account (column D) and the carrying value of the liability (column E) are shown as of each semiannual interest payment date.

The original issuance price of the bonds ($937,689) is entered at the top of column E. This represents the carrying value of the liability throughout the first six-month interest period. The semiannual interest payment, shown in column A, is $4\frac{1}{2}$% (one-half of the original contract rate) of the $1,000,000 face value of the bond issue. The semiannual cash interest payment does not change over the life of the bonds. The interest expense shown in column B, however, *changes every period.* This expense is always a *constant percentage* of the carrying value of the liability as of the end of the preceding period. The "constant percentage" is the effective interest rate of the bond issue. The bonds have an effective annual interest rate of 10%, indicating a semiannual rate of 5%. Thus, the effective interest expense for the first six-month period is $46,884 (5% of $937,689). The discount amortization for period 1 is the difference between this effective interest expense and the contract rate of interest paid to bondholders.

After the discount is reduced by $1,884 at the end of period 1, the carrying value of the bonds in column E *increases* by $1,884 (from $937,689 to $939,573). In period 2, the effective interest expense is determined by multiplying the effective semiannual interest rate of 5% by this new carrying value of $939,573 (5% × $939,573 = $46,979).

Semiannual interest expense may be recorded every period directly from the data in the amortization table. For example, the entry to record bond interest expense at the end of the first six-month period is:

Bond Interest Expense	46,884	
Discount on Bonds Payable		1,884
Cash		45,000

To record semiannual interest payment and amortize discount for six months.

Similarly, interest expense at the end of the *fifteenth* six-month period would be recorded by the following entry:

Bond Interest Expense	48,731	
Discount on Bonds Payable		3,731
Cash		45,000

To record semiannual interest payment and amortize discount for six months.

When bond discount is amortized, the carrying value of the liability for bonds payable *increases* every period toward the maturity value. Since the effective interest expense in each period is a constant percentage of this increasing carrying value, the interest expense also increases from one period to the next. This is the basic difference between the effective interest method and straight-line amortization.

Sale of bonds at a premium. Let us now change our illustration by assuming that the $1,000,000 issue of 9%, 10-year bonds is sold on May 1 at a price of $1,067,952, resulting in an effective interest rate of 8% annually (4% per six-month interest period). An amortization table for this bond issue follows:

In this amortization table, the interest expense for each six-month period is equal to 4% of the carrying value at the beginning of that period. This amount of interest expense is less than the amount of cash being paid to bondholders, illustrating that the effective interest rate is less than the contract rate.

Amortization Table for Bonds Sold at a Premium
($1,000,000, 10-year bonds, 9% interest payable semiannually,
sold at $1,067,952 to yield 8% compounded semiannually)

Six-Month Interest Period	(A) Interest Paid Semiannually ($4\frac{1}{2}$% of Face Value)	(B) Effective Semiannual Interest Expense (4% of Bond Carrying Value)	(C) Premium Amortization (A − B)	(D) Bond Premium Balance	(E) Carrying Value of Bonds, End of Period ($1,000,000 + D)
Issue date				$67,952	$1,067,952
1	$45,000	$42,718	$2,282	65,670	1,065,670
2	45,000	42,627	2,373	63,297	1,063,297
3	45,000	42,532	2,468	60,829	1,060,829
4	45,000	42,433	2,567	58,262	1,058,262
5	45,000	42,330	2,670	55,592	1,055,592
6	45,000	42,224	2,776	52,816	1,052,816
7	45,000	42,113	2,887	49,929	1,049,929
8	45,000	41,997	3,003	46,926	1,046,926
9	45,000	41,877	3,123	43,803	1,043,803
10	45,000	41,752	3,248	40,555	1,040,555
11	45,000	41,622	3,378	37,177	1,037,177
12	45,000	41,487	3,513	33,664	1,033,664
13	45,000	41,347	3,653	30,011	1,030,011
14	45,000	41,200	3,800	26,211	1,026,211
15	45,000	41,408	3,952	22,259	1,022,259
16	45,000	40,890	4,110	18,149	1,018,149
17	45,000	40,726	4,274	13,875	1,013,875
18	45,000	40,555	4,445	9,430	1,009,430
19	45,000	40,377	4,623	4,807	1,004,807
20	45,000	40,193*	4,807	-0-	1,000,000

* In the last period, interest expense is equal to interest paid to bondholders minus the remaining balance of the bond premium. This compensates for the accumulated effects of rounding amounts.

Based upon this amortization table, the entry to record the interest payment and amortization of the premium for the first six months of the bond issue is:

Amortization of premium decreases interest expense

Bond Interest Expense...	42,718	
Premium on Bonds Payable...	2,282	
Cash...		45,000

To record semiannual interest payment and amortization of premium.

As the carrying value of the liability declines, so does the amount recognized as bond interest expense.

Year-end adjusting entries. Since the amounts recognized as interest expense change from one period to the next, we must refer to the appropriate interest period in the amortization table to obtain the dollar amounts for use in year-end adjusting entries. To illustrate, consider our example of the bonds sold at a premium on May 1. The entry shown above records interest and amortization of the premium through November 1. If the company keeps its accounts on a calendar-year basis, two months' interest has accrued as of December 31, and the following adjusting entry is made at year-end:

<table>
<tr><td style="text-align:right">Year-end
adjustment</td><td>Bond Interest Expense . . . .</td><td style="text-align:right">14,209</td><td></td></tr>
<tr><td></td><td>Premium on Bonds Payable . . . .</td><td style="text-align:right">791</td><td></td></tr>
<tr><td></td><td>   Bond Interest Payable . . . .</td><td></td><td style="text-align:right">15,000</td></tr>
<tr><td></td><td colspan="3">To record two months' accrued interest and amortize one-third of the premium
for the interest period.</td></tr>
</table>

This adjusting entry covers one-third (two months) of the second interest period. Consequently, the amounts shown as bond interest expense and amortization of premium are *one-third* of the amounts shown in the amortization table for the second interest period. Similar adjusting entries must be made at the end of every accounting period while the bonds are outstanding. The dollar amounts of these adjusting entries will vary, however, because the amounts of interest expense and premium amortization change in every interest period. The amounts applicable to any given adjusting entry will be the appropriate fraction of the amounts for the interest period then in progress.

Following the year-end adjusting entry illustrated above, the interest expense and premium amortization on May 1 of the second year, are recorded as follows:

<table>
<tr><td style="text-align:right">Interest payment
following
year-end
adjustment</td><td>Bond Interest Expense . . . .</td><td style="text-align:right">28,418</td><td></td></tr>
<tr><td></td><td>Bond Interest Payable . . . .</td><td style="text-align:right">15,000</td><td></td></tr>
<tr><td></td><td>Premium on Bonds Payable . . . .</td><td style="text-align:right">1,582</td><td></td></tr>
<tr><td></td><td>   Cash . . . .</td><td></td><td style="text-align:right">45,000</td></tr>
<tr><td></td><td colspan="3">To record semiannual interest payment, a portion of which had been accrued,
and amortize remainder of premium applicable to interest period.</td></tr>
</table>

Retirement of bonds payable

Bonds are sometimes retired before the maturity date. The principal reason for retiring bonds early is to relieve the issuing corporation of the obligation to make future interest payments. If interest rates decline to the point that a corporation can borrow at an interest rate below that being paid on a particular bond issue, the corporation may benefit from retiring those bonds and issuing new bonds at a lower interest rate.

Most bond issues contain a call provision, permitting the corporation to redeem the bonds by paying a specified price, usually a few points above par. Even without a call provision, the corporation may retire its bonds before maturity by purchasing them in the open market. If the bonds can be purchased by the issuing corporation at less than their *carrying value,* a gain is realized on the retirement of the debt.

If the bonds are reacquired by the issuing corporation at a price in excess of their carrying value, a loss must be recognized. The FASB has ruled that these gains and losses, if *material* in amount, should be shown separately in the income statement as extraordinary items.[6]

For example, assume that the Briggs Corporation has outstanding a $1 million bond issue with unamortized premium in the amount of $20,000. The bonds are callable at 105 and the company exercises the call provision on 100 of the bonds, or 10% of the issue. The entry would be as follows:

Bonds called at price above carrying value

Bonds Payable..	100,000	
Premium on Bonds Payable...	2,000	
Loss on Retirement of Bonds	3,000	
Cash		105,000

To record retirement of $100,000 face value of bonds called at 105.

The carrying value of each of the 100 called bonds was $1,020, whereas the call price was $1,050. For each bond called the company incurred a loss of $30, or a total loss of $3,000. Note that when 10% of the total issue was called, 10% of the unamortized premium was written off.

If bonds remain outstanding until the maturity date, the discount or premium will have been completely amortized and the accounting entry to retire the bonds (assuming that interest is paid separately) will consist of a debit to Bonds Payable and a credit to Cash.

One year before the maturity date, the bonds payable should be reclassified from long-term debt to a current liability in the balance sheet if payment is to be made from current assets rather than from a *bond sinking fund.*

Bond sinking fund

To make a bond issue attractive to investors, corporations may agree to create a sinking fund, exclusively for use in paying the bonds at maturity. A bond sinking fund is created by setting aside a specified amount of cash at regular intervals. The cash is usually deposited with a trustee, who invests it and adds the earnings to the amount of the sinking fund. The periodic deposits of cash plus the earnings on the sinking fund investments should cause the fund to equal approximately the amount of the bond issue by the maturity date. When the bond issue approaches maturity, the trustee sells all the securities in the fund and uses the cash proceeds to pay the holders of the bonds. Any excess cash remaining in the fund will be returned to the corporation by the trustee.

A bond sinking fund is not included in current assets because it is not available for payment of current liabilities. The cash and securities comprising the fund are usually shown as a single amount under a caption such as Long-Term Investments, which is placed just below the current asset section. Interest earned on sinking fund securities constitutes revenue to the corporation.

[6] *FASB Statement No. 4,* "Reporting Gains and Losses from Extinguishment of Debt" (Stamford, Conn.: 1975).

Conversion of bonds payable into capital stock

Convertible bonds represent a popular form of financing, particularly during periods when capital stock prices are rising. The conversion feature gives bondholders an opportunity to profit from a rise in the market price of the issuing company's capital stock while still maintaining their status of creditors rather than stockholders. Because of this potential gain, convertible bonds generally carry lower interest rates than nonconvertible bonds.

The conversion ratio is typically set at a price above the current market price of the capital stock at the date the bonds are authorized. For example, if capital stock has a current market price of $42 a share, the **conversion price** might be set at $50 per share, thus enabling a holder of a $1,000 par value convertible bond to exchange the bond for 20 shares of capital stock.[7] Let us assume that $5 million of such bonds are issued at par, and that some time later when the capital stock has risen in price to $60 per share, the holders of 100 bonds decide to convert their bonds into capital stock. The conversion transaction would be recorded as follows:

Conversion of bonds into capital stock

Convertible Bonds Payable	100,000	
Capital Stock		100,000

To record the conversion of 100 bonds into 2,000 shares of capital stock.

No gain or loss is recognized by the issuing corporation upon conversion of bonds; the carrying value of the bonds is simply assigned to the capital stock issued in exchange.[8] If the bonds had been issued at a price above or below face value, the unamortized premium or discount relating to the bonds would be written off at the time of conversion in order to assign the carrying value of the bonds to the capital stock.

Conversion of bonds from the investor's viewpoint

Investors do not always convert their investment in convertible bonds into capital stock as soon as the market value of the capital stock they would receive rises above the $1,000 maturity value of their bonds. As the bonds easily can be converted into capital stock, their market value **rises right along** with that of the capital stock.

● **CASE IN POINT** ● Walgreen Co. has an outstanding issue of bonds payable in which each bond is convertible into 247.98 shares of the company's capital stock. Recently the company's capital stock was selling at $40 per share, indicating a market value for 247.98 shares of $9,919.20. The market value of the convertible bonds was quoted at 992, even though the bonds mature at a price of only 100 in 1991.

---

[7] $1,000 ÷ $50 conversion price = 20 shares of capital stock.

[8] Our illustrated entry assumes that the capital stock has neither a par value nor a stated value. If the capital stock had a designated par value, the entry would include a credit to an account entitled **Paid-in Capital in Excess of Par.** The concepts of par value and of paid-in capital in excess of par value are discussed in Chapter 12.

In fact, there may be several good reasons for **not** converting an investment in bonds into capital stock. First, the periodic interest payments received from the investment in bonds may exceed the dividends that would be received from the shares of capital stock into which the bonds could be converted. Second, an investment in bonds has less **downside risk** than an investment in capital stock. (The term "downside risk" means the threat of possible loss to the investor from a drop in market price.) Bonds ultimately mature and are redeemed by the issuing corporation at their maturity value (usually $1,000 per bond). Capital stock, on the other hand, has no maturity value. The price of a company's capital stock may decline dramatically even though the company is not in such financial difficulty that it might default upon its obligations to bondholders.

In conclusion, when are the owners of convertible bonds likely to exchange their bonds for shares of capital stock? The exchange point is reached when the dividends that would be received from the capital stock **exceed the interest payments** currently being received from the investment in bonds. When the capital stock dividends increase to this level, the bondholders can increase their cash receipts by converting their bonds into shares of capital stock.

LEASES

6 Explain the accounting treatment of operating leases and of capital leases.

A company may purchase the assets needed in its business operations or, as an alternative, it may lease them. A **lease** is a contract in which the lessor gives the lessee the right to use an asset for a specified period of time in exchange for periodic rental payments. The **lessor** is the owner of the property; the **lessee** is a tenant or renter. Examples of assets frequently acquired by lease include automobiles, building space, computers, and equipment.

Operating leases

When the lessor gives the lessee the right to use leased property for a limited period of time, but retains the usual risks and rewards of ownership, the contract is known as an **operating lease.** An example of an operating lease is a contract leasing office space in an office building. If the building increases in value, the **lessor** (owner) can receive the benefits of this increase by either selling the building or increasing the rental rate once the lease term has expired. On the other hand, if the building declines in value, the lessor bears the loss.

In accounting for an operating lease, the lessor views the monthly lease payments received as rental revenue, and the lessee regards these payments as rental expense. No asset or liability (other than a short-term liability for accrued rent payable) relating to the lease appears in the lessee's balance sheet. Thus, operating leases are sometimes termed **off-balance-sheet financing.**

Capital leases

Some lease contracts are intended to provide financing to the lessee for the eventual purchase of the property, or provide the lessee with use of the property over most of its useful life. These lease contracts are called **capital leases** (or financing leases). In contrast to an operating lease, a capital lease transfers most of the risks and rewards of ownership from the lessor to the **lessee.** Assume, for example, that City Realty leases a new automobile for a period of three years. Also assume that at the end of the lease, title to the automobile transfers to City Realty at no additional cost. Clearly, City Realty is not merely "renting" the use of the automobile; rather, it is using the lease agreement as a means of financing the purchase of the car.

From an accounting viewpoint, capital leases are regarded as **essentially equivalent to a sale** of the property by the lessor to the lessee, even though title to the leased property has not been transferred. Thus, a capital lease should be recorded by the lessor as a **sale** of property and by the lessee as a **purchase.** In such lease agreements, an appropriate interest charge usually is added to the regular sales price of the property in determining the amount of the lease payments.

Some companies frequently use capital lease agreements as a means of financing the sale of their products to customers. In accounting for merchandise "sold" through a capital lease, the lessor debits Lease Payments Receivable and credits Sales for an amount equal to the **present value of the future lease payments.**[9] In most cases, the present value of these future payments is equal to the regular sales price of the merchandise. In addition, the lessor transfers the cost of the leased merchandise from the Inventory account to the Cost of Goods Sold account (assuming a perpetual inventory system is in use). When lease payments are received, the lessor should recognize an appropriate portion of the payment as representing interest revenue and the remainder as a reduction in Lease Payments Receivable.

When equipment is acquired through a capital lease, the lessee should debit an asset account, Leased Equipment, and credit a liability account, Lease Payment Obligation, for the present value of the future lease payments. Lease payments made by the lessee are allocated between Interest Expense and a reduction in the liability, Lease Payment Obligation. No rent expense is involved. The asset account, Leased Equipment, is depreciated over the life of the equipment rather than the life of the lease. (The journal entries used in the accounting for a capital lease are illustrated in Appendix A.)

Distinguishing between capital leases and operating leases. The FASB requires that a lease which meets any one of the following criteria be accounted for as a capital lease.[10]

1 The lease transfers ownership of the property to the lessee at the end of the lease term.

---

[9] We have elected to record the present value of the future lease payments by a single debit entry to Lease Payments Receivable. An alternative is to debit Lease Payments Receivable for the total amount of the future payments and to credit Discount on Lease Payments Receivable, a contra-asset account, for the unearned finance charges included in the contractual amount. Either approach results in the lessor recording a net receivable equal to the present value of the future lease payments.

[10] *FASB Statement No. 13,* "Accounting for Leases" (Stamford, Conn.: 1976), pp. 9–10.

2 The lease contains a "bargain purchase option."

3 The lease term is equal to 75% or more of the estimated economic life of the leased property.

4 The present value of the minimum lease payments amounts to 90% or more of the fair value of the leased property.

Only those leases which meet **none** of the above criteria may be accounted for as operating leases.

OTHER LONG-TERM LIABILITIES

Mortgage notes payable

Purchases of real estate and certain types of equipment often are financed by the issuance of mortgage notes payable. When a mortgage note is issued, the borrower pledges title to specific assets as collateral for the loan. If the borrower defaults on the note, the lender may foreclose upon these assets. Mortgage notes usually are payable in equal monthly installments. These monthly installments may continue until the loan is completely repaid, or the note may contain a "due date" at which the remaining unpaid balance of the loan must be repaid in a single, lump-sum payment.

A portion of each monthly payment represents interest on the unpaid balance of the loan and the remainder of the monthly payment reduces the amount of the liability (Mortgage Payable). Since the liability is being **reduced each month,** the portion of each successive payment representing interest will **decrease,** and the portion of the payment going toward repayment of the liability will **increase.** To illustrate, assume that on June 30 a company issues a $100,000 mortgage note to finance the purchase of a warehouse. The note bears interest at the annual rate of 12% (or 1% per month) and will be paid in monthly installments of $1,201 over a period of 15 years. The following partial amortization table shows the allocation of the first three monthly payments between interest and principal (amounts are rounded to the nearest dollar):

	Payment Date	(A) Monthly Payment	(B) Monthly Interest Expense (1% of Unpaid Balance)	(C) Reduction in Mortgage Payable (A − B)	(D) Balance of Mortgage Payable
Monthly pay-	June 30 — Issue date				$100,000
ments on a	July 31	$1,201	$1,000	$201	99,799
mortgage note	Aug. 31	1,201	998	203	99,596
	Sept. 30	1,201	996	205	99,391

The entry to record the first monthly mortgage payment on July 31 would be:

Payment is allocated between interest and principal

Interest Expense	1,000	
Mortgage Payable	201	
Cash		1,201

To record interest expense and reduction in principal included in July 31 mortgage payment.

That portion of the mortgage which will be paid off within one year (the sum of column C for the next 12 months) should be classified in the balance sheet as a *current liability*. The caption used for this current liability may be "Current Portion of Long-Term Debt." The remaining balance of the mortgage payable should appear as a long-term liability.

Pension plan

A pension plan is a contract between a company and its employees under which the company agrees to pay retirement benefits to eligible employees. An employer company usually meets its obligations under a pension plan by making regular payments into a *pension fund* managed by a *trustee.* This type of arrangement is called a *funded pension plan.*

The employer's payments to the trustee are recorded by a debit to Pension Expense and a credit to Cash. The trustee invests the money received and assumes responsibility for paying benefits to retired employees. If an appropriate balance is maintained in the pension fund, *no liability need appear* in the employer's balance sheet.

There are a number of complex accounting issues relating to pension plans. These issues will be discussed in more advanced accounting courses.

END-OF-CHAPTER REVIEW

Summary of learning objectives

1 Describe the typical characteristics of corporate bonds.

Corporate bonds are transferrable long-term notes payable. Each bond usually has a face amount of $1,000 (or a multiple of $1,000), receives interest payments semiannually, and must be redeemed at its face amount at a specified maturity date. By issuing thousands of bonds at one time, the corporation is able to borrow millions of dollars from many different investors.

2 Explain the tax advantage of raising capital by issuing bonds instead of stock.

The principal advantage of issuing bonds rather than stock is that interest payments to bondholders are *deductible for income tax purposes,* whereas dividends to stockholders are not.

3 Discuss the relationship between interest rates and bond prices.

Prices of outstanding bonds vary inversely with interest rates. As interest rates rise, prices of existing bonds fall. Conversely, as interest rates fall, bond prices rise.

4 Explain how bond discount or premium affects the cost of borrowing.

When bonds are issued at a discount, the maturity value of the bonds will exceed the amount originally borrowed. Thus, the discount may be viewed as an interest charge included in the maturity value of the bonds. Amortization of this discount over the life of the bond issue *increases* periodic interest expense. When bonds are issued at a premium, the maturity value of the bonds will be less than the amount originally borrowed. Thus, amortization of bond premium *reduces* the periodic interest expense.

5 Amortize bond discount or premium by the straight-line and effective interest methods.

When the straight-line method is used, an *equal portion* of discount or premium is amortized each period. When the effective interest method is used, bond interest expense is computed by multiplying the carrying value of the bonds by the *effective interest rate.* The amount of discount or premium amortized is the *difference* between the interest expense computed in this manner and the amount of interest paid to bondholders.

6 Explain the accounting treatment of operating leases and of capital leases.

Operating leases are essentially rental agreements; the lessor recognizes rental revenue and the lessee recognizes rent expense. Capital leases, on the other hand, are treated by the lessor as a sale of the related asset and by the lessee as a purchase.

Key terms introduced or emphasized in chapter 11

Amortization of discount or premium on bonds payable. The process of systematically writing off a portion of bond discount to increase interest expense or writing off a portion of bond premium to decrease interest expense each period the bonds are outstanding.

Bond sinking fund. Cash set aside by the corporation at regular intervals (usually with a trustee) to be used to pay the bonds at maturity.

Capital lease. A lease contract which, in essence, finances the eventual purchase by the lessee of leased property. The lessor accounts for a capital lease as a sale of property; the lessee records an asset and a liability equal to the present value of the future lease payments. Also called a *financing lease.*

Contract interest rate. The contractual rate of interest printed on bonds. The contract interest rate, applied to the face value of the bonds, determines the amount of the annual cash interest payments to bondholders. Also called the *nominal interest rate.*

Convertible bond. A bond which may be exchanged (at the bondholders' option) for a specified number of shares of the company's capital stock.

Discount on bonds payable. Amount by which the face amount of the bond exceeds the price received by the corporation at the date of issuance. Indicates that the contractual rate of interest is lower than the market rate of interest.

Effective interest method of amortization. A method of amortizing bond discount or premium which causes bond interest expense to be a constant percentage of the carrying value of the liability.

Effective interest rate. The actual rate of interest expense to the borrowing corporation, taking into account the contractual cash interest payments and the discount or premium to be amortized.

Lessee. The tenant, user, or renter of leased property.

Lessor. The owner of property leased to a lessee.

Off-balance-sheet financing. An arrangement in which the use of resources is financed without the obligation for future payments appearing as a liability in the balance sheet. An operating lease is a common example of off-balance-sheet financing.

Operating lease. A lease contract which is in essence a rental agreement. The lessee has the use of the leased property, but the lessor retains the usual risks and rewards of ownership. The periodic lease payments are accounted for as rent expense by the lessee and as rental revenue by the lessor.

Pension fund. A fund managed by an independent trustee into which an employer company makes periodic payments. The fund is used for the purpose of paying retirement benefits to company employees.

Premium on bonds payable. Amount by which the issuance price of a bond exceeds the face value. Indicates that the contractual rate of interest is higher than the market rate.

Present value of a future amount. The amount of money that an informed investor would pay today for the right to receive the future amount, based upon a specific rate of return required by the investor.

Underwriter. An investment banking firm which handles the sale to investors of a corporation's issue of bonds payable or of capital stock.

Demonstration problem

On June 30, 1990, Laser Graphics issued $4,000,000 face value of 10-year, $9\frac{1}{2}\%$ bonds payable at a price of $103\frac{1}{4}$, resulting in an effective annual rate of interest of 9%. The semiannual interest payment dates are June 30 and December 31, and the bonds mature on June 30, 2000. The company maintains its accounts on a calendar-year basis and amortizes bond premium by the effective interest method.

Instructions

a Prepare the required journal entries (with explanations) on:
  (1) June 30, 1990, to record the sale of the bonds.
  (2) December 31, 1990, for payment of interest and amortization of premium on bonds. (Use one compound entry.)
  (3) June 30, 2000 for payment of interest, amortization of the remaining premium, and to retire the bonds. Assume that the carrying value of the bonds at the beginning of this last six-month interest period is $4,009,569.

b Show how the accounts, Bonds Payable and Premium on Bonds Payable, would appear on the balance sheet at December 31, 1990.

Solution to demonstration problem

a   **General Journal**

(1)
1990

June 30	Cash	4,130,000	
	Bonds Payable		4,000,000
	Premium on Bonds Payable....................		130,000
	To record sale of $9\frac{1}{2}\%$, 10-year bonds at $103\frac{1}{4}$.		

(2)

Dec. 31	Bond Interest Expense	185,850	
	Premium on Bonds Payable	4,150	
	Cash..		190,000

To record semiannual interest payment and amortize premium:

Interest payment ($4,000,000 × $9\frac{1}{2}$% × $\frac{1}{2}$)....$190,000

Interest expense ($4,130,000 × 9% × $\frac{1}{2}$)......185,850

Premium amortization ....$ 4,150

(3)

2000

June 30	Bond Interest Expense	180,431	
	Premium on Bonds Payable	9,569	
	Cash..		190,000

To record semiannual interest payment and amortize remaining balance of premium ($4,009,569 − $4,000,000 = $9,569).

30	Bonds Payable	4,000,000	
	Cash..		4,000,000

To retire bonds on maturity date.

b

LASER GRAPHICS
Partial Balance Sheet
December 31, 1990

Long-term liabilities:

$9\frac{1}{2}$% bonds payable, due June 30, 2000	$4,000,000	
Add: Premium on bonds payable	125,850	$4,125,850

ASSIGNMENT MATERIAL

Review questions

1 Distinguish between the two terms in each of the following pairs:
   a Mortgage bond; debenture bond
   b Contract (or nominal) interest rate; effective interest rate
   c Callable bond; convertible bond
   d Coupon bond; registered bond

2 K Company has decided to finance expansion by issuing $10 million of 20-year debenture bonds and will ask a number of underwriters to bid on the bond issue. Discuss the factors that will determine the amount bid by the underwriters for these bonds.

3 Briefly explain the income tax advantage of raising capital by issuing bonds rather than by selling capital stock.

4 Bell Company pays federal income taxes at a rate of 30% on taxable income. Compute the company's annual after-tax cost of borrowing on a 10%, $5 million bond issue. Express this after-tax cost as a percentage of the borrowed $5 million.

5 The following excerpt is taken from an article in a leading business periodical: "In the bond market high interest rates mean low prices. Bonds pay out a fixed percentage of their face value, usually $1,000; an 8% bond, for instance, will pay $80 a year. In order for its yield to rise to 10%, its price would have to drop to $800." Give a critical evaluation of this quotation.

6 Discuss the advantages and disadvantages of a *call provision* in a bond contract from the viewpoint of (a) the bondholder and (b) the issuing corporation.

7 Some bonds now being bought and sold by investors on organized securities exchanges were issued when interest rates were much lower than they are today. Would you expect these bonds to be trading at prices above or below their face values? Explain.

8 The 6% bonds of Central Gas & Electric are selling at a market price of 72, whereas the 6% bonds of Interstate Power are selling at a price of 97. Does this mean that Interstate Power has a better credit rating than Central Gas & Electric? Explain. (Assume current long-term interest rates are in the 11 to 13% range.)

9 Explain why the effective rate of interest differs from the contract rate when bonds are issued (a) at a discount and (b) at a premium.

10 When the effective interest method is used to amortize bond discount or premium, the amount of bond interest expense will differ in each period from that of the preceding period. Explain how the amount of bond interest expense changes from one period to another when the bonds are issued (a) at a discount and (b) at a premium.

11 Explain why the effective interest method of amortizing bond discount or premium is considered to be theoretically preferable to the straight-line method.

12 What is a *convertible bond?* Discuss the advantages and disadvantages of convertible bonds from the standpoint of (a) the investor and (b) the issuing corporation.

13 What situation or condition is most likely to cause the holders of convertible bonds to convert their bonds into shares of common stock? (Do not assume that the bonds have been called or that they are about to mature.)

14 Explain how the lessee accounts for an operating lease and capital lease. Why is an operating lease sometimes called *off-balance-sheet financing?*

15 A friend of yours has just purchased a house and has incurred a $50,000, 11% mortgage, payable at $476.17 per month. After making the first monthly payment, he received a receipt from the bank stating that only $17.84 of the $476.17 had been applied to reducing the principal amount of the loan. Your friend computes that at the rate of $17.84 per month, it will take over 233 years to pay off the $50,000 mortgage. Do you agree with your friend's analysis? Explain.

16 Ortega Industries has a fully funded pension plan. Each year, pension expense runs in excess of $10 million. At the present time, employees are entitled to receive pension benefits with a present value of $125 million. Explain what liability, if any, Ortega Industries should include in its balance sheet as a result of this pension plan.

Exercises

Exercise 11-1
Accounting terminology

Listed below are nine technical accounting terms introduced in this chapter:

Amortization of bond discount	**Amortization of bond premium**	**Effective interest method of amortization**
Capital lease	**Present value**	**Effective interest rate**
Operating lease	**Debenture**	**Contract interest rate**

Each of the following statements may (or may not) describe one of these technical terms. For each statement, indicate the accounting term described, or answer "None" if the statement does not correctly describe any of the terms.

    a The interest rate which determines the dollar amount of the semiannual payments to bondholders.

    b A lease which requires the lessee to record both a depreciable asset and a long-term liability.

    c The amount that a knowledgeable investor would pay today for the right to receive a given amount of cash at a given future date. Always *less* than the future amount.

    d The going market rate of interest at the time that bonds are issued.

    e A bond in which past interest payments are in default.

    f A lease agreement which does not require the lessee to include any long-term lease payment obligation in its balance sheet.

    g An adjusting entry which reduces the amount of semiannual interest expense below the amount of the semiannual cash payment to bondholders.

    h Amortizing bond discount or premium in a manner that causes the amount of interest expense to remain the same in every period in which bonds are outstanding.

Exercise 11-2
Bond interest
(bonds issued at par)

On March 31, Wayne Corporation received authorization to issue $50,000,000 of 12%, 30-year debenture bonds. Interest payment dates were March 31 and September 30. The bonds were all issued at par on May 31, two months after the interest date printed on the bonds.

Instructions

    a Prepare the journal entry at May 31, to record the sale of the bonds.

    b Prepare the journal entry at September 30, to record the semiannual bond interest payment.

    c Prepare the adjusting entry at December 31, to record bond interest accrued since September 30.

Exercise 11-3
Amortizing
bond/discount
and premium:
straight-line
method

North Company issued $40 million of 11%, 10-year bonds on January 1. Interest is payable semiannually on June 30 and December 31. The bonds were sold to an underwriting group at 105.

South Company issued $40 million of 10%, 10-year bonds on January 1. Interest is payable semiannually on June 30 and December 31. The bonds were sold to an underwriting group at 95.

Prepare journal entries to record all transactions during the year for (a) the North Company bond issue and (b) the South Company bond issue. Assume that both companies amortize bond discount or premium by the straight-line method at each interest payment date.

Exercise 11-4
Basic entries for
a bond issue:
issuance, interest
payment, and
retirement

La Paloma issued $10,000,000 of 15-year, $10\frac{1}{2}$% bonds on July 1, 1990, at $98\frac{1}{2}$. Interest is due on June 30 and December 31 of each year, and the bonds mature on June 30, 2005. The fiscal year ends on December 31; bond discount is amortized by the straight-line method. Prepare the following journal entries:

    a July 1, 1990, to record the issuance of the bonds.

    b December 31, 1990, to pay interest and amortize the bond discount (make two entries).

    c June 30, 2005, to pay interest, amortize the bond discount, and retire the bonds at maturity (make three entries).

Exercise 11-5
Partial retire-
ment of a bond
issue

The following liability appears on the balance sheet of the Sunrise Company on December 31, 1990 (notice that the bonds mature in 15 years):

Long-term liabilities:

Bonds payable, 11%, due Dec. 31, 2005	$20,000,000	
Premium on bonds payable	420,000	$20,420,000

On January 1, 1991, 25% of the bonds are retired at 98. Interest had been paid on December 31, 1990.

a Record the retirement of $5,000,000 of bonds on January 1, 1991.
b Record the interest payment for the six months ending December 31, 1991, and the amortization of the premium on December 31, 1991, assuming that amortization is recorded by the straight-line method *only at the end of each year.*

Exercise 11-6
Amortizing bond
discount:
effective interest
method

On April 1, Basin Corporation issued $1,000,000 of 10-year, 9% bonds payable and received proceeds of $937,689, resulting in an effective interest rate of 10%. Interest is payable on September 30 and March 31. The effective interest method is used to amortize bond discount; an amortization table for this bond issue is illustrated on page 435.

Instructions. Prepare the necessary journal entries (rounding all amounts to the nearest dollar) on:

a April 1, to record the issuance of the bonds
b September 30, to record the payment of interest and amortization of discount at the first semiannual interest payment date
c December 31, to accrue bond interest expense through year-end
d March 31, to record the payment of interest and amortization of bond discount at the second semiannual interest payment date

Exercise 11-7
Using an amorti-
zation table

Crown Point Corporation issued on the authorization date $1,000,000 of 10-year, 9% bonds payable and received proceeds of $1,067,952, resulting in an effective interest rate of 8%. The premium is amortized by the effective interest method; the amortization table for this bond issue is illustrated on page 437. Interest is payable semiannually.

Instructions

a Show how the liability for the bonds would appear on a balance sheet prepared immediately after issuance of the bonds.
b Show how the liability for the bonds would appear on a balance sheet prepared after 14 semiannual interest periods (three years prior to maturity).
c Show the necessary calculations to determine interest expense by the effective interest method for the *second* six-month period, the premium amortized at the end of that second period, and the cash interest payment. Your calculations should include use of the effective interest rate and also the contractual rate. Round all amounts to the nearest dollar.

Exercise 11-8
Conversion of
bonds into capital
stock

Brand Corporation issued $5,000,000 of 7%, 10-year convertible bonds dated December 31, at a price of 98. Semiannual interest payment dates were June 30 and December 31. The conversion rate was 20 shares of $1 par common stock for each $1,000 bond. Four years later on December 31, bondholders converted $2,000,000 face value of bonds into common stock. Assume that unamortized discount on this date amounted to $60,000 for the entire bond issue. Prepare a journal entry to record the conversion of the bonds.

Problems

Problem 11-1
Bond interest
(bonds issued at
par)

Texas Bus & Tractor Co. obtained authorization to issue $12,000,000 face value of 10% 20-year bonds, dated April 30, 1990. Interest payment dates were October 31 and April 30. Issuance of the bonds did not take place until July 31, 1990. On this date all the bonds were sold at a price of 100 plus three months' accrued interest.

Instructions. Prepare the necessary entries in general journal form on:

    a July 31, 1990, to record the issuance of the bonds
    b October 31, 1990, to record the first semiannual interest payment on the bond issue
    c December 31, 1990, to accrue bond interest expense through year-end
    d April 30, 1991, to record the second semiannual interest payment

Problem 11-2
Amortizing bond
discount and
premium:
straight-line
method

On September 1, 1990, American Farm Equipment issued $9 million in 9% debenture bonds. Interest is payable semiannually on March 1 and September 1, and the bonds mature in 10 years. Company policy is to amortize bond discount or premium by the straight-line method at each interest payment date; the company's fiscal year ends at December 31.

Instructions

    a Make the necessary adjusting entries at December 31, 1990, and the journal entry to record the payment of bond interest on March 1, 1991, under each of the following assumptions:
        (1) The bonds were issued at 98.
        (2) The bonds were issued at 103.
    b Compute the net bond liability at December 31, 1990, under assumptions (1) and (2) above.

Problem 11-3
Comprehensive
problem:
straight-line
amortization

Country Recording Studios obtained the necessary approvals to issue $6 million of 10%, 10-year bonds, dated March 1, 1989. Interest payment dates were September 1 and March 1. Issuance of the bonds did not occur until June 1, 1989. On this date, the entire bond issue was sold to an underwriter at a price which included three months' accrued interest. Country Recording Studios follows the policy of amortizing bond discount or premium by the straight-line method at each interest date as well as for year-end adjusting entries at December 31.

Instructions

    a Prepare all journal entries necessary to record the issuance of the bonds and bond interest expense during 1989, assuming that the sales price of the bonds on June 1 was $6,618,000, including accrued interest. (Note that the bonds will be outstanding for a period of only *9 years and 9 months.*)
    b Assume that the sales price of the bonds on June 1 had been $5,799,000, including accrued interest. Prepare journal entries for 1989 parallel to those in part a above.
    c Show the proper balance sheet presentation of the liability for bonds payable (including accrued interest) in the balance sheet prepared at December 31, *1993,* assuming that the original sales price of the bonds (including accrued interest) had been:
        (1) $6,618,000, as described in part a
        (2) $5,799,000, as described in part b

Problem 11-4
Effective interest
method: bonds
issued at discount

Arcades R Fun maintains its accounts on a calendar-year basis. On June 30, 1990, the company issued $6,000,000 face value of 7.6% bonds at a price of 97¼, resulting in an effective rate of interest of 8%. Semiannual interest payment dates are June 30 and December 31. Bond discount is amortized by the effective interest method. The bonds mature on June 30, 2000.

Instructions

a Prepare the required journal entries on:

(1) June 30, 1990, to record the sale of the bonds.

(2) December 31, 1990, to pay interest and amortize the discount using the effective interest method.

(3) June 30, 2000, to pay interest, amortize the discount, and retire the bonds. Assume that at the beginning of this last interest period, the carrying value of the bonds is $5,988,462. (Use a separate journal entry to show the retirement of the bonds.)

b Show how the accounts, Bonds Payable and Discount on Bonds Payable, should appear on the balance sheet at December 31, 1990.

Problem 11-5
Preparing and using an amortization table

On December 31, 1989, Glenview Hospital sold a $10,000,000 face value, 10%, 10-year bond issue to an underwriter at a price of 94. This price results in an effective annual interest rate of 11%. Interest is payable semiannually on June 30 and December 31. Glenview Hospital amortizes bond discount by the effective interest method.

Instructions

a Prepare an amortization table for the first two years (four interest periods) of this bond issue. Round all amounts to the nearest dollar and use the following column headings for your table:

Six-Month Interest Period	(A) Interest Paid Semi-Annually ($10,000,000 × 5%)	(B) Effective Semi-Annual Interest Expense (Carrying Value × 5½%)	(C) Discount Amortization (B − A)	(D) Bond Discount Balance	(E) Carrying Value of Bonds, End of Period ($10,000,000 − D)

b Using the information from your amortization table, prepare all journal entries necessary to record issuance of the bonds and bond interest for 1990. (Use a compound entry for interest payment and amortization of bond discount at each semiannual interest payment date.)

c Show the proper balance sheet presentation of Bonds Payable and Discount on Bonds Payable at December 31, 1991.

Problem 11-6
Preparing and using an amortization table

On December 31, 1989, Roadside Inns sold an $8,000,000, 9½%, 12-year bond issue to an underwriter at a price of 103¼. This price results in an effective annual interest rate of 9%. The bonds were dated December 31, and the interest payment dates were June 30 and December 31. Roadside Inns follows a policy of amortizing the bond premium by the effective interest method at each semiannual payment date.

Instructions

a Prepare an amortization table for the first two years (four interest periods) of the life of this bond issue. Round all amounts to the nearest dollar and use the following column headings:

Six-Month Interest Period	(A) Interest Paid Semi-Annually ($8,000,000 × 4¾%)	(B) Effective Semi-Annual Interest Expense (Carrying Value × 4½%)	(C) Premium Amortization (A − B)	(D) Bond Premium Balance	(E) Carrying Value of Bonds, End of Period ($8,000,000 + D)

b Using the information in your amortization table, prepare all journal entries necessary to record the issuance of bonds and the bond interest expense during 1990.

c Show the proper balance sheet presentation of the liability for bonds payable at December 31, 1991.

Problem 11-7
Comprehensive
problem: effec-
tive interest
method

Crescent Bay Gas & Electric, on September 1, 1990, issued $9,000,000 par value, $8\frac{1}{2}\%$, 10-year bonds payable with interest dates of March 1 and September 1. The company maintains its accounts on a calendar-year basis and follows the policy of amortizing bond discount and bond premium by the effective interest method at the semiannual interest payment dates as well as at the year-end adjusting of the accounts.

Instructions

a Prepare the necessary journal entries to record the following transactions, assuming that the bonds were sold for $8,700,000, a price resulting in an effective annual interest rate of 9%.

(1) Sale of the bonds on September 1, 1990.

(2) Adjustment of the accounts at December 31, 1990, for accrued interest and amortization of a discount.

(3) Payment of bond interest and amortization of discount on March 1, 1991.

b Assume that the sales price of the bonds on September 1, 1990, had been $9,300,000, resulting in an effective annual interest rate of 8%. Prepare journal entries parallel to those called for in a above at the dates of September 1, 1990; December 31, 1990; and March 1, 1991.

c State the amounts of bond interest expense for 1990 and the **net** amount of the liability for the bonds payable at December 31, 1990, under the independent assumptions set forth in both a and b above. Show your computations.

Problem 11-8
Capital leases: a
comprehensive
problem

Custom Truck Builders frequently uses long-term lease contracts to finance the sale of its trucks. On November 1, 19__, Custom Truck Builders leased to Interstate Van Lines a truck carried in the perpetual inventory records at $33,520. The terms of the lease call for Interstate Van Lines to make 36 monthly payments of $1,400 each, beginning on November 30, 19__. The present value of these payments, after considering a built-in interest charge of 1% per month, is equal to the regular $42,150 sales price of the truck. At the end of the 36-month lease, title to the truck will transfer to Interstate Van Lines.

Instructions

a Prepare journal entries in the accounts of Custom Truck Builders on:

(1) November 1 to record the sale financed by the lease and the related cost of goods sold. (Debit Lease Payments Receivable for the $42,150 present value of the future lease payments.)

(2) November 30, to record receipt of the first $1,400 monthly payment. (Prepare a compound journal entry which allocates the cash receipt between interest revenue and reduction of Lease Payments Receivable. The portion of each monthly payment recognized as interest revenue is equal to 1% of the balance of the account Lease Payments Receivable, at the beginning of that month. Round all interest computations to the nearest dollar.)

(3) December 31, to record receipt of the second monthly payment.

b Prepare journal entries for 19__ in the accounts of Interstate Van Lines on:

(1) November 1, to record acquisition of the leased truck.

(2) November 30, to record the first monthly lease payment. (Determine the portion of the payment representing interest expense in a manner parallel to that described in part a.)

(3) December 31, to record the second monthly lease payment.

(4) December 31, to recognize depreciation on the leased truck through year-end. Compute depreciation expense by the straight-line method, using a 10-year service life and an estimated salvage value of $6,150.

c Compute the net carrying value of the leased truck in the balance sheet of Interstate Van Lines at December 31, 19__.

d Compute the amount of Interstate $\overline{V}$an Lines' lease payment obligation at December 31, 19__.

Business decision cases

**Case 11-1
Convertible
bonds: the
investor's per-
spective**

In April of a recent year, the convertible $8\frac{1}{4}$% bonds of Joseph E. Seagram & Sons, Limited, were selling at a quoted market price of 118. Each $1,000 bond was convertible into 26.49 shares of Seagram Co. Ltd. common stock, which was selling at a price of $41 per share. The common stock pays a cash dividend of $0.80 per share.

Instructions. Assume that you own 100 of Seagram's convertible bonds ($100,000 face value, in total). Under the conditions described above, would it be profitable for you to convert your 100 bonds into 2,649 shares of the company's common stock? Explain the reasons for your answer.

**Case 11-2
Accounting for
leases**

At the beginning of the current year, Cable TV entered into the two long-term lease agreements described below:

Building lease. Leased from Lamden Properties the use of an office building for a period of five years. The monthly lease payments are based upon the square footage of the building and increase by 5% each year. The estimated useful life of the building is 40 years.

Satellite lease. Leased from SpaceNet, Inc., the use of a communications satellite for a period of five years. The monthly payments are intended to pay SpaceNet the current sales price of the satellite, plus a reasonable charge for interest. At the end of the lease, ownership of the satellite will transfer to Cable TV at no additional cost. The estimated useful life of the satellite is 15 years.

Instructions. Answer each of the following questions as they relate to the building lease. After answering all four questions, answer them again as they relate to the satellite lease.

a Is this agreement an operating lease or a capital lease? Why?

b Will this lease result in any assets or liabilities being included in Cable TV's future balance sheets? If so, identify these assets and liabilities.

c Indicate the nature of any expenses that will appear in Cable TV's future income statements as a result of the lease, and indicate the number of years for which the expense will be incurred.

d Briefly explain how the *lessor* should account for this lease agreement, including the receipt of future lease payments. Indicate whether the lessor should recognize depreciation on the leased asset.

Chapter 12
Ownership equity:
single proprietorships,
partnerships, and corporations

CHAPTER PREVIEW

Chapter 12 compares and contrasts the three most common forms of business organization—single proprietorships, partnerships, and corporations. We stress the basic characteristics of each form of organization, and the accounting for transactions between the business and its owners. Attention also is focused upon the problem of dividing partnership net income among the partners. The remainder of the chapter emphasizes the nature of corporations and the various elements of stockholders' equity. The concept of par value is explained, and the issuance of capital stock at a price above par is illustrated. Preferred stock is contrasted with common stock. Other topics include stock issued for assets other than cash, conversion of preferred stock into common, donated capital, and subscriptions to capital stock.

After studying
this chapter
you should be
able to meet
these Learning
Objectives:

1 Explain how the accounts and the financial statements of a single proprietorship differ from those of a corporation.
2 Describe the basic characteristics of a partnership.
3 Account for the formation of a partnership.
4 Divide the net income of a partnership in accordance with the partnership contract.
5 Discuss the advantages and disadvantages of organizing a business as a corporation.
6 Explain the rights of stockholders and the role of corporate directors and officers.
7 Account for the issuance of capital stock in exchange for cash or other assets.
8 Discuss the features of preferred stock and of common stock.
9 Account for subscriptions to capital stock and for donated capital.

Assume that you are planning to start a new business. How would you choose the form of business organization? Most people choose a single proprietorship—this simple form of business unit is far more numerous than partnerships or corporations. In a recent year the federal Bureau of the Census reported the existence of more than 12 million single proprietorships, compared with less than 3 million corporations, and something over 1 million partnerships. The popularity of the single proprietorship is explained in large part by the ease and relatively low cost of its formation.

The other side of the coin is that almost every *large* business is a corporation. In recent years the annual revenue of General Motors has exceeded $100 billion, Exxon has reported revenue over $80 billion, and IBM over $50 billion. The revenue of the 10 largest companies exceeds the combined revenue of all the country's 12 million single proprietorships. Thus, in appraising the structure and size of our economy, we can say that the corporation is clearly the dominant form of business organization.

SINGLE PROPRIETORSHIPS

1 Explain how the accounts and the financial statements of a single proprietorship differ from those of a corporation.

Any unincorporated business owned by one person is called a single proprietorship. This form of organization is common among small retail stores, farms, service businesses, and professional practices. Most of these businesses, however, tend to be relatively small.

An important characteristic of the single proprietorship is that, from a *legal* viewpoint, the business and its owner are not regarded as separate entities. Thus, the owner is *personally liable* for the debts of the business. If the business becomes insolvent, creditors can force the owner to sell his or her personal assets to pay the business debts.

From an accounting viewpoint, however, a single proprietorship is regarded as an entity *separate from the other affairs of its owner.* For example, assume that Jill Green owns two single proprietorships—a gas station and a shoe store. The assets, liabilities, revenue, and expenses relating to the gas station would not appear in the financial statements of the shoe store. Also, Green's personal assets, such as her house, furniture, and savings account, would not appear in the financial statements of either business entity.

Accounting for the owner's equity in a single proprietorship

A balance sheet for a single proprietorship shows the entire ownership equity as a single dollar amount without any effort to distinguish between the amount originally invested by the owner and the later increase or decrease in owner's equity as a result of profitable or unprofitable operations. A corporation must maintain separate accounts for capital stock and retained earnings, because distributions to owners in the form of dividends cannot legally exceed the earnings of the corporation. In an unincorporated business, however, the owner is free to withdraw assets from the business at any time and in any amount.

The accounting records for a single proprietorship do not include accounts for capital stock, retained earnings, or dividends. Instead of these accounts, a *capital* account and a *drawing* account are maintained for the owner.

The owner's capital account. In a single proprietorship, the title of the capital account includes the name of the owner, as, for example, *John Jones, Capital.* The capital account is credited with the amount of the proprietor's original investment in the business and also with any subsequent investments. When the accounts are closed at the end of each accounting period, the Income Summary account is closed into the owner's capital account. Thus the capital account is credited with the net income earned (or debited with the net loss incurred). Withdrawals by the proprietor during the period are debited to a drawing account, which later is closed into the capital account.

The owner's drawing account. A withdrawal of cash or other assets by the owner reduces the owner's equity in the business and could be recorded by debiting the owner's capital account. However, a clearer record is created if a separate Drawing account is maintained. This drawing account (entitled, for example, *John Jones, Drawing*) replaces the Dividends account used by a corporation.

The drawing account is debited for any of the following transactions:

1 Withdrawals of cash or other assets. If the proprietor of a clothing store, for example, withdraws merchandise for personal use, the Drawing account is debited for the cost of the goods withdrawn. The offsetting credit is to the Purchases account (or to Inventory if a perpetual inventory system is maintained).
2 Payment of the proprietor's personal bills out of the business bank account.
3 Collection of an account receivable of the business, with the cash collected being retained personally by the proprietor.

Withdrawals by the proprietor (like dividends to stockholders) are not an expense of the business. Expenses are incurred for the purpose of generating revenue, and a withdrawal of cash or other assets by the proprietor does not have this purpose.

Closing the accounts

The revenue and expense accounts of a single proprietorship are closed into the Income Summary account in the same way as for a corporation. The Income Summary account is then closed to the proprietor's Capital account, rather than to a Retained Earnings account. To complete the closing of the accounts, the balance of the Drawing account is transferred into the proprietor's Capital account.

Financial statements for a single proprietorship

The balance sheet of a single proprietorship differs from that of a corporation principally in the owner's equity section. To see how ownership equity appears in the balance sheet of a single proprietorship and also in the balance sheet of a corporation, you may wish to review the illustration in Chapter 1 (page 20).

A *statement of owner's equity* may be prepared in a form similar to the statement of retained earnings used by a corporation. The statement of owner's equity, however, shows additional investments made by the owner as well as the earnings retained in the business. An illustration follows:

JONES INSURANCE AGENCY
Statement of Owner's Equity
For the Year Ended December 31, 19__

Note that withdrawals may exceed net income

John Jones, capital, Jan. 1, 19__	$ 80,400
Add: Additional investments	10,000
Net income for year	30,500
Subtotal	$120,900
Less: Withdrawals	34,000
John Jones, capital, Dec. 31, 19__	$ 86,900

The *income statement* of a proprietorship differs from that of a corporation in two significant respects. First, the income statement for a single proprietorship does not include any salary expense representing managerial services rendered by the owner. One reason for not including a salary to the owner-manager is the fact that individuals in such a position are able to set their own salaries at any amount they choose. The use of an unrealistic salary to the proprietor would tend to destroy the significance of the income statement as a device for measuring the earning power of the business. It is more logical to regard the owner-manager as working to earn the entire net income of the business rather than working for a salary.

A second distinctive feature of the income statement of a single proprietorship is the absence of any income taxes expense. Unlike a corporation, which must file a corporate income tax return and pay substantial income taxes, a single proprietorship is not subject to income taxes. It is exempt from income taxes because it is not considered to be a legal entity separate from its owner. However, the owner of an unincorporated business must include the net income earned by the business on his or her individual income tax return along with any taxable income from other sources. Notice that the owner of an unincorporated business must pay income taxes upon the *entire net income* of the business, regardless of the amount withdrawn during the year.

PARTNERSHIPS

A partnership is an unincorporated business jointly owned by two or more people. This is a popular form of organization, widely used in all types of small business and also in the professions. Partnerships are popular because they provide a convenient, inexpensive means of combining the capital and the special abilities of two or more persons. The Uniform Partnership Act, which has been adopted by most states, defines a partnership as "an association of two or more persons to carry on, as co-owners, a business for profit." Often a partnership is referred to as a firm; the name of the firm frequently includes the word "company," as, for example, Adams, Barnes, and Company.

Significant features of a partnership

2 Describe the basic characteristics of a partnership

Before taking up the accounting problems peculiar to partnerships, it will be helpful to consider briefly some of the distinctive characteristics of the partnership form of organization. These characteristics (such as limited life and unlimited liability) all stem from the basic point that a partnership is not a separate legal entity in itself but merely a voluntary association of individuals.

Ease of formation. A partnership can be created without any legal formalities. When two or more persons agree to become partners, such agreement constitutes a contract and a partnership is automatically created. The contract should be in writing in order to lessen the chances for misunderstanding and future disagreement.

Limited life. A partnership may be ended at any time by the death or withdrawal of any member of the firm. Other factors which may bring an end to a partnership include the bankruptcy or incapacity of a partner, or the completion of the project for which the partnership was formed. The admission of a new partner or the retirement of an existing member means an end to the old partnership, although the business may be continued by the formation of a new partnership.

Mutual agency. Each partner acts as an agent of the partnership, with authority to enter into contracts. The partnership is bound by the acts of any partner as long as these acts are within the scope of normal operations. The factor of mutual agency suggests the need for exercising great caution in the selection of a partner. To be in partnership with an irresponsible person or one lacking in integrity is an intolerable situation.

Unlimited liability. Each partner is personally responsible for all the debts of the firm. The lack of any ceiling on the liability of a partner may deter a wealthy person from entering a partnership.

A new member joining an existing partnership may or may not assume liability for debts incurred by the firm prior to his or her admission. A partner withdrawing from membership must give adequate public notice of withdrawal; otherwise the former partner may be held liable for partnership debts incurred subsequent to his or her withdrawal. The retiring partner remains liable for partnership debts existing at the time of withdrawal unless the creditors agree to a release of this obligation.

Co-ownership of partnership property and profits. When a partner invests a building, inventory, or other property in a partnership, he or she does not retain any personal right to the assets contributed. The property becomes jointly owned by all partners. Each member of a partnership also has an ownership right in the profits.

Advantages and disadvantages of a partnership

Perhaps the most important advantage of most partnerships is the opportunity to bring together sufficient capital to carry on a business. The opportunity to combine special skills, as, for example, the specialized talents of an engineer and an accountant, may also induce individuals to join forces in a partnership. To form a partnership is much easier and less expensive than to organize a corporation. Members of a partnership enjoy more freedom from government regulation and more flexibility of action than do the owners of a corporation. The partners may withdraw funds and make business decisions of all types without the necessity of formal meetings or legalistic procedures.

Operating as a partnership *may* in some cases produce income tax advantages as compared with doing business as a corporation. The partnership itself is not a legal entity and does not have to pay income taxes as does a corporation, although the individual partners pay taxes on their respective shares of the firm's income.

Offsetting these advantages of a partnership are such serious disadvantages as limited life, unlimited liability, and mutual agency. Furthermore, if a business is to require a large amount of capital, the partnership is a less effective device for raising funds than is a corporation. Many persons who invest freely in common stocks of corporations are unwilling to enter a partnership because of the unlimited liability imposed on partners.

Limited partnerships

In recent years a large number of businesses have been organized as "limited partnerships." This form of organization is used for businesses which provide tax sheltered income to investors, such as real estate syndications and oil drilling ventures. However, limited partnerships are not appropriate for businesses in which the owners intend to be active managers. Recent tax legislation has also reduced greatly the income tax advantages formerly available to investors in limited partnerships.

A limited partnership must have at least one *general partner* as well as one or more *limited partners.* The general partners are partners in the traditional sense, with unlimited liability for the debts of the business and the right to make managerial decisions. The limited partners, however, are basically *investors* rather than traditional partners. They have the right to participate in profits of the business, but their liability for losses is limited to the amount of their investment. Also, limited partners do not actively participate in management of the business. Thus, the concepts of unlimited liability and mutual agency apply only to the general partners in a limited partnership.

In this chapter, we emphasize the characteristics and accounting practices of conventional partnerships rather than limited partnerships. Limited partnerships are discussed in depth in courses on business law and federal income taxes.

The partnership contract

Although a partnership can be formed by an oral agreement, it is highly desirable that a written partnership agreement be prepared, summarizing the partners' mutual understanding on such points as:

1 Names of the partners, and the duties and rights of each
2 Amount to be invested by each partner including the procedure for valuing any noncash assets invested or withdrawn by partners
3 Methods of sharing profits and losses
4 Withdrawals to be allowed each partner

Partnership accounting

Partnership accounting is similar to that in a single proprietorship, except that separate capital and drawing accounts are maintained for each partner. A distinctive feature of partnership accounting is that the net income (or net loss) of the business must be divided among the partners in the manner specified by the partnership agreement.

3 Account for the formation of a partnership

Opening the accounts of a new partnership. When a partner contributes assets other than cash, a question always arises as to the value of such assets. The valuations assigned to noncash assets should be their *fair market values* at the date of transfer to the partnership. The valuations assigned must be agreed to by all the partners.

To illustrate the opening entries for a newly formed partnership, assume that on January 1, John Blair and Melinda Cross, who operate competing retail stores, decide to form a partnership by consolidating their two businesses. A capital account will be opened for each partner and credited with the agreed valuation of the *net assets* (total assets less total liabilities) that partner contributes. The journal entries to open the accounts of the partnership of Blair and Cross are as follows:

Entries for formation of partnership

Cash	40,000	
Accounts Receivable	60,000	
Inventory	90,000	
Accounts Payable		30,000
John Blair, Capital		160,000
To record the investment by John Blair in the partnership of Blair and Cross.		

Cash	10,000	
Land	60,000	
Building	100,000	
Inventory	60,000	
Accounts Payable		70,000
Melinda Cross, Capital		160,000
To record the investment by Melinda Cross in the partnership of Blair and Cross.		

The values assigned to assets in the accounts of the new partnership may be quite different from the amounts at which these assets were carried in the accounts of their previous owners. For example, the land contributed by Cross and valued at $60,000 might have appeared in her accounting records at a cost of $20,000. The building which she contributed was valued at $100,000 by the partnership, but it might have cost Cross only $80,000 some years ago and might have been depreciated on her records to a net value of $60,000. Assuming that market values of land and buildings had risen sharply while Cross owned this property, it is only fair to recognize the **_current market value_** of these assets at the time she transfers them to the partnership and to credit her capital account accordingly. Depreciation of the building in the partnership accounts will be based on the assigned value of $100,000 at the date of acquisition by the partnership.

Withdrawals and additional investments. Partners may make withdrawals of cash or other partnership assets at any time; there is no need for a formal "declaration" as with dividends paid by a corporation. The amounts withdrawn need not be the same for all partners. The withdrawal of cash or other assets by a partner is recorded by debiting that partner's drawing account. If a partner invests additional assets in the business, the investment is recorded by crediting the partner's capital account.

Closing the accounts at year-end. The revenue and expense accounts of a partnership are closed into the Income Summary account in the same way as for a corporation. The balance of the Income Summary account is then closed into the partners' capital accounts, in accordance with the profit-sharing provisions of the partnership agreement. If the partnership agreement does not specify how profits are to be divided, the law requires that any profits or losses be divided equally among the partners.

Let us assume that Blair and Cross have agreed to share profits equally and that the partnership earns net income of $60,000 during its first year of operations. The entry to close the Income Summary account would be as follows:

Closing Income Summary: profits shared equally	Income Summary... 60,000	
	John Blair, Capital	30,000
	Melinda Cross, Capital...	30,000
	To divide net income for 19__ in accordance with partnership agreement to share profits equally.	

The next step in closing the accounts is to transfer the balance of each partner's drawing account to his or her capital account. Assuming that withdrawals during the year amounted to $24,000 for Blair and $16,000 for Cross, the entry at December 31 to close the drawing accounts is as follows:

Closing the drawing accounts to capital accounts	John Blair, Capital 24,000	
	Melinda Cross, Capital 16,000	
	John Blair, Drawing	24,000
	Melinda Cross, Drawing.......................................	16,000
	To transfer debit balances in partners' drawing accounts to their respective capital accounts.	

Income statement for a partnership. The income statement for a partnership differs from that of a single proprietorship in only one respect: a final section may be added to show the division of the net income between the partners, as illustrated below for the firm of Blair and Cross. The income statement of a partnership is consistent with that of a single proprietorship in showing no income taxes expense and no salaries expense relating to services rendered by partners.

BLAIR AND CROSS
Income Statement
For the Year Ended December 31, 19__

Note distribution	Sales		$600,000
of net income	Cost of goods sold:		
	Inventory, Jan. 1	$150,000	
	Purchases..	460,000	
	Cost of goods available for sale	$610,000	
	Less: Inventory, Dec. 31...............................	210,000	
	Cost of goods sold		400,000
	Gross profit on sales		$200,000
	Operating expenses:		
	Selling expenses...	$100,000	
	General & administrative expenses	40,000	140,000
	Net income		$ 60,000
	Distribution of net income:		
	To John Blair (50%)......................................	$ 30,000	
	To Melinda Cross (50%)................................	30,000	$ 60,000

Statement of partners' capitals. The partners will usually want an explanation of the change in their capital accounts from one year-end to the next. A financial statement called a *statement of partners' capitals* is prepared to show this information and is illustrated below for the partnership of Blair and Cross:

BLAIR AND CROSS
Statement of Partners' Capitals
For the Year Ended December 31, 19__

		Blair	Cross	Total
Changes in	Investment, Jan. 1 19__	$160,000	$160,000	$320,000
capital accounts	Add: Additional investment.........................	10,000	10,000	20,000
during the year	Net income for the year...........................	30,000	30,000	60,000
	Subtotals..	$200,000	$200,000	$400,000
	Less: Drawings...................................	24,000	16,000	40,000
	Balances, Dec. 31, 19__	$176,000	$184,000	$360,000

The balance sheet of Blair and Cross would show the capital balance for each partner, as well as the total capital of $360,000.

Partnership profits and income taxes

Partnerships are not required to pay income taxes. However, a partnership is required to file an information tax return showing the amount of the partnership net income, and the share of each partner in the net income. Partners must include their shares of the partnership profit (after certain technical adjustments) on their individual income tax returns. Partnership net income is thus taxable to the partners individually in the year in which it is earned. The income tax rules applicable to investment in a partnership are quite complex; those complexities are appropriate to advanced accounting courses.

Note that partners report and pay tax on their respective shares of the profits earned by the partnership during the year and not on the amounts which they have drawn out of the business during the year. ***The net income of the partnership is taxable to the partners each year,*** even though there may have been no withdrawals. This treatment is consistent with that accorded a single proprietorship.

Alternative methods of dividing partnership net income

4 Divide the net income of a partnership in accordance with the partnership contract

In the preceding illustration, the partners divided net income equally. Partners, however, can share net income in any way they agree upon. Factors that the partners might consider in arriving at an equitable plan to divide net income include: (1) the amount of capital invested by each partner, (2) the amount of time devoted to the business by each partner, and (3) any other contribution by a partner to the success of the business.

Differences in the amounts of capital invested by partners suggest that allowing interest on invested capital may be a desirable first step in dividing partnership net income. Differences in the amount and value of personal services contributed by partners may warrant the authorization of different salaries as a second step in dividing net income. Keep in mind that a particular partner may have experience, business contacts, or special skills which can be of great value to the firm. For these reasons, it is common to find partnership agreements providing for an allowance to each partner for interest on capital invested, a salary for personal services rendered, and a fixed ratio for dividing any residual net income or loss.

To illustrate, assume that the partnership of Adams and Barnes earned $97,000 (before interest and salary allowances to partners) in Year 1 and that they had agreed to share net income as follows:

1 Salary allowances of $24,000 per year to Adams and $48,000 per year to Barnes. (Partners' salaries are merely a device for sharing net income and are not necessarily withdrawn from the business.)
2 Interest at 15% on beginning capitals to be allowed to each partner. Beginning capital balances for Adams and Barnes amounted to $100,000 and $40,000, respectively.
3 Any amount in excess of the foregoing salary and interest allowances to be divided equally.

In accordance with the terms of this agreement, the net income of $97,000 would be divided between Adams and Barnes as follows:

Division of Net Income

	Adams	Barnes	Income Allocated
Net income to be divided			$ 97,000
Salaries to partners.....................................	$24,000	$48,000	(72,000)
Remaining income after salaries			$ 25,000
Interest on beginning capitals:			
Adams ($100,000 × 15%)............................	15,000		
Barnes ($40,000 × 15%).............................		6,000	
Total allocated as interest.......................			(21,000)
Remaining income after salaries and interest			$ 4,000
Allocated in a fixed ratio:			
Adams (50%)	2,000		
Barnes (50%)		2,000	(4,000)
Total share to each partner	41,000	56,000	-0-

Profit sharing; salaries, interest, and fixed ratio as basis

The journal entry to close the Income Summary account in this case will be:

Income Summary...	97,000	
Lynn Adams, Capital		41,000
Dale Barnes, Capital..		56,000
To close the Income Summary account by crediting each partner with authorized salary, interest at 15% on beginning capital, and dividing the remaining profits equally.		

Authorized salaries and interest in excess of net income. In the preceding example the total of the authorized salaries and interest was $93,000 and the net income to be divided was $97,000. Suppose that the net income had been only $75,000; how should the division have been made?

If the partnership contract provides for salaries and interest on invested capital, these provisions are to be followed even though the net income for the year is less than the total of the authorized salaries and interest. If the net income of the firm of Adams and Barnes amounted to only $75,000, this amount would be divided between the partners as shown below.

The residual loss of $18,000 is divided equally because the partnership contract states that profits and losses are to be divided equally after providing for salaries and interest.

Division of Net Income

	Adams	Barnes	Income Allocated
Net income to be divided.............................			$ 75,000
Salaries to partners	$24,000	$48,000	(72,000)
Remaining income after salaries.......................			$ 3,000
Interest on beginning capitals:			
Adams ($100,000 × 15%)...........................	15,000		
Barnes ($40,000 × 15%)............................		6,000	
Total allocated as interest			(21,000)
Remaining income (loss) after salaries and interest			$(18,000)
Allocated in a fixed ratio:			
Adams (50%)......................................	(9,000)		
Barnes (50%).....................................		(9,000)	18,000
Total share to each partner	$30,000	$45,000	$ -0-

Authorized salaries and interest may exceed net income

Other aspects of partnership accounting

The foregoing discussion of partnership accounting is by no means exhaustive. The admission of a new partner to the partnership, the withdrawal of a partner, and the liquidation of a partnership, for example, may raise some very complex accounting issues. These issues are primarily of interest to advanced accounting students and for that reason are not included in this introductory text.

CORPORATIONS

Nearly all large businesses and many small ones are organized as corporations. There are many more single proprietorships and partnerships than corporations, but in dollar volume of business activity, corporations hold an impressive lead. Why is the corporation the most common form of organization for large businesses? One reason is that corporations obtain their equity capital by issuing shares of capital stock. Since a corporation may issue a vast number of these shares, it may amass the combined savings of a great number of investors. Thus, the corporation is an ideal means of obtaining the capital necessary to finance large-scale operations. Because of the prominent role of corporations in our economy, it is important for everyone with an interest in business, economics, or politics to have an understanding of corporations and their accounting practices.

What is a corporation?

A corporation is a legal entity having an existence separate and distinct from that of its owners. In the eyes of the law, a corporation is an artificial person having many of the rights and responsibilities of a real person.

A corporation, as a separate legal entity, may own property in its own name. Thus, the assets of a corporation belong to the corporation itself, not to the stockholders. A corporation has legal status in court, that is, it may sue and be sued as if it were a person. As a legal entity, a corporation enters into contracts, is responsible for its own debts, and pays income taxes on its earnings.

Advantages of the corporate form of organization

5 Discuss the advantages and disadvantages of organizing a business as a corporation.

The corporation offers a number of advantages not available in other forms of organization. Among these advantages are the following:

1 *No personal liability for stockholders.* Creditors of a corporation have a claim against the assets of the corporation, not against the personal property of the stockholders. Thus, the amount of money which stockholders risk by investing in a corporation is *limited to the amount of their investment.* To many investors, this is the most important advantage of the corporate form.

2 *Ease of accumulating capital.* Ownership of a corporation is evidenced by transferable *shares of stock.* The sale of corporate ownership in units of one or more shares permits both large and small investors to participate in ownership of the business. Some corporations actually have more than a million individual stockholders. For this reason, large corporations are often said to be *publicly owned.* Of course not all corporations are large. Many small businesses are organized as corporations and are owned by a limited number of stockholders. Such corporations are said to be *closely held.*

3 *Ownership shares are readily transferable.* Shares of stock may be sold by one investor to another without dissolving or disrupting the business organization. The shares of most large corporations may be bought or sold by investors in organized markets, such as the *New York Stock Exchange.* Investments in these shares have the advantage of *liquidity,* because investors may easily convert their corporate ownership into cash by selling their stock.

4 *Continuous existence.* A corporation is a separate legal entity with a perpetual existence. The continuous life of the corporation despite changes in ownership is made possible by the issuance of transferable shares of stock. By way of contrast, a partnership is a relatively unstable form of organization which is dissolved by the death or retirement of any of its members. The continuity of the corporate entity is essential to most large-scale business activities.

5 *Professional management.* The stockholders own the corporation, but they do not manage it on a daily basis. To administer the affairs of the corporation, the stockholders elect a *board of directors.* The directors, in turn, hire a president and other corporate officers to manage the business. There is no mutual agency in a corporation; thus, an individual stockholder has no right to participate in the management of the business unless he or she has been hired as a corporate officer.

Disadvantages of the corporate form of organization

Among the disadvantages of the corporation are:

1 **Heavy taxation.** The income of a partnership or a single proprietorship is taxable only as personal income to the owners of the business. The income of a corporation, on the other hand, is subject to income taxes which must be paid by the corporation. The combination of federal and state corporate income taxes often takes from one-third to one-half of a corporation's before-tax income. If a corporation distributes its earnings to stockholders, the stockholders must pay personal income taxes on the amounts they receive. This practice of first taxing corporate income to the corporation and then taxing distributions of that income to the stockholders is sometimes called **double taxation.**

2 **Greater regulation.** A corporation comes into existence under the terms of state laws and these same laws may provide for considerable regulation of the corporation's activities. For example, the withdrawal of funds from a corporation is subject to certain limits set by law. Federal laws administered by the Securities and Exchange Commission require large corporations to make extensive public disclosure of their affairs.

3 **Separation of ownership and control.** The separation of the functions of ownership and management may be an advantage in some cases but a disadvantage in others. On the whole, the excellent record of growth and earnings in most large corporations indicates that the separation of ownership and control has benefited rather than injured stockholders. In a few instances, however, a management group has chosen to operate a corporation for the benefit of insiders. The stockholders may find it difficult in such cases to take the concerted action necessary to oust the officers.

Formation of a corporation

A corporation is created by obtaining a corporate **charter** from the state in which the company is to be incorporated. To obtain a corporate charter, an application called the **articles of incorporation** is submitted to the state corporations commissioner or other designated official. Once the charter is obtained, the stockholders in the new corporation hold a meeting to elect **directors** and to pass **bylaws** as a guide to the company's affairs. The directors in turn hold a meeting at which officers of the corporation are appointed.

Organization costs. The formation of a corporation is a much more costly step than the organization of a partnership. The necessary costs include the payment of an incorporation fee to the state, the payment of fees to attorneys for their services in drawing up the articles of incorporation, payments to promoters, and a variety of other outlays necessary to bring the corporation into existence. These costs are charged to an intangible asset account called Organization Costs. In the balance sheet, organization costs appear under the "Other assets" caption, as illustrated on page 483.

The incurring of these organization costs leads to the existence of the corporate entity; consequently, the benefits derived from these costs may be regarded as extending over the entire life of the corporation. Since the life of a corporation may continue indefinitely, one might argue that organization costs are an asset with an unlimited life. However, present income tax rules permit organization costs to be written off over a period of five years or more; consequently, most companies elect to write off organization costs over a five-year period. Accountants have been willing to accept this practice, because organization costs are not material in amount. The accounting principle of **materiality** permits departures from theoretical concepts on the grounds of convenience if the practice in question will not cause any material distortion of net income.

6 Explain the rights of stockholders and the role of corporate directors and officers.

Rights of stockholders. The ownership of stock in a corporation usually carries the following basic rights:

1 To vote for directors, and thereby to be represented in the management of the business. The approval of a majority of stockholders may also be required for such important corporate actions as mergers and acquisitions, the selection of independent auditors, the incurring of long-term debts, the establishment of stock option plans, or the splitting of capital stock into a larger number of shares.

   When a corporation issues both common stock and preferred stock, voting rights generally are granted only to the holders of common stock. These two different types of capital stock will be discussed in detail later in this chapter.

2 To share in profits by receiving **dividends** declared by the board of directors. Stockholders in a corporation cannot make withdrawals of company assets, as an owner of an unincorporated business may do.

3 To share in the distribution of assets if the corporation is liquidated. When a corporation ends its existence, the creditors of the corporation must first be paid in full; any remaining assets are divided among stockholders in proportion to the number of shares owned.

4 To subscribe for additional shares in the event that the corporation decides to increase the amount of stock outstanding. This **preemptive right** entitles stockholders to maintain their percentages of ownership in the company by subscribing, in proportion to their present stockholdings, to any additional shares issued. In many cases, however, stockholders agree to waive their preemptive rights in order to grant more flexibility to management in issuing stock.

Stockholders' meetings are usually held once a year. Each share of stock is entitled to one vote. In large corporations, these annual meetings are usually attended by relatively few persons, often by less than 1% of the stockholders. Prior to the meeting, the management group will request stockholders who do not plan to attend in person to send in **proxy statements** assigning their votes to the existing management. Through this use of the proxy system, management may secure the right to vote as much as, perhaps, 90% or more of the total outstanding shares.

Functions of the board of directors. The primary functions of the board of directors are to manage the corporation and to protect the interests of the stockholders. At this level, management may consist principally of formulating policies and reviewing acts of the officers. Specific duties of the directors include declaring dividends, setting the salaries of officers, reviewing the system of internal control with the internal auditors and with the company's independent auditors, authorizing officers to arrange loans from banks, and authorizing important contracts of various kinds.

In recent years increasing importance has been given to the inclusion of outside directors on the boards of large corporations. The term *outside directors* refers to individuals who are not officers of the company and who thus have a view independent of that of corporate officers.

Functions of corporate officers. Corporate officers are the top level of the professional managers appointed by the board of directors to run the business. These officers usually include a president or chief executive officer (CEO), one or more vice-presidents, a controller, a treasurer, and a secretary. A vice-president is often made responsible for the sales function; other vice-presidents may be given responsibility for such important functions as personnel, finance, and production.

The responsibilities of the controller, treasurer, and secretary are most directly related to the accounting phase of business operation. The *controller,* or chief accounting officer, is responsible for the maintenance of adequate internal control and for the preparation of accounting records and financial statements. Such specialized activities as budgeting, tax planning, and preparation of tax returns are usually placed under the controller's jurisdiction. The *treasurer* has custody of the company's funds and is generally responsible for planning and controlling the company's cash position. The *secretary* represents the corporation in many con-

Typical corporate organization

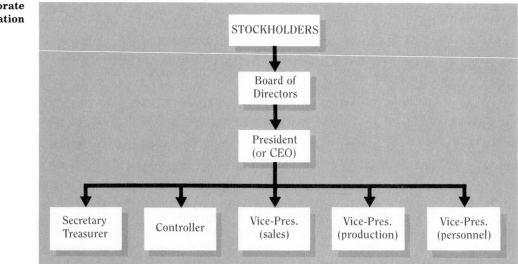

tractual and legal matters and maintains minutes of the meetings of directors and stockholders. Another responsibility of the secretary is to coordinate the preparation of the annual report, which includes the financial statements and other information relating to corporate activities. In small corporations, one officer frequently acts as both secretary and treasurer. The organization chart on page 470 indicates lines of authority extending from stockholders to the directors to the president and other officers.

Authorization and issuance of capital stock

In previous chapters we have seen that corporations use separate owners' equity accounts (Capital Stock and Retained Earnings) to represent (1) the capital invested by the stockholders (called **paid-in capital**) and (2) the capital acquired and retained through profitable operations **(earned capital).** Up to this point we have assumed that all paid-in capital may be recorded in a single ledger account entitled Capital Stock. In this chapter we will see that a corporation may issue several different types of capital stock. In these situations, additional ledger accounts are necessary to indicate the various types of capital investments by stockholders.

The articles of incorporation specify the number of shares of each type of capital stock which a corporation is authorized to issue and the **par value,** if any, per share. Large issues of capital stock to be offered for sale to the general public must be approved by the SEC as well as by state officials. The corporation may choose not to issue immediately all the authorized shares; in fact, it is customary to secure authorization for a larger number of shares than presently needed. In future years, if more capital is needed, the previously authorized shares will be readily available for issue; otherwise, the corporation would be forced to apply to the state for permission to increase the number of authorized shares.

Par value

The chief significance of par value is that it represents the **legal capital** per share, that is, the amount below which stockholders' equity cannot be reduced except by (1) losses from business operations or (2) legal action taken by a majority vote of stockholders. A dividend cannot be declared by a corporation if such action would cause the stockholders' equity to fall below the par value of the outstanding shares. Par value, therefore, may be regarded as a minimum cushion of equity capital existing for the protection of creditors.

Par value may be $1 per share, $5, $100, or any other amount decided upon by the corporation. The par value of the stock is **no indication of its market value;** the par value merely indicates the amount per share to be entered in the Capital Stock account. The par value of most common stocks is relatively low. Polaroid Corporation common stock, for example, has a par value of $1; Sears, Roebuck & Co. common stock has a par value of 75 cents; and Avon Products has a par value of 50 cents per common share. The market value of all these securities is far above their par value.

7 Account for the issuance of capital stock in exchange for cash or other assets.

Issuance of par value stock. Mere authorization of a stock issue does not bring an asset into existence, nor does it give the corporation any capital. The obtaining of authorization from the state for a stock issue merely affords a legal opportunity to obtain assets through the sale of stock.

When par value stock is *issued,* the Capital Stock account is credited with the par value of the shares issued, regardless of whether the issuance price is more or less than par. Assuming that 10,000 shares of $10 par value stock have been authorized and that 6,000 of these authorized shares are issued at a price of $10 each, Cash would be debited and Capital Stock would be credited for $60,000. When stock is sold for more than par value, the Capital Stock account is credited with the par value of the shares issued, and a separate account, Paid-in Capital in Excess of Par Value, is credited for the excess of selling price over par. If, for example, the issuance price is $15, the entry is as follows:

Stockholders' investment in excess of par value

Cash 90,000		
Capital Stock..		60,000
Paid-in Capital in Excess of Par Value		30,000
Issued 6,000 shares of $10 par value stock at a price of $15 a share.		

The amount received in excess of par value **does not represent a profit** to the corporation. It is part of the invested capital and it will be added to the capital stock on the balance sheet to show the total paid-in capital. The stockholders' equity section of the balance sheet is illustrated below. (The existence of $10,000 in retained earnings is assumed in order to have a complete illustration.)

Corporation's capital classified by source

Stockholders' equity:

Capital stock, $10 par value, authorized 10,000 shares, issued and outstanding 6,000 shares	$ 60,000
Paid-in capital in excess of par value	30,000
Total paid-in capital	$ 90,000
Retained earnings	10,000
Total stockholders' equity	$100,000

If stock is issued by a corporation for less than par, the account Discount on Capital Stock should be debited for the difference between the issuance price and the par value. The issuance of stock at a discount is seldom encountered; it is illegal in many states.

Market price of common stock

The preceding sections concerning the issuance of stock at prices above and below par value raise a question as to how the market price of stock is determined. The price which the corporation sets on a new issue of stock is based on several factors including (1) an appraisal of the company's expected future earnings, (2) the probable dividend rate per share, (3) the present financial position of the company, and (4) the current state of the investment market.

After the stock has been issued, the price at which it will be traded among investors will rise and fall in response to all the forces of the marketplace. The market price per share will tend to reflect the progress of the company, with primary emphasis being placed on earnings and dividends. At this point in our discussion, the significant fact to emphasize is that market price is not related to par value, and that it tends to reflect investors' expectations of future earnings and dividends.

Stock issued for assets other than cash

Corporations generally sell their capital stock for cash and use the cash to buy the various types of assets needed in the business. Sometimes, however, a corporation may issue shares of its capital stock in a direct exchange for land, buildings, or other assets. Stock may also be issued in payment for services rendered by attorneys and promoters in the formation of the corporation.

When a corporation issues capital stock in exchange for services or for assets other than cash, the transaction should be recorded at the current **market value** of the goods or services received. For some types of assets such as land or buildings, the services of a firm of professional appraisers may be useful in establishing current market value. Often, the best evidence as to the market value of these goods or services is the market value of the shares issued in exchange. For example, assume that a company issues 10,000 shares of its $1 par value common stock in exchange for land. Competent appraisers may have differing opinions as to the market value of the land. But let us assume that the company's stock is currently selling on a stock exchange for $90 per share. It is logical to say that the cost of the land to the company is $900,000, the market value of the shares issued in exchange.

Once the valuation has been decided, the entry to record the issuance of the stock in exchange for the land is as follows:

How were dollar amounts determined?

Land	900,000	
Common Stock		10,000
Paid-in Capital in Excess of Par Value		890,000

To record the issuance of 10,000 shares of $1 par value common stock in exchange for land. Current market value of stock ($90 per share) used as basis for valuing the land.

No-par stock

In an earlier period of the history of American corporations, all capital stock had par value, but in more recent years state laws have permitted corporations to choose between par value stock and no-par value stock. However, most companies which issue no-par capital stock establish a stated value per share. From an accounting viewpoint, stated value and par value mean the same thing—both terms designate the legal capital per share and the amount to be credited to the Capital Stock account.

Assume that a corporation is organized in a state which permits the board of directors to establish a ***stated value*** on no-par stock, and that the board passed a resolution setting the stated value per share at $5. If a total of 40,000 shares were issued at $20 per share, the journal entry to record the issuance would be:

Note stated value per share

Cash	800,000	
Capital Stock		200,000
Paid-in Capital in Excess of Stated Value		600,000

Issued 40,000 shares of no-par value capital stock at $20 each. Stated value set by directors at $5 per share.

In the absence of a stated value, the entire proceeds on the sale of stock ($800,000) would be credited to the Capital Stock account and would be viewed as legal capital not subject to withdrawal.

Preferred stock and common stock

8 Discuss the features of preferred stock and of common stock.

In order to appeal to as many investors as possible, a corporation may issue more than one kind of capital stock. The basic type of capital stock issued by every corporation is called ***common stock.*** Common stock has the four basic rights previously mentioned. Whenever these rights are modified, the term ***preferred stock*** (or sometimes Class B Common) is used to describe this second type of capital stock. A few corporations issue two or more classes of preferred stock, each class having certain distinctive features designed to interest a particular type of investor. In summary, we may say that every business corporation has common stock; a good many corporations also issue preferred stock; and some companies have two or more types of preferred stock.

Common stock may be regarded as the basic, residual element of ownership. It carries voting rights and, therefore, is the means of exercising control over the business. Common stock has unlimited possibilities of increasing in value; during periods of business expansion the market prices of common stocks of some leading corporations may rise to many times their former values. On the other hand, common stocks lose value more rapidly than other types of securities when corporations encounter periods of unprofitable business.

The following stockholders' equity section illustrates the balance sheet presentation for a corporation having both preferred and common stock; note that the item of retained earnings is not divided between the two groups of stockholders.

Balance sheet presentation

Stockholders' equity:

12% cumulative preferred stock, $100 par value, authorized 100,000 shares, issued 50,000 shares	$ 5,000,000
Common stock, $5 par value, authorized 3 million shares, issued 2 million shares	10,000,000
Retained earnings	3,500,000
Total stockholders' equity	$18,500,000

Characteristics of preferred stock

Most preferred stocks have the following distinctive features:

1 Preferred as to dividends
2 Preferred as to assets in event of the liquidation of the company
3 Callable at the option of the corporation
4 No voting power

Another important but less common feature is a clause permitting the ***conversion*** of preferred stock into common at the option of the holder. Preferred stocks vary widely with respect to the special rights and privileges granted. Careful study of the terms of the individual preferred stock contract is a necessary step in the evaluation of any preferred stock.

Stock preferred as to dividends. Stock preferred as to dividends is entitled to receive each year a dividend of specified amount before any dividend is paid on the common stock. The dividend is usually stated as a dollar amount per share. Some preferred stocks state the dividend preference as a ***percentage of par value.*** For example, a 9% preferred stock with a par value of $100 per share would mean that $9 must be paid yearly on each share of preferred stock before any dividends were paid on the common.

● **CASE IN POINT** ● Consolidated Edison has three issues of preferred stock which are publicly traded on the New York Stock Exchange. The first issue is a $5 preferred stock, which pays annual dividends of $5 per share. The other two issues include a 4.65% preferred and a 6% preferred. As both of these issues have $100 par values, they pay annual dividends of $4.65 and $6.00 per share, respectively.

Dividends on all three issues of preferred stock must be paid in full before Consolidated Edison pays any dividend on its common stock.

The holders of preferred stock have no assurance that they will always receive the indicated dividend. A corporation is obligated to pay dividends to stockholders only when the board of directors declares a dividend. Dividends must be paid on preferred stock before anything is paid to the common stockholders, but if the corporation is not prospering, it may decide not to pay dividends on either preferred or common stock. For a corporation to pay dividends, profits must be earned and cash must be available. However, preferred stocks in general offer ***more assurance of regular dividend payments*** than do common stocks.

Cumulative preferred stock. The dividend preference carried by most preferred stocks is a ***cumulative*** one. If all or any part of the regular dividend on the preferred stock is omitted in a given year, the amount omitted is said to be ***in arrears*** and must be paid in a subsequent year before any dividend can be paid on the common stock. Assume that a corporation was organized January 1, 1988 with 10,000 shares of $8 cumulative preferred stock and 50,000 shares of common stock.

Dividends paid in 1988 were at the rate of $8 per share on preferred stock and $2 per share on common. In 1989, earnings declined sharply and the only dividend paid was $2 per share on the preferred stock. No dividends were paid in 1990. What is the status of the preferred stock at December 31, 1990? Dividends are in arrears in the amount of $14 a share ($6 omitted during 1989 and $8 omitted in 1990). On the entire issue of 10,000 shares of preferred stock, the dividends in arrears amount to $140,000.

Dividends in arrears *are not listed among the liabilities of a corporation, because no liability exists until a dividend is declared by the board of directors.* Nevertheless, the amount of any dividends in arrears on preferred stock is an important factor to investors and should always be *disclosed.* This disclosure is usually made by a note accompanying the balance sheet such as the following:

Footnote disclosure of dividends in arrears

Note 6: Dividends in arrears

As of December 31, 1990, dividends on the $8 cumulative preferred stock were in arrears to the extent of $14 per share and amounted in total to $140,000.

In 1991, we shall assume that the company earned large profits and wished to pay dividends on both the preferred and common stocks. Before paying a dividend on the common, the corporation must pay the $140,000 in arrears on the cumulative preferred stock *plus* the regular $8 a share applicable to the current year. The preferred stockholders would, therefore, receive a total of $220,000 in dividends in 1991; the board of directors would then be free to declare dividends on the common stock.

For a *noncumulative* preferred stock, any unpaid or omitted dividend is lost forever. Because of this factor, investors view the noncumulative feature as an unfavorable element, and very few noncumulative preferred stocks are issued.

Stock preferred as to assets. Most preferred stocks carry a preference as to assets in the event of liquidation of the corporation. If the business is terminated, the preferred stock is entitled to payment in full of its par value or a higher stated liquidation value before any payment is made on the common stock. This priority also includes any dividends in arrears.

Callable preferred stock. Most preferred stocks include a *call provision.* This provision grants the issuing corporation the right to repurchase the stock from the stockholders at a stipulated *call price.* The call price is usually slightly higher than the par value of the stock. For example, $100 par value preferred stock may be callable at $105 or $110 per share. In addition to paying the call price, a corporation which redeems its preferred stock must pay any dividends in arrears. A call provision gives a corporation flexibility in adjusting its financial structure, for example, by eliminating a preferred stock and replacing it with other securities if future growth of the company makes such change advantageous.

Convertible preferred stock. In order to add to the attractiveness of preferred stock as an investment, corporations sometimes offer a ***conversion privilege*** which entitles the preferred stockholders to exchange their shares for common stock in a stipulated ratio. If the corporation prospers, its common stock will probably rise in market value, and dividends on the common stock will probably increase. The investor who buys a convertible preferred stock rather than common stock has greater assurance of regular dividends. In addition, through the conversion privilege, the investor is assured of sharing in any substantial increase in value of the company's common stock.

As an example, assume that Remington Corporation issued a 9%, $100 par, convertible preferred stock on January 1, at a price of $100 a share. Each share was convertible into four shares of the company's $10 par value common stock at any time. The common stock had a market price of $20 a share on January 1, and an annual dividend of $1 a share was being paid. During the next few years, Remington Corporation's earnings increased, the dividend on the common stock was raised to an annual rate of $3, and the market price of the common stock rose to $40 a share. At this point the preferred stock would have a market value of ***at least $160,*** because it could be converted at any time into four shares of common stock with a market value of $40 each. In other words, the market value of a convertible preferred stock will tend to move in accordance with the price of the common.

When the dividend rate is increased on the common stock, some holders of the preferred stock may convert their holdings into common stock in order to obtain a higher cash return on their investments. If the holder of 100 shares of the preferred stock presented these shares for conversion, Remington Corporation would make the following journal entry:

Conversion of preferred stock into common

9% Convertible Preferred Stock	10,000	
Common Stock		4,000
Paid-in Capital in Excess of Par Value.............................		6,000
To record the conversion of 100 shares of preferred stock, par $100, into 400 shares of $10 par value common stock.		

Note that the issue price recorded for the 400 shares of common stock is based upon the carrying value of the preferred stock in the accounting records, not upon market prices at the date of conversion.

Participating clauses in preferred stock. Since participating preferred stocks are very seldom issued, discussion of them will be brief. A fully participating preferred stock is one which, in addition to the regular specified dividend, is entitled to participate with the common stock in any additional dividends paid. For example, a $5 participating preferred stock would be entitled to receive $5 a share before the common stock received anything. After $5 a share had been paid to the preferred stockholders, a $5 dividend could be paid on the common stock. If the company desired to pay an additional dividend to the common, say, an extra $3 per share, the preferred stock would also be entitled to receive an extra $3 dividend. In brief, a fully participating preferred stock participates dollar for dollar with the common stock in any dividends paid in excess of the stated rate on the preferred stock.

It is important to remember that most preferred stocks are *not* participating. Although common stock dividends may increase year after year if the corporation prospers, the dividends on most preferred stocks are fixed in amount. A $6 preferred stock, unless it is participating, *will never pay an annual dividend in excess of $6.*

Market price of preferred stock

Investors buy preferred stocks primarily to receive the dividends that these stocks pay. But what happens to the market price of an 8% preferred stock, originally issued at a par value of $100, if government policies and other factors cause long-term interest rates to rise to, say, 15 or 16%? If investments offering a return of 16% are readily available, investors will no longer pay $100 for a share of preferred stock which provides a dividend of only $8 per year. Thus, the market price of the preferred stock will fall to about half of its original issue price, or about $50 per share. At this market price, the stock offers a 16% return (called the *dividend yield*) to an investor purchasing the stock ($8 per year ÷ $50 = 16%). However, if the prevailing long-term interest rates should again decline to the 8% range, the market price of an 8% preferred stock should rise to approximately par value.

In conclusion, the market price of preferred stock *varies inversely with interest rates.* As interest rates rise, preferred stock prices decline; as interest rates fall, preferred stock prices rise.

● **CASE IN POINT** ● The preceding point is illustrated by the performance of Philadelphia Electric's $9\frac{1}{2}$%, $100 par value, preferred stock as interest rates have fluctuated over the past decade:

	Long-Term Interest Rates*	Stock Price
September 1978	$9\frac{1}{2}$%	$ 99
August 1981	$15\frac{1}{4}$%	60
March 1983	$12\frac{1}{2}$%	76
April 1985	$13\frac{1}{2}$%	68
August 1987	$9\frac{3}{4}$%	102

* The long-term interest rates cited in this example are the market yields of federally insured 30-year fixed rate mortgages.

The underwriting of stock issues

When a large amount of stock is to be issued, the corporation will probably utilize the services of an investment banking firm, frequently referred to as an *underwriter.* The underwriter guarantees the issuing corporation a specific price for the stock and makes a profit by selling the stock to the investing public at a higher price. The corporation records the issuance of the stock at the net amount received from the underwriter. The use of an underwriter assures the corporation that the entire stock issue will be sold without delay, and the entire amount of funds to be raised will be available on a specific date.

Subscriptions to capital stock

9 Account for subscriptions to capital stock and for donated capital.

Small corporations sometimes sell stock on a subscription plan, in which the investor agrees to pay the subscription price at a future date or in a series of installments. When the subscription contract is signed, Stock Subscriptions Receivable is debited and Capital Stock Subscribed is credited. Later, as installments are collected, the entry is a debit to Cash and a credit to Stock Subscriptions Receivable. When the entire subscription price has been collected, the stock certificates are issued. The issuance of the stock is recorded by debiting Capital Stock Subscribed and crediting Capital stock. The following illustration demonstrates the accounting procedures for stock subscriptions.

In this example, 10,000 shares of $10 par value capital stock are subscribed at a price of $15. Subscriptions for 6,000 of these shares are then collected in full. A partial payment is received on the other 4,000 shares.

Subscription price above par

Stock Subscriptions Receivable	150,000	
Capital Stock Subscribed		100,000
Paid-in Capital in Excess of Par Value		50,000
Received subscriptions for 10,000 shares of $10 par value stock at price of $15 a share.		

When the subscriptions for 6,000 shares are collected in full, certificates for 6,000 shares will be issued. The following entries are made:

Certificates issued for fully paid shares

Cash	90,000	
Stock Subscriptions Receivable.................................		90,000
Collected subscriptions in full for 6,000 shares at $15 each.		
Capital Stock Subscribed..	60,000	
Capital Stock...		60,000
Issued certificates for 6,000 fully paid $10 par value shares.		

The subscriber to the remaining 4,000 shares paid only half of the amount of the subscription but promised to pay the remainder within a month. Stock certificates will not be issued until the subscription is collected in full, but the partial collection is recorded by the following entry:

Partial collection of subscription

Cash	30,000	
Stock Subscriptions Receivable.................................		30,000
Collected partial payment on subscription for 4,000 shares.		

From the corporation's point of view, Stock Subscriptions Receivable is a current asset, which ordinarily will be collected within a short time. If financial statements are prepared between the date of obtaining subscriptions and the date of issuing the stock, the Capital Stock Subscribed account is regarded as legal capital and will appear in the stockholders' equity section of the balance sheet.

Donated capital

On occasion, a corporation may receive assets as a gift. To increase local employment, for example, some cities have given corporations the land upon which to build factories. When a corporation receives such a gift, both total assets and total stockholders' equity increase by the market value of the assets received. *No profit is recognized when a gift is received;* the increase in stockholders' equity is regarded as paid-in capital. The receipt of a gift is recorded by debiting the appropriate asset accounts and crediting an account entitled **Donated Capital.** Donated capital appears in the stockholders' equity section of the balance sheet, as illustrated on page 483.

Stockholder records in a corporation

A large corporation with shares listed on the New York Stock Exchange usually has millions of shares outstanding and several hundred thousand stockholders. Each day many stockholders sell their shares; the buyers of these shares become new members of the company's family of stockholders. An investor purchasing stock in a corporation receives a ***stock certificate*** from the company indicating the number of shares acquired. If the investor later sells these shares, this stock certificate must be surrendered to the corporation for cancellation before a new certificate is issued to the new owner of the shares.

A corporation must have an up-to-date record of the names and addresses of this constantly changing army of stockholders so that it can send dividend checks, financial statements, and voting forms to the right people. Also, the corporation must make sure that old stock certificates are canceled as new ones are issued so that no excess certificates become outstanding.

Stockholders' ledger. When there are numerous stockholders, it is not practical to include a separate account for each stockholder in the general ledger. Instead, a single controlling account entitled Capital Stock appears in the general ledger, and a subsidiary stockholders' ledger is maintained. This ledger contains a record for each individual stockholder. Entries in the stockholders' ledger are made in number of shares rather than in dollars. Thus, each stockholders' account shows the number of shares owned, and the dates of acquisitions and sales. This record enables the corporation to send each stockholder a single dividend check, even though the stockholder may have acquired several stock certificates at different dates.

A corporation which has one or more issues of preferred stock outstanding (as well as common stock), will maintain a separate set of stockholders' records for each issue.

Stock transfer agent and stock registrar. Companies with shares traded on organized stock exchanges must engage an independent stock transfer agent and stock registrar to maintain their stockholder records and to control the issuance of stock certificates. These transfer agents and registrars usually are large banks or trust companies.[1] When stock certificates are to be transferred from one owner to another, the old certificates are sent to the transfer agent, who cancels them, makes the necessary entries in the stockholders' ledger, and prepares a new certificate for the new owner of the shares. This new certificate then must be registered with the stock registrar before it represents valid and transferable ownership of stock in the corporation.

Small, closely-held corporations generally do not use the services of independent registrars and transfer agents. In these companies, the stockholder records usually are maintained by the corporate secretary. To prevent the accidental or fraudulent issuance of an excessive number of stock certificates, even a small corporation should require that each certificate be signed by at least two designated corporate officers.

Retained earnings or deficit

Capital provided to a corporation by stockholders in exchange for shares of either preferred or common stock is called paid-in capital, or contributed capital. The second major type of stockholders' equity is retained earnings. The amount of the Retained Earnings account at any balance sheet date represents the accumulated earnings of the company since the date of incorporation, minus any losses and minus all dividends distributed to stockholders.

For a corporation with $1,000,000 of paid-in capital and $600,000 of retained earnings, the stockholders' equity section of the balance sheet may appear as follows:

Paid-in capital and earned capital

Stockholders' equity:

Capital stock, $10 par value, 100,000 shares authorized, 20,000 shares issued ...	$ 200,000
Paid-in capital in excess of par value..	800,000
Total paid-in capital...	$1,000,000
Retained earnings..	600,000
Total stockholders' equity	$1,600,000

[1] Regulations of the New York Stock Exchange now allow a single bank or trust company to act as both stock transfer agent and stock registrar for the same corporation. Traditionally, these functions were performed by two separate institutions.

If this same company had been unprofitable and incurred losses of $300,000 since its organization, the stockholders' equity section of the balance sheet would be as follows:

Paid-in capital reduced by losses incurred

Stockholders' equity:

Capital stock, $10 par value, 100,000 shares authorized, 20,000 shares issued ...	$ 200,000
Paid-in capital in excess of par value..	800,000
Total paid-in capital..	$1,000,000
Less: Deficit..	300,000
Total stockholders' equity	$ 700,000

This second illustration tells us that $300,000 of the original $1,000,000 invested by stockholders has been lost. The total paid-in capital in both illustrations remains at the fixed amount of $1,000,000, the stockholders' original investment. The term *deficit* indicates a negative amount of retained earnings.

Balance sheet for a corporation illustrated

A fairly complete balance sheet for a corporation is illustrated on page 483. Note the inclusion in this balance sheet of liabilities for income taxes payable and dividends payable. Note also that the caption for each capital stock account indicates the type of stock, the par value per share, and the number of shares authorized and issued. The caption for preferred stock also indicates the dividend rate, call price, and other important features.

END-OF-CHAPTER REVIEW

Summary of chapter learning objectives

1 Explain how the accounts and the financial statements of a single proprietorship differ from those of a corporation.

The balance sheet of a single proprietorship shows the entire ownership equity as a single dollar amount, whereas a corporation balance sheet shows separately the amount of paid-in capital and the amount of retained earnings. The income statement of a single proprietorship does not include salary to owner or income taxes among the expenses. These differences arise from the fact that a corporation is a legal entity separate from its owner. The ledger accounts of a single proprietorship do not include accounts for capital stock, retained earnings, or dividends. Instead, a capital account and a drawing account are maintained for the owner.

2 Describe the basic characteristics of a partnership.

A partnership is a voluntary association of two or more persons who agree to combine their efforts and resources to carry on as co-owners a business for profit. Among the basic characteristics is *ease of formation.* The partnership agreement should specify the capital contributions of each partner and a plan for sharing profits. Another characteristic is the *limited life* of a partnership. The admission of a new partner, as well as the withdrawal or death of a partner, dissolves a partnership. Each partner can act as agent for the firm *(mutual agency)* and each partner is *personally responsible* for all debts of the firm.

DEL MAR CORPORATION
Balance Sheet
December 31, 1990

Assets

Current assets:

Cash	$ 305,600
Accounts receivable (net of allowance for doubtful accounts)	1,105,200
Subscriptions receivable: Common stock	110,000
Inventories (lower of FIFO cost or market)...............................	1,300,800
Short-term prepayments...	125,900
Total current assets...	$2,947,500

Plant and equipment:

Land	$ 900,000	
Buildings and equipment (net of accumulated depreciation)	4,033,000	4,933,000
Other assets: Organization costs		14,000
Total assets		$7,894,500

Liabilities & Stockholders' Equity

Current liabilities:

Accounts payable	$ 998,100
Income taxes payable..	324,300
Dividends payable...	109,700
Interest payable..	20,000
Total current liabilities..	$1,452,100
Long-term liabilities: Bonds payable, 12%, due Oct. 1, 2010...................	1,000,000
Total liabilities	$2,452,100

Stockholders' equity:

Cumulative 8% preferred stock, $100 par, callable at $104, authorized and issued 10,000 shares.............................	$1,000,000	
Common stock, $1 par, authorized 1,000,000 shares, issued 600,000 shares...	600,000	
Common stock subscribed, 20,000 shares	20,000	
Paid-in capital in excess of par: common	2,070,000	
Donated capital	210,000	
Total paid-in capital..	$3,900,000	
Retained earnings...	1,542,400	
Total stockholders' equity...		5,442,400
Total liabilities & stockholders' equity		$7,894,500

3 Account for the formation of a partnership.

When a partnership is formed by partners contributing cash and/or other assets to the firm, these investments are recorded by debiting asset accounts and crediting the partners' capital accounts. For noncash assets, the amount should be the *fair market value* at the date of transfer to the partnership. When two or more owners of going businesses become partners, the partnership usually assumes the liabilities. The capital accounts are credited with the value of the net assets (assets less total liabilities).

4 Divide the net income of a partnership in accordance with the partnership contract.

The partnership contract should specify how net income or loss is to be divided. If the agreement does not mention profit-sharing, partners will share equally any amount of profit or loss. To recognize differences in the value and amount of personal services rendered by partners, it is common to provide salaries to partners as a step in sharing profits. To compensate for differences in the amounts of capital contributed, interest may be allowed on capital as a further step in sharing profits. Often both salaries and interest allowances are agreed upon, with any residual profit or loss to be divided in a fixed ratio.

5 Discuss the advantages and disadvantages of organizing a business as a corporation.

The primary advantages are: no personal liability of stockholders for the debts of the business, the transferrability of ownership shares, continuity of existence, ability to hire professional management, and the relative ease of accumulating large amounts of capital. The primary disadvantages are: "double taxation" of earnings and greater governmental regulation.

6 Explain the rights of stockholders and the roles of corporate directors and officers.

Stockholders in a corporation normally have the right to elect the board of directors, to share in dividends declared by the directors, to share in the distribution of assets if the corporation is liquidated, and to subscribe to additional shares if the corporation decides to increase the number of shares outstanding.

The directors formulate company policies, review the actions of the corporate officers, and protect the interests of the company's stockholders. Corporate officers are professional managers appointed by the board of directors to manage the business on a daily basis.

7 Account for the issuance of capital stock in exchange for cash or other assets.

When stock is issued for cash, the transaction is recorded by debiting Cash, crediting Capital Stock for the par value of the shares issued, and crediting Paid-In Capital in Excess of Par Value for any additional amounts received. If the stock is issued in exchange for assets other than cash, the transaction is recorded at either the fair market value of the shares issued or the fair market value of the assets received, whichever can be determined more objectively.

8 Discuss the features of preferred stock and of common stock.

Preferred stock has preference over common stock with respect to dividends and to distributions in the event of liquidation. This "preference" means that preferred stockholders must be paid in full before any payments are made to holders of common stock. The dividends on preferred stock usually are fixed in amount. In addition, the stock usually is callable at the option of the issuing corporation, and often has no voting rights. Preferred stocks sometimes have special features, such as being convertible into shares of common stock.

Common stock represents the true "residual ownership" of a corporation. These shares have voting rights and cannot be called. Also, the common stock dividend is not fixed in dollar amount — thus, it may increase or decrease based upon the company's performance.

9 Account for subscriptions to capital stock and for donated capital.

Stock subscriptions represent investors' promises to buy shares of stock at some future date at an agreed upon price. When shares are subscribed, the corporation records a receivable and credits Capital Stock Subscribed. When the receivable is collected and the subscribed shares are issued, the balance of the Capital Stock Subscribed account is transferred to the regular Capital Stock account.

Assets donated to a corporation are recorded in the accounting records at their fair market value. The offsetting credit is to a stockholders' equity account, entitled Donated Capital.

Key terms introduced or emphasized in chapter 12

Board of directors. Persons elected by common stockholders to direct the affairs of a corporation.

Call price. The price to be paid by a corporation for each share of callable preferred stock if the corporation decides to call (redeem) the preferred stock.

Closely held corporation. A corporation owned by a small group of stockholders. The stock of closely held corporations is not traded on stock exchanges.

Common stock. A type of capital stock which possesses the basic rights of ownership including the right to vote. Represents the residual element of ownership in a corporation.

Corporation. A business organized as a legal entity separate from its owners. Chartered by the state with ownership divided into shares of transferable stock. Stockholders are not liable for debts of the corporation.

Deficit. Accumulated losses incurred by a corporation. A negative amount of retained earnings.

Drawing account. The account used to record the withdrawals of cash or other assets by the owner (or owners) of an unincorporated business. Closed at the end of the period by transferring its balance to the owner's capital account.

Limited liability. An important characteristic of the corporate form of organization. The corporation as a separate legal entity is responsible for its own debts; the stockholders are not personally liable for the corporation's debts.

Limited partnership. A partnership which has one or more *limited partners* as well as one or more *general partners*. Limited partnerships are used primarily to attract investment capital from the limited partners for such ventures as exploratory oil drilling and real estate development.

Mutual agency. Authority of each partner to act as agent for the partnership within its normal scope of operations and to enter into contracts which bind the partnership.

No-par stock. Stock without par value. Usually has a stated value which is similar to par value.

Organization costs. Costs incurred to form a corporation.

Paid-in capital. The amounts invested in a corporation by its stockholders.

Par value. The legal capital of a corporation. Also the face amount of a share of capital stock. Represents the minimum amount per share to be invested in the corporation when shares are originally issued.

Preferred stock. A class of capital stock usually having preferences as to dividends and in the distribution of assets in event of liquidation.

Single proprietorship. An unincorporated business owned by one person.

Stated capital. That portion of capital invested by stockholders which cannot be withdrawn. Provides protection for creditors. Also called *legal capital.*

Statement of partners' capitals. An annual financial statement which shows for each partner and for the firm the amounts of beginning capitals, additional investments, net income, drawings, and ending capitals.

Stock certificate. A document issued by a corporation (or its transfer agent) as evidence of the ownership of the number of shares stated on the certificate.

Stock registrar. An independent fiscal agent, usually a large bank, retained by a corporation to provide assurance against overissuance of stock certificates.

Stock transfer agent. A bank or trust company retained by a corporation to maintain its records of capital stock ownership and make transfers from one investor to another.

Stockholders' ledger. A subsidiary record showing the number of shares owned by each stockholder.

Subscriptions to capital stock. Formal promises to buy shares of stock from a corporation with payment at a later date. Stock certificates are delivered when full payment is received.

Underwriter. An investment banking firm which handles the sale of a corporation's stock to the public.

Uniform Partnership Act. Uniform legislation adopted by most states. Governs the formation, operation, and liquidation of partnerships.

Demonstration problem for your review

At the close of the current year, the stockholders' equity section of the Rockhurst Corporation's balance sheet appeared as follows:

Stockholders' equity:

$1.50 preferred stock, $25 par value, authorized 1,500,000 shares:		
Issued	$10,800,000	
Subscribed	5,400,000	$16,200,000
Common stock, no par, $5 stated value, authorized 6,000,000 shares		12,300,000
Paid-in capital in excess of par or stated value:		
On preferred stock	$ 810,000	
On common stock	7,626,000	8,436,000
Retained earnings (deficit)		(600,000)
Total stockholders' equity		$36,336,000

Among the assets of the corporation appears the following item: Subscriptions Receivable: Preferred, $1,123,200.

Instructions. On the basis of this information, write a brief answer to the following questions, showing any necessary supporting computations.

a How many shares of preferred and common stock have been issued?

b How many shares of preferred stock have been subscribed?

c What was the average price per share received (including stock subscribed) by the corporation on its preferred stock?

d What was the average price per share received by the corporation on its common stock?

e What is the average amount per share that subscribers of preferred stock have yet to pay on their subscriptions?

f What is the total paid-in capital including stock subscribed?

g What is the total legal or stated value of the capital stock including stock subscribed?

Solution to demonstration problem

a Preferred stock issued <u>432,000 shares</u> ($10,800,000 ÷ $25)

Common stock issued <u>2,460,000 shares</u> ($12,300,000 ÷ $5)

b Preferred stock subscribed <u>216,000 shares</u> ($5,400,000 ÷ $25)

c Preferred stock par value ($10,800,000 + $5,400,000) $16,200,000

  Paid-in capital in excess of par   810,000

    Total paid-in and subscribed $17,010,000

  Total shares (432,000 + 216,000)   648,000

  Average price per share ($17,010,000 ÷ 648,000 as computed in a

  and b) . . . .   <u>$26.25</u>

d Common stock stated value $12,300,000

  Paid-in capital in excess of par   7,626,000

    Total paid-in $19,926,000

  Total shares (see a)   2,460,000

  Average price per share ($19,926,000 ÷ 2,460,000) . . . .   <u>$8.10</u>

e Subscriptions receivable, preferred . . . . $ 1,123,200

  Shares subscribed   216,000

  Average price per share ($1,123,200 ÷ 216,000) . . . .   <u>$5.20</u>

f <u>$36,936,000</u> (preferred $16,200,000 + common

  $12,300,000 + paid-in capital in excess of par or stated value

  $8,436,000)

g <u>$28,500,000</u> (preferred $16,200,000 + common

  $12,300,000)

ASSIGNMENT MATERIAL

Review questions

1 Jane Miller is the proprietor of a small manufacturing business. She is considering the possibility of joining in partnership with Mary Bracken, whom she considers to be thoroughly competent and congenial. Prepare a brief statement outlining the advantages and disadvantages of the potential partnership to Miller.

2 Compare the right of partners to withdraw assets from a partership with the right of stockholders to receive dividends from a corporation. Explain any significant differences in these rights.

3 Allen and Baker are considering forming a partnership. What do you think are the two most important factors for them to include in their partnership agreement?

4 A real estate development business is managed by two experienced developers and is financed by 50 investors from throughout the state. To allow maximum income tax benefits to the investors, the business is organized as a partnership. Explain why this type of business would probably be a limited partnership rather than a regular partnership.

5 Scott has land having a book value of $50,000 and a fair market value of $80,000 and a building having a book value of $70,000 and a fair market value of $60,000. The land and building become Scott's sole capital contribution to a partnership. What is Scott's capital balance in the new partnership? Why?

6 Partner Susan Reed withdraws $35,000 from a partnership during the year. When the financial statements are prepared at the end of the year, Reed's share of the partnership income is $25,000. Which amount must Reed report on her individual income tax return?

7 What factors should be considered in drawing up an agreement as to the way in which income shall be shared by two or more partners?

8 Is it possible that a partnership agreement containing interest and salary allowances as a step toward distributing income could cause a partnership net loss to be divided so that one partner's capital account would be decreased by more than the amount of the entire partnership net loss? Explain.

9 Partner John Young has a choice to make. He has been offered by his partners a choice between (a) no salary allowance and a one-third share in the partnership income or (b) a salary of $16,000 per year and a one-quarter share of residual profits. Write a brief memorandum explaining the factors he should consider in reaching a decision.

10 Distinguish between corporations and partnerships in terms of the following characteristics:
   a Owners' liability for debts of the business
   b Transferability of ownership interest
   c Continuity of existence
   d Federal taxation on income

11 What are the basic rights of the owner of a share of corporate stock? In what way are these basic rights commonly modified with respect to the owner of a share of preferred stock?

12 Explain the meaning of the term **double taxation** as it applies to corporate profits.

13 Explain the significance of **par value.** Does par value indicate the reasonable market price for a share of stock? Explain.

14 Describe the usual nature of the following features as they apply to a share of preferred stock: (a) cumulative, (b) convertible, and (c) callable.

15 When stock is issued by a corporation in exchange for assets other than cash, accountants face the problem of determining the dollar amount at which to record the transaction. Discuss the factors to be considered and explain their significance.

16 State the classification (asset, liability, stockholders' equity, revenue, or expense) of each of the following accounts:
   a Subscriptions receivable   e Capital stock subscribed
   b Organization costs   f Paid-in capital in excess of par value
   c Preferred stock   g Income taxes payable
   d Retained earnings

17 If the Retained Earnings account has a debit balance, how is it presented in the balance sheet and what is it called?

18 A professional baseball team received as a gift from the city the land upon which to build a stadium. What effect, if any, will the receipt of this gift have upon the baseball team's balance sheet and income statement? Explain.

19 Explain the following terms:
   a Stock transfer agent   c Underwriter
   b Stockholders' ledger   d Stock registrar

Exercises

**Exercise 12-1
Accounting
terminology**

Listed below are nine technical accounting terms introduced or emphasized in this chapter.

Unlimited liability	**Common stock**	**Interest on partners' capitals**
Preferred stock	**Deficit**	**Retained earnings**
Fair market value	**Par value**	**Paid-in capital**

Each of the following statements may (or may not) describe one of these technical terms. For each statement, indicate the accounting term described, or answer "None" if the statement does not correctly describe any of the terms.

a An amount of cash on hand from which dividends may be paid to stockholders.
b The type of capital stock for which the dividend usually is fixed in amount.
c That portion of owners' equity arising from the issuance of capital stock.
d Amounts to be entered in asset accounts of a partnership to record the investment by partners of noncash assets.
e A method of dividing partnership net income to assure that a partner's share will not be less than the prime rate of interest applied to his or her capital account.
f The type of capital stock most likely to increase in value as a corporation becomes increasingly profitable.
g A characteristic of the partnership type of organization which causes many wealthy investors to choose investments in limited partnerships or corporations rather than in regular partnerships.
h An excess of liabilities over paid-in capital.

**Exercise 12-2
Capital and
drawing accounts
of single
proprietor**

John Stewart owns Steamers & Beer, a seafood restaurant organized as a single proprietorship. Explain what effect, if any, recording the following transactions will have upon the balance of Stewart's capital account and drawing account.

a Stewart brings his personal computer from home to use full time in the business.
b Stewart pays a number of his personal bills from the business bank account.
c Stewart hires his daughter to work in the restaurant while she is home from college during semester break. Her salary, paid from the business bank account, is $800.
d Stewart writes a check from his personal bank account to pay a liability of the business.
e At the end of the accounting period, the balance of Stewart's drawing account is closed into his capital account.

**Exercise 12-3
Formation of a
partnership**

A business owned by Megan Rogers was short of cash and Rogers therefore decided to form a partnership with Steve Wilson, who was able to contribute cash to the new partnership. The assets contributed by Rogers appeared as follows in the balance sheet of her business: cash, $500; accounts receivable, $28,900, with an allowance for doubtful accounts of $600; inventory, $36,000; and store equipment, $19,000. Rogers had recorded depreciation of $1,500 during her use of the store equipment in her single proprietorship.

Rogers and Wilson agreed that the allowance for doubtful accounts was inadequate and should be $1,200. They also agreed that a fair value for the inventory was its replacement cost of $42,000 and that the fair value of the store equipment was $15,000. You are to open the partnership accounts by making a general journal entry to record the investment by Rogers.

**Exercise 12-4
Dividing partner-
ship income**

Redmond and Adams, both of whom are CPAs, form a partnership, with Redmond investing $40,000 and Adams $30,000. They agree to share net income as follows:

(1) Interest at 15% on beginning capital balances.

(2) Salary allowances of $50,000 to Redmond and $40,000 to Adams.

(3) Any residual profits or losses to be divided 60% to Redmond and 40% to Adams.

The partnership net income for the first year of operations amounted to $120,500 before interest and salary allowances. Show how this $120,500 should be divided between the two partners. Use a three-column shedule with a separate column for each partner and a column for the total income allocated. List on separate lines the amounts of interest, salaries, and the residual amount divided.

Exercise 12-5
Preparing the stockholders' equity section of a balance sheet

Heritage Corporation was organized on July 1, 19__. The corporation was authorized to issue 10,000 shares of $100 par value, 10% cumulative preferred stock, and 200,000 shares of no-par common stock with a stated value of $5 per share.

All the preferred stock was issued at par and 170,000 shares of the common stock were sold for $31 per share. Prepare the stockholders' equity section immediately after the issuance of the securities but prior to operation of the company.

Exercise 12-6
Computing retained earnings

Wolfe Company has outstanding two classes of $100 par value stock: 5,000 shares of 8% cumulative preferred and 25,000 shares of common. The company had a $50,000 deficit at the beginning of the current year, and preferred dividends had not been paid for two years. During the current year, the company earned $300,000. What will be the balance in retained earnings at the end of the current year, if the company pays a dividend of $2 per share on the common stock?

Exercise 12-7
Dividends: preferred and common

A portion of the stockholders' equity section from the balance sheet of Palermo Corporation appears below:

Stockholders' equity:

Preferred stock, 9% cumulative, $50 par, 40,000 shares authorized and issued ...	$2,000,000
Preferred stock, 12% noncumulative, $100 par, 8,000 shares authorized and issued	800,000
Common stock, $5 par, 400,000 shares authorized and issued	2,000,000
Total paid-in capital........	$4,800,000

Instructions. Assume that all the stock was issued on January 1, 19__, and that no dividends were paid during the first two years of operations. During the third year, Palermo Corporation paid total cash dividends of $736,000.

a Compute the amount of cash dividends paid during the third year to each of the three classes of stock.

b Compute the dividends paid *per share* during the third year for each of the three classes of stock.

Exercise 12-8
Analyzing stockholders' equity

The stockholders' equity section of the balance sheet appeared as follows in a recent annual report of Kona Corporation:

Stockholders' equity:

Capital stock:

$5.50 cumulative preferred stock; no-par value, 300,000 shares authorized, 180,000 shares outstanding, stated at	$ 18,000,000
Common stock; no-par value, 5,000,000 shares authorized, 4,000,000 shares issued, stated at	33,000,000
Retained earnings........	75,800,000
Total stockholders' equity	$126,800,000

Instructions. From this information compute answers to the following questions:

a What is the stated value per share of the preferred stock?

b What was the average issuance price of a share of common stock?

c What is the amount of the total legal capital and the amount of the total paid in capital?

d What is the total amount of the annual dividend requirement on the preferred stock issue?

e Total dividends of $5,200,000 were declared on the preferred and common stock during the year, and the balance in retained earnings at the ***beginning*** of the year had been $65,800,000. What was the amount of net income for the year?

Problems

**Problem 12-1
Single propri-
etorship: use of
capital and
drawing account**

Dean Engineering is a single proprietorship owned by Sharon Dean. During the month of April, Dean's ownership equity was affected by the following events:

Apr. 7 Dean invested an additional $20,000 cash in the business.

Apr. 15 Dean withdrew $6,500 in cash and used the money to pay her personal income taxes.

Apr. 22 Dean collected from J. Barker an $1,800 account receivable of the business and deposited the money in her personal checking account.

Apr. 30 Dean drew a check payable to herself on the business bank account in the amount of $4,000. She had stipulated this amount as her monthly salary as owner-manager of the business.

Apr. 30 The Income Summary account shows a credit balance of $7,200; the accounts of Dean Engineering are closed monthly.

Instructions

a Prepare journal entries for each of the above events in the accounts of Dean Engineering. Include the entries necessary to close the Income Summary account and Dean's drawing account at April 30.

b Prepare a statement of owner's capital for the month ended April 30. Assume that the balance of Dean's capital account on April 1 was $57,800.

**Problem 12-2
Sharing partner-
ship net income:
various methods**

A small nightclub called Comedy Tonight was organized as a partnership with Lewis investing $40,000 and Martin investing $60,000. During the first year, net income amounted to $65,000.

Instructions

a Determine how the $65,000 net income would be divided under each of the following three independent assumptions as to the agreement for sharing profits and losses. Use schedules of the type illustrated in this chapter to show all steps in the division of net income between the partners.

(1) Net income is to be divided in a fixed ratio: 40% to Lewis and 60% to Martin.

(2) Interest at 15% to be allowed on beginning capital investments and balance to be divided equally.

(3) Salaries of $23,000 to Lewis and $33,000 to Martin, interest at 15% to be allowed on beginning capital investments, balance to be divided equally.

b Prepare the journal entry to close the Income Summary account, using the division of net income developed in the last case (a, 3) above.

**Problem 12-3
Dividing partner-
ship profits; and
losses**

Financial Planners has three partners—A, B, and C. During the current year their capital balances were: A, $140,000; B, $100,000; and C, $60,000. The partnership agreement provides that partners shall receive salary allowances as follows: A, none; B, $50,000; and C, $38,000. The partners shall also be allowed 12% annually on their capital balances. Residual profits or loss are to be divided: A, $\frac{1}{2}$; B, $\frac{1}{3}$; and C, $\frac{1}{6}$.

Instructions. Prepare separate schedules showing how income will be divided among the three partners in each of the following cases. The figure given in each case is the annual income or loss available for distribution among the partners.

    a Income of $502,000
    b Income of $73,000
    c Loss of $29,000

**Problem 12-4
Partnerships: a
short comprehen-
sive problem**

The partnership of Kelley and Reed was formed on January 1, when Tom Kelley and Pat Reed agreed to invest equal amounts and to share profits equally. The investment by Kelley consists of $44,000 cash and an inventory of merchandise valued at $76,000. Reed is also to contribute a total of $120,000. However, it is agreed that her contribution will consist of the following assets of her business along with the transfer to the partnership of her business liabilities. The agreed value of the various items as well as their carrying values on Reed's records are listed below:

	Investment by Reed	
	Balances on Reed's Records	Agreed Value
Accounts receivable	$117,600	$117,600
Allowance for doubtful accounts...........................	5,040	8,500
Inventory...	16,600	20,800
Office equipment (net)	16,800	19,500
Accounts payable	37,800	37,800

Reed also contributed enough cash to bring her capital account to $120,000.

Instructions

    a Draft general journal entries to record the investments of Kelley and Reed in the new partnership.
    b Prepare the beginning balance sheet of the partnership (in report form) at the close of business January 1, reflecting the above transfers to the firm.
    c On the following December 31 after one year of operations, the Income Summary account had a credit balance of $92,000 and the Drawing account for each partner showed a debit balance of $36,000. Prepare journal entries to close the Income Summary and the drawing accounts at December 31.
    d Based upon the information developed in parts b and c, prepare a statement of partners' capitals for the year ended December 31. (Begin your statement of partners' capitals with a balance of $120,000 in each partners' capital account as of January 1, 19__. Do not show Reed's initial investment as an "additional investment.")

**Problem 12-5
Preparing the
stockholders' eq-
uity section of a
balance sheet**

Presented below are two separate cases requiring preparation of the stockholders' equity section of a corporate balance sheet.

a Early in 1989, Bell Corporation was formed with authorization to issue 50,000 shares of $1 par value common stock. All shares were issued at a price of $8 per share. The corporation reported a net loss of $82,000 for 1989 and a net loss of $25,000 in 1990. In 1991, net income was $70,000. No dividends were declared in any of the three years.

b Parker Industries was organized early in 1987 and authorized to issue 200,000 shares of $10 par value common and 30,000 shares of $100 par value cumulative preferred stock. All the preferred stock was issued at par and 120,000 shares of common stock were sold for $16 per share.

The preferred stock was callable at 105% of its $100 par value and was entitled to dividends of 10% before any dividends were paid to common. During the first five years of its existence, the corporation earned a total of $3,200,000 and paid dividends of 50 cents per share each year on the common stock.

Instructions. For each of the independent situations described, prepare in good form the stockholders' equity section of the balance sheet as of December 31, 1991. Include a supporting schedule for each case showing your determination of the balane of retained earnings that should appear in the balance sheet.

Problem 12-6
Stockholders' eq-
uity: a short,
comprehensive
problem

Early in the year Roger Gordon and several friends organized a corporation called Mobile Communications, Inc. The corporation was authorized to issue 50,000 shares of $100 par value, 10% cumulative preferred stock and 400,000 shares of $2 par value common stock. The following transactions (among others) occurred during the year:

Jan. 6   Issued for cash 20,000 shares of common stock at $14 per share. The shares were issued to Gordon and 10 other investors.

Jan. 7   Issued an additional 500 shares of common stock to Gordon in exchange for his services in organizing the corporation. The stockholders agreed that these services were worth $7,000.

Jan. 12   Issued 2,500 shares of preferred stock for cash of $250,000.

June 4   Acquired land as a building site in exchange for 15,000 shares of common stock. In view of the appraised value of the land and the progress of the company, the directors agreed that the common stock was to be valued for purposes of this transaction at $15 per share.

Nov. 15   The first annual dividend of $10 per share was declared on the preferred stock to be paid December 20. (Debit Dividends, Preferred Stock; Credit Dividends Payable, Preferred Stock.)

Dec. 20   Paid the cash dividend declared on November 15.

Dec. 31   After the revenue and expenses were closed into the Income Summary account, that account indicated a net income of $106,500.

Instructions

a Prepare journal entries in general journal form to record the above transactions. Include entries at December 31 to close the Income Summary account and the Dividends account.

b Prepare the stockholders' equity section of the Mobile Communications, Inc., balance sneet at December 31.

Problem 12-7
Starting a new
corporation;
includes stock
subscriptions

Pancho's Cantina is the best Mexican restaurant in town — maybe the best anywhere. For years, the restaurant was a single proprietorship owned by Wayne Label. Many of Label's friends and customers had offered to invest in the business if he ever decided to open new locations. So, early this year, Label decided to expand the business. He formed a new corporation, called Pancho's Cantinas, Inc., which planned to issue stock and use the money received to open new Pancho's restaurants in various locations.

The new corporation is authorized to issue 100,000 shares of $2 par value capital stock. In April the corporation entered into the following transactions:

Apr. 1   Received subscriptions from various investors for 25,000 shares of capital stock to be issued at a price of $20 per share.

Apr. 24   Received an invoice from an attorney for $6,200 for services relating to the formation of the new corporation. This invoice is due in 30 days.

Apr. 28   Received $40,000 cash as full payment from Shirley Long, an investor who had subscribed to 2,000 shares of capital stock. A stock certificate was immediately issued to Long for 2,000 shares. (No payments have been received from the subscribers to the other 23,000 shares.)

Apr. 30   Issued 25,000 shares of capital stock to Label in exchange for the assets of the original Pancho's Cantina. These assets and their current market values on this date are listed below:

Inventory	$ 15,000
Land	145,000
Building	210,000
Equipment and fixtures	130,000

Apr. 30   Issued 100 shares of capital stock to Label in exchange for $2,000 cash, thus assuring Label voting control of the corporation even after the other investors pay for their subscribed shares.

The new corporation will begin operation of the original Pancho's Cantina on May 1. Therefore, the corporation had no revenue or expenses relating to restaurant operations during April. No depreciation of plant assets or amortization of organization costs will be recognized until May when operations get under way.

Instructions

a Prepare journal entries to record the April transactions in the accounting records of the new corporation.

b Prepare a classified balance sheet for the corporation as of April 30, 19__.

Problem 12-8
Analysis of stockholders' equity

The year-end balance sheet of Jamestown Corporation includes the following stockholders' equity section (with certain details omitted):

Stockholders' equity:

$7.50 cumulative preferred stock, $100 par value, callable at $110, authorized 30,000 shares	$ 1,800,000
Common stock, $6 par value, authorized 500,000 shares	2,520,000
Paid-in capital in excess of par: common	5,250,000
Donated capital	500,000
Retained earnings	6,400,000
Total stockholders' equity	$16,470,000

Instructions. On the basis of this information, answer the following questions and show any necessary supporting computations:

a How many shares of preferred stock are outstanding?

b What is the total amount of the annual dividend requirement on preferred stock?

c How many shares of common stock are outstanding?

d What was the average issuance price of a share of common stock?

e What is the total legal capital of the corporation?

f What is the total paid-in (or contributed) capital?

g Total dividends of $1,059,000 were declared on the preferred and common stock during the year, and the balance of retained earnings at the beginning of the year was $5,184,000. What was the amount of net income for the year?

**Problem 12-9
Stockholders'
equity: two
challenging cases**

The two independent cases presented below require preparation of the stockholders' equity section of a corporate balance sheet.

Case A. In 1988, Barbara Sterns organized Flowerland, Inc., a chain of retail nurseries. The corporation was authorized to issue 100,000 shares of $2 par value common stock and 10,000 shares of $5 cumulative, no-par value, preferred stock. All the preferred stock was issued for a total of $511,000, and 35,000 shares of common stock were issued at $20 per share. During the first three years of its existence, Flowerland, Inc., earned a total of $352,000 and paid yearly dividends of $1 per share on the common stock, in addition to the regular dividends on the preferred stock. During 1991, however, the corporation incurred a loss of $165,000 and paid no dividends.

Case B. Tom Martinez organized Urban Transport Company in January, 1988. The corporation issued at $15 per share one-half of its 100,000 authorized shares of $5 par common stock. On January 2, 1989, the corporation sold at par the entire 5,000 authorized shares of 8%, $100 par value, cumulative preferred stock. On January 2, 1990, the company again needed money and issued 5,000 shares of an authorized 10,000 shares of $9, no-par, cumulative preferred stock for a total of $494,000. The company suffered losses in its first two years reporting a deficit of $270,000 at the end of 1989. During 1990 and 1991 combined, the company earned a total of $950,000. Dividends of $1 per share were paid on common stock in 1990 and $3.50 per share in 1991.

Instructions. For each of the independent cases described, prepare in good form the stockholders' equity section of the balance sheet at December 31, 1991. Include a supporting schedule for each case showing your determination of the balance of retained earnings at that date.

Business decision cases

**Case 12-1
Factors affecting
the market prices
of preferred and
common stocks**

ADM Labs is a publicly owned company with several issues of capital stock outstanding. Over the past decade, the company has consistently earned modest profits and has increased its common stock dividend annually by 5 or 10 cents per share. Recently the company introduced several new products which you believe will cause future sales and profits to increase dramatically. You also expect a gradual increase in long-term interest rates from their present level of about 11% to, perhaps, 12 or $12\frac{1}{2}$%. Based upon these forecasts, explain whether you would expect to see the market prices of the following issues of ADM capital stock increase or decrease. Explain your reasoning in each answer.

a 10%, $100 par value, preferred stock (currently selling at $90 per share).
b $5 par value common stock (currently paying an annual dividend of $2.50 and selling at $40 per share).
c 7%, $100 par value, convertible preferred stock (currently selling at $125 per share).

**Case 12-2
Whether or not to
incorporate**

Mario Valenti owns Valenti Ford, a successful automobile dealership. For twenty-five years, Valenti has operated the business as a single proprietorship and has acted as both owner and manager. Now, he is seventy years old and is planning on retiring from active management. However, he wants the dealership to stay in the family; his long-term goal is to leave the business to his two children and five grandchildren.

Valenti is wondering whether or not he should incorporate his business. If he were to reorganize Valenti Ford as a corporation, he could then leave an appropriate number of shares of stock to each of his heirs. Otherwise, he could leave the entire business to his heirs to be operated as a partnership. In selecting the appropriate form of business entity, Valenti has formulated the following objectives:

1 *Ownership:* Valenti wants each of his two children to own 25% of the business and each of his five grandchildren to own 10%.

2 *Continuity of existence:* Valenti wants the business to continue indefinitely, even if one or more of the heirs should die or no longer want to participate in ownership.

3 *Management:* When Valenti retires, he plans to give Joe Heinz, a long-time employee, responsibility for managing the business. Although Valenti wants to keep the ownership of the business in the family, he does not believe that any of his family members have the time or experience to manage the business on a daily basis. In fact, Valenti believes that two of his grandchildren simply have no "business sense," and he does not want them to participate in management.

4 *Income taxes:* Valenti wants to organize the business in a manner which will minimize the income taxes to be paid by his heirs. He expects that all the earnings of the business will normally be distributed to its owners on an annual basis.

5 *Owners' personal liability:* Valenti recognizes that an automobile dealership might become liable for vast amounts of money, if, for example, improper repairs caused a customer's car to be involved in an accident. Although the business carries insurance, he wants to be sure that his heirs' equity in the business does not place their personal assets at risk in the event of business losses.

Instructions

a For each of the five numbered paragraphs above, explain how the choice of business organization (partnership or corporation) relates to Valenti's stated objective.

b In light of your analysis in part a above, would you recommend that Valenti reorganize Valenti Ford as a corporation, or leave the business unincorporated so that his heirs may operate it as a partnership?

Chapter 13
Corporations: a closer look

CHAPTER PREVIEW

In this chapter we explore special topics relating primarily to the financial statements of large corporations. The chapter is divided into three major parts. In the first part, we show how an income statement is organized to show certain "unusual" items separately from the income or loss from normal business activities. Also, we emphasize the computation and interpretation of earnings-per-share. In the second part, we look at various stockholders' equity transactions, including cash dividends, stock dividends, stock splits, prior period adjustments, and purchases and sales of treasury stock. In the final section of the chapter, we discuss accounting for investments in stocks and bonds.

Our study of corporate reporting issues is expanded in Appendixes B, C, and D. These appendixes address such topics as investments for purposes of control, international accounting, and disclosing the effects of inflation.

After studying this chapter you should be able to meet these Learning Objectives:	1 **Describe how discontinued operations, extraordinary items, and accounting changes are presented in the income statement.**
	2 **Compute earnings per share.**
	3 **Distinguish between primary and fully diluted earnings per share.**
	4 **Account for stock dividends and stock splits, and explain the probable effect of these transactions upon market price.**
	5 **Define prior period adjustments and explain how they are presented in financial statements.**
	6 **Account for treasury stock transactions.**
	7 **Prepare a statement of stockholders' equity.**
	8 **Account for short-term investments in stocks and bonds.**

497

REPORTING THE RESULTS OF OPERATIONS

The most important aspect of corporate financial reporting, in the view of most stockholders, is the determination of periodic net income. Both the market price of common stock and the amount of cash dividends per share depend to a considerable extent on the current level of earnings (net income). Even more important than the absolute amount of net income is the *trend* of earnings over time.

Developing predictive information

An income statement tells us a great deal about the performance of a company over the past year. For example, study of the income statement makes clear the types and amounts of revenue earned and expenses incurred as well as the amounts of gross profit and net income. But can we expect the income statement for *next year* to indicate about the same level of performance? If the transactions summarized in the income statement for the year just completed were of a normal recurring nature, such as selling merchandise, paying employees, and incurring other normal expenses, we can reasonably assume that the operating results were typical and that somewhat similar results can be expected in the following year. However, in any business, unusual and nonrecurring events may occur which cause the current year's net income to be quite different from the income we should expect the company to earn in the future. For example, the company may have sustained large losses in the current year from an earthquake or some other event which is not likely to recur in the near future.

1 Describe how discontinued operations, extraordinary items, and accounting changes are presented in the income statement.

Ideally, the results of unusual and nonrecurring transactions should be shown in a separate section of the income statement *after* the income or loss from normal business activities has been determined. Income from *normal and recurring* activities presumably should be a more useful figure for *predicting future earnings* than is a net income figure which includes the results of nonrecurring events. The problem in creating such an income statement, however, is in determining which events are so unlikely to recur that they should be excluded from the results of "normal" operations. Three categories of events that require special treatment in the income statement are (1) the results of discontinued operations, (2) extraordinary items, and (3) the cumulative effects of changes in accounting principles.

Reporting unusual items — an illustration

To illustrate the presentation of these items, assume that Ross Corporation operates both a small chain of retail stores and two motels. Near the end of the current year, the company sells both motels to a national hotel chain. In addition, Ross Corporation reports two "extraordinary items" and also changes the method used in computing depreciation expense. An income statement reporting these events appears on the next page.

ROSS CORPORATION
Condensed Income Statement
For the Year Ended December 31, 19__

Net sales		$8,000,000
Costs and expenses:		
Cost of goods sold	$4,500,000	
Selling expenses	1,500,000	
General and administrative expenses	920,000	
Loss on settlement of lawsuit	80,000	
Income taxes (on continuing operations)	300,000	7,300,000
Income from continuing operations		$ 700,000
Discontinued operations:		
Operating loss on motels (net of $90,000 income tax benefit)	$ (210,000)	
Gain on sale of motels (net of $195,000 income taxes)	455,000	245,000
Income before extraordinary items and cumulative effect of		
accounting change		$ 945,000
Extraordinary items:		
Gain on condemnation of land by State Highway Department (net of		
$45,000 income taxes)	$105,000	
Loss from earthquake damage to Los Angeles store (net of $75,000		
income tax benefit)	(175,000)	(70,000)
Cumulative effect of change in accounting principle:		
Effect on prior years' income of change in method of computing de-		
preciation (net of $60,000 applicable income taxes)		140,000
Net income		$1,015,000

The preceding income statement is designed to illustrate the presentation of "unusual events." Rarely, if ever, will all of these types of events appear in the income statement of one company within a single year.

Continuing operations

The first section of the income statement contains only the results of *continuing business activities*—that is, the retail stores. Notice that the income taxes expense shown in this section relates *only to continuing operations*. The income taxes relating to the "special items" are shown separately in the income statement as adjustments to the amounts of these items.

Income from continuing operations. The subtotal *income from continuing operations* measures the profitability of the ongoing operations. This subtotal should be helpful in making predictions of the company's future earnings. For example, if we predict no significant change in the profitability of its retail stores, we would expect Ross Corporation to earn a net income of approximately $700,000 next year.

Discontinued operations

If management enters into a formal plan to sell or discontinue a *segment* of the business, the results of that segment's operations are shown separately in the income statement. This enables users of the financial statements to better evaluate the performance of the company's ongoing (continuing) operations.

Two items are included in the "discontinued operations" section of the income statement: (1) the income or loss from operating the segment prior to its disposal, and (2) the gain or loss on disposal of the segment. Notice also that the income taxes relating to the discontinued operations are *shown separately* from the income tax expense relating to continuing business operations.

Discontinued operations must be a "segment" of the business. To qualify for separate presentation in the income statement, the discontinued operations must represent an *entire segment* of the business. A "segment" of a business is a separate line of business activity or an operation that services a distinct category of customers.

For example, Allstate Insurance Company is a segment of Sears, Roebuck & Co. From time to time, Sears closes individual Allstate offices. Such office closures do *not* qualify as "discontinued operations," because Sears remains in the insurance business. If, however, Sears were to sell the entire Allstate Insurance Company, insurance activities would be shown in Sears' income statement as discontinued operations.

Discontinued operations are not really "unusual.". In recent years, a characteristic of the American economy has been the "restructuring" of many large corporations. As part of this restructuring, corporations often sell one or more segments of the business. Thus, the presence of "discontinued operations" is not uncommon in the income statements of large corporations.

● **CASE IN POINT** ● In one recent year, TWA sold Hilton International, the hotel chain, to Allegis (parent company of United Airlines). Later that year, Allegis disposed of several segments of its business, including Hilton hotels and Hertz rental cars. In the same year, Sears sold its savings bank segment, RJR Nabisco sold its Heublein (wine and spirits) segment, Owens-Illinois sold its forest products division, and Metromedia sold its cellular telephone operations. All in all, several hundred large corporations reported discontinued operations.

Extraordinary items

The second category of events requiring disclosure in a separate section of the income statements is extraordinary items. An extraordinary item is a gain or loss that is *(1) material in amount, (2) unusual in nature, and (3) not expected to recur in the foreseeable future.* By definition, extraordinary items are extremely rare; hence, they seldom appear in financial statements. Examples of extraordinary items include the effects of unusual casualties such as earthquakes or tornadoes; expropriation (seizure) of assets by a governmental agency; and gains or losses that may result from a newly enacted law or from the early retirement of long-term debt.

When a gain or loss qualifies as an extraordinary item, it appears at or near the bottom of the income statement following the subtotal, *Income before Extraordinary Items*. Since the extraordinary item is so unusual, this subtotal is considered necessary to show investors what the net income *would have been* if the unusual event had not occurred. Extraordinary items are shown net of any related income tax effects.

Other "unusual" gains and losses. Some transactions are not typical of normal operations but also do not meet the criteria for separate presentation as extraordinary items. Among such events are losses incurred because of strikes and the gains or losses resulting from sales of plant assets. Such items, if material, should be individually listed as items of revenue or expense, rather than being combined with other items in broad categories such as sales revenue or general and administrative expenses.

In the illustrated income statement of Ross Corporation (page 499), the $80,000 loss resulting from the settlement of a lawsuit was disclosed separately in the income statement but was *not* listed as an extraordinary item. This loss was important enough to bring to the attention of readers of the financial statements, but most lawsuits are not so unusual or infrequent as to be considered extraordinary items.

Changes in accounting principle

The accounting principle of *consistency* means that a business should continue to use the same accounting principles and methods from one period to the next. However, this principle does not mean that a business can *never* make a change in its accounting methods. A change may be made if the effects of the change are *properly disclosed* in the financial statements. Such changes, however, are extremely rare in the published financial statements of large corporations.

The "cumulative effect" of an accounting change. In reporting most changes in accounting principle, the *cumulative effect* of the change upon the income of prior years is shown in the income statement when the change is made. To compute this "cumulative effect," we recompute the income of prior years *as if the new accounting method had always been in use.* The difference between this recomputed net income for past periods and the net income actually reported is the "cumulative effect" of the accounting change.

To illustrate, assume that Ross Corporation has been using the double-declining balance method of depreciation, but decides in the current year to change to the straight-line method. The company determines that if the straight-line method had always been in use, the total net income of prior years would have been $140,000 higher than was actually reported. This $140,000 is the *cumulative effect* of the change in accounting principle and is shown as a separate item in the current year's income statement. Depreciation expense in the current income statement is computed by the straight line method, just as if this method had always been in use.

Changes in principle versus changes in estimate. A change in accounting principle refers to a change in the *method* used to compute financial statements amounts, not to a change in the underlying estimates. For example, a switch from straight-line to another method of computing depreciation is regarded as a change in accounting principle. However, a change in the estimated useful life used to compute depreciation expense is a *change in estimate.* This distinction is an important one. When we change an accounting principle (method), we determine the cumulative effect of the change upon the income reported in prior years. Changes in estimate, however, relate only to the current year and to future years; no effort is made to recompute the income of prior years.

Earnings per share

Perhaps the most widely used of all accounting statistics is *earnings per share* of common stock. Everyone who buys or sells stock in a corporation needs to know the annual earnings per share. Stock market prices are quoted on a per-share basis. If you are considering investing in IBM stock at a price of, say, $120 per share, you need to know the earnings per share and the annual dividend per share in order to decide whether this price is reasonable. In other words, how much earning power and how much dividend income would you be getting for each share you buy?

To compute earnings per share, the annual net income available to the common stockholders is divided by the average number of common shares outstanding. The concept of earnings per share applies *only to common stock;* preferred stock has no claim to earnings beyond the stipulated preferred stock dividends.

Many financial analysts express the relationship between earnings per share and market price per share as a *price-earnings ratio* (p/e ratio). This ratio is computed by dividing the market price per share of common stock by the annual earnings per share.

Weighted-average number of shares outstanding. The simplest example of computing earnings per share is found when a company has issued only common stock and the number of shares outstanding has not changed during the year. In this situation, the net income for the year divided by the number of shares outstanding at year-end equals earnings per share.

In many companies, however, the number of shares of stock outstanding is changed one or more times during the year. When additional shares are issued in exchange for assets during the year, the computation of earnings per share is based upon the *weighted-average* number of shares outstanding.[1]

[1] When the number of shares outstanding changes as a result of a stock split or a stock dividend (discussed later in this chapter), the computation of the weighted-average number of shares outstanding should be adjusted *retroactively* rather than weighted for the period the new shares were outstanding. Earnings per share data for prior years thus will be consistently stated in terms of the current capital structure.

The weighted-average number of shares for the year is determined by multiplying the number of shares outstanding by the fraction of the year that said number of shares outstanding remained unchanged. For example, assume that 100,000 shares of common stock were outstanding during the first nine months of the year and 140,000 shares during the last three months. Assume also that the increase in shares outstanding resulted from the sale of 40,000 shares for cash. The weighted-average number of shares outstanding during the year would be *110,000* determined as follows:

100,000 shares $\times \frac{9}{12}$ of a year..	75,000
140,000 shares $\times \frac{3}{12}$ of a year..	35,000
Weighted-average number of common shares outstanding.........................	110,000

This procedure gives more meaningful earnings per share data than if the total number of shares outstanding at the end of the year were used in the calculations. By using the weighted-average number of shares, we recognize that the proceeds from the sale of the 40,000 shares were available to generate earnings only during the last three months of the year.

Preferred dividends and earnings per share. When a company has preferred stock outstanding, the preferred stockholders participate in net income to the extent of the preferred stock dividends. To determine the earnings *applicable to the common stock,* we must first deduct from net income the amount of any preferred stock dividends. To illustrate, let us assume that Tanner Corporation has 200,000 shares of common stock and 10,000 shares of $6 preferred stock outstanding throughout the year. Net income for the year totals $560,000. Earnings per share of common stock would be computed as follows:

Net income	$560,000
Less: Dividends on preferred stock (10,000 shares $\times$ $6)	60,000
Earnings applicable to common stock..	$500,000
Weighted-average number of common shares outstanding........................	200,000
Earnings per share of common stock ($500,000 $\div$ 200,000 shares)	$2.50

Presentation of earnings per share in the income statement. All publicly owned corporations are required to present earnings per share data in their income statements.[2] If an income statement includes subtotals for *income from continuing operations,* or for *income before extraordinary items,* per-share figures are shown for these amounts as well as for net income. The per share effect of any accounting change also is shown. These additional per-share amounts are computed by substituting the amount of the appropriate subtotal for the net income figure in the preceding calculation.

---

[2] The FASB has exempted closely held corporations (those not publicly owned) from the requirement of computing and reporting earnings per share. See *FASB Statement No. 23,* "Suspension of the Reporting of Earnings per Share and Segment Information by Nonpublic Enterprises" (Stamford, Conn.: 1978).

To illustrate all of the potential per-share computations, we will expand our Tanner Corporation example to include income from continuing operations and income before extraordinary items. We should point out, however, that all of these figures seldom appear in the same income statement. Very few companies have both discontinued operations and an extraordinary item to report in the same year. The following condensed income statement is intended to illustrate the proper format for presenting earnings per share figures and to provide a review of the calculations.

TANNER CORPORATION
Condensed Income Statement
For the Year Ended December 31, 19__

Net sales...		$9,000,000
Cost and expenses (including income taxes on continuing operations).........		8,340,000
Income from continuing operations..		$ 660,000
Loss from discontinued operations (net of income tax benefits)..............		(60,000)
Income before extraordinary items and cumulative effect of accounting change		$ 600,000
Extraordinary loss (net of income tax benefit)..................	$(120,000)	
Cumulative effect of accounting change (net of related income taxes)..	80,000	(40,000)
Net income		$ 560,000
Earnings per share of common stock:		
Earnings from continuing operations.......................................		$3.00[a]
Loss from discontinued operations.......................................		(.30)
Earnings before extraordinary items and cumulative effect of accounting change..		$2.70[b]
Extraordinary loss		(.60)
Cumulative effect of accounting change.....................................		.40
Net earnings..		$2.50[c]

[a] ($660,000 − $60,000 preferred dividends) ÷ 200,000 shares
[b] ($600,000 − $60,000) ÷ 200,000 shares
[c] ($560,000 − $60,000) ÷ 200,000 shares

Interpreting the different per-share amounts. To informed users of financial statements, each of these figures has a different significance. Earnings per share from continuing operations represents the results of continuing and ordinary business activity. This figure is the most useful one for predicting future operating results. *Net earnings* per share, on the other hand, shows the overall operating results of the current year, including any discontinued operations or extraordinary items.

Unfortunately the term *earnings per share* often is used without qualification in referring to various types of per-share data. When using per-share information, it is important to know exactly which per-share statistic is being presented. For example, the price-earnings ratios (market price divided by earnings per share) for common stocks listed on major stock exchanges are reported daily in *The Wall Street Journal* and many other newspapers. Which earnings per share figures are used in computing these ratios? If a company reports an extraordinary gain or loss, the price-earnings ratio is computed using the per-share **earnings before the extraordinary item.** Otherwise, the ratio is based upon **net earnings** per share.

Primary and fully diluted earnings per share

3 Distinguish
between primary
and fully diluted
earnings per
share.

Let us assume that a company has an outstanding issue of preferred stock that is convertible into shares of common stock at a rate of, say, two shares of common for each share of preferred. The conversion of this preferred stock would increase the number of common shares outstanding and might **dilute** (reduce) earnings per share. Any common stockholder interested in the trend of earnings per share will want to know what effect the conversion of the preferred stock would have upon this statistic.

To inform investors of the potential dilution which might occur, two figures are presented for each earnings per share statistic. The first figure, called **primary** earnings per share, is based upon the weighted-average number of common shares actually outstanding during the year. Thus, this figure ignores the potential dilution represented by the convertible preferred stock.[3] The second figure, called **fully diluted** earnings per share, shows the impact that conversion of the preferred stock would have upon primary earnings per share.

Primary earnings per share are computed in the same manner illustrated in our preceding example of Tanner Corporation. Fully diluted earnings per share, on the other hand, are computed on the assumption that all the preferred stock **had been converted into common stock at the beginning of the current year.**[4] (The mechanics of computing fully diluted earnings per share are covered in the intermediate accounting course.)

It is important to remember that fully diluted earnings per share represent a **hypothetical case.** This statistic is computed even though the preferred stock actually was **not** converted during the year. The purpose of showing fully diluted earnings per share is to warn common stockholders of what **could** have happened. When the difference between primary and fully diluted earnings per share becomes significant, investors should recognize the **risk** that future earnings per share may be reduced by conversions of other securities into common stock.

OTHER TRANSACTIONS AFFECTING STOCKHOLDERS' EQUITY

Cash dividends

The prospect of receiving cash dividends is a principal reason for investing in the stocks of corporations. An increase or decrease in the established rate of dividends

---

[3] If certain criteria are met, convertible securities qualify as **common stock equivalents** and enter into the computation of primary earnings per share. Common stock equivalents and other complex issues relating to earnings per share are discussed in intermediate accounting courses and in *APB Opinion No. 15,* "Earnings per Share," AICPA (New York, 1969).

[4] If the preferred stock had been issued during the current year, we would assume that it was converted into common stock on the date it was issued.

will usually cause an immediate rise or fall in the market price of the company's stock. Stockholders are keenly interested in prospects for future dividends and as a group are strongly in favor of more generous dividend payments. The board of directors, on the other hand, is primarily concerned with the long-run growth and financial strength of the corporation; it may prefer to restrict dividends to a minimum in order to conserve cash for purchase of plant and equipment or for other needs of the company. Many of the so-called "growth companies" plow back into the business most of their earnings and pay only very small cash dividends.

The preceding discussion suggests three requirements for the payment of a cash dividend. These are:

1 *Retained earnings.* Since dividends represent a distribution of earnings to stockholders, the theoretical maximum for dividends is the total undistributed net income of the company, represented by the credit balance of the Retained Earnings account. As a practical matter, many corporations limit dividends to somewhere near 40% of annual net income, in the belief that a major portion of the net income must be retained in the business if the company is to grow and to keep pace with its competitors.

2 *An adequate cash position.* The fact that the company reports large earnings does not mean that it has a large amount of cash on hand. Earnings may have been invested in new plant and equipment, or in paying off debts, or in acquiring larger inventory. There is no necessary relationship between the balance in the Retained Earnings account and the balance in the Cash account. The traditional expression of "paying dividends out of retained earnings" is misleading. Cash dividends can be paid only "out of" cash.

3 *Dividend action by the board of directors.* Even though the company's net income is substantial and its cash position seemingly satisfactory, dividends are not paid automatically. A formal action by the board of directors is necessary to declare a dividend.

Dividend dates

Four significant dates are involved in the distribution of a dividend. These dates are:

1 *Date of declaration.* On the day on which the dividend is declared by the board of directors, a liability to make the payment comes into existence.

2 *Date of record.* The date of record always follows the date of declaration, usually by a period of two or three weeks, and is always stated in the dividend declaration. In order to be eligible to receive the dividend, a person must be listed as the owner of the stock on the date of record.

3 *Ex-dividend date.* The ex-dividend date is significant for investors in companies with stocks traded on the stock exchanges. To permit the compilation of the list of stockholders as of the record date, it is customary for the stock to go "ex-dividend" three business days before the date of record. A stock is said to be selling ex-dividend on the day that it loses the right to receive the

upcoming dividend. A person who buys the stock before the ex-dividend date is entitled to receive the dividend; conversely, a stockholder who sells shares before the ex-dividend date does not receive the dividend.

4 **Date of payment.** The declaration of a dividend always includes announcement of the date of payment as well as the date of record. Usually the date of payment comes from two to four weeks after the date of record.

The journal entries to record the declaration and payment of a cash dividend were illustrated in Chapter 3 but are repeated here with emphasis on the date of declaration and date of payment.

Entries made on declaration date and . . .	June 1	Dividends 100,000	
		Dividends Payable	100,000
		To record declaration of a cash dividend of $1 per share on the 100,000 shares of common stock outstanding. Payable July 10 to stockholders of record on June 20.	
. . . on payment date	July 10	Dividends Payable 100,000	
		Cash	100,000
		To record payment of $1 per share dividend declared June 1 to stockholders of record on June 20.	

At the end of the accounting period, a closing entry is required to transfer the debit balance of the Dividends account into the Retained Earnings account. Some companies follow the alternative practice of debiting Retained Earnings when the dividend is declared instead of using a Dividends account. Under either method, the balance of the Retained Earnings account ultimately is reduced by all dividends declared during the period.

Most dividends are paid in cash, but occasionally a dividend declaration calls for payment in assets other than cash. A large distillery once paid a dividend consisting of a bottle of whiskey for each share of stock. When a corporation goes out of existence (particularly a small corporation with only a few stockholders), it may choose to distribute noncash assets to its owners rather than to convert all its assets into cash. Dividends payable in assets other than cash are called *property dividends.*

Liquidating dividends

A *liquidating dividend* occurs when a corporation pays a dividend that *exceeds the balance in the Retained Earnings account.* Thus, the dividend returns to stockholders all or part of their paid-in capital investment. Liquidating dividends are usually paid only when a corporation is going out of existence or is making a permanent reduction in the size of its operations. Normally dividends are paid as a result of profitable operations; stockholders may assume that a dividend represents a distribution of profits unless they are notified by the corporation that the dividend is a return of invested capital.

Stock dividends

4 Account for
stock dividends
and stock splits,
and explain the
probable effect of
these transac-
tions upon
market price.

Stock dividend is a term used to describe a distribution of additional shares of stock to a company's stockholders in proportion to their present holdings. In brief, the dividend is payable in *additional shares of stock* rather than in cash. Most stock dividends consist of additional shares of common stock distributed to holders of common stock, and our discussion will be limited to this type of stock dividend.

An important distinction must be drawn between a cash dividend and a stock dividend. In a *cash dividend,* assets are distributed by the corporation to the stockholders. Thus, a cash dividend reduces both assets and stockholders' equity. In a *stock dividend,* however, *no assets are distributed.* Thus, a stock dividend causes *no change* in assets or in total stockholders' equity. Each stockholder receives additional shares, but his or her total ownership in the corporation is *no larger than before.*

To illustrate this point, assume that a corporation with 2,000 shares of stock is owned equally by James Davis and Susan Miller, each owning 1,000 shares of stock. The corporation declares a stock dividend of 10% and distributes 200 additional shares (10% of 2,000 shares), with 100 shares going to each of the two stockholders. Davis and Miller now hold 1,100 shares apiece, but each still owns one-half of the business. Furthermore, the corporation has not changed; its assets and liabilities and its total stockholders' equity are exactly the same as before the dividend.

Now let us consider the logical effect of this stock dividend upon the market price of the company's stock. Assume that before the stock dividend, the outstanding 2,000 shares had a market price of $110 per share. This price indicates a total market value for the corporation of $220,000 (2,000 shares × $110 per share). As the stock dividend does not change total assets or total stockholders' equity, the total market value of the corporation *should remain $220,000* after the stock dividend. As 2,200 shares are now outstanding, the market price of each share *should fall* to $100 ($220,000 ÷ 2,200 shares). In short, the market value of the stock *should fall in proportion* to the number of new shares issued. Whether the market price per share *will* fall in proportion to a small increase in number of outstanding shares is another matter. The market prices of common stocks are influenced by many different factors.

Reasons for issuing stock dividends. Although stock dividends cause no change in total assets or total stockholders' equity, they are popular both with management and with stockholders. Management likes stock dividends because they do not cost anything (other than administrative costs) — the corporation does not have to surrender any assets. Stockholders enjoy stock dividends because often the market price of the stock *does not fall enough* to fully reflect the increased number of shares. While this failure of the stock price to fall proportionately is not logical, it is nonetheless a common phenomenon. In such cases, the stock dividend actually does increase the total market value of the corporation and of each stockholder's investment.

Entries to record a stock dividend. In accounting for *small* stock dividends (say, less than 20%), the *market value* of the new shares is transferred from the Retained Earnings accounts to the paid-in capital accounts. This process sometimes is called **capitalizing** retained earnings. The overall effect is the same as if the dividend had been paid in cash, and the stockholders had immediately reinvested the cash in the business in exchange for additional shares of stock. Of course, no cash actually changes hands — the new shares of stock are sent directly to the stockholders.

To illustrate, assume on June 1, Aspen Corp. has outstanding 100,000 shares of $5 par value common stock with a market value of $22 per share. On this date, the company declares a 10% stock dividend, distributable on July 15 to stockholders of record on June 20. The entry at June 1 to record the **declaration** of this dividend is:

Declaration of a stock dividend; note use of market price of stock

Retained Earnings..	220,000	
Stock Dividend to Be Distributed..................................		50,000
Paid-in Capital from Stock Dividends		170,000

Declared a 10% stock dividend consisting of 10,000 shares (100,000 shares × 10%) of $5 par value common stock, market price $22 per share. Distributable July 15 to stockholders of record on June 20.

The Stock Dividend to Be Distributed account is **not a liability,** because there is no obligation to distribute cash or any other asset. If a balance sheet is prepared between the date of declaration of a stock dividend and the date of distribution of the shares, this account, as well as Paid-in Capital from Stock Dividends, should be presented in the stockholders' equity section of the balance sheet.

Notice that the Retained Earnings account was debited for the **market value** of the shares to be issued (10,000 shares × $22 per share = $220,000). Notice also that **no change** occurs in the total amount of stockholders' equity. The amount removed from the Retained Earnings account was simply transferred into two other stockholders' equity accounts.

On July 15, the entry to record the **distribution** of the dividend shares is:

Distribution of a stock dividend

Stock Dividend to Be Distributed...	50,000	
Common Stock..		50,000

Distributed 10,000 share stock dividend declared June 1.

Large stock dividends (for example, those in excess of 20 to 25%) should be recorded by transferring **only the par or stated value** of the dividend shares from the Retained Earnings account to the Common Stock account. Large stock dividends generally have the effect of proportionately reducing the market price of the stock. For example, a 100% stock dividend would reduce the market price by about 50%, because twice as many shares would be outstanding. A 100% stock dividend is very similar to the 2 for 1 **stock split** discussed in the following section of this chapter.

Stock splits

A corporation may split its stock by increasing the number of outstanding shares of common stock and reducing the par or stated value per share in proportion. The purpose of the split is to reduce substantially the market price of the common stock, with the intent of making the stock more attractive to investors.

For example, assume that Pelican Corporation has outstanding 1 million shares of $10 par value stock. The market price is $90 per share. The corporation now reduces the par value from $10 to $5 per share and increases the number of shares from 1 million to 2 million. This action would be called a 2 for 1 stock split. A stockholder who owned 100 shares of the stock before the split would own 200 shares after the split. Since the number of outstanding shares has been doubled without any change in total assets or total stockholders' equity, the market price of the stock should drop from $90 to approximately $45 a share.

A stock split does not change the balance of any ledger account; consequently, the transaction may be recorded merely by *memoranda entries* in the general journal and in the Common Stock account. For Pelican Corporation, these memoranda entries might read:

Memorandum entry to record a stock split

Sept. 30   **Memorandum: Issued additional 1 million shares of common stock in a 2 for 1 stock split. Par value reduced from $10 per share to $5 per share.**

The description of common stock also is changed in the balance sheet to reflect the lower par value and the greater number of shares outstanding.

Stock may be split in any desired ratio. Among the more common ratios are 2 for 1, 3 for 2, and 3 for 1. The determining factor is the number of shares needed to bring the price of the stock into the desired trading range. For example, assume that a stock is selling at a price of $150 per share, and that management wants to reduce the price to approximately $30 per share. This objective may be accomplished with a *5 for 1* stock split ($150 ÷ 5 = $30).

Distinction between stock splits and large stock dividends. What is the difference between a 2 for 1 stock split and a 100% stock dividend? There is very little difference; both will double the number of outstanding shares without changing total stockholders' equity, and both will serve to cut the market price of the stock in half. The stock dividend, however, will cause a transfer from the Retained Earnings account to the Common Stock account equal to the par or stated value of the dividend shares, whereas the stock split does not change the dollar balance of any account.

After an increase in the number of shares as a result of a stock split or stock dividend, earnings per share are computed in terms of the increased number of shares. In presenting five- or ten-year summaries, the earnings per share for earlier years are *retroactively revised* to reflect the increased number of shares currently outstanding and thus make the trend of earnings per share from year to year a valid comparison.

Retained earnings

Throughout this textbook, the term retained earnings is used to describe the portion of stockholders' equity derived from profitable operations. Retained earnings is increased by earning net income and is reduced by the declaration of dividends.

In addition to a balance sheet and an income statement, a complete set of financial statements includes a statement of retained earnings and a statement of cash flows. The statement of cash flows will be discussed in Chapter 14; a statement of retained earnings is illustrated below:

SHORE LINE CORPORATION
Statement of Retained Earnings
For the Year Ended December 31, 1990

Retained earnings, December 31, 1989.		$600,000
Net income		180,000
Subtotal		$780,000
Less: Cash dividends:		
Preferred stock ($5 per share)	$ 17,500	
Common stock ($1 per share).	55,300	
10% stock dividend	140,000	212,800
Retained earnings, December 31, 1990.		$567,200

Prior period adjustments

5 Define prior period adjustments and explain how they are presented in financial statements.

On occasion, a company may discover that a material error was made in the measurement of net income in a prior year. Since net income is closed into the Retained Earnings account, an error in reported net income will cause an error in the amount of retained earnings shown in all subsequent balance sheets. When such errors come to light, they should be corrected. The correction, called a ***prior period adjustment***, is shown in the ***statement of retained earnings*** as an adjustment to the balance of retained earnings at the beginning of the current year. The amount of the adjustment is shown net of any related income tax effects.

To illustrate, assume that late in 1990 Shore Line Corporation discovers that it failed to record depreciation on certain assets in 1989. After considering the income tax effects of this error, the company finds that the net income reported in 1989 was overstated by $35,000. Thus, the current balance of retained earnings ($600,000 at December 31, 1989) also is overstated by $35,000. Correction of this error will appear in the 1990 statement of retained earnings as follows:

SHORE LINE CORPORATION
Statement of Retained Earnings
For the Year Ended December 31, 1990

Notice the adjustment to beginning retained earnings

Retained earnings, December 31, 1989:		
As originally reported		$600,000
Less: Prior period adjustment for error in recording 1989 depreciation		
expense (net of $15,000 income taxes)		(35,000)
As restated.		$565,000
Net income.		180,000
Subtotal.		$745,000
Less: Cash dividends:		
Preferred stock ($5 per share).	$ 17,500	
Common stock ($1 per share)	55,300	
10% stock dividend.	140,000	212,800
Retained earnings, December 31, 1990		$532,200

Prior period adjustments rarely appear in the financial statements of large, publicly owned corporations. The financial statements of these corporations are audited annually by certified public accountants and are not likely to contain material errors which subsequently will require correction by prior period adjustments. Such adjustments are much more likely to appear in the financial statements of closely held corporations that are not audited on an annual basis.

Restrictions of retained earnings. Some portion of retained earnings may be restricted because of various contractual agreements. A "restriction" of retained earnings prevents a company from declaring a dividend that would cause retained earnings to fall below a designated level. Most companies disclose restrictions of retained earnings in notes accompanying the financial statements. For example, a company with retained earnings of $10 million might include the following note in its financial statements:

Footnote disclosure of restrictions placed on retained earnings

Note 7: Restriction of retained earnings

As of December 31, 19__, certain long-term debt agreements prohibited the declaration of cash dividends that would reduce the amount of retained earnings below $5,200,000. Retained earnings not so restricted amounted to $4,800,000.

Treasury stock

Corporations frequently reacquire shares of their own capital stock by purchase in the open market. Paying out cash to reacquire shares will reduce the assets of the corporation and reduce the stockholders' equity by the same amount. One reason for such purchases is to have stock available to reissue to officers and employees under bonus plans. Other reasons may include a desire to increase the reported earnings per share or to support the current market price of the stock.

Treasury stock may be defined as shares of a corporation's own capital stock that have been issued and later *reacquired by the issuing company,* but that have not been canceled or permanently retired. Treasury shares may be held indefinitely or may be issued again at any time. Shares of capital stock held in the treasury are not entitled to receive dividends, to vote, or to share in assets upon dissolution of the company. In the computation of earnings per share, shares held in the treasury are not regarded as outstanding shares.

Recording purchases of treasury stock

6 Account for treasury stock transactions.

Purchases of treasury stock should be recorded by debiting the Treasury Stock account with the cost of the stock.[5] For example, if Torrey Corporation reacquires 1,500 shares of its own $5 par stock at a price of $100 per share, the entry is as follows:

[5] State laws may prescribe different methods of accounting for treasury stock transactions. In this text, we illustrate only the widely used "cost method."

Treasury stock recorded at cost

```
Treasury Stock ...................................................  150,000
     Cash .......................................................          150,000
Purchased 1,500 shares of $5 par treasury stock at $100 per share.
```

Note that the Treasury Stock account is debited for the **cost** of the shares purchased, not their par value.

Treasury stock not an asset. When treasury stock is purchased, the corporation is eliminating part of its stockholder's equity by a payment to one or more stockholders. The purchase of treasury stock should be regarded as a **reduction of stockholders' equity,** not as the acquisition of an asset. For this reason, the Treasury Stock account should appear in the balance sheet **as a deduction in the stockholders' equity section.**[6] The presentation of treasury stock in a corporate balance sheet is illustrated on page 517.

Reissuance of treasury stock

When treasury shares are reissued, the Treasury Stock account is credited for the cost of the shares reissued and Paid-in Capital from Treasury Stock Transactions is debited or credited for any difference between **cost** and the reissue price. To illustrate, assume that 1,000 of the treasury shares acquired by Torrey Corporation at a cost of $100 per share are now reissued at a price of $115 per share. The entry to record the reissuance of these shares at a price above cost would be:

Reissued at a price above cost

```
Cash ...........................................................  115,000
     Treasury Stock...............................................          100,000
     Paid-in Capital from Treasury Stock Transactions ..................          15,000
Sold 1,000 shares of treasury stock, which cost $100,000 at a price of $115
per share.
```

If treasury stock is reissued at a price below cost, paid-in capital from previous treasury stock transactions is reduced (debited) by the excess of cost over the reissue price. To illustrate, assume that Torrey Corporation reissues its remaining 500 shares of treasury stock (cost $100 per share) at a price of $90 per share. The entry would be:

Reissued at a price below cost

```
Cash ...........................................................  45,000
Paid-in Capital from Treasury Stock Transactions .........................  5,000
     Treasury Stock...............................................          50,000
Sold 500 shares of treasury stock, which cost $50,000 at a price of $90 each.
```

[6] Despite a lack of theoretical support, a few corporations do classify treasury stock as an asset, on the grounds that the shares could be sold for cash just as readily as shares owned in another corporation. The same argument could be made of treating unissued shares as assets. Treasury shares are basically the same as unissued shares, and an unissued share of stock is definitely not an asset.

If there is no paid-in capital from previous treasury stock transactions, the excess of the cost of the treasury shares over the reissue price may be recorded as a debit in any other paid-in capital account.

No profit or loss on treasury stock transactions. Note that *no gain or loss is recognized on treasury stock transactions,* even when the shares are reissued at a price above or below cost. A corporation earns profits by selling goods and services to outsiders, not by issuing or reissuing shares of its own capital stock. When treasury shares are reissued at a price above cost, the corporation receives from the new stockholder a larger amount of paid-in capital than was eliminated when the corporation acquired the treasury shares. Conversely, if treasury shares are reissued at a price below cost, the corporation ends up with less paid-in capital as a result of the purchase and reissuance of the shares. Thus, any changes in stockholders' equity resulting from treasury stock transactions are regarded as changes in *paid-in capital* and are *not* included in the measurement of net income.

Restriction of retained earnings for treasury stock owned. Purchases of treasury stock, like cash dividends, are distributions of assets to the stockholders in the corporation. Many states have a legal requirement that distributions to stockholders (including purchases of treasury stock) cannot exceed the balance in the Retained Earnings account. Therefore, retained earnings usually is restricted by an amount equal to the cost of any shares held in the treasury.

Statement of stockholders' equity

7 Prepare a statement of stockholders' equity.

Many corporations expand their statement of retained earnings to show the changes during the year in all of the stockholders' equity accounts. This expanded statement, called a *statement of stockholders' equity,* is illustrated on the following page.

The top line of this statement shows the beginning balance in each stockholders' equity account. All of the transactions affecting these accounts during the year then are listed in summary form, along with the related changes in the balances of specific stockholders' equity accounts. The bottom line of the statement shows the ending balance in each stockholders' equity account and should agree with the amounts shown in the year-end balance sheet.

A statement of stockholders' equity is not a required financial statement. However, it is widely used as a substitute for the *statement of retained earnings* because it presents a more complete description of the transactions affecting stockholders' equity. Notice that the Retained Earnings column of this statement contains the same items shown in the statement of retained earnings illustrated on page 511.

Book value per share of common stock

Since each stockholder's equity in a corporation is determined by the number of shares he or she owns, an accounting measurement of interest to many stock-

SHORE LINE CORPORATION
Statement of Stockholders' Equity
For the Year Ended December 31, 1990

	5% Convertible Preferred Stock ($100 Par Value)	Common Stock ($10 Par Value)	Paid-in Capital in Excess of Par Value	Retained Earnings	Treasury Stock	Total Stockholders' Equity
Balances, December 31, 1989	$400,000	$200,000	$300,000	$600,000	$ -0-	$1,500,000
Prior period adjustment (net of $15,000 income taxes)				(35,000)		(35,000)
Issuance of common stock: 5,000 shares @ $52		50,000	210,000			260,000
Conversion of 1,000 shares of preferred stock into 3,000 shares of common stock	(100,000)	30,000	70,000			
Distributed 10% stock dividend (2,800 shares of common stock; market price $50 per share)		28,000	112,000	(140,000)		
Purchased 1,000 shares of common stock for the treasury at a price of $47 per share					(47,000)	(47,000)
Net income.............				180,000		180,000
Cash dividends:						
Preferred stock ($5 per share)				(17,500)		(17,500)
Common stock ($2 per share)				(55,300)		(55,300)
Balances, December 31, 1990	$300,000	$308,000	$692,000	$532,200	$(47,000)	$1,785,200

holders is book value per share of common stock. Book value per share is equal to the ***net assets*** represented by one share of stock. The term ***net assets*** means total assets minus total liabilities; in other words, net assets are equal to total stockholders' equity. Thus in a corporation which has issued common stock only, the book value per share is computed by dividing total stockholders' equity by the number of shares outstanding.

For example, assume that a corporation has 4,000 shares of capital stock outstanding and the stockholders' equity section of the balance sheet is as follows:

How much is
book value per
share?

Capital stock, $1 par value	$ 4,000
Paid-in capital in excess of par value	40,000
Retained earnings	76,000
Total stockholders' equity	$120,000

The book value per share is $30; it is computed by dividing the stockholders' equity of $120,000 by the 4,000 shares of outstanding stock. In computing book value, we are not concerned with the number of authorized shares but merely with the outstanding shares, because the total of the outstanding shares represents 100% of the stockholders' equity.

Book value when a company has both preferred and common stock. Book value is computed only for common stock. If a company has both preferred and common stock outstanding, the computation of book value per share of common stock requires two steps. First, the redemption value or call price of the entire preferred stock issue and any dividends in arrears are deducted from total stockholders' equity. Second, the remaining amount of stockholders' equity is divided by the number of common shares outstanding to determine book value per common share. This procedure reflects the fact that the common stockholders are the residual owners of the corporate entity.

To illustrate, assume that the stockholders' equity of Video Company at December 31 is as follows:

8% preferred stock, $100 par, callable at $110.	$1,000,000
Common stock, no-par; $10 stated value; authorized 100,000 shares, issued and outstanding 50,000 shares.	500,000
Paid-in capital in excess of par value.	750,000
Retained earnings.	130,000
Total stockholders' equity	$2,380,000

Because of a weak cash position, Video Company has paid no dividends during the current year. As of December 31, dividends in arrears on the cumulative preferred stock total $80,000.

All the capital belongs to the common stockholders, except the $1.1 million call price ($110 × 10,000 shares) applicable to the preferred stock and the $80,000 of dividends in arrears on preferred stock. The calculation of book value per share of common stock can therefore be made as follows:

Total stockholders' equity		$2,380,000
Less: Equity of preferred stockholders:		
Call price of preferred stock	$1,100,000	
Dividends in arrears	80,000	1,180,000
Equity of common stockholders		$1,200,000
Number of common shares outstanding		50,000
Book value per share of common stock ($1,200,000 ÷ 50,000)		$24

To some extent, book value is used in evaluating the reasonableness of the market price of a stock. However, it must be used with great caution; the fact that a stock is selling at less than book value does not necessarily indicate a bargain.

Book value is a historical concept, representing the amounts invested by stockholders plus the amounts earned and retained by the corporation. If a stock is selling at a price well **above book value,** investors believe that management has created a business worth substantially more than the historical cost of the resources entrusted to its care. This, in essence, is the sign of a successful corporation. If the excess of market price over book value becomes very great, however, investors should consider whether the company's prospects really justify a market price so much above the underlying book value of the shares.

On the other hand, if the market price of a stock is **less than book value,** investors believe that the company's resources are worth less than their historical amounts when under the control of current management. Thus, the relationship between book value and market price is one measure of investors' confidence in a company's management.

Illustration of a stockholders' equity section

The following illustration of a stockholders' equity section of a balance sheet includes some of the items discussed in this chapter. For illustrative purposes, we also show the computation of book value per share. (This computation is not shown in an actual balance sheet.) You should be able to explain the nature and origin of each account and disclosure printed in black.

Stockholders' Equity

Capital stock:

8% Preferred stock, $100 par value, call price $110 per share, authorized and issued 2,000 shares		$200,000
Common stock, $5 par value, authorized 100,000 shares, issued 32,000 shares (of which 2,000 are held in the treasury)		160,000
Additional paid-in capital:		
Paid-in capital in excess of par: common stock	$240,000	
Paid-in capital from stock dividends	50,000	
Paid-in capital from treasury stock transactions	10,000	300,000
Total paid-in capital		$660,000
Retained earnings (of which $50,000, an amount equal to the cost of treasury stock owned, is not available for dividends)		210,000
Subtotal		$870,000
Less: Treasury stock (2,000 shares of common, at cost)		50,000
Total stockholders' equity		$820,000

* Book value per share: $820,000 − (2,000 preferred shares × $110) = $600,000 equity of common stockholders; $600,000 ÷ 30,000 outstanding common shares = $20 per share.

INVESTMENTS IN CORPORATE SECURITIES

In the last several chapters, we have described corporate securities (stocks and bonds) from the viewpoint of the issuing corporation. Let us now look at these securities from the viewpoint of the investor.

Marketable securities

The term **marketable securities** refers primarily to U.S. government bonds and to the bonds and stocks of large corporations. These securities are traded on organized securities exchanges, such as the New York Stock Exchange. Thus, they are easily purchased or sold at quoted market prices. Investments in marketable securities earn a return for the investor, yet are almost as liquid as cash itself. For this reason, marketable securities are listed in the balance sheet second among current assets, immediately after cash.

To qualify as a current asset, an investment in marketable securities must be readily marketable. **Readily marketable** means immediately salable at a quoted market price. In addition, management must be **willing** to use the invested funds to pay current liabilities. Investments which are not readily marketable, or which management intends to hold on a long-term basis, are **not** current assets. Such investments should be shown in the balance sheet just below the current asset section under the caption, Long-Term Investments.

Some investors own enough of a company's common stock to influence or control the company's activities through the voting rights of the shares owned. Such large holdings of capital stock create important business relationships between the investor and the issuing corporation. Since investments of this type cannot be sold without disturbing these relationships, they are not considered "marketable" securities. **Investments for purposes of control** are discussed in Appendix B.

Quoted market prices. The market prices of most marketable securities are quoted daily by brokerage houses and in the financial pages of major newspapers. The market prices of stocks are quoted in terms of dollars per share. As illustrated in Chapter 11, bond prices are stated as a percentage of the bond's maturity value, which is usually $1,000. Thus, a bond with a quoted price of **102** has a market value of **$1,020** ($1,000 × 102%).

Accounting for marketable securities

8 Account for short-term investments in stocks and bonds.
Accounting principles differ somewhat between investments in marketable **equity** securities (stocks) and in marketable **debt** securities (bonds). For this reason, separate controlling accounts are used in the general ledger for each type of investment. For each controlling account, a subsidiary ledger is maintained which shows for each security owned the acquisition date, total cost, number of shares (or bonds) owned, and the cost per share (or bond). This subsidiary ledger provides the information necessary to determine the amount of gain or loss when an investment in a particular stock or bond is sold.

The principal distinction in accounting for investments in stocks and in bonds is that **interest on bonds accrues** from day to day. An investor in bonds must account for this accrued interest when the bonds are purchased, at the end of each accounting period, and when the bonds are sold. Dividends on stock, however, **do not accrue.**

Bond interest payments. The amount of interest paid to bondholders is equal to a stated percentage of the bond's maturity value. Thus, the owner of a 10% bond would receive $100 interest ($1,000 × 10%) every year. Since bond interest usually is paid semiannually, the bondholder would receive two semiannual interest payments of $50 each.

When bonds are purchased between interest dates, the purchaser pays the quoted market price for the bond **plus** the interest accrued since the last interest payment date. By this arrangement the new owner becomes entitled to receive in full the next semiannual interest payment. An account called Bond Interest Receivable should be debited for the amount of interest purchased.

Marketable debt securities (bonds)

To illustrate the accounting entries for an investment in bonds, assume that on August 1 an investor purchases ten 9%, $1,000 bonds of Rider Co. which pay interest on June 1 and December 1. The investor buys the bonds on August 1 at a price of 98 (or $9,800), plus a brokerage commission of $50 and two months' accrued interest of $150 ($10,000 × 9% × $\frac{2}{12}$ = $150). The brokerage commission is viewed as part of the cost of the bonds. However, the accrued interest receivable at the time of purchase must be accounted for separately. Therefore, the entry made by the investor on August 1 is:

Separate account for accrued bond interest purchased		
Marketable Debt Securities	9,850	
Bond Interest Receivable.	150	
Cash.		10,000

Purchased ten 9% bonds of Rider Co. for $9,800 plus a brokerage commission of $50 and two months' accrued interest.

On December 1, the semiannual interest payment date, the investor will receive an interest check for $450, which will be recorded as follows:

Note portion of interest check earned		
Cash	450	
Bond Interest Receivable		150
Bond Interest Revenue		300

Received semiannual interest on Rider Co. bonds.

The $300 credit to Bond Interest Revenue represents the amount actually earned during the four months the bonds were owned by the investor (9% × $10,000 × $\frac{4}{12}$ = $300).

If the investor's accounting records are maintained on a calendar-year basis, the following adjusting entry is required at December 31 to record bond interest earned since December 1:

Bond Interest Receivable..	75	
Bond Interest Revenue		75

To accrue one month's interest earned (Dec. 1–Dec. 31) on Rider Co. bonds ($10,000 × 9% × $\frac{1}{12}$ = $75).

Amortization of bond discount or premium from the investor's viewpoint. We have discussed the need for the corporation issuing bonds payable to amortize any bond discount or premium to measure correctly the bond interest expense. But what about the *purchaser* of the bonds? When an investment in bonds is classified as a current asset, the investor usually *does not* amortize discount or premium. The justification for this practice is the accounting principle of *materiality*. Given that the investment may be held for but a short period of time, amortization of bond discount or premium probably will not have a material effect upon reported net income. When an investment in bonds will be held for the long term, however, the investor should amortize discount or premium. Amortization of a discount will increase the amount of interest revenue recognized by the investor; amortization of a premium will reduce the amount of interest revenue recognized.

Marketable equity securities (stocks)

Since dividends on stock do not accrue, the *entire cost* of purchasing stock (including brokerage commissions) is debited to the Marketable Equity Securities account. Dividend revenue usually is recognized when the dividend check arrives; the entry consists of a debit to Cash and a credit to Dividend Revenue. No adjusting entries are needed to recognize dividend revenue at the end of an accounting period.

Additional shares of stock received in stock splits or stock dividends *are not income* to the stockholder, and only a *memorandum entry* is used to record the increase in the number of shares owned. The *cost basis per share* is decreased, however, because of the larger number of shares comprising the investment after receiving additional "free" shares from a stock split or a stock dividend.

As an example, assume that an investor paid a total of $7,200 (commission included) for 100 shares of stock. Thus, cost per share was $72. Later the investor received 20 additional shares as a stock dividend. The cost per share is thereby reduced to $60 a share, computed by dividing the total cost of $7,200 by the 120 shares owned after the 20% stock dividend. The memorandum entry to be made in the general journal would be as follows:

July 10 Memorandum: Received 20 additional shares of Delta Co. common stock as a result of 20% stock dividend. Now own 120 shares with a cost basis of $7,200, or $60 per share.

Gains and losses from sales of investments

The sale of an investment in **stocks** is recorded by debiting Cash for the amount received and crediting the Marketable Equity Securities account for the cost of the securities sold. Any difference between the proceeds of the sale and the cost of the investment is recorded by a debit to Loss on Sale of Marketable Securities or by a credit to Gain on Sale of Marketable Securities.

At the date of sale of an investment in **bonds,** any interest which has accrued since the last interest payment date (or year-end) should be recognized as interest revenue. For example, assume that 10 bonds of the Elk Corporation carried in the accounts of an investor at $9,600 are sold at a price of 94, plus accrued interest of $90, and less a brokerage commission of $50. The gain or loss may be computed as follows:

Proceeds from sale ($9,400 + $90 − $50).	$9,440
Less: Proceeds representing interest revenue.	90
Sales price of investment in bonds	$9,350
Cost of investment in bonds.	9,600
Loss on sale	$ 250

This sale should be recorded by the following journal entry:

Investment in bonds sold at a loss		
Cash	9,440	
Loss on Sale of Marketable Securities.	250	
Marketable Debt Securities.		9,600
Bond Interest Revenue		90
Sold 10 bonds of Elk Corporation at 94 and accrued interest of $90, less broker's commission of $50.		

Balance sheet valuation of marketable securities

Although the market price of a bond may fluctuate from day to day, we can be reasonably certain that when the maturity date arrives the market price will be equal to the bond's maturity value. Stocks, on the other hand, do not have maturity values. When the market price of stock declines, there is no way we can be certain whether the decline will be temporary or permanent. For this reason, different valuation standards are applied in accounting for investments in marketable **debt** securities and investments in marketable **equity** securities.

Valuation of marketable debt securities. A short-term investment in bonds is generally carried in the accounting records at **cost** and a gain or loss is recognized when the investment is sold. If bonds are held as a long-term investment and the difference between the cost of the investment and its maturity value is substantial, the valuation of the investment is adjusted each year by amortization of the discount or premium.

Valuation of marketable equity securities. The market price of stocks may rise or fall dramatically during an accounting period.

● **CASE IN POINT** ● In a single day, the market price of IBM's capital stock dropped over $31 per share, falling from $135 to $103.25. Of course, this was not a "typical" day. The date — October 19, 1987 — will long be remembered as "Black Monday." On this day, stock prices around the world suffered the greatest one-day decline in history. Those stocks listed on the New York Stock Exchange lost about 20% of their total value in six hours. Given that annual dividends on these stocks amounted to about 2% of market value, this one-day "market loss" was approximately equal to the loss by investors of all dividend revenue for a period of 10 years.

An investor who sells an investment at a price above or below cost will recognize a gain or loss on the sale. But what if the investor continues to hold securities after a significant change in their market value? In this case, should any gain or loss be recognized in the financial statements?

Lower-of-cost-or-market

The FASB has stated that a portfolio of marketable equity securities should be shown in the investor's balance sheet at the ***lower of*** the portfolio's total cost or current market value. If the market value of the portfolio ***falls below cost,*** the decline in value is ***reported as a loss*** in the investor's income statement. Recoveries in the market value of the portfolio are reported in the income statement as gains, but only as the market value rises back up to cost. Increases in market value above cost are ***not shown*** in the income statement.

The lower-of-cost-or-market rule produces ***conservative results*** in both the balance sheet and the income statement. In the balance sheet, the portfolio of securities is shown at the lowest justifiable amount — that is, the lower of its cost or its market value. In the income statement, declines in market value below cost immediately are recognized as losses. Increases in market value above cost, however, are not recognized until the securities are sold.[7]

The lower-of-cost-or-market rule involves many mechanical and theoretical issues which are appropriately deferred to later accounting courses.

Income tax rules for marketable securities. The lower-of-cost-or-market rule is not used in determining income subject to income tax. The only gains or losses recognized for income tax purposes are realized gains and losses resulting from sale of an investment.

---

[7] This discussion assumes that the portfolio of marketable equity securities is classified as a current asset. If the portfolio is classified as a long-term investment, the gains and losses from price fluctuations when market price is below cost are not reported in the income statement. Instead, the net decline in market value is reported as a separate item in the stockholders' equity section of the balance sheet.

END-OF-CHAPTER REVIEW

Summary of chapter learning objectives

1 Describe how discontinued operations, extraordinary items, and accounting changes are presented in the income statement.

Each of these "unusual" items is shown in a separate section of the income statement, after determination of the income or loss from ordinary and continuing operations. Each special item is shown net of any related income tax effects.

2 Compute earnings per share.

Net earnings per share is computed by dividing the income applicable to the common stock by the weighted average number of common shares outstanding. If the income statement includes subtotals for income from continuing operations, or for income before extraordinary items, per share figures are shown for these amounts as well as for net income.

3 Distinguish between primary and fully diluted earnings per share.

Fully diluted earnings per share must be computed only for companies that have outstanding securities convertible into shares of common stock. In such situations, the computation of primary earnings per share is based upon the number of common shares actually outstanding during the year. The computation of fully diluted earnings, however, is based upon the potential number of common shares outstanding if the various securities were converted into common shares. The purpose of showing fully diluted earnings is to warn investors of the extent to which conversions of securities could dilute primary earnings per share.

4 Account for stock dividends and stock splits, and explain the probable effect of these transactions upon market price.

Small stock dividends are recorded by transferring the market value of the additional shares to be issued from retained earnings to the appropriate paid-in capital accounts. (Large stock dividends—over 20 or 25%—are recorded at par value, rather than market value.) A stock split, on the other hand, is recorded only by a memorandum entry indicating that the number of outstanding shares have been increased and that the par value per share has been reduced proportionately. Both stock dividends and stock splits increase the number of shares outstanding, but neither transaction changes total stockholders' equity. Therefore, both stock dividends and stock splits should reduce the market price per share in proportion to the number of additional shares issued.

5 Define prior period adjustments and explain how they are presented in financial statements.

A prior period adjustment is an entry to correct an error in the amount of net income reported in a prior year. As the income of the prior year has already been closed into retained earnings, the error is corrected by debiting or crediting the Retained Earnings account. Prior period adjustments appear in the statement of retained earnings, not in the income statement for the current period.

6 Account for treasury stock transactions.

Purchases of treasury stock are recorded by debiting a contra-equity account, entitled Treasury stock. No profit or loss is recorded when the treasury shares are reissued at a price above or below cost. Rather, any difference between the reissuance price and the cost of the shares is debited or credited to a paid-in capital account.

7 Prepare a statement of stockholders' equity.

This expanded version of the statement of retained earnings explains the changes during the year in each stockholders' equity account. It is not a required financial statement, but is often prepared instead of a statement of retained earnings. The statement lists the beginning balance in each stockholders' equity account, explains the nature and the amount of each change, and thus computes the ending balance in each equity account.

8 Account for short-term investments in stocks and bonds.

Investments in stocks and bonds are initially recorded at cost, and gains or losses from changes in the market value of the investments are recognized when the investments are sold. Interest revenue from an investment in bonds is recognized as it accrues. Dividend revenue from stocks, however, does not accrue. Rather, it is recognized when the dividends are actually received. Short-term investments in bonds generally appear in the balance sheet at cost; a portfolio of short-term investments in stocks, on the other hand, is valued at the lower of total cost or market value.

Key terms introduced or emphasized in chapter 13

Book value. The stockholders' equity represented by each share of common stock. Computed by dividing the common stockholders' equity by the number of common shares outstanding.

Date of record. The date on which a person must be listed as a shareholder in order to be eligible to receive a dividend. Follows the date of declaration of a dividend by two or three weeks.

Discontinued operations. The net operating results (revenue and expenses) of a segment of a company which has been or is being sold.

Earnings per share. Net income applicable to the common stock divided by the weighted-average number of common shares outstanding during the year.

Ex-dividend date. A date three days prior to the date of record specified in a dividend declaration. A person buying a stock prior to the ex-dividend date also acquires the right to receive the dividend. The three-day interval permits the compilation of a list of stockholders as of the date of record.

Extraordinary items. Transactions and events that are material in dollar amount, unusual in nature, and occur infrequently; for example, a large earthquake loss. Such items are shown separately in the income statement after the determination of Income before Extraordinary Items.

Fully diluted earnings per share. Earnings per share computed under the assumption that all convertible securities had been converted into additional common shares at the beginning of the current year. The purpose of this hypothetical computation is to warn common stockholders of the risk that future earnings per share might be diluted by the conversion of other securities into common stock.

Lower-of-cost-or-market (LCM). The conservative practice of valuing a portfolio of marketable equity securities in the balance sheet at the lower of total cost or current market value.

Marketable securities. Investments in stocks (equity securities) and bonds (debt securities). A highly liquid investment that may be sold at any time. Classified as a current asset second only to cash in liquidity.

Portfolio. A group of investment securities that receive similar accounting treatment and balance sheet classification. An investor's holdings of marketable *equity* securities and of marketable *debt* securities are considered two separate portfolios. In addition, the investor may have both a long-term and a short-term portfolio in each category.

Price-earnings ratio. Market price of a share of common stock divided by annual earnings per share.

Primary earnings per share. Net income applicable to the common stock divided by weighted-average number of common shares outstanding during the year.

Prior period adjustment. A correction of a material error in the earnings reported in the financial statements of a prior year. Prior period adjustments are recorded directly in the Retained Earnings account and are not included in the income statement of the current period.

Segment of a business. Those elements of a business that represent a separate and distinct line of business activity or that service a distinct category of customers.

Statement of retained earnings. A basic financial statement explaining the change during the year in the amount of retained earnings. May be expanded into a *statement of stockholders' equity.*

Statement of stockholders' equity. An expanded version of a *statement of retained earnings.* Summarizes the changes during the year in all stockholders' equity accounts. Not a required financial statement, but widely used as a substitute for the statement of retained earnings.

Stock dividend. A distribution of additional shares to common stockholders in proportion to their holdings.

Stock split. An increase in the number of shares outstanding with a corresponding decrease in par value per share. The additional shares are distributed proportionately to all common shareholders. Purpose is to reduce market price per share and encourage wider public ownership of the company's stock. A 2 for 1 stock split will give each stockholder twice as many shares as previously owned.

Treasury stock. Shares of a corporation's stock which have been issued and then reacquired, but not canceled.

Demonstration problem for your review

The stockholders' equity of Sutton Corporation at January 1, 19__, is shown below:

Stockholders' equity:

Common stock, $10 par, 100,000 shares authorized, 40,000 shares issued.......	$ 400,000
Paid-in capital in excess of par: common stock	200,000
Total paid-in capital..	$ 600,000
Retained earnings...	1,500,000
Total stockholders' equity	$2,100,000

Transactions affecting stockholders' equity during the year are as follows:

Mar. 31　A 5 for 4 stock split proposed by the board of directors was approved by vote of the stockholders. The 10,000 new shares were distributed to stockholders.

Apr. 1　The company purchased 2,000 shares of its common stock on the open market at $37 per share.

July 1　The company reissued 1,000 shares of treasury stock at $45 per share.

July 1　Issued for cash 20,000 shares of previously unissued $8 par value common stock at a price of $45 per share.

Dec. 1　A cash dividend of $1 per share was declared, payable on December 30, to stockholders of record at December 14.

Dec. 22　A 10% stock dividend was declared; the dividend shares to be distributed on January 15 of the following year. The market price of the stock on December 22 was $48 per share.

The net income for the year ended December 31, 19__, amounted to $177,000, after an extraordinary loss of $35,400 (net of related income tax benefits).

Instructions

  a Prepare journal entries (in general journal form) to record the transactions relating to stockholders' equity that took place during the year.

  b Prepare the lower section of the income statement for the year, beginning with the ***income before extraordinary items*** and showing the extraordinary loss and the net income. Also illustrate the presentation of earnings per share in the income statement, assuming that earnings per share is determined on the basis of the ***weighted-average*** number of shares outstanding during the year.

Solution to demonstration problem

a   **General Journal**

Mar. 31	Memorandum: Stockholders approved a 5 for 4 stock split. This action increased the number of shares of common stock outstanding from 40,000 to 50,000 and reduced the par value from $10 to $8 per share. The 10,000 new shares were distributed.		
Apr. 1	Treasury Stock	74,000	
	Cash		74,000
	Acquired 2,000 shares of treasury stock at $37 per share.		
July 1	Cash..	45,000	
	Treasury Stock.......................................		37,000
	Paid-in Capital from Treasury Stock Transactions		8,000
	Sold 1,000 shares of treasury stock at $45 per share.		
1	Cash..	900,000	
	Common Stock, $8 par		160,000
	Paid-in Capital in Excess of Par: Common Stock		740,000
	Issued 20,000 shares of previously unissued $8 par value stock for cash of $45 per share.		
Dec. 1	Dividends...	69,000	
	Dividends Payable.....................................		69,000
	To record declaration of cash dividend of $1 per share on 69,000 shares of common stock outstanding (1,000 shares in treasury are not entitled to receive dividends).		

Note: Entry to record the payment of the cash dividend is not shown here since the action does not affect the stockholders' equity.

22	Retained Earnings	331,200	
	Stock Dividends to Be Distributed.......................		55,200
	Paid-in Capital from Stock Dividends		276,000
	To record declaration of 10% stock dividend consisting of 6,900 shares of $8 par value common stock to be distributed on Jan. 15 of next year.		

31	Income Summary	177,000	
	Retained Earnings.....................................		177,000
	To close Income Summary account.		

31	Retained Earnings	69,000	
	Dividends		69,000
	To close Dividends account.		

b

SUTTON CORPORATION
Partial Income Statement
For Year Ended December 31, 19___

Income before extraordinary items..	$212,400
Extraordinary loss (net of income tax benefits)	(35,400)
Net income..	$177,000

Earnings per share.*

Income before extraordinary items..	$3.60
Extraordinary loss...	(0.60)
Net income..	$3.00

* On 59,000 weighted-average number of shares of common stock outstanding during 19___ , determined as follows:

Jan. 1 – Mar. 31: (40,000 + 10,000 shares issued pursuant to a 5 for 4 split) $\times \frac{1}{4}$ of year.....	12,500
Apr. 1 – June 30: (50,000 − 2,000 shares of treasury stock) $\times \frac{1}{4}$ of year	12,000
July 1 – Dec. 31: (50,000 + 20,000 shares of new stock − 1,000 shares of treasury stock) $\times \frac{1}{2}$ of year...	34,500
Weighted-average number of shares outstanding	59,000

ASSIGNMENT MATERIAL

Review questions

1 What is the purpose of arranging an income statement to show subtotals for *Income from Continuing Operations* and for *Income before Extraordinary Items?*

2 Pappa Joe's owns 30 pizza parlors and a minor league baseball team. During the current year, the company sold three of its pizza parlors and closed another when the lease on the building expired. Should any of these events be classified as "discontinued operations" in the company's income statement? Explain.

3 Define *extraordinary items.* Give three examples of losses which qualify as extraordinary items and three examples of losses which would not be classified as extraordinary.

4 In past years, the management of St. Thomas Medical Supply had consistently estimated the allowance for doubtful accounts at 2% of total accounts receivable. In the current year, management estimated that uncollectible accounts would equal 4% of accounts receivable. Should the uncollectible accounts expense of prior years be recomputed in order to show in the income statement the cumulative effect of this change in accounting estimate?

5 Both the *cumulative effect of a change in accounting principle* and a *prior period adjustment* affect the income of past accounting periods. Distinguish between these two items and explain how each is shown in the financial statements.

6 In the current year, Garden Products decided to switch from use of an accelerated method of depreciation to the straight-line method. Will the cumulative effect of this change in accounting principle increase or decrease the amount of net income reported in the current year? Explain.

7 Explain how each of the following is computed:
a Price-earnings ratio
b Primary earnings per share
c Fully diluted earnings per share

8 Throughout the year, Gold Seal Co. had 4 million shares of common stock and 120,000 shares of convertible preferred stock outstanding. Each share of preferred is convertible into four shares of common. What number of shares should be used in the computation of (a) primary earnings per share, and (b) fully diluted earnings per share?

9 A financial analyst notes that Baxter Corporation's earnings per share have been rising steadily for the last five years. The analyst expects the company's net income to continue to increase at the same rate as in the past. In forecasting future primary earnings per share, what special risk should the analyst consider if Baxter's primary earnings are significantly larger than its fully diluted earnings?

10 Explain the significance of the following dates relating to dividends: date of declaration, date of record, date of payment, ex-dividend date.

11 What is the purpose of a *stock split?*

12 Distinguish between a *stock split* and a *stock dividend.* Is there any reason for the difference in accounting treatment of these two events?

13 What are *prior period adjustments?* How are they presented in financial statements?

14 Identify three items that may appear in a statement of retained earnings as changes in the amount of retained earnings.

15 A *statement of stockholders' equity* sometimes is called an "expanded" statement of retained earnings. Why?

16 What is *treasury stock?* Why do corporations purchase their own shares? Is treasury stock an asset? How should it be reported in the balance sheet?

17 In many states, the corporation law requires that retained earnings be restricted for dividend purposes to the extent of the cost of treasury shares. What is the reason for this legal rule?

18 What does *book value per share* of common stock represent? Does it represent the amount common stockholders would receive in the event that the corporation were liquidated? Explain briefly.

19 How is book value per share of common stock computed when a company has both preferred and common stock outstanding?

20 What would be the effect, if any, on book value per share of common stock as a result of each of the following independent events: (a) a corporation obtains a bank loan; (b) a dividend is declared (to be paid in the next accounting period); and (c) a corporation issues additional shares of common stock as a stock dividend.

21 If an investor buys a bond between interest dates, he or she pays as a part of the purchase price the accrued interest since the last interest date. On the other hand, if the investor buys a share of common or preferred stock, no "accrued dividend" is added to the quoted price. Explain why this difference exists.

22 Why must an investor who owns numerous marketable securities maintain a marketable securities subsidiary ledger?

23 In the current asset section of its balance sheet, Delta Industries shows marketable securities at a market value $120,000 below cost. If the market value of these securities rises by $190,000 during the next accounting period, how large a gain (if any) should Delta Industries include in its next income statement? Explain fully.

24 How does the financial reporting requirement of valuing marketable securities at the lower-of-cost-or-market value compare with *income tax rules* concerning marketable securities?

Exercises

Exercise 13-1
Accounting
terminology

Listed below are nine technical accounting terms introduced in this chapter:

Prior period adjustment	Fully diluted earnings per share	Primary earnings per share
Date of record	Book value per share	P/e ratio
Stock split	Extraordinary item	Stock dividend

Each of the following statements may (or may not) describe one of these technical terms. For each statement, indicate the accounting term described, or answer "None" if the statement does not correctly describe any of the terms.

a A gain or loss which is material in amount, unusual in nature, and not expected to recur in the foreseeable future.

b A hypothetical figure, showing the result which would have occurred if all of the securities convertible into common stock had been converted at the beginning of the current year.

c A statistic expressing a relationship between the current market value of a share of common stock and the underlying earnings per share.

d The date upon which the declaration of a cash dividend is recorded in the accounting records.

e An adjustment to the beginning balance of retained earnings to correct an error previously made in the measurement of net income.

f A distribution of additional shares to stockholders which does not change total stockholders' equity or the par value per share.

g The stockholders' equity represented by each share of common stock.

Exercise 13-2
Reporting
discontinued
operations

During the current year, SunSports, Inc., operated two business segments: a chain of surf and dive shops and a small chain of tennis shops. The tennis shops were not profitable and were sold near year-end to another corporation. SunSports' operations for the current year are summarized below. The first two captions, "Net sales" and "Costs and expenses," relate only the company's continuing operations.

Net sales	$9,600,000
Costs and expenses (including applicable income taxes)	8,600,000
Operating loss from tennis shops (net of income tax benefit)	160,000
Loss on sale of tennis shops (net of income tax benefit)	290,000

The company had 100,000 shares of a single class of capital stock outstanding throughout the year.

Instructions. Prepare a condensed income statement for the year. At the bottom of the statement, show any appropriate earnings-per-share figures.

Exercise 13-3
Reporting an ex-
traordinary item

For the year ended December 31, Union Chemical had net sales of $4,500,000, costs and other expenses (including income taxes) of $4,030,000, and an extraordinary loss (net of income tax) of $200,000. Prepare a condensed income statement (including earnings per share), assuming that 200,000 shares of common stock were outstanding throughout the year.

Exercise 13-4
Computing
earnings-per-
share: charges in
number of shares
outstanding

In the year just ended, Sunshine Citrus earned net income of $9,020,000. The company has issued only one class of capital stock, of which 1 million shares were outstanding at January 1. Compute the company's earnings per share under each of the following *independent* assumptions:

a No change occurred during the year in the number of shares outstanding.
b On October 1, the company issued an additional 100,000 shares of capital stock in exchange for cash.
c On July 1, the company distributed an additional 100,000 shares of capital stock as a 10% stock dividend. (No additional shares are issued on October 1.)

Exercise 13-5
Computing
earnings-per-
share: effect of
preferred stock

The net income of Carriage Trade Clothiers amounted to $3,750,000 for the current year. Compute the amount of earnings per share assuming that the shares of capital stock outstanding throughout the year consisted of:

a 300,000 shares of $10 par value common stock and no preferred stock.
b 200,000 shares of 9%, $100 par value, cumulative preferred stock and 300,000 shares of $5 par value common stock.

Exercise 13-6
Cash dividends,
stock dividends,
and stock splits

Glass Corporation has 500,000 shares of $5 par value capital stock outstanding. You are to prepare the journal entries to record the following transactions:

Apr. 30 Distributed an additional 500,000 shares of capital stock in a 2 for 1 stock split. Par value per share was reduced from $5 to $2.50.
June 1 Declared a cash dividend of 60 cents per share.
July 1 Paid the 60-cent cash dividend to stockholders.
Aug. 1 Declared a 5% stock dividend. Market price of stock was $19 per share.
Sept. 10 Issued 50,000 shares pursuant to the 5% stock dividend.
Dec. 1 Declared a 50% stock dividend. Market price of stock was $23 per share.

Exercise 13-7
Effect of stock
dividends on
stock price

Jiffy Tool Co. has a total of 40,000 shares of common stock outstanding and no preferred stock. Total stockholders' equity at the end of the current year amounts to $3 million and the market value of the stock is $84 per share. At year-end, the company declares a stock dividend of one share for each five shares held. If all parties concerned clearly recognize the nature of the stock dividend, what should you expect the market price per share of the common stock to be on the ex-dividend date?

Exercise 13-8
Recording
treasury stock
transactions

Cable Transmissions engaged in the following transactions involving treasury stock:

Nov. 10 Purchased for cash 12,500 shares of treasury stock at a price of $30 per share.
Dec. 4 Reissued 5,000 shares of treasury stock at a price of $33 per share.
Dec. 22 Reissued 4,000 shares of treasury stock at a price of $29 per share.

Instructions

a Prepare general journal entries to record these transactions.
b Compute the amount of retained earnings that should be restricted because of the treasury stock still owned at December 31.

Exercise 13-9
Computing book
value

Presented below is the information necessary to compute the net assets (stockholders' equity) and book value per share of common stock for Ringside Corporation:

8% cumulative preferred stock, $100 par (callable at $110)	$200,000
Common stock, $5 par, authorized 100,000 shares, issued 60,000 shares	300,000
Paid-in capital in excess of par	452,800
Deficit...	131,800
Dividends in arrears on preferred stock, 1 full year...............................	16,000

Instructions

    a Compute the amount of net assets (stockholders' equity).

    b Compute the book value per share of common stock.

Exercise 13-10
Investment in
bonds

Yamato Company purchased as a short-term investment $50,000 face value of the 9% bonds of Lorenzo, Inc., on March 31 of the current year, at a total cost of $50,625, including interest accrued since January 1. Interest is paid by Lorenzo, Inc., on June 30 and December 31. On July 31, four months after the purchase, Yamato Company sold the bonds and interest accrued since July 1 for a total price of $50,525.

    Prepare in general journal form all entries required in the accounting records of Yamato Company relating to the investment in Lorenzo, Inc., bonds. (Commissions are to be ignored.)

Exercise 13-11
Investment in
stocks

Prepare the journal entries in the accounting records of Axel Masters, Inc., to record the following transactions. Include a memorandum entry on July 9 to show the change in the cost basis per share.

Jan. 7 Purchased as a temporary investment 1,000 shares of Reed Company common stock at a price of $52 per share, plus a brokerage commission of $500.

Feb. 12 Received a cash dividend of $1 per share on the investment in Reed Company stock.

July 9 Received an additional 50 shares of Reed Company common stock as a result of a 5% stock dividend.

Aug. 14 Sold 500 shares of Reed Company common stock at a price of $55 per share, less a brokerage commission of $290.

Problems

Problem 13-1
Discontinued
operations and
extraordinary
items

Sea Quest Corporation operated both a fleet of commercial fishing vessels and a chain of six seafood restaurants. The restaurants continuously lost money and were sold to a large restaurant chain near year-end. The operating results of Sea Quest Corporation for the year ended December 31, 19__ are shown below:

Continuing operations (fishing fleet):	
Net sales	$23,000,000
Costs and expenses (including related income taxes).......................	20,100,000
Other data:	
Operating loss of restaurants (net of income tax benefit)	1,540,000
Gain on sale of restaurant properties (net of income taxes)..................	460,000
Extraordinary loss (net of income tax benefits)	720,000

The extraordinary loss resulted from the expropriation of a fishing vessel by a foreign government.

  Sea Quest Corporation had 500,000 shares of a single class of capital stock outstanding throughout the year.

Instructions. Prepare a condensed income statement including proper presentation of the discontinued restaurant operations and the extraordinary loss. Include all appropriate earnings-per-share figures. (A condensed income statement is illustrated on page 504.)

Problem 13-2
Format of an income statement and a statement of retained earnings

Shown below is data relating to the operations of Ocean Transport Corp. during 1990:

Continuing operations:

Net sales	$14,000,000
Costs and expenses (including applicable income taxes).....................	12,200,000

Other data:

Operating income during 1990 on segment of the business discontinued near year-end (net of income taxes)	150,000
Loss on disposal of discontinued segment (net of income tax benefit).........	450,000
Extraordinary loss (net of income tax benefit)	520,000
Cumulative effect of change in accounting principle (increase in net income, net of applicable income taxes)...	90,000
Prior period adjustment (increase in 1988 depreciation expense, net of income tax benefit)...	100,000
Cash dividends declared ($3 per share)	600,000

Instructions

a Prepare a condensed income statement for 1990, including earnings per share statistics. Use a format similar to that illustrated on page 504. Ocean Transport had 200,000 shares of a single class of capital stock outstanding throughout the year.

b Prepare a statement of retained earnings for the year ended December 31, 1990. As originally reported, retained earnings at December 31, 1989 amounted to $4,300,000.

Problem 13-3
Reporting the results of operations: a comprehensive problem

Katherine McCall, the accountant for Alternative Energy Systems, was injured in a skiing accident, and the following income statement was prepared by a temporary employee with little knowledge of accounting:

ALTERNATIVE ENERGY SYSTEMS
Income Statement
For the Year Ended December 31, 1990

Net sales...		$5,400,000
Gain on sale of treasury stock..		30,000
Excess of issuance price over par value of capital stock		120,000
Operating income from segment of business discontinued during the year (net of income taxes)...		200,000
Cumulative effect of change in accounting principle (net of income taxes)		75,000
Total revenue		$5,825,000
Less:		
Prior period adjustment (net of income tax benefit)..............	$ 250,000	
Cost of goods sold	2,480,000	
Selling expenses...	1,160,000	
General and administrative operations	820,000	
Income taxes (on continuing operations)......................	270,000	
Extraordinary loss (net of income tax benefit)	230,000	
Loss on sale of discontinued segment (net of income tax benefit) .	450,000	
Dividends declared on capital stock...........................	300,000	5,960,000
Net loss...		$ 135,000

The captions and the dollar amounts of the listed items are correct. The errors lie in the arrangement of the items and the fact that some of the items do not belong in an income statement.

Instructions

a Prepare a corrected income statement using the format illustrated on page 504. Include at the bottom of your income statement all appropriate earnings per share figures. Assume that throughout the year the company had outstanding a weighted average of 50,000 shares of a single class of capital stock.

b Prepare a statement of retained earnings. Assume that retained earnings at December 31, 1989, were originally reported at $2,300,000.

Problem 13-4
Preparation of a statement of stockholders' equity

Shown below is a summary of the transactions affecting the stockholders' equity in Sonoma Valley Corporation during the year ended December 31, 1990:

Prior period adjustment (net of income tax benefit)	$ (50,000)
Issuance of common stock: 10,000 shares of $10 par value capital stock at @ $62 per share	620,000
Distribution of 5% stock dividend (6,000 shares, market price $60 per share)	360,000
Purchased 1,000 shares of treasury stock @ $58	(58,000)
Reissued 500 shares of treasury stock at a price of $64 per share	32,000
Net income	510,000
Cash dividends declared ($1 per share)	126,000

At the beginning of 1990, the company had outstanding *110,000 shares* of $10 par value capital stock.

Instructions. Prepare a statement of stockholders' equity for the year ended December 31, 1990. Use the column headings and the beginning balances shown below. (Notice that all types of paid-in capital in excess of par value are combined into a single column.)

	Capital Stock ($10 Par Value)	Paid-in Capital in Excess of Par	Retained Earnings	Treasury Stock	Total Stockholders' Equity
Balances, January 1, 19__	$1,100,000	$1,800,000	$900,000	$ -0-	$3,800,000

Problem 13-5
Effects of stock dividends, stock splits, and treasury stock transactions

At the beginning of the year, Hydro-Spa Co. has total stockholders' equity of $660,000 and 20,000 outstanding shares of a single class of capital stock. During the year, the corporation completes the following transactions affecting its stockholders' equity accounts:

Jan. 10 A 10% stock dividend is declared and distributed. (Market price, $40 per share.)

Mar. 15 The corporation acquires 1,000 shares of its own capital stock at a cost of $40.50 per share.

May 30 All 1,000 shares of the treasury stock are reissued at a price of $44.90 per share.

July 31 The capital stock is split, two shares for one.

Dec. 15 The board of directors declares a cash dividend of $1.10 per share, payable on January 15.

Dec. 31 Net income of $127,600 (equal to $2.90 per share) is reported for the year ended December 31.

Instructions. Compute the amount of total stockholders' equity, the number of shares of capital stock outstanding, and the book value per share following each successive transaction. Organize your solution as a three-column schedule with separate column headings for (1) Total Stockholders' Equity, (2) Number of Shares Outstanding, and (3) Book Value per Share.

Problem 13-6
Recording stock
dividends and
treasury stock
transactions

The stockholders' equity of Precious Metals at January 1, 19__ is as follows:

Stockholders' equity:

Common stock, $5 par value, 500,000 shares authorized, 240,000 issued	$1,200,000
Paid-in capital in excess of par: common stock	4,065,000
Total paid-in capital.	$5,265,000
Retained earnings.	1,610,000
Total stockholders' equity	$6,875,000

During the year the following transactions relating to stockholders' equity occurred:

Jan. 15   Paid a $1 per share cash dividend declared in December of the preceding year. This dividend was properly recorded at the declaration date and was the only dividend declared during the preceding year.

June 10   Declared a 5% stock dividend to stockholders of record on June 30, to be distributed on July 15. At June 10, the market price of the stock was $35 per share.

July 15   Distributed the stock dividend declared on June 10.

Aug. 4   Purchased 4,200 shares of treasury stock at a price of $30 per share.

Oct. 15   Reissued 2,200 shares of treasury stock at a price of $32 per share.

Dec. 10   Reissued 1,000 shares of treasury stock at a price of $28.50 per share.

Dec. 15   Declared a cash dividend of $1 per share to be paid on January 15 to stockholders of record on December 31.

Dec. 31   Closed the Income Summary account and the Dividends account into Retained Earnings. The Income Summary account showed net income of $780,000.

Instructions

a Prepare in general journal form the entries necessary to record these transactions.

b Prepare the stockholders' equity section of the balance sheet at December 31, 19__. Include a note following your stockholders' equity section indicating any portion of retained earnings which is not available for dividends. Also include a supporting schedule showing your computation of the balance of retained earnings at year-end.

c Comment on whether Precious Metals increased or decreased the total amount of cash dividends declared during the year in comparison with dividends declared in the preceding year.

Problem 13-7
Investments in
marketable debt
securities

On April 1, 1990, Imperial Motors purchased $60,000 face value of the 10% bonds of Crest Theatres, Inc., at a price of 96 plus accrued interest. The bonds pay interest semiannually on March 1 and September 1.

Instructions

a In general journal form, prepare the entries required in 1990 to record:
(1) Purchase of the bonds on April 1
(2) Receipt of the semiannual interest payment on September 1
(3) Adjustment of the accounts at December 31 for bond interest earned since September 1. (Imperial Motors adjusts and closes its accounts annually, using the calendar year.)

b Assume that on January 31, 1991, Imperial Motors sells the entire investment in Crest Theatre bonds for $57,850 plus accrued interest. Prepare the entries to:
(1) Accrue bond interest earned from December 31, 1990 through the date of sale
(2) Record the sale of the bonds on January 31

Problem 13-8
Investments in
marketable
equity securities

During the current year, Overnight Air Freight (OAF) engaged in the following transactions relating to marketable securities:

Feb. 28 Purchased 1,000 shares of National Products common stock for $54.50 per share plus a broker's commission of $500.

Mar. 15 National Products paid a cash dividend of 50 cents per share which had been declared on February 20 payable on March 15 to stockholders of record on March 6.

May 31 National Products distributed a 10% stock dividend.

Nov. 15 National Products distributed additional shares as the result of a 2 for 1 stock split.

Dec. 5 OAF sold 600 shares of its National Products stock at $27 per share, less a broker's commission of $150.

Dec. 10 National Products paid a cash dividend of 25 cents per share. Dividend was declared November 20 payable December 10 to stockholders of record on November 30.

Instructions. Prepare journal entries to account for this investment in OAF's accounting records. Include memorandum entries when appropriate to show changes in the **cost basis per share.**

Business decision cases

Case 13-1
Forecasting
future earnings
(or Life without
Baseball

Midwestern Publishing, Inc., publishes two newspapers and until recently owned a professional baseball team. The baseball team had been losing money for several years and was sold at the end of 1990 to a group of investors who plan to move it to a larger city. Also in 1990, Midwestern suffered an extraordinary loss when its Raytown printing plant was damaged by a tornado. The damage has since been repaired. A condensed income statement is shown below:

MIDWESTERN PUBLISHING, INC.
Income Statement
For the Year Ended December 31, 1990

Net revenue		$41,000,000
Costs and expenses		36,500,000
Income from continuing operations		$ 4,500,000
Discontinued operations:		
Operating loss on baseball team	$(1,300,000)	
Gain on sale of baseball team	4,700,000	3,400,000
Income before extraordinary items		$ 7,900,000
Extraordinary loss:		
Tornado damage to Raytown printing plant		600,000
Net income		$ 7,300,000

Instructions. On the basis of this information, answer the following questions. Show any necessary computations and explain your reasoning.

a What would Midwestern's net income have been for 1990 if it **had not** sold the baseball team?

b Assume that for 1991, you expect a 7% increase in the profitability of Midwestern's newspaper business, but had projected a $2,000,000 operating loss for the baseball team if Midwestern had continued to operate the team in 1991. What amount would you forecast as Midwestern's 1991 net income *if the company had continued to own and operate the baseball team?*

c Given your assumptions in part b, but given that Midwestern **did** sell the baseball team in 1990, what would you forecast as the company's estimated net income for 1991?

Case 13-2
Using earnings
per share
statistics

For many years American Studios has produced television shows and operated several FM radio stations. Late in the current year, the radio stations were sold to Times Publishing, Inc. Also during the current year, American Studios sustained an extraordinary loss when one of its camera trucks caused an accident in an international grand prix auto race. Throughout the current year, the company had 3 million shares of common stock and a large quantity of convertible preferred stock outstanding. Earnings per share reported for the current year were as follows:

	Primary	Fully Diluted
Earnings from continuing operations	$8.20	$6.80
Earnings before extraordinary items.	$6.90	$5.50
Net earnings.	$3.80	$2.40

Instructions

a Briefly explain why American Studios reports fully diluted earnings per share amounts as well as earnings per share computed on a primary basis. What is the purpose of showing investors the fully diluted figures?

b What was the total dollar amount of the extraordinary loss sustained by American Studios during the current year?

c Assume that the price-earnings ratio shown in the morning newspaper for American Studios' common stock indicates that the stock is selling at a price equal to 10 times the reported earnings per share. What is the approximate market price of the stock?

d Assume that you expect both the revenue and expenses involved in producing television shows to increase by 10% during the coming year. What would you forecast as the company's net earnings per share (primary basis) for the coming year under each of the following independent assumptions? (Show your computations and explain your reasoning.)

(1) **None** of the convertible preferred stock is converted into common stock during the coming year.

(2) **All** of the convertible preferred stock is converted into common stock at the beginning of the coming year.

Part Four: Comprehensive Problem Review Session

A review session — also an opportunity for students to make oral presentations.

Listed below are 10 selected topics from Part Four of this textbook. You are to discuss briefly each assigned topic as if you were an instructor conducting a review session before an examination. Your discussion should address each point listed below the topic.

Many instructors assign different parts of this problem to different students. Ask your instructor which parts of the problem you are to prepare. Also ask whether you should prepare your discussion in writing or make an oral presentation to the class.

Written discussions should be limited to two or three handwritten pages per topic. (No working papers are provided, as written discussions may be prepared on ordinary paper.) Oral presentations should be limited to 10 minutes per topic. You may use the blackboard or prepare other visual aids to accompany an oral presentation.

Topic 1: notes payable

— Two forms of note.
— Nature of the Discount on Notes Payable account.
— Using the data in *Exercise 10-2,* illustrate the journal entries at December 31 and the balance sheet presentation for each type of note.
— Economic substance of transaction with each form of note.

Topic 2: payrolls and payroll taxes

— Subdivision of duties to create adequate internal control.
— Deductions from employees' pay and payroll taxes.
— Concept of rate and base in computing FICA and unemployment taxes.
— Journal entries to record payrolls.(Use data from *Exercise 10-7.*)

Topic 3: bonds payable; straight-line amortization of discount and premium

— Purpose of issuing bonds, characteristics of bonds, tax advantages.
— Relationship of bond prices to market interest rates.
— Reasons that bonds may be issued at a discount or premium.
— Accounting for bonds payable. (Illustrate using the straight-line method of amortization and data from *Exercise 11-3*).

Topic 4: comparison of the straight-line and effective interest methods of amortizing bond discount and bond premium

—Straight-line method. (Illustrate using data provided below.)
—Theoretical shortcoming in the straight-line method.
—Effective interest method. (Illustrate using data below.)
—Preferable method; FASB requirements.

Data for illustrations: On January 1, issued $9,000,000 face value, $8\frac{1}{2}\%$, 10-year bonds payable. The bonds were issued for a total price of $8,700,000, resulting in an effective rate of interest of 9%.

Topic 5: single proprietorships

—Basic characteristics of single proprietorships.
—Differences between the income statements of single proprietorships and corporations.
—Owner's capital and drawing accounts. (Illustrate with data from *Problem 12-1,* part a).

Topic 6: partnerships

—Basic characteristics of partnerships.
—Limited partnerships.
—Use of partners' capital and drawing accounts.
—The need for a partnership contract.
—Dividing partnership income among partners. (Illustrate using data from *Exercise 12-4.*)

Topic 7: capital stock

—Par or stated value.
—Issuance of stock for cash and other assets.
—Features of preferred stock and of common stock.
—Book value per share. (Illustrate using data from *Exercise 13-9.*)
—Factors affecting market value of preferred stock and of common stock.

Topic 8: reporting unusual and nonrecurring items

—Explain the nature of discontinued operations, extraordinary items, and the cumulative effect of an accounting change.
—Using data from *Problem 13-2,* illustrate the income statement presentation of the above items (omit earnings per share).
—Prior period adjustments.

Topic 9: earnings per share

—Nature of the statistic
—Computations when preferred stock also is outstanding. (Illustrate using data from *Exercise 13-5,* part b.)
—Changes in the number of common shares outstanding. (Illustrate using data from *Exercise 13-4,* parts b and c.)

—Required per-share figures when the income statement includes discontinued operations and/or extraordinary items.

—Primary and fully diluted earnings per share.

Topic 10: investments in marketable securities

—Nature of marketable securities.

—Accounting for investments in marketable debt securities. (Illustrate using data from *Exercise 13-10.*)

—Accounting for marketable equity securities. (Illustrate using data from *Exercise 13-11.*)

—Balance sheet valuation of investments in stocks and bonds.

Part Five	Special reports and analysis of accounting information

Chapter 14	Measuring cash flows
Chapter 15	Analysis of financial statements
Chapter 16	Income taxes and business decisions

Our last three chapters cover several special topics relating to the use, understanding, and interpretation of accounting information. The first chapter shows how balance sheet and income statement information are combined to form a new financial statement — the statement of cash flows. In the final two chapters, we discuss the analysis of financial statements by investors and the all-too-practical topic of income taxes.

Chapter 14
Measuring cash flows

CHAPTER PREVIEW

In this chapter we introduce the third major financial statement — a statement of cash flows. First, we illustrate this financial statement and explain its purpose and usefulness. Next, we describe the three basic classifications of cash flows and emphasize the long-run importance of generating a positive net cash flow from operations. In the remainder of the chapter, we show step-by-step how a statement of cash flows can be developed from accrual-basis accounting records. Both the direct and indirect methods of determining net cash flow from operating activities are illustrated.

After studying this chapter you should be able to meet these Learning Objectives:

1 **Explain the purposes and usefulness of a statement of cash flows.**
2 **Describe how cash transactions are classified within a statement of cash flows.**
3 **Compute the major cash flows relating to operating activities.**
4 **Explain why net income differs from net cash flow from operating activities.**
5 **Compute the cash flows relating to investing and financing activities.**
6 **Explain how noncash investing and financing activities are disclosed in a statement of cash flows.**

In Chapter 1, we introduced two key financial objectives of every business organization: *operating profitably* and *staying solvent.* Operating profitably means increasing the amount of the owners' equity through the activities of the business; in short, providing the owners with a satisfactory return on their investment. Staying solvent means being able to pay the debts and obligations of the business as they come due.

An income statement is designed to measure the success or failure of the business in achieving its objective of profitable operations. To some extent, a balance sheet shows whether or not the business is solvent. It shows, for example, the nature and amounts of current assets and current liabilities. From this information, users of the financial statements may compute such measures of solvency as the current ratio and the amount of working capital.

However, assessing the ability of a business to remain solvent involves more than just evaluating the liquid resources on hand at the balance sheet date. How much cash does the company receive during a year? What are the sources of these cash receipts? What expenditures are made each year for operations, and for investing and financing activities? To answer these questions, companies prepare a third major financial statement showing the sources and uses of liquid resources during the accounting period.

Until recently, the financial statement showing the sources and uses of liquid resources was called a *statement of changes in financial position.* Informally, this statement was often termed a *funds statement.* In preparing a funds statement, companies were permitted to define "liquid resources" in several different ways. Some companies prepared funds statements showing the sources and uses of cash. Other companies, however, prepared funds statements showing the sources and uses of working capital or some other type of "liquid resources." As a result of these alternative definitions of "funds," the statements of changes in financial position prepared by different companies varied greatly in content. This created difficulties for investors in comparing the funds statements of different companies.

To solve this problem, the FASB stated that beginning in 1988 all companies should discontinue the statement of changes in financial position and, instead, prepare a *statement of cash flows.* The FASB provides considerably more guidance as to the form and content of the new statement of cash flows than it did for the old funds statement. To avoid confusion between the old "funds statement" and the new statement of cash flows, the FASB has asked companies to *avoid* the use of the word "funds" in the new statement.

STATEMENT OF CASH FLOWS

Purpose of the statement

1 Explain the purposes and usefulness of a statement of cash flows. The basic purpose of a statement of cash flows is to provide information about the *cash receipts* and *cash payments* of a business entity during the accounting period. (The term *cash flows* includes both cash receipts and cash payments.) In addition, the statement is intended to provide information about all the *investing* and *financing* activities of the company during the period. Thus, a statement of cash flows should assist investors, creditors, and others in assessing such factors as:

1 The company's ability to generate positive cash flows in future periods
2 The company's ability to meet its obligations and to pay dividends
3 The company's need for external financing
4 Reasons for differences between the amount of net income and the related net cash flow from operations
5 Both the cash and noncash aspects of the company's investment and financing transactions for the period
6 Causes of the change in the amount of cash shown in the balance sheets at the beginning and end of the period

Example of a statement of cash flows

An example of a statement of cash flows is illustrated below. Cash outflows are shown in brackets.

ALLISON CORPORATION
Statement of Cash Flows
For the Year Ended December 31, 19__

Cash flows from operating activities:

Cash received from customers.................................	$ 870,000	
Interest and dividends received...............................	10,000	
Cash provided by operating activities......................................		$ 880,000
Cash paid to suppliers and employees.........................	$(764,000)	
Interest paid	(28,000)	
Income taxes paid	(38,000)	
Cash disbursed for operating activities....................................		(830,000)
Net cash flow from operating activities.......................................		$ 50,000

Cash flows from investing activities:

Purchases of marketable securities............................	$ (65,000)	
Proceeds from sales of marketable securities...................	40,000	
Loans made	(17,000)	
Collections on loans..	12,000	
Purchases of plant assets....................................	(160,000)	
Proceeds from sales of plant assets...........................	75,000	
Net cash used by investing activities		(115,000)

Cash flows from financing activities:

Proceeds from short-term borrowing...........................	$ 45,000	
Payments to settle short-term debts	(55,000)	
Proceeds from issuing bonds payable	100,000	
Proceeds from issuing capital stock	50,000	
Dividends paid	(40,000)	
Net cash provided by financing activities.....................................		100,000

Net increase (decrease) in cash		$ 35,000
Cash and cash equivalents, beginning of year		40,000
Cash and cash equivalents, end of year......................................		$ 75,000

Two supplementary schedules accompany a statement of cash flows. The first reports any "noncash" investing and financing transactions, such as the purchase of land by issuing capital stock or a note payable. The second schedule itemizes and explains the differences between net income and the net cash flow from operating activities. These supplementary schedules are illustrated and explained later in this chapter.

Classification of cash flows

2 Describe how
cash transactions
are classified
within a state-
ment of cash
flows.

Notice that the cash flows shown in the statement are grouped into three major categories: (1) *operating activities,* (2) *investing activities,* and (3) *financing activities.*[1] We will now look briefly at the way cash flows are classified among these three categories.

Operating activities. All cash flows *other than* those associated with investing and financing activities are classified as operating activities. Cash flows from operating activities include:

Cash Receipts	**Cash Payments**
Collections from customers for sales of goods and services	Payments to suppliers of merchandise and services, including payments to employees
Interest and dividends received	Payments of Interest
Other receipts from operations, as, for example, proceeds from settlement of litigation	Payments of income taxes
	Other expenditures relating to operations, as, for example, payments in settlement of litigation

Notice that receipts and payments of interest are classified as operating activities, not as investing or financing activities.

Investing activities. Cash flows relating to investing activities include:

Cash Receipts	**Cash Payments**
Cash proceeds from selling investments or plant assets	Payments to acquire investments or plant assets
Cash proceeds from collecting principal amounts on loans	Amounts advanced to borrowers

Financing activities. Cash flows classified as financing activities include the following:

Cash Receipts	**Cash Payments**
Proceeds from both short-term and long-term borrowing	Repayments of amounts borrowed (excluding interest payments)
Cash received from owners (as, for example, from issuing stock)	Payments to owners, such as cash dividends

[1] A fourth classification, "Effects of changes in exchange rates on cash," is used in the cash flow statements of companies with holdings of foreign currency. This fourth classification will be discussed in the intermediate accounting course.

Using this information, we will now illustrate the steps in preparing Allison Corporation's statement of cash flows and also a supporting schedule disclosing the "noncash" investing and financing activities. In our discussion, we will often refer to these items of "Additional information" by citing the paragraph numbers shown in parentheses.

Cash flows from operating activities

3 Compute the major cash flows relating to operating activities.

The FASB has taken the position that cash flow from operations should generally reflect the cash effects of transactions entering into the determination of net income. Therefore, the net cash flow from operations is equal to cash receipts from customers, plus investment income received (interest and dividends), less cash payments for purchases of merchandise and for expenses. To determine cash flow from operations, we must *convert the company's accrual-basis measurements of revenue and expenses to the cash basis.* The techniques for converting net sales, investment income, cost of goods sold, and expenses from the accrual basis to the cash basis are illustrated and explained below. For emphasis, those amounts that appear in the statement of cash flows are shown in black.

Cash received from customers. To the extent that sales are made for cash, there is no difference between the amount of cash received from customers and the amount recorded as sales revenue. Differences do arise, however, when sales are made on account. If accounts receivable have increased during the year, credit sales have exceeded collections of accounts receivable. Therefore, we must *deduct the increase* in accounts receivable over the year from net sales in order to determine the amount of cash received. If accounts receivable have decreased over the year, collections of these accounts must have exceeded credit sales. Therefore, we must *add the decrease* in accounts receivable to net sales to determine the amount of cash received. The relationship between cash received from customers and net sales is summarized below:

$$\text{Cash received} \atop \text{from customers} = {\text{Net} \atop \text{sales}} \left\{ {+ \text{ decrease in accounts receivable} \atop \text{or} \atop - \text{ increase in accounts receivable}} \right\}$$

The increase or decrease in accounts receivable is determined simply by comparing the year-end balance in the account to its balance at the beginning of the year.

In our Allison Corporation example, paragraph (1) of the Additional information tells us that accounts receivable have *increased* by $30,000 during the year. The income statement shows net sales for the year of $900,000. Therefore, the amount of cash received from customers may be computed as follows:

Net sales (accrual basis)	$900,000
Less: Increase in accounts receivable	30,000
Cash received from customers	$870,000

Interest and dividends received. Our next objective is to determine the amounts of cash collected during the year as dividends and interest. As explained in paragraph **(2)** of the Additional information, dividend revenue is recorded on the cash basis. Therefore, the $3,000 shown in the income statement also represents the amount of cash received as dividends.

Interest revenue, on the other hand, is recognized on the accrual basis. We have already shown how to convert one type of revenue, net sales, from the accrual basis to the cash basis. We may use the same approach in converting interest revenue from the accrual basis to the cash basis. Our formula for converting net sales to the cash basis may be modified to convert interest revenue to the cash basis as follows:

$$\begin{matrix} \text{Interest} \\ \text{received} \end{matrix} = \begin{matrix} \text{Interest} \\ \text{revenue} \end{matrix} \left\{ \begin{matrix} + \text{ decrease in interest receivable} \\ \text{or} \\ - \text{ increase in interest receivable} \end{matrix} \right\}$$

The income statement for Allison Corporation shows interest revenue of $6,000, and paragraph **(2)** states that the amount of accrued interest receivable has **decreased** by $1,000 during the year. Thus, the amount of cash received as interest may be computed as follows:

Interest revenue (accrual basis).	$6,000
Add: Decrease in accrued interest receivable	1,000
Interest received (cash basis)	$7,000

The amounts of interest and dividends received in cash are combined for presentation in the statement of cash flows:

Interest received (cash basis)	$ 7,000
Dividends received (cash basis)	3,000
Interest and dividends received.	**$10,000**

Cash payments for merchandise and for expenses

The next item in the statement of cash flows, "Cash paid to suppliers and employees," includes all cash payments for purchases of merchandise and for operating expenses (all expenses other than interest and income taxes). Payments of interest and income taxes are listed as a separate item in the statement. The amounts of cash paid for purchases of merchandise and for operating expenses are computed separately.

Cash paid for purchases of merchandise. The relationship between cash payments for purchases of merchandise and the cost of goods sold depends upon the changes during the period in inventory and in accounts payable to suppliers of merchandise. This relationship may be stated as follows:

$$\begin{matrix} \text{Cash payments} \\ \text{for purchases} \end{matrix} = \begin{matrix} \text{Cost of} \\ \text{goods sold} \end{matrix} \left\{ \begin{matrix} + \text{ increase in} \\ \text{inventory} \\ \text{or} \\ - \text{ decrease in} \\ \text{inventory} \end{matrix} \right\} \text{ and } \left\{ \begin{matrix} + \text{ decrease in} \\ \text{accounts payable} \\ \text{or} \\ - \text{ increase in} \\ \text{accounts payable} \end{matrix} \right\}$$

Using information from the Allison Corporation income statement and paragraph **(3)**, the cash payments for purchases may be computed as follows:

Cost of goods sold	$500,000
Add: Increase in inventory	10,000
Net purchases (accrual basis)	$510,000
Less: Increase in accounts payable to suppliers	15,000
Cash payments for purchases of merchandise	$495,000

Let us review the logic behind this computation. If a company is increasing its inventory, it will be **buying more merchandise than it sells** during the period; furthermore, if the company is increasing its account payable to merchandise creditors, it is **not paying cash** for all of these purchases.

Cash payments for expense. Expenses, as shown in the income statement, represent the cost of goods and services used up during the period. However, the amounts shown as expenses may differ significantly from the cash payments made during the period. Consider, for example, depreciation expense. Recording depreciation expense **requires no cash payment,** but it does increase total expenses measured on the accrual basis. Thus, in converting accrual-basis expenses to the cash basis, we must deduct depreciation expense and any other "noncash" expenses from our accrual-basis operating expenses. The other "noncash" expenses — expenses not requiring cash outlays — include amortization of intangible assets and amortization of bond discount.

A second area of difference arises from short-term timing differences between the recognition of expenses and the actual cash payments. Expenses are recorded in accounting records when the related goods or services are used. However, the cash payments for these expenses might occur (1) in an earlier period, (2) in the same period, or (3) in a later period. Let us briefly consider each case:

1 If payment is made in advance, the payment creates an asset, termed a prepaid expense, or, in our formula, a "prepayment."
2 If payment is made in the same period, no problem arises because the cash payment is equal to the amount of expense.
3 If payment is made in a later period, the payment reduces a liability for an accrued expense payable.

The relationships between cash payments and accrual-basis expenses are summarized below:

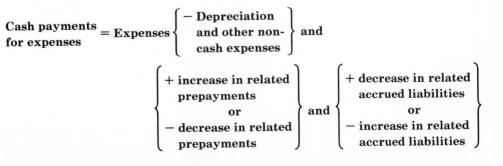

In a statement of cash flows, cash payments for interest and for income taxes are shown separately from cash payments for operating expenses. Using data from Allison Corporation's income statement and from paragraph **(4),** we may compute the company's cash payments for operating expenses as follows:

Operating expenses (including depreciation)		$300,000
Less: Noncash expenses (depreciation)		40,000
Subtotal		$260,000
Add: Increase in short-term prepayments	$3,000	
Decrease in accrued liabilities	6,000	9,000
Cash payments for operating expenses		$269,000

Cash paid to suppliers and employees. The caption used in our cash flow statement, "Cash paid to suppliers and employees," includes both cash payments for purchases and for operating expenses. This cash outflow may now be computed as follows:

Cash payments for purchases of merchandise	$495,000
Cash payments of operating expenses	269,000
Cash payments to suppliers and employees	$764,000

Cash payments for interest and taxes. Interest expense and income taxes expense may be converted to cash payments with the same formula we used to convert operating expenses. Allison Corporation's income statement shows interest expense of $35,000, and paragraph **(5)** states that the liability for interest payable *increased* by $7,000 during the year. Thus, the amount of cash paid for interest expense may be computed as follows:

Interest expense	$35,000
Less: Increase in related accrued liability	7,000
Interest paid	$28,000

Using information from Allison Corporation's income statement and paragraph **(6),** the cash payments for income taxes may be computed as follows:

Income taxes expense	$36,000
Add: Decrease in related accrued liability	2,000
Income taxes paid	$38,000

Let us review the logic behind these two computations. The fact that the liability for interest payable increased during the year indicates that not all of the interest expense was paid in cash. To achieve a decrease in its liability for income taxes payable, Allison Corporation must have made cash payments to the government in excess of its income tax expense for the current year.

A quick review. We have now shown the computation of each cash flow relating to Allison Corporation's operating activities. Previously we illustrated a complete statement of cash flows for the company. For your convenience, we will again show the operating activities section of that statement, illustrating the information developed in the preceding paragraphs.

Cash flows from operating activities:

Cash received from customers.	$ 870,000	
Interest and dividends received.	10,000	
Cash provided by operating activities		$ 880,000
Cash paid to suppliers and employees	$(764,000)	
Interest paid	(28,000)	
Income taxes paid	(38,000)	
Cash disbursed for operating activities.		(830,000)
Net cash flow from operating activities.		$ 50,000

Differences between net income and net cash flow from operations

4 Explain why net income differs from net cash flow from operating activities. Allison Corporation reported net income of $65,000, but net cash flow from operations of only $50,000. What caused this $15,000 difference?

The answer, in short, is many things. First, **depreciation expense** reduces net income but does not affect net cash flow. Next, all the adjustments that we made to net sales, cost of goods sold, and expenses represented short-term **timing differences** between net income and the underlying net cash flow from operating activities. Finally, **nonoperating gains and losses** may cause substantial differences between net income and net cash flow from operations.

Nonoperating gains and losses may result from sales of plant assets, marketable securities, and other investments; or from the retirement of long-term debt. These gains and losses affect the cash flows relating to investing or financing activities, not the cash flows from operating activities.

An alternative method of reporting operating cash flows. In this textbook, we use the **direct method** of reporting net cash flow from operations. The direct method identifies the major operating cash flows, using such captions as "Cash received from customers," and "Cash paid to suppliers and employees."

The FASB **recommends use of the direct method** for reporting cash flow from operations; however, it also permits the use of an alternative approach, termed the **indirect method.**

The indirect method of computing net cash flow from operations will be explained in the intermediate accounting course. However, a brief illustration of this method appears later in this chapter.

Cash flows from investing activities

5 Compute the cash flows relating to investing and financing activities. Paragraphs **(7)** through **(9)** in the Additional Information for our Allison Corporation example provide most of the information necessary to determine the cash flows from investing activities. In the following discussion, we will illustrate the presentation of these cash flows and also explain the sources of the information contained in the numbered paragraphs.

Much information about investing activities can be obtained simply by looking at the changes in the related asset accounts during the year. Debit entries in these accounts represent purchases of the assets, or cash outlays. Credit entries represent sales of the assets, or cash receipts. However, credit entries in asset accounts represent only the *cost (or book value)* of the assets sold. To determine the cash proceeds from these sales transactions, we must adjust the amount of the credit entries for any gains or losses recognized on the sales.

Purchases and sales of securities. To illustrate, consider paragraph **(7)** which summarizes the debit and credit entries to the Marketable Securities account. As explained earlier in this chapter, the $65,000 in debit entries represent purchases of marketable securities. The $44,000 in credit entries represent the cost of marketable securities sold during the period. However, the income statement shows that these securities were sold at a $4,000 loss. Thus, the cash proceeds from these sales amounted to only $40,000 ($44,000 cost, minus $4,000 loss on sale). In the statement of cash flows, these investing activities are summarized as follows:

Purchases of marketable securities . . . . $(65,000)
Proceeds from sales of marketable securities . . . . $ 40,000

Loans made and collected. Paragraph **(8)** provides all the information necessary to summarize the cash flows from making and collecting loans:

Loans made . . . . $(17,000)
Collections on loans . . . . $ 12,000

This information comes directly from the Notes Receivable account. Debit entries in the account represent new loans made during the year; credit entries indicate collections on outstanding notes (loans). (Collections of interest are credited to the Interest Revenue account and are included among the cash receipts from operating activities.)

6 Explain how noncash investing and financing activities are disclosed in a statement of cash flows.

Cash paid to acquire plant assets. Paragraph **(9)** states that Allison Corporation purchased plant assets during the year for $200,000, paying $160,000 in cash and issuing a long-term note payable for the $40,000 balance. Notice that *only the $160,000 cash payment* appears in the statement of cash flows. However, one objective of this financial statement is to show all of the company's *investing and financing activities* during the year. Therefore, the *noncash aspects* of these transactions are shown in a supplementary schedule, as follows:

Supplementary Schedule A: Noncash Investing and Financing Activities

Purchases of plant assets. $200,000
Less: Portion financed through issuance of long-term debt.   40,000
Cash paid to acquire plant assets **$160,000**

This supplementary schedule should accompany the statement of cash flows.

Proceeds from sales of plant assets. Assume that an analysis of the plant asset accounts shows net credit entries totaling $44,000 in the year. ("Net credit entries" means all credit entries, net of related debits to accumulated depreciation when assets were sold). These "net credit entries" represent the *book value* of plant assets sold during the year. However, the income statement shows that these assets were sold at a ***gain of $31,000***. Therefore, the ***cash proceeds*** from sales of plant assets amounted to $75,000, as shown below:

Book value of plant assets sold	$44,000
Add: Gain on sales of plant assets	31,000
Proceeds from sales of plant assets	$75,000

Cash flows from financing activities

Cash flows from financing activities are determined by analyzing the debit and credit changes recorded in the related balance sheet accounts during the period. In a sense, cash flows from financing activities are more easily determined than those relating to investing activities, because financing activities seldom involve gains or losses.[4] Thus, we generally do not have to adjust the debit or credit changes in the balance sheet accounts in order to determine the related cash flows.

Credit changes in such accounts as Notes Payable and the accounts for long-term debt and paid-in capital usually indicate cash receipts; debit changes indicate cash payments.

Short-term borrowing transactions. To illustrate, consider paragraph **(10)** which provides the information indicating the following cash flows:

Proceeds from short-term borrowing	$ 45,000
Payments to settle short-term debts	$(55,000)

Is it possible to determine the proceeds of short-term borrowing transactions throughout the year without carefully reviewing the cash receipts journals? The answer is ***yes*** — easily. The proceeds from short-term borrowing are equal to the ***sum of the credit entries*** in the short-term Notes Payable account. Payments to settle short-term debts are equal to the ***sum of the debit entries*** in this account.

Proceeds from issuing bonds payable and capital stock. Paragraph **(11)** states that Allison Corporation received cash of $100,000 by issuing bonds payable. This amount was determined by adding the credit entries in the Bonds Payable account. The Bonds Payable account included no debit entries during the year; thus, no bonds were retired.

Paragraph **(12)** states that during the year Allison Corporation issued capital stock for $50,000. The proceeds from issuing stock are equal to the credit entries made in the stockholders' equity accounts Capital Stock and Paid-in Capital in Excess of Par Value.

Cash dividends paid to stockholders. Paragraph **(13)** states that Allison Company declared and paid cash dividends of $40,000 during the year. In practice, most corporations pay cash dividends in the same year in which these dividends are declared. In these situations, the cash payments are equal to the related debit entries in the Retained Earnings account.

---

[4] An early retirement of debt is the only financing transaction that may result in a gain or a loss.

If the balance sheet includes a liability for dividends payable, the amounts debited to Retained Earnings represent dividends **declared** during the period, which may differ from the amount of dividends **paid.** To determine cash dividends paid, we must adjust the amount of dividends declared by adding any decrease (or subtracting any increase) in the Dividends Payable account over the period.

Relationship of the cash flow statement to the balance sheet

The final section in the statement of cash flows illustrates the relationship between this statement and two successive balance sheets. The amount of cash (including cash equivalents) is listed as an asset in the balance sheet at both the beginning and end of the current period. The statement of cash flows explains in detail the increase or decrease in this asset during the period.

To illustrate, paragraph **(14)** of our Additional information states that the amounts of cash (including cash equivalents) shown in the beginning and ending balance sheets are $40,000 and $75,000, respectively. Thus, during the year, this asset **increased by $35,000.** Notice that this $35,000 increase agrees with the sum of the cash flows listed in our cash flow statement.

The relationship between cash flows and the beginning and ending balance sheet amounts is summarized in the last three lines of the statement of cash flows, as shown below:

Net increase (decrease) in cash and cash equivalents............................	$35,000
Cash and cash equivalents, beginning of year....................................	40,000
Cash and cash equivalents, end of year..	$75,000

The statement of cash flows: a second look

We have now explained the computation of each cash flow included in Allison Corporation's statement of cash flows. To summarize our discussion we again illustrate the statement of cash flows, along with the two required supplementary schedules.

In this second illustration, we list the net cash flow from operating activities as a single "line item" and show the supporting computations in a supplementary schedule. These supporting computations, shown in schedule B, illustrate the indirect method of reporting net cash flow from operating activities. While the FASB recommends use of the direct method, the indirect method is an allowable alternative.

Supplementary schedules accompanying a statement of cash flows. The two supplementary schedules illustrated on the following page should accompany the statement of cash flows regardless of whether the direct or indirect method is used in computing net cash flow from operating activities.

Schedule A shows the "noncash" effects of investing and financing activities. The purpose of this schedule is to assist readers of the financial statements in understanding all of the company's investing and financing activities.

Schedule B reconciles net income with the net cash flow from operating activities. This information assists readers of the statements in understanding the differences between net income and cash flow. A discussion of the computations shown in this schedule is appropriately deferred to a later accounting course.

ALLISON CORPORATION
Statement of Cash Flows
For the Year Ended December 31, 19__

Cash flows from operating activities:		
Net cash flow from operating activities (see supplementary schedule B)		$ 50,000
Cash flows from investing activities:		
Purchases of marketable securities.	$ (65,000)	
Proceeds from sales of marketable securities.	40,000	
Loans made	(17,000)	
Collections on loans.	12,000	
Cash paid to acquire plant assets (see supplementary schedule A).	(160,000)	
Proceeds from sales of plant assets	75,000	
Net cash used by investing activities		(115,000)
Cash flows from financing activities:		
Proceeds from short-term borrowing.	$ 45,000	
Payments to settle short-term debts	(55,000)	
Proceeds from issuing bonds payable	100,000	
Proceeds from issuing capital stock	50,000	
Dividends paid	(40,000)	
Net cash provided by financing activities.		100,000
Net increase (decrease) in cash		$ 35,000
Cash and cash equivalents, beginning of year		40,000
Cash and cash equivalents, end of year.		$ 75,000

Supplementary Schedule A: Noncash Investing and Financing Activities

Purchases of plant assets	$ 200,000
Less: Portion financed through issuance of long-term debt.	40,000
Cash paid to acquire plant assets	$ 160,000

Supplementary Schedule B: Net Cash Flow from Operating Activities

Net income		$ 65,000
Add: Depreciation expense		40,000
Decrease in accrued interest receivable		1,000
Increase in accounts payable		15,000
Increase in accrued liabilities		7,000
Nonoperating loss on sales of marketable securities		4,000
Subtotal.		$ 132,000
Less: Increase in accounts receivable	$ 30,000	
Increase in inventory.	10,000	
Increase in prepayments	3,000	
Decrease in accrued liabilities.	8,000	
Nonoperating gain on sales of plant assets.	31,000	82,000
Net cash flow from operating activities.		$ 50,000

END-OF-CHAPTER REVIEW

Summary of chapter learning objectives

1 Explain the purposes and usefulness of a statement of cash flows.

The purposes of a statement of cash flows are to provide information about the cash receipts and cash payments of the entity, and also about its investing and financing activities. Readers of financial statements use this information to assess the solvency of a business and to evaluate its ability to generate positive cash flows in future periods, pay dividends, and finance growth.

2 Describe how cash transactions are classified within a statement of cash flows.

Cash flows are classified into the categories of (1) operating activities, (2) investing activities, and (3) financing activities. Receipts and payments of interest are classified as operating activities.

3 Compute the major cash flows relating to operating activities.

The major operating cash flows are (1) cash received from customers, (2) interest and dividends received, (3) cash paid to suppliers and employees, (4) interest paid, and (5) income taxes paid. These cash flows are computed by converting the income statement amounts for revenue, cost of goods sold, and expenses from the accrual basis to the cash basis. This is done by adjusting the income statement amounts for changes occurring over the period in related balance sheet accounts.

4 Explain why net income differs from net cash flow from operating activities.

Net income differs from net operating cash flow for several reasons. One reason is "noncash" expenses, such as depreciation and the amortization of intangible assets. These expenses, which require no cash outlays, reduce net income but do not affect net cash flow. Another reason is the many timing differences existing between the recognition of revenue and expense and the occurrence of the underlying cash flows. Finally, nonoperating gains and losses enter into the determination of net income, but the related cash flows are classified as investing or financing activities, not operating activities.

5 Compute the cash flows relating to investing and financing activities.

Cash flows from investing and financing activities can be determined by examining the entries in the related asset and liability accounts, along with any related gains or losses shown in the income statement. Debit entries in asset accounts represent purchases of assets (an investing activity). Credit entries in asset accounts represent the cost of assets sold. (However, the amount of these credit entries must be adjusted by any gains or losses recognized on these sales transactions.)

Debit entries to liability accounts represent repayment of debt, while credit entries represent borrowing. Both types of transactions are classified as financing activities. Other financing activities include the issuance of stock (indicated by credits to the paid-in capital accounts) and payment of dividends (indicated by debit entries in the Retained Earnings account).

6 Explain how noncash investing and financing activities are disclosed in a statement of cash flows.

One purpose of the statement of cash flows is to provide information about all investing and financing activities. Therefore, if these activities have "noncash" elements, such as the issuance of capital stock in exchange for land, the noncash aspects of the transactions are disclosed in a supplementary schedule that accompanies the statement of cash flows.

Key terms introduced or emphasized in chapter 14

Accrual basis. A method of summarizing operating results in terms of revenue earned and expenses incurred, rather than cash receipts or cash payments.

Cash basis. A method of summarizing operating results in terms of cash receipts and cash payments, rather than revenue earned or expenses incurred.

Cash equivalents. Highly liquid short-term investments, such as Treasury bills, money market funds, and commercial paper. For purposes of preparing a statement of cash flows, money held in cash equivalents is still viewed as "cash." Thus, transfers between a bank account and cash equivalents are not considered receipts or disbursements of cash.

Cash flows. A term describing both cash receipts (inflows) and cash payments (outflows).

Financing activities. Transactions such as borrowing, repaying borrowed amounts, raising equity capital, or making distribution to owners. The cash effects of these transactions are reported in the financing activities section of a statement of cash flows.

Investing activities. Transactions involving acquisitions or sales of investments or plant assets. The cash aspects of these transactions are shown in the investing activities section of a statement of cash flows. Noncash aspects of these transactions are disclosed in a supporting schedule to this financial statement.

Operating activities. Transactions entering into the determination of net income, with the exception of gains and losses relating to financing or investing activities. The category includes such transactions as selling goods or services, earning investment income, and incurring costs and expenses. The cash effects of these transactions are reflected in the operating activities section of a statement of cash flows.

Statement of cash flows. A financial statement designed to provide information about the cash receipts, cash payments, investing activities, and financing activities of a business. Useful in evaluating the solvency of the business.

Demonstration problem for your review

You are the chief accountant for American Modem. Your assistant has prepared an income statement for the current year, and also has developed the following "Additional information" by analyzing changes in the company's balance sheet accounts.

AMERICAN MODEM
Income Statement
For the Year Ended December 31, 19__

Revenue:		
Net sales..		$4,900,000
Interest income		260,000
Gain on sales of plant assets..		20,000
Total revenue and gains		$5,180,000
Costs and expenses:		
Cost of goods sold	$2,600,000	
Operating expenses (including depreciation of $400,000)..........	1,650,000	
Interest expense	200,000	
Income taxes..	190,000	
Loss on sales of marketable securities	60,000	
Total costs, expenses, and losses		4,700,000
Net income..		$ 480,000

Additional information. Information about changes in the company's balance sheet accounts over the year is summarized below:

(1) Accounts receivable decreased by $100,000.
(2) Accrued interest receivable increased by $25,000.
(3) Inventory increased by $200,000 and accounts payable to suppliers of merchandise increased by $160,000.
(4) Short-term prepayments of operating expenses decreased by $15,000, and accrued liabilities for operating expenses increased by $80,000.
(5) The liability for accrued interest payable decreased by $8,000 during the year.
(6) The liability for accrued income taxes payable increased by $18,000 during the year.
(7) The following schedule summarizes the total debit and credit entries during the year in other balance sheet accounts:

	Debit Entries	Credit Entries
Marketable securities	$ 200,000	$170,000
Notes receivable (cash loans made to others)	210,000	290,000
Plant assets (see paragraph 8)	1,300,000	50,000
Notes payable (short-term borrowing)	650,000	420,000
Capital stock		50,000
Paid-in Capital in Excess of Par Value		750,000
Retained earnings (see paragraph 9 below)	300,000	480,000

(8) The $50,000 in credit entries to the plant asset accounts are net of any debits to accumulated depreciation when plant assets were retired. Thus, the $50,000 in credit entries represents the **book value** of all plant assets sold or retired during the year.
(9) The $300,000 debit to retained earnings represents dividends declared and paid during the year. The $480,000 credit entry represents the net income shown in the income statement.
(10) All investing and financing activities were cash transactions.
(11) Cash and cash equivalents amounted to $300,000 at the beginning of the year, and to $390,000 at year-end.

Instructions. You are to prepare a statement of cash flows for the current year, following the format illustrated on page 545. Place brackets around dollar amounts representing cash outlays. Show separately your computations of the following amounts:

(1) Cash received from customers.
(2) Interest received.
(3) Cash paid to suppliers and employees.
(4) Interest paid.
(5) Income taxes paid.
(6) Proceeds from sales of marketable securities.
(7) Proceeds from sales of plant assets.
(8) Proceeds from issuing capital stock.

Solution to demonstration problem

AMERICAN MODEM
Statement of Cash Flows
For the Year Ended December 31, 19__

Cash flows from operating activities:

Cash received from customers **(1)**.	$ 5,000,000	
Interest received **(2)**.	235,000	
Cash provided by operating activities		$5,235,000
Cash paid to suppliers and employees **(3)**	$(3,795,000)	
Interest paid **(4)**	(208,000)	
Income taxes paid **(5)**	(172,000)	
Cash disbursed for operating activities		(4,175,000)
Net cash flow from operating activities		$ 1,060,000

Cash flows from investing activities:

Purchases of marketable securities	$ (200,000)	
Proceeds from sales of marketable securities **(6)**	110,000	
Loans made	(210,000)	
Collections on loans.	290,000	
Cash paid to acquire plant assets	(1,300,000)	
Proceeds from sales of plant assets **(7)**	70,000	
Net cash used by investing activities.		(1,240,000)

Cash flow from financing activities:

Proceeds from short-term borrowing.	$ 420,000	
Payments to settle short-term debts	(650,000)	
Proceeds from issuing capital stock **(8)**	800,000	
Dividends paid	(300,000)	
Net cash provided by financing activities		270,000

Net increase (decrease) in cash.		$ 90,000
Cash and cash equivalents, beginning of year.		300,000
Cash and cash equivalents, end of year		$ 390,000

Supporting computations:

(1) Cash received from customers:

Net sales		$ 4,900,000
Add: Decrease in accounts receivable		100,000
Cash received from customers.		$ 5,000,000

(2) Interest received:

Interest revenue		$ 260,000
Less: Increase in accrued interest receivable		25,000
Interest received.		$ 235,000

(3) Cash paid to suppliers and employees:

Cash paid for purchases of merchandise:

Cost of goods sold		$ 2,600,000
Add: Increase in inventory		200,000
Net purchases		$ 2,800,000
Less: Increase in accounts payable to suppliers		160,000
Cash paid for purchases of merchandise		$ 2,640,000

Cash paid for operating expenses:

Operating expenses		$ 1,650,000
Less: Depreciation (a "noncash" expense)	$400,000	
Decrease in prepayments	15,000	
Increase in accrued liabilities for operating expenses.	80,000	495,000
Cash paid for operating expenses		$ 1,155,000
Cash paid to suppliers and employees ($2,640,000 + $1,155,000)		$ 3,795,000

(4) Interest paid:

Interest expense		$ 200,000
Add: Decrease in accrued interest payable		8,000
Interest paid		$ 208,000

(5) Income taxes paid:

Income taxes expense		$190,000
Less: Increase in accrued income taxes payable		(18,000)
Income taxes paid		$ 172,000

(6) Proceeds from sales of marketable securities:

Cost of marketable securities sold (credit entries to the Marketable Securities account)		$ 170,000
Less: Loss reported on sales of marketable securities		60,000
Proceeds from sales of marketable securities		$ 110,000

(7) Proceeds from sales of plant assets:

Book value of plant assets sold (paragraph 8)		$ 50,000
Add: Gain reported on sales of plant assets		20,000
Proceeds from sales of plant assets		$ 70,000

(8) Proceeds from issuing capital stock:

Amounts credited to the Capital Stock account		$ 50,000
Add: Amounts credited to Paid-in Capital in Excess of Par Value		750,000
Proceeds from issuing capital stock		$ 800,000

ASSIGNMENT MATERIAL

Review questions

1 A recent headline in the business section of a newspaper referred to the statement of cash flows as a "new" financial statement. Why?

2 Why does the FASB ask companies not to use the term "funds" in a statement of cash flows?

3 Briefly state the purposes of a statement of cash flows.

4 Two supplementary schedules usually accompany a statement of cash flows. Briefly explain the content of these schedules.

5 Give two examples of cash receipts and two examples of cash payments which fall into each of the following classifications:
   a Operating activities.
   b Investing activities.
   c Financing activities.

6 Why are payments and receipts of interest classified as operating activities rather than as financing or investment activities?

7 Define **cash equivalents** and list three examples.

8 During the current year, Delta Corporation transferred $300,000 from its bank account into a money market fund. Will this transaction appear in a statement of cash flows? If so, in which section? Explain.

9 In the long run, is it more important for a business to have positive cash flows from its operating activities, investing activities, or financing activities? Why?

10 Of the three types of business activities summarized in a cash flow statement, which type is **least** likely to show a positive net cash flow in a successful, growing business? Explain your reasoning.

11 The items and amounts listed in a balance sheet and an income statement correspond to specific accounts in a company's ledger. Is the same true about the items and amounts in a statement of cash flows? Explain.

12 Briefly explain two different approaches that an accountant might follow in preparing a statement of cash flows from the accounting records of a small business.

13 SuperBoard, Inc., had net sales for the year of $550,000. Accounts receivable increased from $100,000 at the beginning of the year to $145,000 at year-end. Compute the amount of cash collected during the year from customers.

14 Describe the types of cash payments summarized by the caption, "Cash paid to suppliers and employees."

15 Identify three factors that may cause net income to differ from net cash flow from operating activities.

16 Briefly explain the difference between the direct and indirect methods of computing net cash flows from operating activities. Which method results in the higher net cash flow?

17 Are cash payments of accounts payable viewed as operating activities or investing activities? Referring to the statement of cash flows illustrated on page 545, state the caption that includes amounts paid on accounts payable.

18 Discount Club acquired land by issuing $500,000 worth of capital stock. No cash changed hands in this transaction. Will the transaction be disclosed in the company's statement of cash flows? Explain.

19 The only transaction recorded in the plant asset accounts of Rogers Corporation in the current year was a $150,000 credit to the Land account. Assuming that this credit resulted from a cash transaction, does this entry indicate a cash receipt or a cash payment? Should this $150,000 amount appear in the statement of cash flows, or is some adjustment necessary?

20 During the current year, the following credit entries were posted to the paid-in capital accounts of Moser Shipyards:

| Capital Stock.. | $10,000,000 |
| Paid-in Capital in Excess of Par Value .... | 98,500,000 |

Explain the type of cash transaction that probably caused these credit changes, and illustrate the presentation of this transaction in a statement of cash flows.

21 At the beginning of the current year, Polar Corporation had dividends payable of $1,000,000. During the current year, the company declared cash dividends of $4,800,000, of which $1,200,000 appeared as a liability at year-end. Determine the amount of cash dividends **paid** during the year.

Exercises

Exercise 14-1
Accounting terminology

Listed below are nine technical accounting terms introduced in this chapter:

Statement of cash flows	Operating activities	Cash flows
Income statement	Investing activities	Accrual basis
Cash equivalents	Financing activities	Cash basis

Each of the following statements may (or may not) describe one of these technical terms. For each statement, indicate the accounting term described, or answer "None" if the statement does not correctly describe any of the terms.

a The financial statement that best describes the profitability of a business which receives most of its revenue in cash.
b Transactions involving the issuance and repayment of debt, investments by owners, and distributions to owners.
c A method of accounting that summarizes operating results in terms of cash receipts and cash payments.
d The financial statement that shows the financial position of the business at a particular date.
e An asset consisting of investments in corporate stocks and bonds.
f The section of a statement of cash flows summarizing the cash effects of most transactions that enter into the determination of net income.
g A term describing both cash receipts and cash payments.

Exercise 14-2
Computing cash flows

An analysis of the Marketable Securities controlling account of Dexter Labs shows the following entries during the year:

Balance, January 1	$220,000
Debit entries	60,000
Credit entries...	(75,000)
Balance, December 31	$205,000

In addition, the company's income statement includes a $29,000 gain on sales of marketable securities. None of the company's marketable securities is considered a cash equivalent.

Compute the amounts that should appear in the statement of cash flows as:

a Purchases of marketable securities.
b Proceeds from sales of marketable securities.

**Exercise 14-3
Comparing net
sales and cash
receipts**

During the current year, Great Look made cash sales of $220,000 and credit sales of $460,000. During the year, accounts receivable decreased by $24,000.

  a Compute for the current year the amounts of:
    (1) Net sales.
    (2) Cash received from collecting accounts receivable.
    (3) Cash received from customers.
  b Write a brief statement explaining why cash received from customers differs from the amount of net sales.

**Exercise 14-4
Computing cash
paid for
purchases of
merchandise**

The general ledger of NitroTech provides the following information relating to purchases of merchandise:

	End of Year	Beginning of Year
Inventory..	$720,000	$780,000
Accounts payable to merchandise suppliers........................	530,000	500,000

The company's cost of goods sold during the year was $2,460,000.

Instructions

  a Compute the amount of cash payments made during the year to suppliers of merchandise.
  b Assume that NitroTech maintains a cash payments journal identical in design to the one illustrated on page 240 in Chapter 6 of this text. How might you determine the amounts of cash paid to suppliers of merchandise from this journal? (Identify the relevant column totals in your answer.)

**Exercise 14-5
Reporting
lending activities
and interest
revenue**

During the current year, Otay Savings and Loan Association made new loans of $12,000,000. In addition, the company collected $36,000,000 from borrowers, of which $31,000,000 was interest revenue. Explain how these cash flows will appear in the company's statement of cash flows, indicating the classification and the dollar amount of each cash flow.

**Exercise 14-6
Disclosing
"noncash" in-
vesting and
financing
activities**

During the current year, Nordic Co. purchased a factory from Fisher Industries. The journal entry made to record this transaction is shown below:

Land	300,000	
Buildings...	650,000	
Equipment	1,800,000	
Mortgage Payable		1,900,000
Cash		850,000

Purchased factory from Fisher Industries.

This was Nordic Co.'s only purchase of plant assets during the year. Nordic Co. prepares a supplementary schedule to its statement of cash flows for the purpose of disclosing any "noncash" aspects of investing and financing activities.

Instructions

  a Prepare the supplementary schedule to disclose the "noncash" aspects of this transaction. Follow the general format illustrated on page 556.
  b Illustrate the presentation of this transaction in Nordic Co.'s statement of cash flows. Begin your illustration by indicating the section of the statement (operating, investing, or financing activities) in which this transaction will appear.

Exercise 14-7
Format of a statement of cash flows

The accounting staff of Cajun Chef has assembled the following information for the year ended December 31, 19__:

Cash and cash equivalents, beginning of year	$38,600
Cash and cash equivalents, end of year	57,600
Cash paid to acquire plant assets	19,000
Proceeds from short-term borrowing	10,000
Loans made to others	5,000
Collections on loans (excluding interest)	4,000
Interest and dividends received	12,000
Cash received from customers	815,000
Proceeds from sales of plant assets	7,000
Dividends paid	80,000
Cash paid to suppliers and employees	635,000
Interest paid	9,000
Income taxes paid	81,000

Using this information, prepare a formal statement of cash flows. Include a proper heading for the financial statement, and classify the given information into the categories of operating activities, investing activities, and financing activities. Place brackets around the dollar amounts of all cash outlays.

Problems

Problem 14-1
Classifying cash flows

Fifteen business transactions of Chung Lin Communications are listed below:

  a Made payments on accounts payable to merchandise suppliers.
  b Issued bonds payable for cash; management plans to use this cash in the near future to modernize production facilities.
  c Sold marketable securities at a loss.
  d Collected principal amounts due on a loan (a notes receivable).
  e Collected interest due on the note receivable described in d, above.
  f Collected an account receivable from a customer.
  g Transferred cash from a money market fund into the payroll bank account.
  h Used the cash received in b, above, for the purpose of modernizing production facilities.
  i Made a semiannual interest payment on bonds payable.
  j Made a year-end adjusting entry to recognize depreciation expense.
  k Paid salaries to employees in the accounting and finance departments.
  l Paid a dividend declared in the prior year.
  m Declared a dividend to be paid early next year.
  n At year-end, purchased for cash an insurance policy covering the next two years.
  o Purchased short-term Treasury bills for cash.

Instructions. Most of the preceding transactions should be included among the activities summarized in a statement of cash flows. For each transaction that should be included in this statement, indicate whether the transaction should be classified as an operating activity, investing activity, or financing activity. If the transaction should *not be included* in the current year's statement of cash flows, briefly explain why not.

Problem 14-2
Reporting
investing
activities

An analysis of the income statement and the balance sheet accounts of Olympic Shoes at December 31 provides the following information:

Income statement items:

Gain on sale of plant assets	$ 8,000
Loss on sales of marketable securities	4,000

Analysis of balance sheet accounts:

Marketable Securities account:

Debit entries	$31,000
Credit entries	22,000

Notes Receivable account:

Debit entries	30,000
Credit entries	34,000

Plant and equipment accounts:

Debit entries to plant asset accounts	65,000
Credit entries to plant asset accounts	70,000
Debit entries to accumulated depreciation accounts	50,000

Additional information

(1) Except as noted in (4), below, payments and proceeds relating to investing transactions were made in cash.

(2) The marketable securities are not cash equivalents.

(3) All notes receivable relate to cash loans, not to receivables from customers.

(4) Purchases of new equipment during the year ($65,000) were financed by paying $25,000 in cash and issuing a long-term note payable for $40,000.

(5) Debits to the accumulated depreciation account are made whenever depreciable plant assets are retired. Thus, the book value of plant assets retired during the year was $20,000 ($70,000 − $50,000).

Instructions

a Prepare the ***Investing activities*** section of a statement of cash flows. Show supporting computations for the amounts of (1) proceeds from sales of marketable securities, and (2) proceeds from sales of plant assets. Place brackets around amounts representing cash outflows.

b Prepare the supporting schedule that should accompany the statement of cash flows in order to disclose the "noncash" aspects of the company's investing and financing activities.

Problem 14-3
Reporting
operating
activities

The following data have been taken from the accounting records of Lam Electronics Corp. at December 31:

	End of Year	Beginning of Year
Balance sheet accounts:		
Accounts receivable...	$ 600,000	$720,000
Accrued interest receivable	6,000	4,000
Inventories...	800,000	765,000
Short-term prepayments	20,000	15,000
Accounts payable (merchandise suppliers)	570,000	562,000
Accrued operating expenses payable	65,000	94,000
Accrued interest payable......................................	21,000	12,000
Accrued income taxes payable.................................	22,000	35,000
Income statement amounts:		
Net sales	2,950,000	
Dividend income..	104,000	
Interest revenue	70,000	
Cost of goods sold..	1,550,000	
Operating expenses...	980,000	
Interest expense...	185,000	
Income taxes expense.......................................	110,000	

Additional information

(1) Dividend revenue is recognized on the cash basis. All other income statement amounts are recognized on the accrual basis.
(2) Operating expenses include depreciation expense of $115,000.

Instructions. Prepare a partial statement of cash flows, including only the operating activities section of the statement. Use the format and captions illustrated on page 545, and place brackets around numbers representing cash payments. Show supporting computations for the amounts of:

(1) Cash received from customers.
(2) Interest and dividends received.
(3) Cash paid to suppliers and employees.
(4) Interest paid.
(5) Income taxes paid.

Problem 14-4
Preparing a
statement of cash
flows

The accounting staff of FastFax Corp. has assembled the following information for the year ended December 31, 19__:

Cash sales	$ 700,000
Credit sales	1,100,000
Collections on accounts receivable	900,000
Cash transferred from the money market fund to the general bank account	250,000
Interest and dividends received	50,000
Purchases (all on account)	1,000,000
Payments on accounts payable to merchandise suppliers	850,000
Cash payments for operating expenses	550,000
Interest paid.	120,000
Income taxes paid.	70,000
Loans made.	250,000
Collections on loans (excluding receipts of interest)	150,000
Cash paid to acquire plant assets.	2,000,000
Book value of plant assets sold	350,000
Loss on sales of plant assets	40,000
Proceeds from issuing bonds payable.	1,800,000
Dividends paid.	60,000
Cash and cash equivalents, beginning of year	68,000
Cash and cash equivalents, end of year	78,000

Instructions. Prepare a statement of cash flows in the format illustrated on page 545. Place brackets around amounts representing cash outflows. Many of the items above will be listed in your statement without change. However, you will have to combine certain given information to compute the amounts of (1) collections from customers, (2) cash paid to suppliers and employees, and (3) proceeds from sales of plant assets. (Hint: Not every item listed above is used in preparing a statement of cash flows.)

Problem 14-5
Preparing a
statement of cash
flows: a compre-
hensive problem

You are the chief accountant for Radley's Giftpacks, Inc. Your assistant has prepared an income statement for the current year, and has also developed the following "Additional information" by analyzing changes in the company's balance sheet accounts.

RADLEY'S GIFTPACKS, INC.
Income Statement
For the Year Ended December 31, 19__

Revenue:		
Net sales.		$1,400,000
Interest revenue.		10,000
Gain on sales of marketable securities		17,000
Total revenue and gains		$1,427,000
Costs and expenses:		
Cost of goods sold.	$810,000	
Operating expenses (including depreciation of $25,000)	420,000	
Interest expense.	11,000	
Income taxes	50,000	
Loss on sales of plant assets.	6,000	
Total costs, expenses, and losses		1,297,000
Net income		$ 130,000

Additional information. Information about changes in the company's balance sheet accounts over the year is summarized below:

(1) Accounts receivable increased by $20,000.
(2) Accrued interest receivable decreased by $1,000.
(3) Inventory decreased by $30,000 and accounts payable to suppliers of merchandise decreased by $8,000.
(4) Short-term prepayments of operating expenses increased by $3,000, and accrued liabilities for operating expenses decreased by $4,000.
(5) The liability for accrued interest payable increased by $2,000 during the year.
(6) The liability for accrued income taxes payable decreased by $7,000 during the year.
(7) The following schedule summarizes the total debit and credit entries during the year in other balance sheet accounts:

	Debit Entries	Credit Entries
Marketable securities...	$ 30,000	$ 19,000
Notes receivable (cash loans made to others)	22,000	14,000
Plant assets (see paragraph 8 below)	200,000	18,000
Notes payable (short-term borrowing)	46,000	41,000
Capital stock		10,000
Paid-in Capital in Excess of Par Value.............................		80,000
Retained earnings (see paragraph 9 below)	60,000	130,000

(8) The $18,000 in credit entries to the plant asset accounts are net of any debits to accumulated depreciation when plant assets were retired. Thus, the $18,000 in credit entries represents the book value of all plant assets sold or retired during the year.
(9) The $60,000 debit to retained earnings represents dividends declared and paid during the year. The $130,000 credit entry represents the net income shown in the income statement.
(10) All investing and financing activities were cash transactions.
(11) Cash and cash equivalents amounted to $82,000 at the beginning of the year, and to $52,000 at year-end.

Instructions. You are to prepare a statement of cash flows for the current year, following the format illustrated on page 545. Place brackets around dollar amounts representing cash outlays. Show separately your computations of the following amounts:

(1) Cash received from customers.
(2) Interest received.
(3) Cash paid to suppliers and employees.
(4) Interest paid.
(5) Income taxes paid.
(6) Proceeds from sales of marketable securities.
(7) Proceeds from sales of plant assets.
(8) Proceeds from issuing capital stock.

Business decision cases

This case is based upon the statement of cash flows for Allison Corporation, illustrated on page 545. You are to use this statement to evaluate the company's ability to continue paying the current level of dividends — $40,000 per year. The following information also is available:

(1) The net cash flow from operating activities shown in the statement is relatively "normal" for Allison Corporation. In fact, net cash flows from operating activities have not varied by more than a few thousand dollars in any of the last three years.

(2) The net outlay for investing activities was unusually high, because the company modernized its production facilities during the year. The "normal" investing cash outflow is about $45,000 per year, the amount required to replace existing plant assets as they are retired. Over the long run, marketable securities transactions and lending transactions have a very small impact upon Allison's net cash flow from investing activities.

(3) The net cash flow from financing activities was unusually large in the current year, because of the issuance of bonds payable and capital stock. These securities were issued to finance the modernization of the production facilities. In a typical year, financing activities include only short-term borrowing transactions and payments of dividends.

Instructions

a Based solely upon the company's past performance, do you feel that the $40,000 annual dividend payments are secure? That is, does the company appear able to pay this amount in dividends every year without putting any strain on its cash position? Do you think it more likely that Allison Corporation will increase or decrease the amount of dividends that it pays? Explain fully.

b Should any of the "unusual" events appearing in the statement of cash flows for the current year affect your analysis of the company's ability to pay future dividends? Explain.

It is late summer and National Motors, an auto manufacturer, is facing a financial crisis. A large issue of bonds payable will mature next March, and the company must issue stock or new bonds to raise the money to retire this debt. Unfortunately, profits and cash flows have been declining over recent years. Management fears that if cash flows and profits do not improve in the current year, the company will not be able to raise the capital needed to pay off the maturing bonds. Therefore, members of management have made the following proposals to improve the cash flows and profitability that will be reported in the financial statements dated this coming December 31.

(1) Switch from the LIFO method to the FIFO method of valuing inventories. Management estimates that the FIFO method will result in a lower cost of goods sold, but in higher income taxes for the current year. However, the additional income taxes will not actually be paid until early next year.

(2) Switch from the sum-of-the-years' digits method of depreciation to the straight-line method, and also lengthen the useful lives over which assets are depreciated. (These changes would be made only for financial reporting purposes, not for income tax purposes.)

(3) Pressure dealers to increase their inventories — in short, buy more cars. (The dealerships are independently owned; thus, dealers are the "customers" to whom National Motors sells automobiles.) It is estimated that this strategy could increase sales for the current year by 5%. However, any additional sales in the current year would be almost entirely offset by fewer sales to dealers in the following year.

(4) Require dealers to pay for purchases more quickly. Currently, dealers must pay for purchases of autos within 60 days. Management is considering reducing this period to 30 days.

(5) Pass up cash discounts offered for prompt payment (i.e., 2/10, n/30) and do not pay any bills until the final due date.

(6) Borrow at current short-term interest rates (about 10%) and use the proceeds to pay off long-term debt bearing an interest rate of 13%.

(7) Substitute stock dividends for the cash dividends currently paid on capital stock.

Instructions

a Prepare a schedule with four columns. The first column is to be headed "Proposals," and contains the paragraph numbers of the seven proposals listed above. The next three columns are to be headed with the following financial statement captions: (1) Net income, (2) Net cash flow from operating activities, and (3) Cash.

   For each of the seven proposals in the left column, indicate whether you expect the proposal to "Increase," "Decrease," or have "No Effect" in the current year upon each of the financial statement captions listed in the next three columns.

b For each of the seven proposals, write a short paragraph explaining the reasoning behind your answers to part a.

Chapter 15
Analysis and interpretation of financial statements

CHAPTER PREVIEW

In many of the preceding chapters we have been concerned with preparing a set of financial statements. In this chapter we start with the completed financial statements and concentrate on methods of analyzing and interpreting the information they contain. Our goal is to determine whether a company is gaining or losing ground in the unending struggle for profitability and solvency. We explore the techniques for comparing a company's present financial position with its position a year ago and for comparing this year's earnings with last year's earnings. We also compare a company's performance with that of other companies in the industry. Various types of analysis are presented to meet the special needs of common stockholders, long-term creditors, preferred stockholders, and short-term creditors.

After reading this chapter you should be able to meet these Learning Objectives:

1 Put the dollar amount of a company's net income into perspective by relating it to the company's sales, assets, and stockholders' equity.
2 Describe several sources of financial information about a business.
3 Explain the uses of dollar and percentage changes, trend percentages, and component percentages.
4 Discuss the "quality" of a company's earnings, assets, and working capital.
5 Analyze financial statements from the viewpoints of common stockholders, creditors, and others.
6 Compute the ratios widely used in financial statement analysis and explain the significance of each.

575

Financial statements are the instrument panel of a business enterprise. They constitute a report on managerial performance, attesting to managerial success or failure and flashing warning signals of impending difficulties. To read a complex instrument panel, one must understand the gauges and their calibration to make sense out of the array of data they convey. Similarly, one must understand the inner workings of the accounting system and the significance of various financial relationships to interpret the data appearing in financial statements. To a reader with a knowledge of accounting, a set of financial statements tells a great deal about a business enterprise.

The annual financial statements of large corporations are used by a number of different groups: stockholders, creditors, government agencies, union officials, politicians, and financial analysts, among others. What assurance do these people have that the information in these financial statements is reliable and is presented in accordance with generally accepted accounting principles? The answer is that these corporations are ***audited*** by independent firms of certified public accountants.

An audit is a thorough investigation of every item, dollar amount, and disclosure which appears in the financial statements. After completing the audit, the CPAs express their opinion as to the ***fairness*** of the financial statements. This opinion, called the ***auditors' report,*** is published with the financial statements in the company's annual report to its stockholders. A report by a CPA firm might read as follows:

To the Board of Directors and Stockholders
XYZ Company

Independent Auditors' Report

We have audited the accompanying balance sheet of XYZ Company as of December 31, 19___, and the related statements of income, retained earnings, and cash flow for the year then ended. These financial statements are the responsibility of the Company's management; our responsibility is to express an opinion based on our audit.

We conducted our audit in accordance with generally accepted auditing standards. Those standards require planning and performing the audit to provide reasonable assurance about whether the financial statements are free of material misstatement. An audit includes examining, on a test basis, evidence supporting the amounts and disclosures in the financial statements. An audit also includes assessing the accounting principles used and significant estimates made by management, as well as evaluating the overall financial statement presentation. We believe that our audit provides a reasonable basis for our opinion.

In our opinion, the financial statements referred to above present fairly, in all material respects, the financial position of XYZ Company as of December 31, 19___, and the results of its operations and its cash flows for the year then ended in conformity with generally accepted accounting principles.

Springfield, Mo.
January 29, 19___

Blue, White & Company

Certified Public Accountants

What is your opinion of the level of corporate profits?

1 Put the dollar amount of a company's net income into perspective by relating it to the company's sales, assets, and stockholders' equity.

As a college student who has completed (or almost completed) a course in accounting, you have a much better understanding of corporate profits than do people who have never studied accounting. The level of earnings of large corporations is a controversial topic, a favorite topic in many political speeches and at cocktail parties. Many of the statements one reads or hears from these sources are emotional rather than rational, and fiction rather than fact. Public opinion polls show that the public believes the average manufacturing company has an after-tax profit of about 30% of sales, when in fact such profit has been **about 5% of sales** in recent years. A widespread public belief that profits are six times the actual rate may lead to some unwise legislation.

● **CASE IN POINT** ● General Motors in an annual report a few years ago showed a net income of $321 million. This profit may sound like a huge amount, but it was only one-half of 1% of GM's sales. Thus, of every dollar received as revenue, only $\frac{1}{2}$ cent represented profit for GM. On a $10,000 car, this was a profit of $50. Actually, earning only $321 million in a year must be regarded as very poor performance for a corporation the size of General Motors. Shortly afterward, however, GM enjoyed its best year ever, and set new records for both sales and earnings. Net income was $4.5 billion and represented about $5\frac{1}{2}$ cents profit on each dollar of sales. That was a profit of $550 on a $10,000 automobile.

An in-depth knowledge of accounting does not enable you to say at what level corporate earnings **should be;** however, a knowledge of accounting does enable you to read audited financial statements that show what the level of corporate earnings **actually is.** Moreover, you are aware that the information in published financial statements of corporations has been audited by CPA firms and has been reviewed in detail by government agencies, such as the Securities and Exchange Commission and the IRS. Consequently, you know that the profits reported in these published financial statements are reasonably reliable; they have been determined in accordance with generally accepted accounting principles and verified by independent experts.

Some specific examples of corporate earnings . . . and losses

Not all leading corporations earn a profit every year. For the seven years from 1981 through 1987, Pan American Airways reported a net loss each year. The total loss for these years exceeded $1\frac{1}{2}$ billion. During a good part of the last decade, much of the airline industry operated at a loss. Net losses were incurred in one or more years by such well-known companies as American Airlines, Continental, TWA, Western, and United Airlines.

The oil companies have been particularly subject to criticism for so-called excessive profits, so let us briefly look at the profits of Exxon, the world's largest oil company. A recent annual report of Exxon (audited by Price Waterhouse) shows that profits amounted to a little over $4 billion. Standing alone, that figure seems enormous — but we need to look a little farther. The total revenue of Exxon was over $103 billion, so net income amounted to approximately 4% of sales. On the other hand, income taxes, excise taxes, and other taxes levied upon Exxon amounted to more than $21 billion, or about 5 times as much as the company's profit. Thus, taxation represents a far greater portion of the cost of a gallon of gasoline than does the oil company's profit.

There are many ways of appraising the adequacy of corporate earnings. Certainly, earnings should be compared with total assets and with invested capital as well as with sales. In this chapter we shall look at a number of ways of evaluating corporate profits and solvency.

Sources of financial information

2 Describe several sources of financial information about a business.

For the most part, our discussion will be limited to the kind of analysis that can be made by "outsiders" who do not have access to internal accounting records. Investors must rely to a considerable extent on financial statements in published annual and quarterly reports. In the case of large publicly owned corporations, additional information is filed with the Securities and Exchange Commission and is available to the public. Financial information about most large corporations is also published by Moody's Investors Service, Standard & Poor's Corporation, and stock brokerage firms.

Bankers are usually able to secure more detailed information by requesting it as a condition for granting a loan. Trade creditors may obtain financial information for businesses of almost any size from credit-rating agencies such as Dun & Bradstreet, Inc.

Comparative financial statements

Significant changes in financial data are easy to see when financial statement amounts for two or more years are placed side by side in adjacent columns. Such a statement is called a *comparative financial statement.* The amounts for the most recent year are usually placed in the left-hand money column. Both the balance sheet and the income statement are often prepared in the form of comparative statements. A highly condensed comparative income statement covering three years is shown below.

BENSON CORPORATION
Comparative Income Statement
For the Years Ended December 31, 1991, 1990, and 1989
(in thousands of dollars)

	1991	1990	1989
Condensed three-year income statement Net sales	$600	$500	$400
Cost of goods sold	370	300	235
Gross profit	$230	$200	$165
Expenses	194	160	115
Net income	$ 36	$ 40	$ 50

Tools of analysis

3 Explain the
uses of dollar and
percentage
changes, trend
percentages, and
component
percentages.
Few figures in a financial statement are highly significant in and of themselves. It is their relationship to other quantities, or the amount and direction of change that is important. Analysis is largely a matter of establishing significant relationships and pointing up changes and trends. Four widely used analytical techniques are (1) dollar and percentage changes, (2) trend percentages, (3) component percentages, and (4) ratios.

Dollar and percentage changes

The dollar amount of change from year to year is significant, but expressing the change in percentage terms adds perspective. For example, if sales this year have increased by $100,000, the fact that this is an increase of 10% over last year's sales of $1 million puts it in a different perspective than if it represented a 1% increase over sales of $10 million for the prior year.

The dollar amount of any change is the difference between the amount for a *comparison* year and for a *base* year. The percentage change is computed by dividing the amount of the change between years by the amount for the base year. This is illustrated in the tabulation below, using data from the comparative income statement above.

| | In Thousands | | | Increase or (Decrease) | | | |
| | | | | 1991 over 1990 | | 1990 over 1989 | |
	Year 1991	Year 1990	Year 1989	Amount	%	Amount	%
Net sales	$600	$500	$400	$100	20%	$100	25%
Net income.............	36	40	50	(4)	(10%)	(10)	(20%)

Dollar and percentage changes

Although net sales increased $100,000 in both 1990 and 1991, the percentage of change differs because of the shift in the base from 1989 to 1990. These calculations present no problems when the figures for the base year are positive amounts. If a negative amount or a zero amount appears in the base year, however, a percentage change cannot be computed. Thus if Benson Corporation had incurred a net loss in 1990, the percentage change in net income from 1990 to 1991 could not have been calculated.

Evaluating percentage changes in sales and earnings. Computing the percentage changes in sales, gross profit, and net income from one year to the next gives insight into a company's rate of growth. If a company is experiencing growth in its economic activities, sales and earnings should increase at *more than the rate of inflation.* Assume, for example, that a company's sales increase by 6% while the general price level rises by 10%. It is probable that the entire increase in sales may be explained by inflation, rather than by an increase in sales volume. In fact, the company may well have sold fewer goods than in the preceding year.

In measuring the dollar or percentage change in **quarterly** sales or earnings, it is customary to compare the results of the current quarter with those of the **same quarter in the preceding year.** Use of the same quarter of the preceding year as the base period prevents our analysis from being distorted by seasonal fluctuations in business activity.

Percentages become misleading when the base is small. Percentage changes may create a misleading impression when the dollar amount used as a base is unusually small. Occasionally we hear a television newscaster say that a company's profits have increased by a very large percentage, such as 900%. The initial impression created by such a statement is that the company's profits must now be excessively large. But assume, for example, that a company had net income of $100,000 in its first year; that in the second year net income drops to $10,000, and that in the third year, net income returns to the $100,000 level. In this third year, net income has increased by $90,000, representing a 900% increase over the profits of the second year. What needs to be added is that this 900% increase in profits in the third year **exactly offsets** the 90% decline in profits in the second year.

Few people realize that a 90% decline in earnings must be followed by a 900% increase just to get back to the starting point.

● **CASE IN POINT** ● In the third quarter of 1979, General Motors earned $21.4 million, as compared with $527.9 million in the third quarter of 1978. This represented a 96% decline in third quarter profits, computed as follows:

Decline in profits ($527.9 − $21.4) $506.5
Base period earnings (third quarter, 1978) $527.9
Percentage decrease ($506.5 ÷ $527.9)........................... 96%

How much of an increase in profits would be required in the third quarter of 1980 for profits to return to the 1978 level? Many people erroneously guess 96%. However, the correct answer is an astounding 2,367%, computed as follows:

Required increase to reach 1978 profit level (from $21.4 to $527.9) ... $506.5
Base period earnings (third quarter, 1979) .... $ 21.4
Required percentage increase ($506.5 ÷ $21.4).................... 2,367%

Unfortunately for GM, the company's 1980 profits did not return to 1978 levels. Instead, the company lost a record-setting $567 million in the third quarter of 1980.

Trend percentages

The changes in financial statement items from a base year to following years are often expressed as **trend percentages** to show the extent and direction of change. Two steps are necessary to compute trend percentages. First, a base year is selected and each item in the financial statements for the base year is given a weight of 100%. The second step is to express each item in the financial statements for following years as a percentage of its base-year amount. This computation consists of dividing an item such as Sales in the years after the base year by the amount of Sales in the base year.

For example, assume that 1987 is selected as the base year and that Sales in the base year amounted to $300,000 as shown below. The trend percentages for Sales are computed by dividing the Sales amount of each following year by $300,000. Also shown in the illustration are the yearly amounts of net income. The trend percentages for net income are computed by dividing the Net Income amount for each following year by the base-year amount of $15,000.

	1992	1991	1990	1989	1988	1987
Sales............	$450,000	$360,000	$330,000	$320,000	$312,000	$300,000
Net income.......	22,950	14,550	21,450	19,200	15,600	15,000

When the computations described above have been made, the trend percentages will appear as shown below.

	1992	1991	1990	1989	1988	1987
Sales............	150%	120%	110%	107%	104%	100%
Net income.......	153%	97%	143%	128%	104%	100%

The above trend percentages indicate a very modest growth in sales in the early years and accelerated growth in 1991 and 1992. Net income also shows an increasing growth trend with the exception of the year 1991, when net income declined despite a solid increase in sales. This variation could have resulted from an unfavorable change in the gross profit margin or from unusual expenses. However, the problem was overcome in 1992 with a sharp rise in net income. Overall the trend percentages give a picture of a profitable growing enterprise.

As another example, assume that sales are increasing each year, but that the cost of goods sold is increasing at a faster rate. This means that the gross profit margin is shrinking. Perhaps the increases in sales are being achieved through excessive price cutting. The company's net income may be declining even though sales are rising.

Component percentages

Component percentages indicate the **relative size** of each item included in a total. For example, each item on a balance sheet could be expressed as a percentage of total assets. This shows quickly the relative importance of current and noncurrent assets as well as the relative amount of financing obtained from current creditors, long-term creditors, and stockholders. By computing component percentages for several successive balance sheets, we can see which items are increasing in importance and which are becoming less significant.

Common size income statement. Another application of component percentages is to express all items on an income statement as a percentage of net sales. Such a statement is called a common size income statement. A condensed income statement in dollars and in common size form is illustrated on page 582.

Income Statement

	Dollars		Component Percentages	
	1991	1990	1991	1990
Net sales	$1,000,000	$600,000	100.0%	100.0%
Cost of goods sold	700,000	360,000	70.0	60.0
Gross profit on sales......................	$ 300,000	$240,000	30.0%	40.0%
Expenses (including income taxes)	250,000	180,000	25.0	30.0
Net income..............................	$ 50,000	$ 60,000	5.0%	10.0%

Are the year-to-year changes favorable?

Looking only at the component percentages, we see that the decline in the gross profit rate from 40 to 30% was only partially offset by the decrease in expenses as a percentage of net sales, causing net income to decrease from 10 to 5% of net sales.

Ratios

A ratio is a simple mathematical expression of the relationship of one item to another. Ratios may be stated several ways. To illustrate, let us consider the current ratio, which expresses the relationship between current assets and current liabilities. If current assets are $100,000 and current liabilities are $50,000, we may say either that the current ratio is 2 to 1 (which is written as 2:1), or that current assets are 200% of current liabilities. Either statement correctly summarizes the relationship—that is, that current assets are twice as large as current liabilities.

   If a ratio is to be useful, the two amounts being compared must be logically related. Our interpretation of a ratio often requires investigation of the underlying data.

Comparative data in annual reports of major corporations

The annual reports of major corporations usually contain a comparative balance sheet covering two years and a comparative income statement for three years. Supplementary schedules showing sales, net income, and other key amounts are often presented for periods of five to 10 years. Shown below are selected items from an annual report of Sears, Roebuck showing some interesting trends for a five-year period.

SEARS, ROEBUCK & CO.
($ millions, except per common share data)

	1986	1985	1984	1983	1982
Revenues	$44,281	$40,715	$38,828	$35,883	$30,020
Net income	1,351	1,303	1,455	1,342	861
Net income per share	$3.62	$3.53	$4.01	$3.80	$2.46
Dividends per share.........	$1.76	$1.76	$1.76	$1.52	$1.36
Market price (high–low)	50–36	41–31	40–29	45–27	32–16
Price-earnings ratio (high–low)	14–10	12–9	10–7	12–7	13–6

Standards of comparison

In using dollar and percentage changes, trend percentages, component percentages, and ratios, financial analysts constantly search for some standard of comparison against which to judge whether the relationships that they have found are favorable or unfavorable. Two such standards are (1) the past performance of the company and (2) the performance of other companies in the same industry.

Past performance of the company. Comparing analytical data for a current period with similar computations for prior years affords some basis for judging whether the position of the business is improving or worsening. This comparison of data over time is sometimes called *horizontal* or *trend* analysis, to express the idea of reviewing data for a number of consecutive periods. It is distinguished from *vertical* or *static* analysis, which refers to the review of the financial information for only one accounting period.

In addition to determining whether the situation is improving or becoming worse, horizontal analysis may aid in making estimates of future prospects. Because changes may reverse their direction at any time, however, projecting past trends into the future is always a somewhat risky statistical pastime.

A weakness of horizontal analysis is that comparison with the past does not afford any basis for evaluation in absolute terms. The fact that net income was 2% of sales last year and is 3% of sales this year indicates improvement, but if there is evidence that net income *should be* 7% of sales, the record for both years is unfavorable.

Industry standards. The limitations of horizontal analysis may be overcome to some extent by finding some other standard of performance as a yardstick against which to measure the record of any particular firm.[1] The yardstick may be a comparable company, the average record of several companies in the same industry, or some predetermined standard.

Suppose that Y Company suffers a 5% drop in its sales during the current year. The discovery that the sales of all companies in the same industry fell an average of 20% would indicate that this was a favorable rather than an unfavorable performance. Assume further that Y Company's net income is 2% of net sales. Based on comparison with other companies in the industry, this would be substandard performance if Y Company were a manufacturer of commercial aircraft, but it would be a satisfactory record if Y Company were a grocery chain.

When we compare a given company with its competitors or with industry averages, our conclusions will be valid only if the companies in question are reasonably comparable. Because of the large number of diversified companies formed in recent

[1] For example, the Robert Morris Associates publishes *Annual Statement Studies* which contains detailed data obtained from 27,000 annual reports grouped in 223 industry classifications. Assets, liabilities, and stockholders' equity are presented as a percentage of total assets; income statement amounts are expressed as a percentage of net sales; and key ratios are given (expressed as the median for each industry, the upper quartile, and the lower quartile). Measurements, within each of the 223 industry groups, are grouped according to the size of the firm. Similarly, Dun & Bradstreet, Inc., annually publishes *Key Business Ratios* in 125 lines of business divided by retailing, wholesaling, manufacturing, and construction. A total of 14 ratios is presented for each of the 125 industry groups.

years, the term *industry* is difficult to define, and companies that fall roughly within the same industry may not be comparable in many respects. For example, one company may engage only in the marketing of oil products; another may be a fully integrated producer from the well to the gas pump, yet both are said to be in the "oil industry."

Quality of earnings

4 Discuss the "quality" of a company's earnings, assets, and working capital.

Profits are the lifeblood of a business entity. No entity can survive for long and accomplish its other goals unless it is profitable. On the other hand, continuous losses will drain assets from the business, consume owners' equity, and leave the company at the mercy of creditors. In assessing the prospects of a company, we are interested not only in the total *amount* of earnings but also in the *rate* of earnings on sales, on total assets, and on owners' equity. In addition, we must look at the *stability* and *source* of earnings. An erratic earnings performance over a period of years, for example, is less desirable than a steady level of earnings. A history of increasing earnings is preferable to a "flat" earnings record.

A breakdown of sales and earnings by *major product lines* is useful in evaluating the future performance of a company. Publicly owned companies include with their financial statements supplementary schedules showing sales and profits by product line and by geographical area. These schedules assist financial analysts in forecasting the effect upon the company of changes in consumer demand for particular types of products.

Financial analysts often express the opinion that the earnings of one company are of higher quality than earnings of other similar companies. This concept of *quality of earnings* arises because each company management can choose from a variety of accounting principles and methods, all of which are considered generally acceptable. A company's management often is under heavy pressure to report rising earnings, and accounting policies may be tailored toward this objective. We have already pointed out the impact on current reported earnings of the choice between the LIFO and FIFO methods of inventory valuation and the choice of depreciation policies. In judging the quality of earnings, the financial analyst should consider whether the accounting principles and methods selected by management lead to a conservative measurement of earnings or tend to inflate reported earnings.

Quality of assets and the relative amount of debt

Although a satisfactory level of earnings may be a good indication of the company's long-run ability to pay its debts and dividends, we must also look at the composition of assets, their condition and liquidity, the relationship between current assets and current liabilities, and the total amount of debt outstanding. A company may be profitable and yet be unable to pay its liabilities on time; sales and earnings may appear satisfactory but plant and equipment may be deteriorating because of poor maintenance policies; valuable patents may be expiring; substantial losses may be in prospect from slow-moving inventories and past-due receivables. Companies with large amounts of debt often are vulnerable to increases in interest rates.

Impact of inflation

During a period of significant inflation, financial statements prepared in terms of historical costs do not reflect fully the economic resources or the real income (in terms of purchasing power) of a business enterprise. The FASB recommends that companies include in their annual reports supplementary schedules showing the effects of inflation upon their financial statements. Inclusion of these supplementary disclosures is voluntary, not mandatory. Many companies do **not** include these supplementary schedules because of the high cost of developing this information. The effects of inflation on financial statements are discussed further in Appendix D.

Illustrative analysis for Seacliff Company

Keep in mind the above discussion of analytical principles as you study the illustrative financial analysis which follows. The basic information for our analysis is

SEACLIFF COMPANY
Condensed Comparative Balance Sheet*
December 31, 1991 and December 31, 1990

	1991	1990	Increase or (Decrease) Dollars	%	Percentage of Total Assets 1991	1990
Assets						
Current assets..................................	$390,000	$288,000	$102,000	35.4	41.1	33.5
Plant and equipment (net)	500,000	467,000	33,000	7.1	52.6	54.3
Other assets (loans to officers).................	60,000	105,000	(45,000)	(42.9)	6.3	12.2
Total assets	$950,000	$860,000	$ 90,000	10.5	100.0	100.0
Liabilities & Stockholders' Equity						
Liabilities:						
Current liabilities	$112,000	$ 94,000	$ 18,000	(19.1)	11.8	10.9
12% long-term note payable	200,000	250,000	(50,000)	(20.0)	21.1	29.1
Total liabilities	$312,000	$344,000	$ (32,000)	(9.3)	32.9	40.0
Stockholders' equity:						
9% preferred stock, $100 par, callable at 105....	$100,000	$100,000			10.5	11.6
Common stock, $50 par	250,000	200,000	$ 50,000	25.0	26.3	23.2
Paid-in capital in excess of par...............	70,000	40,000	30,000	75.0	7.4	4.7
Retained earnings...........................	218,000	176,000	42,000	23.9	22.9	20.5
Total stockholders' equity	$638,000	$516,000	$122,000	23.6	67.1	60.0
Total liabilities & stockholders' equity	$950,000	$860,000	$ 90,000	10.5	100.0	100.0

* In order to focus attention on important subtotals, this statement is highly condensed and does not show individual asset and liability items. These details will be introduced as needed in the text discussion. For example, a list of Seacliff Company's current assets and current liabilities appears on page 594.

SEACLIFF COMPANY

Comparative Income Statement

For the Years Ended December 31, 1991 and December 31, 1990

	1991	1990	Increase or (Decrease) Dollars	%	Percentage of Net Sales 1991	1990
Net sales	$900,000	$750,000	$150,000	20.0	100.0	100.0
Cost of goods sold	530,000	420,000	110,000	26.2	58.9	56.0
Gross profit on sales	$370,000	$330,000	$ 40,000	12.1	41.1	44.0
Operating expenses:						
Selling expenses:	$117,000	$ 75,000	$ 42,000	56.0	13.0	10.0
General and administrative expenses	126,000	95,000	31,000	32.6	14.0	12.7
Total operating expenses	$243,000	$170,000	$ 73,000	42.9	27.0	22.7
Operating income	$127,000	$160,000	$ (33,000)	(20.6)	14.1	21.3
Interest expense	24,000	30,000	(6,000)	(20.0)	2.7	4.0
Income before income taxes	$103,000	$130,000	$ (27,000)	(20.8)	11.4	17.3
Income taxes	28,000	40,000	(12,000)	(30.0)	3.1	5.3
Net income	$ 75,000	$ 90,000	$ (15,000)	(16.7)	8.3	12.0
Earnings per share of common stock (see page 587)	$13.20	$20.25	$(7.05)	(34.8)		

SEACLIFF COMPANY

Statement of Retained Earnings

For the Years Ended December 31, 1991 and December 31, 1990

	1991	1990	Increase or (Decrease) Dollars	%
Retained earnings, beginning of year	$176,000	$115,000	$61,000	53.0
Net income	75,000	90,000	(15,000)	(16.7)
	$251,000	$205,000	$46,000	22.4
Less: Dividends on common stock	$ 24,000	$ 20,000	$ 4,000	20.0
Dividends on preferred stock	9,000	9,000		
	$ 33,000	$ 29,000	$ 4,000	13.8
Retained earnings, end of year	$218,000	$176,000	$42,000	23.9

contained in a set of condensed two-year comparative financial statements for Seacliff Company shown on the following pages. Summarized statement data, together with computations of dollar increases and decreases, and component percentages where applicable, have been compiled. For convenience in this illustration, relatively small dollar amounts have been used in the Seacliff Company financial statements.

Using the information in these statements, let us consider the kind of analysis that might be of particular interest to (1) common stockholders, (2) long-term creditors, (3) preferred stockholders, and (4) short-term creditors.

Analysis by common stockholders

5 Analyze financial statements from the viewpoints of common stockholders, creditors, and others.

Common stockholders and potential investors in common stock look first at a company's earnings record. Their investment is in shares of stock, so *earnings per share and dividends per share* are of particular interest.

Earnings per share of common stock. As indicated in Chapter 13, earnings per share of common stock are computed by dividing the income applicable to the common stock by the weighted average number of shares of common stock outstanding during the year. Any perferred dividend requirements must be subtracted from net income to determine income applicable to common stock, as shown in the following computations for Seacliff Company:

Earnings per Share of Common Stock

		1991	1990
Earnings related to number of common shares outstanding	Net income..	$75,000	$90,000
	Less: Preferred dividend requirements...........................	9,000	9,000
	Income applicable to common stock .... (a)	$66,000	$81,000
	Shares of common stock outstanding, during the year.......... (b)	5,000	4,000
	Earnings per share of common stock (a ÷ b).....................	$13.20	$20.25

Dividend yield and price-earnings ratio. Dividends are of prime importance to some stockholders, but a secondary factor to others. In other words, some stockholders invest primarily to receive regular cash income, while others invest in stocks principally with the hope of securing capital gains through rising market prices. If a corporation is profitable and retains its earnings for expansion of the business, the expanded operations should produce an increase in the net income of the company and thus tend to make each share of stock more valuable.

In comparing the merits of alternative investment opportunities, we should relate earnings and dividends per share to the *market value* of the stock. Dividends per share divided by market price per share determines the *yield* rate of a company's stock. Dividend yield is especially important to those investors whose objective is to maximize the dividend revenue from their investments.

Earnings performance of common stock is often expressed as a *price-earnings ratio* by dividing the market price per share by the annual earnings per share. Thus, a stock selling for $60 per share and earning $5 per share in the year just ended may be said to have a price-earnings ratio of 12 times earnings ($60 ÷ $5). The price-earnings ratio of the 30 stocks included in the Dow-Jones Industrial Average has varied widely in recent years, ranging from a low of about 6 for the group to a high of about 20.

The outlook for future earnings is a major factor influencing a company's price-earnings ratio. Companies with track records of rapid growth may sell at price-earnings ratios of perhaps 20 to 1, or even higher. Companies with stable earnings or earnings expected to decline in future years often sell at price-earnings ratios below 10 to 1.

Assume that the 1,000 additional shares of common stock issued by Seacliff on January 1, 1991 received the full dividend of $4.80 paid in 1991. When these new shares were issued, Seacliff Company announced that it planned to continue indefinitely the $4.80 dividend per common share currently being paid. With this assumption and the use of assumed market prices of the common stock at December 31, 1990 and December 31, 1991, earnings per share and dividend yield may be summarized as follows:

Earnings and Dividends per Share of Common Stock

	Date	Assumed Market Value per Share	Earnings per Share	Price-Earnings Ratio	Dividends per Share	Dividend Yield, %
Earnings and dividends related to market price of common stock	Dec. 31, 1990..............	$125	$20.25	6	$5.00	4.0
	Dec. 31, 1991..............	100	13.20	8	4.80	4.8

The decline in market value during 1991 presumably reflects the decrease in earnings per share. Investors appraising this stock at December 31, 1991, would consider whether a price-earnings ratio of 8 and a dividend yield of 4.8% represented a satisfactory situation in the light of alternative investment opportunities. They would also place considerable weight on estimates of the company's prospective future earnings and the probable effect of such estimated earnings on the market price of the stock and on dividend payments.

Book value per share of common stock. The procedures for computing book value per share were fully described in Chapter 13 and will not be repeated here. We will, however, determine the book value per share of common stock for the Seacliff Company:

Book Value per Share of Common Stock

		1991	1990
Why did book value per share increase?	Total stockholders' equity......................................	$638,000	$516,000
	Less: Equity of preferred stockholders (1,000 shares at call price of $105)	105,000	105,000
	Equity of common stockholders............................. (a)	$533,000	$411,000
	Shares of common stock outstanding .... (b)	5,000	4,000
	Book value per share of common stock (a ÷ b)	$106.60	$102.75

Book value indicates the net assets represented by each share of stock. This statistic is often helpful in estimating a reasonable price for a company's stock, especially for small corporations whose shares are not publicly traded. However, if a company's future earnings prospects are unusually good or unusually poor, the market price of its shares may differ significantly from their book value.

Revenue and expense analysis. The trend of earnings of Seacliff Company is unfavorable and stockholders will want to know the reasons for the decline in net income. The comparative income statement on page 586 shows that despite a 20% increase in net sales, net income fell from $90,000 in 1990 to $75,000 in 1991, a decline of 16.7%. As a percentage of net sales, net income fell from 12% to only 8.3%. The primary causes of this decline were the increases in selling expenses (56.0%), in general and administrative expenses (32.6%), and in the cost of goods sold (26.2%), all of which exceeded the 20% increase in net sales.

Let us assume that further investigation reveals Seacliff Company decided in 1991 to reduce its sales prices in an effort to generate greater sales volume. This would explain the decrease in gross profit rate from 44% to 41.1% of net sales. Since the dollar amount of gross profit increased $40,000 in 1991 the strategy of reducing sales prices to increase volume would have been successful if there had been little or no increase in operating expenses. However, operating expenses rose by $73,000, resulting in a $33,000 decrease in operating income.

The next step is to find which expenses increased and why. An investor may be handicapped here, because detailed operating expenses are not usually shown in published financial statements. Some conclusions, however, can be reached on the basis of even the condensed information available in the comparative income statement for Seacliff Company shown on page 586.

The substantial increase in selling expenses presumably reflects greater selling effort during 1991 in an attempt to improve sales volume. However, the fact that selling expenses increased $42,000 while gross profit increased only $40,000 indicates that the cost of this increased sales effort was not justified in terms of results. Even more disturbing is the increase in general and administrative expenses. Some growth in administrative expenses might be expected to accompany increased sales volume, but because some of the expenses are fixed, the growth generally should be *less than proportional* to any increase in sales. The increase in general and administrative expenses from 12.7 to 14% of sales would be of serious concern to informed investors.

Management generally has greater control over operating expenses than over revenue. The **operating expense ratio** is often used as a measure of management's ability to control its operating expenses. The unfavorable trend in this ratio for Seacliff Company is shown below.

Operating Expense Ratio

		1991	1990
Operating expenses	(a)	$243,000	$170,000
Net sales	(b)	$900,000	$750,000
Operating expense ratio (a ÷ b)		27.0%	22.7%

Does a higher operating expense ratio indicate higher net income?

If management were able to increase the sales volume while at the same time increasing the gross profit rate and decreasing the operating expense ratio, the effect on net income could be quite dramatic. For example, if in 1992 Seacliff Company can increase its sales by 11% to $1,000,000, increase its gross profit rate from 41.1 to 44%, and reduce the operating expense ratio from 27 to 24%, its operating income will increase from $127,000 to $200,000 ($1,000,000 − $560,000 − $240,000), an increase of over 57%.

Return on investment (ROI)

The rate of return on investment (often called ROI) is a test of management's efficiency in using available resources. Regardless of the size of the organization, capital is a scarce resource and must be used efficiently. In judging the performance of branch managers or of company-wide management, it is reasonable to raise the question: What rate of return have you earned on the resources under your control? The concept of return on investment can be applied to a number of situations: for example, evaluating a branch, a total business, a product line, or an individual investment. A number of different ratios have been developed for the ROI concept, each well suited to a particular situation. We shall consider the return on total assets and the return on common stockholders' equity as examples of the return on investment concept.

Return on assets. An important test of management's ability to earn a return on funds supplied from all sources is the rate of return on total assets.

The income figure used in computing this ratio should be **_operating income,_** since interest expense and income taxes are determined by factors other than the efficient use of resources. Operating income is earned throughout the year and therefore should be related to the **_average_** investment in assets during the year. The computation of this ratio for Seacliff Company is shown below:

Percentage Return on Assets

			1991	1990
Earnings related to investment in assets	Operating income	(a)	$127,000	$160,000
	Total assets, beginning of year	(b)	$860,000	$820,000
	Total assets, end of year	(c)	$950,000	$860,000
	Average investment in assets [(b + c) ÷ 2]	(d)	$905,000	$840,000
	Return on total assets (a ÷ d)		14%	19%

This ratio shows that earnings per dollar of assets invested have fallen off in 1991. Before drawing conclusions as to the effectiveness of Seacliff's management, however, we should consider the trend in the return on assets earned by other companies of similar kind and size.

Return on common stockholders' equity. Because interest and dividends paid to creditors and preferred stockholders are fixed in amount, a company may earn a greater or smaller return on the common stockholders' equity than on its total assets. The computation of return on stockholders' equity for Seacliff Company is shown below:

Return on Common Stockholders' Equity

		1991	190
Net income.		$ 75,000	$ 90,000
Less: Preferred dividend requirements		9,000	9,000
Net income applicable to common stock.	(a)	$ 66,000	$ 81,000
Common stockholders' equity, beginning of year	(b)	$416,000	$355,000
Common stockholders' equity, end of year.	(c)	$538,000	$416,000
Average common stockholders' equity [(b + c) ÷ 2].	(d)	$477,000	$385,500
Return on common stockholders' equity (a ÷ d)		13.8%	21.0%

Does the use of leverage benefit common stockholders?

In both years, the rate of return on common stockholders' equity was higher than the rate of interest paid to long-term creditors or the dividend rate paid to preferred stockholders. This result was achieved through the favorable use of leverage.

Leverage

The term *leverage* means operating a business with borrowed money. If the borrowed capital can be used in the business to earn a return *greater* than the cost of borrowing, then the net income and the return on common stockholders' equity will *increase.* In other words, if you can borrow money at 12% and use it to earn 20%, you will benefit by doing so. However, leverage can act as a "double-edged sword"; the effects may be favorable or unfavorable to the holders of common stock. If the rate of return on total assets should fall *below* the average rate of interest on borrowed capital, leverage will *reduce* net income and the return on common stockholders' equity. In this situation, paying off the loans that carry high interest rates would appear to be a logical move. However, most companies do not have enough cash to retire long-term debt on short notice. Therefore, the common stockholders may become "locked in" to the unfavorable effects of leverage.

In deciding how much leverage is appropriate, the common stockholders should consider the *stability* of the company's return on assets as well as the relationship of this return to the average cost of borrowed capital. If a business incurs so much debt that it becomes unable to meet the required interest and principal payments, the creditors may force liquidation or reorganization of the business.

Equity ratio. One indicator of the amount of leverage used by a business is the equity ratio. This ratio measures the proportion of the total assets financed by stockholders, as distinguished from creditors. It is computed by dividing total stockholders' equity by total assets. A *low* equity ratio indicates an extensive use of leverage, that is, a large proportion of financing provided by creditors. A high equity ratio, on the other hand, indicates that the business is making little use of leverage.

The equity ratio at year-end for Seacliff is determined as follows:

Equity Ratio

		1991	1990
Total stockholders' equity .... (a)		$638,000	$516,000
Total assets (or total liabilities & stockholders' equity) .... (b)		$950,000	$860,000
Equity ratio (a ÷ b)		67.2%	60.0%

Proportion of assets financed by stockholders

Seacliff Company has a higher equity ratio in 1991 than in 1990. Is this favorable or unfavorable?

From the viewpoint of the common stockholder, a low equity ratio will produce maximum benefits if management is able to earn a rate of return on assets greater than the rate of interest paid to creditors. However, a low equity ratio can be very unfavorable if the return on assets falls below the rate of interest paid to creditors. Since the return on total assets earned by Seacliff Company has declined from 19% in 1990 to a relatively low 14% in 1991, the common stockholders probably would **not** want to risk a low equity ratio. The action by management in 1991 of retiring $50,000 in long-term liabilities will help to protect the common stockholders from the unfavorable effects of leverage if the rate of return on assets continues to decline.

Analysis by long-term creditors

Bondholders and other long-term creditors are primarily interested in three factors: (1) the rate of return on their investment, (2) the firm's ability to meet its interest requirements, and (3) the firm's ability to repay the principal of the debt when it falls due.

Yield rate on bonds. The yield rate on bonds or other long-term indebtedness cannot be computed in the same manner as the yield rate on shares of stock, because bonds, unlike stocks, have a definite maturity date and amount. The ownership of a 12%, 10-year bond represents the right to receive $120 each year for 10 years plus the right to receive $1,000 at the end of 10 years. If the market price of this bond is $950, the yield rate on an investment in the bond is the rate of interest that will make the present value of these two contractual rights equal to $950. *The yield rate varies inversely with changes in the market price of the bond.* If interest rates rise, the market price of existing bonds will fall; if interest rates decline, the price of bonds will rise. If the price of a bond is above maturity value, the yield rate is less than the bond interest rate; if the price of a bond is below maturity value, the yield rate is higher than the bond interest rate.

Number of times bond interest earned. Bondholders feel that their investments are relatively safe if the issuing company has enough income to cover its interest requirements by a wide margin.

A common measure of debt safety is the ratio of income available for the payment of interest to the annual interest expense, called **number of times interest earned.** This computation for Seacliff Company would be:

Number of Times Interest Earned

			1991	1990
Operating income (before interest and income taxes)............	(a)	$127,000	$160,000
Annual interest expense	(b)	$ 24,000	$ 30,000
Times interest earned (a ÷ b).................................		5.3	5.3

The ratio remained unchanged at a satisfactory level during 1991. A ratio of 5.3 times interest earned would be considered strong in many industries. In the electric utilities industry, for example, the interest coverage ratio for the leading companies presently averages about 3, with the ratios of individual companies varying from 2 to 6.

Debt ratio. Long-term creditors are interested in the amount of debt outstanding in relation to the amount of capital contributed by stockholders. The *debt ratio* is computed by dividing total liabilities by total assets, shown below for Seacliff Company.

Debt Ratio

		1991	1990
Total liabilities...	(a)	$312,000	$344,000
Total assets (or total liabilities & stockholders' equity)............	(b)	$950,000	$860,000
Debt ratio (a ÷ b)		32.8%	40.0%

What portion of
total assets is
financed by debt?

From a creditor's viewpoint, the lower the debt ratio (or the higher the equity ratio) the better, since this means that stockholders have contributed the bulk of the funds to the business, and therefore the margin of protection to creditors against a shrinkage of the assets is high.

Analysis by preferred stockholders

Some preferred stocks are convertible into common stock at the option of the holder. However, many preferred stocks do not have the conversion privilege. If a preferred stock is convertible, the interests of the preferred stockholders are similar to those of common stockholders. If a preferred stock is not convertible, the interests of the preferred stockholders are more like those of long-term creditors.

Preferred stockholders are interested in the yield on their investment. The yield is computed by dividing the dividend per share by the market value per share. The dividend per share of Seacliff Company preferred stock is $9. If we assume that the market value at December 31, 1991, is $60 per share, the yield rate at that time would be 15% ($9 ÷ $60).

The primary measurement of the safety of an investment in preferred stock is the ability of the firm to meet its preferred dividend requirements. The best test of this ability is the ratio of the net income available to pay the preferred dividend to the amount of the annual dividend, as follows:

Times Preferred Dividends Earned

		1991	1990
Net income available to pay preferred dividends............... (a)		$75,000	$90,000
Annual preferred dividend requirements........................ (b)		$ 9,000	$ 9,000
Times dividends earned (a ÷ b)		8.3	10

Is the preferred dividend safe?

Although the margin of protection declined in 1991, the annual preferred dividend requirement still appears well protected.

As previously discussed in Chapter 12 (page 478) the market price of a preferred stock tends to vary inversely with interest rates. When interest rates are moving up, preferred stock prices tend to decline; when interest rates are dropping, preferred stock prices rise.

Analysis by short-term creditors

Bankers and other short-term creditors share the interest of stockholders and bondholders in the profitability and long-run stability of a business. Their primary interest, however, is in the current position of the firm — its ability to generate sufficient funds (working capital) to meet current operating needs and to pay current debts promptly. Thus the analysis of financial statements by a banker considering a short-term loan, or by a trade creditor investigating the credit status of a customer, is likely to center on the working capital position of the prospective debtor.

Amount of working capital. The details of the working capital of Seacliff Company are shown below:

SEACLIFF COMPANY
Comparative Schedule of Working Capital
As of December 31, 1991 and December 31, 1990

	1991	1990	Increase or (Decrease) Dollars	%	Percentage of Total Current Items 1991	1990
Current assets:						
Cash.....................................	$ 38,000	$ 40,000	$ (2,000)	(5.0)	9.7	13.9
Receivables (net).........................	117,000	86,000	31,000	36.0	30.0	29.9
Inventories...............................	180,000	120,000	60,000	50.0	46.2	41.6
Prepaid expenses.........................	55,000	42,000	13,000	31.0	14.1	14.6
Total current assets......................	$390,000	$288,000	$102,000	35.4	100.0	100.0
Current liabilities:						
Notes payable to creditors	$ 14,600	$ 10,000	$ 4,600	46.0	13.1	10.7
Accounts payable.........................	66,000	30,000	36,000	120.0	58.9	31.9
Accrued liabilities........................	31,400	54,000	(22,600)	(41.9)	28.0	57.4
Total current liabilities...................	$112,000	$ 94,000	$ 18,000	19.1	100.0	100.0
Working capital...........................	$278,000	$194,000	$ 84,000	43.3		

The amount of working capital is measured by the ***excess of current assets over current liabilities.*** Thus, working capital represents the amount of cash, near-cash items, and cash substitutes (prepayments) on hand after providing for payment of all current liabilities.

This schedule shows that current assets increased $102,000, while current liabilities rose by only $18,000, with the result that working capital increased $84,000.

Quality of working capital. In evaluating the debt-paying ability of a business, short-term creditors should consider the quality of working capital as well as the total dollar amount. The principal factors affecting the quality of working capital are (1) the nature of the current assets and (2) the length of time required to convert these assets into cash.

The preceding schedule shows an unfavorable shift in the composition of Seacliff Company's working capital during 1991; cash decreased from 13.9 to 9.7% of current assets, while inventory rose from 41.6 to 46.2%. Inventory is a less liquid resource than cash. Therefore, the quality of working capital is not as liquid as in 1990. ***Turnover ratios*** may be used to assist short-term creditors in estimating the time required to turn assets such as inventories and receivables into cash.

Inventory turnover. The cost of goods sold figure on the income statement represents the total cost of all goods that have been transferred out of inventories during any given period. Therefore the relationship between cost of goods sold and the average balance of inventories maintained throughout the year indicates the number of times that inventories "turn over" and are replaced each year.

Ideally we should total the inventories at the end of each month and divide by 12 to obtain an average inventory. This information is not always available, however, and the nearest substitute is a simple average of the inventory at the beginning and at the end of the year.

Assuming that only beginning and ending inventories are available, the computation of inventory turnover for Seacliff Company may be illustrated as follows:

Inventory Turnover

		1991	1990
Cost of goods sold..	(a)	$530,000	$420,000
Inventory, beginning of year		$120,000	$100,000
Inventory, end of year		$180,000	$120,000
Average inventory	(b)	$150,000	$110,000
Average inventory turnover per year (a ÷ b).....................		3.5 times	3.8 times
Average number of days to sell inventory (divide 365 days by inventory turnover)..		104 days	96 days

What does inventory turnover mean?

The trend indicated by this analysis is unfavorable, since the length of time required for Seacliff Company to turn over (sell) its inventory is increasing. A high inventory turnover and a low gross profit rate frequently go hand in hand. This, however, is merely another way of saying that if the gross profit rate is low, a high volume of business is necessary to produce a satisfactory return on total assets.

Short-term creditors generally regard a high inventory turnover as a good sign, indicating that the inventory is readily marketable.

Accounts receivable turnover. The turnover of accounts receivable is computed by dividing net credit sales by the average balance of accounts receivable. Ideally, a monthly average of receivables should be used, and only sales on credit should be included in the sales figure. For illustrative purposes, we shall assume that Seacliff Company sells entirely on credit and that only the beginning and ending balances of receivables are available:

Accounts Receivable Turnover

		1991	1990
Net sales on credit	(a)	$900,000	$750,000
Receivables, beginning of year		$ 86,000	$ 80,000
Receivables, end of year		$117,000	$ 86,000
Average receivables	(b)	$101,500	$ 83,000
Receivable turnover per year (a ÷ b)		8.9 times	9.0 times
Average number of days to collect receivables (divide 365 days by receivable turnover)		41 days	41 days

Are customers paying promptly?

There has been no significant change in the average time required to collect receivables. The interpretation of the average age of receivables depends upon the company's credit terms and the seasonal activity immediately before year-end. For example, if the company grants 30-day credit terms to its customers, the above analysis indicates that accounts receivable collections are lagging. If the terms are for 60 days, however, collections are being made ahead of schedule.

In Chapter 5 we defined the term *operating cycle* as the average time period between the purchase of merchandise and the conversion of this merchandise back into cash. In other words, the merchandise acquired for inventory is gradually converted into accounts receivable by selling goods to customers on credit, and these receivables are converted into cash through the process of collection. The word *cycle* refers to the circular flow of capital from cash to inventory to receivables to cash again.

The *operating cycle* in 1991 was approximately 145 days, computed by adding the 104 days required to turn over inventory and the average 41 days required to collect receivables. This compares to an operating cycle of only 137 days in 1990, computed as 96 days to dispose of the inventory plus 41 days to collect the resulting receivables. From the viewpoint of short-term creditors, the shorter the operating cycle, the higher the quality of the borrower's working capital. Therefore, these creditors would regard the lengthening of Seacliff Company's operating cycle as an unfavorable trend.

Current ratio. The current ratio (current assets divided by current liabilities) expresses the relationship between current assets and current liabilities. As debts come due, they must be paid out of current assets. Therefore, we want to compare the amount of current assets with the amount of current liabilities. The current ratio indicates a company's short-run, debt-paying ability. It is a measure of liquidity and of solvency. A strong current ratio provides considerable assurance that a company will be able to meet its obligations coming due in the near future. The current ratio for Seacliff Company is computed as follows:

Current Ratio

		1991	1990
Total current assets	(a)	$390,000	$288,000
Total current liabilities	(b)	$112,000	$ 94,000
Current ratio (a ÷ b)		3.5	3.1

Does this indicate satisfactory debt-paying ability?

A widely used rule of thumb is that a current ratio of 2 to 1 or better is satisfactory. By this standard, Seacliff Company's current ratio appears quite strong. Creditors tend to feel that the higher the current ratio the better. From a managerial point of view, however, there is an upper limit. Too high a current ratio may indicate that capital is not being used productively in the business.

Use of both the current ratio and the amount of working capital helps to place debt-paying ability in its proper perspective. For example, if Company X has current assets of $200,000 and current liabilities of $100,000 and Company Y has current assets of $2,000,000 and current liabilities of $1,900,000, each company has $100,000 of working capital, but the current position of Company X is clearly superior to that of Company Y. The current ratio for Company X is quite satisfactory at 2 to 1, but Company Y's current ratio is very low — only slightly above 1 to 1.

As another example, assume that Company A and Company B both have current ratios of 3 to 1. However, Company A has working capital of $20,000 and Company B has working capital of $200,000. Although both companies appear to be good credit risks, Company B would no doubt be able to qualify for a much **larger** bank loan than would Company A.

Quick ratio. Because inventories and prepaid expenses are further removed from conversion into cash than other current assets, a statistic known as the **quick ratio** is sometimes computed as a supplement to the current ratio. The quick ratio compares the highly liquid current assets (cash, marketable securities, and receivables) with current liabilities. Seacliff Company has no marketable securities; its quick ratio is computed as follows:

Quick Ratio

		1991	1990
Quick assets (cash and receivables)	(a)	$155,000	$126,000
Current liabilities	(b)	$112,000	$ 94,000
Quick ratio (a ÷ b)		1.4	1.3

A measure of liquidity

Here again the analysis reveals a favorable trend and a strong position. If the credit periods extended to customers and granted by creditors are roughly equal, a quick ratio of 1.0 or better is considered satisfactory.

Summary of analytical measurements

6 Compute the ratios widely used in financial statement analysis and explain the significance of each.

The basic ratios and other measurements discussed in this chapter and their significance are summarized below.

The student should keep in mind the fact that the full significance of any of these ratios or other measurements depends on the *direction of its trend* and its *relationship to some predetermined standard* or industry average.

Ratio or Other Measurement	Method of Computation	Significance
1 Earnings per share of common stock	$$\frac{\text{Net income} - \text{preferred dividends}}{\text{Shares of common outstanding}}$$	Gives the amount of earnings applicable to a share of common stock.
2 Dividend yield	$$\frac{\text{Dividend per share}}{\text{Market price per share}}$$	Shows the rate earned by stockholders based on current price for a share of stock.
3 Price-earnings ratio	$$\frac{\text{Market price per share}}{\text{Earnings per share}}$$	Indicates if price of stock is in line with earnings.
4 Book value per share of common stock	$$\frac{\text{Common stockholders' equity}}{\text{Shares of common outstanding}}$$	Measures the recorded value of net assets behind each share of common stock.
5 Operating expense ratio	$$\frac{\text{Operating expenses}}{\text{Net sales}}$$	Indicates management's ability to control expenses.
6 Return on assets	$$\frac{\text{Operating Income}}{\text{Average investment in assets}}$$	Measures the productivity of assets regardless of capital structure.
7 Return on common stockholders' equity	$$\frac{\text{Net income} - \text{preferred dividends}}{\text{Average common stockholders' equity}}$$	Indicates the earning power of common stock equity.
8 Equity ratio	$$\frac{\text{Total stockholders' equity}}{\text{Total assets}}$$	Shows the protection to creditors and the extent of leverage being used.
9 Number of times interest earned	$$\frac{\text{Operating income}}{\text{Annual interest expense}}$$	Measures the coverage of interest requirements, particularly on long-term debt.

Ratio or Other Measurement	Method of Computation	Significance
10 Debt ratio	$\dfrac{\text{Total liabilities}}{\text{Total assets}}$	Indicates the percentage of assets financed through borrowing; it shows the extent of leverage being used.
11 Times preferred dividends earned	$\dfrac{\text{Net income}}{\text{Annual preferred dividends}}$	Shows the adequacy of current earnings to pay dividends on preferred stock.
12 Working capital	Current assets − current liabilities	Measures short-run debt-paying ability.
13 Inventory turnover	$\dfrac{\text{Cost of goods sold}}{\text{Average inventory}}$	Indicates marketability of inventory and reasonableness of quantity on hand.
14 Accounts receivable turnover	$\dfrac{\text{Net sales on credit}}{\text{Average receivables}}$	Indicates reasonableness of accounts receivable balance and effectiveness of collections.
15 Current ratio	$\dfrac{\text{Current assets}}{\text{Current liabilities}}$	Measures short-run debt-paying ability.
16 Quick ratio	$\dfrac{\text{Quick assets}}{\text{Current liabilities}}$	Measures the short-term liquidity of a firm.

END-OF-CHAPTER-REVIEW

Summary of chapter learning objectives

1 Put the dollar amount of a company's net income into perspective by relating it to the company's sales, assets, and stockholders' equity.

To judge the adequacy of a corporation's net income, we need to relate the dollar amount of net income to the company's annual sales, to the amount of its assets, and to the stockholders' equity. A net income of $1,000,000 may represent very good earnings or very poor earnings depending upon the size of operations and amounts invested.

2 Describe several sources of financial information about a business.

Sources of information about a listed corporation include the company's published annual report, quarterly reports, data available from the SEC, stock brokerage firms, financial periodicals such as Moody's Investor Service, and Standard & Poor's Corporation, investment advisory services, and credit agencies.

3 Explain the uses of dollar and percentage changes, trend percentages, and component percentages.

Analysis of financial statements should indicate whether a company's earnings and solvency are on the upgrade or are deteriorating. The dollar change in any item is the difference between the amount for a *comparison* year and for a *base* year. The percentage change is computed by dividing the change between years by the amount for the base year. Trend percentages are useful to compare performance in each of a series of years with a selected base year. Thus, the rate of growth in sales is revealed by trend percentages. Component percentages indicate the relative size of each item included in a total. Thus, each item on a balance sheet may be expressed as a percentage of total assets. Each item on an income statement may be expressed as a percentage of net sales.

4 Discuss the "quality" of a company's earnings, assets, and working capital.

The concept of "quality" of earnings exists because each company management can choose from a variety of accounting principles and methods all of which are considered generally accepted. For example, the choice between straight-line depreciation and accelerated depreciation leads to different reported earnings. In judging the quality of earnings, the financial analyst considers whether the accounting principles and methods selected by management lead to a conservative measurement of earnings or tend to inflate earnings. The trend of earnings, their stability, and source are also significant in judging quality of earnings. The quality of assets and of working capital may reflect a well-maintained plant, long-run patents, a strong current position and liquidity of working capital.

5 Analyze financial statements from the viewpoints of common stockholders, creditors, and others.

Investors in *common stocks* are interested in earnings per share, price-earnings ratios, and dividend yields. These items help an investor to determine whether the current market price per share is excessive or undervalued. *Long-term creditors* are interested in the rate of return and the ability of the company to meet its obligations both as to interest on debt and repayment of principal. *Short-term creditors* are primarily interested in a company's ability to pay its current debts promptly. This quality of short-run solvency is measured by the current ratio, quick ratio, and the amount and liquidity of working capital. *Management* is interested in all the ratios mentioned above, and also has a strong interest in the efficiency of operations as measured by the return on investment (ROI) and the use of leverage.

6 Compute the ratios widely used in financial statement analysis and explain the significance of each.

The ratios widely used in financial statement analysis, the methods of computation, and the significance of each ratio are summarized in the table on pages 598–599.

Key terms introduced or emphasized in chapter 15

Comparative financial statements. Financial statement data for two or more successive years placed side by side in adjacent columns to facilitate study of changes.

Component percentage. The percentage relationship of any financial statement item to a total including that item. For example, each type of asset as a percentage of total assets.

Horizontal analysis. Comparison of the change in a financial statement item such as inventories during two or more accounting periods.

Leverage. Refers to the practice of financing assets with borrowed capital. Extensive leverage creates the possibility for the rate of return on common stockholders' equity to be substantially above or below the rate of return on total assets. When the rate of return on total assets exceeds the average cost of borrowed capital, leverage increases net income and the return on common stockholders' equity. However, when the return on total assets is less than the average cost of borrowed capital, leverage reduces net income and the return on common stockholders' equity. Leverage is also called *trading on the equity.*

Quality of assets. The concept that some companies have assets of better quality than others, such as well-balanced composition of assets, well-maintained plant and equipment, and receivables that are all current. A lower quality of assets might be indicated by poor maintenance of plant and equipment, slow-moving inventories with high danger of obsolescence, past-due receivables, and patents approaching an expiration date.

Quality of earnings. Earnings are said to be of high quality if they are stable, the source seems assured, and the methods used in measuring income are conservative. The existence of this concept suggests that the range of alternative but acceptable accounting principles may still be too wide to produce financial statements that are comparable.

Rate of return on investment (ROI). The overall test of management's ability to earn a satisfactory return on the assets under its control. Numerous variations of the ROI concept are used such as return on total assets, return on total equities, etc.

Ratios. See pages 598 and 599 for list of ratios, methods of computation, and significance.

Trend percentages. The purpose of computing trend percentages is to measure the increase or decrease in financial items (such as sales, net income, cash, etc.) from a selected base year to a series of following years. For example, the dollar amount of net income each year is divided by the base year net income to determine the trend percentage.

Vertical analysis. Comparison of a particular financial statement item to a total including that item, such as inventories as a percentage of current assets, or operating expenses in relation to net sales.

Demonstration problem for your review

The accounting records of King Corporation showed the following balances at the end of 1990 and 1991:

	1991	1990
Cash..	$ 35,000	$ 25,000
Accounts receivable (net)......................................	91,000	90,000
Inventory	160,000	140,000
Short-term prepayments	4,000	5,000
Investment in land	90,000	100,000
Equipment...	880,000	640,000
Less: Accumulated depreciation	(260,000)	(200,000)
Total..	$1,000,000	$ 800,000

	1991	1990
Accounts payable..	$ 105,000	$ 46,000
Income taxes payable and other accrued liabilities...............	40,000	25,000
Bonds payable—8%.......................................	280,000	280,000
Premium on bonds payable....................................	3,600	4,000
Capital stock, $5 par	165,000	110,000
Retained earnings	406,400	335,000
Total...	$1,000,000	$ 800,000
Sales (net of discounts and allowances).......................	$2,200,000	$1,600,000
Cost of goods sold..	1,606,000	1,120,000
Gross profit on sales	$ 594,000	$ 480,000
Expenses (including $22,400 interest expense).................	(336,600)	(352,000)
Income taxes...	(91,000)	(48,000)
Net income	$ 166,400	$ 80,000

Cash dividends of $40,000 were paid and a 50% stock dividend was distributed early in 1991. All sales were made on credit at a relatively uniform rate during the year. Inventory and receivables did not fluctuate materially. The market price of the company's stock on December 31, 1991, was $86 per share; on December 31, 1990, it was $43.50 (before the 50% stock dividend distributed in 1991).

Instructions. Compute the following for 1991 and 1990.

(1) Quick ratio
(2) Current ratio
(3) Equity ratio
(4) Debt ratio
(5) Book value per share of capital stock (based on shares outstanding after 50% stock dividend in 1991)
(6) Earnings per share of capital stock
(7) Price-earnings ratio
(8) Gross profit percentage
(9) Operating expense ratio
(10) Net income as a percentage of net sales
(11) Inventory turnover (Assume an average inventory of $150,000 for both years.)
(12) Accounts receivable turnover (Assume average accounts receivable of $90,000 for 1990.)
(13) Times bond interest earned (before interest expense and income taxes)

Solution to demonstration problem

	1991	1990
(1) Quick ratio:		
$126,000 ÷ $145,000	.9 to 1	
$115,000 ÷ $71,000		1.6 to 1
(2) Current ratio:		
$290,000 ÷ $145,000	2 to 1	
$260,000 ÷ $71,000		3.7 to 1

	1991	1990

(3) Equity ratio:

$571,400 ÷ $1,000,000 .... 57%

$445,000 ÷ $800,000 .... 56%

(4) Debt ratio:

$428,600 ÷ $1,000,000 .... 43%

$355,000 ÷ $800,000 .... 44%

(5) Book value per share of capital stock:

$571,400 ÷ 33,000 shares................................. $17.32

$445,000 ÷ 33,000* shares $13.48

(6) Earnings per share of capital stock

$166,400 ÷ 33,000 shares................................. $5.04

$80,000 ÷ 33,000* shares $2.42

(7) Price-earnings ratio:

$86 ÷ $5.04... 17 times

$43.50 ÷ 1.5* = $29, adjusted market price; $29 ÷ $2.42........ 12 times

(8) Gross profit percentage:

$594,000 ÷ $2,200,000 .... 27%

$480,000 ÷ $1,600,000 .... 30%

(9) Operating expense ratio:

($336,600 − $22,400) ÷ $2,200,000 .... 14%

($352,000 − $22,400) ÷ $1,600,000 .... 20.6%

(10) Income as a percentage of net sales:

$166,400 ÷ $2,200,000 .... 7.6%

$80,000 ÷ $1,600,000 .... 5%

(11) Inventory turnover:

$1,606,000 ÷ $150,000 .... 10.7 times

$1,120,000 ÷ $150,000 .... 7.5 times

(12) Accounts receivable turnover:

$2,200,000 ÷ $90,500 .... 24.3 times

$1,600,000 ÷ $90,000 .... 17.8 times

(13) Times bond interest earned:

($166,400 + $22,400 + $91,000) ÷ $22,400 .... 12.5 times

($80,000 + $22,400 + $48,000) ÷ $22,400 .... 6.7 times

* Adjusted retroactively for 50% stock dividend.

ASSIGNMENT MATERIAL

Review questions

1 a What groups are interested in the financial affairs of publicly owned corporations?

   b List some of the more important sources of financial information for investors.

2 In financial statement analysis, what is the basic objective of observing trends in data and ratios? Suggest some other standards of comparison.

3 In financial analysis, what information is produced by computing a ratio that is not available in a simple observation of the underlying data?

4 Distinguish between *trend percentages* and *component percentages.* Which would be better suited to analyzing the change in sales over a term of several years?

5 "Although net income declined this year as compared with last year, it increased from 3% to 5% of net sales." Are sales increasing or decreasing?

6 Differentiate between *horizontal* and *vertical* analysis.

7 Assume that Chemco Corporation is engaged in the manufacture and distribution of a variety of chemicals. In analyzing the financial statements of this corporation, why would you want to refer to the ratios and other measurements of companies in the chemical industry? In comparing the financial results of Chemco Corporation with another chemical company, why would you be interested in the accounting procedures used by the two companies?

8 Explain how the following accounting practices will tend to raise or lower the quality of a company's earnings. (Assume the continuance of inflation.)
a Adoption of an accelerated depreciation method rather than straight-line depreciation.
b Adoption of fifo rather than lifo for the valuation of inventories.
c Adoption of a 7-year life rather than a 10-year life for the depreciation of equipment.

9 What single ratio do you think should be of greatest interest to:
a a banker considering a short-term loan?
b a common stockholder?
c an insurance company considering a long-term mortgage loan?

10 Modern Company earned a 16% return on its total assets. Current liabilities are 10% of total assets. Long-term bonds carrying a 13% coupon rate are equal to 30% of total assets. There is no preferred stock. Is this application of leverage favorable or unfavorable from the viewpoint of Modern Company's stockholders?

11 In deciding whether a company's equity ratio is favorable or unfavorable, creditors and stockholders may have different views. Why?

12 Company A has a current ratio of 3 to 1. Company B has a current ratio of 2 to 1. Does this mean that A's operating cycle is longer than B's? Why?

13 An investor states, "I bought this stock for $50 several years ago and it now sells for $100. It paid $5 per share in dividends last year so I'm earning 10% on my investment." Criticize this statement.

14 Company C experiences a considerable seasonal variation in its business. The high point in the year's activity comes in November, the low point in July. During which month would you expect the company's current ratio to be higher? If the company were choosing a fiscal year for accounting purposes, how would you advise them?

15 Both the inventory turnover and accounts receivable turnover increased from 10 times to 15 times from Year 1 to Year 2, but net income decreased. Can you offer some possible reasons for this?

16 Is the rate of return on investment (ROI) intended primarily to measure liquidity, solvency, or some other aspect of business operations? Explain.

17 Mention three financial amounts to which corporate profits can logically be compared in judging their adequacy or reasonableness.

18 Under what circumstances would you consider a corporate net income of $1,000,000 for the year as being unreasonably low? Under what circumstances would you consider a corporate profit of $1,000,000 as being unreasonably high?

Exercises

Exercise 15-1
Accounting terminology

Listed below are nine technical accounting terms introduced in this chapter.

Trend percentages	Leverage	Inventory turnover
Vertical analysis	Yield	Operating cycle
Return on assets	Quick ratio	Price-earnings ratio

Each of the following statements may (or may not) describe one of these technical terms. For each statement, indicate the accounting term described, or answer "None" if the statement does not correctly describe any of the terms.

a Buying assets with money raised by borrowing or by issuing preferred stock.
b The proportion of total assets financed by stockholders, as distinguished from creditors.
c Market price per common share divided by earnings per common share.
d Changes in financial statement items from a base year to following years expressed as a percentage of the base year amount and designed to show the extent and direction of change.
e Dividends per share divided by market price per share.
f Average time period between the purchase of merchandise and the conversion of this merchandise back into cash.
g Comparison of a particular financial statement item to a total including that item.
h Net sales divided by average inventory.
i Comparison of highly liquid current assets (cash, marketable securities, and receivables) with current liabilities.

Exercise 15-2
Percentage changes

Selected information taken from financial statements of Lopez Company for two successive years is shown below. You are to compute the percentage change from 1990 to 1991 whenever possible.

	1991	1990
a Notes payable	$360,000	$300,000
b Cash	82,400	80,000
c Sales	990,000	900,000
d Accounts receivable	132,000	150,000
e Marketable securities	-0-	100,000
f Retained earnings	30,000	(30,000)
g Notes receivable	20,000	-0-

Exercise 15-3
Intuition vs. calculation

NICO Corporation had net income of $2,000,000 in its first year. In the second year, net income decreased by 80%. In the third year, due to an improved business environment, net income increased by 350%.

Instructions

a Prior to making any computations, do you think NIKO's net income was higher or lower in the third year than in the first year?
b Compute NICO's net income for the second year and for the third year. Do your computations support your initial response in part a?

Exercise 15-4
Trend percentages

Compute **trend percentages** for the following items taken from the financial statements of Raybar, Inc., over a five-year period. Treat 1987 as the base year. State whether the trends are favorable or unfavorable.

	1991	1990	1989	1988	1987
Sales	$440,000	$380,000	$310,000	$300,000	$250,000
Cost of Goods Sold	$308,000	$247,000	$198,000	$186,000	$150,000

Exercise 15-5
Common size income statements

Prepare **common size** income statements for Bell Company, a single proprietorship, for the two years shown below by converting the dollar amounts into percentages. For each year, sales will appear as 100% and other items will be expressed as a percentage of sales. (Income taxes are not involved as the business is not incorporated.) Comment on whether the changes from 1990 to 1991 are favorable or unfavorable.

	1991	1990
Sales...	$600,000	$500,000
Cost of goods sold	384,000	325,000
Gross profit	$216,000	$175,000
Operating expenses	168,000	145,000
Net income...	$ 48,000	$ 30,000

Exercise 15-6
Computing ratios

A condensed balance sheet for Magnet Corporation prepared at the end of the year appears below.

Assets		Liabilities & Stockholders' Equity	
Cash	$ 26,000	Notes payable	$ 60,000
Accounts receivable............	90,000	Accounts payable	100,000
Inventory	200,000	Long-term liabilities	140,000
Prepaid expenses..............	10,000	Capital stock, $10 par...........	200,000
Plant & equipment (net)	399,000	Retained earnings..............	250,000
Other assets	25,000		
Total	$750,000	Total	$750,000

During the year the company earned a gross profit of $324,000 on sales of $1,080,000. Accounts receivable, inventory, and plant assets remained almost constant in amount throughout the year. From this information, compute the following:

    a Current ratio
    b Quick ratio
    c Working capital
    d Equity ratio
    e Accounts receivable turnover (all sales were on credit)
    f Inventory turnover
    g Book value per share of capital stock.

Exercise 15-7
Ratios for a retail store

Selected financial data for Silverwoods, a retail store, appear below. Since monthly figures are not available, the average amounts for inventories and for accounts receivable should be based on the amounts shown for the beginning and end of 1991.

	1991	1990
Sales (terms 2/10, n/30)	$420,000	$300,000
Cost of goods sold	315,000	225,000
Inventory at end of year	54,000	60,000
Accounts receivable at end of year	62,000	47,000

Compute the following for 1991:

a Gross profit percentage
b Inventory turnover
c Accounts receivable turnover

Exercise 15-8
Current ratio, debt ratio, and earnings per share

Selected items from successive annual reports of Rayco appear below.

	1991	1990
Total assets (40% of which are current)	$500,000	$340,000
Current liabilities	$ 90,000	$100,000
Bonds payable, 12%	150,000	65,000
Capital stock, $10 stated value	150,000	150,000
Retained earnings	110,000	25,000
Total liabilities & stockholders' equity	$500,000	$340,000

Dividends of $5,000 were declared and paid in 1991. Compute the following:

a Current ratio for 1990 and 1991
b Debt ratio for 1990 and 1991
c Earnings per share for 1991

Exercise 15-9
Ratio analysis for two similar companies

Selected data from the financial statements of X Company and Y Company for the year just ended are shown below. Assume that for both companies dividends declared were equal in amount to net earnings during the year and therefore stockholders' equity did not change. The two companies are in the same line of business.

	X Company	Y Company
Total liabilities	$ 400,000	$ 200,000
Total assets	1,600,000	800,000
Sales (all on credit)	3,200,000	2,400,000
Average inventory	480,000	280,000
Average receivables	400,000	200,000
Gross profit as a percentage of sales	40%	30%
Operating expenses as a percentage of sales	38%	26%
Net income as a percentage of sales	2%	4%

Compute the following for each company:

a Net income
b Net income as a percentage of stockholders' equity
c Accounts receivable turnover
d Inventory turnover

Problems

The following information was developed from the financial statements of Pioneer Waterbeds. At the beginning of 1991, the company's former supplier went bankrupt, and the company began buying merchandise from another supplier.

	1991	1990
Gross profit on sales	$280,000	$315,000
Income before income taxes......................................	64,000	70,000
Net income..	48,000	52,500
Net income as a percentage of net sales..........................	6.0%	7.5%

Instructions

a Compute the net sales for each year.
b Compute the cost of goods sold in dollars and as a percentage of net sales for each year.
c Compute operating expenses in dollars and as a percentage of net sales for each year. (Income taxes expense is not an operating expense.)
d Prepare a condensed comparative income statement for 1990 and 1991. Include the following items: Net sales, cost of goods sold, gross profit, operating expenses, income before income taxes, income taxes expense, and net income. Omit earnings per share statistics.
e Identify the significant favorable trends and unfavorable trends in the performance of Pioneer Waterbeds. Comment on any unusual changes.

Harvest King manufactures and distributes farm equipment. Shown below are the income statement for the company and a common size summary for the industry in which the company operates. (Note: Notice that the percentages in the right-hand columns are **not** for Harvest King, but are average percentages for the industry.)

	Harvest King	Industry Average
Sales (net)	$8,000,000	100%
Cost of goods sold	5,040,000	58%
Gross profit on sales	$2,960,000	42%
Operating expenses:		
Selling...	$ 960,000	10%
General and administrative	1,120,000	15%
Total operating expenses	$2,080,000	25%
Operating income	$ 880,000	17%
Income taxes..	420,000	8%
Net income..	$ 460,000	9%
Return on stockholders' equity	10%	18%

Instructions

a Prepare a two-column common size income statement. The first column should show for Harvest King all items expressed as a percentage of net sales. (Round all figures to the nearest whole percent.) The second column should show as an industry average the percentage data given in the problem. The purpose of this common size statement is to compare the operating results of Harvest King with the average for the industry.

b Comment specifically on differences between Harvest King and the industry average with respect to gross profit on sales, selling expenses, general and administrative expenses, operating income, income taxes, net income, and return on stockholders' equity. Suggest possible reasons for the more important disparities.

Problem 15-3
Ratios; consider advisability of incurring long-term debt

At the end of the year, the following information was obtained from the accounting records of Craftsman Clocks.

Sales (all on credit)	$900,000
Cost of goods sold..	585,000
Average inventory (FIFO method)	117,000
Average accounts receivable...	100,000
Interest expense...	15,000
Income taxes	28,000
Net income	53,000
Average investment in assets	600,000
Average stockholders' equity..	265,000

Instructions. From the information given, compute the following:

a Inventory turnover.
b Accounts receivable turnover.
c Total operating expenses. (Interest expense and income taxes are nonoperating expenses.)
d Gross profit percentage.
e Return on average stockholders' equity.
f Return on average assets.
g Craftsman Clocks has an opportunity to obtain a long-term loan at an annual interest rate of 11% and could use this additional capital at the same rate of profitability as indicated above. Would obtaining the loan be desirable from the viewpoint of the stockholders? Explain.

Problem 15-4
Leverage: an alternate problem to 15-3

At the end of the year, the following information was obtained from the accounting records of Santa Fe Boot Co.

Sales (all on credit)	$800,000
Cost of goods sold..	480,000
Average inventory (FIFO method)	120,000
Average accounts receivable...	80,000
Interest expense...	6,000
Income taxes	8,000
Net income for the year...	36,000
Average investment in assets	500,000
Average stockholders' equity..	400,000

The company declared no dividends of any kind during the year and did not issue or retire any capital stock.

Instructions. From the information given, compute the following for the year.

a Inventory turnover.
b Accounts receivable turnover.
c Total operating expenses. (Interest expense is a nonoperating expense.)
d Gross profit percentage.
e Return on average stockholders' equity.
f Return on average assets.
g Santa Fe Boot Co. has an opportunity to obtain a long-term loan at an annual interest rate of 12% and could use this additional capital at the same rate of profitability as indicated above. Would obtaining the loan be desirable from the viewpoint of the stockholders? Explain.

Problem 15-5
Analysis and interpretation from viewpoint of short-term creditor

Shown below are selected financial data for Hill Corporation and for Valley Company at the end of the current year.

	Hill Corporation	Valley Company
Net credit sales	$480,000	$595,000
Cost of goods sold	420,000	412,500
Cash	12,000	35,000
Accounts receivable (net)	60,000	70,000
Inventory	168,000	82,500
Current liabilities	80,000	75,000

Assume that the year-end balances shown for accounts receivable and for inventory also represent the average balances of these accounts throughout the year.

Instructions

a For each company, compute the following:
  (1) Working capital.
  (2) Current ratio.
  (3) Quick ratio.
  (4) Number of times inventory turned over during the year and the average number of days required to turn over inventory.
  (5) Number of times accounts receivable turned over during the year and the average number of days required to collect accounts receivable. (Round to the nearest day.)
  (6) Operating cycle.
b From the viewpoint of a short-term creditor, comment upon the relative *quality* of each company's working capital. To which company would you prefer to sell $15,000 in merchandise on a 30-day open account?

Problem 15-6
Effects of
transactions on
various ratios

Listed in the left-hand column below is a series of business transactions and events relating to the activities of Potomac Mills. Opposite each transaction is listed a particular ratio used in financial analysis:

Transaction	Ratio
(1) Purchased inventory on open account.	Quick ratio
(2) A larger physical volume of goods was sold at smaller unit prices.	Gross profit percentage
(3) Corporation declared a cash dividend.	Current ratio
(4) An uncollectible account receivable was written off against the allowance account	Current ratio
(5) Issued additional shares of common stock and used proceeds to retire long-term debt.	Debt ratio
(6) Paid stock dividend on common stock, in common stock.	Earnings per share
(7) Conversion of a portion of bonds payable into common stock. (Ignore income taxes.)	Times interest charges earned
(8) Appropriated retained earnings.	Rate of return on stockholders' equity
(9) During period of rising prices, company changed from FIFO to LIFO method of inventory pricing.	Inventory turnover
(10) Paid a previously declared cash dividend.	Debt ratio
(11) Purchased factory supplies on open account.	Current ratio (assume that ratio is greater than 1 : 1)
(12) Issued shares of capital stock in exchange for patents.	Equity ratio

Instructions. What effect would each transaction or event have on the ratio listed opposite to it; that is, as a result of this event would the ratio increase, decrease, or remain unchanged? Your answer for each of the 12 transactions should include a brief explanation.

Problem 15-7
Analysis and in-
terpretation from
viewpoint of
common stock-
holders and of
bondholders

The following financial information for Continental Transfer Co. and American Van Lines (except market price per share of stock) is stated in ***thousands of dollars.*** The figures are as of the end of the current year. The two companies are in the same industry and are quite similar as to operations, facilities, and accounting methods. Assume that both companies pay income taxes equal to 50% of income before income taxes.

Assets	Continental Transfer Co.	American Van Lines
Current assets	$ 97,450	$132,320
Plant and equipment	397,550	495,680
Less: Accumulated depreciation	(55,000)	(78,000)
Total assets	$440,000	$550,000

Liabilities & Stockholders' Equity

Current liabilities	$ 34,000	$ 65,000
Bonds payable, 12%, due in 15 years.........................	120,000	100,000
Capital stock, no par..	150,000	200,000
Retained earnings	136,000	185,000
Total liabilities & stockholders' equity......................	$440,000	$550,000
Analysis of retained earnings:		
Balance, beginning of year...................................	$125,200	$167,200
Net income for the year......................................	19,800	37,400
Dividends	(9,000)	(19,600)
Balance, end of year	$136,000	$185,000
Market price of capital stock, per share......................	$30	$61
Number of shares of capital stock outstanding.................	6 million	8 million

Instructions

a Compute for each company:

(1) The number of times bond interest was earned during the current year. (Remember to use *available income* rather than net income in determining the coverage of interest expense. Add back to net income both income taxes and bond interest.)

(2) The debt ratio.

b In the light of the information developed in a above, write a paragraph indicating which company's bonds you think would trade in the market at the higher price. Which would probably provide the higher yield? Explain how the ratios developed influence your answer. (It may be assumed that the bonds were issued several years ago and are traded on an organized securities exchange.)

c For each company compute the dividend yield, the price-earnings ratio, and the book value per share. (Show supporting computations to determine dividends per share. Remember that dollar amounts in the problem are in thousands of dollars, that is, three zeros omitted.) In determining the price-earnings ratios, you must first compute earnings per share. Show this computation in a supporting note.

d Express an opinion, based on the data developed in c above, as to which company's stock is a better investment at the present market price.

Business decision cases

Case 15-1
Figures don't lie

Holiday Greeting Cards is a local company organized late in July of 1990. The company's net income for each of its first six calendar quarters of operations is summarized below. The amounts are stated in thousands of dollars.

	1991	1990
First quarter (January through March)	$ 253	—
Second quarter (April through June)	308	—
Third quarter (July through September).......................	100	$ 50
Fourth quarter (October through December)...................	450	500
Total for the calendar year..................................	$1,111	$550

Glen Wallace reports the business and economic news for a local radio station. On the day that Holiday Greeting Cards released the above financial information, you heard Wallace make the following statement during his broadcast: "Holiday Greeting Cards enjoyed a 350% increase in its profits for the fourth quarter, and profits for the entire year were up by over 100%."

Instructions

a Show the computations that Wallace probably made in arriving at his statistics. (Hint: Wallace did not make his computations in the manner recommended in this chapter. His figures, however, can be developed from the financial data above.)

b Do you believe that Wallace's percentage changes present a realistic impression of Holiday Greeting Cards' rate of growth in 1991? Explain.

c What figure would you use to express the percentage change in Holiday's fourth quarter profits in 1991? Explain why you would compute the change in this manner.

Case 15-2
Evaluation of recent developments

Presented below are three independent situations. Following each situation, we identify two or three groups of investors. You are to prepare a separate evaluation of the situation from the perspective of each of these investor groups. In your evaluation, indicate whether the recent developments described in the situation should be viewed as favorable, unfavorable, or not of much importance to the group. Explain the reasons for your conclusion.

Situation 1. During each of the last 10 years, Reese Corporation has increased the common stock dividend per share by about 10%. Total dividends now amount to $9 million per year, consisting of $2 million paid to preferred stockholders and $7 million paid to common stockholders. The preferred stock is cumulative but not convertible. Annual net income had been rising steadily until two years ago, when it peaked at $44 million. Last year, increased competition caused net income to decline to $37 million. Management expects income to stabilize around this level for several years. This year, Reese Corporation issued bonds payable. The contract with bondholders requires Reese Corporation to limit total dividends to not more than 25% of net income.

Instructions. Evaluate this situation from the perspective of:

a Common stockholders
b Preferred stockholders

Situation 2. Reynolds Labs develops and manufactures pharmaceutical products. The company has been growing rapidly during the past 10 years, due primarily to having discovered, patented, and successfully marketed dozens of new products. Profits have increased annually by 30% or more. The company pays no dividend, but has a very high price-earnings ratio. Due to its rapid growth and large expenditures for research and development, the company has experienced occasional cash shortages. To solve this problem, Reynolds has decided to improve its cash position by (1) requiring customers to pay for products purchased on account from the company in 30 days instead of 60 days, and (2) reducing expenditures for research and development by 20%.

Instructions. Evaluate this situation from the perspective of:

a Short-term creditors
b Common stockholders

Situation 3. Metro Utilities has outstanding 16 issues of bonds payable, with interest rates ranging from $5\frac{1}{2}$% to 14%. The company's return on assets consistently averages 12%. Almost every year, the company issues additional bonds to finance growth, to pay maturing bonds, or to call outstanding bonds when advantageous. During the current year, long-term interest rates have fallen dramatically. At the beginning of the year, these rates were between 12% and 13%; now, however, they are down to between 8% and 9%. Management currently is planning a large $8\frac{1}{2}$% bond issue.

Instructions. Evaluate this situation from the perspective of:

    a Holders of $5\frac{1}{2}$% bonds, maturing in 11 years but callable now at 103
    b Holders of 14% bonds, maturing in 23 years but callable now at 103
    c Common stockholders

Part Five: Comprehensive Problem
American Home Products Corporation

Analysis of the financial statements of a publicly owned corporation.

The purpose of this Comprehensive Problem is to acquaint you with the financial statements of a publicly owned company. The financial statements included in the 1985 annual report of American Home Products Corporation (the Company) were selected because they illustrate many of the financial reporting issues discussed in this textbook. Notice that several pages of explanatory notes are included with the basic statements. These explanatory notes supplement the condensed information in the financial statements and are intended to carry out the generally accepted accounting principle of adequate disclosure.

The Company's 1985 annual report originally included statements of changes in working capital, rather than a statement of cash flows. The FASB now requires companies to prepare statements of cash flow. To illustrate the new reporting requirements, we have substituted a statement of cash flows for the original statements of changes in working capital. This statement of cash flows was prepared by the textbook authors using the techniques described in Chapter 14. (Had this statement been prepared by the Company, certain items might have been classified differently.) We have shown a statement of cash flows only for 1985; sufficient data was not available to prepare comparative statements for 1984 and 1983.

This Comprehensive Problem is subdivided into three parts. ***Part 1*** is designed to familiarize you with the content of these financial statements. ***Part 2*** requires analysis from the viewpoint of a short-term creditor, and ***Part 3,*** from the perspective of a stockholder. As indicated in the instructions, some portions of Parts 1 and 3 relate to material covered in Appendix D.

Consolidated Balance Sheets

American Home Products Corporation and Subsidiaries

December 31,	1985	1984
Assets	*(In thousands)*	
Cash and cash equivalents	$ 915,021	$ 767,980
Accounts receivable less allowances (1985—$21,737, and 1984—$20,070)	695,270	641,147
Inventories	575,504	529,391
Deferred taxes and other current assets.	89,767	89,576
Total Current Assets	2,275,562	2,028,094
Investments at cost which approximates market	30,471	17,464
Property, plant and equipment:		
Land.	33,678	29,248
Buildings	494,074	427,704
Machinery and equipment	879,166	778,308
	1,406,918	1,235,260
Less accumulated depreciation	547,504	465,637
	859,414	769,623
Intangibles.	193,465	182,851
Other assets	36,299	46,898
	$3,395,211	$3,044,930
Liabilities		
Loans payable to banks	$ 8,229	$ 9,885
Accounts payable and accrued expenses	603,042	526,777
Accrued federal and foreign taxes on income	50,631	51,719
Total Current Liabilities	661,902	588,381
Deferred compensation payable under Management Incentive Plan	63,322	70,526
Deferred taxes	46,142	12,395
Other noncurrent liabilities	332,087	285,044
Stockholders' Equity		
$2 convertible preferred stock, par value $2.50 per share	246	280
Common stock, par value $.33⅓ per share	50,296	50,667
Additional paid-in capital	245,352	187,338
Retained earnings	2,091,438	1,959,723
Currency translation adjustments	(95,574)	(109,424)
Total Stockholders' Equity	2,291,758	2,088,584
	$3,395,211	$3,044,930

Consolidated Statements of Income
American Home Products Corporation and Subsidiaries

Years Ended December 31,	1985	1984	1983
	(In thousands except per share amounts)		
Net sales	$4,684,742	$4,485,470	$4,273,299
Other income, net	59,578	82,936	56,707
	4,744,320	4,568,406	4,330,006
Cost of goods sold	1,837,119	1,799,537	1,759,095
Selling, administrative and general expense	1,695,963	1,594,404	1,491,204
	3,533,082	3,393,941	3,250,299
Income before federal and foreign taxes on income	1,211,238	1,174,465	1,079,707
Provision for taxes on income:			
Federal	380,401	394,259	358,829
Foreign	113,697	124,378	130,032
	494,098	518,637	488,861
Income from continuing operations	717,140	655,828	590,846
Businesses sold:			
Income, net of taxes	—	19,754	36,387
Gain on sales, net of taxes	—	56,500	—
	—	76,254	36,387
Provision for impairment of investments in certain foreign locations	—	(50,000)	—
Net income	$ 717,140	$ 682,082	$ 627,233
Net Income Per Share of Common Stock:			
Continuing operations	$ 4.70	$ 4.26	$ 3.77
Businesses sold	—	.13	.23
Gain on sales of businesses	—	.37	—
Provision for impairment of investments in certain foreign locations	—	(.33)	—
Net income per share	$ 4.70	$ 4.43	$ 4.00

Consolidated Statements

American Home Products Corporation and Subsidiaries

Years Ended December 31,	1985	1984	1983
Retained Earnings		*(In thousands)*	
Balance, beginning of year	$1,959,723	$1,933,968	$1,746,610
Net income	717,140	682,082	627,233
	2,676,863	2,616,050	2,373,843
Cash dividends declared:			
$2 convertible preferred stock	207	237	277
Common stock	441,659	406,181	374,814
	441,866	406,418	375,091
Cost of treasury stock acquired, less amounts charged to capital	143,559	249,909	64,784
	585,425	656,327	439,875
Balance, end of year	$2,091,438	$1,959,723	$1,933,968
Additional Paid-in Capital			
Balance, beginning of year	$ 187,338	$ 155,684	$ 104,417
Excess over par value of common stock issued	57,747	40,198	46,766
Miscellaneous, net	267	(8,544)	4,501
Balance, end of year	$ 245,352	$ 187,338	$ 155,684
Currency Translation Adjustments			
Balance, beginning of year	$ 109,424	$ 93,046	$ 59,732
Aggregate translation adjustments for the year	(13,850)	49,349	33,314
Cumulative translation adjustments related to businesses sold	—	(17,786)	—
Cumulative translation adjustments related to foreign investments deconsolidated	—	(15,185)	—
Balance, end of year	$ 95,574	$ 109,424	$ 93,046

Consolidated statement of cash flows*
American home products corporation and subsidiaries

Year Ended December 31, 1985

	(In Thousands)

Cash flows from operating activities:

Cash received from customers	$ 4,630,619	
Interest and dividends received.	49,744	
Cash provided by operating activities		$ 4,680,363
Cash paid to suppliers and employees.	$(3,413,556)	
Interest paid	(95)	
Income taxes paid	(461,439)	
Cash disbursed for operating activities		(3,875,090)
Net cash flow from operating activities		$ 805,273

Cash flows from investing activities:

Purchases of investments.	$ (13,007)	
Cash paid to acquire plant assets	(199,509)	
Proceeds of sales from plant assets.	22,863	
Net cash used by investing activities.		(189,653)

Cash flows from financing activities:

Repayment of short-term borrowing	$ (1,656)	
Proceeds from issuance of long-term debt	47,043	
Dividends paid	(441,866)	
Repurchase of capital stock (net)	(85,950)	
Miscellaneous.	13,850	
Net cash used by financing activities		(468,579)
Net increase (decrease) in cash.		$ 147,041
Cash and cash equivalents, December 31, 1984		767,980
Cash and cash equivalents, December 31, 1985		$ 915,021

* Not included in the Company's original annual report. See introductory comments on page 615.

Notes to Consolidated Financial Statements

1. Summary of Significant Accounting Policies:
Principles of consolidation: The accompanying consolidated financial statements include the accounts of the Company and its subsidiaries with the exception of those subsidiaries described in Note 3 which are accounted for on a cash basis.

Inventories are valued at the lower of cost or market. Inventories valued under the last-in, first-out (LIFO) method amounted to $298,731,000 at December 31, 1985 and $281,437,000 at December 31, 1984. Current value exceeded LIFO value by $67,596,000 and $67,618,000 at the 1985 and 1984 year-ends. The remaining inventories continue to be valued under the first-in, first-out (FIFO) or average method.

Inventories at December 31 consist of:

	1985	1984
	(In thousands)	
Finished goods	$283,774	$262,739
Work in progress	90,784	73,548
Materials and supplies	200,946	193,104
	$575,504	$529,391

Property, plant and equipment is carried at cost. Depreciation is provided over the estimated useful lives of the related assets, principally on the straight-line method.

Intangible assets at December 31, 1985 include goodwill, representing the excess of cost over net assets of businesses acquired by purchase, as well as patents, trademarks, formulae and sales rights. Intangible assets acquired after October 31, 1970, totalling $154,733,000, are being amortized on the straight-line method based on their estimated useful lives not exceeding forty years. The balance of $38,732,000 is not being amortized since the Company believes there has been no diminution in value of these assets.

Research and development costs from continuing operations amounted to $217,304,000 in 1985, $183,733,000 in 1984 and $158,780,000 in 1983.

Reclassifications: Certain amounts in the 1984 balance sheet have been reclassified to conform with the 1985 presentation.

2. Businesses Sold: In 1984, the Company completed the sales of its Ekco Housewares, Ekco Products and Dupli-Color businesses and its majority interest in The Prestige Group PLC. The aggregate proceeds on these sales were $338,200,000 in cash and notes and convertible preferred stock valued at $10,000,000. Net sales of these businesses were $318,829,000 and $482,357,000 in 1984 and 1983. Net income was $19,754,000 and $36,387,000 net of taxes of $14,669,000 and $25,367,000 in 1984 and 1983, respectively.

3. Provision for Impairment of Investment in Certain Foreign Locations: In 1984, the Corporation recorded a charge of $50,000,000 recognizing the impairment of its investment in its subsidiaries in South America, except for its investment in Brazil. The provision was made after determining that the continued imposition of constraints such as dividend restrictions, exchange controls, price controls and import restrictions in these countries so severely impede management's control of the economic performance of the businesses that continued inclusion of these subsidiaries in the consolidated financial statements is inappropriate. The Company is continuing to operate these businesses, which for the most part are self-sufficient; however, the investments have been deconsolidated and earnings are recorded on a cash basis. Net sales from these operations aggregated $97,790,000, $95,084,000, and $100,845,000 in 1985, 1984 and 1983, respectively. Net income included in the consolidated statements of income was approximately $2,200,000 for 1985 and approximately $2,000,000 for 1984 and 1983.

4. Other Noncurrent Liabilities include provisions for loss contingencies relating to taxes, general and product liability and worker's compensation claims. Also included under this caption are provisions for severance payments to foreign employees, foreign income taxes payable after one year, and noncurrent debt which includes $40,000,000 of privately placed Adjustable Rate Industrial Revenue Bonds 1983 Series A due December 1, 2018. The effective annual interest rate on the bonds is 8.21% per annum through November 30, 1988 after which date the rate will be reset annually unless the Company elects to establish a fixed rate to be paid for the remaining term of the bonds.

5. Capital Stock: There were 210,000,000 shares of common stock and 5,000,000 shares of preferred stock authorized at December 31, 1985. Of the authorized preferred shares, there is a series of 112,844 shares (98,333 outstanding) which is designated as $2 convertible preferred stock. Each share of the $2 series is convertible at the option of the holder into four and one-half shares of common stock. This series may be called for redemption at $60 per share plus accrued dividends if the market price of the common stock is at least $13.33 per share. In the event of involuntary liquidation, the liquidation value of this series would exceed its par value by $50 per share ($57.50 in voluntary liquidation).

Changes in outstanding common shares during 1985, 1984 and 1983 are summarized as follows:

	1985	1984	1983
	(In thousands)		
Balance, beginning of year	152,002	155,870	155,858
Issued for stock options and deferred compensation	1,499	1,175	1,373
Conversions of preferred stock (13,000 shares in 1985, 19,000 shares in 1984 and 21,000 in 1983)	61	84	94
Purchase of shares for Treasury	(2,678)	(5,127)	(1,512)
Other	5	—	57
Balance, end of year (excludes treasury shares— 18,032,000 in 1985, 16,858,000 in 1984 and 12,906,000 in 1983)	150,889	152,002	155,870

6. Stock Options:

6. Stock Options: The Company has four Stock Option Plans—1985, 1980, 1978, and 1972. Under the 1980 Plan, a maximum of 7,000,000 shares and under the 1985, 1978 and 1972 Plans, a maximum of 3,000,000 shares for each Plan may be sold at prices not less than 100 percent of the fair market value at the date of option grant. The 1985, 1980 and 1978 Plans provide for the granting of incentive stock options as defined under the Economic Recovery Tax Act of 1981. No additional options may be granted under the 1972 Plan. Under the 1985, 1980 and 1978 Plans, grants may be made to selected officers and employees of non-qualified options with a ten-year term or incentive stock options with a term not exceeding ten years.

The Stock Option Plans provide for the granting of Stock Appreciation Rights (SAR's) subject to certain conditions and limitations to holders of options under these plans. SAR's permit the optionee to surrender an exercisable option for an amount equal to the excess of the market price of the common stock over the option price when the right is exercised. Transactions involving the Plans are summarized as follows:

	1985	1984
Option Shares		
Outstanding January 1	5,247,452	3,554,221
Granted	1,269,265	2,825,160
Cancelled	(161,171)	(183,742)
Exercised and surrendered for SAR's (1985—$27.25 to $54.13 per share)	(1,304,858)	(948,187)
Outstanding December 31	5,050,688	5,247,452
Exercisable December 31 (1985—$27.25 to $54.13 per share)	3,807,223	2,516,452

	1985	1984
Stock Appreciation Rights		
Outstanding January 1	698,350	433,750
Granted	50,900	405,000
Cancelled	(7,800)	(12,800)
Exercised (1985—$29.75 to $54.13 per share)	(242,500)	(127,600)
Outstanding December 31	498,950	698,350
Exercisable December 31 (1985—$29.75 to $54.13 per share)	483,450	285,850

At December 31, 1985, 3,646,020 shares were available for future grants under the 1985, 1980 and 1978 Plans.

7. Income Taxes: Deferred taxes are provided for certain items of revenue and expense when the timing of their recognition for financial statement and income tax purposes differs. The net result of these timing differences is such that taxes currently payable are $113,362,000, $33,488,000 and $31,100,000 less than the provisions for federal and foreign income taxes in 1985, 1984 and 1983, respectively.

Deferred tax benefits result principally from the recording of certain reserves which are not currently deductible for tax purposes. Deferred tax credits result principally from the use, for tax purposes, of accelerated depreciation and, in 1985, the installment method for reporting certain sales and tax deductible payments made to a Voluntary Employees' Beneficiary Association trust for the payment of certain employee benefits. Payments made to the VEBA ($78,500,000) are included in cash and cash equivalents and will be used to pay employee benefits in 1986. Deferred tax benefits of $59,267,000 and $61,975,000 were classified as current assets at December 31, 1985 and 1984. At December 31, 1985, current deferred tax credits of $76,855,000 were included in "accounts payable and accrued expenses." At December 31, 1984, the current deferred tax credit amount was insignificant.

The Company's effective tax rate was 40.8%, 44.2% and 45.3% in 1985, 1984 and 1983, respectively. In 1985, the effective tax rate was lower than the statutory rate primarily as a result of manufacturing earnings of the Company's Puerto Rico operation being taxed at rates lower than the statutory rate.

Investment tax credits, which are not material, are accounted for as a reduction of income tax expense in the year the related assets are placed in service. Income taxes are not provided on the undistributed earnings of foreign subsidiaries and affiliates as such tax amounts are not significant.

8. Management Incentive Plan: The Company's Management Incentive Plan provides for cash and deferred contingent common stock awards to key employees. The maximum shares issuable under the plan are 6,000,000 common shares of which 3,502,670 shares have been awarded through December 31, 1985. Deferred contingent common stock awards plus accrued dividends for a total of 1,449,964 shares were outstanding at December 31, 1985. Awards for 1985 amounted to $14,188,000 which included deferred contingent common stock of $8,384,000 (133,196 shares). Awards for 1984 amounted to $12,676,000 which included deferred contingent common stock of $7,530,000 (147,060 shares). Awards for 1983 amounted to $13,724,000 which included deferred contingent common stock of $8,260,000 (165,282 shares).

9. Employee Benefit Plans:

Pension plans: The Company and its subsidiaries sponsor various retirement plans for most full-time employees. Total pension expense for continuing operations for 1985, 1984 and 1983 was $26,165,000, $20,775,000 and $16,833,000. It has been the Company's policy to fund all current and prior service costs under these retirement plans, and all liabilities for accrued vested and non-vested benefits have been fully funded. All such liabilities under the United States and major foreign plans have been guaranteed by financial institutions.

Postretirement benefits: The Company provides postretirement health care and life insurance benefits for retired employees. Most full-time employees become eligible for these benefits after attaining specified age and service requirements. The cost of these programs, $4,946,000 in 1985 and $4,589,000 in 1984, is recognized as expense as claims are paid.

10. Net Income Per Share of common stock is based on the average number of common shares and common share equivalents outstanding during the year assuming full conversion of preferred stock: 152,610,000 shares in 1985, 154,057,000 shares in 1984 and 156,684,000 shares in 1983.

11. Contingencies: The Company is involved in various legal proceedings including product liability suits of a nature considered normal to its business.

It is the opinion of the Company that although the outcome of the litigation cannot be predicted with any certainty, the ultimate liability to the Company will not have a material adverse effect on the Company's consolidated financial position.

12. Company Data By Industry Segment

(Millions of dollars)

	Prescription Drugs & Medical Supplies	Packaged Medicines	Food & Household Products	Corporate	Consolidated Totals
Net sales to customers					
1985	$2,523.5	$ 642.1	$1,519.1	—	$4,684.7
1984	2,416.8	598.8	1,469.9	—	4,485.5
1983	2,278.1	584.0	1,411.2	—	4,273.3
Operating income before taxes					
1985	$ 768.4	$ 158.2	$ 232.5	$ 52.1	$1,211.2
1984	765.5	142.0	207.4	59.6	1,174.5
1983	713.9	151.4	187.0	27.4	1,079.7
Total assets at December 31,					
1985	$1,722.7	$ 183.9	$ 526.5	$ 962.1	$3,395.2
1984	1,519.1	158.6	472.5	894.7	3,044.9
1983	1,418.8	151.1	453.5	712.7	2,736.1
Depreciation expense					
1985	$ 58.4	$ 5.9	$ 21.6	$ 1.2	$ 87.1
1984	55.6	5.3	17.9	0.9	79.7
1983	51.5	4.6	16.1	0.9	73.1
Capital expenditures					
1985	$ 111.0	$ 12.1	$ 49.7	$ 6.5	$ 179.3
1984	100.0	13.1	28.5	0.3	141.9
1983	134.8	13.2	39.4	0.2	187.6

Company Data By Geographic Segment   *(Millions of dollars)*

	United States	Canada and Latin America	Europe and Africa	Other Foreign	Consolidated Totals
Net sales to customers					
1985	$3,636.9	$ 387.1	$ 513.3	$ 147.4	$4,684.7
1984	3,435.9	366.7	537.0	145.9	4,485.5
1983	3,178.3	399.1	558.6	137.3	4,273.3
Operating income before taxes					
1985	$1,001.9	$ 78.7	$ 113.8	$ 16.8	$1,211.2
1984	931.6	97.4	121.9	23.6	1,174.5
1983	828.2	100.4	130.3	20.8	1,079.7
Total assets at December 31,					
1985	$2,722.0	$ 201.1	$ 347.4	$ 124.7	$3,395.2
1984	2,472.1	183.4	289.9	99.5	3,044.9
1983	2,131.6	205.1	297.4	102.0	2,736.1

Transactions between industry and geographic segments are not material. Foreign exchange adjustments, which are included in Operating income before taxes in this note and in Other income, net, in the Consolidated Statements of Income on page 33 resulted in net charges to income of $30.1 million in 1985, $16.1 million in 1984 and $22.9 million in 1983. For a description of the products in each industry segment, see the foldout following page 4.

Report of Independent Public Accountants

To the Board of Directors and Shareholders of
American Home Products Corporation:

We have examined the consolidated balance sheets of American Home Products Corporation (a Delaware corporation) and subsidiaries as of December 31, 1985 and 1984, and the related consolidated statements of income, retained earnings, additional paid-in capital, currency translation adjustments and changes in working capital for each of the three years in the period ended December 31, 1985. Our examinations were made in accordance with generally accepted auditing standards and, accordingly, included such tests of the accounting records and such other auditing procedures as we considered necessary in the circumstances.

In our opinion, the consolidated financial statements referred to above present fairly the financial position of American Home Products Corporation and subsidiaries as of December 31, 1985 and 1984, and the results of their operations and changes in working capital for each of the three years in the period ended December 31, 1985, in conformity with generally accepted accounting principles applied on a consistent basis.

New York, N.Y.,   Arthur Andersen & Co.
January 21, 1986.

Inflation Information

The following Consolidated Supplementary Inflation-Adjusted Income Statement reflects the effect on income from continuing operations of restating (1) cost of goods sold to cost of inventories at the time of sale and (2) depreciation expense based on the average of asset replacement costs at the beginning and end of the year.

Consolidated Supplementary Inflation-Adjusted Income Statement

Year Ended December 31, 1985	As Reported in the Primary Statements	Adjusted for Changes in Specific Prices (Current Cost)
	(In thousands except per share amounts)	
Net sales and other operating revenues	$4,744,320	$4,744,320
Cost of goods sold	1,837,119	1,859,470
Selling, administrative and general expense	1,695,963	1,702,555
Provision for income taxes	494,098	494,098
Income from continuing operations	$ 717,140	$ 688,197
Income per common share of stock from continuing operations	$ 4.70	$ 4.51
Depreciation expense included in cost of goods sold and selling, administrative and general expense	$ 87,126	$ 111,319

Five-Year Comparison of Selected Supplementary Financial Data Adjusted for the Effects of Changing Prices

(Average 1985 Dollars)

Years Ended December 31,	1985	1984	1983	1982	1981
	(Dollars in thousands except per share amounts)				
Net sales and other operating revenues from continuing operations	$4,744,320	$4,731,406	$4,675,361	$4,486,718	$4,211,635
Current Cost Information:					
Net income from continuing operations	688,197	653,894	616,800	553,484	517,521
Net income per common share from continuing operations	4.51	4.25	3.95	3.54	3.31
Increase (decrease) in specific prices net of changes in general price level	(1,940)	4,763	16,036	52,049	(39,173)
Net assets at year-end	2,627,193	2,482,568	2,601,901	2,465,377	2,316,436
Cumulative translation adjustment	123,753	144,360	129,928	78,768	—
Loss from decline in purchasing power of net monetary assets held	25,746	22,154	16,636	13,436	52,691
Cash dividends declared per common share	2.90	2.73	2.59	2.39	2.25
Market price per common share at year-end	61.88	51.76	52.81	49.30	41.79
Average consumer price index	322.2	311.1	298.4	289.1	272.4

Other 1985 Inflation-Adjusted Data

	(In thousands)
Loss from decline in purchasing power of net monetary assets held	$ 25,746
Increase in specific prices (current cost) of inventories and property, plant, and equipment held during the year [1]	$ 61,000
Effect of increase in general price level	62,940
Decrease in specific prices net of changes in general price level	$ (1,940)[2]
Translation adjustment	$(20,607)[3]

The above data are based on the translate-restate method (that is, after translation and based on the U.S. C.P.I.-U.).

[1] At December 31, 1985 current cost of inventories was $633,630 and current cost of property, plant and equipment, net of accumulated depreciation, was $1,165,295.

[2] The decrease in specific prices (current cost) restated in average 1985 dollars to eliminate the effect of inflation as measured by the U.S. Consumer Price Index for all Urban Consumers.

[3] The effect of changes in the exchange rates during the year on equity of foreign hard currency companies measured in current cost at average 1985 dollars.

Part 1   Published financial statements include not only the statements themselves, but also notes, an auditor's report, and unaudited data showing the effects of inflation. The purpose of this problem is to acquaint you with the form and content of these materials.

Instructions

Answer each of the following questions and briefly explain where in the statements, notes, auditor's report, or inflation-adjusted data you located the information used in your answer.

a   Write out the total dollar amount of the Company's net sales in 1985 using words rather than numbers. (Hint: Most dollar amounts in the financial statements are not expressed in units of $1.)

b   The comparative financial statements include two balance sheets and three income statements. Were all of these financial statements audited by a firm of independent accountants? Name the firm that audited some or all of these statements.

c   What was the total dollar amount of the Company's liabilities at December 31, 1985? (Express in numbers.)

d   What was the total amount of dividends declared by the Company in 1983? In 1984? In 1985?

e   In the valuation of inventories, did the company use LIFO, FIFO, average cost, or several different methods?

f   Is the company a defendant in any lawsuits? If so, are these lawsuits expected to have a material adverse effect upon the Company's financial position?

g   In the notes to the financial statements, the Company's net sales are classified into "industry segments." Identify the three "industry segments" into which sales are classified. What percentage of 1985 net sales fall into the "Prescription Drugs & Medical Supplies" classification?

h*   What was the Company's Income from Continuing Operations in 1985 computed on a basis of *current costs* rather than historical costs? What was the Company's total depreciation expense for 1985 computed on a current cost basis?

i*   What was the net amount of gain or loss in *purchasing power* experienced by the Company as a result of holding net monetary assets (or having net monetary liabilities) during 1985?

Part 2   Assume that in early 1986 you are the credit manager of a company which sells chemicals used in the manufacture of medical supplies. American Home Products wants to make credit purchases from your company of between $10 million and $20 million per month, with payment due in 60 days.

Instructions

a   As part of your credit investigation, compute the following from American Home Products' financial statements:

(1) Current ratio at December 31, 1985. (Express as a decimal and round to one decimal place; e.g., 2.1 to 1.)

(2) Quick ratio at December 31, 1985. (Round as in item 1, above.)

(3) Working capital at December 31, 1985. (Express in thousands of dollars.)

(4) Inventory turnover in 1985 (rounded to one decimal place), and the average number of days required to sell the inventory (rounded to the nearest day, using your turnover figure which was rounded to one decimal place).

* Relates to disclosures discussed in Appendix D.

(5) Accounts receivable turnover in 1985 and the average number of days required to collect accounts receivable. (Assume that all net sales are made on account; round as in item 4, above.)

(6) The company's operating cycle, stated in days.

(7) The excess (or shortfall) of the Company's **net cash flow from operations** over (below) the sum of (a) net cash used for investing activities and (b) dividends paid to stockholders.

b Your company assigns each customer one of the four credit ratings listed below. Assign a credit rating to American Home Products and write a memorandum explaining your decision. (In your memorandum, you may use any of your computations in part a, and may refer to other information in American Home Products' financial statements.)

Possible Credit Ratings

A *Outstanding.* Little or no risk of inability to pay. For customers in this category, we fill any reasonable order, without imposing a credit limit. The customer's credit is reevaluated annually.

B *Good.* Customer has good debt paying ability, but is assigned a credit limit which is reviewed every six months. Orders above the established credit limit are accepted only on a cash basis.

C *Marginal.* Customer appears sound, but credit should be extended only on a 30-day basis with a relatively low credit limit. Credit status and credit limit are reevaluated every 90 days.

D *Unacceptable.* Customer does not qualify for credit.

Part 3 Assume that you are an investment advisor who publishes a monthly newsletter with recommendations on buying and selling common stocks. One of the common stocks you will evaluate this month is American Home Products. It is now early 1986, and the price of the company's stock is $65.80 per share.

Instructions

a As a starting point in your investigation, compute the following. (Follow the company's practice of stating all dollar amounts in thousands, except for per-share amounts. Round percentage computations to 1/10 of 1%.)

(1) Price-earnings ratio. (Use 1985 earnings and the current market price of $65.80 per share.)

(2) Dividend yield on the common stock. (1985 dividends amounted to $2.90 per share; use the current market price of $65.80 per share.)

(3) Return on average total assets in 1985. (Use Income before Federal and Foreign Taxes on Income ($1,211,238) as "operating income" in this computation.)

(4) Return on average total stockholder's equity in 1985. (Express net income as a percentage of average total stockholders' equity. We will ignore the claims of preferred stockholders, as these claims are not material in dollar amount.)

(5) Equity ratio.

(6) Prepare trend percentages for (a) net sales, (b) net income, and (c) net earnings per share for the three years from 1983 through 1985. Use 1983 as the base year, in which each statistic will be 100%. (See pages 580–581 for an illustration of trend percentages. Round computations to the nearest 1 percent.)

b In recent years, American Home Products has consistently followed a policy of increasing each year the cash dividend per share paid to holders of the common stock. Write a memorandum evaluating the Company's ability to continue this policy. As a basis for this memorandum, review the trends in the Company's net income and earnings per share, and also review the statement of cash flows.

c Write a brief memorandum on the topic of leverage as it relates to American Home Products. Does the company make extensive use of long-term debt financing? Assuming that long-term interest rates are about 9%, would the use of long-term debt as a means of financing future growth be desirable from the viewpoint of common stockholders?

d Write a brief memorandum on the "quality" of the company's earnings. As a basis for this memorandum, review trends in the comparative income statements and in the major product lines shown in note 12. If you have studied Appendix D, also review and comment upon the Company's inflation-adjusted income statement, which follows the auditor's report.

e Write a statement for your newsletter in which you recommend that your clients take one of the following actions with respect to American Home Products' common stock:

Buy (Your most positive recommendation; you think the market price of the stock will go up.)

Sell (Your most negative recommendation; you feel that the stock is overpriced and will fall in value.)

Hold (A relatively neutral position; you feel that the stock is priced at a fair value with good but not exceptional prospects.)

Explain the reasoning behind your recommendation.

In addition to the information developed in other parts of this problem, your recommendation should consider the following facts about the economic environment in early 1986:

(1) The stock market is in the midst of a strong rally, in which the p/e ratios of stocks with strong growth potential are rising to the 15 to 20 range. Stocks with modest growth potential are selling at prices between 8 and 12 times earnings.

(2) Interest rates are falling to the lowest level in a decade.

(3) Dividend yields for growth-oriented companies range from zero to 5%; for slow-growth companies, yields are from 6 to 10%.

f Look up the current price of American Home Products' common stock in the financial pages of a newspaper. How did your recommendation work out in the long run?

Chapter 16
Income taxes and business decisions

CHAPTER PREVIEW

For many college students, this chapter may be their only academic exposure to the truly remarkable system known as federal income taxes. The early part of the chapter presents a brief history and rationale of the federal tax structure, including the Tax Reform Act of 1986. This introduction stresses the pervasive influence of income taxes upon economic activity. The next section portrays the basic process of determining taxable income and the tax liability for individual taxpayers. The income tax computations for a small corporation are also explained and illustrated. The final section of the chapter gives students an understanding of the important role that tax planning can play in the affairs of individuals and also in the decision-making of a business entity.

After studying this chapter you should be able to meet these Learning Objectives:

1 Describe the history of the federal income tax and the highlights of the Tax Reform Act of 1986.
2 Discuss the advantages of the cash basis of accounting for preparation of individual income tax returns.
3 State the formula for determining the taxable income of an individual.
4 Explain the recent changes in the taxation of capital gains and losses.
5 Contrast the determination of taxable income for a corporation with that for an individual.
6 Discuss the concept of interperiod income tax allocation.
7 Explain how tax planning is used in choosing the form of business organization and the capital structure.

Tax Reform Act of 1986

The United States Congress spent much of the year 1986 in writing a new tax bill — a bill that brought sweeping changes in income tax rules and rates. Although annual changes in the income tax laws have become normal practice, the changes made by the Tax Reform Act of 1986 were the most drastic in the history of the federal income tax. Annual changes however, will continue. In fact, this 1986 bill prescribed changes in rules and rates effective in 1987, further changes in 1988, and still more changes in 1989. In other words, the drastic changes created by the 1986 law are being phased in over a period of years. In this book we have utilized the changes brought into being by the new tax legislation emphasizing those which became effective in 1988. The three most striking characteristics of recent tax legislation are the lowering of tax rates, the elimination of numerous deductions, and a shifting of the tax burden from individuals to corporations.

1 Describe the history of the federal income tax and the highlights of the Tax Reform Act of 1986.

Income tax returns are based on accounting information. In many respects this information is consistent with the accounting concepts we have discussed in earlier chapters. However, the measurement of **taxable income** includes some unique principles and computations which differ from those used for published financial statements. An understanding of the unique aspects of taxable income can assist an individual or a business in minimizing the amount of income taxes owed.

Tax planning versus tax evasion

Individuals who plan their business affairs in a manner that will result in the lowest possible income tax are acting rationally and legally. They are using the techniques called **tax planning.** In the words of a distinguished jurist, Judge Learned Hand:

> Over and over again courts have said that there is nothing sinister in so arranging one's affairs as to keep taxes as low as possible. Everybody does so, rich or poor, and all do right, for nobody owes any public duty to pay more than the law demands: taxes are enforced exactions, not voluntary contributions. To demand more in the name of morals is mere cant.

To reduce and to postpone income taxes are the goals of tax planning. Almost every business decision involves a choice among alternative courses of action with different tax consequences. For example, should we lease or buy business automobiles; should we obtain needed capital by issuing bonds or preferred stock; should we use straight-line depreciation or an accelerated method? Some of these alternatives will lead to much lower income taxes than others. Tax planning, therefore, means **determining in advance the income tax effect** of every proposed business action and then making business decisions which will lead to the smallest tax liability. Tax practice is an important element of the services furnished to clients by CPA firms. This tax work includes not only the computing of taxes and preparing of tax returns, but also tax planning.

Tax planning must begin early. Unfortunately, some wait until the end of the year and then, faced with the prospect of paying a large amount of income tax, ask their accountants what can be done to reduce the tax liability. If we are to arrange transactions in a manner that will lead to the minimum income tax liability, the tax planning must be carried out *before* the date of a transaction, not after it is an accomplished fact. Because it is important for everyone to recognize areas in which tax savings may be substantial, a few of the major opportunities for tax planning are discussed in the final section of this chapter.

Newspaper stories tell us each year of some taxpayers who have deliberately understated their taxable income by failing to report a portion of income received or by claiming fictitious deductions such as an excess number of personal exemptions. Such purposeful understatement of taxable income is called *tax evasion* and is, of course, illegal. On the other hand, *tax avoidance* (the arranging of business and financial affairs in a manner that will minimize tax liability) is entirely legal.

The critical importance of income taxes

Taxes levied by federal, state, and local governments are a significant part of the cost of operating a typical household, as well as a business enterprise. Every manager who makes business decisions, and every individual who makes personal investments, urgently needs some knowledge of income taxes. A general knowledge of income taxes will help any business manager or owner to benefit more fully from the advice of the professional tax accountant.

Some understanding of income taxes will also aid the individual citizen in voting intelligently, because a great many of the issues decided in every election have tax implications. Such issues as pollution, inflation, foreign policy, and employment are quite closely linked with income taxes. For example, the offering of special tax incentives to encourage businesses to launch massive programs to reduce pollution is one approach to protection of the environment.

In terms of revenue generated, the four most important kinds of taxes in the United States are *income taxes, sales taxes, property taxes,* and *excise taxes.* Income taxes exceed all others in terms of the amounts involved, and they also exert a pervasive influence on all types of business decisions. For this reason we shall limit our discussion to the basic federal income tax rules applicable to individuals, partnerships, and corporations.

Income taxes are usually determined from information contained in accounting records. The amount of income tax is computed by applying the appropriate tax rates (as set by federal, state, and some local governments) to *taxable income.* As explained later in this chapter, *taxable income* is not necessarily the same as *accounting income* even though both are derived from the accounting records. Business managers can influence the amount of taxes they pay by their choice of form of business organization, methods of financing, and alternative accounting methods. Thus income taxes are inevitably an important factor in reaching business decisions.

The federal income tax: history and objectives

The present federal income tax dates from the passage of the Sixteenth Amendment to the Constitution in 1913.[1] This amendment, only 30 words in length,[2] removed all questions of the constitutionality of income taxes and paved the way for the more than 50 revenue acts passed by Congress since that date. In 1939 these tax laws were first combined into what is known as the Internal Revenue Code. The administration and enforcement of the tax laws are duties of the Treasury Department, operating through a division known as the Internal Revenue Service (IRS). The Treasury Department publishes its interpretation of the tax laws in Treasury regulations; the final word in interpretation lies with the federal courts.

Originally the purpose of the federal income tax was simply to obtain revenue for the government. And at first, the tax rates were quite low — by today's standards. In 1913 a married person with taxable income of $15,000 would have been subject to a tax rate of 1%, resulting in a tax liability of $150. The maximum federal income tax rate in 1913 was 7%. During the 1970s, the maximum tax rate had risen to 70%; and for most of the 1980s the top rate was 50%. Recent Congressional action lowered the top rate to 28% beginning with the year 1988.

The purpose of federal income tax now includes several goals apart from raising revenue. Examples of these other goals are: influencing the rate of economic growth, encouraging full employment, combatting inflation, favoring small businesses, and redistributing national income on a more equal basis.

Classes of taxpayers

In the eyes of the income tax law, there are four major classes of taxpayers: **individuals, corporations, estates,** and **trusts.** A business organized as a single proprietorship or as a partnership is not taxed as a separate entity; its income is taxed directly to the individual proprietor or partners, **whether or not the income is withdrawn from the business.** However, a partnership must file an **information return** showing the computation of total partnership net income and the allocation of this income among the partners.

A single proprietor reports his or her income from ownership of a business on an individual tax return (Form 1040); the members of a partnership include on their individual income tax returns their respective shares of the partnership net income. Of course, an individual's income tax return must include not only any business income from a proprietorship or partnership, but also any interest, dividends, salary, or other forms of income received.

A corporation is a separate taxable entity; it must file a corporate income tax return (Form 1120) and pay a tax on its annual taxable income. In addition,

---

[1] A federal income tax was proposed as early as 1815, and an income tax law was actually passed and income taxes collected during the Civil War. This law was upheld by the Supreme Court, but it was repealed when the need for revenue subsided after the war. In 1894 a new income tax law was passed, but the Supreme Court declared this law invalid on constitutional grounds.

[2] It reads "The Congress shall have power to lay and collect taxes on incomes, from whatever source derived, without apportionment among the several States, and without regard to any census or enumeration."

individual stockholders must report dividends received from corporations as part of their personal taxable income. The taxing of corporate dividends has led to the charge that there is "double taxation" of corporate income — once to the corporation and again when it is distributed to stockholders. This double impact of tax is particularly apparent when a corporation is owned by one person or one family.

To illustrate, let us use the tax rates in effect during the early 1980s to consider the tax impact on one dollar of corporate earnings. The *income before taxes* earned by a corporation was (in general) subject to a federal corporate income tax rate of 46%. First, the corporation paid 46%, or 46 cents, out of the dollar to the Internal Revenue Service. That left 54 cents for the corporation. Next, assume that the 54 cents was distributed as dividends to individual stockholders. The dividend was taxable to the stockholders personally at rates varying from 12 to 50%, depending on their individual tax brackets. Thus, the 54 cents of after-tax income to the corporation could be reduced by 50%, or 27 cents of individual income tax, leaving 27 cents of the original dollar for the shareholder. In summary, *federal income taxes could take as much as 73 cents out of a dollar earned by a corporation and distributed as a dividend to a shareholder.* The remaining 27 cents could be reduced further by state income taxes. This example would, of course, appear less extreme if we used the lower rates set for 1988.

Special and complex rules apply to the determination of taxable income for estates and trusts. These rules will not be discussed in this chapter.

INCOME TAXES: INDIVIDUALS

Cash basis of accounting for income tax returns

2 Discuss the advantages of the cash basis of accounting for preparation of individual income tax returns.

Almost all *individual* income tax returns are prepared on the cash basis of accounting. Many small service-type business concerns and professional firms also choose to prepare their tax returns on the cash basis. Revenue is recognized when collected in cash; expenses (except depreciation) are recognized when a cash payment is made. The cash basis (as prescribed in IRS rules) does not permit expenditures for plant and equipment to be deducted in the year of purchase. These capital expenditures are capitalized and depreciated for tax purposes. Also, the income tax laws do not permit use of the cash basis by companies in which inventories and the sale of merchandise are significant factors.

Although the cash basis of accounting does not measure income satisfactorily in the context of generally accepted accounting principles, it has much merit in the area of taxation. From the government's viewpoint, the logical time to collect tax on income is when the taxpayer receives the income in cash. At any earlier date, the taxpayer may not have the cash to pay income taxes; at any later date; the cash may have been used for other purposes.

The cash basis is advantageous for the individual taxpayer and for service-type businesses for several reasons. It is relatively simple, and requires a minimum of records. The income of most individuals comes in the form of salaries, interest, and dividends. At the end of each year, an individual receives from his or her employer a W-2 form showing the salary earned and income tax withheld during the year. This report is prepared on a cash basis without any accrual of unpaid wages. Persons receiving interest or dividends also receive from the paying companies Form 1099 showing amounts received for the year. Thus, most individuals are provided with ***reports prepared on a cash basis*** for use in preparing their individual tax returns.

The cash basis has other advantages for the individual taxpayer and for many professional firms and service-type businesses. It often permits tax savings by individuals who deliberately shift the timing of revenue and expense transactions from one year to another. For example, a dentist whose taxable income is higher than usual in the current year may decide in December to delay billing patients until January 1, and thus postpone the receipt of gross income to the next year. The timing of ***expense payments*** near year-end is also controllable by a taxpayer using the cash basis. A taxpayer who has received a bill for a deductible expense item in December may choose to pay it before or after December 31 and thereby influence the amount of taxable income in each year.

Any taxpayer who maintains a set of accounting records may ***elect*** to use the accrual basis in preparing a tax return, but very few taxpayers (individual or corporate) choose to do so if they are eligible to use the cash basis.

Tax rates

All taxes may be characterized as progressive, proportional, or regressive with respect to any given base. A ***progressive*** tax becomes a larger portion of the base as that base increases. Federal income taxes are ***progressive*** with respect to income, since a higher tax ***rate*** applies as the amount of taxable income increases. A ***proportional*** tax remains a constant percentage of the base no matter how that base changes. For example, a 6% sales tax remains a constant percentage of sales regardless of changes in the dollar amount of sales. A ***regressive*** tax becomes a smaller percentage of the base as the base increases. Regressive taxes, however, are extremely rare.

Keep in mind that tax rates have been changed many times in the past and no doubt will continue to be changed in the future. The present tax structure for individuals provides for only two brackets of 15% and 28%. The 15% rate is applicable to all taxable income of single individuals up to $17,850, and the 28% rate to income above that amount. For married couples filing joint returns, the 15% rate applies to taxable income up to $29,750. The 28% rate applies to taxable income above that amount.

1988 Tax Rate Schedules

	Taxable Income	Tax Rate
Single taxpayers:	First $17,850	15%
	Amount over $17,850	28%*
Married taxpayers filing joint returns:	First $29,750	15%
	Amount over $29,750	28%*

* High-income taxpayers are subject to surtaxes which cause some portion of their income to be taxed at an effective rate of 33%. These surtaxes are discussed on pages 640 and 641.

Example: Find the tax for a single person having taxable income of $25,000.

Answer:		
Tax on first $17,850 at 15%		$2,677.50
Tax on $7,150 excess at 28%		2,002.00
Tax on $25,000 for a single person		$4,679.50

The top rate of 28% stipulated in the current law is perhaps misleading, because high-income taxpayers must pay a rate of 33% on a portion of their income. This 33% effective rate results from adding a 5% surcharge to the 28% rate. The purpose of this 5% surcharge is to deny high-income taxpayers any benefit from the 15% rate. The result is that high-income taxpayers are required to pay an average tax rate of 28% on their entire taxable income.

Income tax formula for individuals

3 State the formula for determining the taxable income of an individual.

The federal government supplies standard income tax forms on which taxpayers are guided to a proper computation of their taxable income and the amount of the tax. It is helpful to visualize the computation in terms of an income tax formula as diagrammed on the next page. The sequence of material on income tax forms differs somewhat from the arrangement in this formula. However, it is easier to understand the structure and logic of the federal income tax by referring to the tax formula rather than to tax forms.

Total income and gross income

Total income as defined for tax purposes is a very broad concept that includes in the words of the law, "all income from whatever source derived." ***Gross income*** is computed by deducting from ***total income*** certain items excluded by the tax laws; the leading example is interest received on state and municipal bonds. A concise definition of gross income is "all income not excluded by law." Gross income therefore includes salaries, commissions, bonuses, dividends, interest, rent, and gains from sale of securities, real estate, and other property. To determine whether any given income item is included in gross income, one must ask, "Is there a provision in the tax law excluding this item of income from gross income?" Among the items ***excluded from gross income*** by statute are interest on state and municipal bonds, gifts and inheritances, life insurance proceeds, workmen's compensation, social security benefits (subject to certain limits), the portion of receipts from annuities that represents return of cost, pensions to veterans, and compensation for actual damages.

Among the items of miscellaneous income which must be ***included*** in gross income are prizes and awards won, tips received, and gains from sale of personal property. The fact that income arises from an illegal transaction does not keep it from being taxable.

General Federal Income Tax Formula for Individuals

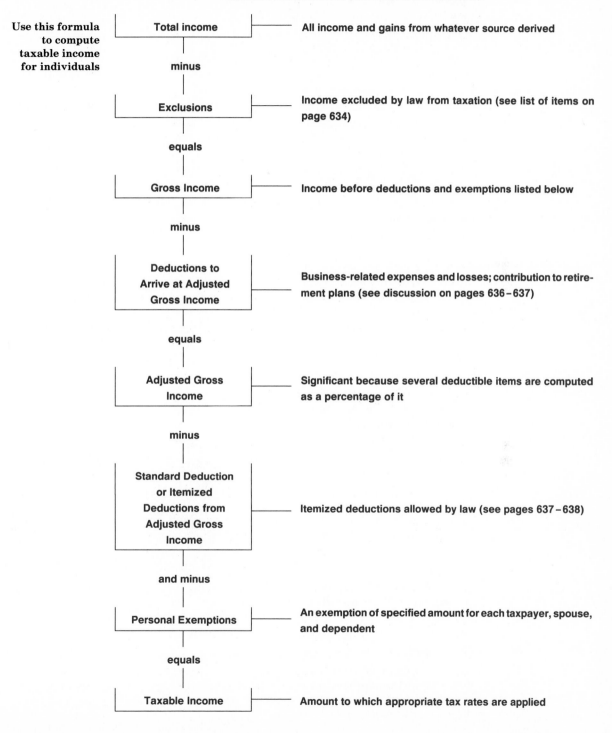

Use this formula
to compute
taxable income
for individuals

Total income ———— All income and gains from whatever source derived

minus

Exclusions ———— Income excluded by law from taxation (see list of items on page 634)

equals

Gross Income ———— Income before deductions and exemptions listed below

minus

Deductions to Arrive at Adjusted Gross Income ———— Business-related expenses and losses; contribution to retirement plans (see discussion on pages 636–637)

equals

Adjusted Gross Income ———— Significant because several deductible items are computed as a percentage of it

minus

Standard Deduction or Itemized Deductions from Adjusted Gross Income ———— Itemized deductions allowed by law (see pages 637–638)

and minus

Personal Exemptions ———— An exemption of specified amount for each taxpayer, spouse, and dependent

equals

Taxable Income ———— Amount to which appropriate tax rates are applied

Deductions to arrive at adjusted gross income

Some of the more common deductions from **gross income** in computing **adjusted gross income** are listed below.

1 **Business expenses of a single proprietorship.** These include all ordinary and necessary expenses of carrying on a trade, business, or profession (other than as an employee). For the actual tax computation, business expenses are deducted from business revenue, and net business income is then included in adjusted gross income on the proprietor's tax return.

2 **Expenses attributable to rental properties.** The owner of rental property, such as an apartment building, incurs a variety of operating expenses. Depreciation, property taxes, repairs, maintenance, interest on indebtedness related to property, and other expenses incurred in connection with the earning of rental income are allowed as a deduction. This means that only the **net income** derived from rental property is included in adjusted gross income.

3 **Losses from the sale of property used in business.** Any loss resulting from the sale of property used in a trade or business may be deducted against other items of gross income.[3]

4 **Net capital losses.** Up to $3,000 of **net capital losses** may be deducted to arrive at adjusted gross income. Capital gains and losses are discussed on pages 639–640.

5 **Contributions to retirement plans: IRA and Keogh plans.** A retirement plan known as IRA (Individual Retirement Arrangement) is one that you set up yourself. The present tax law permits a person who is not covered by an employer pension plan to contribute up to $2,000 a year to an IRA and to deduct this contribution in arriving at adjusted gross income. At a 28% tax rate, this deduction creates an immediate tax saving of 28% × $2,000 or $560. Persons covered by an employer-sponsored retirement plan and with high incomes may not take a deduction for an IRA contribution. However, they may still choose to make an annual IRA contribution without claiming a deduction, because the earnings from an IRA plan accumulate tax-free until retirement, and therefore grow more rapidly than most investments.

If you are self-employed, a Keogh H.R. 10 plan is a valuable device for reducing your income taxes and building assets for retirement. Individuals who are self-employed are permitted to deduct from gross income the amounts they contribute to a Keogh plan. The present limit on such contributions is the lower of $30,000 or 15% of your annual earnings. The amounts contributed, plus earnings on the fund assets, are not taxable until the taxpayer retires and begins making withdrawals from the fund. The Keogh plan is intended to provide self-employed persons with opportunities similar to those of persons employed by companies with pension plans. A self-employed person may

---

[3] Losses arising from the sale of personal property, such as a home or personal automobile, are not deductible. On the other hand, gains from the sale of personal property are taxable. This appears inconsistent, until one realizes that a loss on the sale of personal property usually reflects depreciation through use, which is a personal expense.

contribute to both an IRA and a self-employed retirement plan. However, the IRA contribution will be deductible only if income is within specified limits.

6 *Other deductions to arrive at adjusted gross income.* Among other deductions are alimony paid, and penalty on early withdrawals from long-term savings deposits.

Adjusted gross income. By deducting from gross income the various items described in the preceding section, we arrive at a very significant total called *adjusted gross income.* This amount is significant because several deductible items such as medical expense and contributions are limited by their percentage relationship to adjusted gross income. For example, medical expense is deductible only to the extent it *exceeds* $7\frac{1}{2}\%$ of adjusted gross income.

Deductions from adjusted gross income

Taxpayers have a choice with respect to deductions from adjusted gross income. They may choose to take a lump-sum *standard deduction,* or they may choose to *itemize* their deductions, in which case they can deduct a number of expenses specified in the tax law as itemized deductions.

Standard deduction. Most taxpayers choose to take the standard deduction from adjusted gross income rather than to itemize their deductions by listing such items as mortgage interest payments and state income taxes. Effective in 1988, the amounts of the standard deduction were increased substantially to the following levels: $5,000 for married couples filing jointly, $4,400 for heads of households, and $3,000 for single taxpayers. These amounts will continue to be adjusted annually for inflation. Originally the standard deduction was based on the concept that everyone could claim some deductions and the computation of a person's tax liability could be simplified by providing the option of a standard deduction. Now, however, a major reason for the recent large increases in the standard deduction appears to be a desire to free millions of lower-income individuals from paying any income tax.

Does it pay to itemize? Should you itemize your deductions or claim the standard deduction? If you can qualify to itemize your deductions, it pays to do so. To find out if you qualify, add up your deductible expenses to see if the total exceeds the standard deduction. If it does, you will save taxes by itemizing. If the total is less than the standard deduction, you will benefit by claiming the standard deduction.

Itemized deductions. The major types of itemized deductions allowable under the Tax Reform Act of 1986 are described below.

1 *Mortgage interest.* Interest on mortgages on a first and a second home continue to be deductible. However, consumer interest charges, as on credit cards, auto loans, and boat loans, were phased out during the years from 1988 through 1990.

2 **Taxes.** State income taxes and taxes by local government on real estate and personal property continue to be deductible. Sales taxes no longer may be deducted. No federal taxes qualify as itemized deductions.

3 **Contributions.** Contributions by individuals to charitable, religious, educational, and certain nonprofit organizations are deductible within certain limits, but only for taxpayers who itemize deductions. In other words, a taxpayer who takes the standard deduction cannot also take deductions for charitable contributions. Gifts to friends, relatives, and other persons are not deductible.

4 **Medical expenses.** Medical and dental expenses may be deducted only to the extent that they exceed $7\frac{1}{2}\%$ of adjusted gross income.

5 **Casualty losses.** Losses in excess of $100 from any fire, storm, earthquake, theft, or other sudden, unexpected, or unusual causes are deductible only to the extent that they exceed 10% of adjusted gross income. For example, assume that a taxpayer with adjusted gross income of $45,000 sustains an uninsured fire loss of $10,100. First, we eliminate $100 of the loss, leaving the amount of $10,000. Next, we reduce the loss by 10% of the adjusted gross income of $45,000, a reduction of $4,500. This leaves $5,500 as the net deduction from adjusted gross income in arriving at the amount subject to tax.

6 **Miscellaneous deductions.** Such items as union dues, investment expenses, professional journals, and deductions for employee business expenses are allowable only to the extent that they exceed 2% of adjusted gross income.

Personal exemptions

A deduction from adjusted gross income is allowed for one or more **personal exemptions,** as well as for the standard deduction discussed above. An unmarried individual is entitled to one personal exemption, provided that he or she is not listed as a dependent on some other person's tax return. In addition, a taxpayer can claim a personal exemption for each dependent.

For 1988, the personal exemption is $1,950; for 1989, it is $2,000. An indexing plan provides for an annual inflation adjustment thereafter. As a matter of convenience in illustrations and problems in this book, we assume the round amount of $2,000 for each personal exemption.

The term **dependent** means a person who (1) receives over one-half of his or her support from the taxpayer, (2) is closely related to the taxpayer or lives in the taxpayer's home, (3) has gross income during the year of less than the current exemption amount unless he or she is a child of the taxpayer and is under 19 years of age or is a full-time student, (4) meets a citizenship test, and (5) does not file a joint return. For any dependent five years of age or more, the taxpayer must list the dependent's social security number. To summarize the tax savings from personal exemptions (using 1989 amounts), we can say that each personal exemption reduces taxable income by $2,000. With a tax rate of 28%, the tax saving is $560, computed as $2,000 × 28%.

Taxable income — individuals

We have now traced the steps required to determine the taxable income of an individual: In brief, this process includes:

1 Computation of total income
2 Exclusion of certain items specified by law to determine gross income
3 Deduction of business-related expenses to arrive at adjusted gross income
4 Deduction of the standard deduction (or itemized deductions) and personal exemptions to arrive at the key figure of taxable income.

The concept of taxable income is important because it is the amount to which the appropriate tax rate is applied to determine the tax liability.

Capital gains and losses

4 Explain the recent changes in the taxation of capital gains and losses.

Certain kinds of property are defined under the tax laws as capital assets. Common examples are investments in securities and real estate (including a personal residence). A gain from the sale of a capital asset occurs if the sales price exceeds the basis of the property sold. A capital loss occurs if the sales price is less than the basis of the asset. In general, the **basis** of purchased property is its cost reduced by accumulated depreciation.

Capital gains and losses are classified as long-term when the investor owns the asset for more than six months. In the past, long-term capital gains received special favorable tax treatment. The tax on such gains was only 40% as high as the tax on an equal amount of income from other sources, such as salaries, interest, or dividends received. In other words, in 1986 and prior years, 60% of a long-term capital gain was not subject to tax. The rationale underlying the favorable treatment of capital gains was to encourage investment capital to flow into new growth industries and thus to stimulate the economy. However, the Tax Reform Act of 1986 eliminated favorable treatment for capital gains. It is still necessary to identify capital gains and losses and to report them separately, because only a limited portion of net capital losses can be deducted from other income.

Limited deductibility of capital losses. Not every investment is a winner, thus investors have capital losses as well as capital gains. The term *net short-term gains* means short-term gains in excess of short-term losses. Net short-term gains have for years been taxed the same as ordinary income. Capital losses, whether long-term or short-term, are deductible against capital gains. If total capital losses exceed capital gains, however, individual taxpayers may deduct net capital losses against other income up to a maximum of $3,000 a year. To illustrate the limitation on deducting capital losses, let us assume that an individual incurred a capital loss of $100,000 and also had an annual salary of $50,000. He or she would have adjusted gross income of $47,000. The unused capital loss could be carried forward and offset against capital gains, if any, in future years, or against other income at the rate of

$3,000 a year. Thus, a great many years might be required to offset the $100,000 loss against other income.

Business plant and equipment. Buildings, machinery, and other depreciable property used in a trade or business are not capital assets under the tax law. This means that a net loss realized on the sale or disposal of such business property is fully deductible.

Computing the tax liability

After determining the amount of taxable income, we are ready to compute the gross tax liability. For a single taxpayer with taxable income less than $43,150, we apply the 15% rate to the first $17,850, and then the 28% rate to the excess above $17,850. For example, assume that Edward Jones is single and has taxable income of $22,850. The computation produces a tax of $4,078 (rounded to the nearest dollar) as shown below.

Taxable Income		Tax Rate		Tax
$17,850	×	.15	=	$2,678
5,000	×	.28	=	1,400
$22,850				$4,078

For a married couple filing a joint return, we apply the 15% rate to the first $29,750 of taxable income, and then the 28% rate to the excess above $29,750. For example, assume that John and Mary Smith have taxable income of $60,000. The computation produces a tax (rounded to the nearest dollar) of $12,933, as shown below.

Taxable Income		Tax Rate		Tax
$29,750	×	.15	=	$ 4,463
30,250	×	.28	=	8,470
$60,000				$12,933

Surtaxes. For single persons with taxable income above $43,150 (and for married couples with taxable income above $71,900), one or two surtaxes are imposed and the calculations become more complex. The purpose of the first surtax of 5% is to take back the benefit derived by the taxpayer from using the lower 15% rate on the first layer of taxable income. This "rate" surtax is 5% of the amount by which a single person's taxable income exceeds $43,150, up to a maximum surtax amount of $2,321. For married couples, the rate surcharge is 5% of the amount by which taxable income exceeds $71,900, up to a maximum surtax amount of $3,867.50. The result of this rate surcharge is that higher-income taxpayers must pay tax of 28% on their entire taxable incomes.

Another 5% surcharge designed to take back the benefit of the personal exemption is imposed upon higher-income taxpayers. This surcharge equals 5% of the amount by which the taxable income of a single person exceeds $89,560. For married couples, the surtax is 5% of the excess of taxable income over $149,250. The maximum dollar amount of the surcharge is $546 for each personal exemption shown on the tax returns of both single taxpayers and married couples. For example, the maximum surcharge for a married couple with two dependent children would be 4 × $546 or $2,184. One conclusion which might be drawn from the creation of the two surcharges described above is that the new tax structure is somewhat more progressive in nature than is suggested by the much discussed rates of 15% and 28%.

Tax credits. The gross tax liability as computed by the methods described above is reduced by subtracting any tax credits. Note that a tax credit is subtracted directly from the tax owed, whereas a deduction (as for charitable contributions) is subtracted from adjusted gross income and thus leads to a smaller amount of taxable income to which the tax rate is applied. Tax credits were important to many individuals and to virtually every business prior to the Tax Reform Act of 1986. Under the present tax law, however, most types of tax credits have been eliminated. The few remaining tax credits include a credit for qualifying low-income taxpayers and a small credit for certain child care expenses of working parents.

Tax prepayments. The most common example of tax prepayments is the withholding of income taxes from a person's salary. Another common example is the quarterly payment of estimated income taxes on dividend income or interest income not subject to withholding. The gross tax liability computed at the end of the year is reduced by subtracting these tax prepayments. The remaining amount is the *net tax liability* — the amount to be paid with the tax return.

Quarterly payments of estimated tax

We have seen that the federal income tax law stresses a pay-as-you-go system for all taxpayers. The tax must be paid as the taxpayer receives income during the year. There are two methods of carrying out the pay-as-you-go principle: one is *withholding* and the other is payment of *estimated taxes* on a current basis.

Income in the form of salaries has long been subject to withholding. However, for self-employed persons, such as doctors, dentists, and owners of small unincorporated business concerns, there is no salary and no withholding. Other examples of income on which no withholding occurs are interest, dividends, rental income, and capital gains.

To equalize the treatment of self-employed persons and salaried employees, the tax law requires persons having taxable income not subject to withholding to pay *estimated taxes* in advance quarterly installments. One-quarter of the current year's estimated income tax must be paid by April 15 and the remainder in three equal quarterly installments. Thus, a self-employed person may write two checks to the IRS on April 15; one for any balance due with last year's tax return and one for one-quarter of the estimated tax for the current year.

Tax returns, tax refunds, and payment of the tax

The tax return must be filed within $3\frac{1}{2}$ months after the close of the taxable year. Most taxpayers are on a calendar-year basis; therefore, the deadline for filing is April 15. However, the taxpayer has the alternative of paying the tax due at April 15 and requesting an extension of time to August 15 for filing of the return.

Withholding makes the system work. Without the withholding feature, the present income tax system would probably be unworkable. The high rate of income taxes would pose an impossible collection problem if employees received their total earnings in cash and were later called upon at the end of the year to pay the government a major portion of a year's salary.

The amounts withheld from an employee's salary for income tax can be considered as payments on account. If the amount of income tax as computed by preparing a tax return at the end of the year is less than the amount withheld during the year; the taxpayer is entitled to a refund. On the other hand, if the tax as computed at year-end is more than the amount withheld, the taxpayer must pay the additional amount with the tax return.

The deceptive lure of a tax refund check. Most American taxpayers receive tax refunds each year. Apparently these 60 million or more persons so enjoy receiving a refund check that they are willing to have the government withhold excessive amounts of tax from their paychecks throughout the year. The IRS reports that millions of individual taxpayers declare fewer personal exemptions than they expect to claim at year-end. The result is over-withholding of billions of dollars on which the government pays no interest. It is interesting that even during periods of inflation and high interest rates, American taxpayers would choose to have the government hold their money throughout the year with no interest in order to be paid back at year-end in dollars worth less in purchasing power than when earned.

Computation of individual income tax illustrated

The computation of the federal income tax for Mary and John Reed is illustrated below.

In this example it is assumed that the Reeds provide over one-half the support of their two children. John Reed is a practicing attorney who received $81,000 in gross fees from his law practice and incurred $32,000 of business expenses. Mary Reed earned $24,400 during the year as a CPA working for a national firm of accountants. During the year, $4,000 was withheld from her salary for federal income taxes. Just before the end of the year, John Reed contributed $3,000 to a Keogh retirement plan. The Reeds received $700 interest on municipal bonds, and $1,120 interest on savings accounts. Dividends received on stock jointly owned amounted to $7,240. During the year, stock purchased several years ago by John

Reed for $2,600 was sold for $3,600, net of brokerage fees, thus producing a $1,000 long-term capital gain.

The Reeds have total itemized deductions of $12,920, including contributions, mortgage interest expense, property taxes, etc. They paid a total of $8,000 on their declaration of estimated tax during the year. In this illustration, as in the problems at the end of the chapter, we have for convenience used the amount of $2,000 for each personal exemption.

MARY AND JOHN REED
Illustrative Federal Income Tax Computation

Gross income (excluding $700 interest on municipal bonds):

Gross fees from John Reed's law practice	$81,000	
Less: Expenses incurred in law practice	32,000	
Net income from law practice		$49,000
Salary received by Mary Reed		24,400
Dividends received		7,240
Interest received		1,120
Long-term capital gain		1,000
Gross income		$82,760
Deductions to arrive at adjusted gross income:		
Contribution to Keogh retirement plan		3,000
Adjusted gross income		$79,760
Deductions from adjusted gross income:		
Itemized deductions	$12,920	
Personal exemptions (4 × $2,000)	8,000	$20,920
Taxable income.		$58,840

Computation of tax (using the 15% and 28% brackets indicated for 1988):		
Tax on $29,750 at 15%	$ 4,463	
Tax on $29,090 at 28%	8,145	
Total tax.		$12,608
Less: Quarterly payments of estimated tax and amounts withheld:		
Quarterly payments of estimated tax	$ 8,000	
Tax withheld from salary	4,000	12,000
Tax to be paid with return		$ 608

On the basis of these facts, the taxable income for the Reeds is shown to be $58,840, and the total tax is $12,608. Taking withholdings and quarterly payments of estimated tax into account, the Reeds have already paid income taxes of $12,000 and thus owe $608 at the time of filing their tax return.

Alternative Minimum Tax

You may have read newspaper stories about a few individuals with very high incomes who were able, through extensive use of tax shelters, tax preferences, and various loopholes, to avoid paying any income tax. Although such cases are extremely rare, they create strong adverse reaction by the public and by Congress. One goal of the Tax Reform Act of 1986 was to assure that every person with a large income pays a significant amount of income tax. The approach taken was to strengthen the Alternative Minimum Tax (AMT). This minimum tax requires that you add back to adjusted gross income a long list of deductions (such as state income tax) and tax preferences (such as accelerated depreciation). The total resulting from these adjustments is your Alternative Minimum Tax income. You apply a 21% rate to this total. If your Alternative Minimum Tax is higher than your tax under the regular computation, you must pay the Alternative Minimum Tax.

Partnerships

Partnerships are not taxable entities. Although a partnership pays no income tax, it must file an ***information return*** showing the computation of net income or loss and the share of net income or loss allocable to each partner. The partners must include in their personal tax returns their respective shares of the net income or loss of the partnership.

INCOME TAXES: CORPORATIONS

Taxation of corporations

5 Contrast the determination of taxable income for a corporation with that for an individual.

A corporation is a separate taxable entity. Our discussion is focused on the general business corporation and does not cover certain other types of corporations for which special tax treatment applies. Every corporation, unless specifically exempt from taxation, must file an income tax return whether or not it has taxable income or owes any tax.

The earning of taxable income inevitably creates a liability to pay income taxes. This liability and the related charge to expense must be entered in the accounting records before financial statements are prepared. The following journal entry is typical:

```
Income Taxes Expense ................................................  60,000
        Income Taxes Payable .........................................          60,000
To record corporate income taxes for the current period.
```

Corporation tax rates

The Tax Reform Act of 1986 reduced the top corporate tax rate from 46% to 34% and continued the practice of allowing lower rates for small companies. The following table shows the three brackets provided by the current law.

Corporate Income Tax Rates

Taxable Income	Rates
Up to $50,000	15%
Over $50,000 but not over $75,000	25%
Over $75,000	34%

The benefits from the 15% and 25% tax rates on the first two layers of corporate income are phased out for larger companies with earnings over $100,000. The 5% surtax applies to taxable earnings between $100,000 and $335,000.

To illustrate, let us compute the tax for a corporation with taxable income of $1,000,000.

	Taxable Income	Tax Rate	Tax
First	$ 50,000	15%	$ 7,500
Next	25,000	25%	6,250
Next	25,000	34%	8,500
Next	235,000	39%*	91,650
Next	665,000	34%	226,100
Total	$1,000,000		$340,000

* Includes a 5% surtax designed to deny high-income corporations any benefit from the lower tax rates on the first $75,000 of corporate income.

In looking over the above table, notice that the total tax of $340,000 is exactly 34% of the entire $1,000,000 of taxable income. This proves that the use of the 5% surtax has nullified the benefits of the 15% and 25% rates for this corporation. Any corporation with taxable income of $335,000 or more pays tax at a flat rate of 34%.

Taxable income of corporations

In many respects, the taxable income of corporations is computed by following the same concepts we employ in preparing an income statement. The starting point is total revenue. From this amount, we deduct ordinary and necessary business expenses. However, as explained later in this chapter, net income determined by generally accepted accounting principles usually differs from taxable income. The difference is caused by specific rules in the tax laws which prescribe for certain items of revenue and expense a treatment different from that called for by GAAP. Another difference is the fact that from time to time, Congress makes drastic changes in the rules for determining taxable income. Some of the special factors to be considered in preparing a corporation tax return are considered below.

1 **Dividends received.** The dividends received by a corporation on its investments in stocks of other corporations are included in gross income, but 80% of such dividends can be deducted from gross income. As a result, only 20% of dividend income is taxable to the receiving corporation.

2 *Capital gains and losses.* The net capital gains of corporations are taxed as ordinary income. Thus, rates may vary from 15% to 34%. Capital gains are treated the same as any other form of income in determining the extent, if any, to which the 5% surtax is applied. Corporations may deduct capital losses only by offsetting them against capital gains.

3 *Other variations from taxation of individuals.* The concept of adjusted gross income is not applicable to a corporation. There is no standard deduction and no personal exemption. Gross income minus the deductions allowed to corporations equal *taxable income.*

4 *Repeal of the Investment Tax Credit.* For many years in the past, businesses were eligible for an Investment Tax Credit, often equal to as much as 10% of the cost of new equipment. The Investment Tax Credit (ITC) is no longer in effect; however, the possibility of its reinstatement remains. This is not the first time the Investment Tax Credit has been eliminated. In the past the elimination of the ITC was followed by its reinstatement. Present congressional concern over budget deficits suggests that Congress will look closely at the tax laws. Issues such as favorable treatment for capital gains and tax credits to stimulate investment will probably be among the topics considered.

5 *Alternative Minimum Tax.* A major political reason for passage of the Tax Reform Act of 1986 was that a few large corporations had paid little or no income tax in certain years. The new bill contains a strong new minimum tax designed to prevent such extremes of tax avoidance. The starting point in calculating the Alternative Minimum Tax is the corporation's regular taxable income. This amount is adjusted by recalculating various deductions and deferrals, such as deferred gain on installment sales and any excess of income reported to stockholders over reported taxable income. A 20% minimum tax (AMT) is applied to this recalculated base. The minimum tax must be paid if it is higher than the tax calculated by regular procedures.

Illustrative tax computation for corporation

Shown on the next page is an income statement for Stone Corporation, along with a separate supporting schedule for the tax computation. In this supporting schedule, we compute the amount of income taxes to appear in the income statement and also show the payments of estimated tax, thus arriving at the amount of tax payable with the tax return.

Accounting income versus taxable income

6 Discuss the concept of interperiod income tax allocation.

In the determination of **accounting income,** the objective is to measure business operating results as accurately as possible in accordance with generally accepted accounting principles. **Taxable income,** on the other hand, is a legal concept governed by statute and subject to sudden and frequent change by Congress. In setting the rules for determining taxable income, Congress is interested not only in meeting the revenue needs of government but in achieving certain public policy objectives. Since accounting income and taxable income are determined with dif-

STONE CORPORATION
Income Statement
For the Year Ended December 31, 19__

Revenue:			
Sales.			$800,000
Dividends received from domestic corporations			20,000
Total revenue			$820,000
Expenses:			
Cost of goods sold		$537,000	
Other expenses (includes capital loss of $13,000)		100,000	637,000
Income before income taxes.			$183,000
Income taxes expense.			53,450
Net income			$129,550

SCHEDULE A
Computation of Income Tax

Income before income taxes.		$183,000
Add back: Items not deductible for tax purposes:		
Capital loss deducted as operating expense		13,000
Subtotal.		$196,000
Deduct: Dividends received credit ($20,000 × 80%)		16,000
Taxable income		$180,000

Income tax:			
15% of first $50,000		$ 7,500	
25% of next $25,000		6,250	
34% of next $25,000		8,500	
39% of $80,000 (includes 5% surtax)		31,200	
Total income tax.			$ 53,450
Deduct: Quarterly payments of estimated tax			50,000
Balance of tax payable with tax return			3,450

ferent purposes in mind, it is not surprising that they often differ by material amounts.

Differences between taxable income and accounting income may result from special tax rules which are unrelated to accounting principles.

1 Some items included in accounting income are not taxable. For example, interest on state or municipal bonds is excluded from taxable income.

2 Some business expenses are not deductible. The Tax Reform Act of 1986 bans the reserve method of determining the amount of the deduction for bad debts. Only the direct write-off method is accepted for use by taxpayers other than certain banks.

3 Special deductions in excess of actual business expenses are allowed some taxpayers. For example, depletion deductions in excess of actual cost are allowed taxpayers in some mining industries.

In addition, the *timing* of the recognition of certain revenue and expenses under tax rules differs from that under accounting principles. Some items of income received in advance may be taxed in the year of receipt while certain accrued expenses may not be deductible for income tax purposes until they are actually paid in cash.

Alternative accounting methods offering possible tax advantages

There are many examples of elective methods which postpone income taxes. Taxpayers engaged in exploration of natural resources may use a one-year write-off of the costs of drilling for oil and gas rather than capitalizing these costs for later depreciation. Ranchers may treat the cost of cattle feed as expense in the year of purchase rather than in the year the feed is consumed.

The accelerated cost recovery system (ACRS) created by Congress in 1981 replaced for tax purposes the useful-life depreciation concept which had been followed since the beginning of the federal income tax. For some types of plant and equipment, depreciation under ACRS is based on a recovery period shorter than useful life. The Tax Reform Act of 1986 provided less liberal write-offs (especially of real estate) but retained the ACRS approach. This arbitrary shorter recovery period is not in accordance with generally accepted accounting principles; consequently a different amount of depreciation expense based on useful life will appear in financial statements. Thus, another factor exists to cause taxable income to differ from accounting income. Under present tax laws, taxpayers have the option of using straight-line depreciation rather than the rapid write-off provided by ACRS. However, taxpayers generally choose for income tax purposes those accounting methods which cause expenses to be recognized as soon as possible and revenue to be recognized as late as possible.

Interperiod income tax allocation

We have seen that differences between generally accepted accounting principles and income tax rules can be material. Some businesses might consider it more convenient to maintain their accounting records in conformity with the tax rules, but the result would be to distort financial statements. It is clearly preferable to maintain accounting records by the principles that produce relevant information about business operations. The data contained in the records can then be adjusted by use of work sheets to arrive at taxable income.

When a corporation follows one method in its accounting records and financial statements but uses a different method for its income tax return, a financial reporting problem arises. The difference in method will usually have the effect of postponing the recognition of income on the tax return (either because an expense deduction is accelerated or because revenue recognition is postponed). The question is whether the income tax expense to appear in the financial statements should be accrued when the income is recognized in the accounting records, or when it is actually subject to taxation.

To illustrate the problem, let us consider a very simple case. Suppose the Pryor Company has before-tax accounting income of $600,000 in each of two years. However, the company takes as a tax deduction in the first year an expense of $200,000 which is reported for accounting purposes in the second year. The company's accounting income, taxable income, and the actual income taxes due (assuming an average tax rate of 34%) are shown below.

	1st Year	2d Year
Accounting income (before income taxes)	$600,000	$600,000
Taxable income	400,000	800,000
Actual income taxes due each year at 34% rate	136,000	272,000

Let us assume the Pryor Company reports as an expense in its income statement each year the amount of income taxes due for that year. The effect on reported net income as shown in the company's financial statements would be as follows:

	1st Year	2d Year
Company reports actual taxes Accounting income (before income taxes)	$600,000	$600,000
Income taxes expense (amount actually due)	136,000	272,000
Net income	$464,000	$328,000

The readers of Pryor Company's income statement might well wonder why the same $600,000 accounting income before income taxes in the two years produced such widely varying amounts of tax expense and net income.

To deal with this distortion between pretax income and after-tax income, an accounting policy known as *interperiod income tax allocation* is required for financial reporting purposes.[5] Briefly, the objective of income tax allocation is to accrue income taxes in relation to accounting income, whenever differences between accounting and taxable income are caused by differences in the *timing* of revenue or expenses. In the Pryor Company example, this means we would report in the first year income statement a tax expense based on $600,000 of accounting income even though a portion of this income ($200,000) will not be subject to income tax until the second year. The effect of this accounting procedure is demonstrated by the following journal entries to record the income tax expense in each of the two years:

Entries to record income tax allocation

1st Year	Income Taxes Expense	204,000	
	Current Income Tax Liability		136,000
	Deferred Income Tax Liability		68,000
	To record current and deferred income taxes at 34% of accounting income of $600,000.		

[5] For a more complete discussion of tax allocation procedures, see *APB Opinion No. 11*, "Accounting for Income Taxes," AICPA (New York: 1967).

2nd Year	Income Taxes Expense......................................	204,000	
	Deferred Income Tax Liability	68,000	
	Current Income Tax Liability		272,000
	To record income taxes of 34% of accounting income of $600,000		
	and to record actual income taxes due.		

Using tax allocation procedures, Pryor Company's financial statements would report net income during the two-year period as follows:

	1st Year	2d Year
Company uses tax allocation procedure		
Income before income taxes.......................................	$600,000	$600,000
Income taxes expense (tax allocation basis)	204,000	204,000
Net income..	$396,000	$396,000

In this example, the difference between taxable income and accounting income (caused by the accelerated deduction of an expense) was fully offset in a period of two years. In practice, differences between accounting and taxable income may persist over extended time periods and deferred tax liabilities may accumulate to significant amounts. For example, in a recent balance sheet of Sears, Roebuck and Co., deferred taxes of almost $2.5 billion were reported. This huge deferral of tax payments resulted from the use of the installments sales method for income tax purposes while reporting the net income in financial statements by the usual accrual method.

In contrast to the example for the Pryor Company in which income taxes were deferred, income taxes *may be prepaid* when taxable income exceeds accounting income because of timing differences. The portion of taxes paid on income deferred for accounting purposes would be reported as prepaid taxes in the balance sheet. When the income is reported as earned for accounting purposes in a later period, the *prepaid taxes are recognized as tax expense* applicable to the income currently reported but *taxed in an earlier period.*[6]

TAX PLANNING

Federal income tax laws have become so complex that detailed tax planning is now a way of life for most business firms. Almost all companies today engage professional tax specialists to review the tax aspects of major business decisions and to develop plans for legally minimizing income taxes. We will now consider some areas in which tax planning may offer substantial benefits.

---

[6] A good example of this treatment is found in the annual report of the Ford Motor Company. A recent balance sheet showed "Income Taxes Allocable to the Following Year," $206.5 million, as a current asset. This large prepaid tax came about as a result of estimated car warranty expense being deducted from revenue in the period in which cars were sold; for income tax purposes, this expense is deductible only when it is actually incurred.

Form of business organization

7 Explain how tax planning is used in choosing the form of business organization and the capital structure.

Tax factors should be carefully considered at the time a business is organized. As a single proprietor or partner, a business owner will pay taxes at individual rates, ranging currently from 15 to 33% (including surtax), on the business income earned in any year *whether or not it is withdrawn from the business.* Corporations, on the other hand, are taxed on earnings at rates varying from 15 to 39% (including surtax). In determining taxable income, corporations deduct salaries paid to owners for services but cannot deduct dividends paid to stockholders. Both *salaries and dividends* are taxable income to the persons receiving them.

These factors must be weighed in deciding in any given situation whether the corporate or noncorporate form of business organization is preferable. There is no simple rule of thumb, even considering only these basic differences. To illustrate, suppose that Able, a married man, starts a business which he expects will produce, before any compensation to himself and before income taxes, an average annual income of $80,000. Able plans to withdraw $20,000 yearly from the business. The combined corporate and individual taxes under the corporate and single proprietorship form of business organization are summarized below.

Form of Business Organization

		Corporation	Single Proprietorship
Business income		$80,000	$80,000
Salary to Able...		20,000	
Taxable income		$60,000	$80,000
Corporate Tax:			
15% of first $50,000	$7,500		
25% of next $10,000...........................	2,500	10,000	
Net income		$50,000	$80,000
Combined corporate and individual tax:			
Corporate tax on $60,000 income*.......................		$10,000	
Individual tax—joint return			
On Able's $20,000 salary...............................		3,000	
On Able's $80,000 business income			$18,938
Total tax on business income...........................		$13,000	$18,938

* Able's personal exemptions and deductions have been ignored, on the assumption that his other income equals personal exemptions and deductions. We have rounded amounts to the nearest dollar.

Under these assumptions, the formation of a corporation is favorable from an income tax viewpoint. If the business is incorporated, the combined tax on the corporation and on Able personally will be $13,000. If the business is not incorporated, the tax will be $18,938, or almost 50% more. The key to the advantage indicated for choosing the corporate form of organization is that Able did not take much of the earnings out of the corporation.

If Able decides to operate as a corporation, the $50,000 of net income retained in the corporation will be taxed to Able as ordinary income **when and if** it is distributed as dividends. In other words, Able cannot get the money out of the corporation without paying personal income tax on it. An advantage of the corporation as a form of business organization is that Able can **postpone** payment of a significant amount of tax as long as the earnings remain invested in the business.

If all earnings of the business are to be withdrawn. Now let us change one of our basic assumptions and say that Able plans to withdraw all net income from the business each year. Under this assumption the single proprietorship form of organization would be better than a corporation from an income tax standpoint. If the business is incorporated and Able again is to receive a $20,000 salary plus dividends equal to the $50,000 of corporate net income, the total tax will be much higher. The corporate tax of $10,000 plus personal tax of $15,733 (based on $20,000 salary and $50,000 in dividends) would amount to $25,733. This is considerably higher than the $18,938 which we previously computed as the tax liability if the business operated as a proprietorship.

We have purposely kept our example as short as possible. You can imagine some variations which would produce different results. Perhaps Able might incorporate and set his salary at, say, $75,000 instead of $20,000. If this salary were considered reasonable by the IRS, the corporation's taxable income would drop to $5,000 rather than the $60,000 used in our illustration. This and other possible assumptions should make clear that the choice between a corporation and a single proprietorship requires careful consideration of a number of factors in each individual case. Both the marginal rate of tax to which individual business owners are subject and the extent to which profits are to be withdrawn are always basic issues in studying the relative advantages of one form of business organization over another.

Under certain conditions, small, closely held corporations may elect to be Subchapter S corporations, in which case the corporation pays no tax but the individual shareholders are taxed directly on the corporation's earnings.

Tax planning in the choice of financial structure

In deciding upon the best means of raising capital to start or expand a business, consideration should be given to income taxes. Different forms of business financing produce different amounts of tax expense. Interest paid on debt, for example, is **fully deductible** in computing taxable income, but dividends paid on preferred or common stock are not. This factor operates as a strong incentive to finance expansion by borrowing.

Let us assume that a corporation subject to a 39% marginal tax rate needs $100,000 to invest in productive assets on which it can earn a 20% annual return. If the company obtains the needed money by issuing $100,000 in 14% preferred stock, it will earn **after taxes** only $12,200, which is not even enough to cover the $14,000 preferred dividend. (This after-tax amount is computed as $20,000 income less taxes at 39% of $20,000.)

Now let us assume, on the other hand, that the company borrowed $100,000 at 14% interest. The additional gross income would be $20,000 but interest expense of $14,000 would be deducted, leaving taxable income of $6,000. The tax on the $6,000 at 39% would be $2,340, leaving after-tax income of $3,660. Analysis along these lines is also needed in choosing between debt financing and financing by issuing common stock.

The choice of financial structure should be considered from the viewpoint of investors, especially in the case of a small, closely held corporation.

● **CASE IN POINT** ● The owners of a small incorporated business decided to invest an additional $100,000 in the business to finance expanding operations. They were undecided whether to make a $100,000 loan to the corporation or to purchase $100,000 worth of additional capital stock. Finally, the owners turned to a CPA firm for advice. The CPAs suggested that the loan would be better because the $100,000 cash invested could be returned by the corporation at the maturity date of the loan without imposing any individual income tax on the owners. The loan could be arranged to mature in installments or at a single fixed date. Renewal of the note could be easily arranged if desired.

On the other hand, if the $100,000 investment were made by purchase of additional shares of capital stock, the return of these funds to the owners would be more difficult. If the $100,000 came back to the owners in the form of dividends, a considerable portion would be consumed by individual income taxes. If the corporation repurchased $100,000 worth of its stock from the owners, the retained earnings account would become restricted by this amount. In summary, the CPAs pointed out that it is easier for persons in control of a small corporation to get their money back if the investment takes the form of a loan rather than the purchase of additional capital stock.

Tax shelters

A tax shelter is an investment which produces a loss for tax purposes in the near term but hopefully proves profitable in the long run. The reason for seeking a tax loss is to offset this loss against other income and, by so doing, lower both taxable income and the income tax owed for the current year. Near the close of each year, many newspaper advertisements offer an opportunity to invest in a program which promises to reduce the investor's present tax liability yet produce future profits. These programs have a particular appeal to persons in high tax brackets who face the prospect of paying much of a year's net income as taxes.

A limited partnership organization has often been used for tax shelter ventures, so that each investor may claim his or her share of the immediate losses. Typical of the types of ventures are oil and gas drilling programs and real estate investments offering high leverage and accelerated depreciation. The real estate limited partnership appears to have been virtually wiped out by the Tax Reform Act of 1986, but no doubt the promoters of tax shelters will find new loopholes to exploit. A principal appeal of real estate tax shelters has been their use of rapid depreciation to produce losses in early years of the partnership. The change in the law drastically curtails rapid depreciation. A major goal of the Tax Reform Act of 1986 was to curtail or eliminate tax shelters in general. Among the heaviest blows to tax shelters were: (1) the elimination of favorable treatment of long-term capital gains; (2) the strengthening of the Alternative Minimum Tax to catch investors deeply involved in sheltering income; and (3) the change to less liberal depreciation. The depreciation of rental residential property is limited to the straight-line method over a period of 27.5 years and other real estate to 31.5 years.

Unfortunately, many so-called tax shelters have proved to be merely unprofitable investments, in which the investors saved taxes but lost larger amounts of capital. A sound approach to tax shelters should probably be based on the premise that if an investment does not appear **worthwhile without the promised tax benefits, it should be avoided.**

Some tax shelters, on the other hand, are not of a high-risk nature. State and municipal bonds offer a modest rate of interest which is tax exempt. Investment in real estate with deductions for mortgage interest, property taxes, and depreciation will often show losses which offset other taxable income, yet eventually prove profitable because of rising market value, especially in periods of inflation.

END-OF-CHAPTER REVIEW

Summary of learning objectives

1 Describe the history of the federal income tax and the highlights of the Tax Reform Act of 1986.

The federal income tax when established in 1913 called for very low rates and was intended only for the purpose of raising revenue for the government. Since then tax rates have soared, reaching levels as high as 70% in some years. The purposes have broadened to include such objectives as stimulating the economy, protecting the environment, and enforcing a more equal distribution of the national income. The Tax Reform Act of 1986 was the most drastic revision of the tax laws in many years. Its sweeping changes included relieving millions of low-income taxpayers from paying any income tax, the lowering of tax rates for individuals and corporations, the elimination of many types of deductions, and a shifting of the tax burden from individuals to corporations.

2 Discuss the advantages of the cash basis of accounting for preparation of individual income tax returns.

The cash basis of accounting means that revenue is recognized when received in cash and expenses (except depreciation) are recognized when paid. From the government's viewpoint, the use of the cash basis facilitates collection of taxes, because the taxpayer is required to pay the tax as cash from revenue becomes available. From the taxpayer's viewpoint, the cash basis requires a minimum of record keeping. Yearly amounts of income from salaries, interest, and dividends are reported to individual taxpayers on a cash basis by means of Forms W-2 and 1099. The cash basis also permits tax savings by individuals who deliberately shift the timing of revenue and expense transactions from one year to another. Thus, the taxpayer who will incur a deductible expense near the year-end can choose whether to pay it before or after December 31, and, by this choice, influence the amount of taxable income in each year. In general, the strategy is to accelerate expenses and delay receipt of revenue.

3 State the formula for determining the taxable income of an individual.

A formula for determining the taxable income for individual taxpayers consists of the following steps in gathering and organizing tax data.

a Compute *total income.*	Consists of all income and gains from whatever source derived.
b Subtract *exclusions.*	Items which the law says are not taxable, such as interest on municipal bonds.
c Compute *gross income.*	A subtotal representing total income minus exclusions.
d Subtract *deductions.*	Gross income is reduced by such items as business expenses, and contributions to retirement plans.
e Compute *adjusted gross income.*	Consists of gross income minus deductions.
f Subtract *standard deduction* or *itemized deductions.*	Itemized deductions include mortgage interest paid, property taxes, and charitable contributions.
g Subtract *personal exemptions.*	An exemption of specified amount for each taxpayer, spouse, and dependent.
h Compute *taxable income.*	Amount to which the tax rates are applied.

4 Explain the recent changes in the taxation of capital gains and losses.

For a great many years, government encouraged taxpayers to invest in capital assets such as securities and real estate. The encouragement was in the form of favorable tax treatment of long-term capital gains. This policy was ended by the Tax Reform Act of 1986, which provided that capital gains should be taxed as ordinary income. In other words, capital gains are no longer a goal of tax planning.

5 Contrast the determination of taxable income for a corporation with that for an individual.

Among the points of difference are (a) a separate tax schedule with different rates and brackets; (b) no concept of adjusted gross income, and no standard deduction or personal exemption; (c) only 20% of dividends received by a corporation treated as taxable; and (d) no deduction by a corporation of *net* capital losses.

6 Discuss the concept of interperiod income tax allocation.

The purpose of income tax allocation is to accrue income tax expense in the income statement in relation to the accounting income shown in that statement. Without income tax allocation, the differences between GAAP and income tax rules would often cause the income tax expense for a given year to be unrelated to the accounting income of that year.

7 Explain how tax planning is used in choosing the form of business organization and the capital structure.

An important decision in tax planning is whether a business will achieve tax benefits by incorporating rather than operating as a single proprietorship or partnership. The decision will vary from case to case depending on such factors as the tax bracket of the owners as individual taxpayers, and the intent of the owners to withdraw earnings from the corporation in the form of dividends as opposed to retaining earnings in the corporation to facilitate growth of the business.

In deciding on a capital structure, the owners of a busines should be aware that interest on debt such as bonds and notes payable is deductible in arriving at taxable income, but dividends paid on common or preferred stock are not.

Key terms introduced or emphasized in chapter 16

Accelerated cost recovery system (ACRS). An accelerated depreciation method for income tax purposes for depreciable assets acquired after 1980. This method is used in income tax returns but not in financial statements prepared in accordance with generally accepted accounting principles.

Adjusted gross income. A subtotal in an individual's tax return computed by deducting from gross income any business-related expenses and other deductions authorized by law. A key figure to which many measurements are linked.

Capital asset. Stocks, bonds, and real estate not used in a trade or business.

Capital gain or loss. The difference between the cost basis of a capital asset and the amount received from its sale.

Cash basis of accounting. Revenue is recorded when received in cash and expenses are recorded in the period in which payment is made. Widely used for individual tax returns and for tax returns of professional firms, farms, and service-type businesses. Gives taxpayers a degree of control over taxable income by deliberate timing of collections and payments. Not used in most financial statements because it fails to match revenue with related expenses.

Declaration of estimated tax. Self-employed persons and others with income not subject to withholding must file by April 15 each year a declaration of estimated tax for the current year and must make quarterly payments of such tax.

Gross income. All income and gains from whatever source derived unless specifically excluded by law, such as interest on state and municipal bonds.

Interperiod tax allocation. Allocation of income tax expense among accounting periods because of timing differences between accounting income and taxable income. Causes income tax expense reported in financial statements to be in logical relationship to accounting income.

Itemized deductions. Personal expenses deductible from adjusted gross income, such as mortgage interest, property taxes, contributions, and medical expenses and casualty losses in excess of certain amounts.

Marginal tax rate. The rate to which a taxpayer is subject on the top dollar of income received.

Personal exemption. A deduction of specified amount from adjusted gross income for the taxpayer, the taxpayer's spouse, and each dependent.

Standard deduction. A specified amount to be deducted from adjusted gross income. An alternative to listing itemized deductions, such as mortgage interest and property taxes.

Tax credit. An amount to be subtracted from the tax itself. Examples are the earned income credit and the credit for child-care expenses.

Tax planning. A systematic process of minimizing income taxes by considering in advance the tax consequences of alternative business or investment actions. A major factor in choosing the form of business organization and capital structure, in lease-or-buy decisions, and in timing of transactions.

Tax shelters. Investment programs designed to show losses in the short term to be offset against other taxable income, but offering the hope of long-run profits.

Taxable income. The computed amount to which the appropriate tax rate is to be applied to arrive at the tax liability.

Demonstration problem for your review

Mike and Peggy Stevens, a married couple, had items of income and expense for the year as shown below.

Salaries ($30,000 each)	$60,000
Consulting fees earned by Mike (net of expenses)	9,200
Dividends	580
Interest on bonds of State of Maine	252
Capital gains	3,900
Unused capital loss carryover from preceding year	2,100
Proceeds from life insurance policy upon death of relative	10,000
Payment by Mike to an IRA. (Neither Mike nor Peggy is covered by an employer-sponsored pension plan)	2,000
Casualty loss, interest, taxes, and other expenditures (see list below)	52,040

Theft of furniture while on vacation	$ 2,200
Interest on home mortgage	2,630
Medical expenses	1,120
Insurance on home	252
Income taxes withheld (federal)	14,000
Payments of estimated tax	2,000
Charitable contributions	200
Sales taxes	500
Property taxes on home	1,100
State income taxes	1,900
Clothes, food, and other living expenses	26,138
Total (as listed above)	$52,040

Instructions. Compute the taxable income and the income tax liability for Mike and Peggy Stevens who file a joint return. Use a format similar to that illustrated on page 643 but list itemized deductions in detail. Your solution should show the various elements of gross income, any deduction needed to arrive at adjusted gross income, itemized deductions, personal exemptions, and taxable income, followed by a section for computation of tax. Use the tax rate information for married taxpayers filing joint returns (page 640). Add a note identifying any items listed in the problem which are not deductible.

Solution to demonstration problem

Joint Return for Mike and Peggy Stevens

Gross Income:

Salaries ($30,000 each)		$60,000
Consulting fees earned (net of expenses).............		9,200
Dividends.......................................		580
Capital gains	$ 3,900	
Unused capital loss carryover from last year	(2,100)	1,800
Gross income...................................		$71,580

Deductions to arrive at adjusted gross income:

Payment to an IRA................................		2,000
Adjusted gross income...........................		$69,580

Deductions from adjusted gross income:

Itemized deductions:

Interest on home mortgage	$ 2,630	
Charitable contributions	200	
Property taxes on home	1,100	
State income taxes	1,900	
Total itemized deductions	$ 5,830	
Personal exemptions (2 × $2,000)	4,000	9,830
Taxable income....................................		$59,750

Computation of tax:

Tax on first $29,750 at 15%........................		$ 4,463
Tax on next $30,000 at 28%		8,400
Total tax		$12,863
Less: Income tax withheld.................	$14,000	
Payments of estimated tax	2,000	16,000
Amount to be refunded		$ 3,137

Note: Interest on bonds of the State of Maine and the proceeds on the life insurance policy are not taxable. Medical expenses are below $7\frac{1}{2}\%$ of adjusted gross income and are not deductible. Casualty losses (after elimination of the first $100) are deductible only to the extent they exceed 10% of adjusted gross income. The casualty loss of $2,200 incurred by Mike and Peggy Stevens, therefore, is not deductible. Insurance premiums paid on a home and clothes, food, and other living expenses are not deductible. Sales taxes are no longer deductible.

ASSIGNMENT MATERIAL

Review questions

1 The increase in the standard deduction by the Tax Reform Act of 1986 was primarily of benefit to those individuals who usually did not itemize their deductions. Do you agree with this statement? Explain.

2 What is meant by the expression "tax planning"?

3 What are the four major classes of taxpayers under the federal income tax law?

4 It has been claimed that corporate income is subject to "double taxation." Explain the meaning of this expression.

5 Taxes are characterized as *progressive, proportional,* or *regressive* with respect to any given base. Describe an income tax rate structure that would fit each of these characterizations.

6 State whether you agree with the following statements and explain your reasoning.
   a A person in a very high tax bracket who makes a cash contribution to a college will reduce his or her tax liability by more than the amount of the gift.
   b Newspaper stories occasionally tell of very wealthy individuals who are so deeply involved in tax sheltered ventures that they are not required to pay any income tax. Does the Tax Reform Act of 1986 deal with such situations? Explain.

7 State in equation form the federal income tax formula for individuals, beginning with total income and ending with taxable income.

8 List some differences between the tax rules for corporations and the tax rules for individuals.

9 What are some objectives of the federal income tax structure other than providing revenue for the government?

10 Explain the difference between *tax avoidance* and *tax evasion,* and give an example of each.

11 Peggy Bame, M.D., files her income tax return on a cash basis. During the current year she collected $12,600 from patients for medical services rendered in prior years, and billed patients $77,000 for services rendered this year. She has accounts receivable of $16,400 relating to this year's billings at the end of the year. What amount of gross income from her practice should Bame report on her tax return?

12 Joe Gilmore, a single man, files his income tax return on a cash basis. During the current year $800 of interest was credited to him on his savings account; he withdrew his interest on January 18 of the following year. No other interest and no dividends were received by Gilmore.

   In December of the current year Gilmore purchased some business equipment having an estimated service life of 10 years. He also paid a year's rent in advance on certain business property on December 29 of the current year. Explain how these items would be treated on Gilmore's income tax return for the current year.

13 Which of the following is not a capital asset according to the Internal Revenue Code? (a) an investment in General Motors stock; (b) a personal residence; (c) equipment used in the operation of a business; (d) an investment in Krugerrands (gold coins).

14 An individual with a yearly salary of $20,000 had a capital loss of $25,000. To what extent, if any, could this capital loss be offset against the salary in computing taxable income? Explain.

15 Even when a taxpayer uses the accrual method of accounting, taxable income may differ from accounting income. Give four examples of differences between the tax treatment and accounting treatment of items that are included in the determination of income.

16 Under what circumstances is the accounting procedure known as ***income tax allocation*** appropriate? Explain the purpose of this procedure.

17 List some tax factors to be considered in deciding whether to organize a new business as a corporation or as a partnership.

18 Explain how the corporate income tax makes debt financing in general more attractive than financing through the issuance of preferred stock.

19 The depreciation expense computed by Zane Company under the accelerated cost recovery system (ACRS) appeared in the tax return as $150,000. In the accounting records and financial statements, Zane's depreciation was computed on the straight-line basis and amounted to $100,000. Under interperiod tax allocation procedures, would Zane Company's balance sheet show prepaid income taxes or deferred income taxes? Explain.

20 Some of the decisions that business owners must make in organizing and operating a business will affect the amount of income taxes to be paid. List some of these decisions which affect the amount of income taxes legally payable.

Exercises

Exercise 16-1
Accounting terminology

Listed below are nine technical accounting terms introduced in this chapter:

Alternative Minimum Tax	Itemized deductions	Tax credit
Adjusted gross income	Tax shelter	Personal exemption
Interperiod tax allocation	Reserve method	Cash basis of accounting

Each of the following statements may (or may not) describe one of these technical terms. For each statement, indicate the accounting term described, or answer "None" if the statement does not correctly describe any of the terms.

a Important to individual taxpayers who pay large amounts of state income tax, and make large charitable contributions.

b An amount subtracted from the gross tax liability.

c Assures that profitable corporations and high-income individuals do not escape taxation altogether through any combination of tax shelters and tax preferences.

d A subtotal in an individual's tax return, computed by deducting from gross income any business-related expenses, contributions to retirement plans, and other deductions authorized by law.

e Revenue recorded when received in cash and expenses recorded in period payment is made.

f Income tax recognized each period as a constant percentage of net sales.

g An investment program designed to show losses in the short run to be offset against other taxable income, but offering the hope of long-run profits.

h Causes income tax expense reported in financial statements to be in logical relationship to accounting income.

i A method of accounting for bad debts no longer permitted in determining taxable income.

Exercise 16-2
Impact of the Tax
Reform Act of
1986

Explain briefly the impact of the Tax Reform Act of 1986 on each of the following:

a Tax rates on individuals
b Tax rates on corporations
c Capital gains of individuals
d The standard deduction and low-income taxpayers

Exercise 16-3
Gross income:
items to include
and items to
exclude

You are to consider the income tax status of the items listed below. List the numbers 1 to 15 on your answer sheet. For each item state whether it is *included in gross income* or *excluded from gross income* for federal income tax on individuals. Add explanatory comments if needed.

(1) Inheritance of ranch from estate of deceased uncle
(2) Amount received as damages for injury in automobile accident
(3) Tips received by waiter
(4) Pension received by veteran from U.S. government for military service
(5) Dividends received on investment in Ford Motor stock
(6) Trip to London received by employee as award for outstanding performance
(7) Rent received on personal residence while on an extended European tour
(8) First prize of $14,000,000 won in California state lottery
(9) Gain on the sale of a 1953 Jaguar purchased 10 years ago
(10) Proceeds of life insurance policy received on death of spouse
(11) Share of income from partnership in excess of drawings
(12) Gain on sale of Super Bowl tickets by season ticket holder
(13) Interest received on bonds of state of Texas
(14) Value of U.S. Savings Bonds received as a gift
(15) Salary received from corporation by a stockholder who owns directly or indirectly all of the corporation's capital stock

Exercise 16-4
Is it deductible?

You are to determine the deductibility status, for federal income tax purposes, of each of the items listed below. List the numbers 1 to 10 on your answer sheet. For each item state whether the item *is deducted to arrive at adjusted gross income; deducted from adjusted gross income;* or *not deductible.*

(1) Sales taxes
(2) Medical expense of $2,000 incurred by a taxpayer with adjusted gross income of $50,000
(3) State income tax paid
(4) Property taxes paid on personal residence
(5) Interest paid on mortgage on personal residence
(6) Loss on sale of equipment used in a business
(7) Capital loss on sale of an investment in securities
(8) Contribution to a Keogh H.R.10 retirement plan
(9) Payment to an IRA
(10) Damage by storm to motorboat used for pleasure

Exercise 16-5
Computing
taxable income

Listed below is income tax data for Arthur and Jane Brown, a married couple filing a joint tax return. You are to compute the *taxable income,* using *only* the relevant data.

Total income, including gifts, inheritances, interest on municipal bonds, etc.	$56,000
Exclusions (gifts, inheritances, interest on municipal bonds, etc.)	8,300
Deductions to arrive at adjusted gross income	1,700
Itemized deductions	7,100
Personal exemptions ($2,000 each)	4,000
Income taxes withheld from salary	7,300

Exercise 16-6
Computing tax on individuals

Use the tax rate information on page 640 to compute the tax for each of the following. Round amounts to the nearest dollar.

	Taxable Income
a Single taxpayer	$24,000
b Married couple filing joint return	$48,050

Exercise 16-7
Computing tax liability of a corporation

Raintree Corporation reports the following income for the year.

Income from operations.	$260,000
Capital gain.	90,000

In computing the tax, assume that corporate tax rates are as follows:

On first $50,000 of taxable income	15%
On second $25,000 of taxable income	25%
On taxable income over $75,000	34%
A surtax on taxable income between $100,000 and $335,000	5%

Compute Raintree's tax liability for the year.

Exercise 16-8
Interperiod tax allocation

Mission Bay Corporation deducted on its tax return for 1989 an expense of $100,000 which was not recognized as an expense for accounting purposes until 1990. The corporation's accounting income before income taxes in each of the two years was $525,000. The company uses tax allocation procedures.

   a Prepare the journal entries required at the end of 1989 and 1990 to record income tax expense. To compute the tax, multiply the entire amount of taxable income by 34%.
   b Prepare a two-column schedule showing the net income to appear on the financial statements for 1989 and 1990, assuming that tax allocation procedures are used. Also prepare a similar schedule on the assumption that tax allocation procedures are not used.

Problems

Problem 16-1
Computing the tax: joint return

Jack and Marian Wood, a married couple, file a joint income tax return and claim one exemption each, plus two exemptions for dependents. Both Jack and Marian are employed; each earns an annual salary of $24,000. During the year, Jack contributed $2,000 to an IRA. This contribution is fully deductible because neither Jack nor Marian is covered by an employer-sponsored pension plan. The following information has been gathered by Jack and Marian in getting ready to prepare their tax return. Assume the standard deduction is $5,000.

Federal income taxes withheld from salaries.	$ 4,800
Payments of estimated tax	2,200
Itemized deductions.	4,200
Total income (including $48,000 salaries, $800 in municipal bond interest, and $11,200 income from other sources)	60,000
Payment to an IRA	2,000
Personal exemptions ($2,000 × 4)	8,000

Instructions

a Compute gross income.
b Compute adjusted gross income.
c Compute taxable income.
d Compute the amount of tax remaining to be paid or the refund to be claimed.

Problem 16-2
Determining adjusted gross income and taxable income

The following two cases are independent of each other. The instructions for preparing your solutions appear at the end of the second case.

Case A. John Roberts, a free-lance writer, had total income of $80,000 for the year just ended. This amount included $1,600 of interest on municipal bonds; the remainder was from self-employment. During the year Roberts contributed $9,000 to a Keogh H.R.10 retirement plan. His itemized deductions amounted to $8,090 and he was entitled to one personal exemption of $2,000.

Case B. Ann Mason, an attorney conducting her own law practice, uses the accrual basis of accounting in maintaining accounting records and preparing financial statements. However, for income tax purposes, she uses the cash basis of accounting. During the current year, her business net income (computed on an accrual basis) was $75,400. Between the beginning and end of the current year, her financial statements showed that receivables from clients increased by $12,000, and current liabilities for rent and other operating expenses decreased by $6,800. The net income for the business included $1,200 of interest received on municipal bonds.

Mason has a personal savings account to which $720 in interest was credited during the year, none of which was withdrawn from the bank. In addition to business expenses taken into account in computing the net income of her law practice, Mason has $1,360 in deductions to arrive at adjusted gross income. Her personal exemption amounts to $2,000 and her itemized deductions are $5,790.

Instructions. For each of the two cases described above, prepare a separate schedule showing in appropriate order all the steps necessary to determine the taxpayer's *adjusted gross income* and the *taxable income* for the year. For Case B, your solution would show: (1) business net income (accrual basis), (2) the increases and/or decreases for conversion to the cash basis, (3) the amount of business net income on a cash basis, and (4) the steps to determine taxable income.

Problem 16-3
Joint return: a comprehensive problem

Ralph and Jennifer Lane own a hardware store and an apartment building. They file a joint income tax return. Assume that the net income from the hardware store is self-employment income divided equally between Ralph and Jennifer. (Income from the apartment building is considered investment income rather than earned income.)

The Lanes furnish over one-half the support of their son who attends college and who earned $2,560 in part-time jobs and summer employment. They also support Ralph's father, who is eighty years old and has no taxable income of his own.

The depreciation basis of the apartment building is $160,000; depreciation is recorded at the rate of 4% per year on a straight-line basis. During the current year, the Lanes had the following cash receipts and cash expenditures applicable to the hardware business, the apartment building, other investments, and personal activities.

Cash receipts:

Cash withdrawn from hardware store (net income, $48,000)	$36,000
Gross rentals from apartment building	28,800
Cash dividends on stock owned jointly	2,760
Interest on River City bonds	976
Received from sale of stock purchased two years ago for $10,000	16,000
Received from sale of motorboat purchased three years ago for $4,792 and used entirely for pleasure	2,712

Cash expenditures:

Expenditures relating to apartment building:

Interest on mortgage	7,200
Property taxes	4,720
Insurance (one year)	560
Utilities	2,368
Repairs and maintenance	3,872
Gardening	640

Other cash expenditures:

Mortgage interest on residence	3,160
Property taxes on residence	1,700
Insurance on residence	400
State income tax paid	1,900
State sales taxes	700
Charitable contributions	1,200
Medical expenses	1,376
Payment by Ralph to a Keogh H.R.10 plan	3,000
Payment by Jennifer to an IRA	2,000
Payments on declaration of estimated tax for current year	7,000

Instructions

a Determine the amount of taxable income Ralph and Jennifer Lane would report on their federal income tax return for the current year. In your computation of taxable income, first list the net income of the hardware business. Second, show the revenue and expenses of the apartment building and the amount of net income from this source. Third, show the data for dividends and capital gains. After combining the above amounts and appropriate deductions to determine adjusted gross income, list the itemized deductions and personal exemptions to arrive at taxable income. Assume that the personal exemption is $2,000 each.

b Compute the income tax liability for Ralph and Jennifer Lane using the tax rate information on page 640. Indicate the amount of tax due (or refund to be received).

Problem 16-4
Corporation tax
return

Riverbend Corporation had total revenue for the year of $304,000. Included in this amount were dividends of $6,000 received from domestic corporations. Expenses of the company for the year were as follows:

Advertising expense	$ 18,800
Depreciation expense	6,400
Property taxes expense	4,500
Rent expense	34,000

Salaries expense	110,000
Travel expense	8,400
Utilities expense	6,900

Instructions

a Prepare an income statement for the corporation. Show Dividends Received as a separate item following Income from Operations. Reference the amount for Income Tax Expense to a separate supporting schedule as called for in b below.

b Compute Riverbend's total income tax for the year in a schedule which begins with "Income before income taxes," and shows all details of the tax computation.

**Problem 16-5
Interperiod income tax allocation**

The following summary amounts reflect the operations of Dunleer Corporation for the year 1989.

Net sales	$1,185,000
Cost of goods sold	630,000
Selling expenses	100,000
Administrative expenses	50,000

In addition to the selling expenses shown above, Dunleer Corporation incurred a cost of $65,000 during the year for a sales promotion campaign for a new line of products. The $65,000 cost of this sales campaign will be deducted in computing taxable income for 1989, but the company has chosen to defer this $65,000 expenditure for accounting purposes so that it may be charged against revenue during 1990 when sales of the new product line will be reflected in revenue. The company will follow tax allocation procedures in reporting the income taxes expense in the income statement during 1989.

In 1990, revenue was $1,400,000. The total of cost of goods sold and expenses (including the $65,000 of sales promotion cost deferred from 1989 amounted to $1,000,000.

Instructions

a Prepare an income statement for Dunleer Corporation for 1989. In a separate supporting schedule, show your computation of the provision for federal income taxes for 1989. In computing the tax, use the short-cut method of multiplying the entire taxable income by 34%.

b Prepare the journal entry which should be made to record Dunleer's current income taxes expense, the current income tax liability, and the deferred income tax liability at the end of 1989.

c Prepare the journal entry needed at December 31, 1990, to record the company's current income taxes expense for 1990. (Again, use the short-cut method to compute income tax expense.)

Business decision cases

**Case 16-1
Investors choose between debt and equity**

Bill and Hannah Bailey own a successful small company, Bailey Corporation. The outstanding capital stock consists of 1,000 shares of $100 par value, of which 400 shares are owned by Bill and 600 by Hannah. In order to finance a new branch operation, the corporation needs an additional $100,000 in cash. Bill and Hannah have this amount on deposit with a savings and loan association and intend to put these personal funds into the corporation in order to establish the new branch. They will either arrange for the corporation to issue to them at par an additional 1,000 shares of stock, or they will make a loan to the corporation at an interest rate of 12%.

Income before taxes of the corporation has been consistently averaging $150,000 a year, and annual dividends of $64,000 have been paid regularly. It is expected that the new branch will cause *income before taxes* to increase by $30,000. If new common stock is issued to finance the expansion, the total annual dividend of $64,000 will be continued unchanged. If a loan of $100,000 is arranged, the dividend will be reduced by $12,000, the amount of annual interest on the loan.

Instructions

a From the standpoint of the individual income tax return which Bill and Hannah file jointly, would there be any savings as between the stock issuance and the loan? Explain.

b From the standpoint of getting their money out of the corporation (assuming that the new branch is profitable), should Bill and Hannah choose capital stock or a loan for the infusion of new funds to the corporation?

c Prepare a two-column schedule, with one column headed If New Stock is Used and the other headed If Loan Is Used. For each of these proposed methods of financing, show (1) the present corporate income *before taxes;* (2) the corporate income *before taxes* after the expansion; (3) the corporate income taxes after the expansion; and (4) the corporate net income after the expansion.

Case 16-2
Tax advantage:
single proprietor-
ship versus
corporation

Gary and Joy Allen, a married couple, are in the process of organizing a business which is expected to produce, before any compensation to the Allens and before income taxes, an income of $72,000 per year. In deciding whether to operate as a single proprietorship or as a corporation, the Allens are willing to make the choice on the basis of the relative income tax advantage under either form of organization.

The Allens file a joint return, have no other dependents, and have itemized deductions of $8,800 for the year.

If the business is operated as a single proprietorship, the Allens expect to withdraw the entire income of $72,000 each year. Of this $72,000 total, the amount of $42,000 is considered a fair payment for the personal services rendered by the Allens, that is, $21,000 each.

If the business is operated as a corporation, the Allens will own all the shares; they will pay themselves salaries of $21,000 each and will withdraw as dividends the entire amount of the corporation's net income after income taxes.

It may be assumed that the accounting income and the taxable income for the corporation would be the same and that the personal exemption is $2,000. Mr. and Mrs. Allen have only minor amounts of nonbusiness income, which may be ignored.

Instructions. Determine the relative income tax advantage to the Allens of operating either as a single proprietorship or as a corporation, and make a recommendation as to the form of organization they should adopt. Use the individual (joint return) and corporate tax rate information given on pages 640 and 645.

To provide a basis for this recommendation, you should prepare two schedules: one for operation as a single proprietorship, and one for operation as a corporation.

In the first schedule, compute the total income tax on the Allens' joint personal return when the business is operated as a proprietorship. Also show the Allens' disposable income, that is, the amount withdrawn minus personal income tax.

In the second schedule, compute the corporate income tax and the amount remaining for dividends. Also compute the Allens' *personal* income tax if the corporate form of business entity is used. From these two steps, you can determine the Allens' disposable income under the corporate form of operation.

Appendix A
Applications of present value

Several preceding chapters have included brief references to the concept of present value in discussions of the valuation of certain assets and liabilities. The purpose of this appendix is to discuss this concept more fully and also to demonstrate the use of present value tables as an aid to making present value computations. In addition, the appendix summarizes in one location the various applications of the present value concept which have been discussed throughout the book. These applications include the valuation of notes payable, estimation of goodwill, computation of bond prices, and accounting for capital lease transactions.

After studying this appendix you should be able to meet these Learning Objectives:

1 **Explain the concept of present value.**
2 **Identify the three factors that affect the present value of a future amount.**
3 **Compute the present value of a future amount and of an annuity using present value tables.**
4 **Discuss accounting applications of the present value concept.**

The concept of present value

1 Explain the concept of present value.

The concept of present value has many applications in accounting, but it is most easily explained in the context of evaluating investment opportunities. In this context, the present value of an expected future cash receipt is the amount that a knowledgeable investor would pay **today** for the right to receive that future amount. The present value is always **less** than the future amount, because the investor will expect to earn a return on the investment. The amount by which the future cash receipt exceeds its present value represents the investor's profit; in short, this difference may be regarded as **interest revenue** included in the future amount.

2 Identify the three factors that affect the present value of a future amount.

The present value of a particular investment opportunity depends upon three factors: (1) the expected dollar amount to be received in the future, (2) the length of time until the future amount will be received, and (3) the rate of return (called the **discount rate**) required by the investor. The process of determining the present value of a future cash receipt or payment is called **discounting** the future amount.

667

To illustrate the present value concept, assume that a specific investment is expected to result in a $1,000 cash receipt at the end of one year. An investor requiring a 10% annual rate of return would be willing to pay $909 today (computed as $1,000 ÷ 1.10) for the right to receive this future amount. This computation may be verified as follows (amounts rounded to the nearest dollar):

Amount to be invested (present value)	$ 909
Required return on investment ($909 × 10%).....................................	91
Amount to be received in one year (future value)	$1,000

If the $1,000 is to be received **two years** in the future, the investor would pay only $826 for the investment today [($1,000 ÷ 1.10) ÷ 1.10]. This computation may be verified as follows (amounts rounded to the nearest dollar):

Amount to be invested (present value)	$ 826
Required return on investment in first year ($826 × 10%)	83
Amount invested after one year..	$ 909
Required return on investment in second year ($909 × 10%)	91
Amount to be received in two years (future value)	$1,000

The amount that our investor would pay today, $826, is the **present value** of $1,000 to be received two years later, discounted at an annual rate of 10%. The $174 difference between the $826 present value and the $1,000 future amount may be regarded as the return (interest revenue) to be earned by the investor over the two-year period.

Present value tables

Although we can compute the present value of future amounts by a series of divisions as illustrated above, a more convenient method is available. We can use a **table of present values** to find the present value of $1 at a specified discount rate and then multiply that value by the future amount. For example, in **Table 1** on the next page, the present value of $1 to be received in two years, discounted at an annual rate of 10%, is $0.826. If we multiply .826 by the expected future cash receipt of $1,000, we get an answer of $826, the same amount produced by the series of divisions in our previous illustration.

Selecting an appropriate discount rate

The **discount rate** may be viewed as the investor's required rate of return. All investments involve some degree of risk that actual future cash flows may turn out to be less than expected. Investors usually will expect a rate of return which justifies taking this risk. Under today's market conditions, investors require annual returns of between 6% and 9% on low-risk investments, such as government bonds and certificates of deposit. For relatively high-risk investments, such as the introduction of a new product line, investors may expect to earn an annual return of perhaps 15% or more.

TABLE 1
Present Values of $1 Due in *n* Periods*

Number of Periods (*n*)	1%	1½%	5%	6%	10%	12%	15%	20%
					Discount Rate			
1	.990	.985	.952	.943	.909	.893	.870	.833
2	.980	.971	.907	.890	.826	.797	.756	.694
3	.971	.956	.864	.840	.751	.712	.658	.579
4	.961	.942	.823	.792	.683	.636	.572	.482
5	.951	.928	.784	.747	.621	.567	.497	.402
6	.942	.915	.746	.705	.564	.507	.432	.335
7	.933	.901	.711	.665	.513	.452	.376	.279
8	.923	.888	.677	.627	.467	.404	.327	.233
9	.914	.875	.645	.592	.424	.361	.284	.194
10	.905	.862	.614	.558	.386	.322	.247	.162
20	.820	.742	.377	.312	.149	.104	.061	.026
24	.788	.700	.310	.247	.102	.066	.035	.013

* The present value of $1 may be computed by the formula $p = 1/(1 + i)^n$, where p is the present value of $1, i is the discount rate, and n is the number of periods until the future cash flow will occur. Amounts in this table have been rounded to three decimal places and are shown for a limited number of periods and discount rates.

In addition to the amount of risk involved, the "appropriate" discount rate for determining the present value of a specific investment depends upon the investor's cost of capital and the returns available from other investment opportunities. When a higher discount rate is used, the resulting present value will be lower and the investor, therefore, will be interested in the investment only at a lower price.

Discounting annual cash flows

3 Compute the present value of a future amount and of an annuity using present value tables.

Let us now assume that an investment is expected to produce an annual net cash flow of $10,000 for each of the next three years. If Camino Company expects a 12% return on this type of investment, it may compute the present value of these cash flows as follows:

Year	Expected Net Cash Flow	×	Present Value of $1 Discounted at 12%	=	Present Value of Net Cash Flows
1	$10,000		.893		$ 8,930
2	10,000		.797		7,970
3	10,000		.712		7,120
Total present value of the investment					$24,020

This analysis indicates that the present value of the expected net cash flows from the investment, discounted at an annual rate of 12%, amounts to $24,020. This is the maximum amount that Camino Company could afford to pay for this investment and still expect to earn the 12% required rate of return.

In the preceding schedule, we multiplied each of the expected annual cash flows by the present value of $1 in the appropriate future period, discounted at 12% per year. The present values of the annual cash flows were then added to determine the total present value of the investment. Separately discounting each annual cash flow to its present value is necessary only when the cash flows vary in amount from one year to the next. Since the annual cash flows in our example are **uniform in amount,** there are two easier ways to compute the total present value.

One way is to add the three decimal figures representing the present value of $1 in the successive years (.893 + .797 + .712) and then to multiply this total (2.402) by the $10,000 annual cash flow. This approach produces the same result ($10,000 × 2.402 = $24,020) we obtained by determining the present value of each year's cash flow separately and adding the results.

An even easier approach to determining the present value of uniform annual cash flows is to refer to an **annuity table,** which shows the present value of **$1 to be received periodically** for a given number of periods. An annuity table is shown below:

TABLE 2
Present Value of $1 to Be Received Periodically for n Periods

Number of Periods (n)	1%	1½%	5%	6%	10%	12%	15%	20%
1	0.990	0.985	0.952	0.943	0.909	0.893	0.870	0.833
2	1.970	1.956	1.859	1.833	1.736	1.690	1.626	1.528
3	2.941	2.912	2.723	2.673	2.487	2.402	2.283	2.106
4	3.902	3.854	3.546	3.465	3.170	3.037	2.855	2.589
5	4.853	4.783	4.329	4.212	3.791	3.605	3.352	2.991
6	5.795	5.697	5.076	4.917	4.355	4.111	3.784	3.326
7	6.728	6.598	5.786	5.582	4.868	4.564	4.160	3.605
8	7.652	7.486	6.463	6.210	5.335	4.968	4.487	3.837
9	8.566	8.361	7.108	6.802	5.759	5.328	4.772	4.031
10	9.471	9.222	7.722	7.360	6.145	5.650	5.019	4.192
20	18.046	17.169	12.462	11.470	8.514	7.469	6.259	4.870
24	21.243	20.030	13.799	12.550	8.985	7.784	6.434	4.937

Note that the present value of $1 to be received periodically (annually) for three years, discounted at 12% per year, is 2.402. Thus, $10,000 received annually for three years, discounted at 12%, is $24,020 ($10,000 × 2.402).

Discount periods of less than one year

The interval between regular periodic cash flows is termed the **discount period.** In our preceding examples we have assumed annual cash flows and, therefore, discount periods of one year. Often a note or a contract may call for cash payments on a more frequent basis, such as monthly, quarterly, or semiannually. The illustrated present value tables can be used with discount periods of any length, **but the discount rate must relate to the time interval of the discount period.** Thus, if we use the annuity table to find the present value of a series of monthly cash payments, the discount rate must be expressed as a monthly interest rate.

To illustrate, assume that StyleMart purchases merchandise from Western Fashions, issuing in exchange a $9,600 note payable to be paid in 24 monthly installments of $400 each. StyleMart should record this transaction at the **present value** of the note. If a reasonable **annual** interest rate for this type of note is 12%, we should discount the monthly cash payments at the **monthly** rate of 1%. The annuity table shows the present value of $1 to be received (or paid) for 24 monthly periods, discounted at 1% per month, is 21.243. Thus, the present value of the installment note issued by StyleMart is $8,497 ($400 × 21.243, rounded to the nearest dollar).

Accounting applications of the present value concept

Accounting applications of the concept of present value have been discussed at appropriate points throughout this textbook. We will now demonstrate these applications with examples which make use of our present value tables.

4 Discuss accounting applications of the present value concept.

Valuation of notes payable (Chapter 10). When a note payable does not bear a realistic stated rate of interest, a portion of the face amount of the note should be regarded as representing an interest charge. The amount of this interest charge can be determined by **discounting the note to its present value** using as a discount rate a realistic rate of interest.

To illustrate, consider our preceding example in which StyleMart purchases merchandise from Western Fashions by issuing an installment note payable with a face amount of $9,600 and no stated rate of interest. The present value of this note, discounted at the realistic market interest rate of 1% per month, is $8,497. The difference between the $9,600 face amount of the note and its present value of $8,497 is $1,103, which represents the interest charge included in the face amount. StyleMart should use the **present value** of the note in determining the cost of the merchandise and the amount of the related net liability, as shown by the following entry:

Purchases.	8,497	
Discount on Notes Payable.	1,103	
Notes Payable.		9,600

Purchased merchandise by issuing a 24-month installment note payable with a 1% monthly interest charge included in the face amount.

Assuming that StyleMart uses the effective interest method to amortize the discount on the note, the entry to record the first monthly payment and the related interest expense is as follows:

Notes Payable	400	
Interest Expense	85	
Discount on Notes Payable		85
Cash..		400

To record first monthly payment on installment note payable and recognize one month's interest expense ($8,497 × 1%, rounded to nearest dollar).

Estimating the value of goodwill (Chapter 9). The asset goodwill may be defined as the ***present value*** of expected future earnings in excess of the normal return on net identifiable assets. One method of estimating goodwill is to estimate the annual amounts by which earnings are expected to exceed a normal return and then to discount these amounts to their present value.

For example, assume that John Reed is negotiating to purchase a small but very successful business. In addition to paying the fair market value of the company's net identifiable assets, Reed is willing to pay an appropriate amount for goodwill. He believes that the business will probably earn at least $40,000 in excess of "normal earnings" in each of the next five years. If Reed requires a 20% annual return on purchased goodwill, he would be willing to pay $119,640 for this expected five-year $40,000 annuity, computed as follows: $40,000 × 2.991 (from Table 2) = $119,640.

Market prices of bonds (Chapter 11). The market price of bonds may be regarded as the ***present value*** to bondholders of the future principal and interest payments. To illustrate, assume that a corporation issues $1,000,000 face value of 9%, 10-year bonds when the going market rate of interest is 10%. Since bond interest is paid semiannually, we must use 20 ***semiannual*** periods as the life of the bond issue and a 5% ***semiannual*** market rate of interest in our present value calculations. The expected issuance price of this bond issue may be computed as follows:

Present value of future principal payments:
  $1,000,000 due after 20 semiannual periods, discounted at 5% per period:
    $1,000,000 × .377 (from Table 1, page 669) $377,000
Present value of future interest payments:
  45,000 per period ($1,000,000 × 9% × ½) for 20 semiannual periods, discounted at
    5%: $45,000 × 12.462 (from Table 2, page 670)............................. <u>560,790</u>
Expected issuance price of bond issue*....................................... <u>$937,790</u>

* The terms of this bond issue correspond with those of the bond issue illustrated in the amortization table on page 435 in Chapter 11. In the amortization table, however, the issuance price of the bonds is $937,689, or $101 less than indicated by our computations above. The difference results from our rounding the present value of $1 to only three decimal places. Rounding to three decimal places may cause an error of up to $500 per $1 million.

Capital leases (Chapter 11). A capital lease is regarded as a sale of the leased asset by the lessor to the lessee. At the date of this sale, the lessor recognizes sales revenue equal to the ***present value*** of the future lease payments receivable, discounted at a realistic rate of interest. The lessee also uses the present value of the future payments to determine the cost of the leased asset and the valuation of the related liability.

To illustrate, assume that on December 1, Kelly Grading Co. enters into a capital lease contract to finance the purchase of a bulldozer from Midwest Tractor Sales. The terms of the lease call for 24 monthly payments of $7,000 each, beginning on December 31. These lease payments include an interest charge of $1\frac{1}{2}\%$ per month. At the end of the 24-month lease, title to the bulldozer will pass to Kelly Grading Co.

The annuity table on page 670 shows that the present value of $1 to be received monthly for 24 months, discounted at $1\frac{1}{2}\%$ per month, is 20.030. Therefore, the present value of the 24 future lease payments is $7,000 × 20.030, or $140,210. Kelly Grading Co. (the lessee) should use this present value in determining the cost of the bulldozer and the amount of the related liability, as shown in the following entry:

Entry by lessee

Leased Equipment	140,210	
Lease Payment Obligation		140,210

To record acquisition of bulldozer from Midwest Tractor Sales on a capital lease. Lease terms call for 24 monthly payments of $7,000, which include a $1\frac{1}{2}\%$ monthly interest charge.

Note that the cost assigned to the leased equipment is only $140,210, even though Kelly Grading Co. must actually pay $168,000 ($7,000 × 24 payments) over the life of the lease. The difference between these two amounts, $27,790, will be recognized by Kelly Grading Co. as interest expense over the next 24 months.

Midwest Tractor Sales (the lessor) should also use the present value of the future lease payments in determining the sales price of the bulldozer and the amount of the related receivable. Assuming that the bulldozer was carried in the perpetual inventory records at a cost of $110,000, the entry to record the sale is:

Entry by lessor

Lease Payments Receivable (net)	140,210	
Cost of Goods Sold...	110,000	
Inventory...		110,000
Sales..		140,210

Financed sale of bulldozer to Kelly Grading Co. using a capital lease. Terms call for 24 monthly payments of $7,000 including a $1\frac{1}{2}\%$ monthly interest charge. Gross amount of the receivable is $168,000, of which $27,790 is unearned interest.

ASSIGNMENT MATERIAL

Problems

Problem A-1
Use of present
value tables

Use the tables on pages 669 and 670 to determine the present value of the following cash flows:

    a $10,000 to be paid annually for seven years, discounted at an annual rate of 10%.

    b $7,300 to be received today, assuming that money can be invested to earn 15% annually.

    c $800 to be paid monthly for 24 months, with an additional "balloon payment" of $25,000 due at the end of the twenty-fourth month, discounted at a monthly interest rate of $1\frac{1}{2}$%.

    d $35,000 to be received annually for the first three years, followed by $11,000 to be received annually for the next two years (total of five years in which payments are made), discounted at an annual rate of 12%.

Problem A-2
Present value
and bond prices

On June 30 of the current year, Rural Gas & Electric Co. issued $40,000,000 face value, 11%, 10-year bonds payable, with interest dates of December 31 and June 30. The bonds were issued at a discount, resulting in an effective semiannual interest rate of 6%. The company maintains its accounts on a calendar-year basis and amortizes the bond discount by the effective interest method.

Instructions

    a Compute the issuance price for the bond issue which will result in an effective semiannual interest rate of 6%. (Hint: Discount both the interest payments and the maturity value over 20 semiannual periods.)

    b Prepare all journal entries necessary to record the issuance of the bonds and bond interest expense during the current year, assuming that the sales price of the bonds on June 30 was the amount you computed in part a.

Problem A-3
Valuation of a
note payable

On December 1, Showcase Interiors purchased a shipment of furniture from Colonial House by paying $15,000 cash and issuing an installment note payable in the face amount of $48,000. The note is to be paid in 24 monthly installments of $2,000 each. Although the note makes no mention of an interest charge, the rate of interest usually charged to Showcase Interiors in such transactions is $1\frac{1}{4}$% per month.

Instructions

    a Compute the present value of the note payable, using a discount rate of $1\frac{1}{4}$% per month.

    b Prepare the journal entries in the accounts of Showcase Interiors on:

        (1) December 1, to record the purchase of the furniture (debit Purchases).

        (2) December 31, to record the first $2,000 monthly payment on the note and to recognize interest expense for one month by the effective interest method. (Round interest expense to the nearest dollar.)

    c Show how the liability for this note would appear in the balance sheet at December 31. (Assume that the note is classified as a current liability.)

Problem A-4
Discounting lease
agreements to
present value

Metropolitan Transit District plans to acquire a large computer system by entering into a long-term lease agreement with the computer manufacturer. The manufacturer will provide the computer system under either of the following lease agreements:

Five-year lease. MTD is to pay $2,500,000 at the beginning of the lease (delivery date) and $1,000,000 annually at the end of each of the next five years. At the end of the fifth year, MTD may take title to the system for an additional payment of $3,000,000.

Ten-year lease. MTD is to pay $2,000,000 at the beginning of the lease and $900,000 annually at the end of the next 10 years. At the end of the tenth year, MTD may take title for an additional payment of $1,300,000.

Under either proposal, MTD will buy the computer at the end of the lease. MTD is a governmental agency which does not seek to earn a profit and is not evaluating alternative investment opportunities. However, MTD does attempt to minimize its costs and it must borrow the money to finance either lease agreement at an annual interest rate of 10%.

Instructions

  a Determine which lease proposal results in the lower cost for the computer system when the future cash outlays are discounted at an annual interest rate of 10%.
  b Prepare a journal entry to record the acquisition of the computer system under the lease agreement selected in part a. This journal entry will include the initial cash payment to the computer manufacturer required at the beginning of the lease.

Appendix B
Investments for
purposes of control

This appendix addresses situations in which one corporation owns enough of another corporation's voting stock to influence the operations of the owned company. The first topic discussed is the equity method—an accounting technique employed when the investor is able to influence, but not totally control, the activities of the investee. The major topic of the appendix, however, is the preparation of consolidated financial statements when a parent company owns enough stock in a subsidiary corporation to exercise complete control. Consolidated statements portray the parent company and its subsidiaries as if the affiliated corporations were a single economic entity.

1 **Account for an investment in common stock by the equity method.**
2 **Explain how a parent company "controls" its subsidiaries.**
3 **Describe the distinctive feature of consolidated financial statements.**
4 **Explain why intercompany transactions must be eliminated as a step in preparing consolidated financial statements.**
5 **Prepare a consolidated balance sheet.**

As discussed in Chapter 13, a portfolio of marketable securities may include investments in common stock. Marketable securities generally are classified as current assets, and the investor recognizes cash dividends received as investment income. Some investors, however, may own enough of a company's common stock to ***influence or control*** that company's activities through the voting rights of the shares owned. Such large holdings of common stock create an important business relationship between the investor and the issuing company (called the ***investee***). Since investments of this type cannot be sold without disrupting this relationship, they are not included in the portfolio of marketable securities. Such investments are shown in the balance sheet under the caption Long-Term Investments, which follows the current asset section.

If an investor is able to exercise significant influence over the investee's management, dividends paid by the investee may no longer be a good measure of the investor's income from the investment. This is because the investor may influence the investee's dividend policy. In such cases, dividends paid by the investee are likely to reflect the ***investor's*** cash needs and income tax considerations, rather than the profitability of the investment.

For example, assume that Sigma Company owns all the common stock of Davis Company. For three years Davis Company is very profitable but pays no dividends, because Sigma Company has no need for additional cash. In the fourth year, Davis Company pays a large cash dividend to Sigma Company despite operating at a loss for that year. Clearly, it would be misleading for Sigma Company to report no investment income while the company it owns is operating profitably, and then to show large investment income in a year when Davis Company incurred a net loss.

The investor does not have to own 100% of the common stock of the investee to exercise a significant degree of control. An investor with much less than 50% of the voting stock may have influence or even effective control, since the remaining shares are not likely to vote as an organized block. In the absence of other evidence (such as another large stockholder), ownership of ***20% or more*** of the investee's common stock is viewed as giving the investor significant influence over the investee's policies and operations. In such cases, the investor should account for the investment by using the ***equity method.***

The equity method

1 Account for an investment in common stock by the equity method.

When the equity method is used, an investment in common stock is first recorded at cost but later is adjusted each year for changes in the stockholders' equity in the investee. As the investee earns net income, the stockholders' equity in the company increases. An investor using the equity method recognizes its ***proportionate share of the investee's net income*** as an increase in the carrying value of its investment. A proportionate share of a net loss reported by the investee is recognized as a decrease in the investment.

When the investee pays dividends, the stockholders' equity in the company is reduced. The investor, therefore, treats dividends received from the investee as a conversion of the investment into cash, thus reducing the carrying value of the investment. Investments accounted for by the equity method are ***not*** adjusted to the lower of cost or market value. In effect, the equity method causes the carrying value of the investment to rise and fall with changes in the book value of the shares.

Illustration of the equity method. Assume that Cove Corporation purchases 25% of the common stock of Bay Company for $200,000, which corresponds to the underlying book value. During the following year, Bay Company earns net income of $120,000 and pays dividends of $80,000. Cove Corporation would account for its investment as follows:

Investment in Bay Company	200,000	
Cash		200,000

To record acquisition of 25% of the common stock of Bay Company.

Investment in Bay Company	30,000	
Investment Income..		30,000

To increase the investment for 25% share of net income earned by Bay
Company (25% × $120,000).

Cash	20,000	
Investment in Bay Company....................................		20,000

To reduce investment for dividends received from Bay Company (25% ×
$80,000).

The net result of these entries by Cove Corporation is to increase the carrying
value of the investment in Bay Company account by $10,000. This corresponds to
25% of the increase reported in Bay Company's retained earnings during the period
[25% × ($120,000 − $80,000) = $10,000].

In this illustration of the equity method, we have made several simplifying
assumptions: (1) Cove Corporation purchased the stock of Bay Company at a price
equal to the underlying book value; (2) Bay Company had issued common stock
only and the number of shares outstanding did not change during the year; and (3)
there were no intercompany transactions between Cove Corporation and Bay
Company. If we were to change any of these assumptions, the computations in
applying the equity method would become more complicated. Application of the
equity method in more complex situations is discussed in advanced accounting
courses.

CONSOLIDATED FINANCIAL STATEMENTS

Parent and subsidiary companies

2 Explain how a parent company "controls" its subsidiaries.

A corporation which owns **all or a majority** of another corporation's capital
stock is called a **parent** company, and the corporation which is wholly owned or
majority-held is called a **subsidiary**.[1] Through the voting rights of the owned
shares, the parent company can elect the board of directors of the subsidiary
company and thereby control the subsidiary's resources and activities. In effect,
the **affiliated companies** (the parent and its subsidiaries) function as a **single
economic unit** controlled by the directors of the parent company. This relationship is illustrated in the following diagram:

For simplicity, our illustration shows a parent company with only two subsidiaries. It is not unusual, however, for a parent company to own and control a dozen
or more subsidiaries.

[1] Ownership of a **majority** of a company's voting stock means holding at least 50% plus one share.

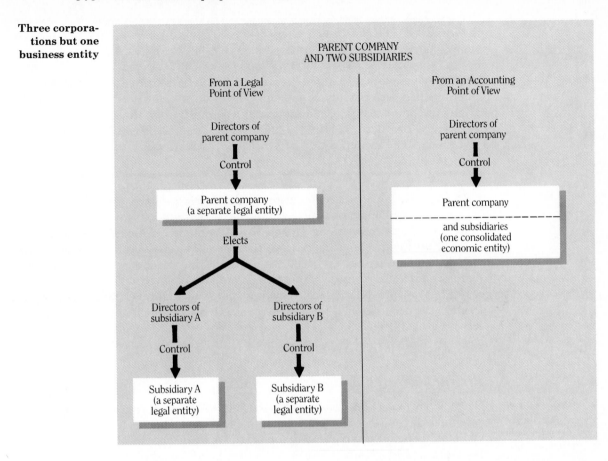

There are a number of economic, legal, and income tax advantages which encourage large business organizations to operate through subsidiaries rather than through a single legal entity. Although we think of Sears, General Electric, or IBM as single companies, each of these organizations is really a parent company with many subsidiaries. Since the parent company in each case controls the resources and activities of its subsidiaries, it is logical for us to consider an organization such as IBM as one *economic* entity.

Growth through the acquisition of subsidiaries

A parent company may acquire another corporation as a subsidiary by purchasing more than 50% of the other corporation's voting stock. The purchase of one corporation by another may be termed a *merger,* a *business combination,* an *acquisition,* or a *takeover.* The acquisition of new subsidiaries is a fast and effective way for a company to grow, to diversify into new product lines, and to acquire new technology. In one recent year, more than 2,500 existing corporations were acquired by other companies at a total cost of over $120 billion.

● **CASE IN POINT** ● Just a few of the large business combinations in recent years: Chevron Corporation greatly increased the size of its oil reserves by acquiring as a subsidiary one of its largest competitors, Gulf Corporation. R. J. Reynolds, a tobacco company, expanded its product line by acquiring the well-known food company, Nabisco Brands. Mobil Oil went into the department store business by acquiring the giant retailer, Montgomery Ward. Eli Lilly, a manufacturer of pharmaceutical products, acquired a "high tech" medical research company called Hybritech, Inc., in hopes that Hybritech's research will lead to important new pharmaceutical products.

The acquisition of one corporation by another is, perhaps, the largest and most interesting of all business transactions. Such transactions may involve billions of dollars, bidding wars among prospective buyers, and dramatic increases in the value of a sought-after company's capital stock. Sometimes a company borrows vast amounts of money and acquires a corporation much larger than itself, thus doubling or tripling the size of the parent company overnight. For example, ABC, a major television network, recently was acquired by Capital Communications, Inc. Prior to the acquisition, Capital Communications was about one-fourth the size of ABC.

Financial statements for a consolidated economic entity

3 Describe the distinctive feature of consolidated financial statements. Because the parent company and its subsidiaries are separate legal entities, separate financial statements are prepared for each company. In the **separate** financial statements of the parent company, the subsidiaries appear only as an asset classified as a long-term investment. Since the affiliated companies function as a single economic unit, the parent company also prepares **consolidated financial statements** which show the financial position and operating results of the **entire group of companies.** It is these consolidated financial statements which are of greatest interest to the investing public and which are included in the parent company's annual report to its stockholders.

In consolidated financial statements, the parent company and its subsidiaries are viewed as **one business entity.** The distinctive feature of these statements is that the assets, liabilities, revenue, and expenses of **two or more separate legal entities** are combined in a single set of financial statements. For example, the amount shown as cash in a consolidated balance sheet is the total of the cash owned by all of the affiliated companies. Liabilities of the parent and subsidiary companies also are combined. Similarly, in a consolidated income statement, the revenue and expenses of the affiliated companies are combined to show the operating results of the consolidated economic entity.

Stockholders and creditors of the parent company have a vital interest in the financial results of all operations under the parent company's control, including those conducted by subsidiaries. Therefore, it is the consolidated financial statements which are included in the parent company's annual and quarterly reports to stockholders. (The separate financial statements of certain major subsidiaries sometimes are presented in footnotes to the consolidated financial statements.)[2]

There are many interesting accounting issues involved in the preparation of consolidated financial statements. A brief introduction to some of these issues is provided in the following section of this chapter. However, **no special problems are posed in reading a set of consolidated financial statements.** The number of separate legal entities within the consolidated organization is an unimportant detail. For most purposes, consolidated financial statements may be interpreted as if the parent companies and its subsidiaries **were just one organization.**

Methods of consolidation

The purchase of an entire corporation usually is a very big investment. To accumulate the money necessary to buy another corporation, the parent company often needs to issue capital stock or bonds payable. If the parent company pays cash or issues debt securities to purchase the other corporation's capital stock, the business combination is accounted for by the **purchase method.**

A second method of accounting for a business combination is called a **pooling of interests.** The pooling method may be appropriate if the stock of a subsidiary is acquired in direct exchange for shares of the parent company's capital stock.[3] A key aspect of such a transaction is that the former stockholders of the subsidiary **become stockholders in the parent corporation.** The vast majority of business combinations are viewed as purchases, rather than poolings. In this textbook, we shall illustrate only the purchase method accounting for business combinations. The special case of a pooling-of-interests will be covered in more advanced accounting courses.

Consolidated financial statements are prepared by combining the amounts that appear in the separate financial statements of the parent and subsidiary companies. In the combining process, however, certain adjustments are made to **eliminate the effects of intercompany transactions** and thus to reflect the assets, liabilities, and stockholders' equity as those of a single economic entity.

4 Explain why intercompany transactions must be eliminated as a step in preparing consolidated financial statements.

Intercompany transactions. The term **intercompany transactions** refers to transactions between affiliated companies. These transactions may include, for example, the sale of merchandise, the leasing of property, and the making of loans.

[2] In the past, some subsidiaries were omitted from the consolidated financial statements because the subsidiaries were engaged in business activities substantially different from those of the parent company. New rules, however, require every subsidiary controlled by the parent company to be included in the consolidated statements unless this control will be temporary. In this case, the investment in the subsidiary is shown in the balance sheet at cost and is classified as a long-term investment.

[3] In addition to the parent company issuing only common stock in exchange for the subsidiary's shares, other specific criteria must be met for the affiliation to qualify as a pooling of interests. For example, at least 90% of the subsidiary's stock must be acquired within one year following the beginning of negotiations. For a more complete discussion of the differences between a purchase and a pooling of interests, see *APB Opinion No. 16,* "Business Combinations," AICPA (New York: 1970).

When the affiliated companies are viewed separately, these transactions may create assets and liabilities for the individual companies. However, when the affiliated companies are viewed as a single business entity, these assets and liabilities are merely the result of internal transfers within the business organization and should not appear in the consolidated financial statements.

For example, if a subsidiary borrows money from the parent company, a note payable will appear as a liability in the balance sheet of the subsidiary company and a note receivable will appear as an asset in the separate balance sheet of the parent. When the two companies are viewed as a single consolidated entity, however, this "loan" is nothing more than a transfer of cash from one part of the business to another. Transferring assets between two parts of a single business entity does not create either a receivable or a payable for that entity. Therefore, the parent company's note receivable and the subsidiary's note payable should not appear in the consolidated financial statements.

Preparing consolidated financial statements. Separate accounting records are maintained for each company in an affiliated group, but no accounting records are maintained for the consolidated entity. The amounts shown in consolidated financial statements *do not come from a ledger;* they are determined on a *working paper* by combining the amounts of like items on the financial statements of the affiliated companies. For example, the inventories of all the affiliated companies are combined into one amount for inventories. Entries to eliminate the effects of intercompany transactions are made *only* on this working paper. These elimination entries are *not recorded in the accounting records* of either the parent company or its subsidiaries.

Consolidation at the date of acquisition

5 Prepare a consolidated balance sheet.

To illustrate the basic principles of consolidation, we will now prepare a consolidated balance sheet. Assume that on January 1, Post Corporation purchases for cash 100% of the capital stock of Sun Company at its book value of $300,000. (The shares are purchased from Sun Company's former stockholders.) Also on this date, Post Corporation lends $40,000 cash to Sun Company, receiving a note as evidence of the loan. Immediately after these two transactions, the separate balance sheet accounts of Post Corporation and Sun Company are as shown in the following working paper:

Intercompany eliminations

Before the balance sheet amounts of Post Corporation and Sun Company are combined, entries are made in the working paper to eliminate the effects of intercompany transactions. Intercompany eliminations may be classified into three basic types:

1 Elimination of intercompany stock ownership
2 Elimination of intercompany debt
3 Elimination of intercompany revenue and expenses

POST CORPORATION AND SUBSIDIARY
Working Paper—Consolidated Balance Sheet
January 1, 19__ (Date of Acquisition)

	Post Corporation	Sun Company	Intercompany Eliminations		Consolidated Balance Sheet
			Debit	Credit	
Cash	60,000	45,000			105,000
Notes receivable	40,000			(b) 40,000	
Accounts receivable (net)	70,000	50,000			120,000
Inventories	110,000	95,000			205,000
Investment in Sun Company	300,000			(a) 300,000	
Plant & equipment (net)	210,000	180,000			390,000
Totals	790,000	370,000			820,000
Notes payable		40,000	(b) 40,000		
Accounts payable	125,000	30,000			155,000
Capital stock—Post Corporation	400,000				400,000
Capital stock—Sun Company.........		200,000	(a) 200,000		
Retained earnings—Post Corporation..	265,000				265,000
Retained earnings—Sun Company		100,000	(a) 100,000		
Totals	790,000	370,000	340,000	340,000	820,000

Explanation of elimination:
(a) To eliminate the Investment in Sun Company against Sun Company's stockholders' equity.
(b) To eliminate intercompany note receivable against related note payable.

The first two types of eliminations are illustrated in our example of Post Corporation and Sun Company. The elimination of intercompany revenue and expenses will be discussed later in this appendix.

To understand the need for elimination entries, we must adopt the viewpoint of the consolidated entity, in which Post Corporation and Sun Company are regarded as two departments within a single company.

Entry (a): Elimination of intercompany stock ownership. The purpose of entry (a) in the illustrated working paper is to eliminate from the consolidated balance sheet both the asset account and the stockholders' equity accounts representing the parent company's ownership of the subsidiary.

Post Corporation's ownership interest in Sun Company appears in the *separate* balance sheets of both corporations. In the parent's balance sheet, this ownership interest is shown as the asset, Investment in Sun Company. In the separate balance sheet of the subsidiary, the parent company's ownership interest is represented by the stockholders' equity accounts, Capital Stock and Retained Earnings. In the *consolidated* balance sheet, however, this "ownership interest" is neither an asset nor a part of stockholders' equity.

From the viewpoint of the single consolidated entity, *there are no stockholders in Sun Company.* "Stockholders" are outside investors who have an ownership interest in the business. All of Sun Company's capital stock is "internally owned" by another part of the consolidated entity. A company's "ownership" of its own stock does not create either an asset or stockholders' equity. Therefore the asset account, Investment in Sun Company, and Sun Company's related stockholders' equity accounts must be eliminated from the consolidated balance sheet.

Entry (b): Elimination of intercompany debt. When Post Corporation loaned $40,000 to Sun Company, the parent company recorded a note receivable and the subsidiary recorded a note payable. This "receivable" and "payable" exist only when Post Corporation and Sun Company are viewed as two separate entities. When both corporations are viewed as a single company, this "loan" is merely a transfer of cash from one part of the business to another. Such internal transfers of assets do not create either a receivable or a payable for the consolidated entity. Therefore, entry (b) is made to eliminate Post Corporation's note receivable and Sun Company's note payable from the consolidated balance sheet.

After the necessary eliminations have been entered in the working paper, the remaining balance sheet amounts of Post Corporation and Sun Company are combined to determine the assets, liabilities, and stockholders' equity of the consolidated entity. The following consolidated balance sheet is then prepared from the working paper.

POST CORPORATION AND SUBSIDIARY
Consolidated Balance Sheet
January 1, 19__

Assets

Note stockholders' equity is that of the parent company

Current assets:	
Cash	$105,000
Accounts receivable (net)	120,000
Inventories	205,000
Total current assets	$430,000
Plant & equipment (net)	390,000
Total assets	$820,000

Liabilities & Stockholders' Equity

Current liabilities:		
Accounts payable		$155,000
Stockholders' equity:		
Capital stock	$400,000	
Retained earnings	265,000	
Total stockholders' equity		665,000
Total liabilities & stockholders' equity		$820,000

Acquisition of subsidiary's stock at a price above book value

When a parent company purchases a controlling interest in a subsidiary, it usually pays a price for the shares in excess of their book value.[4] We cannot ignore a difference between the cost of the parent company's investment and the underlying book value of these shares. In consolidation, the parent's investment is offset against the stockholders' equity accounts of the subsidiary, and if the two amounts are not equal, we must determine what the difference between them represents.

To illustrate, assume that C Company purchases all of the outstanding shares of D Company for $980,000. At the date of acquisition, D Company's balance sheet shows total stockholders' equity of $700,000, consisting of capital stock of $300,000 and retained earnings of $400,000. In preparing the elimination entry on the working papers for a consolidated balance sheet, we must determine what to do with the $280,000 difference between the price paid, $980,000, and the stockholders' equity of D Company, $700,000.

Why would C Company pay a price in excess of book value for D Company's stock? C Company's management must believe that either (1) the fair market value of certain specific assets of D Company (such as land or buildings) is in excess of book value, or (2) D Company's future earnings prospects are so favorable as to justify paying $280,000 for D Company's unrecorded *goodwill.*

If we assume that the $280,000 represents unrecorded goodwill, the entry in the working papers to eliminate C Company's investment account against the stockholders' equity accounts of D Company would be:

Elimination entry when price paid for shares of subsidiary exceeds their book value	Capital Stock — D Company.	300,000	
	Retained Earnings — D Company	400,000	
	Goodwill	280,000	
	Investment in D Company (C Company's asset account).		980,000
	To eliminate the cost of C Company's 100% interest in D Company against D's stockholders' equity accounts and to recognize D Company's unrecorded goodwill.		

(Although we have shown this entry in general journal form, it actually would be made only in the Intercompany Eliminations columns of the working paper for a consolidated balance sheet.)

The $280,000 of goodwill will appear as an asset in the consolidated balance sheet.[5] This asset will be amortized to expense over its useful life.

---

[4] The parent company also might acquire the shares of the subsidiary at a price below book value. This situation will be discussed in an advanced accounting course.

[5] If specific assets of D Company had been undervalued, the $280,000 would be allocated to increase the valuation of those assets in the consolidated working papers. The revaluation of specific assets is beyond the scope of our introductory discussion.

Less than 100% ownership in subsidiary

If a parent company owns a majority interest in a subsidiary but less than 100% of the outstanding shares, a new kind of ownership equity known as the *minority interest* will appear in the consolidated balance sheet. This minority interest represents the ownership interest in the subsidiary held by stockholders other than the parent company.

When there are minority stockholders, only the portion of the subsidiary's stockholders' equity owned by the parent company is eliminated. The remainder of the stockholders' equity of the subsidiary is included in the consolidated balance sheet under the caption Minority Interest.

To illustrate, assume that on December 31, Park Company purchases 75% of the outstanding capital stock of Sims Company for $150,000 cash, an amount equal to the book value of the stock acquired. The working paper to prepare a consolidated balance sheet on the date that control of Sims Company is acquired appears below:

PARK COMPANY AND SUBSIDIARY
Working Paper—Consolidated Balance Sheet
December 31, 19__ (Date of Acquisition)

	Park Company	Sims Company	Intercompany Eliminations Debit	Intercompany Eliminations Credit	Consolidated Balance Sheet
Cash	200,000	50,000			250,000
Other assets................................	500,000	210,000			710,000
Investment in Sims Company...................	150,000			(a) 150,000	
Totals	850,000	260,000			960,000
Liabilities	250,000	60,000			310,000
Capital stock — Park Company	500,000				500,000
Capital stock — Sims Company.................		120,000	(a) 90,000 (b) 30,000		
Retained earnings — Park Company..............	100,000				100,000
Retained earnings — Sims Company		80,000	(a) 60,000 (b) 20,000		
Minority interest (25% of $200,000)				(b) 50,000	50,000
Totals	850,000	260,000	200,000	(b) 200,000	960,000

Explanation of elimination:
(a) To eliminate Park Company's investment in 75% of Sims Company's stockholders' equity.
(b) To classify the remaining 25% of Sims Company's stockholders' equity as a minority interest.

Entry (a) in this working paper offsets Park Company's asset, Investment in Sims Company, against 75% of Sims Company's capital stock and retained earnings. The purpose of this entry is to eliminate intercompany stock ownership from the assets and stockholders' equity shown in the consolidated balance sheet. Entry (b) reclassifies the remaining 25% of Sims Company's capital stock and retained earnings into a special stockholders' equity account entitled Minority Interest. The

FASB has recommended that the minority interest appear in the stockholders' equity section of the consolidated balance sheet as shown below:[6]

Stockholders' equity:	
Capital stock	$500,000
Minority interest	50,000
Retained earnings	100,000
Total stockholders' equity	$650,000

Minority interest. Why is the minority interest shown separately in the consolidated balance sheet instead of being included in the amounts shown for capital stock and retained earnings? The reason for this separate presentation is to distinguish between the ownership equity of the controlling stockholders and the equity of the minority stockholders.

The stockholders in the parent company own the controlling interest in the consolidated entity. Because these stockholders elect the directors of the parent company, they control the entire group of affiliated companies. The minority interest, however, has **no control** over any of the affiliated companies. Because they own shares only in a subsidiary, they cannot vote for the directors of the parent company. Also, they can never outvote the majority stockholder (the parent company) in electing the directors or establishing the policies of the subsidiary.

The minority stockholders receive 25% of the dividends declared by Sims Company but do not participate in dividends declared by the parent company. The controlling stockholders, on the other hand, receive all the dividends declared by Park Company but do not receive dividends declared by the subsidiary.

Consolidated income statement

A consolidated income statement is prepared by combining the revenue and expense accounts of the parent and subsidiary. Revenue and expenses arising from **intercompany transactions** are eliminated because they reflect transfers of assets from one affiliated company to another and do not change the net assets from a consolidated viewpoint.

Elimination of intercompany revenue and expenses. Some of the more common examples of intercompany items that should be eliminated in preparing a consolidated income statement are:

1 Sales to affiliated companies
2 Cost of goods sold resulting from sales to affiliated companies
3 Interest expense on loans from affiliated companies

---

[6] Some companies emphasize the limited ownership of the minority stockholders by showing the minority interest as a liability or placed between the liabilities section and the stockholders' equity section of the consolidated balance sheet. However, the FASB supports the classification of minority interest as stockholders' equity. See *FASB Statement of Financial Accounting Concepts No. 3,* "Elements of Financial Statements of Business Enterprise" (Stamford, Conn.: 1980), para. 179.

4 Interest revenue on loans made to affiliated companies

5 Rent or other revenue received for services rendered to affiliated companies

6 Rent or other expenses paid for services received from affiliated companies

Because of the complexity of the intercompany eliminations, the preparation of a consolidated income statement and a consolidated statement of retained earnings are topics appropriately deferred to an advanced accounting course.

Accounting for investment in corporate securities: a summary

In this chapter, we have discussed investments in marketable securities, investments accounted for by the equity method, and investments in subsidiaries which are shown in the financial statements on a consolidated basis. The accounting treatment of an investment in stock depends primarily upon the ***degree of control*** which the investor is able to exercise over the issuing corporation. These relationships are summarized below:

Degree of Control	General Practice
1 Controlling interest (ownership of more than 50% of voting stock)	The assets, liabilities, revenue, and expenses of controlled subsidiaries are combined with those of the parent company in consolidated financial statements.
2 Influential but noncontrolling interest (ownership of between 20% and 50% of voting stock)	Show as a long-term investment, accounted for by the equity method.
3 Noninfluential interest (ownership of less than 20% of voting stock)	Show as a marketable security (may be classified as a current asset or long-term investment). Portfolio of marketable equity securities is valued at lower of total cost or market.

ASSIGNMENT MATERIAL

Problems

**Problem B-1
Accounting terminology**

Listed below are nine technical accounting terms introduced or emphasized in this appendix:

Consolidated financial statements	Intercompany debt	Elimination of intercompany
Parent company	Minority interest	transactions
Goodwill	Investee	Equity method
		Subsidiary

Each of the following statements may (or may not) describe one of these technical terms. For each statement, indicate the accounting term described, or answer "None" if the statement does not correctly describe any of the terms.

a A separate legal entity owned and controlled by another corporation.

b An accounting procedure which is a necessary step in preparing consolidated financial statements, but which does not involve making entries in the ledger accounts.

c A single set of financial statements showing the assets, liabilities, revenue, and expenses of all companies in a given industry.

d A corporation which owns at least 20% of the voting shares of another company, but which does not have controlling interest in that company.

e Procedures used to account for an investment which gives a corporate investor significant influence over the policies of another corporation.

f An unrecorded asset that often explains why a parent company pays far more than book value to acquire the capital stock of a subsidiary.

g The equity in a subsidiary held by stockholders other than the parent company.

Problem B-2
The equity
method

On January 1, 1989, City Broadcasting purchases 25% of the common stock of News Service, Inc., for $250,000, which corresponds to the underlying book value. News Service, Inc., has issued common stock only. At December 31, News Service, Inc., reported net income for the year of $140,000 and paid cash dividends of $60,000. City Broadcasting uses the equity method to account for this investment.

Instructions

a Prepare all journal entries in the accounting records of City Broadcasting relating to the investment during 1989.

b During 1990, News Service, Inc., reports a net loss of $110,000 and pays no dividends. Compute the carrying value of City Broadcasting's investment in News Service, Inc., at the **end of 1990.**

Problem B-3
Computing
consolidated
amounts

Selected account balances from the separate balance sheets of Adams Corporation and its wholly owned subsidiary, Baker Company, are shown below:

	Adams Corporation	Baker Company	Consolidated Balances
Accounts receivable............................	$ 300,000	$ 170,000	$
Accrued rent receivable — Adams Corporation....		6,000	
Investment in Baker Company...................	1,740,000		
Accounts payable..............................	310,000	150,000	
Accrued expenses payable.....................	11,000		
Bonds payable................................	1,400,000	900,000	
Capital stock	2,000,000	1,000,000	
Retained earnings.............................	1,220,000	740,000	

Adams Corporation owes Baker Company $6,000 in accrued rent payable and Baker Company owes Adams Corporation $30,000 on account for services rendered.

Instructions. Indicate the amount that should appear in the consolidated balance sheet for each of these selected accounts. If the account would not appear in the consolidated balance sheet, enter -0- as the consolidated account balance. Show supporting computations.

Problem B-4
Preparing a con-
solidated balance
sheet; minority
interest

On June 30, P Company purchased 70% of the stock of S Company for $420,000 in cash. The separate condensed balance sheets immediately after the purchase are shown below:

	P Company	S Company
Cash..	$ 130,000	$ 90,000
Investment in S Company	420,000	
Other assets	2,250,000	710,000
	$2,800,000	$800,000
Liabilities	$ 600,000	$200,000
Capital stock	1,200,000	400,000
Retained earnings..	1,000,000	200,000
	$2,800,000	$800,000

Instructions. Prepare a consolidated balance sheet immediately after P Company acquired control of S Company.

Problem B-5
Preparing a con-
solidated balance
sheet

On June 30, 19__, Marina Restaurants paid $1 million cash to acquire all the outstanding capital stock of Pelican Pier. Immediately *before* this acquisition, the condensed separate balance sheets of the two companies were as shown below. (As these balance sheets were prepared immediately *before* the acquisition, the current assets of Marina Restaurants still include the $1 million in cash which will be paid to acquire Pelican Pier.)

Assets	Marina Restaurants	Pelican Pier
Current assets...	$1,980,000	$ 320,000
Plant and equipment.......................................	1,620,000	900,000
Total assets...	$3,600,000	$1,220,000

Liabilities & Stockholders' Equity		
Current liabilities..	$ 540,000	$ 180,000
Long-term debt..	1,300,000	200,000
Capital stock	600,000	300,000
Retained earnings	1,160,000	540,000
Total liabilities & stockholders' equity	$3,600,000	$1,220,000

The excess of the $1 million purchase price over the book value of Pelican Pier's shares is regarded as payment for Pelican Pier's unrecorded goodwill.

Instructions. Prepare a consolidated balance sheet for Marina Restaurants and its newly acquired subsidiary (Pelican Pier) on June 30, 19__, the date of acquisition.

Problem B-6
Working papers
for a consolidated
balance sheet;
includes minority
interest

The balance sheet accounts for Entertainment Tonight and Charlie's Pub at December 31 appear below:

Assets	Entertainment Tonight	Charlie's Pub
Cash	$ 55,000	$ 20,000
Accounts receivable	85,000	5,000
Inventories	60,000	45,000
Investment in Charlie's Pub stock (equity method).	133,000	
Plant and equipment	274,000	195,000
Accumulated depreciation	(50,000)	(35,000)
Total assets	$557,000	$230,000

Liabilities & Stockholders' Equity

	Entertainment Tonight	Charlie's Pub
Accounts payable	$ 65,000	$ 40,000
Common stock, no par value	300,000	100,000
Retained earnings	192,000	90,000
Total liabilities & stockholders' equity	$557,000	$230,000

Additional information

(1) Entertainment Tonight owns 70% of the capital stock of Charlie's Pub, which was purchased for cash at a price equal to its book value.
(2) Charlie's Pub owes Entertainment Tonight $6,000 in accrued rent payable. This amount is included in the accounts payable of the subsidiary and the accounts receivable of the parent company.

Instructions. Prepare a working paper for a consolidated balance sheet at December 31, 19__. Use the form illustrated on page 686. Include at the bottom of the working paper explanations of the elimination entries.

Appendix C
International accounting and foreign currency translation

This appendix addresses some special accounting issues encountered by companies which conduct part of their business in foreign countries or in foreign currencies. First, we discuss the meaning of currency exchange rates and the reasons that cause these rates to fluctuate. The accounting for purchases and sales of merchandise in transactions that span national boundaries is illustrated and explained. Special attention is given to gains and losses caused by fluctuations in exchange rates.

After studying this appendix you should be able to meet these Learning Objectives:

1 **Translate an amount of foreign currency into the equivalent number of U.S. dollars.**
2 **Explain why exchange rates fluctuate and what is meant by a "strong" or a "weak" currency.**
3 **Compute the gain or loss on a receivable or payable stated in terms of a foreign currency when exchange rates fluctuate.**
4 **Explain how fluctuations in foreign exchange rates affect companies with receivables or with payables stated in terms of foreign currencies.**

From what geographical area does Bank of America — the largest bank in California — earn most of its revenue? The answer is abroad — that is, from its operations in foreign countries. Bank of America is not alone in its pursuit of business on a worldwide basis. Most large corporations, such as Exxon, IBM, Volkswagen, and Sony, do business in many countries. Coca-Cola, for example, has operations in more than 150 countries throughout the world. Companies that do business in more than one country often are described as *multinational* corporations. The extent to which foreign sales contributed to the revenue of several well-known multinational corporations in a recent year is shown below:

Company	Headquarters	Total Revenue (in Millions)	% Earned from Foreign Operations
Nestles	Switzerland	$13,626	97.2
Sony	Japan	4,528	74.5
Exxon	USA	97,173	71.4
Volkswagen	W. Germany	15,427	67.9
Bank of America	USA	14,955	53.8
British Petroleum	Great Britain	51,353	52.3
IBM	USA	34,364	44.6
Coca-Cola	USA	6,250	42.7

Most large and well-known multinational corporations are headquartered in the highly industrialized countries, such as the United States, Japan, Great Britain, and the countries of Western Europe. Virtually every country, however, has many companies that engage in international business activity.

What is international accounting?

Accounting for business activities that span national borders comprises the field of international accounting. In this appendix, we emphasize accounting for transactions with foreign companies. We also briefly discuss some of the problems of preparing consolidated financial statements for American-based companies with subsidiaries located in foreign countries. Our discussion is limited to basic concepts; the details and complexities of international accounting will be covered in advanced accounting courses.

Foreign currencies and exchange rates

One of the principal problems in international accounting arises because every country uses a different currency. Assume, for example, that a Japanese company sells merchandise to an American corporation. The Japanese company will want to be paid in Japanese currency—yen, but the American company's bank account contains U.S. dollars. Thus, one currency must be converted into another.

Most banks participate in an international currency exchange, which enables them to buy foreign currencies at the prevailing *exchange rate.* Thus, our American corporation can pay its liability to the Japanese company through the international banking system. The American company will pay its bank in dollars. The bank will then use these dollars to purchase the required amount of yen on the international currency exchange and will arrange for delivery of the yen to the Japanese company's bank.[1]

---

[1] Alternatively, the American company may send the Japanese company a check (or a bank draft) stated in dollars. The Japanese company can then arrange to have the dollars converted into yen through its bank in Japan.

Exchange rates. A currency exchange rate is the ratio at which one currency may be converted into another. Thus, the exchange rate may be viewed as the "price" of buying units of foreign currency, stated in terms of the domestic currency (which for our purpose is U.S. dollars). Exchange rates fluctuate daily, based upon the worldwide supply and demand for particular currencies. The current exchange rate between the dollar and most major currencies is published daily in the financial press. For example, a few of the exchange rates recently listed in ***The Wall Street Journal*** are shown below:

Country	Currency	Exchange Rate (in Dollars)
Britain	Pound (£)	$1.7730
France	French franc (FF)	.1772
Japan	Yen (¥)	.0080
Mexico	Peso ($)	.0005
West Germany	Deutsche mark (DM)	.5974

1 Translate an amount of foreign currency into the equivalent number of U.S. dollars.

Exchange rates may be used to determine how much of one currency is equivalent to a given amount of another currency. Assume that the American company in our preceding example owes the Japanese company 1 million yen (expressed ¥1,000,000). How many dollars are needed to settle this obligation, assuming that the current exchange rate is $.0080 per yen? To restate an amount of foreign currency in terms of the equivalent amount of U.S. dollars, we multiply the foreign currency amount by the exchange rate, as illustrated below:[2]

Amount Stated in Foreign Currency		Exchange Rate (in Dollars)		Equivalent Number of U.S. Dollars
¥1,000,000	×	$.0080 per yen	=	$8,000

This process of restating an amount of foreign currency in terms of the equivalent number of dollars is called ***translating*** the foreign currency.

2 Explain why exchange rates fluctuate and what is meant by a "strong" or a "weak" currency.

Why exchange rates fluctuate. An exchange rate represents the "price" of one currency, stated in terms of another. These prices fluctuate, based upon supply and demand, just as do the prices of gold, silver, soybeans, and other commodities. When the demand for a particular currency exceeds supply, the price (exchange rate) rises. If supply exceeds demand, the exchange rate falls.

What determines the demand and supply for particular currencies? In short, it is the quantities of the currency that traders and investors seek to buy or to sell. Buyers of a particular currency include purchasers of that country's exports and

---

[2] To convert an amount of dollars into the equivalent amount of a foreign currency, we would ***divide*** the dollar amount by the exchange rate. For example, $8,000 ÷ $.0080 per yen = ¥1,000,000.

foreign investors seeking to invest in the country's capital markets. Sellers of a currency include companies within the country that are importing goods from abroad and investors within the country who would prefer to invest their funds abroad. Thus, two major factors in the demand and supply for a currency are (1) the ratio of the country's imports to its exports, and (2) the real rate of return available in the country's capital markets.

To illustrate the first of these points, let us consider Japan and Great Britain. Japan exports far more than it imports. As a result, Japan's customers must buy yen in the international currency market in order to pay for their purchases. This creates a strong demand for the yen and has caused its price (exchange rate) to rise relative to most other currencies. Great Britain, on the other hand, imports more than it exports. Thus, British companies must sell British pounds in order to acquire the foreign currencies needed to pay for their overseas purchases. This has increased the supply of pounds in the currency markets, and the price of the pound has declined substantially over the last several decades.

The second factor — the international attractiveness of a country's capital markets — depends upon both political stability and the country's interest rates relative to its internal rate of inflation. When a politically stable country offers high interest rates relative to inflation, foreign investors will seek to invest their funds in that country. First, however, they must convert their funds into that country's currency. This demand tends to raise the exchange rate for that currency. High interest rates relative to the internal rate of inflation were the major reason for the strength of the U.S. dollar during the early 1980s. More recently, however, lower interest rates in the United States, along with large trade deficits (imports in excess of exports), have caused the value of the dollar to fall relative to other currencies.

Exchange rate "jargon." In the financial press, currencies are often described as "strong," "weak," or as rising or falling against one another. For example, an evening newscaster might say that "A strong dollar rose sharply against the weakening British pound, but fell slightly against the Japanese yen and the Swiss franc." What does this mean about exchange rates?

To understand such terminology, we must remember that an exchange rate is simply the price of one currency *stated in terms of another currency.* Throughout this appendix, we refer to the prices of various foreign currencies stated in terms of U.S. dollars. In other countries, however, the U.S. dollar is a foreign currency, and its price is stated in terms of the local (domestic) currency.

To illustrate, consider our table from *The Wall Street Journal,* which shows the exchange rate for the Japanese yen to be $.0080. At this exchange rate, ¥125 is equivalent to $1 (¥125 × $.0080 per yen = $1). Thus, while we would say that the exchange rate for the Japanese yen is $.0080, the Japanese would say that the exchange rate for the U.S. dollar is ¥125.

Now let us assume that the exchange rate for the yen (stated in dollars) rises to $.0082. At this exchange rate, ¥122 is approximately equivalent to $1 (¥122 × $.0082 = $1). In the United States, we would say that the exchange rate for the yen has *risen* from $.0080 to $.0082. In Japan, however, they would say that the exchange rate for the dollar has **fallen** from ¥125 to ¥122. In the financial press, it might be said that "the yen has risen against the dollar," or that "the dollar has fallen against the yen." The two statements mean the same thing — that the yen has become more valuable relative to the dollar.

Now let us return to our original phrase, "A strong dollar rose sharply against the weakening British pound, but fell slightly against the Japanese yen and the Swiss franc." When exchange rates are stated in terms of U.S. dollars, this statement means that the price (exchange rate) of the British pound fell sharply, but the prices of the Japanese yen and the Swiss franc rose slightly. A currency is described as "strong" when its exchange rate is rising relative to most other currencies and as "weak" when its exchange rate is falling.

Accounting for transactions with foreign companies

3 Compute the gain or loss on a receivable or payable stated in terms of a foreign currency when exchange rates fluctuate.

When an American company buys or sells merchandise in a transaction with a foreign company, the transaction price may be stipulated either in U.S. dollars or in units of the foreign currency. If the price is stated in **dollars,** the American company encounters no special accounting problems. The transaction may be recorded in the same manner as are similar transactions with domestic suppliers or customers.

If the transaction price is stated in terms of the **foreign currency,** the American company encounters two accounting problems. First, since the American company's accounting records are maintained in dollars, the transaction price must be translated into dollars before the transaction can be recorded. The second problem arises when (1) the purchase or sale is made **on account,** and (2) the exchange rate **changes** between the date of the transaction and the date that the account is paid. This fluctuation in the exchange rate will cause the American company to experience either a gain or a loss in the settlement of the transaction.

Credit purchases with prices stated in a foreign currency. Assume that on August 1 an American company buys merchandise from a British company at a price of 10 thousand British pounds (£10,000), with payment due in 60 days. The exchange rate on August 1 is $1.80 per British pound. The entry on August 1 to record this purchase (assuming use of the periodic inventory system) is shown below:

Purchases	18,000	
Accounts Payable		18,000

To record the purchase of merchandise from a British company for £10,000 when the exchange rate is $1.80 per pound (£10,000 × $1.80 = $18,000).

Let us now assume that by September 30, when the £10,000 account payable must be paid, the exchange rate has fallen to $1.78 per British pound. If the American company had paid for the merchandise on August 1, the cost would have been $18,000. On September 30, however, only $17,800 is needed to pay off the £10,000 liability (£10,000 × $1.78 = $17,800). Thus, **the decline in the ex-**

change rate has saved the company $200. This savings is recorded in the accounting records as a *Gain on Fluctuations in Foreign Exchange Rates.* The entry on September 30 to record payment of the liability and recognition of this gain would be:

Accounts Payable	18,000	
Cash..		17,800
Gain on Fluctuations in Foreign Exchange Rates		200

To record payment of £10,000 liability to British company and to recognize gain from decline in exchange rate:

Original liability (£10,000 × $1.80)	$18,000
Amount paid (£10,000 × $1.78)	17,800
Gain from decline in exchange rate...........................	$ 200

Now let us assume that instead of declining, the exchange rate had *increased* from $1.80 on August 1 to $1.83 on September 30. Under this assumption, the American company would have to pay $18,300 in order to pay off the £10,000 liability on September 30. Thus, the company would be paying *$300 more* than if the liability had been paid on August 1. This additional $300 cost was caused by the increase in the exchange rate and should be recorded as a loss. The entry on September 30 would be:

Accounts Payable	18,000	
Loss on Fluctuations in Foreign Exchange Rates.........................	300	
Cash..		18,300

To record payment of £10,000 liability to British company and to recognize loss from increase in exchange rate:

Original liability (£10,000 × $1.80)	$18,000
Amount paid (£10,000 × $1.83)	18,300
Loss from increase in exchange rate	$ 300

In summary, having a liability that is fixed in terms of a foreign currency results in a gain for the debtor if the exchange rate falls between the date of the transaction and the date of payment. The gain results because fewer dollars will be needed to repay the debt than had originally been owed. An increase in the exchange rate, on the other hand, causes the debtor to incur a loss. In this case, the debtor will have to spend more dollars than had originally been owed in order to purchase the foreign currency needed to pay the debt.

Credit sales with prices stated in a foreign currency. A company that makes credit sales at prices stated in a foreign currency also will experience gains or losses from fluctuations in the exchange rate. To illustrate, let us change our preceding example to assume that the American company *sells* merchandise on August 1 to the British company at a price of £10,000. We shall again assume that the exchange rate on August 1 is $1.80 per British pound and that payment is due in 60 days. The entry on August 1 to record this sale is:

Accounts Receivable	18,000	
Sales		18,000

To record sale to British company with sales price set at £10,000 (£10,000 ×
$1.80) = $18,000. To be collected in 60 days.

In 60 days (September 30), the American company will collect from the British
company the U.S. dollar equivalent of £10,000. If the exchange rate on September
30 has fallen to $1.78 per pound, the American company will collect only $17,800
(£10,000 × $1.78 = $17,800) in full settlement of its account receivable. Since the
receivable had originally been equivalent to $18,000, the decline in the exchange
rate has caused a loss of $200 to the American company. The entry to be made on
September 30 is:

Cash	17,800	
Loss on Fluctuations in Foreign Exchange Rates.	200	
Accounts Receivable.		18,000

To record collection of £10,000 receivable from British company and to
recognize loss from fall in exchange rate since date of sale:

Original sales price (£10,000 × $1.80).	$18,000
Amount received (£10,000 × $1.78).	17,800
Loss from decline in exchange rate.	$ 200

Now consider the alternative case, in which the exchange rate rises from $1.80 at
August 1 to $1.83 at September 30. In this case, the British company's payment of
£10,000 will convert into $18,300, creating a gain for the American company. The
entry on September 30 would then be:

Cash	18,300	
Accounts Receivable.		18,000
Gain on Fluctuations in Foreign Exchange Rates		300

To record collection of £10,000 receivable from British company and to
recognize gain from increase in exchange rate:

Original sales price (£10,000 × $1.80).	$18,000
Amount received (£10,000 × $1.83).	18,300
Gain from increase in exchange rate.	$ 300

Adjustment of foreign receivables and payables at the balance sheet date.
We have seen that fluctuations in exchange rates may cause gains or losses for
companies with accounts payable or receivable in foreign currencies. The fluctuations in the exchange rates occur on a daily basis. For convenience, however, the
company usually waits until the account is paid or collected before recording the
related gain or loss. An exception to this convenient practice occurs at the end of
the accounting period. An *adjusting entry* must be made to recognize any gains
or losses that have accumulated on any foreign payables or receivables through the
balance sheet date.

To illustrate, assume that on November 10 an American company buys equipment from a Japanese company at a price of 10 million yen (¥10,000,000), payable on January 10 of the following year. If the exchange rate is $.0080 per yen on November 10, the entry to record the purchase would be:

Equipment	80,000	
Accounts Payable		80,000

To record purchase of equipment from Japanese company at a price of
¥10,000,000, payable January 10 (¥10,000,000 × $.0080 = $80,000).

Now assume that on December 31, the exchange rate has fallen to $.0077 per yen. At this exchange rate, the American company's account payable is equivalent to only $77,000 (¥10,000,000 × $.0077). Gains and losses from changes in exchange rates are recognized in the period *in which the change occurs.* Therefore, the American company should make an adjusting entry to restate its liability at the current dollar-equivalent and to recognize any related gain or loss. This entry, which would be dated December 31, is as follows:

Accounts Payable	3,000	
Gain on Fluctuations in Foreign Exchange Rates		3,000

To adjust balance of ¥10,000,000 account payable to amount indicated by
year-end exchange rate:

Original account balance...	$80,000
Adjusted balance (¥10,000,000 × $.0077)	77,000
Required adjustment	$ 3,000

Similar adjustments should be made for any other accounts payable or receivable at year-end that are fixed in terms of a foreign currency.

If the exchange rate changes again between the date of this adjusting entry and the date that the American company pays the liability, an additional gain or loss must be recognized. Assume, for example, that on January 10 the exchange rate has risen to $.0078 per yen. The American company must now spend $78,000 to buy the ¥10,000,000 needed to pay its liability to the Japanese company. Thus, the rise in the exchange rate has caused the American company a $1,000 loss since year-end. The entry to record payment of the account on January 10 would be:

Accounts Payable	77,000	
Loss on Fluctuations in Foreign Exchange Rates..........................	1,000	
Cash...		78,000

To record payment of ¥10,000,000 payable to Japanese company and to
recognize loss from rise in exchange rate since year-end:

Account payable, December 31	$77,000
Amount paid, January 10.....................................	78,000
Loss from increase in exchange rate	$ 1,000

Gains and losses from fluctuations in foreign exchange rates should be shown in the income statement following the determination of income from operations. This treatment is similar to that accorded to gains and losses from the sale of plant assets or investments.

Currency fluctuations—who wins and who loses?

4 Explain how fluctuations in foreign exchange rates affect companies with receivables or payables stated in terms of foreign currencies.

Gains and losses from fluctuations in exchange rates are sustained by companies (or individuals) that have either payables or receivables that are *fixed in terms of a foreign currency.* American companies that import foreign products usually have large foreign liabilities. Companies that export American products to other countries are likely to have large receivables stated in foreign currencies.

As foreign exchange rates (stated in dollars) fall, American-based importers will gain and exporters will lose. When a foreign exchange rate falls, the foreign currency becomes **less expensive.** Therefore, importers will have to spend fewer dollars to pay their foreign liabilities. Exporters, on the other hand, will have to watch their foreign receivables become worth fewer and fewer dollars.

When foreign exchange rates rise, this situation reverses. Importers will lose, because more dollars are required to pay the foreign debts. Exporters will gain, because their foreign receivables become equivalent to an increasing number of dollars.

Exchange rates and competitive prices. Up to this point, we have discussed only the gains and losses incurred by companies that have receivables or payables stated in terms of a foreign currency. However, fluctuations in exchange rates change the **relative prices** of goods produced in different countries. Exchange rate fluctuations may make the prices of a country's products more or less competitive both at home and to customers throughout the world. Even a small store with no foreign accounts receivable or payable may find its business operations greatly affected by fluctuations in foreign exchange rates.

Consider, for example, a small store in Kansas that sells an American-made brand of television sets. If foreign exchange rates fall, which happens when the dollar is strong, the price of foreign-made television sets will decline. Thus, the store selling American-made television sets may have to compete with stores selling imported television sets at lower prices. Also, a strong dollar makes American goods *more expensive to customers in foreign countries.* Thus, an American television manufacturer will find it more difficult to sell its products abroad.

The situation reverses when the dollar is weak—that is, when foreign exchange rates are relatively high. A weak dollar makes foreign imports more expensive to American consumers. Also, a weak dollar makes American products less expensive to customers in foreign countries.

In summary, we may say that a strong U.S. dollar *helps companies that produce or sell foreign goods.* A weak dollar, on the other hand, *gives a competitive advantage to companies that sell American products.*

Consolidated financial statements that include foreign subsidiaries

In Appendix B, we discussed the principles of preparing consolidated financial statements. These statements view the operations of the parent company and its subsidiaries as if the affiliated companies were a single business entity. Several special accounting problems arise in preparing consolidated financial statements when subsidiaries operate in foreign countries. First, the accounting records of the foreign subsidiaries must be translated into U.S. dollars. Second, the accounting principles in use in the foreign countries may differ significantly from American generally accepted accounting principles.

These problems pose interesting challenges to professional accountants and will be addressed in later accounting courses. Readers of the financial statements of American-based corporations, however, **need not be concerned with these technical issues.** The consolidated financial statements of these companies are expressed in U.S. dollars and conform to American generally accepted accounting principles.

ASSIGNMENT MATERIAL

Review questions

1 Translate the following amounts of foreign currency into an equivalent number of U.S. dollars using the exchange rates in the table on page 694:
  a £300,000
  b ¥275,000
  c DM25,000

2 Assume that an American company makes a purchase from a West German company and agrees to pay a price of 2 million deutsche marks.
  a How will the American company determine the cost of this purchase for the purpose of recording it in the accounting records?
  b Briefly explain how an American company can arrange the payment of deutsch marks to a West German company.

3 A recent newspaper shows the exchange rate for the British pound at $1.78 and for the yen at $.0083. Does this indicate that the pound is a stronger currency than the yen? Explain.

4 Identify two factors that tend to make the exchange rate for a country's currency rise.

5 Explain how an increase in a foreign exchange rate will affect a U.S. company that makes:
  a Credit sales to a foreign company at prices stated in the foreign currency.
  b Credit purchases from a foreign company at prices stated in the foreign currency.
  c Credit sales to a foreign company at prices stated in U.S. dollars.

6 You are the purchasing agent for an American business that purchases merchandise on account from companies in Mexico. The exchange rate for the Mexican peso has been falling against the dollar and the trend is expected to continue for at least several months. Would you prefer that the prices for purchases from the Mexican companies be specified in U.S. dollars or in Mexican pesos? Explain.

7 CompuTech is an American-based multinational corporation. Foreign sales are made at prices set in U.S. dollars, but foreign purchases are often made at prices stated in foreign currencies. If the exchange rate for the U.S. dollar has risen against most foreign currencies throughout the year, would CompuTech have recognized primarily gains or losses as a result of exchange rate fluctuations? Explain.

Problems

Problem C-1
Currency fluctuations: who wins and who loses?

Indicate whether each of the companies or individuals in the following independent cases would benefit more from a strong U.S. dollar (relatively low foreign exchange rates) or a weak U.S. dollar (relatively high foreign exchange rates). Provide a brief explanation of your reasoning.

a An American tourist visiting England.
b A small store that sells American-made video recorders in Toledo, Ohio. The store has no foreign accounts receivable or payable.
c Toyota (a Japanese auto manufacturer).
d The Mexico City dealer for Caterpillar tractors (made in the U.S.).
e Boeing (an American aircraft manufacturer that sells many planes to foreign customers).
f A Nikon camera store in Beverly Hills, California. (Nikon cameras are made in Japan.)

Problem C-2
Gains and losses from exchange rate fluctuations

Europa-West is an American corporation that purchases automobiles from European manufacturers for distribution in the United States. A recent purchase involved the following events:

Nov. 12 Purchased automobiles from West Berlin Motors for DM2,000,000, payable in 60 days. Current exchange rate, $.5975 per deutsche mark. (Europa-West uses the perpetual inventory system; debit the Inventory account.)

Dec. 31 Made year-end adjusting entry relating to the DM2,000,000 account payable to West Berlin Motors. Current exchange rate, $.6150 per deutsche mark.

Jan. 11 Issued a check to World Bank for $1,220,000 in full payment of the account payable to West Berlin Motors.

Instructions

a Prepare in general journal form the entries necessary to record the preceding events.
b Compute the exchange rate (price) of the deutsche mark in U.S. dollars on January 11.

Problem C-3
Gains and losses from rate fluctuations: an alternative problem

IronMan, Inc., is an American company that manufactures exercise machines and also distributes several lines of imported bicycles. Selected transactions of the company are listed below:

Oct. 4 Purchased manufacturing equipment from Rhine Mfg. Co., a West German company. The purchase price was DM150,000, due in 60 days. Current exchange rate, $.6000 per deutsche mark. (Debit the Equipment account.)

Oct. 18 Purchased 4,000 racing bicycles from Ninja Cycles, a Japanese company, at a price of ¥80,000,000. Payment is due in 90 days; the current exchange rate is $.0080 per yen. (IronMan uses the perpetual inventory system; debit the Inventory account.)

Nov. 15 Purchased 1,000 touring bicycles from Royal Lion Ltd., a British corporation. The purchase price was £199,500, payable in 30 days. Current exchange rate, $1.80 per British pound.

Dec. 3 Issued check to First Bank for the U.S. dollar-equivalent of DM150,000 in
payment of the account payable to Rhine Mfg. Co. Current exchange rate,
$.6150 per deutsche mark.

Dec. 15 Issued check to First Bank for dollar-equivalent of £199,500 in payment of
the account payable to Royal Lion Ltd. Current exchange rate, $1.77 per
British pound.

Instructions

a Prepare entries in general journal form to record the preceding transactions.

b Prepare the December 31 adjusting entry relating to the account payable to Ninja
Cycles. The year-end exchange rate is $.0082 per Japanese yen.

Problem C-4
A comprehensive
problem on
exchange rate
fluctuations

Wolfe Computer is an American company that manufactures portable personal computers. Many of the components for the computer are purchased abroad, and the
finished product is sold in foreign countries as well as in the United States. Among the
recent transactions of Wolfe are the following:

Oct. 28 Purchased from Mitsutonka, a Japanese company, 20,000 disc drives. The
purchase price was ¥200,000,000, payable in 30 days. Current exchange
rate, $.0082 per yen. (Wolfe uses the perpetual inventory method; debit the
Inventory of Raw Materials account.)

Nov. 9 Sold 700 personal computers to the Bank of England for £510,000, due in 30
days. The cost of the computers, to be debited to the Cost of Goods Sold
account, was $518,000. Current exchange rate, $1.75 per British pound.
(Use one compound journal entry to record the sale and the cost of goods
sold. In recording the cost of goods sold, credit Inventory of Finished
Goods.)

Nov. 27 Issued a check to Inland Bank for $1,720,000 in full payment of account
payable to Mitsutonka.

Dec. 2 Purchased 10,000 amber monitors from German Optical for DM1,200,000,
payable in 60 days. Current exchange rate, $.6000 per deutsche mark. (Debit
Inventory of Raw Materials.)

Dec. 9 Collected dollar equivalent of £510,000 from the Bank of England. Current
exchange rate, $1.73 per British pound.

Dec. 11 Sold 10,000 personal computers to Computique, a French retail chain, for
FF75,000,000, due in 30 days. Current exchange rate, $.1700 per French
franc. The cost of the computers, to be debited to Cost of Goods Sold and
credited to Inventory of Finished Goods, is $7,400,000.

Instructions

a Prepare in general journal form the entries necessary to record the preceding
transactions.

b Prepare the adjusting entries needed at December 31 for the DM1,200,000 account
payable to German Optical and the FF75,000,000 account receivable from Computique. Year-end exchange rates, $.5950 per deutsche mark and $.1710 per French
franc. (Use a separate journal entry to adjust each account balance.)

c Compute the unit sales price of computers in U.S. dollars in either the November 9
or December 11 sales transactions. (The sales price is the same in each transaction.)

d Compute the exchange rate for the yen, stated in U.S. dollars, on November 27.

Appendix D
Accounting for the effects of inflation

The objective of this appendix is to introduce methods of adjusting accounting information for the effects of inflation. We illustrate and explain how net income is measured under the alternative assumptions of constant dollars and current costs. We also discuss gains and losses in purchasing power and show how data from prior years can be restated in terms of current dollars. Throughout our discussion, emphasis is placed upon the interpretation of information adjusted for the effects of inflation.

After studying this appendix you should be able to meet these Learning Objectives:

1 **Define inflation.**
2 **Explain why the use of historical costs during periods of inflation may overstate profits.**
3 **Distinguish between the constant dollar and current cost approaches to measuring net income.**
4 **Use a price index to restate historical costs to an equivalent number of current dollars.**
5 **Explain why holding monetary items may cause gains or losses in purchasing power.**

Throughout this textbook, we have seen how the *cost principle* influences the valuation of assets and the measurement of expenses. Depreciation expense, for example, is based upon the *cost* of the related asset. In periods of sustained inflation, however, historical costs soon lose their relevance and may even become misleading as measurements of economic value. For this reason, accountants, business managers, investors, tax authorities, and other decision makers have long been interested in methods of adjusting accounting information for the effects of inflation.

What is inflation?

1 Define inflation.

Inflation may be defined either as an increase in the general price level or as a decrease in the purchasing power of the dollar. The **general price level** is the

704

weighted average of the prices of all goods and services in the economy. Changes in the general price level are measured by a ***general price index*** with a base year assigned a value of 100. The index compares the level of current prices with that of the base year. Assume, for example, that 1990 is the base year. If prices rise by 10% during 1991, the price index at the end of 1991 will be 110. At the end of 1999, the price index might be 200, indicating that the general price level had doubled since 1990.

The most widely recognized measure of the general price level in the United States is the Consumer Price Index (CPI), published monthly by the Bureau of Labor Statistics. For many years, the base year of the Consumer Price Index was 1967. In May 1983, the CPI passed the 300 level, indicating that prices (on the average) had tripled since 1967. (Note: In 1988, the Consumer Price Index was restated using 1986 as a base year.)

We often hear statements such as "Today's dollar is worth only 33 cents." The "worth" or "value" of a dollar lies in its ability to buy goods or services. This "value" is called ***purchasing power.*** The reciprocal of the general price index (100 divided by the current level of the index) represents the purchasing power of the dollar in the current year ***relative to that in the base year.*** For example, the reciprocal of the CPI in May 1983, was $100 \div 300$, or $.33\frac{1}{3}$. Therefore, we might say that $1 in 1983 was equivalent in purchasing power to about 33 cents in 1967.

What effect do material changes in general price levels, and thus changes in the value of money, have on accounting measures? By combining transactions measured in dollars of various years, the accountant in effect ignores changes in the size of the measuring unit. For example, suppose that a company purchases land for $200,000 and 10 years later sells this land for $400,000. Using the dollar as a measuring unit, we would recognize a gain of $200,000 ($400,000 sales price — $200,000 cost) on the sale of the land. But if prices doubled during that 10-year period and the value of money was cut in half, we might say that the company was ***no better off*** as a result of buying and selling this land. The $400,000 received for the land after 10 years represents the same command over goods and services as $200,000 did when invested in the land 10 years earlier.

We have experienced persistent inflation in the United States for over 40 years; more importantly, the forces which have been built into our economic and political institutions almost guarantee that inflation will continue. The only question is how severe the inflationary trend will be. Our traditional accounting process is based upon the assumption of a stable dollar. This cost-based system works extremely well in periods of stable prices; it works reasonably well during prolonged but mild inflation; but it loses virtually all meaning if inflation becomes extreme.

Profits — fact or illusion?

2 Explain why the use of historical costs during periods of inflation may overstate profits.

Corporate profits are watched closely by business managers, investors, and government officials. The trend of these profits plays a significant role in the allocation of the nation's investment resources, in levels of employment, and in national economic policy. As a result of the ***stable monetary assumption,*** however, a strong argument may be made that much of the corporate profit reported today is an illusion.

In the measurement of business income, a distinction must be drawn between *profit* and the *recovery of costs.* A business earns a profit only when the value of goods sold and services rendered (revenue) *exceeds* the value of resources consumed in the earning process (costs and expenses). Accountants have traditionally assigned "values" to resources consumed in the earning process by using historical dollar amounts. Depreciation expense, for example, may be based upon prices paid to acquire assets 10 or 20 years ago.

When the general price level is rising rapidly, such historical costs may significantly understate the current *economic value* of the resources being consumed. If costs and expenses are understated, it follows that reported profits are overstated. In other words, the stable monetary assumption may lead to reporting *illusory* profits; much of the net income reported by business enterprises actually may be a return of costs.

● **CASE IN POINT** ● In a recent year, Exxon Corporation appeared to be one of the most profitable companies in the world, reporting net income of $4 billion, 186 million. But when the giant oil company's income statement was adjusted for the effects of inflation, the profits vanished — instead, there appeared a net loss of $296 million. What happened? Did Exxon operate at a profit or a loss? The accounting concepts discussed in this appendix should shed some light on these interesting questions.

Two approaches to "inflation accounting"

3 Distinguish between the constant dollar and the current cost approaches to measuring net income.

Two alternative approaches to modifying our accounting process to cope with inflation have received much attention. These two approaches are:

1 *Constant dollar accounting.* Under this approach, historical costs in the financial statements are adjusted to the *number of current dollars representing an equivalent amount of purchasing power.* Thus, all amounts are expressed in units (current dollars) of equal purchasing power. Since a general price index is used in restating the historical costs, constant dollar accounting shows the effects of changes in the *general* price level. Constant dollar accounting is also called *general price level* accounting.

2 *Current cost accounting.* This method differs from constant dollar accounting in that assets and expenses are shown in the financial statements at the current cost to *replace* those specific resources. The *current replacement cost* of a specific asset may rise or fall at a different rate from the general price level. Thus, current cost accounting shows the effects of *specific price changes,* rather than changes in the general price level.

To illustrate these approaches to "inflation accounting" assume that in Year 1 you purchased 1,000 pounds of sugar for $100 when the general price index was at 100. Early in Year 2, you sold the sugar for $108 when the general price index was at 110 and the replacement cost of 1,000 pounds of sugar was $104. What is the amount of your profit or loss on this transaction? The amount of profit or loss determined under current accounting standards (unadjusted historical cost) and the two "inflation accounting" alternatives is shown below:

	Unadjusted Historical Cost	Adjusted for General Inflation (Constant Dollars)	Adjusted for Changes in Specific Prices (Current Costs)
Revenue......................	$108	$108	$108
Cost of goods sold.............	100	110	104
Profit (loss)....................	$ 8	$ (2)	$ 4

Which "cost" of goods sold is most realistic?

Under each method, an amount is deducted from revenue to provide for recovery of cost. However, the value assigned to the "cost" of goods sold differs under each of the three approaches.

Unadjusted historical cost. This method is used in current accounting practice. The use of unadjusted historical cost is based upon the assumption that the dollar is a stable unit of measure. Profit is determined by comparing sales revenue with the *historical cost* of the asset sold. In using this approach to income determination, accountants assume that a business is as well off when it has recovered its *original dollar investment,* and that it is better off whenever it recovers more than the original number of dollars invested in any given asset.

In our example of buying and selling sugar, the profit figure of $8 shows *how many dollars* you came out ahead. However, this approach ignores the fact that Year 1 dollars and Year 2 dollars are *not equivalent in terms of purchasing power.* It also ignores the fact that the $100 deduction intended to provide for the recovery of cost is not sufficient to allow you to *replace* the 1,000 pounds of sugar.

Constant dollar accounting. When financial statements are adjusted for changes in the general price level, historical amounts are restated as the number of current dollars *equivalent in purchasing power* to the historical cost. Profit is determined by comparing revenue with the *amount of purchasing power* (stated in current dollars) originally invested.

The general price index tells us that $110 in Year 2 is equivalent in purchasing power to the $100 invested in sugar in Year 1. But you do not have $110 in Year 2; you received only $108 dollars from the sale of the sugar. Thus, you have sustained a *$2 loss in purchasing power.*

Current cost accounting. In current cost accounting, profit is measured by comparing revenue with the *current replacement cost* of the assets consumed in the earning process. The logic of this approach lies in the concept of the going concern. What will you do with the $108 received from the sale of the sugar? If you are going to continue in the sugar business, you will have to buy more sugar. At current market prices, it will cost you $104 to replace 1,000 pounds of sugar; the remaining $4, therefore, is designated as profit.

Current cost accounting recognizes in the income statement the costs which a going concern actually has to pay to replace its expiring assets. The resulting profit figure, therefore, closely parallels the maximum amount which a business could distribute to its owners and still be able to maintain the present size and scale of its operations.

Which approach correctly measures net income? The answer to this question is that **all three** methods correctly measure net income, but each method is based upon a different definition of "cost" and, therefore, of "net income." Thus, the important question becomes *"Which approach provides the most useful information for making the decision at hand?"* The answer to this question may vary from one decision to the next.

Disclosing the effects of inflation in financial statements

In past years, large corporations were required to include with their financial statements **supplementary schedules** disclosing the effects of inflation. As the rate of inflation declined in the United States, the FASB reduced these disclosure requirements. Today, disclosure of the effects of inflation is no longer required. However, the FASB encourages companies to make **voluntary** disclosures and provides guidelines for these disclosures. Also, the FASB has stated that if the rate of inflation increases, these disclosures may again become mandatory.

A complete discussion of the FASB's disclosure guidelines is beyond the scope of the introductory course. However, everyone who makes use of accounting information should have some understanding of the effects of inflation upon accounting measurements. Therefore, our discussion will focus upon the following basic concepts:

1 Net income measured in constant dollars
2 Gains and losses in purchasing power caused by owning monetary assets and by having liabilities
3 Net income on a current cost basis
4 Comparative data expressed in constant dollars

The value of understanding these concepts extends well beyond reading and interpreting financial statements. An understanding of these concepts is of great value to every economic decision maker.

"INFLATION ACCOUNTING" — AN ILLUSTRATION

The following illustration is typical of the supplementary schedules used to disclose (1) net income measured in constant dollars, (2) gain or loss in purchasing power, and (3) net income measured using current costs. (These three items are printed in black and identified by the numbered arrows.)

Supplement to the financial statements:

COLEMAN COMPANY
Income Statement Adjusted for Changing Prices
For the Year Ended December 31, 19X5

	As Reported in the Primary Statements	Adjusted for General Inflation (Constant Dollars)*	Adjusted for Changes in Specific Prices (Current Costs)
Net Sales...............................	$600,000	$600,000	$600,000
Costs and expenses:			
Cost of goods sold......................	$360,000	$370,000	$391,500
Depreciation expense	60,000	80,000	90,000
Other expenses	130,000	130,000	130,000
Total................................	$550,000	$580,000	$611,500
Net income	$ 50,000 ① →	$ 20,000 ③ →	$(11,500)
Net gain from decline in purchasing power of net amounts owed	② →	$ 8,000	

* Stated in dollars of average purchasing power during 19X5.

We shall now use the information in this illustration to demonstrate further the concepts of constant dollar and current cost accounting and to interpret these disclosures from the viewpoint of the financial statement user.

Net income measured in constant dollars

4 Use a price index to restate historical costs to an equivalent number of current dollars.

A basic problem with the use of historical costs for measuring income is that revenue and expenses may be stated in dollars having different amounts of purchasing power. Sales revenues, for example, is recorded in current-year dollars. Depreciation expense, on the other hand, is based upon dollars spent to acquire assets in past years. As previously emphasized, dollars in the current year and dollars of past years are not equivalent in terms of purchasing power.

In a constant dollar income statement, expenses based on "old" dollars are **restated** at the number of current dollars representing the equivalent amount of purchasing power. When all revenue and expenses are stated in units of similar purchasing power, we can see whether the business is gaining or losing in terms of the amount of purchasing power it controls.

To restate a historical amount in terms of an equivalent number of current dollars, we multiply the historical amount by the ratio of the current price level to the historical price level, as illustrated below:

$$\text{Historical cost} \times \frac{\text{Average price index for current period}}{\text{Index at date of historical cost}} = \frac{\text{Equivalent number}}{\text{of current dollars}}$$

For example, assume that land was purchased for $100,000 when the price index stood at **100.** If the price index is now **170,** we may find the number of current dollars equivalent to the **purchasing power** originally invested in the land by multiplying the $100,000 historical cost by **170/100.** The result, $170,000, represents the number of current dollars **equivalent in purchasing power** to the 100,000 historical dollars.

Price index levels for our illustration. The following changes in the general price index are assumed in our Coleman Company illustration:

Date	Price Index
Beginning of 19X3 (acquisition date for depreciable assets)	150
End of 19X4	180
Average price level for 19X5*	200
End of 19X5	216
Rate of inflation for 19X5†	20%

* The "average" price level for the year is computed as a monthly average and need not lie exactly halfway between the price levels at the beginning and end of the year.

† The inflation rate is computed by dividing the increase in the price index over the year by the price index at the beginning of the year: $(216 - 180) \div 180 = 20\%$.

In restating historical dollars to current dollars, we shall use the **average price level** for 19X5 (200) to represent the purchasing power of current dollars.[1]

Not all amounts are restated. Compare the constant dollar and historical cost income statements of Coleman Company for 19X5 (page 709). Note that only two items — depreciation expense and the cost of goods sold — have been restated in the constant dollar statement. Sales revenue and expenses other than depreciation consist of transactions occurring during the current year. Therefore, these amounts are **already** stated in current dollars. We need to adjust to current dollars only those expenses which are based on costs incurred in past years.

Restating depreciation expense. Assume that Coleman Company's depreciation expense all relates to equipment purchased early in **19X3** when the price level was **150.** The equipment cost $600,000 and is being depreciated over 10 years by the straight-line method. Since the average price level in 19X5 is 200, the **purchasing power** originally invested in this equipment is equivalent to **$800,000 current dollars** ($600,000 \times \frac{200}{150} = $800,000). Thus, the amount of **purchasing power** expiring in 19X5, stated in current dollars, is **$80,000** ($800,000 \div 10 years).

---

[1] An acceptable alternative is to use the year-end price level to represent the purchasing power of current dollars. However, use of the year-end price level means that all income statement amounts, including revenue and expense transactions conducted during the current year, must be restated. For this reason, the average price level for the current year is more widely used.

A shortcut approach is simply to restate the historical depreciation expense, as follows:

Historical Dollars		Conversion Ratio		Equivalent Current Dollars
$60,000	×	200/150	=	$80,000

Since depreciable assets are long-lived, the price level prevailing when the assets were acquired may be substantially different from the current price level. In such cases, the amount of depreciation expense recognized becomes one of the most significant differences between historical dollar and current dollar financial statements.

Restating the cost of goods sold. During 19X5, Coleman Company sold merchandise with a historical cost of $360,000. Assume that $90,000 of these goods came from the beginning inventory, acquired at the end of *19X4* when the price level was *180;* the remaining $270,000 of these goods were purchased during 19X5. The restatement of the cost of goods sold to average dollars is shown below:

	Historical Dollars		Conversion Ratio		Equivalent Current Dollars
Beginning inventory	$ 90,000	×	200/180	=	$100,000
Purchased in 19X5	270,000		*		270,000
Cost of goods sold	$360,000				$370,000

* No adjustment necessary—amount already is stated in current dollars.

Interpreting the constant dollar income statement

The basic difference between historical dollar and constant dollar income statements is the unit of measure. Historical dollar income statements use the dollar as a basic unit of measure. The unit of measure in constant dollar income statements is the *purchasing power of the current dollar.*

A conventional income statement shows how many dollars were added to owner's equity from the operation of the business. Identifying a dollar increase in owner's equity as "income" implies that owners are better off when they recover more than the original number of dollars they invested. No attention is given to the fact that a greater number of dollars may still have less purchasing power than was originally invested.

A *constant dollar* income statement shows whether the *inflow of purchasing power* from current operations is larger or smaller than the *purchasing power consumed* in the effort to generate revenue. In short, the net income figure tells us whether the amount of purchasing power controlled by the business has increased or decreased as a result of operations.

Gains and losses in purchasing power

5 Explain why
holding monetary
items may cause
gains *or* losses
in purchasing
power.

Constant dollar accounting introduces a new consideration in measuring the effects of inflation upon a business: gains and losses in purchasing power from holding monetary items. **Monetary items** are those assets and liabilities representing claims to a **fixed number of dollars.** Examples of monetary assets are cash, notes receivable, and accounts receivable; most liabilities are monetary, including notes payable and accounts payable.

Holding monetary assets during a period of rising prices results in a **loss** of purchasing power because the value of the money is falling. In contrast, owing money during a period of rising prices gives rise to a **gain** in purchasing power because debts may be repaid using dollars of less purchasing power than those originally borrowed.

To illustrate, assume that Coleman Company held $30,000 in cash throughout 19X5, while the price level rose 20% (from 180 to 216). By the end of the year, this $30,000 cash balance will have lost 20% of its purchasing power, as demonstrated by the following analysis:

Number of dollars needed at year-end to represent the same purchasing power as $30,000 at the beginning of the year ($30,000 × 216/180)	$36,000
Number of dollars actually held at year-end	30,000
Loss in purchasing power as a result of holding monetary assets	$ 6,000

We can also compute this $6,000 loss simply by multiplying the amount of the monetary assets held throughout the year by the 20% inflation rate: $30,000 × 20% = $6,000.)

A similar analysis is applied to any monetary liabilities. Assume, for example, that Coleman Company has a $70,000 note payable outstanding throughout 19X5. The resulting gain in purchasing power is computed as follows:

Number of dollars at year-end representing the same purchasing power as $70,000 owed at beginning of year ($70,000 × 216/180)	$84,000
Number of dollars actually owed at year-end	70,000
Gain in purchasing power as a result of owing a fixed number of dollars	$14,000

Thus, during 19X5 Coleman Company has experienced an **$8,000 net gain in purchasing power** ($14,000 gain — $6,000 loss), because its monetary liabilities were greater than its monetary assets. The disclosure of this net gain is illustrated in the supplementary schedule on page 709 (arrow number **2**).

Interpreting the net gain or loss in purchasing power

In determining the total change in the purchasing power represented by owners' equity, we must consider **both** the amount of constant dollar net income **and** the amount of any gain or loss resulting from holding monetary items. Thus, the purchasing power of the owners' equity in Coleman Company increased by $28,000 during 19X5 ($20,000 net income + $8,000 gain in purchasing power from monetary items).[2]

The purchasing power gain from monetary items is shown separately from the determination of net income to emphasize the special nature of this gain. The income statement shows the purchasing power created or lost *as a result of business operations.* The $8,000 net gain in purchasing power, however, is caused entirely by the *effect of inflation* upon the purchasing power of monetary assets and liabilities. A business that owns monetary assets or owes money may have a purchasing power gain or loss *even if it earns no revenue and incurs no expenses.*

In evaluating the effect of inflation upon a particular business, we must consider the effect of inflation upon operations and its effects upon the monetary assets and liabilities of the business. If a business must maintain high levels of cash or accounts receivable from customers, we should recognize that inflation will continually erode the purchasing power of these assets. On the other hand, if a business is able to finance its operations with borrowed capital, inflation will benefit the company by allowing it to repay smaller amounts of purchasing power than it originally borrowed.

Net income on a current cost basis

Constant dollar accounting does not abandon historical costs as the basis for measurement but simply *expresses these costs in terms of the current value of money.* Current cost accounting, on the other hand, does represent a departure from the historical cost concept. The term "current cost" usually refers to the *current replacement cost* of assets. In a current cost income statement, expenses are stated at the estimated cost to *replace the specific assets* sold or used up. Thus, current cost accounting involves *estimates of current market values,* rather than adjustments to historical costs for changes in the general price level.

Of course, the replacement cost of an asset may fluctuate during the year. Since a cost such as depreciation expense occurs continually *throughout* the year, current cost measurements are based on the *average* replacement cost during the year, not on the replacement cost at year-end.

To illustrate, assume that the replacement cost of Coleman Company's equipment was estimated to be $850,000 at the beginning of 19X5 and $950,000 at year-end. Current cost depreciation expense should be based upon the *$900,000 average replacement cost* of the equipment during the year. Since the equipment has a 10-year life, the depreciation expense appearing in the current cost income statement (page 709) is *$90,000* ($900,000 ÷ 10 years).

---

[2] Some readers may notice that our net gain is stated in end-of-19X5 dollars. To be technically consistent with the other constant dollar data on page 712, this net gain should be restated in dollars of average purchasing power for 19X5. The gain can be restated as follows: $8,000 \times \frac{200}{216} = \$7,407$. We have ignored this restatement because it is not material in dollar amount and is an unnecessary refinement for an introductory discussion.

Now let us consider the determination of the cost of goods sold on a current cost basis. All we need to know is (1) how many units of inventory were sold during the year, and (2) the **average replacement cost** of these units during the year. If Coleman Company sold 145,000 units during the year, and the average replacement cost was $2.70 per unit, the cost of goods sold would be $391,500 on a current cost basis (145,000 units × $2.70). Note that the historical cost of units in the company's beginning inventory does not enter into the current cost computation.

Interpreting a current cost income statement

A current cost income statement does **not** measure the flow of general purchasing power in and out of the business. Rather, it shows whether a company earns enough revenue to **replace** the goods and services used up in the effort to generate that revenue. The resulting net income figure closely parallels **distributable profit** — the maximum amount that the business can distribute to its owners and still maintain the present size and scale of its operations.

Unfortunately, the financial statements of large corporations show that many companies in industries vital to our economy are reporting profits measured on a historical cost basis but are incurring large **losses** according to their supplementary current cost disclosures. Companies in the steel industry and utilities industry provide excellent examples. What does this mean to an informed reader of financial statements? In short, it means that these companies do not earn sufficient revenue to maintain their productive capacity. In the long run, they must either obtain capital from other sources or scale down the size of their operations.

Expressing comparative data in dollars of constant purchasing power

To assist decision makers in evaluating trends, data for a series of years often are expressed in dollars of constant purchasing power. For example, the FASB recommends that companies disclose five-year summaries of such key statistics as net sales, income from continuing operations (on a current cost basis), purchasing power gains and losses, earnings per share (on a current cost basis), cash dividends per share, and the market price per share of common stock at year-end. These summaries are to be expressed in dollars of constant purchasing power.

Let us use a short example to illustrate the concept of expressing comparative data in constant dollars. Assume that Wheelhouse Restaurants includes in its annual financial statements supplementary schedules measuring net income on a current cost basis. The earnings per share shown in these schedules (also on a current cost basis) in each of the last five years are shown below. Also shown is the per-share price of the company's common stock at the end of each year.

Data as Originally Reported

	19X5	19X4	19X3	19X2	19X1
Earnings per share (based on current cost net income)	$ 5.40	$ 4.72	$ 4.20	$ 3.66	$ 3.30
Year-end stock price	63.00	57.60	52.50	47.40	44.00

At first glance, it appears that both earnings and the price of the company's stock have increased steadily each year. Now, however, let us consider the changes during these years in the general price level.

Assume that the average level of the general price index for each year is as follows:

	19X5	19X4	19X3	19X2	19X1
Average level of price index.....................	180	160	140	120	110

Using this price index, we may restate our annual figures in the equivalent number of current year dollars:

Data Restated in Constant (19X5) Dollars

	19X5	19X4	19X3	19X2	19X1
Earnings per share (based on current cost net income)..................	$ 5.40[e]	$ 5.31[d]	$ 5.40[c]	$ 5.49[b]	$ 5.40[a]
Year-end stock price................	63.00[j]	64.80[i]	67.50[h]	71.10[g]	72.00[f]

Computations:

Earnings per share:	Year-end stock price:
[a] $3.30 × 180/110	[f] $44.00 × 180/110
[b] $3.66 × 180/120	[g] $47.40 × 180/120
[c] $4.20 × 180/140	[h] $52.50 × 180/140
[d] $4.72 × 180/160	[i] $57.60 × 180/160
[e] No adjustment necessary	[j] No adjustment necessary

Interpreting comparative data stated in constant dollars

The amounts in this second schedule are stated in **units of equal purchasing power**—namely, 19X5 dollars. Thus, the schedule indicates the relative amounts of purchasing power earned each year and the purchasing power represented by the year-end stock price.

This schedule paints a very different picture of the company's "growth" than did our original five-year summary. The amount of purchasing power earned each year has remained about the same, rather than "increasing steadily." In short, the increases appearing in the first schedule resulted from inflation, not from economic growth. Our constant dollar analysis also reveals that the purchasing power represented by the market value of the company's stock has **declined** each year since 19X1.

ASSIGNMENT MATERIAL

Review questions

1 Define inflation.

2 Evaluate the following statement: "During a period of rising prices, the conventional income statement overstates net income because the amount of depreciation recorded is less than the value of the service potential of assets consumed."

3 Define **monetary assets** and indicate whether a gain or loss results from the holding of such assets during a period of rising prices.

4 Why is it advantageous to be in debt during an inflationary period?

5 How does **constant dollar** accounting differ from **current cost** accounting? For which one would the Consumer Price Index be used?

6 Alpha Company sells pocket calculators which have been decreasing in cost while the general price level has been rising. Explain why Alpha Company's cost of goods sold on a constant dollar basis and on a current cost basis would be higher or lower than on a historical cost basis.

7 The latest financial statements of Boston Manufacturing Co. indicate that income measured in terms of constant dollars is much lower than income measured in historical dollars. What is the most probable explanation for this large difference?

8 What conclusion would you draw about a company that consistently shows large net losses when its income is measured on a current cost basis?

Exercises

Exercise D-1
Effects of changing price levels

Empire Company paid $500,000 cash in 1986 to acquire land as a long-term investment. At this time, the general price level stood at 100. In 1990, the general price index stands at 140, but the price of land in the area in which Empire Company invested has doubled in value. Rental receipts for grazing and farming during the five-year period were sufficient to pay all carrying charges on the land.

Empire Company prepares a constant dollar income statement and discloses purchasing power gains and losses as supplementary information to its cost-based financial statements.

a How much, if any, purchasing power gain or loss relating to the land will be included in the supplementary disclosures over the five-year period? (Assume the land is still owned at the end of 1990).

b Assume the land is sold in 1990 for $685,000. Compute the gain or loss on the sale on a basis of (1) historical cost and (2) constant dollars.

Exercise D-2
Monetary items: gains and losses in purchasing power

Three companies started business with $600,000 at the beginning of the current year when the general price index stood at 120. The First Company invested the money in a note receivable due in four years; the Second Company invested its cash in land; and the Third Company purchased a building for $1,800,000, assuming a liability for the unpaid balance of $1,200,000. The price level stood at 140 at the end of the year. Compute the purchasing power gain or loss on monetary items for each company during the year.

Exercise D-3
Cost of goods sold using constant dollars and current costs

For the current year, PhotoMart computed the cost of goods sold for the Presto, its biggest-selling camera, as follows (historical cost, FIFO basis):

	Units	×	Unit Cost	=	Total
From beginning inventory	400		$40.00		$16,000
From current year purchases	1,700		42.00		71,400
Cost of goods sold	2,100				$87,400

The beginning inventory of Presto cameras had been acquired when the general price index stood at 320. During the current year, the average level of the price index was 350, and the average replacement cost of Prestos was $42.

Compute the cost of goods sold for Presto cameras in the current year on:

a A constant dollar basis
b A current cost basis

Exercise D-4
Depreciation
using constant
dollars and
current costs

Western Showcase purchased equipment for $300,000 in 19X3 when the general price index stood at 120. The company depreciates the equipment over 15 years by the straight-line method, with no estimated salvage value. In 19X7, the general price level is 180 and the estimated replacement cost of the equipment is $468,000.

Compute the amount of depreciation expense for 19X7 on:

a A historical cost basis
b A constant dollar basis
c A current cost basis

Problems

Problem D-1
Profits: now you
see them . . .
now you don't

Shown below is a supplementary schedule which appeared in a recent annual report of Chevron Corporation (in millions of dollars):

	As Reported in the Primary Statements	Current Cost
Revenues..	$29,207	$29,207
Costs and Expenses		
Cost of products sold and operating expenses	21,835	22,281
Depreciation, depletion and amortization	1,388	2,630
Taxes other than on income	2,469	2,469
Interest and debt expense..........................	961	961
Provision for taxes on income......................	1,020	1,020
Net Income (Loss)................................	$ 1,534	$ (154)

Instructions. Use this supplementary schedule to answer each of the following questions. Explain the reasoning behind your answers.

a Was Chevron's revenue sufficient to recover the original number of dollars invested in the goods and services consumed during the year?
b Was Chevron's revenue sufficient to replace the goods and services consumed in the effort to generate revenue during the year?
c What do you think is the principal reason for the large difference between the amounts of net income (or net loss) computed under the alternative measurement techniques of historical cost and current cost?

Problem D-2
Interpreting con-
stant dollars and
current costs

The following schedule was developed from information contained in a recent annual report of Ralston Purina Company:

Income Statement Adjusted for Changing Prices
(in millions of dollars)

	As Reported in the Primary Statements	Adjusted for General Inflation (Constant Dollars)	Adjusted for Changes in Specific Prices (Current Costs)
Net sales.....................................	$4,980.1	$4,980.1	$4,980.1
Costs and expenses:			
Cost of goods sold..........................	$3,652.8	$3,664.0	$3,642.3
Depreciation expense	108.7	168.2	174.4
Other expenses	975.9	975.9	975.9
Total......................................	$4,737.4	$4,808.1	$4,792.6
Net income (loss)............................	$ 242.7	$ 172.0	$ 187.5
Gain from decline in purchasing power of net amounts owed		$ 20.3	

Instructions. Use the supplementary schedule to answer each of the following questions. Explain the reasoning behind your answers.

a Was the replacement cost of the products sold by Ralston Purina rising or falling during the year?

b Has the replacement cost of the company's depreciable assets increased faster or more slowly than the general price level since these assets were acquired?

c Were the average monetary assets held by the company during the year greater or smaller than the average monetary liabilities owed?

d What was the total change in the purchasing power of the owners' equity in the business during the year?

e Assuming that this was a typical year, are the company's earnings sufficient to maintain the present size and scope of current operations on a long-term basis?

Problem D-3
Interpreting con-
stant dollar and
current cost
disclosures—
an alternate to
Problem D-2

The following supplementary schedule appears with the financial statements of Lager-bier for the current year.

Income Statement Adjusted for Changing Prices
(in thousands of dollars)
For the Year Ended December 31, 19__

	As Reported in the Primary Statements	Adjusted for General Inflation (Constant Dollars)	Adjusted for Changes in Specific Prices (Current Costs)
Net sales.....................................	$600,000	$600,000	$600,000
Costs and expenses:			
Cost of goods sold..........................	$300,000	$315,000	$310,000
Depreciation expense	50,000	65,000	95,000
Other expenses	210,000	210,000	210,000
Total.....................................	$560,000	$590,000	$615,000
Net Income	$ 40,000	$ 10,000	$ (15,000)
Loss from decline in purchasing power of net			
monetary assets owned		$ 18,000	

Instructions. Explain the reasoning behind your answer to each of the following questions:

  a Has the replacement cost of the company's inventory increased faster or more slowly than the general price level during the year?
  b Has the replacement cost of the company's depreciable assets increased faster or more slowly than the general price level since these assets were acquired?
  c Were the average monetary assets held by the company during the year greater or smaller than the average monetary liabilities owed?
  d What was the total change in the purchasing power of the owners' equity in this business during the year?
  e Assuming that this is a typical year, are the company's earnings sufficient to maintain the present size and scope of its operations on a long-term basis?

Problem D-4
Expressing
comparative data
in constant
dollars

Shown below is the per-share price of the common stock of Southwest Gas & Electric at the end of each of the last four years:

	19X5	19X4	19X3	19X2	19X1
Year-end stock price	$69.00	$65.00	$60.50	$56.70	$50.00

Instructions

  a Based solely upon the above data and ***without regard*** to changes in the general price level, briefly comment upon the apparent trend in the price of the company's stock. In your comments, indicate the total ***percentage change*** in the price of the stock over the four-year period from the end of 19X1 to the end of 19X5.
  b Prepare a schedule in which the ending stock prices for each year are all stated in terms of the purchasing power of the dollar in 19X5. Use the following price index in preparing this constant dollar analysis. Show supporting computations.

	19X5	19X4	19X3	19X2	19X1
Average level of price index	150	125	110	105	100

c Based upon the schedule prepared in part b, comment upon the trends in price of the company's stock. In your comments, indicate the total percentage change in the purchasing power represented by one share over the four-year period from the end of 19X1 to the end of 19X5.

Problem D-5
Constant dollars
and current
costs: a compre-
hensive problem

Sandy Malone, the president of Sandstone Art Company, has asked you to prepare constant dollar and current cost income statements to supplement the company's financial statements. The company's accountant has provided you with the following data:

Income Statement—Historical Cost
For the Year Ended December 31, 19__

Net sales		$840,000
Costs and expenses:		
Cost of goods sold	$420,000	
Depreciation expense	60,000	
Other expenses	320,000	
Total costs and expenses		800,000
Net income		$ 40,000

Other Data

(1) Changes in the general price index during the current year were as follows:

	Price Index
Beginning of current year	120
Average for current year	130
End of current year.	138
Rate of inflation [(138 − 120) ÷ 120]	15%

Amounts in the constant dollar income statement are to be expressed in current-year dollars of average purchasing power.

(2) The company sells a single product and uses the first-in, first-out method to compute the cost of goods sold. The historical cost of goods sold includes the following unit sales at the following costs:

	Units	×	Average Unit Costs	=	Total
From beginning inventory	10,000		$6.00		$ 60,000
From current-year-purchases	56,250		6.40		360,000
Cost of goods sold	66,250		6.34		$420,000

The $60,000 beginning inventory was purchased when the general price index stood at 120. (It is not necessary to know total purchases or ending inventory for the current year.)

(3) The company's depreciable assets consist of equipment acquired five years ago when the price index stood at 75. The equipment cost $900,000 and is being depreciated over a 15-year life by the straight-line method with no estimated salvage value.

   The estimated replacement cost of the equipment was $1,200,000 at the beginning of the current year and $1,260,000 at year-end.

(4) Throughout the current year, the company has owned monetary assets of $180,000 and has owed monetary liabilities of $320,000.

Instructions. Prepare a supplementary schedule in the format illustrated on page 709. Include comparative income statements prepared on the bases of historical costs, constant dollars, and current costs. Also show the net gain or loss from holding monetary items. Include supporting computations for the (1) cost of goods sold—constant dollar basis, (2) depreciation expense—constant dollar basis, (3) net gain or loss in purchasing power from holding monetary items, (4) cost of goods sold—current cost basis, and (5) depreciation expense—current cost basis.

Index

Accelerated cost recovery system (ACRS), 364–365, 648, 656
Accelerated depreciation methods, 361, 377
Accountant(s):
certified public (CPA), 8, 30
controller as, 9
opinion on financial statements, 8, 576, 623
tax services of, 8–9
Accounting:
accrual basis of, 111, 113, 140, 551–558, 561
as basis for business decisions, 13
cash basis of, 111, 113, 551–558, 632–633, 656, 561
cost, 10
(See also Current-cost accounting)
defined, 4
financial, 9, 12, 30
governmental, 10–11
as language of business, 4
management, 10, 30
payroll (see Payroll accounting)
primary business objectives and, 12–13
private, 9–10
purpose and nature of, 4–5
Accounting applications of the computer, 245–246
Accounting cycle, 61–62, 66, 109–110, 159
with computer-based system, 62–64
diagram of, 64, 155
Accounting entity concept, 16, 680–681
Accounting equation, 21–22, 29
Accounting information, 5–7
classifying, 5
communicating, 6–7
recording, 5
user-oriented character of, 6–7
using, 6–7
Accounting period, 85, 113, 129–130
Accounting principles, 11–12, 30
authoritative support for, 12
changes in, 501–502

Accounting principles (Cont.)
generally accepted (see Generally accepted accounting principles)
international, 692–701
Accounting procedures:
in a computer-based system, 62–64
in a manual system, 61–62
Accounting systems:
computer-based, (see Computer-based accounting systems)
diagram of, 64
manual (see Manual accounting systems)
Accounts:
chart of, 51
contra-asset, 98, 113, 281, 297
contra-liability, 398, 412, 429
controlling, 231–233, 248
defined, 43, 66
drawing, 457, 461, 485
financial statement order, 51–52, 66, 95–96
ledger (see Ledger accounts)
normal balance of, 51
sequence of, 51–52, 66, 95–96
T, 43
valuation, 281
Accounts payable:
classification of, in balance sheet, 201–202, 396
defined, 19
subsidiary ledger for, 232–233, 248
Accounts receivable, 280–289
aging of, 284–286, 296, 298
analysis of, 289
on balance sheet, classification of, 280
internal controls, 289
recovery of accounts previously written off, 283–284
subsidiary ledger for, 232–233, 248
turnover in, 596
uncollectible (see Uncollectible accounts)
Accrual of interest, 137–138
Accrual basis of accounting, 111, 113, 140, 561

Accrual basis of accounting (Cont.)
conversion of, to cash basis, 551–558
Accrued expenses:
adjusting entries for, 131, 136–139
defined, 159
Accrued revenue:
adjusting entries for, 131, 139–140
defined, 159
Accumulated depreciation, 97–98, 113, 357–359
not a fund of cash, 358
Acquisition of subsidiaries, 679–680
ACRS (accelerated cost recovery system), 364–365, 648, 656
Adjusted gross income, 637, 656
Adjusted trial balance, 99, 113
Adjusting entries:
and the accrual basis of accounting, 140
for accrued expenses, 136–139
for accrued revenue, 139–140
characteristics of, 131
defined, 113
for depreciation, 97–98, 134
four main types of, 131
reason for, 130–131
from work sheet, 150–151
Adjustment of foreign receivables and payables at balance sheet date, 698–700
After-closing trial balance, 109–110, 113, 154
Aging of accounts receivable, 284–285, 296, 298
AICPA (American Institute of Certified Public Accountants), 8, 12, 29, 313, 318
Allowance for doubtful accounts, 281–286, 296
Alternative Minimum Tax, 656
corporate, 646
personal, 643–644
American Accounting Association, 12
American Airlines, 577
American Express credit card, 288
American Home Products Corporation, 615–627

American Institute of Certified
  Public Accountants (AICPA), 8,
  12, 29, 313, 318
Amortization:
  of bond premium or discount,
    430–432
  defined, 445
  effective interest method,
    434–438, 445
  effective interest rate, 434–436
    442, 445
  from investor's viewpoint, 520
  straight-line method, 430–431,
    433–434
  theoretical considerations on,
    433–434
  of discount on notes payable, 399,
    411
  of intangible assets, 371, 377
Analysis of financial statements,
    575–599
  accounts receivable turnover, 596
  book value per share of common
    stock, 588–589, 598
  common size income statement,
    581–582
  by common stockholders, 587–592
  comparative data in annual
    reports of major corporations,
    581
  comparative financial statements,
    578, 600, 616–618
  component percentages in, 581, 600
  debt ratio, 593, 599
  dividend yield and price-earnings
    ratio, 587–588, 598
  dollar and percentage changes in,
    579–580
  earnings per share of common
    stock, 502–505, 524, 587, 598
  equity ratio, 591–592, 598
  evaluating percentage changes in
    sales and earnings, 579–580
  illustrative analysis, 585–598
  impact of inflation on, 585, 708
  industry standards for, 583–584
  inventory turnover, 595–596, 599
  leverage, 591, 601
  by long-term creditors, 592–593
  operating cycle, 201, 206, 596
  past performance of the company,
    583
  percentages misleading when base
    is small, 580

Analysis of financial statements
    (Cont.)
  by preferred stockholders, 593–594
  price-earnings ratio, 587–588, 598
  quality of assets in, 584, 595, 601
  quality of earnings in, 584, 601
  quick ratio, 597–599
  ratios in, 582, 601
  return on assets, 590, 598
  return on common stockholders'
    equity, 590–591, 598
  return on investment (ROI),
    590–591, 601
  revenue and expenses analysis,
    589–590
  by short-term creditors, 594–598
  sources of financial information,
    578
  standards of comparison for, 583
  summary of analytical measure-
    ments used in, 598–599
  times interest earned, 592–593,
    598
  tools of, 579
  trend percentages, 580–581, 601
  working capital, amount and
    quality, 594–595
  yield rate on bonds, 592
Arthur Andersen & Co., 623
Articles of incorporation, 468
Assets:
  capital stock issuance for, other
    than cash, 473
  current, 201, 205, 595
  defined, 16, 29
  fixed (see Plant and equipment)
  intangible (see Intangible assets)
  quality of, 584, 595, 601
  rules of debit and credit, 45, 88–89
  tangible, 353
  treasury stock not an asset, 513
  valuation of, 16–17, 30, 313–315,
    318, 354, 518, 521–522
  (See also specific types of assets)
Audit report, 576, 623
Auditing:
  of corporations, 576
  defined, 8, 29
  internal, 9, 223
Auditors' report on financial
    statements, 8, 576, 623
Average-cost method of inventory
    valuation, 321, 338
Avon Products, 471

Bad debts (see Uncollectible
    accounts)
Balance sheet:
  account form, 15
  analysis of (see Analysis of
    financial statements)
  classification of, 199–202
  comparative, 578, 616–618
  consolidated, 616, 680–687
  corporation, illustrated, 482–483,
    616
  defined, 15–16, 29
  effects of business transactions
    upon, 22, 29
  nature and purpose of, 15–16
  report form, 102
  stockholders' equity section on,
    20–21, 517
  use by outsiders, 27
Bank checking accounts:
  control features of, 270–271,
    276–279
  miscellaneous charges on, 277
  NSF checks, 276, 297
  reconciliation of, 276–279, 296
  service charges for, 276
  statement of, 275
Bank of America, 692–693
Bank reconciliation, 276–279, 296
Bankers, 27, 594–598
Beginning inventory, 186–187
"Black Monday," 522
Board of directors, 470, 485
Bond premium and discount,
    429–433
  amortization of (see Amortization,
    of bond premium or discount)
Bonds:
  convertible, 440–441, 445
  coupon, 425
  debenture, 424–425
  defined, 422–423
  effect of bond financing on
    holders of capital stock, 591
  income on investments in, 519–520
  interest on: entries to record
    earned, 519–520
    payment of, 519
    purchase of bonds between
      interest dates, 519
  maturity value of, 423, 521
  mortgage, 424
  registered, 425
  serial, 425